Edited by
James E. Elias, Ph.D.
Vern L. Bullough, R.N., Ph.D.
Veronica Elias, Ph.D.
& Gwen Brewer, Ph.D.
Foreword by
Joycelyn Elders, M.D.
*Former Surgeon General of the United States*

# Prostitution

## On Whores,
## Hustlers,
## and Johns

 Prometheus Books
59 John Glenn Drive
Amherst, New York 14228-2197

Published 1998 by Prometheus Books

01 00 99 98 97     5 4 3 2 1

Library of Congress Cataloging-in-Publication Data

Prostitution : on whores, hustlers, and johns / edited by James E. Elias . . . [et al.]
    p.    cm.
  Includes bibliographical references.
  ISBN 1–57392–229–3 (cloth : alk. paper)
  1. Prostitution. 2. Prostitutes—Social conditions. 3. Male prostitution. 4. Pimps.
I. Elias, James.
HQ117.P769     1998
306.74—dc21                                                          98–33520
                                                                        CIP

Printed in the United States of America on acid-free paper.

# DEDICATION

To sex workers everywhere who are struggling for even a minimal level of rights granted to others; to those who live in the shadows and on the margins of society, often feeling alienated and alone. We hope that their cries for recognition and justice will be heard.

# CONTENTS

## 1. History, Anthropology, and Some Recommendations for Prostitutes by "One Who Knows"

8 **Prostitution**

# 2. Celebrated Whores: Their Stories of Law Enforcement and the Media

# 3. The Johns

# 4. Rent Boys, Hustlers, and She-Males

# 5. Prostitution on the American Frontier and the Current Scene

# 6. Feminist Perspectives

# 9. The Struggle over Legal Issues

# Appendices

# ACKNOWLEDGMENTS

The editors would like to extend thanks to the College of Social and Behavioral Sciences; Information and Technological Resources; the Department of Sociology; and the administration of California State University, Northridge, for their support of the Center for Sex Research. In particular, we are grateful to Dean William Flores and Chair Harvey Rich, along with numerous faculty members of the Center for Sex Research, and to Vice Provost Susan C. Curzon and Special Collections Archivist Tony Gardner, who provided an evening with the Special Collection in Human Sexuality. We also thank Valdis Volkovskis of the psychology department, who provided technical support and supervision, and the numerous student volunteers who contributed to this successful endeavor.

A conference such as International Conference on Prostitution '97 could not have been presented without the work of COYOTE (Call Off Your Old Tired Ethics), especially that of co-chair Norma Jean Almodovar. The timely help of the founder of COYOTE, Margo St. James, was significant in making the conference a success. We gratefully acknowledge the untiring work of Rene Blake, chair of the art exhibit and Amanda, chair of the "Hooker's Ball." We thank the sex workers from around the world who traveled to Los Angeles for this conference, and who brought with them their intense commitment to eradicating the oppression of sex workers everywhere and the judicial, legal, and legislative personnel who participated and who added considerably to the substance of the discussions.

The support of our cosponsoring agencies, the Society for the Scientific Study of Sexuality, the American Association of Sex Educators and Counselors, and the Network of Sex Work Projects and Affiliated Sex Worker Organizations, was invaluable. Mr. Jim Dunn and his staff at the Air Tel Plaza Hotel, through their professionalism and cooperation, helped greatly to ensure the success of the International Conference on Prostitution.

Special thanks are extended to the editors and staff of Prometheus Books, who worked with us on the completion of this book, particularly Steven Mitchell, Kathy Deyell, and Eugene O'Connor.

Without all of the above the conference and the book would not have been possible.

# Foreword

# ON PROSTITUTION

## JOYCELYN ELDERS, M.D.

We live in a society where women are trained to have "private virtue." That's what it's all about, you know—the virtue of women. In fact, we train our girls to be virgins, but we want our young men to be studs. And I wonder whom we think our studs are having sex with. Women are trained for "private virtue" and men are trained for public power. That's what a lot of the laws that we have that criminalize women are all about. And those are some of the things on which we need to work. We arrest prostitutes, but we never say much about the johns. We never say anything about our sons, fathers, grandfathers, politicians, preachers, and doctors who are having sex with the sex workers.

We've allowed our politicians to engage in what I call "vaginal politics" for a long time. Just think of all the laws that are on our books and that our politicians argue about in relation to abortion. I've said many times that I've never known any woman in need of an abortion who was not already pregnant. Why don't we deal with the real issues? We talk about women's reproductive rights and we talk about sex workers. We talk about spreading disease and things of that sort, but then when we check, the facts are that there is no difference in the disease rates among the sex workers and the rest of the population. But you would expect that because sex is their business and they are very well informed about keeping themselves healthy through safe sex.

The rest of us walk around and we don't talk about sex because we're afraid that if we talk about it, our young people will do it. Well, they're already doing it. All we have to do is look out in our society and see what happens to so many of our young people.

I want you to know that I loved being your surgeon general. I loved every minute of it. And I also want to tell you that if I had it all to do over again, I would do it the same way. Many times when I was out talking about safe sex

15

and using condoms, I was labeled, if you remember, "The Condom Queen." I would remind people that I would put a crown on my head and sleep in it if everyone who needed to use a condom was using one when they needed to. Human immunodeficiency virus (HIV), the disease that causes AIDS, is rampant in our community, especially among our young people and among our minority people. Fifty-seven percent of the women with HIV are black women, and 20-plus percent are Hispanic women. In fact, 75 percent of the women with HIV are minority women and they make up less than 20 percent of the population. These real issues occur because of poor education—because of the things we've often been taught. You know where it all started. It started at church. We have our ministers up there in the pulpit, preaching to the choir and the congregation when they really need to be out in the streets dealing with the real problems that our society faces.

We are in a society where we are more interested, if you will, in bedroom laws than boardroom laws. We are out there passing all of these laws related to sexuality, and many of our politicians say "I'm really a conservative," but they are conservatives in the bedroom and they are liberals when it comes to the boardroom. When I was speaking at an AIDS conference and brought up the word "masturbation," you would have thought the world had never heard of masturbation. If they had never heard of it, then they shouldn't have known what I was talking about. We know from the data that have been gathered that 95-plus percent of men masturbate, 80 percent of women masturbate, and the rest lie. I think we know that we've got a real problem with AIDS out there that we've got to deal with. But I said, "One of the things I know is that this country talked more about masturbation in December 1994 than they ever had before or since." Now it's all right to mention masturbation in polite conversation.

Then when people asked me, "Are you talking about teaching kids to masturbate?" I said, "Don't you know that nobody needs to teach anybody how to masturbate?!" So I don't know why we need to have all this conversation about teaching them how to do it. Anybody who has ever seen a baby with its diapers off knows that. I'm just saying that we need to be realistic and to stop telling our children they'll go blind, they'll go crazy, or hair will grow on their hands. We've got to begin to be honest about those kinds of issues.

The other thing that I think we need to ask is Why do people go into prostitution? Most of the men and women who become sex workers do so because they're having trouble with money. They're really doing it to stay out of poverty or because they're poor. So poverty is often the cause of prostitution and I think we need to deal with that. I'm not saying that that eliminating poverty is the only cure, but I think it is very significant. Some of the studies show that as the economy goes down, prostitution of both men and women goes up. When we start cutting Aid to Families with Dependent Children (AFDC), we find more AFDC moms being arrested for prostitution. We've known for many years that many women marry just for money. To me, that's one more form of prostitution. We as women have to go out and really get involved and work on these issues.

The one thing that I think we all agree on is that our children and youth who are made to become prostitutes are really being molested by our society. None of us supports childhood prostitution. In Asian countries, more than a million children are being sold into prostitution, usually by poor families. Some of them are very young children, six and seven years of age. Regardless of the situation, most sexually abused children are manipulated by disparities in wealth and power. Western sex offenders exploit the economic hardships in pursuit of their criminal desires. We've known that. Look at our army. You know we placed our army camps next to certain areas where women would be available for the men. We admit that, but we've got to make people respect the idea that if two consenting adults choose to have sex, that should be none of our business.

Nobody should be forced into prostitution or into having sex. Let me tell you a fact. Eighty-four percent of the girls fourteen and under who become pregnant were abused by somebody in their own home. Eighty-four percent! Sixty-six and two-thirds percent of all the teenagers who become pregnant have been abused at some time during their life. We spend billions of dollars in this country trying to prosecute prostitution, which is sex between consenting adults, and we do nothing about the abuse of children. Many children in this country and around the world are exploited for profit and unhealthy criminal desires. I feel that we need to begin to spend those funds not on trying to prosecute sex between consenting adults, but on making sure that all children will have the opportunity to grow up healthy, educated, motivated, and with hope for the future.

I, frankly, don't care who's sleeping in Lincoln's bedroom. But *I do care* that many children have been forced to sleep in someone else's bed where they didn't want to sleep. I feel that we've got to begin to do something about the problems that are going on. We've all worked so hard talking about welfare and welfare reform. Why don't we do something about the "corporate welfare" that's going on? Look at the "savings and loan welfare," the "bank welfare," "corporate welfare." We pay big business to grow tobacco then we turn around and we pay the health maintenance organizations (HMOs) for taking care of the tobacco industry's dying victims. So I'm saying that we, our government, has been a part of exploiting young people. We refuse to make sure that all people have access to health care. We say every criminal has a right to consult a lawyer, but we don't feel that every sick person has the right to see a doctor. I feel that if we could make sure that all people have the opportunity to be taken care of we wouldn't need to set up special programs to make sure we take care of sex workers. Sex workers would be able to choose to go to their doctor and get proper care.

We think about who's sleeping in Mr. Lincoln's bed. I bet he would love to know why we have so many people in this country who don't even have a bed in which to sleep. We control 25 percent of the world's wealth and have only 5 percent of the world's population; yet we can't feed and house our own people. We have children in America who will only be members of what I call the "5 H Club": children who are Hungry—every night we have 5 million children who go to bed hungry—then Home-less; Health-less; Hug-less; and Hope-less. That's a real problem.

Why are we so upset about sex workers selling sexual acts to consenting adults? We say that they are selling their bodies, but how different is that from what athletes do? They're selling their bodies. Models? They're selling their bodies. Actors? They're selling their bodies. We do with our bodies what we see fit. We live in a free country. Those, I feel, are things we need to think about and deal with.

We know that many American women are in difficulty, and we know that if they're black or transgendered, the problems are worse. Immigrants have still greater problems. If you become a sex worker and you're arrested twice, you'll become labeled a criminal. You can lose your child, and I don't have to go into how you're treated.

So what are we going to do? What do we need to do about it? I read the report that San Francisco did on its sex workers. I thought the most awful thing that I read in that report was the idea of taking condoms away from sex workers. Can you believe that? Our country does many stupid things. When we start criminalizing disease or medical problems, we start making mistakes. Just think, we don't furnish clean needles because we say, "Well, if we furnish clean needles that says we support legalization of drugs." Furnishing clean needles doesn't mean you support drug legalization, it means that you want to prevent death and disease.

Then we say, if youth have condoms, that's evidence of their intent to have sex. About ten years ago, I was telling high school students (girls), "Don't ever go out on a date with some guy that you like without a condom in your purse, because he might say 'I don't have one.' Then you can say, 'Well, that's fine. I've got one.'" We have to really make sure that we deal up front and openly with sex and talk about it so our children will learn and know how to negotiate when the time comes. It's too late to learn when you're in the backseat of a car. We taught them what to do in driver's education. We taught them what to do in the front seat, now we need to teach them what to do in the backseat.

It's very important to recognize that every time you have sex with somebody, you're not really having sex with one person; you're having sex with all the people in their history. Sometimes you're having sex with up to 537 different people. You really can't tell by looking if someone has HIV. So I bemoan the fact that we are not out there promoting safe sex. We're not educating people to be safe because we're not making condoms available. They should be available everywhere. Condoms cost health departments five to ten cents apiece or less. I had a woman call me one time and she said, "Dr. Elders, I just can't possibly consider using my tax dollars to pay for condoms." I said, "Ma'am, I buy condoms for a nickel a dozen." They were almost giving them to us at the health department. I said, "We spend more than 100 million dollars a year on AFDC, or food stamps and Medicaid for teenagers who give birth to children. I said, "How many condoms, at a nickel a dozen, do you think $100 million will buy?" She said, "Thank you, Dr. Elders."

You have to make people come down and deal with reality. People don't complain about all the money we spend on defense. I really wasn't very smart when I was surgeon general. I really should've given the money for condoms to the defense department and then they wouldn't have said they were giving them out for sex purposes. They would've said they were giving them out to protect the people from disease and pregnancy. We have all these guns and you've never heard the defense department say they give out guns and weapons to kill people. They say they give them out to protect our country. So I say we have to learn to be smarter in how we approach many of these issues.

We've got to stop criminalizing public health. We've got to make sure our young people and all our people understand safe sex, understand that they must use a condom, not sometimes, but each and every time. We've got to make sure that if they don't use a condom, they certainly can use creams or jellies or vaginal contraceptive film. But we haven't taught our young people that. People say all the time, "Dr. Elders, creams, jellies, film—they won't protect against HIV." I think all of the data we have that says otherwise. They are the best protection we've got. Nothing provides a 100 percent guarantee against disease—except no sex—but we are sexual beings.

The size of a sperm allows it to pass through a hole about 300 nanometers (nm).* Gonorrhea and syphilis can penetrate at 900 nm. The HIV virus is approximately 125 nm and hepatitis B is about 12 nm. They test condoms; they really make certain that they will protect for even smaller particles such as molecules. Condoms are very safe in protection against both pregnancy and also against HIV.

If we decriminalize prostitution, sex workers would not be vulnerable to pimps, drug dealers, extortionists, and others who profit off of the illegality of prostitution. Crimes of violence such as assault, rape, kidnapping, burglaries, and so on could be dealt with in the normal course of events, and women could report them rather than continue to be abused. I feel that we must begin to deal with this issue related to prostitution.

It's time to become advocates for sound public policy related to sexuality. We have a lot of poor public policy out there. We've got poor public policy in

---

*A nanometer is one-millionth of a millimeter.

regards to drugs. We've got poor public policy in regards to sex. Any time we start relating to human issues or social issues, we start making all of these laws and I've never known one of them that has decreased anything. We need to develop a master plan by which society can begin to deal with these human welfare issues.

So, think of sexuality and think of what we need to do. We've got sex workers who are often denied access to health care. So are 44 million other Americans. We've got to make health service available to all of our people. We've got to continue to have outreach workers so that they can begin to help deal with many of these issues. We've got to educate—the community, the schools, and professionals. Educate our people. Educate the investigators of all the different departments so they'll know what to do. Educate our police department. We as women will have to give up our pedestal rights for our rights as women. We've got to be unified and united around sexuality issues.

We've got to make sure that we insure the rights of sex workers and stop the enforcement of unfair sex laws, but we've got to have zero tolerance for child prostitution. We've got to make sure that we go out and support the rights of consenting adults to do what they feel they need to do. We've got to be aware of the problem. We've got to be advocates for the problem. We've got to develop a plan of action that's right for this country. And you, here, will be the leaders. You've got to be the leaders. You've got to be leaders who are willing to lead. We've got too many leaders who go out and find out which way the wind is blowing and jump out in front. We've got enough of those. We've got to have some real leaders. You've got to be involved. We've all got to be involved. We need to begin to look at how we can go about decriminalizing all aspects of adult prostitution.

To do it, we've got to have three things, what I call the "tools of commitment." There's a great big difference between being committed and being concerned. When you are concerned about the problem, it's negotiable; when you are committed, it's not negotiable. The tools you have to give are your time, your talents, and your treasures—i.e., the money from your pocket. These are the "three T's," the tools of commitment.

# A Note about This Book

The Center for Sex Research at California State University, Northridge (CSUN), and the Los Angeles chapter of COYOTE (Call Off Your Old Tired Ethics) sponsored the International Conference on Prostitution in Los Angeles in March 1997. The purpose of the conference was to bring together workers in the sex industry and academic researchers to exchange ideas and findings about prostitution, both male and female. This book grew out of the conference. It is not an official proceedings, but rather a selection of thinking about prostitution from a variety of perspectives. The conference was originally planned and organized by Bonnie Bullough, James Elias, Vern Bullough, and Norma Jean Almodovar. Bonnie Bullough, however, died early in the planning process and the conference was dedicated to her. Norma Jean was assisted for her part by a number of professional sex workers, and much of the success in attracting professional sex workers was due to her and her coworkers. Vern Bullough and James Elias also had wide contacts with professional sex workers and invited many of the presenters but concentrated for the most part on the academic research portion of the presentations. They also received considerable help from their academic colleagues at CSUN, particularly from the other members of the Center for Sex Research. Collaboration between the sex workers and academics generally was excellent, and strong bonds were formed between many of them. There was also, however, considerable tension among the three organizers as the demands for funds exceeded what we could raise, and there were more services than the university was willing to contribute to. Still the conference remained a remarkable achievement, and for many academics it marked a significant alteration in their perspectives. In general it lessened the suspicion between academics and the professional sex workers.

The book is organized into sections, each with a separate introduction. We tried to intersperse studies and reports by sex workers with those by academics (and it should be noted that some of the academics had experience as sex workers). We believe the result is unique. Setting the stage for the conference is a historical sociological paper by Bonnie Bullough and Vern L. Bullough examining the research and changing interpretations of prostitution up to the time of the conference itself, and looking at some of the questions that have been asked and how the answers have differed.

# INTRODUCTION

## FEMALE PROSTITUTION: CURRENT RESEARCH AND CHANGING INTERPRETATIONS

### BONNIE BULLOUGH AND VERN L. BULLOUGH

Until recently, prostitution has been a subject that has engendered considerable emotion but little scholarly or scientific research. Much of the traditional writing on the topic has been moralistic and condemnatory while promising forgiveness to those prostitutes who changed their ways. An almost equal portion of the writing has been what might be called erotic or pornographic. In fact, the very word "pornography" comes from the Greek *pornographos,* meaning writings of the prostitutes or writing about prostitutes.

The lack of serious scholarly research has allowed misinformation to circulate about the extent, nature, and causes of prostitution. Occasionally, there were serious studies of prostitution, but only in the past three decades has there been a significant increase in the number of such studies. Unfortunately, many of these are still based more on rhetoric than fact (Bullough, Eleano, Deacon, and Bullough 1977; Bullough and Sentz 1992).

The emergence of more scholarly studies in recent decades can be linked to two factors: (1) the massive public information campaign about AIDS, and (2) the renewed interest in the topic brought about by feminists. In terms of the kind of research of most interest to sexologists, feminist-oriented scholars, both female and male, have been far more important in bringing about a better understanding of prostitution than the AIDS campaign.

## A Brief Historical Background

Prostitution has often been called the world's oldest profession but it might be more accurate to say that in a male-dominated world, prostitution was almost the only way that many women lacking a husband, father, or brother to support or protect them were able to survive. It is perhaps the most extreme form of a double standard and has been justified by the male establishment as a way of preserving the virginity of their daughters and separating the "good women" (the proper wife and mother) from the "bad women" (those who served male sexual needs). Even Saint Augustine (354–439), the fountainhead of Western Christian morals, argued that prostitution was a necessity. This, in spite of the fact that Augustine stated there was nothing more sordid, more full of shame, more void of modesty than prostitutes, brothels, and other such "evils." If these were removed, however, society, he claimed, would be polluted with lust and established patterns of sexual relationship would be endangered, i.e., males might turn to other males. Prostitutes, however, were to be excluded from the Church as long as they continued to sell their bodies, although they were to be welcomed as repentant sinners when they abandoned prostitution (Bullough and Bullough 1987, 70). In fact, many former prostitutes came to be granted sainthood in the Middle Ages including Mary Magdalene, the model for all such saints.

Much of Western history can be read as a history of this ambivalence toward the prostitute and female prostitution. This is indicated by both the widespread toleration of the practice during much of this history and a toleration of the practice interspersed with periodic condemnation and even attempts to abolish it. Mostly, however, Western societies have tried to regulate prostitution and control its excesses.

Many other societies, particularly those with less hostility to sex than Christianity, were less ambivalent about prostitution. Many of the ancient religions recognized and gave a special role to prostitutes, and prostitution today is more openly accepted and practiced in many parts of the world than it is in the United States. This chapter concentrates primarily on prostitution in the Western world which, in spite of growing secularization, still continues to hold to the ambivalent ideas associated with traditional Christian culture.

## Who Is a Prostitute?

The ambivalence complicates the problem of defining who is a prostitute, a problem that has been debated since Saint Augustine. Havelock Ellis, a pioneer in the scientific investigation of sex, defined a prostitute as "a person who makes it a profession to gratify the lust of various persons of the opposite or the same sex" (1936, 225–26). This definition has the advantage of including both sexes but leaves unanswered the question of when prostitution becomes an occupation. Does a person who sells his or her body for lustful purposes a single time become a prostitute, or is he or she so labeled after ten times, or after a hundred? Saint Jerome, one of the early Christian Church Fathers, held that a prostitute was a woman who served the sexual urges of many, but he never bothered to define what he meant by "many." Other churchmen concerned with the ambiguity inherent in Jerome's definition attempted to be more specific but this only added to the confusion. One commentator on canon law held that a woman could be called a prostitute if she served from forty to sixty different men, while another, Johannes Teutonicus, in 1605, suggested that to be called a prostitute a woman must have had sex with a minimum of 23,000. How seriously he took his own definition is debatable because elsewhere he used the number forty (Bullough and Bullough 1987).

As far as police records are concerned, a prostitute is a person who has been charged, arrested, or convicted of prostitution, but this ignores some of the more successful prostitutes who have never run afoul of the law. Some investigators into prostitution have argued that a key to determining whether a person is or is not a prostitute is the emotional involvement and the pleasure she or he gained from the client. It has traditionally been believed that most prostitutes were emotionally uninvolved with their clients and received little physical pleasure themselves, but this might not always be the case and many might well get emotional satisfaction. In short, many have struggled with definitions, and any discussion of prostitution is dependent upon definition. Perhaps the most comprehensive was that offered by Iwan Bloch at the beginning of the twentieth century. Bloch held that prostitution was a distinct form of extramarital sexual activity characterized by being more or less promiscuous, was seldom without reward, and was a form of professional commercialism for the purpose either of intercourse or of other forms of sexual activities and allurement, resulting in due time in the formation of a special type (Bloch 1912, 1:38). This inclusive description applies to both male and female prostitutes and is broad enough to include the mistress, since she is a recognizable type and engages in sex or allurement for the rewards attached to it. Bloch's definition is the one generally used in this paper, but any definition presents problems since different societies have different standards. It is the social evaluation and legal determination of a society that give prostitution a special status.

# The Extent of Female Prostitution and Current Changes

One of the first steps in examining any so-called social problem is to determine its extent (Bullough 1965). Where prostitution is concerned, there has always been a significant amount of misinformation since the available figures represent either the (a) inscribed women in countries where regulation exists or existed, or (b) women convicted for soliciting. Both of these prevalence figures are inaccurate because even in those countries where prostitution has been or is legally regulated, only a portion of women actually practicing prostitution were or are listed on the official rolls. Missing are the clandestine, part time, and amateur prostitutes, as well as most of those of higher status. Arrest figures are also extremely misleading because they tend to concentrate on the low-status prostitute, fluctuate with the views of individual magistrates or police response to public opinion, and change from region to region because of attitudes and traditions. Prevalence figures are also dependent on what is classified as prostitution because there is little agreement on anything but the more blatant forms of solicitation and definitions change from jurisdiction to jurisdiction.

Still, when these weaknesses have been pointed out, official figures represent a necessary beginning and it is to be hoped they can be supplemented as research progresses. The pioneer effort to define the extent of prostitution was made in 1836 by the French physician Alexandre Jean Baptiste Parent-Duchâtelet, who should be regarded as a founder of modern social and behavioral science research on sexual issues (Bullough 1994). In examining the police register in Paris, where prostitution was controlled by the municipal government, Parent-Duchâtelet found that there were 3,558 prostitutes in the city, which in the 1830s had a population of approximately 785,000. This meant that roughly 5 percent of the women between fifteen and twenty-five years of age were registered prostitutes. Comparing this number with those on the register in 1814 (total population of approximately 700,000), he found that the number of registered prostitutes had increased but not more rapidly than the population (1836, 1:28–38). The replication of his study in 1854 showed that the prostitute population continued to increase in proportion to the city's growth.

From these studies, a baseline estimation can be derived for the extent of prostitution in a large urban area. Such a baseline, however, has its limitations because some prostitutes were inscribed only for short periods, and those not placed on the lists were not counted. We know from other sources that there were many of the latter kind of prostitutes, some of them of quite high status. Taking these limitations into account, the Paris studies suggest that probably somewhere between a minimum of 5 and a maximum of 15 percent of the young female population engaged in some kind of prostitution either for shorter or longer periods. Prior to this, and unfortunately even afterward, there has been tremendous variation in the estimates of the extent of prostitution. Typical of such estimates was the one made by Michael Ryan for London in the middle of the nineteenth century. Ryan followed the form set by Parent-Duchâtelet, but because there was no official register of prostitutes, his data were based much more on guesswork and his figures were accordingly much more suspect. He estimated that there were some 80,000 prostitutes in London, two-thirds of them between fifteen and twenty years of age (Ryan 1839). This figure must be regarded as either pure fantasy or the result of a much broader definition of what constituted prostitution, so broad in fact that it was relatively meaningless (Ryan 1839). Using Ryan's figures, a skeptical commissioner of metropolitan police estimated that since the total female population of greater London at that time was 769,628, of whom 78,962 were between fifteen and twenty, Ryan's claim would have made almost every woman between fifteen and twenty a prostitute (Wardlaw 1843). Ryan's far-fetched estimates were for the nineteenth century, and yet similar estimates have been circulated for twentieth-century cities without any real attempt to analyze the source. Ben L. Reitman, for example, estimated that there were 100,000 prostitutes in Chicago in 1930, although the basis for his estimate is unclear (Restman 1931).

Fortunately, current historical research has tended to validate the ranges derived from the work of Parent-Duchâtelet. It should be added that one of the major foci of the current generation of researchers has been on the history of prostitution and more than four hundred historical studies of prostitution have been published in the past twenty-five or thirty years, many of them derived from Ph.D. dissertations (Bullough and Sentz 1992). These authors have worked to fine-tune past estimates. Based on their conclusions, it now seems evident that there was a much higher proportion of the female population engaged in prostitution in the nineteenth and early twentieth centuries than there is now.

Timothy F. Gilfoyle's 1992 examination of prostitution in New York City between 1790 and 1920 is an example of one of the better studies conducted in recent years. Gilfoyle estimated that 10 to 15 percent of all young women in New York City in the nineteenth century were prostitutes, either temporarily or on a long-term basis (Gilfoyle 1992, 59). Prostitution for much of the period was the second largest business in New York in terms of money generated (tailoring was first). This is probably true of most other major European and American cities, and his estimates, it is hoped, bring a touch of reality to other nineteenth-century estimates. If prostitution in New York City can be regarded as a business, it is worth noting that it brought in more income than any of the major developing industries such as ironmaking, soap manufacture, distilleries, bakeries, and printing. It generated more than four times as much income as the brewing industry, three times as much as the hat and cap manufacturing industry, and twice as much as boiler and steam engine sales (Gilfoyle 1992, 126). Using Gilfoyle's figures as representative of other cities in the United States and Europe at that time, prostitution has to be visualized as one of the major occupations for young women. Most, however, were engaged in it for only short periods of time, and almost all had left it by the age of thirty.

Gilfoyle also emphasized that prostitution was a major form of sex release for males for much of the nineteenth century. He writes that by the midcentury mark, "journalists and doctors were convinced that sex with prostitutes was the norm for young male New Yorkers" (Gilfoyle 1992, 403). Walt Whitman, no stranger to New York City's netherworld, wrote that "the plain truth is that nineteen out of twenty of the mass of American young men, who live in or visit the great cities, are more or less familiar with houses of prostitution and customers in them (Gilfoyle 1992, 403).

A large number of married men, perhaps a majority of both the poor and the wealthy, also visited the houses. They were social gathering places, and their ubiquity and availability might have been a factor in decreasing the size of families during the century before information about contraception became more widespread.

The extent of prostitution and the proportion of males utilizing prostitutes distinguish recent generations of Americans (and other citizens of modern industrialized countries) from those of the historical past. This change was first noted by Alfred Kinsey and his associates. They reported that on the basis of their sample that 69 percent of the total white male population in the United States had had some kind of sexual experience with a prostitute. Many of their respondents, however, had a single or at most two experiences with a prostitute and no more than 15 percent of them had ever had such relations more than a few times a year. Kinsey et al. estimated that contact with prostitutes amounted to between 3.5 and 4 percent of total sexual experience. By far the largest proportion of those males turning to prostitutes for sexual services were unmarried—bachelors, divorcees, or widowers (Kinsey, Pomeroy, and Martin 1948, 595–609).

More importantly, in terms of the changes taking place in prostitution, the Kinsey group found that younger men in the sample were less likely to have visited prostitutes than their fathers had been at their age. This decline has continued. Samuel and Cynthia Janus in their quantitative study of sexual practices reported that 20 percent of their male sample had had sex involving a monetary exchange (Janus and Janus 1993). Interestingly, they found that married, middle-aged, and middle-income males constituted the group more likely to turn to prostitutes, and the percentages who had visited a prostitute seemed to remain the same across income levels. They also found that roughly 5 percent of their female sample had participated in sex involving monetary exchange although they did not particularly identify these women as prostitutes. Interestingly, they found that women whose incomes were over $50,000 were much more likely to engage in sex for money than women who earned less or than those who earned more than $100,000 (345–48).

The Janus figures were higher than those reported in the more carefully drawn representative sample examined by Laumann, Gagnon, Michael, and Michaels, who reported that only 16 percent of the men surveyed had ever paid for sex (Laumann et al. 1994). This latter study also emphasized the continuing generational change taking place. Seven percent of the men who came of age in 1950 had their first sexual encounter with a prostitute, compared to 1.5 percent of those who came of age in the late 1980s (Michael et al. 1994, 63, 95). The survey did not ask female participants whether they identified themselves as a prostitute, but 2 percent of the women said they had had sex with someone they picked up and 7.2 percent with a person they knew less than two days. The prostitute is most likely to come from these groups (Laumann et al. 1994, 399). It should be noted, however, that this study included men who had served in the Korean and Vietnam wars, so many of the prostitutes might well have come from overseas.

These mostly American statistics, we believe, can be replicated in many of the Western industrialized countries. The statistics, however, are very different in many of the developing countries such as Thailand and the Philippines, where prostitution is much more widespread and the patronage probably approaches nineteenth-century American figures. In many such countries the availability of prostitutes has become part of the tourist economy, and the money paid to prostitutes is an important part of the national income (*The Economist* 1996; Baker 1995; Hodgson 1994; Levan 1994; Maardh 1994; Nyland 1995; Smolenski 1995).

Although the existence of tourist prostitution can in part be explained by differing cultural attitudes toward prostitution and about sex in general than those prevailing in the West, we think other factors are also at work. The economic and social conditions in these countries that are undergoing radical changes similar to those which took place in nineteenth-century America undoubtedly encourage a higher level of prostitution, if only because most of these countries have a dominant male hierarchy and wide acceptance of a double standard.

## Prostitution and the Military

That attitudes toward prostitution can change in countries where prostitution was once widespread is emphasized by the Japanese apologies for their use of enforced prostitution during World War II. The Japanese military, recognizing the need for male sexual outlets, but also wanting to exert control over their troops, established brothels for them, a not uncommon occurrence in past wars. But where does one get the women to "serve"? In earlier days armies traveled with large number of camp followers, many of them "wives" of the troops, while others were involved with a number of different men. These women not only offered sexual services but also did laundry, the cooking, and, until the time of Florence Nightingale, often took care of the sick and wounded. Armies in earlier years were highly dependent upon such women.

Modern armies, however, have greater control of their troops. The Japanese solution avoided troops' intermingling with conquered civilian populations but to get the large supply of women necessary for large concentrations of military personnel, they forced thousands of women into prostitution. A disproportionate number of such women were Korean or from other areas that the Japanese had conquered, but usually the prostitutes were not local to the area where they were "stationed." Not until fifty years after the war ended did some of these women make their case public, and they are now demanding and receiving compensation. It is important to note that such demands were made as the Japanese have been reassessing the role of women in their own society (Boling 1995; Hicks and Shapiro 1995), emphasizing, as if it needed to be emphasized, the importance of a feminist voice.

The Japanese military, however, were perhaps only less diplomatic than other countries in the way they recruited prostitutes for their troops because sexual satisfaction of soldiers and sailors has always been a problem of concern to the military; in fact, contact with prostitutes tends to increase during major wars simply because highly localized areas have large concentrations of males with only a limited number of females. In a sense, the American public has generally avoided facing such issues, because actual warfare on American soil has not occurred since the Civil War. In that war, the military spent considerable time regulating prostitution, and many women, having lost their homes, their loved ones, and any other means of providing for themselves, as well as for purely patriotic or other personal reasons, turned to prostitution. Emphasizing this Civil War solution is the widespread acceptance of the term "hooker," which many texts state was derived from the activities of Union general Joseph Hooker in providing women for his troops.*

In American expeditions abroad, the military has generally relied on short-term leaves for R & R (rest and recreation), leaves not long enough for the individuals to make it back to the States but long enough to get "refreshed." Little is said publicly about what takes place, but the army makes certain the individual soldier is provided with condoms and told about the necessity of taking appropriate prophylactic steps. This procedure was adopted after other alternatives had failed. In fact, in the initial appearances of the American Expeditionary Forces in France during the First World War, public pressure on the government to keep "our boys pure" had made the army loath to deal with prostitution publicly as a source of sexual services for soldiers overseas. The inevitable result was mass outbreaks of sexually transmitted diseases among the troops. This was only brought under control when

---

*Not all agree with this derivation of the term, but the fact that it is part of folklore indicates the widespread acceptance of the sexual needs of the military.

the military adopted the example of their French hosts in controlling prostitution and emphasizing prophylactics. In later wars in countries like Japan, Germany, the Philippines, Vietnam, Thailand, Cambodia, and other areas where American troops fought or were assigned, the American military developed favored areas for rest and relaxation, a euphemism for areas where there were available supplies of women (Bullough and Bullough 1987; Sturdevant and Stolzfus 1993). In fact, it was American troops during the Korean and Vietnam wars who laid the foundation for what became tourist prostitution in countries like Thailand, Vietnam, Cambodia, and the Philippines, although other factors also contributed to the development of prostitution as a business as well.

## Who Becomes a Prostitute?

Prostitution remains widespread not only in some of the countries where Americans had their R & R centers, but in many other areas of the world as well. Unfortunately, in many of them women can still be sold into prostitution by their families (Barry 1995). Many of those so sold are children and this is also true in those countries engaged in tourist prostitution. Involuntary prostitution is not a new problem but one recognized under the old League of Nations, which did some of its most important work in researching and publicizing involuntary prostitution (Bullough and Bullough 1987). The United Nations kept on with these investigations, but the continued existence of involuntary prostitution remains a serious problem.

Even in advanced countries and regions some kinds of prostitution are not the free choice that this chapter has described. Women might only rarely be sold into prostitution in countries such as the United States, but many individuals such as drug addicts are more or less forced to turn to prostitution to survive and maintain their habit (Graham and Wisch 1994; Miller 1995). We do not regard them as really free agents. Moreover, even in the United States, there are children who turn to the only way they know to make money, by selling themselves.

Excluding these kinds of involuntary prostitution from discussion, it appears that while various countries and regions have their own special tradition (Davis 1993), voluntary prostitution has many similarities. Until recently, scholarly interpretations of why women entered prostitution emphasized either sociological or psychological factors. Parent-Duchâtelet (1836) again set the pattern when he replaced the religious explanation (i.e., women as sinners) with a sociological one. He found that the inscribed prostitute of Paris was in her late teens or early twenties, illiterate, poor, probably illegitimate or from a broken family, and likely to have been a prostitute for only a short time and willing to leave it if something better turned up. These concepts, sometimes using other terminologies such as "dispossessed," "dislocated," and "helpless," appeared in many other studies (Parent-Duchâtelet 1913; Kneeland 1913; League of Nations 1943; Miner 1916; Sanger 1858; Woolston 1921).

Because economic causes were given so much emphasis in these early studies, a great deal of interest was focused upon the early Soviet claims that prostitution had disappeared in the new Soviet Union. The Communist explanation for this disappearance was simple, essentially that the chief cause of prostitution—capitalism—had been eliminated. The Soviet revolutionaries had abolished the more overt forms of prostitution, including brothels, and as far as the Soviet writers (and many outside observers) were concerned this eliminated prostitution (Bronner 1936). Despite such claims, however, prostitution continued to exist in the Union of Soviet Socialist Republics but in more subtle forms (Gunther 1957; Salisbury 1959). Because housing was a problem, overnight trains often served as temporary meeting places, and hotels became favored places of assignation, as did many of the workers' recreation centers on the Black Sea. In the summer months, the prostitute plied her trade in the public parks and other centers of outdoor activity. Obviously there were more factors involved in turning to prostitution than simply economic survival.

Other studies of prostitutes offered a number of common factors in the backgrounds of prostitutes besides poor living conditions and unhealthy neighborhoods. These included neglected homes, inadequate education, low levels of intelligence, ignorance of sexual matters or early coercive sex experiences (including incest), and a whole combination of personal and environmental factors. The remarkable thing about the social and economic findings, however, is not that women with such backgrounds became prostitutes, but that so many from the same background did not. To complicate the understanding of prostitution, these studies usually ignored the upper class prostitute and all prostitutes who did not have a police record or who were not widely identified as prostitutes.

Perhaps because of the contradictory conclusions derived from social and economic explanations, there came to be greater emphasis on exploring the psychopathology of the prostitute. Probably the first writer to discuss psychological aspects of prostitution was Havelock Ellis (1936), who argued that there had to be psychological factors involved because the economic motivations were insufficient to explain prostitution. Ellis also cast doubt on the thesis that the prostitute was an exceptionally libidinous woman, an explanation that also had been advanced previously.

Other psychological, but particularly psychiatric, writers expanded on this notion. Karl Abraham (1942, 361) carried Ellis's idea about the lack of sexuality in the prostitute even further by arguing, without much empirical evidence, that it was only when a woman could not enjoy the sex act with one partner that she felt compelled to change partners constantly. In other words, she became a female Don Juan. The prostitute avenged herself on every man by demonstrating that the sex act that was so important to him meant very little to her; she was thus unconsciously, or perhaps consciously, humiliating all men by having intercourse with any and all customers.

Encouraging further exploration of psychopathology was the sociologist Kingsley Davis (1937), who theorized that the prostitute, at least in Western society, was not only being paid for her sexual services, but for a loss of social standing as well. This implied that women who turned to prostitution ipso facto became social outcasts, condemned by the moral systems of modern Western societies, and an exploration of psychopathology was necessary to explain why.

Unfortunately, investigators (mostly psychoanalysts) based their findings on a few clients or occasional chance observations and generalized from their own psychoanalytic assumptions to explain all cases of prostitution. Edward Glover (1945, 4) theorized that the prostitute suffered from hostility toward her mother and acute disappointment with her father, was sexually frigid, had an unconscious hostility toward males, and exhibited lesbian "tendencies." For a time the concept of latent lesbianism was extremely popular among psychoanalytic interpreters of prostitution. Perhaps the extreme was reached by Frank Caprio and Donald Brenner (1961), who argued that prostitution was a defense mechanism against lesbian desires—desires that had forced the prostitute to turn to a pseudoheterosexuality rather than take overt homosexual action.

Conscious of the limitation of the sample size of prostitutes involved in earlier psychoanalytic studies, Harold Greenwald (1958) gathered his data from some twenty call girls, but his conclusions, based on Freudian notions, posited that the primary predisposing factor in a prostitute's background was a history of severe maternal deprivation. This loss of mother love caused the child to turn increasingly to her father for affection. Usually the father failed to give the necessary emotional support, and this led the girl to turn eventually to self-abasement in an attempt to hurt her parents. Prostitution then came to represent a search for security, for the warmth and love that the adult woman did not receive as a child.

Another psychoanalytic study, this time based on twelve cases, was that of French psychoanalyst Maryse Choisy (1961), who earlier in her career had spent a month as a waitress in a French brothel gathering material for a newspaper series (1960). She theorized that the union of the prostitute with the client was one of mutual debasement in which both partners expressed their aggression and hostility in a sadomasochistic relation, with the woman seeking revenge on her father and the man on his mother. Choisy even regarded the money that changed hands in such a relationship as a symbol of contempt.

The difficulty with her analysis is the same as that which befell the research of other psychoanalysts: she generalized on insufficient evidence in order to make her conclusions fit in with a particular theory. On what basis could Choisy, for example, argue that the exchange of money was a sign of mutual contempt, while Greenwald (1958) regarded it as a search for security, and Sandor Ferenczi (1916), an earlier psychiatric writer who touched on the topic, theorized it was closely connected with the anal desires of the child?

The obvious problem with the psychoanalytic studies such as these is that the samples are very small and the assumptions made about sexuality are difficult, if not impossible, to prove. Those who have examined prostitution from other perspectives suggest that the psychoanalysts might well have been operating under erroneous assumptions. Wardell Pomeroy (1965), for example, in a study of 175 white prostitutes found that they were not the frigid women portrayed in much of the then-current literature, but were sexually very responsive with their customers. Furthermore, this particular group of prostitutes reported that they received considerable satisfaction from being able to please their customers.

Others who have conducted large-scale research on prostitution have not always agreed. One of best of such studies was by the anonymous English author of *Women of the Streets,* edited by C. H. Rolph (1955). Her study involved a statistical sampling of 150 streetwalkers, plus a smaller number of in-depth studies. The author found that there were radical personality and status differences among streetwalkers, usually regarded as the lowest class of prostitutes. The more well-to-do street-walkers, those who worked in the better sections of London, were more likely to be charming, educated, and seemingly sympathetic, while those who worked in the poorer neighborhoods were more socially embittered and more obviously out to get the best of their customers. All of the prostitutes, the author found, were alienated from society, and despite widespread popular belief to the contrary, worked hard at their jobs. Although they were often generous, they were also, for the most part, untruthful and spiteful. None of the women felt that she worked for pleasure, and on the whole, all tended to transfer their guilt feelings to their customers: that is, the prostitute rationalized that she was earning her wages while her customer was deceiving his wife or otherwise acting in a dishonest fashion.

Those still looking for psychopathological answers have come up with ones different from earlier generations. James and Davis (1982), for example, found that unplanned events often precipitated an individual into prostitution. Obviously one event over which females lack control is child sexual abuse. Researchers J. James and J. Meyerding (1978) found in their study that prostitutes were much more likely to have suffered from abusive childhood sexual experiences such as incest and rape than did the women in their control group. They examined some eight different potentially unplanned events in the lives of both prostitutes and a control group and concluded that unplanned events or contingencies may have weakened conventional controls on behavior. R. J. Stoller (1988) probably would have agreed with such an analysis but added that erotic "aberrations" such as prostitution are the result of aesthetic choices based on nuances. Exner, Wylie, and Leura (1977), utilizing a variety of psychological tests on streetwalkers, concluded that, as a group, they were less mature and more dependent than their control group counterparts. R. Rubenstein (1980) compared thirty-two prostitutes with thirty-two nonprostitute women and reported that the prostitutes had less accessibility to an attachment figure and more separation experiences than the comparison group. Prostitutes also had earlier sexual encounters than the comparison group. Certainly, childhood experiences are important, and several studies including a Czech one (Sepova and Nedoma 1972) have emphasized the importance of the family milieu and childhood influences in the development of a prostitute. What seems to be hinted at in some studies is the importance of a girl's self-image. Many of the studies emphasize that prostitution tends to be related to low self-esteem to an even greater extent than the more violent types of delinquency (Tamura 1984).

Still, when all is said and done, no single factor stands out as causal in a woman becoming a prostitute. As researchers and therapists have continued to search for answers, multivariate explanations that de-emphasize the psychopathological aspects of prostitution and look upon it as any other occupation have found favor. As is the case with most occupations, many factors seem to be involved, and often serendipitous factors contribute. E. G. Armstrong (1981), in fact, has argued that there is no basis for a distinction between conventional behavior and that of prostitutes. Some women somehow come to be identified, either by themselves or others, as prostitutes, and as they immerse themselves in the subculture, they become more accepting of such a label (Bell 1976). Prostitution then simply becomes another occupation with its own rewards and liabilities, and prostitutes choose or accept theirs as much as anyone chooses a trade or profession (Carmen and Moody 1985; James 1976).

# Some Problems

Missing from almost all of the reported studies of prostitution is an examination of the patrons, i.e., the males who purchase prostitutes' services. Because prostitution involves at least two people—the prostitute and her customer—an explanation of prostitution should also require an examination of the patrons and their needs. Unfortunately, although it is often generalized that many customers of prostitutes in countries like the United States are individuals with special sexual needs ranging from voyeurism to sadomasochistic desires, we pay little attention to how these needs would be satisfied without the availability of prostitutes. Martha Stein (1974) broke important ground in this area but there has been little further progress. Her survey of 1,230 men who visited call girls found that, regardless of their sexual desires, the men wanted their sex needs met conveniently, professionally, and without any obligation except a monetary one. Some reported that they enjoyed at least a temporary illusion of love or friendly involvement, but it was the convenience of having someone meet their particular sexual needs that mattered the most.

This emphasizes the importance of recognizing that prostitution is unusual among the various stigmatized sexual behaviors because it is one of the few that is almost uniquely a female deviance. At least this is the claim of K. E. Rosenblum (1975), and if it is a female deviance and not an especially sexual one, it can best be understood by looking at the role and status of women both in the past and in contemporary society. This, in fact, is what feminists have been doing.

# Feminism and Prostitution

Because women have a potential for sexual enjoyment at least equal to men, we have to conclude that male prostitution serving a female clientele is not as prevalent either because it is physiologically more difficult or because its relative scarcity is tied to other norms, values, and power systems in society and to differences in the sexes. Although it is a physiological fact that the necessity of male tumescence creates problems for multiple incidents of intercourse in comparatively short periods of time, thus limiting the number of potential customers seen in any one day, most of the higher-paid female prostitutes also limit the number of clients in any one time period. Moreover, the refractory period is comparatively short in the younger male and has not proved to be an impenetrable barrier for male homosexual prostitutes. It is also important to emphasize that both male and female prostitutes engage in a variety of sexual practices that do not demand that they themselves have an orgasm. Moreover, the arousal period in women takes longer and can be prolonged until the male is able to perform once again. In effect, social factors must be involved, and in our opinion these are closely related to the traditional dominance of men over women. The various expressions of such dominance include the conceptualization of women as property and the double standard. If this hypothesis is accepted, then prostitution can be seen as a symptom of the victimization and subordination of women or, in the case of male homosexual prostitutes, the victimization of the paid partner.

Prostitution is also based on the culturally supported assumption that men enjoy, need, and desire sex more than women. Although this belief has little to do with the actual physiological responses to sex, what is accepted as social reality remains a powerful force in sexual relationships. Moreover, to perpetuate the assumption, elaborate systems of reward and punishment have been developed emphasizing the shortage—or at least giving the illusion of a shortage—of willing female sex partners. In those periods when traditional barriers broke down, contemporary male writers seemed perfectly willing to label every woman who was the least bit promiscuous as a prostitute. Women, on the other hand, by preserving their chastity, have forced men to bargain for sex either through contractual arrangements such as marriage or concubinage, or on a direct fee-for-service basis. Although there have been periods in the past when there were either long-term or short-term shortages of women, there were also shortages socially created by polygamy and preference for male children (which might have increased female mortality). It was the real or believed shortage that led church fathers such as Saint Augustine to justify prostitution as essential for societal survival (Bullough and Bullough 1987). To put it bluntly, it was a man-made world, and the purpose of women was to serve the male as sexual partner, wife, and mother. Laws were passed that brought women under the control of a man—father, husband, brother, or other male. Woman's subordination in the past was compounded by lack of educational opportunities, the denial of political power, and the emphasis on women's biological inferiority. This coincided with her mission to be mother, wife, and "preserver" of morality (Bullough 1964; Bullough and Bullough 1978; Bullough and Bullough 1987).

The emergence of feminist scholarship has given rise to new views of prostitution. What the feminist approach attempts to do is to look at the subject from the woman's point of view, rather than the more traditional one that, perhaps unconsciously, was really a male viewpoint. Women in the past had few opportunities for employment outside the family setting, and prostitution was one of the major occupations available (Bullough, Shelton and Slavin 1988; Finnegan 1979; Gibson 1986; S. Pomeroy 1975; Rosen 1982; Rossiaud 1988). Many of the prostitutes in the past were slaves, including many who were sold into prostitution by their families as young women. Still others, faced with hungry infants or their own starvation, found few other viable alternatives.

Women in many parts of the world still face little choice, and it is the issue of choice that concerns feminists. There is, however, no single feminist interpretation because woman's role and place in society can be interpreted from many diverse points of view, and men can also learn to use a feminist approach. Some feminists, such as Andrea Dworkin (1987), would deny that prostitution, no matter how defined, could be accepted as a free choice by any woman. Dworkin, however, would claim the same lack of freedom for any kind of heterosexual intercourse, even that which takes place within the marriage relationship. Certainly, in the past, Dworkin's argument had greater truth than today, because there was often little difference between the sexual obligation of a wife and the selling of services by a prostitute; by law a woman was required to provide sexual services to her husband whether she wanted to or not, and in return for this she received support, financial and otherwise. The prostitute simply demanded cash up front (Bullough and Bullough 1987).

Prostitution, from this point of view, represents an extreme case of sexual stratification in which the commodization of female sexuality contributes to the devaluation and objectification of women (Davis and Stasz 1990; Heyl 1979). The problem then is to empower women and give them greater free choice. The question becomes "What is free choice?"

The issue today is complicated by the fact that prostitutes themselves are involved in the debate and their view is obviously a feminist one, but one radically different from Dworkin's. Only rarely in the past has there been a prostitute writing about what it means to be a prostitute or what is involved in being one. Unfortunately, few have written scholarly articles on the topic, although the number of books by and about prostitutes are increasing, with many emphasizing their acceptance of a life as a sex worker.

Still another feminist view is that of Kathleen Barry, who has done as much as any woman in today's world to bring attention to the lack of choice facing many women who are prostitutes. She classifies involuntary prostitution as female sexual slavery whether it be legalized, regulated, or tolerated (Barry 1979). Involuntary prostitution is defined by Barry as being present in all situations where women or girls cannot change the immediate conditions of their existence; where, regardless of how they got into those conditions, they cannot get out; and where they are subject to sexual violence and exploitation. On this issue she is in agreement with most of the prostitutes we have known and interviewed, and in this respect it represents a core of the feminist viewpoint. Although Barry would like to see prostitution disappear, and hopes it will as women gain more power, she recognizes that it might not, at least in the easily foreseeable future. Her solution, as is ours, is to decriminalize prostitution. She argues that it is only under decriminalization that prostitutes who choose to do so can leave the life without stigma. Barry compares leaving prostitution in this way to the wife who leaves a marriage through divorce.

Decriminalization is also accepted as a goal by most of the organized prostitute groups. The problem comes when women do not have a choice or when they live in a culture that has values different from our own and where their choices are more limited. Traditionally, for example, in Chinese culture, the purchase of women for prostitution was not qualitatively different from the general trade in women that existed in China.

> Among all classes, females were viewed as more disposable than males. Were they not, after all, destined to leave the family hearth when their childhood years were over, belonging no longer to their natal family but to a stranger's

family instead? In times of economic strife, hard-pressed parents sought ways to hasten the departure of females, and a virtual marketing of women developed. Throughout Chinese history, females were limited, restricted and reduced to property. They were purchased as wives and concubines, servants and slaves—and as prostitutes. (Gronewald 1981, 3)

Unfortunately such attitudes toward women are not simply historical, but continue to exist. This helps explain the high rate of prostitution in Thailand, which has been called the "prostitution capital of the world" (Rhodes and Zachman 1991). In a large number of countries where the young are not well protected, many of the prostitutes are little more than children, and the current practice not much different from traditional Chinese ones.

Barry recognizes this problem, and one result of her efforts has been the formation of an international network of feminists against sexual slavery (Barry, Bunch and Castley 1985). The network attempts to combat the involuntary exploitation of women in prostitution everywhere (Barry 1995), removing women from the victim mode and allowing them greater choice.

This is also the main political agenda of prostitutes who have formed organizations for themselves. The group COYOTE (Call Off Your Old Tired Ethics) and similar groups would like to play down the term "prostitution" and broaden the scope of their trade by using the term "Women in the Sex Industry" (Delacoste and Alexander 1988). This term would apply to exotic dancers, actresses in X-rated movies, nude models, those who give erotic massages, telephone sex operators, and a whole host of people (including men) who sell sex. Some of this inclusion is a result of organizational attempts to gain more power, but at the same time it represents a recognition by sex workers of their potential sisters in the feminist movement. Moreover, in the past, most such workers would have been identified as prostitutes. The new inclusive designation emphasizes choice and is an effort toward self-definition. In this sense the organization of the prostitutes is as much a symbolic breakthrough for prostitutes as the "Stonewall Riots" were to the gays and lesbians. The riots resulted in official public notice of what was in fact happening in the gay and lesbian community, namely, that the issues were being defined and the solutions were being advanced by gays and lesbians themselves. In other words, changes were not being suggested or imposed by outsiders but came from within the community itself.

Because sex workers suffer much from public stigmatization of their work, the ability to define what they will and will not do becomes all-important in the path to self-definition and empowerment. This is ultimately what most of the feminists and the authors of this chapter want and desire. COYOTE and other organized groups of prostitutes, however, face a major difficulty in carrying out their political goals aimed at decriminalization, namely, the traditional barriers that exist between the well-educated and upper-level prostitutes (who dominate COYOTE and similar groups) and the low-level streetwalker. Prostitution has always been highly stratified and this stratification is a significant barrier to communication. The organized feminist allies of the prostitutes face this same problem in selling their agenda to women in general because many of the Dworkin-type feminists would deny that prostitutes are feminists. Still, the appearance of organizations and the growth of analytical self-studies by the sex workers give a new dimension to scholarship. Symbolic of this is the International Conference on Prostitution held in 1997 in Northridge (California) in which researchers, feminists, and sex workers came together for the first time, of which one of the results is this book. For perhaps the first time in history there are real opportunities to do in-depth studies of sex workers as they consciously open their ranks to researchers. Since the sex worker title embraces males as well as females, it even becomes possible to extend the studies beyond the sexual boundaries and look at males and females together, highlighting differences and similarities. This has not yet occurred.

One other factor, however, has to be considered in any discussion of prostitution, namely, AIDS. The AIDS debate currently dominates much of the discourse on prostitution, just as the topic of sexually transmitted diseases dominated the discussion of prostitution in the past (Bullough and Bullough 1987). We know from AIDS research that those women who feel they have a choice in what they are doing feel much more in control of their lives and are much more likely to use prophylactics. It is these women who insist on using condoms and who have challenged the assumption that prostitutes are among the main carriers of AIDS. Undoubtedly some prostitutes are carriers, but they need not be, and most of the hundreds of articles about AIDS and prostitution point this out (Chickwem 1987; Day 1988; Khabbaz et al. 1990; Ngugi 1988; Richardson 1988). It is the very lack of empowerment and choice for sex workers that has led to the characterization of Thailand, for example, as a nation committing suicide by HIV infection (Rhodes and Zachman 1991). A major key to controlling the transmission of AIDS is the empowerment of the sex worker, and this can best be accomplished by providing women with more choices, while at the same time recognizing those in the sex industry as simply another category of workers with special problems and needs. At least this seems to be what much of the current research is emphasizing, and many feminists and sex workers agree on this issue.

# Conclusion

Research into prostitution has changed over the past decades, more so than at any time in the past. We now know more about the extent of prostitution and its changing nature in the West and have a better grasp of the reasons some people enter the sex industry. More important, however, with the growth of the prostitute organizations, we have easier access to research subjects. Like research into homosexuality and lesbianism as well as transgender behavior, the existence of a pool of volunteers from the community willing to contribute to research projects both by themselves and by others has greatly added to our knowledge about these areas and offers us greater opportunity for research. The papers in this book represent a sampling of current research and thinking about prostitution.

# References

Abraham, K. 1942. Manifestation of the female castration complex. *Selected Papers*. Translated by D. Bryan and A. Strachey. London: Hogarth Press.

Armstrong, E. G. 1981. The sociology of prostitution. *Sociological Spectrum* 1(1): 91–102.

Baker, C. P. 1995. Child chattel lure tourists for sex. *Insight on the News* 11(11): 11.

Barry, K. 1979. *Female Sexual Slavery*. New York: Prentice-Hall.

———. 1995. *The Prostitution of Sexuality: The Global Exploitation of Women*. New York: New York University Press.

Barry, K., C. Bunch, and S. Castley. 1984. *International Feminism: Networking against Female Sexual Slavery*. New York: Distributed by International Women's Tribune Center.

Bell, R. R. 1976. *Social Deviance: A Substantive Analysis*. Chicago: Dorsey.

Bloch, I. 1912. *Die Prostitution*. 2 vols. Berlin: L. Marcus.

Boling, D. A. 1995. Mass rape, enforced prostitution, and the Japanese Imperial Army. *Columbia Journal of Transnational Law* 32(3): 533 ff.

Bronner, V. 1936. *La lutte contre la prostitution in URSS*. Moscow: n.p.

Bullough, V. L. 1964. *A History of Prostitution*. New York: Basic Books.

———. 1965. Problems and methods for research in prostitution and the behavioral sciences. *Journal of the History of the Behavioral Sciences* 1: 244–52.

———. 1994. *Science and the Bedroom: A History of Sex Research*. New York: Basic Books.

Bullough, V. L., and B. Bullough. 1978. *Illustrated History of Prostitution*. New York: Crown.

———. 1987. *Women and Prostitution*. Amherst, N.Y.: Prometheus Books.

Bullough, V. L., B. Elcano, M. Deacon, and B. Bullough. 1977. *A Bibliography of Prostitution*. New York: Garland.

Bullough, V. L., and L. Sentz. 1992. *Prostitution: A Guide to Sources 1970–1990*. New York: Garland.

Bullough, V. L., B. Shelton, and S. Slavin. 1988. *The Subordinated Sex*. Athens: University of Georgia.

Caprio, F., and D. Brenner. 1961. *Sexual Behavior: Psycho-Legal Aspects*. New York: Citadel Press.

Carmen, A., and H. Moody. 1985. *Working Women: The Subterranean World of Street Prostitution*. New York: Harper and Row.

Chickwem, J. O., et al. 1988. Impact of health education on prostitutes' awareness and attitudes to acquired immune deficiency syndrome. *Public Health* 102(5): 439–45.

Choisy, M. 1960. *A Month among the Girls.* New York: Pyramid Books.

———. 1961. *Psychoanalysis of the Prostitute.* New York: Philosophical Library.

Davis, K. 1937. The sociology of prostitution. *American Sociological Review* 2: 25–32.

Davis, N. 1993. *Prostitution: An International Handbook on Trends, Problems, and Policies.* Westport, Conn.: Greenwood Press.

Davis, N. J., and C. Stasz. 1990. *Social Control of Deviance: A Critical Perspective.* New York: McGraw-Hill.

Day, S. 1988. Prostitute women and AIDS: Anthropology. *AIDS* 260: 421–28.

Dworkin, A. 1987. *Intercourse.* New York: Free Press.

*The Economist.* 1996. Asia—Child prostitution in Cambodia. 338: 59.

Ellis, H. 1936. Sex in relation to society. In *Studies in the Psychology of Sex.* 7 vols. New York: Random House.

Ferenczi, S. 1916. *Contributions to Psychoanalysis.* Boston: Richard G. Badger.

Finnegan, F. 1979. *Poverty and Prostitution: A Study of Victorian Prostitutes in York.* New York: Cambridge University Press.

Gibson, M. 1986. *Prostitution and the State in Italy: 1860–1915.* New Brunswick, N.J.: Rutgers.

Gilfoyle, T. J. 1992. *The City of Eros: New York City, Prostitution, and the Commercialization of Sex, 1790–1920.* New York: W. W. Norton.

Glover, E. 1945. *The Psycho-Pathology of Prostitution.* London: Hogarth Press.

Graham, N., and E. D. Wisch. 1994. Drug use among female arrestees: Onset, patterns, and relationship to prostitution. *Journal of Drug Issues* 24(1–2): 315 ff.

Greenwald, H. 1958. *The Call Girl: A Social and Psychoanalytic Study.* New York: Ballantine Books.

Gronewald, S. 1982. Beautiful merchandise: Prostitution in China 1860–1936. *Women and History* 1: 1–114.

Gunther, J. 1957. *Inside Russia Today.* New York: Harper.

Heyl, B. S. 1979. Prostitution: An extreme case of sexual stratification. In *Criminology of Deviant Women,* edited by F. Adler and R. J. Simon. Boston: Houghton-Mifflin.

Hicks, G., and M. Shapiro. 1995. *The Comfort Women: Japan's Brutal Regime of Enforce Prostitution in the Second World War.* New York: n.d.

Hodgson, D. 1994. Sex tourism and child prostitution in Asia: Legal responses and strategies. *Melbourne University Law Review* 19(3): 512 ff.

James, J. 1976. Motivations for entrance into prostitution. In *Female Offender,* edited by L. Crites. Lexington, Mass.: D.C. Heath.

James, J., and N. J. Davis. 1982. Contingencies in female sexual role deviance: The case of prostitution. *Human Organization* 41(4): 345–50.

James, J., and J. Meyerding. 1978. Early sexual experience as a factor in prostitution. *Archives of Sexual Behavior* 7(10): 31–42.

Johannes Teutonicus. 1605. *Glossa ordinaria* to the *Decretum,* in the version revised by Bartholomaeus Brixiensis (d. 1258). Venice: Apud Iuntas. D. 34. c. 16.

Khabbaz, R. F., et al. 1990. Seroprevalence and risk factors for HTLV–I/H infection among female prostitutes in the United States. *JAMA* 263: 60–64.

Kinsey, A. C., W. B. Pomeroy, and C. E. Martin. 1948. *Sexual Behavior in the Human Male.* Philadelphia: W. B. Saunders.

Kneeland, George J. 1913. *Commercialized Prostitution in New York City.* New York: Century Company.

Laumann, E. O., J. H. Gagnon, R. T. Michael, and S. Michaels. 1994. *The Social Organization of Sexuality.* Chicago: University of Chicago Press.

League of Nations. 1943. *Prevention of Prostitution.* C.26.M.26.1943.IV:25–32.

Levan, P. D. 1994. Curtailing Thailand's child prostitution through an international conscience. *American University Journal of International Law and Policy* 9(3): 869 ff.

Maardh, P. A. 1996. Sex tourism, migratory prostitution and travel sex. *Journal of Obstetrics and Gynecology* 14(supp. 2): S76.

Mayhew, H. 1861–62. *London Labour and the London Poor,* 4 vols. London: Griffin, Bohn.

Michael, R. T., J. H. Gagnon, E. O. Laumann, and G. Kolata. 1994. *Sex in America: A Definitive Survey.* Boston: Little, Brown.

Miller, J. 1995. Gender and power on the streets: Street prostitution in the era of crack cocaine. *Journal of Contemporary Ethnology* 23(4): 427 ff.

Miner, M. E. 1916. *Slavery of Prostitution.* New York: Century.

Ngugi, E. N. 1988. Prevention of transmission of human immunodeficiency virus in Africa: Effectiveness of condom protection and health education among prostitutes. *Lancet* 1(8616): 887–90.

Nyland, B. 1995. Child prostitution and the new Australian legislation on paedophiles in Asia. *Journal of Contemporary Asia* 25: 546 ff.

Parent-Duchâtelet, A. J. B. 1836; reprint, 1937. *De la prostitution dans la ville de Paris.* 2 vols. Paris: J. B. Bailliére.

Pomeroy, S. 1975. *Goddesses, Whores, Wives and Slaves: Women in Classical Antiquity.* New York: Schoken.

Pomeroy, W. B. 1965. Some aspects of prostitution. *Journal of Sex Research* 1(2): 177–87.

Reitman, B. L. 1931. *The Second Oldest Profession.* New York: Vanguard Press.

Rhodes, R., and P. Zachman. 1991. Death in the candy store. *Rolling Stone* 618: 62–71.

Richardson, D. 1988. *Women and AIDS.* New York: Methuen, 1988.

Rolph, C. H., ed. 1955. *Women of the Streets.* London: Seeker and Warburg.

Rosen, R. 1982. *The Lost Sisterhood: Prostitution in America 1900–1918.* Baltimore: Johns Hopkins University Press.

Rosenblum, K. E. 1975. Female deviance and the female sex role: A preliminary investigation. *British Journal of Sociology* 16(2): 169–85.

Rossiaud, J. 1988. *Medieval Prostitution,* translated by L. G. Cochrane. Oxford: Blackwell.

Rubinstein, R. 1980. Female prostitution: Relationship of early separation and sexual experiences. Ph.D. diss. Los Angeles, California School of Professional Psychology.

Ryan, M. 1839. *Prostitution in London with a Comparative View of That in Paris and New York.* London: H. Bailliére.

Salisbury, H. 1959. *New York Times,* September 10.

Sanger, W. 1858. *The History of Prostitution.* New York: Harper and Brothers.

Sipova, I., and K. Nedoma. 1972. Family setting and childhood in socially and sexually depraved women. *Ceskosolvenska-psychiatrie* 68(3): 150–53 (English abstract).

Smolenski, C. 1995. Sex tourism and the sexual exploitation of children: The fight to end child prostitution. *Christian Century* 112(33): 1079 ff.

Stein, M. 1974. *Lovers, Friends, Slaves: Nine Male Sexual Types: Their Psycho-Sexual Trans-actions with Call-Girls.* New York: G. Putnam.

Stoller, R. J. 1988. Aesthetik der erotik. *Zeitschrift für Sexualforschung* 1(4): 351–64.

Sturdivant, S. P., and B. Stoltzfus. 1993. *Let the Good Times Roll: Prostitution and the U.S. Military in Asia.*

Tamura, M. 1984. A pattern analysis of delinquent gangs: I. On the traits of members' personality. *Reports of the National Research Institute of Police Science* 25(1): 34–41.

Wardlaw, R. 1843. *Lectures on Magdelenism.* New York: J. S. Redfield.

Woolston, H. W. 1921. *Prostitution in the United States.* New York: Century.

# 1

# HISTORY, ANTHROPOLOGY, AND SOME RECOMMENDATIONS FOR PROSTITUTES BY "ONE WHO KNOWS"

## Introduction

A disproportionate number of studies of sex workers have had a historical orientation. One reason for this is that many of those interested in changing the laws about prostitution, whether for greater or lesser freedom of sex workers, included much history to justify their recommendations. Not so surprisingly, most (but not quite all) of these early studies were by men who tended to approach the subject of female prostitution (they generally ignored male prostitution) with what can only be called a kind of masculine blindness. The few women who did write about it seemed for the most part to be concerned about the dangers unbridled sexuality had for society, although some of them also expressed sympathy for the prostitute as victim. Many of these female researchers (as well as many of the men) had reservations about female sexuality itself, and it was not until the feminists of the last part of this century could come to terms with female sexuality that they could look at prostitution in a light quite different from most of the researchers of the past, males as well as females.

One of the richest sources of data is, as indicated earlier, the historical records, and looking at prostitution in Spain, India, United States, and France, four women researchers, Elizabeth Clement, Mary Elizabeth Perry, Kathryn Norberg, and Judy Whitehead, open up new vistas about prostitution. The feminist perspective, that is, looking at women as important individuals in their own right, is not limited to those who are females themselves. Men have also attempted to adopt this same perspective and have tried to reorient their viewpoint either in collaboration with women (as the editors of this book have done) or by themselves. This appears in a brief personal account by Wan Yan Hai of interaction with prostitutes in China today, a country struggling to come to terms with the past official denial under Mao of the existence of prostitution and to the reality of prostitution in contemporary China.

No examination of prostitution would be complete without the input of a philosopher. Timothy Madigan examines Immanuel Kant and the contradictions in his views on prostitution. One the problems is societal stigmatization of the prostitute. Picking up on this are two brief summaries on the problems by a well-known sex worker, Annie Sprinkle, who gives forty reasons why whores are her heroes and a twelve-step program for overcoming worker burn-out for sex workers.

# Prostitution and Community in Turn-of-the-Century New York City

## Elizabeth Clement

In early-twentieth-century New York, prostitution made good economic sense for many women. Working women's wages remained extremely low, even by working-class standards, and unemployment often cast women or their family members out of work. Prostitution could provide a way to support families in an uncertain and often brutal economy. And, for a lucky few who could save their wages, prostitution made excellent business sense. As an undercover investigator reported of a woman he met, "she would like to open up a place to do business, but she has no money, she said to us 'With the help of God I think we should make a success by opening a whore house.' "[1] Many women shared her opinion, viewing prostitution as a way to provide for themselves and their families.

This chapter is about the women who chose this path and how they negotiated in a difficult marketplace characterized by profound changes in the social organization, culture, and economics of prostitution between the turn of the century and World War I. I argue that this period witnessed the development of two divergent strands of prostitution. The decline of the brothel led one group of women to explore the commercial possibilities that nonbrothel prostitution in residential working-class neighborhoods offered. Keeping an unprecedented proportion of their wages, these young women began to participate openly in and help develop small commercial networks. At the same time, clandestine prostitutes went another direction. Taking advantage of the anonymity of the city, they practiced prostitution in secret. These women chose to maintain the appearance of sexual morality that enabled them to continue to participate in the moral mainstream of working-class life.

This paper explores the development of these two kinds of prostitution and examines the ways in which women made difficult choices about money,

47

commercialism, and morality. In essence, some women chose to emphasize economic considerations in their decision making, while others favored respectability and reputation. Prostitution at the turn of the century in New York City underwent enormous changes that gave women more autonomy in their decisions and more freedom to exchange sex for money if they chose to do so. In this essay, I will briefly describe these changes in the structure of prostitution and then discuss the way in which women reshaped prostitution and its practices to meet their individual needs.

Throughout most of the nineteenth century, brothels dominated the practice of prostitution in New York City. The most visible and most organized form of prostitution, brothels were the primary site where men could buy and women could sell sex. Although brothels could provide unique economic opportunities for women at the turn of the century, they remained extremely exploitative and occasionally dangerous places for women to work. A few women did save the money they made, but most did not enjoy the profits that their work generated. The brothels' rules about division of payments deprived women of a significant portion of their earnings. All brothels required that women give to the madam half of all money made on tricks. Prostitutes also paid exorbitant prices for room and board and for required medical treatments. When combined, these expenses greatly reduced the remuneration of individual women.

Finally, most brothels, by relying largely on a brass or paper-check system, deliberately limited women's access to cash. Many prostitutes never even handled the money that men paid for their services. Instead, they received a check for each trick. At the end of the week, the madam collected the checks and tallied each woman's earnings against her expenditures. Some women even ended the week in debt to the house. This practice made prostitutes in brothels a dependent population, existing largely in a credit economy, with no real control over their own profits.[2]

On the other hand, brothel prostitution did offer women protection from police harassment and from violent johns. In addition, brothels served as a career path for a few women who could, against the odds, save enough money to open houses of their own. One young woman summed up the benefits and drawbacks of brothel life to an investigator, explaining that "she left the parlor house because there was no money in it, and that girls who were afraid to hustle on the street stayed there" (Investigative Reports 1905–1910). As this woman indicates, brothels provided some safety for women even while they exploited them. Most prostitutes did not become madams because they couldn't save the necessary money. However, the very existence of such a career path for women remained important. The goal of becoming a madam, and the visibility of the few women who did succeed, provided a pattern for other women to follow when the brothels disappeared in the first years of the new century.

Historian Timothy Gilfoyle, in his book *City of Eros,* has argued that brothels failed because the increasing industrialization of New York City's economy made it more profitable for landlords to rent to light industry than to houses of ill repute. As the entertainment districts of New York converted over to industrial areas, brothel owners faced rising rents and decreasing patronage. New York's vibrant entertainment districts gave way to light industry, and the brothels faltered (Gilfoyle 1992).

I do not dispute Gilfoyle's findings. Instead, I seek to illuminate how women responded to the collapse of brothel prostitution, and what factors shaped the choices they made. Perhaps the most important development for women came, ironically, in the form of a new tax law aimed at reducing drinking on the Christian Sabbath. Passed in 1896, the Raines Law attempted to discourage drinking on Sundays by limiting the sale of liquor to hotels that possessed at least ten beds. As with many temperance reforms, the law had unintended consequences. In response to its passage, most saloonkeepers, rather than close on Sundays, divided up their back rooms with partitions, put in ten beds, and began renting them out by the trick to prostitutes and their customers. The Raines Law not only failed to put a dent in the numbers of those who imbibed on Sundays, it but led to a rapid expansion and diffusion of prostitution.[3] These new hotels combined the benefits of brothels with a new freedom that allowed many young women to become independent proprietors in their own right.

Selling sex out of these saloons, prostitutes kept a much greater proportion of their wages than they had previously and began to establish themselves as active participants in the new and decentralized economy of pleasure, vice, and entertainment. Raines Law hotels spread very rapidly. In 1900 they made up a significant proportion of the places in which prostitution was practiced, by 1907 they dominated the trade, and by 1910 brothels had virtually disappeared. Thus, within little more than a decade, shifting land-use patterns, the Raines Law, and most importantly, saloon owners' and prostitutes' response to that law transformed the practice of prostitution in New York City. Diffused throughout the city, prostitution became the province of small proprietors, individual young women or groups of two or three who sold their sexual services from tenements, barrooms, and furnished rooming houses.

As young women freed themselves from brothels, they embarked on careers as business people. Choosing to prostitute out of the new Raines Law hotels, these women established their own businesses, developed client bases, entered into partnership with other local proprietors, and helped each other handle difficult patrons. In essence, they helped create small-scale commercial communities that revolved around the sale of drinks, company, and sex to neighborhood clients. Always used in a multiplicity of ways, New York City's tenements became the primary sites of sexual commerce.

A court transcript from the trial of a Raines Law hotel proprietor in

Brooklyn provides one of the few surviving descriptions of the atmosphere of these establishments. The investigator chronicles what he saw while sitting in the bar. The testimony shows the remarkable extent to which prostitution permeated local bar sociability and the ways in which prostitutes and proprietors worked together to give local men the pleasure and entertainment they wanted. As the investigator reported:

> Deponent observed automatic piano playing in adjoining room, to the music of which two men and two women were dancing in a manner suggestive of sexual intercourse. During the dance the dancers came to a full stop and moved their bodies in a manner suggestive of sexual intercourse. Deponent said to the said Jim Proprietor, while the dance was going, "That is some dance." The said Jim Proprietor replied, "Yes." Deponent also saw an intoxicated man accompanied by a woman on said premises moving to a stairway which led to upper floors. The said Jim Proprietor called out, "Hey, Sam, get a room ready." In a short time the unknown woman returned to the room where the deponent sat, her hair disheveled, and said to the said Jim Proprietor, "I had a hell of a time with him, no more drunken men for me." . . . The unknown woman said to the unknown man, "I don't believe you have a prick," at the same time putting her hand on the private parts of the unknown man's body. The unknown man then said to the said Jim Proprietor who was present, "Hey, Jim, how about it, I haven't got the price of a room." The said Jim Proprietor said, "Giver her a standup—in the corner," indicating a part of the said enclosure. (IR 1915)

This testimony evokes the casual, neighborhood feel of these hotels. Unlike the formal atmosphere of the brothels, these hotels functioned as bars, catering to prostitutes who knew each other and who knew their usual clients. Prostitutes danced and joked with their clients, and they used the time to arouse the men sexually. This stands in sharp contrast to brothel practices, in which madams severely limited the contact between prostitutes and johns, usually to five or ten minutes for sexual intercourse. In this bar, sexual intercourse did not appear to take much more time than that, but the prostitutes had extended social contact with the johns before they went to their rooms.

This scene also indicates the extent to which proprietors made business decisions that, although obviously cutting into their profit margin, helped the neighborhood patrons and prostitutes get what they wanted. In this case, the proprietor waived his room rents and allowed a customer to have a "standup." Clearly, Jim made enough money from the drinks he sold and the other patrons renting rooms that he could afford to allow a steady customer a break now and then. By choosing to forego the bed rent, this proprietor made his customer feel more like a friend. Perhaps this largess increased the possibility that the man would return and spend more of his liquor money in Jim's bar.

In addition, cutting the john a break pleased the prostitute because it insured that she would make her fee, even if it she had to stand up in the hallway to do it. Ultimately Jim's decision made economic sense because prostitution brought him more money through drink sales than it did through bed rents. However, the "standup" was not simply about economics. It also revealed the ways in which prostitutes and proprietors relied on each other. It was their alliances and, in fact, their friendships that made these bars the kind of social space they were. The prostitute who serviced the drunken man demonstrated this best when she complained to Jim about how much she disliked her last trick. Disheveled, tired, and annoyed, she treated Jim like a confidante who could provide a sympathetic audience to a friend fed up with the more upsetting aspects of her job.

The investigator's testimony about events later on in the same evening reinforces the sense of these "hotels" as places where prostitutes and proprietors cooperated to make money and keep patrons happy. The investigator continued:

> About this time deponent observed an unknown man who appeared to be a deaf and dumb mute seated at a table with an unknown woman; the said unknown mute was making motions with his hands to the said unknown woman, whereupon Joseph F. Christie said to the said Jim Proprietor, "the deaf and dumb mute is having a tough time over there making her understand him." The said Jim Proprietor then called out in a loud voice to an unknown woman, "Florence, go over there and help May get him." The unknown woman addressed as Florence left the table where she was seated and sat at the table at which the unknown woman known as May and the deaf and dumb mute sat. About this time deponent observed an unknown woman seated at a table who called out in a loud voice, "Here is the way you say F—," at the same time indicating the deaf and dumb language with her fingers. Shortly thereafter deponent heard the said Joseph F. Christie say to the said Jim Proprietor, "Where did the dummie and the woman go?" and heard the said Jim Proprietor say to the said Joseph Christie, "Oh, she got him, they went upstairs; that damn fool is a married man and lives around the corner." (IR 1915)

Clearly, Jim and the prostitutes working out of his bar knew their regular clients well and worked together to meet their needs and turn a profit. Jim knew both the deaf mute and his family situation. A frequent patron of the bar, the deaf mute had obviously come there for sex before. One of the prostitutes had picked up enough American Sign Language slang to communicate the basic information necessary to conduct her business. Perhaps she had had him as a client in the past, or perhaps she simply learned Sign from previous contacts with him in the neighborhood. What is crucial, however, was that she and Jim cooperated with each other and with the other prostitute to "get him" as a client for the bar.

As this example makes clear, prostitution followed a much looser, more neighborhood-based format in the Raines Law hotels. Using their experience in brothels as a pattern, prostitutes began to establish the conditions under which they liked to work, at the same time eliminating practices they despised. Viewing the prostitutes as a good draw for patrons, proprietors came to easy agreements with the women. After all, their primary desire when they established a "hotel" was to keep selling liquor, not to open a serious sideline business in prostitution. As a result, prostitutes met little resistance from Raines Law hotel owners over how prostitution should be practiced or who should benefit from the profits.

Taking advantage of the egalitarian attitudes of saloon owners, prostitutes bargained small proprietor to small proprietor, and they kept all the money they made from tricks. In addition, they often got a cut of the proprietors' profits on bed rents and liquor sold. In one fairly typical description, the investigator reported that "the prostitutes consist of girls having the privilege of regular soliciting places and street walkers. There are no residents. . . . The man accompanying the disorderly woman pays $2 for the use of the room when he registers as man and wife. In addition he pays the woman. . . . The woman . . . get[s] a percentage of the $2 paid for the room. They also receive a percentage for the amount of drinks which the man is induced to buy" (Investigative Reports 1905–1910).

Understandably, prostitutes working out of Raines Law hotels reaped impressive profits. One investigator reported of the Sans Souci that "the women in this place consider $30 a fair night's work and say that they average from five to ten men every evening" (Investigative Reports 1905–1910). At a time when a working woman's salary in New York State averaged a little over six dollars a week, prostitutes working out of the hotels made far more money than they ever could in any kind of legitimate employment.[4] They also kept far more than any brothel prostitute would see of her earnings.

Prostitutes did like some aspects of brothel prostitution, namely, its relative safety, and they recreated similar relationships with the proprietors of the Raines Law hotels. One investigator summed up the standard agreement concisely when he commented that "proprietor goes bail for the girls" (Wald Papers). Thus, given the extra profits they could retain, and the relative safety they enjoyed, it is not surprising that women left brothels in droves. The presence of Raines Laws hotels provided brothels with visible competition and served to scatter the practice of prostitution into smaller and smaller establishments throughout New York City's working-class neighborhoods.

Raines Law hotels opened up opportunities for other establishments to cater to prostitutes and their clients. As women increasingly chose to work in more casual, less supervised, coercive, or exploitative conditions, prostitution diffused rapidly through the social and commercial space of working-class New York neighborhoods. Candy stores and cigar stores, for example, became important places where prostitutes made contacts with men. These stores already provided essential social space for working-class neighborhoods. The owners of these establishments, seeing profits, readily consented to this trade.

The use of candy stores by prostitutes indicated how integrated they were into other respectable neighborhood institutions. Even more than Raines Law hotels, these stores catered to a very local clientele. Few outsiders ever suspected how diversified their business had become. When prostitution occurred in these stores, the prostitutes usually came to agreements with their owners similar to those they made with Raines Law hotel proprietors. In one description of a candy store, an investigator stated that "$2 [is] the rate for [a] girl, and girls get a percentage on candy sold" (Investigative Reports 1905–1910). Just as prostitutes often got a cut of the alcohol sold in the Raines Law hotels, women working out of candy stores, when they increased business or helped boys and men spend their money, sometimes shared the profits of sales with proprietors.

Like Raines Law hotels, candy and cigar stores functioned within commercial frameworks. The most extreme example of the integration of prostitution into working-class communities, however, occurred when prostitutes worked out of apartments in New York's working-class tenements. Although the city outlawed soliciting and "disorderly" behavior in its rental housing, many women still succeeded in selling sex out of their homes. Working alone or in groups of twos and threes, these women engaged in prostitution amid the clamor of working-class family and neighborhood life.

Examples of tenement prostitution indicate how multi-use most tenements were. Investigators reported prostitutes in buildings that contained a mix of other businesses as well as family and single dwellings. For example, an investigator described one tenement house as "a two story house, on the corner of the house is a grocery store, and on the Oak Street side is a vegetable store and the upper floor is occupied by prostitutes. I saw seven women in short dresses" (Precinct 5—James Slip). Other investigators reported similar mixtures of businesses, vice establishments, and family dwellings. Another man reported "2 story, butcher store; 2 families upstairs; no children; 2 girls at door soliciting" and "4 story and store, saloon; 22 families, 26 children. Prostitutes in lower hall soliciting man. In back room of saloon white and colored men getting policy slip from party writing same" (Precinct 5—James Street).

Many of the women who worked out of these crowded tenements seemed unconcerned about being identified as prostitutes by their neighbors. Women solicited from the side doors and main entrances of tenements, as well as the streets in front of them (Precinct 5—James Slip).[5] However, the relative visibility and openness of this sort of prostitution does not mean that these women did not care about their neighborhoods. In fact, prostitutes functioned as integral parts of the community, relying, as other women did, on networks of friendship to sustain them.

One investigator, for example, reported with some distaste that the disord. women have a new scheme to hide themselves from the police. Every girl has a pimp, so-called husband, and as soon as they move in a house they get acquainted with their neighbors and generally every tenant has children. Finally they take in a child to play with. If a stranger comes in and they don't want to be known as disorder. women they have the child on the arm and the stranger thinks that she is a good woman and . . . if one of their friends comes they give the child back to the parents. (Precinct 11—104 Bowery)

This strategy implies a high level of toleration among the neighboring families. Not only did these families not turn prostitutes in, but they actively participated in protecting the prostitutes who lived in their building. In addition, they did not seem to worry that associating with prostitutes might have detrimental effects on their children. Lending their children to prostitutes for the afternoon, the women in tenements perhaps enjoyed a welcome relief from some of their domestic responsibilities. Rather than trying to expel the prostitutes in their midst, neighbors instead integrated them into networks of working-class female friendship and support.

Many prostitutes in the tenements achieved this acceptance because families knew them before they embarked on a career of prostitution. On Mott Street a neighborhood woman solicited an investigator and brought him to her apartment. Visibly pregnant, she had also had two young sons, one of whom was asleep on the bed. According to the investigator, "she asked me for ten cents and said: 'Come in, I will give you a fuck for the luck of ten cents as you are a nice fellow.' " "She was about 38 years of age," he explained, and "after entering the said room she threw herself on the bed beside the young boy and exposed her person to me for the purpose of prostitution" (Precinct 6). The woman explained that her husband had gone out of the city to look for work and did not support her and her children.

In this case, the prostitute stated explicitly that she engaged in the trade because her husband had left and she needed to care for herself and her children. Her low price indicates that her foray into prostitution was relatively casual and perhaps new. It is unlikely that she prostituted while her husband still lived with the family and could provide for them. Neighbors of this woman probably knew her before she began to prostitute and, more importantly, would have known why she resorted to prostitution. This need-based perspective on prostitution explains why some working-class families accepted prostitutes living in their midst.

Like their middle-class counterparts, most working-class families had no desire to see their daughters grow up to be prostitutes. The large number of parents who brought their girls before the children's court for sexual license clearly indicates that working-class parents had little tolerance for sexual misbehavior.[6] However, working-class families did not routinely shun prostitutes because they did not view prostitution as solely a moral failing. Instead, working-class New Yorkers tended to see prostitution as symptomatic of a profound economic and social crisis in the prostitute's family. From this perspective, women prostituted because they lacked financial support, not because of a potentially contagious moral failing. Although prostitutes may not have set a good example for young children, their mere presence did not directly threaten the morals of young children. As a result, few families ostracized prostitutes, and some allowed prostitutes to "borrow" their children.

In addition, prostitution in this context existed to hold families together. Prostitution resulting from desertion or widowing has often been viewed as a sign of family disintegration. However, I believe that it reflected a desperate attempt to keep families together in the face of economic disaster. Women working out of the tenements, and out of Raines Law hotels as well, often did so to salvage what remained of their families. Many neighbors sympathized with women who prostituted out of great need because they respected the attempt to hold a family together and, if possible, to lift it out of the dire crisis that made prostitution a necessity. The spectacular wages and flexible hours that characterized prostitution made it particularly attractive to women with heavy family responsibilities.

Tenement prostitution clearly exemplified the diffusion of prostitution into working-class residential housing. Small-scale but nonetheless commercial relations permeated the basic fabric of working-class life in New York in this period. Grocery stores, saloons, and vice resorts all thrived amid family housing. Tenement prostitutes solicited openly and often used their earnings to support family members whom other neighbors knew. Integrated into the communities in which they lived, these women worked often as casual prostitutes, but rarely as clandestine ones.

Even while many prostitutes began openly to manage their own businesses in the shelter of Raines Law hotels, other women took advantage of their increasing freedom to work and live independently in the city to engage in clandestine prostitution. The elaborate development of rooming house districts provided opportunities for women to prostitute without being detected by family members, friends, and prospective spouses. Furnished-room houses provided the necessary anonymity for clandestine prostitution. Women working out of furnished rooms made different choices about their lives, diverging significantly from the women who worked openly in neighborhood bars, candy stores, or tenements.

Instead of making the most of their financial opportunities by openly soliciting as independent prostitutes, these women pursued a secretive path that allowed them to seem to adhere to working-class expectations of respectable women's behavior. In essence, women working out of furnished-room houses used the anonymity of the cities to prostitute relatively undetected. In so doing, they blurred the line between moral women and immoral women. Just who was and who could be a prostitute was no longer easy to tell from a woman's clothing, behavior, or location. These clandestine prostitutes deliberately walked a fine line between respectability and immorality, and in the process they began to separate their culture's understanding of certain sexual practices from its moral judgments.

Furnished room prostitutes hid their activities from their neighbors and families in an attempt to benefit from prostitution without paying the price in lost reputation. Landlords who let furnished rooms to prostitutes rarely concerned themselves actively with their tenants' business. They tolerated prostitution in exchange for the higher rents that they could charge.[7] Scattered throughout working-class neighborhoods and industrial districts, furnished rooms provided housing for single men and women who lived and worked independently from their families. Most of the inhabitants had no close family in the city, but some native New Yorkers chose to live in furnished rooms because of the freedom they provided. Living independently reduced, though it did not eliminate, close supervision of the social and sexual lives of young people.

Furnished-room houses, although they often tolerated prostitution, did not carry the moral taint of a saloon or Raines Law hotel. Prostitution in these houses could be quite casual, and many of the female inhabitants pursued prostitution as a profitable side activity rather than a full-time job. In places like these rooming houses, the diffusion of prostitution began to have its most profound social and sexual effects. If Raines Law hotels increased prostitution in neighborhood bars, furnished-room houses made it possible for many women to practice prostitution casually and relatively undetected by police, and sometimes even by neighbors and family members.

Most prostitutes working out of furnished rooms tried to keep their activities somewhat discreet. These young girls usually worked together, pooling resources and sharing profits, safety, and company. As one investigator reported, the "girls here seem new. They go on the streets in neighborhood without hats and are quite timid. . . . Met two girls eating popcorn. One offered some to the investigator. He refused and asked where they were going. They said they were working at shirtwaists. One invited him to go with them to a hotel, the other said their rooms were best" (Investigative Reports 1905–1910).

These young women appeared to be both employed in other work, namely, making shirtwaists, and relatively savvy about the business of prostitution. Although the investigator assessed them as timid and new to the game, they understood enough of prostitution to debate the merits of taking a hotel room or returning with him to their own rooms. Their doubts about the wisdom of prostituting from their rooms indicates that they wanted to keep this side activity a secret from their neighbors.

Some prostitutes kept a low profile because they felt genuine concern for the people in their neighborhoods and did not wish to set a bad example. One woman became outraged in conversation with a man when he callously brushed off her concerns over the visibility of their transactions. Observing the interaction in a bar, the investigator reported that, after some time, one of the men wanted to know why the woman stayed at the bar, instead of taking the investigator home with her. Enraged, she retorted, "I told you once I ain't going to take anybody to my room." "What are you afraid of anyways [*sic*]?" the man asked. "There is always somebody sitting on the stoop at this hour [about 10 o'clock]," she explained, "a bunch of women and children, and I don't want them to see me bring anybody up." Obviously unimpressed, the man replied rather crassly, "thats [*sic*] nothing. I'd screw my own sister if I got the chance." After this provocation, the investigator reported that

> as soon as he said that the woman got mad and said go on get the H__ out of here I got no use for a man that'll say that, why you wouldn't even respect your own mother, she kept swearing at him and get noisy until [*sic*] man came in from bar room and said come on cut out the loud stuff or you'll have to get out of here but she wouldn't quite [*sic*] down so he told her to finish her drink and get out, she finished her drink. . . . I then said to the man that remained at table with me, what's the matter with her? (Brooklyn Investigative Reports 1914–1915)

Although she undoubtedly wished to protect her own reputation, it also seems that the woman did not want her own activities to jeopardize the virtue of the women and children among whom she lived. Rather than cultivating a mercenary attitude, she chastised a potential client for his own disregard for neighborhood and family ties. Her attitude reflects a profound ambivalence about prostitution and its place in working-class residential life. Unlike the tenement prostitutes who clearly did not shrink from soliciting clients from front stoops and doorways, furnished-room prostitutes often wanted to hide their behavior to protect their reputations, and sometimes to reduce the effects it might have on other women and children. This indicates both a fear of exposure and an investment in the moral standards of working-class sexual values.

To conclude, furnished-room prostitution was one avenue that women who needed extra money could take and still maintain some semblance of virtue. These women participated in the transformation of sexual practices that resulted from women's ability to live independently of family. This kind of casual and clandestine prostitution contributed to the incorporation of sexual activity and commercial exchange into heterosexual interactions among working-class people.

The other path prostitutes followed in the years before the war took full advantage of a revolution affecting the public presence of women, as well as their growing importance in commercial activities. Rather than hiding their behavior in the hopes that they could remain in the moral mainstream of working-class communities, these women chose to sell sex openly in their neighborhoods and in that way entered the ranks of small proprietors providing entertainment and services to local consumers. Although World War I would change both forms of prostitution, for the time being women had varied options for exchanging sex for cash. The choices these women made had a profound impact on the commercial economy of working-class neighborhoods, as well as on working-class attitudes toward commercial and sexual values.

# Notes

1. "Precinct 5—James Slip," Box 4, Committee of Fifteen Papers, New York Public Library, Astor, Lenox, and Tilden Collection. In this paper I rely heavily on the Papers of the Committee of Fifteen and the Committee of Fourteen. Both organizations paid working-class investigators to go undercover posing as johns. Uninterested in the lives and fates of individual prostitutes, both committees instead pressured the owners of establishments that tolerated prostitution. This approach did not significantly disrupt the lives of prostitutes, although yielding wonderful accounts of the daily workings of the commercial sex industry in New York City.

2. On the financial arrangements of brothel prostitution in New York City in this period, see "Investigative Reports—untitled—1905–1910," Box 38, Committee of Fourteen Papers, New York Public Library, Astor, Lenox and Tilden Collection; "Precint 5—Batavia Street–Cherry Street," Box 4, Committee of Fifteen; "Precinct 11—118 Mott Street–126 Mott Street," Box 4, Committee of Fifteen; "Precinct 5—James Slip," Box 4, Committee of Fifteen; "Precinct 11—104 Bowery–97 Elizabeth Street," Box 5, Committee of Fifteen. In every extensive report I found on brothels, and even in many partial ones, madams required that their prostitutes be inspected once a week for disease, and that the prostitutes pay for this service out of their own pockets. Madams also required that the girls pay them half of the revenue off the top from the trick. These agreements are so consistent over time that they appear to be an industry-wide practice in a business with very little coordination or oversight.

3. As the Committee of Fourteen concludes, "From the passage of this law dates the immediate growth of one of the most insidious forms of the social evil—the 'Law' hotel. This growth was due to a heavy increase in the penalties for a violation and the expected increased enforcement of the law by state authorities beyond the reach of local influences. To illustrate, the license tax was raised from $200 to $800, and the penalty of the forfeiture of a bond was also added. To escape these drastic penalties for the selling of liquor on Sunday in saloons, saloon keepers created hotels with the required 10 bedrooms, kitchen and dining room. The immediate increase was over 10,000 bedrooms. There being no actual demand for such an increase in hotel accommodations, the proprietors in many instances used them for purposes of assignation or prostitution, to meet the additional expense incurred." Committee of Fourteen Research Committee, *The Social Evil in New York City: A Study of Law Enforcement* (New York: Andrew Kellogg Co., 1910), 39.

4. The Consumer's League of New York estimated that the average wage-earning woman in New York State made $6.54 per week. "Our Working Girls: How They Do It" (Consumers' League of New York, 1910). Microfilmed from the Schlessinger Library, Radcliffe College, Cambridge, Mass. (History of Women: 8608.)

For other data on women's wages in this period see Lynn Y. Weiner, *From Working Girl to Working Mother: The Female Labor Force in the United States, 1820–1980* (Chapel Hill: University of North Carolina Press, 1985), 25.

5. I have found several instances of young women soliciting from tenement house windows. For example, "Two girls were looking out of the window on the 2d floor. I went upstairs, they would not let me in but they call men in." "Precinct 5— Batavia St.–Cherry St." Box 4, Committee of Fifteen Papers. Interestingly, many nineteenth-century brothels placed women in windows to entice male customers. It was a relatively safe way for women to drum up trade, and it is not surprising that when prostitution diffused throughout the city, many prostitutes adopted this practice on their own. In many ways it made even more sense in this context. Women did not have to risk soliciting on the streets. Soliciting from windows proved safer because women could assess the men who responded and decide whether or not to let them into the room. The physical divisions and barriers represented by the windows took the place of the cadets and bouncers that brothels employed.

6. For discussions of parents' concerns over daughters' experimentation with sexuality see Mary Odem, *Delinquent Daughters: Protecting and Policing Adolescent Female Sexuality in the United States, 1885–1920* (Chapel Hill: University of North Carolina Press, 1995), 56–62, 138–39.

7. For tolerance and even expectations of prostitution in furnished-room houses, see "Investigative Reports—untitled—1905–1910," Box 38, Committee of Fourteen Papers and "Investigative Reports—1912," Box 28, Committee of Fourteen Papers.

# References

Brooklyn, Staten Island, Manhattan—Investigative Reports and Related Material, 1914–1915. Box 29, Committee of Fourteen Papers, New York Public Library, Astor, Lenox, and Tilden Collection.

Committe of Fourteen, Research Committee. 1910. *The Social Evil in New York City: A Study of Law Enforcement.* New York: Andrew Kellogg Co.

Consumers' League of New York. 1910. Our working girls: How they do it. Microfilmed from the Schlessinger Library, Radcliffe College, Cambridge, Mass.

Timothy Gilfoyle. 1992. *City of Eros: New York City, Prostitution and the Commercialization of Sex, 1790–1920.* New York: W. W. Norton & Co.

Investigative Reports—1912. Box 28, Committee of Fourteen Papers, New York Public Library, Astor, Lenox, and Tilden Collection.

Investigative Reports—untitled—1905–1910. Box 38, Committee of Fourteen Papers, New York Public Library, Astor, Lenox, and Tilden Collection.

IR—(no title)—1915. Box 29, Committee of Fourteen Papers, New York Public Library, Astor, Lenox, and Tilden Collection.

Odem, Mary. 1995. *Delinquent Daughters: Protecting and Policing Adolescent Female Sexuality in the United States. 1885–1920*. Chapel Hill: University of North Carolina Press.

Precinct 5—Batavia Street–Cherry Street. n.d. Box 4, Committee of Fifteen Papers, New York Public Library, Astor, Lenox, and Tilden Collection.

Precinct 5—James Slip. n.d. Box 4, Committee of Fifteen Papers, New York Public Library, Astor, Lenox, and Tilden Collection.

Precinct 5—James Street–Walter Street. n.d. Box 4, Committee of Fifteen Papers, New York Public Library, Astor, Lenox, and Tilden Collection.

Precinct 6—100 Mott–119 Mulberry. n.d. Box 4, Committee of Fifteen Papers, New York Public Library, Astor, Lenox, and Tilden Collection.

Precinct 11—104 Bowery–97 Elizabeth Street. n.d. Box 5, Committee of Fifteen Papers, New York Public Library, Astor, Lenox, and Tilden Collection.

Precinct 11—118 Mott Street–126 Mott Street. Box 4, Committee of Fifteen Papers, New York Public Library, Astor, Lenox, and Tilden Collection.

Weiner, Lynn L. 1985. *From Working Girl to Working Mother: The Female Labor Force in the United States, 1820–1980*. Chapel Hill: University of North Carolina Press.

Lillian Wald Papers. n.d. Box 91, Columbia University Rare Books and Manuscripts Library.

# Prostitution in Eighteenth-Century Paris: Pages from a Madam's Notebook

## Kathryn Norberg

8 October 1750: a lawyer from the Chatelet court came to my house even though he has a young and beautiful wife; at 4 I turned away a young man because I did not know him; the same day a procuress, Madeleine Bourgeois, brought me a girl of about 15 who is named Elizabeth Grandville; she is from the village of Ceans near Meaux; she says she has been in Paris for a year; she plays the tambourine in cafés; I took her in because she has been possessed (she claims) by three men: one who took her to his apartment but gave her nothing; and two more in the bordello of the said Bourgeois; I gave Madame Bourgeois 18 pounds for this girl because that is what she said she spent to dress her; M Séguier came and stayed all night with Rosette; Monsieur Ducroissant wants me to find him a negress to satisfy his fantasy; my landlord says that I can keep the lease for another few months but I'm worried. (Archives de la Bastille)

Sometime toward the beginning of November 1750, this document came into the hands of René Berryer de Ravenoville, an aristocrat and career state servant who since 1747 was *lieutenant général de police* or head of the Parisian police.[1] For Berryer, this report was a small part of his larger campaign to monitor daily life in Paris. Berryer had created specialized departments within the police, including a Bureaux des Moeurs, which gathered information about banned books, homosexuals, and gambling, in short, any activities that could be placed under the rubric "morals." The surveillance of prostitutes and brothels was a key element in this endeavor. One inspector— Meusnier (1747–1757), then his subordinate Marais (1757–1771)—was charged with the surveillance of "actresses and gallant girls," and both Meusnier and Marais filled pages with witty, sometimes lewd observations about these women.[2] The inspector's work was supplemented by reports from seven eminent bordello madams: Mesdames Baudoin, Montbrun, Desmarets, Héricourt, Dufresne, Carlier, and Dhosmont. These women dutifully provided Berryer with descriptions of bordello routine.[3] In return, Berryer tolerated the women's brothels. He declined to enforce the law that made prostitution illegal and made procuring a felony punishable by whipping, branding, and banishment. For the madams, the reports were the cost of toleration, a tax on their "illegal" business, and a means of currying favor with the omnipotent police chief.

Obviously, the madams' reports were not unmediated, personal memoirs. They were written for Berryer and followed his guidelines. The police chief told the madams to inform him when a cleric entered their bordello; they did.[4] Berryer instructed the women to write down when each client came to the brothel along with his name, residence, status, and length of stay; they did. Berryer told the madams to note all conversation regarding the monarchy, its ministers, religion, and government finance; the women complied. Just why Berryer wanted this wealth of information is unclear. Perhaps he hoped to blackmail these influential men, for the good of the monarchy, or for his protector Madame de Pompadour.[5]

The madams wanted to please Berryer, but they also wanted to protect themselves, so they probably hid as much as they disclosed. Some of the madams' journals are very brief, more like schedules than texts. Madame Dufresne ran a bordello on the second floor of a house on the rue St. Louis near the Tuileries gardens. In her journal she recorded only the bare minimum. "On the June 27," she notes, "Monsieur Bofort [*sic*] chevalier de St. Louis, lieutenant colonel, 60 years of age, residing rue Neuve St. Augustin, had himself whipped very hard by Victoire; he came at 11 in the morning and left at noon" (Archives de la Bastille, 92).

Other journals were more complex, adding some details to the rather monotonous recital of entries and exits.[6] Exceptional in this regard is the notebook with which this paper began, the journal of Madame Dhosmont or Ozmante. Dhosmont's reports fill two hundred and fifty pages in folio, making them the lengthiest of all the madams' reports. They also cover the longest period of time, from October 1747 to October 1757, with only a few weeks missing. Written in clear if plain French, Dhosmont's reports include marginal notes made by inspectors Meusnier or Marais or perhaps Berryer himself.[7]

Berryer was not the first policeman with whom Madame Dhosmont had a relationship. Notes made by Inspector Meusnier indicate that she was already acting as his informant in early 1747. Sometime between May 1747 (when Berryer was appointed) and October of the same year, Dhosmont managed to acquire the supreme protection of the police chief himself. Beginning in the fall of 1747, Madame Dhosmont's notes reveal that she had occasional personal audiences with Berryer.[8] Sometimes she reserved her best information for these occasions, fully aware that a scribe recopied or at least read her reports.[9]

The reports, like these meetings, were a conversation involving two parties, the madam and the (temporarily) silent police chief.[10] Madame Dhosmont definitely tailored her reports to Berryer's specifications and she proved to be an able, even enthusiastic spy. When several regular clients began discussing a gambler, Madame Dhosmont "did everything to determine his identity. I asked what his name was and where he came from pretending that I thought him one of my clients." Such innocent inquiries soon led to more serious snooping. On February 4, 1751, when she found herself in a police commissioner's home, she profited from his momentary absence to read all the letters on his desk. Their contents were duly reported to Berryer (Archives de la Bastille, 311v).

Unfortunately not all days produced such juicy information. Sometimes Dhosmont had little—or nothing—to report. But she scribbled in her notebook, filling in the gaps with domestic incidents and a chronicle of her extensive business dealings. If the cook got married, Dhosmont included it in her reports. If her pensioner or live-in prostitute ran off with the neighbor's valet, she included that too. No detail of her negotiations with other madams, prostitutes, or clients was too trivial to be excluded. On one occasion, Dhosmont was so desperate that she wrote down the story of her life, from birth to the beginning of her relations with Berryer (Archives de la Bastille, 124). The result is a unique document: the only life history written by an eighteenth-century prostitute.

Of course, Madame Dhosmont wrote this autobiography for the police chief, and so she obscures as much as she reveals. Like her fellow madams, Dhosmont had a great deal to hide. But unlike her fellow bawds, she did not seek protection in silence. For her, security lay not in the paucity of words, but in their superfluity. Madame Dhosmont covered her omissions and untruths with a torrent of words. Berryer wanted information, so he got information, be it important or banal, significant or meaningless.

Along the way, the procuress paints a vivid picture of life inside a high-toned bordello. No other document brings us inside the bordello or allows us to examine its operations so carefully. No other document permits us to know a practitioner of the "trade" so well. We can use Dhosmont's reports the way Robert Darnton (1984) used the inspector Emery's files to uncover a world previously ignored. Or, we can combine Madame Dhosmont's text with other documents to construct what Giovanni Levi and his fellow Italian historians call a "micro history." Most importantly, we can use Dhosmont's notebook to see prostitution from a new angle. Usually we have to rely on policemen, moralists, and pornographers to describe the sex market. Though flawed, Madame Dhosmont's journal is the only source that allows us to see eighteenth-century prostitution through the eyes of a sex worker.

# The Madam

Who, then, was Madame Dhosmont? Thanks to the "brief sketch of (her) life" inserted into the report of October 10, 1750, we know something about her from birth to 1747, when she met Berryer.[11] She claims her father came from an elite family that counted magistrates and officers among its members. In fact, her father was a lawyer and her mother the daughter of a tradesman, probably a grocer. Dhosmont came from the merchant-professional class whose members were respectable but far from aristocratic. In her origins, she was very much like the other madams, actresses, and kept women who constituted the elite of Parisian prostitution.[12] She was inferior to most of her clients but infinitely superior by birth and culture to the common streetwalker or bordello prostitute. Among her living relatives, she counted a mother superior at the Carmelite convent on the rue de Grenelle, a *plumassieur du roy*,* and two devout old maids who depended on an inherited annuity for their livelihood (Archives de la Bastille, 124).

The Dhosmonts were respectable but poor. They had lost everything in the collapse of the Law System in 1720, when Dhosmont's father had to flee Paris and buy a minor office (*huissier*) in Charly. There, he and his new wife, Anne Elisabeth Bigor, produced fourteen children despite what Madame Dhosmont describes as an unhappy marriage. Money did not come the family's way so they moved to Chateau-Thierry, where a wealthy relative lived. The Dhosmont couple placed their eight-year-old daughter in the local convent school, but she still participated in their active social life, attending parties and suppers with her parents' friends. The Dhosmonts frequented the best company—magistrates, petty nobles, and high clerics—who were amused and delighted by their loquacious daughter. "By this means," Madame Dhosmont states, "I developed a taste for coquettishness."

At thirteen, Madame Dhosmont accompanied her mother to Paris: "They showed me off everywhere, in Paris and Versailles, everywhere and always in a carriage." The young girl quickly forgot the provinces and was seized by "ambition, a mania that still afflicts me." Paris was where Dhosmont longed to live and when her father died, she moved with her mother to the capital. The family had no money and lived very simply. One of her father's acquaintances, an abbé Paval, took an interest in the family. He offered to sell the father's office if the mother would give the proceeds to her daughter. Shortly thereafter, Monsieur l'abbé gave the family 500 *livres*. "I was very grateful to Monsieur L'abbé," Madame Dhosmont admits, "and I allowed him to call upon us without the slightest scruple." Upon the death of the abbé, Madame Dhosmont made the acquaintance of an aristocrat, a chevalier de St. Louis. "At this

---

*Either a royal feather merchant or a dresser.

point," she says, "I abandoned virtue but very secretly and only because I wanted to buy things and saw no other way of getting money." Madame Dhosmont began to dine with aristocrats and frequent libertine company.

But Dhosmont's mother had other plans: she wanted to marry her daughter to an honest artisan or maybe even a minor officer. But these people, Madame Dhosmont stresses, bored her. Then Dhosmont met a certain Tarlé for whom she developed a genuine "friendship." For eighteen months she enjoyed a true "idyll," "uncontaminated by greed or self interest." But then Tarlé jilted her, and Madame abruptly accepted another man's offer of marriage, "partly out of spite, partly out of good sense." We are never told this man's name or profession. "Three quarters of men are cheats," Dhosmont remarks, and her marriage was sour enough to convince her never to take a lover again.[13] "Never a man, certainly never a husband or lover," she said. "In my business, one cannot afford to be duped; we are here to make dupes of others" (Archives de la Bastille, 211). To escape her dreadful husband, Madame Dhosmont fled to London. There she survived by "selling goods." She stayed for only six months lamenting the weather, the unstylish clothes, the rude inhabitants, the omnipresent beggars, and the bad humor of the English. "The only good thing one can say for this nation," she remarks, "is that the grandees are easily approached." At this point Dhosmont's biography stops. Two weeks' worth of reports have strayed from the file, leaving us in suspense. We may assume, however, that one of those English grandees who were "so easily approached" became Madame Dhosmont's protector and facilitated her transformation from destitute woman into a *fille à la mode*.

When did Dhosmont's "fall" occur? Biographies of whores, which were particularly numerous after the success of *Fanny Hill*, made the prostitute's loss of virginity and her subsequent "descent" into mercenary sex the crucial event in her life.[14] No such turning point exists in Madame Dhosmont's autobiography. She was neither a nymphomaniac nor a victim. No particular man "seduced" her, and although she attributes her drift into prostitution to choice (that is, "ambition"), her bad marriage and straitened circumstances probably opened the door.[15]

When she returned to Paris, Madame Dhosmont almost certainly made her living as a *fille galante* or kept woman. To become a successful procuress required an apprenticeship. Thanks to her background and convent education, Dhosmont was familiar with polite society and upper-class ways. But she needed to cultivate clients, assemble a network of acquaintances, and learn about business and finance. Like all of the procuresses who informed for Berryer, she had probably served some time as a "gallant girl." Madame Baudoin, one of Dhosmont's fiercest rivals, had been a much sought after *fille galante* and Mesdames Dufresne and Montigny had both been kept women in their youth.[16] Madame Dhosmont had probably followed the same path, and there is no reason why she couldn't have continued to "gratify" her clients.

Even by eighteenth-century standards, she was certainly not an old woman: married in 1741, she was probably in her late twenties or early thirties when her journal begins.

## The Bordello

Madame Dhosmont's first bordello was located in an apartment on the rue Jean-Saint-Denis, a classic area of prostitution abutting on the rue St. Honoré. At some point, she moved to the rue des Deux Portes Saint Sauveur farther north and east, and then in 1751 to the rue St. Fiacre near Montmartre, where she remained through 1757. Her place of business was, as best we can tell, rather small. Though she occupied a *maisonette* or small house with a garden on the rue St. Fiacre, she only mentions a few rooms in her reports. We know that the house had a salon, a dining room, a kitchen, and one bedroom—her own. One assumes that there were other bedrooms or at the very least *cabinets*. By working-class standards, this was large. But in comparison to Madame Gourdan's bordello, the most luxurious of the day, which occupied four stories and could sleep fourteen clients, this was small.[17]

Both in its physical setting and its personnel, Dhosmont's house was quite bourgeois. There were servants, though only a few. Dhosmont always employed a cook, two female domestics, and a footman. The cook was a real necessity, for clients frequently dined before or after sex. The cook not only prepared the food, she also ran to the market when a client appeared. Service at table was provided by a footman who also delivered messages (key to the madam's business) and accompanied Dhosmont on her business and social rounds. Two female domestics usually lived in the house. Dhosmont had trouble finding honest and responsible servants so, when a prostitute too old or unattractive to be a pensioner offered her services, Dhosmont took her on as a maid of all work. The arrangement made sense: when there was a rush of clients, the maids pitched in and helped service the customers.

## Pensioners

No more than three prostitutes resided in Madame Dhosmont's bordello at any one time. Usually there was only one but sometimes there were none.[18] Girls were hard to keep: prostitutes in the eighteenth century as today regarded the brothel as the least desirable setting in which to work.[19] Despite the advantages—room and board, security from both the police and violent clients— women only became pensioners, live-in prostitutes, when they were debutantes or financially strapped. Young girls eager to leave their parents often asked to be pensioners. "Today," Dhosmont wrote on March 19, 1751, "Nanette Poisson asked me to take her in, she lives on the rue des Petits Carreaux, 4th story, with her father, a painter, and her mother. . . . Her mother gives her nothing and doesn't care where she lives or with whom. Nanette says that if I don't take her in she will go to Lyon with a man because she does not want to return home" (Archives de la Bastille, 211). Often girls complained that their mothers abused them; sometimes they were beaten by stepfathers. In any event, lacking all resources, these neophytes appealed to the bordello owner. Nanette, as we will see, came to cause Madame Dhosmont some trouble.

Other girls who presented themselves at Madame's door were more experienced but almost as penniless. A certain Mademoiselle Vaudrin appeared on March 13, 1756. She had left another bordello after being "purchased" by a client for 2,000 *livres*. In other words, the client had given Vaudrin this money to pay her outstanding debts to the brothel madam. Instead, Vaudrin had purchased some earrings, bringing the wrath of the bordello owner, the client, and potentially the law down on her head. In desperation, she appealed to Madame Dhosmont, who agreed to take her in on one condition: that she repay at least part of her debt. Madame Dhosmont was scrupulously honest in her business dealings, a quality in which she took great pride (Archives de la Bastille, 143v).

Mademoiselle Vaudrin was only fifteen and the other girls who became pensioners in the Dhosmont establishment were just as young. The average age of the fifty-two women recruited into Madame Dhosmont's bordello in the years between 1750 and 1757 was sixteen.[20] Always, Madame Dhosmont emphasized, it was someone else who had "deflowered the girl." Usually the culprit was a soldier, a childhood friend, or a neighbor. French law levied serious penalties on those who debauched youth, and Madame Dhosmont had no intention of incurring the wrath of the courts. Consequently, she was always careful to inquire into a girl's past and to ask about her parents, for they could be the source of charges of debauchery. "Nanette Poisson," Madame Dhosmont informed Berryer, "claims that her parents 'don't care where (she) lives or whether (she) is near or far from them.' . . . I told her," Dhosmont continues, "that if her father inquired after her, she would have to return to his house." Only a few months later, Nanette's father did indeed surface and Madame Dhosmont quickly dispatched her to another bordello.

Because she feared the trouble a girl's parents could make, Madame Dhosmont had an unstated preference for non-Parisians. Of the fifty-two girls she recruited, only ten were born in the capital. In contrast, 75 percent of the women arrested for streetwalking were native born. As in so many other aspects of her life, Madame Dhosmont may have worried needlessly: not all parents cared about their daughter's virtue or hesitated to profit from her prostitution. "I took on Jannelle, called Janneton," Madame Dhosmont writes. "She is 17 and blonde, blue eyes a little droopy but good natured and small; her father who is a domestic lives in Paris but he's aware of her promiscuity and doesn't refuse the money she gives him; she has been in Paris for three years; she began as a domestic for a minor procuress; then she solicited on the street."

Experience was no bar to entry into Dhosmont's elegant whorehouse but venereal disease definitely was. "I looked at Marthe who presented herself, asking for a position, but she is diseased; I loaned her some money to see a surgeon and told her to return when she was cured." On another occasion, Madame Dhosmont had to let a girl go: "I put Manon on the street: she had a disease; she has been used by too many men; she must go."

Not all girls offered, however, were accepted. "Madame Gris who runs a bordello in the Roule offered a girl named Elise today," Dhosmont writes in 1753. "She was not pretty enough and very ill-spoken and awkward so I sent her back." Good manners as well as good looks were much appreciated by Dhosmont's clients. "I have only Manon with me now who is small, red headed and rather plain; but she is very lively and gay and not lacking in wit." Apparently, Dhosmont's well-heeled clients wanted at least the illusion that they were sleeping with well-born girls. "I gave Monsieur Drevet the English girl but he rejected her angrily at first: she was wearing an apron and he complained that I had offered him an ignorant servant instead of a girl." Monsieur Drevet was appeased, indeed intrigued, when Dhosmont explained that the apron was a part of the English dress. He spent the night with the girl and left her, Madame Dhosmont suspected, a large tip.

Just how much Madame Dhosmont paid her pensioners is unclear. Traditionally, eighteenth-century madams, pimps, and tavern owners appropriated anywhere between one-third and one-half of the prostitutes' earnings.[21] Madame Dhosmont probably took much more: clients paid Madame and she never mentions sharing any money with her pensioners. In fact, no money ever changed hands between the women.[22] On the other hand, she has a lot to say about the money the pensioners owed her. Like bordello owners from ancient Greece to nineteenth-century France, Dhosmont "held" her pensioners by drawing them into debt (Corbin 1984; Adler 1990). Usually a girl came, as Madame Dhosmont put it, "naked." Without fancy clothes she was worthless, so Madame Dhosmont and her fellow bawds bought the girl clothes and put them on a tab. The amount of money expended could be considerable: prostitutes who "sold" a girl to Madame Dhosmont had spent 100 *livres* "to dress the girl" (Archives de la Bastille, 113v). Soon debts for cab fares, new petticoats, and surgeon's fees (for the gonorrhea cure) would be added. As best I can tell, Madame Dhosmont was fairer than many bordello owners: she did not charge for room and board and paid for cabs herself.

Still, relations were strained inside the Dhosmont establishment and girls decamped in the night. "I have told you of Manon Moisson," she writes Berryer. "She ran out leaving me with 200 *livres* unpaid." On another occasion,

Madame writes that "Anne my pensioner left with a domestic in the night," and later, "Victoire disappeared." We know that some madams cultivated familial ties with their pensioners and had themselves called "mama." Others however were despotic and greedy. In the quarter of the Palais Royal, the police had to quell a "rebellion" in a whorehouse: the girls had run amuck and threatened the madam with a knife (Archives de la Police, AA 242).

To our knowledge, no such "revolt" occurred on Madame Dhosmont's premises. Still, her pensioners never stayed very long: no girl (as best I can tell) remained more than six months in her bordello. Some left secretly; others were "purchased" by clients. "Monsieur Brucier has taken a liking to Adelaide and would like to purchase her for 60 *livres* (pounds); he agrees to pay her debts; he wants her all to himself but doesn't have an apartment for her yet so she will stay with me for the time being." Madame Dhosmont facilitated such transactions for they were highly lucrative: rarely did a girl see any of this money because it all went to pay off her "debts." Less profitable was the sudden disappearance of a girl, and in such cases, Madame Dhosmont was quick to lay blame. "Adelaide left today while I was out; I think the domestic of a neighbor persuaded her to go; I'll look into this matter." More often she blamed the girl "who was lazy anyway and I'll get my money back somehow" (Archives de la Bastille, 201v).

Not all of Dhosmont's charges flourished on their own. Adelaide popped up again a year later: she had been bilked of her money by a lover, contracted venereal disease, and had to solicit in the taverns of the boulevard. A stay in the Bicêtre venereal disease hospital had put her even further into debt. In desperation, she returned to Madame Dhosmont, who took her back "seeing as how she is cured." Illiterate, unskilled, and very young, the pensioners had neither the background nor the business acumen to succeed as Madame Dhosmont had.[23] Most likely, these girls experienced prostitution quite differently from the madams or the prostitutes who operated independently out of their own apartments, the so-called gallant girls.

## Gallant Girls

Either because she had trouble keeping girls or because she found it too expensive to do so, Madame relied upon independent prostitutes, whom she called "day girls," to service her clientele. When several clients appeared at once, Madame simply sent her footman to a "gallant girl's" apartment and summoned her to the St. Fiacre bordello. "Monsieur Séguier came with two friends at 4," she writes. "I sent for the Boucher who brought with her a blonde, 18, who lives on the rue St. Honoré" (Archives de la Bastille, 211v). Almost daily, Madame had recourse to independent prostitutes who lived in the *chambre garnie* or furnished rooming houses along the rue St. Honoré or near the Palais Royal. Some had been bordello inmates; some had even spent some time on the street or in the taverns of the Porcherons.[24] But all depended on Madame as a kind of non-mechanized escort service to provide them with tricks and "parties."

"Parties" or suppers at the homes of clients were an important part of Madame's operation. "I sent two girls with Monsieur Tonnelier who is going to dinner at a friend's house," Madame Dhosmont wrote in 1754. Outcalls accounted for more than half of her business, and she frequently sent both pensioners and "day girls" to the homes of clients and their friends. "On (February) 11," she writes, "Monsieur Séguier came to the house and asked for two girls to accompany him to supper with two friends; I gave him Mlle Bonnevaux, who lives on the rue Guillaume with her aunt" (Archives de la Bastille, 147). Sometimes Madame Dhosmont accompanied her girls: "Monsieur Francoeur sent by Monsieur Curis," she writes, "came at nine to ask for some girls to have supper: I took Nanette Poisson and another girl who lives on the rue Mauconseil to the home of Monsieur the baron de la Plaisse where we found Monsieur de Curis, Francoeur, and a fourth gentleman who's [sic] name I never learned" (Archives de la Bastille, 152).

# Procuresses and Pimps

When Madame Dhosmont could not find a girl on her own, she called on one of her fellow madams. "Tonight," Madame Dhosmont notes casually, "I took Mlle Petit also known as Chateauroux, a pensioner of Madame Fleurance, to Monsieur Bouvet's house" (Archives de la Bastille). Madame Fleurance was Dhosmont's closest friend; Fleurance often dined at Dhosmont's house and shared her personal trials (most involving a reprobate lover) with Dhosmont. Consequently, it is far from surprising to see the two women sharing girls. But such arrangements were quite common and Madame regularly traded girls and referred clients to her competitors. "Today," she wrote in 1756, "I took in Yvette who had been with the Baudouin [another famous bawd] for a few months." Madame Dhosmont even accompanied a client "because he had no one else to speak up for him" to the brothel of the famous Madame Paris. She also "accepted girls from the hands" of other procuresses, most often Mesdames Carlier, Montigny, and (of course) Fleurance. On more than one occasion, Madame Dhosmont's clients complained that they had "seen the girl under another name" at another bordello. Only once did Madame Dhosmont run afoul of a fellow procuress, an obscure Mlle Le Febvre who claimed that Dhosmont had failed to pay for a girl. Scrupulous in her business dealings, Dhosmont appealed to inspector Marais, who decided in her favor (Archives de la Bastille, 301v).

Madame Dhosmont usually depended on her fellow madams for girls, but she did not disdain the "merchandise" offered by lowly streetwalkers. "The streetwalker called Duval," she writes, "brought me a girl today who is from the Maubert quarter"; or on another occasion, "the girl Arras who works out of her own rented apartment recommended a blonde who was born in Meaux." Just about any prostitute—streetwalker or kept woman—traded in girls (and boys for that matter) and hoped to make money "selling" a girl to a rich procuress.

Men too participated in this aspect of the sex trade. In a recent synthesis of the history of women, Olwen Hufton states that in early modern Europe "the vice trade was in the hands of women" (1996, 334). Men were certainly active and visible in Madame Dhosmont's world, whether as elite brothel owners or recruiters.[25] "A lackey who barters [*marchander*] women came to see me today," she writes offhandedly "and proposed a certain Hélène." "Monsieur Ginestre," she writes elsewhere, "had this girl in his apartments on the rue St. Honoré." She makes frequent references to lackeys, apartment house owners, and even some artisans who proposed freshly deflowered girls to her. At the same time, several famous bordellos were run by couples like the famous Brissaults.

# The Clients

Still, both in literature and life, women did occupy most of the "managerial" positions in the sex industry, especially at its upper end. Eighteenth-century clients seem to have preferred madams to pimps, probably because women were less likely than men to be drunk or draw their swords. Madame Dhosmont was a well-bred woman who ran a refined establishment. Although she did not attract the most prestigious nobles like the Comte d'Artois or the Duke de Soubise, Madame Dhosmont had a comfortable and respectable clientele that appreciated discretion. Magistrates, financiers, state functionaries, and a few wealthy merchants frequented Dhosmont's bordello. They were men of substance and therefore also of age.[26] Most were probably over forty and some were married. Dhosmont did not welcome young men and when they did come to her establishment she did not hesitate to upbraid them.

Madame Dhosmont's establishment had its regular clients. Monsieur Séguier who came from an old robe family appeared just about every week at the bordello on the rue St. Fiacre. Monsieur Riche de la Popelinière, a financier, also came regularly even though he had a mistress, and so too did Pileur d'Alpigny, a magistrate, and the count de Gouffier, maréchal de camp. About two dozen men formed the nucleus of Dhosmont's clientele and they helped recruit new customers. Word of mouth brought men to Madame's door, and new customers often came with old. Men frequently visited the bordello in groups, introducing a newcomer to the establishment during a supper or afternoon visit. Other times, a regular like Séguier would "recommend" a client as he did with a young cousin. When the cousin failed to pay his bill, Séguier had to reimburse Madame Dhosmont because he had vouched for the young man in the first place. References were desirable but not necessary: virtually every week a man whose name and residence Madame Dhosmont did not know entered the bordello. Was she concealing a client's name or did she actually take the risk of admitting potential spies or informants?

These nameless customers often insisted on remaining incognito. "An Englishman, order of the Garter I think, came today," reports Madame Dhosmont, "but I wasn't able to determine his name or title even though I asked lots of questions." Some of Dhosmont's clients were ashamed to frequent the bordello or at least afraid their habits would be revealed. Every week Madame Dhosmont sent to the house of a magistrate, Monsieur Degbert, "a woman of fifty, small and pretty ugly. . . . This is how he likes it," reports Madame Dhosmont, "for he doesn't want to be suspected in his neighborhood."[27]

For some clients, a visit from a whore or a night in a bordello was shameful. What Madame Dhosmont provided was (relative) discretion and guarantees of good health and absolute tranquility. For these guarantees, clients were willing to pay. Generally, the rates in Madame Dhosmont's establishment fell between 25 and 100 *livres,* the latter sum being so large as to merit considerable comment in Madame's journal. Because a sexual encounter with a streetwalker cost less than one *livre,* Madame Dhosmont was offering very expensive sex indeed. To situate the Dhosmont establishment vis à vis other luxury bordellos, Madame Paris (according to Casanova) expected "6 francs (almost six *livres*) for lunch with a nymph, 12 for dinner and the double to spend the whole night." These prices, he added, were very reasonable (Capon 1905, 33). Sometimes Madame Dhosmont's clients paid a great deal more: when the Duke de Richelieu spent the night with Adelaide, he sent her back with 50 *livres,* a sum large enough to be brought to Berryer's attention. Clients usually paid less, but how much is hard to say. No fixed prices existed at chez Dhosmont (as in Madame Paris's bordello) so clients paid what they liked, but almost invariably 12 *livres* or more, not including the tips that girls usually received. If there was no menu of tariffs, Madame Dhosmont had a clear idea of the floor beneath which no gentleman sank. When inspector Meusnier paid only 12 *sols** for a prostitute, Dhosmont was outraged. When a client gave a girl only 6 *livres* and sent her back to Dhosmont after a night in his apartment, Dhosmont fumed. We may assume that this gentleman was turned away the next time he appeared at Dhosmont's door.

Steady clients were another matter. Madame Dhosmont allowed them to use her premises as a *maison de rendez-vous* or house of assignation. "Monsieur

---

*A *sol* is a copper halfpenny coin.

Molleron brought Mademoiselle Pelissier to my house yesterday while I was out," she writes in 1757. In early September 1755, she "lent Monsieur Mamain the key to my garden because he wanted to meet Madame Leger there between 4 and 6; he gave me 6 *livres* for this service."

## Sex and Business

At this point, the reader may wonder what actually went on in Madame Dhosmont's establishment, that is, behind the bedroom doors. When it comes to sex, Madame has remarkably little to say. Maybe sex was just too routine to be mentioned; maybe she was protecting her clients. In any event, she never engages in the pornographic description and sly innuendo that characterized the reports of inspectors Meusnier and Marais. While these texts bore an uncanny resemblance to the libels and pornographic novels of the mid-eighteenth century, Madame Dhosmont in her reports never uses what Pamela Cheek has called "sexualized language" (1995). She never gloats over the "sexualized bodies" of her prostitutes nor does she attribute to them hyperactive libidos or superior sexual knowledge (as the inspectors did).[28] Even her autobiography, which could easily have resembled *Margot la ravaudeuse* or *Histoire de Marguerite, fille de Suzon*, owes nothing to fiction.[29] Maybe Madame Dhosmont was unfamiliar with the banned books and libertine poetry that elaborated a new, sexualized language. Maybe as a sex worker she just found them irrelevant. In any event, one could read Madame Dhosmont's notebook without realizing that she sold sex.

But then sex was not all Madame Dhosmont offered to her clients. Like many sex workers, she also provided an array of services both emotional and material. Clients came to her house not just for sexual services, but also to dine, to meet with their friends, and to talk to Madame Dhosmont. Her accounts of dinner table conversation make it clear that when Monsieur Séguier and his friends ate supper at her house, she was an active participant in the conversation. "Monsieur Maleval explained to me," she says, "or Monsieur Combé asked me what I thought about this." Madame also offered advice (solicited or not we cannot tell). "When this young man came and asked me for a girl, I told him that he was in no position to maintain a woman and that he should stop gambling too."

Because they almost invariably came in groups, Madame Dhosmont's bordello was something like a clubhouse for certain gentlemen. Monsieur Séguier and his friends Maléval and Combé dined together almost every fortnight at Madame Dhosmont's establishment. When they did not have supper on the rue St. Fiacre, they often went with Madame Dhosmont and a girl to a third friend's house. All in all, a visit to the bordello was not just an occasion for sex. It was a time for camaraderie, for friendship and leisure. Like the Tellier establishment described over a hundred years later by Maupassant, Madame Dhosmont's brothel was a kind of social club, an eighteenth-century version of the fraternity house with Madame Dhosmont as a sort of rococo house mother.

Clients also sought out Madame Dhosmont when they had financial needs. She regularly extended credit to her clients, both for girls and for other purposes. When Monsieur Mezeval, an habitué of the house, had no money, Madame Dhosmont loaned him 6 *livres*, keeping his watch ("which I wanted to refuse") as security (Archives de la Batille, 19 mars 1751). When Monsieur Blanc wanted to sell his mistress's annuity on the secondary market, Madame Dhosmont called for an *agioteur* and money changed hands on the spot (Archives de la Bastille, 112). Madame Dhosmont dealt with much larger transactions too. "A young man came and asked if I could loan him 11 *louis**on a letter of exchange for 1000 *écus* drawn at Rouen and due in a couple of days; I told him that at the moment I could not loan anything; but I told him to go to my friend Madame Berne, a former procuress, who lives on rue Montorgeuil . . . or Madame Thevenin who also once had girls" (Archives de la Bastille, 19 mars 1751). Money lending was clearly one of the occupations— along with running a gambling establishment—to which madams "retired."

Retirement was never far from Madame Dhosmont's mind. "This is not an easy life," she complained to Berryer, "and if you knew what a woman like me has to endure, you would pity me." Madame certainly had problems. One of the worst "curses" a procuress had to endure were bands of young men. Three times during the years between 1752 and 1753, groups of armed men "forced" the door to Madame Dhosmont's establishment and threatened both her life and property. On May 6, 1752, "six young men whom I've never seen before forced their way into my apartment; they found me alone and despite the cordiality with which I treated them they swore and cursed like musketeers. They were badly dressed and turned everything upside down and despite my vigilance they took a pair of sleeves [i.e., a chemise] worth 25 *livres*." A year earlier another band of young men had broken into Dhosmont's establishment, demanded a girl (which she sent for), cut her satin bedclothes to ribbons and then left without paying the prostitute. "I paid her myself," sighed Madame Dhosmont, "glad to be rid of that swine" (Archives de la Bastille).

Worse still were the police inspectors Meusnier and especially Marais. Both slept with prostitutes for nothing and tried to undermine Dhosmont's relationship with Berryer. "Monsieur Marais is not as polite as Monsieur Meusnier," she complained in 1757, and Marais returned the favor by accusing Dhosmont of withholding information and falsifying her reports. "I

---

*A *louis* is a French coin worth twenty gold francs.

do not fail, as Monsieur Marais insinuates," she wrote in an angry letter to Berryer, "to report every cleric who crosses my threshold" (Archives de la Bastille, 334).[30] Negotiating with the police, currying their favor, and maintaining their good will was nerve wracking.

Small wonder that Madame Dhosmont longed to leave her profession. Her goal, she stated, was to purchase a sinecure as a stamp-tax (*papier timbré*) officer. She longed to leave behind the violent gangs, Berryer, and his obnoxious inspectors. The strain of running an illegal business began to show. "I am very worried," "I was very frightened," and "I fear" are phrases that come frequently to her pen. "I cannot allow anyone to take advantage of me," she remarks frequently and she was always on her guard. Madame had no legal recourse so she had to be careful and wary. Clients had to be scrutinized because they might fail to pay her or turn her into the commissioner of the quarter. The "youth" might break in, destroy her property, or bring the commissioner to her door.

Worst of all, Berryer himself might turn on her and condemn her to prison or worse. Madame Dhosmont never complained about girls, fellow madames, or even clients. Obviously, she never complained about Berryer either in her reports because they were addressed to him. But one senses a simmering resentment and scarcely controlled anger. She grovels too much and professes her admiration too fervently. One even suspects her of irony when she says she desires "nothing more than to be in the presence of your Grace." But wit is surely something she would never have risked. She was too vulnerable. Who would not have preferred a quiet life in a boring, provincial stamp-tax office?

Did she get it? It is hard to say, for Madame Dhosmont's chronicle breaks off abruptly on October 28, 1757. In the previous weeks, Dhosmont's establishment had been as busy as ever. A few old clients—Monsieur Séguier and Monsieur Maléval—had disappeared, the first because he had married. Each day at least three men came to the rue St. Fiacre. Madame's financial dealings appear to have prospered for she was now loaning larger sums of money.[31] On October 25, Monsieur Lamiau and Monsieur Camuset, both magistrates, dined with Madame Dhosmont and left after midnight. Thereafter, silence.

On October 27, Henri Bertin de Bellisle replaced the disgraced Berryer as *lieutenant de police*. Madame Dhosmont had the pleasure of outlasting her tormentor, but for how long we do not know. The fall of Berryer both freed her and placed her in a most delicate position. Now she was vulnerable to police harassment and arrest. Chatelet records show that she was not arrested between 1757 and 1770, but it is hard to say if she continued to operate her bordello on the rue St. Fiacre. By 1770, she was definitely gone, for a competitor, Madame Hecquet, had succeeded her at her address. Maybe she continued to sell sex at another location; we have few police records for the period after Berryer's disgrace. Maybe she died of the "illness" occasionally invoked in her final reports. Or maybe she found the sinecure, the stamp-tax position, for which she had always longed and spent the rest of her days in a dull but secure retirement.

# Notes

1. On Berryer see William Allan, *The Police of Paris 1718–1789* (Baton Rouge: Louisiana State University Press, 1979), 300.

2. On the Morals Bureau and the police in general see Erica Marie Bénabou, *La prostitution et la police des moeurs au dix-huitième siècle* (Paris: Editions Perrin, 1987), 96–186.

3. All of this material is in the Archives de la Bastille, 10,253. Fragments by other madams appear in the dossier, and there may have been more extensive report at some time. The police archives were dispersed and damaged on July 14, 1789, and then again because of the fire at the Hotel de Ville during the Commune.

4. Monetary incentives were included: "I met Monsieur Marais," reports Madame Payen, "and he told me I should note all the priests who came to my premises; I said I had none; he added that I would receive 6 *livres* for every priest I reported to him" (Archives de la Bastille).

5. Blackmail was an eighteenth-century policeman's most common tool and it inspired another of the Morals Bureau's activities: the arrest of hundreds of unsuspecting homosexuals who had the misfortune to try to pick up a police decoy in the Tuileries and Luxemburg gardens. See *Les buchers de Sodome* (Paris: Editions du Seuil, 1987).

6. Madame Payen does not fail to note the bad humor and lubricity of police inspector Marais, who "screwed a negress and gave her only 9 *livres*; one has only to be an inspector to imagine you can have a girl for nothing!" (Archives de la Bastille, 50).

7. Dhosmont's journal was probably recopied by an employee of Berryer's secretariat who also provided a list of clients on the lefthand side of the first page of each fortnightly report.

8. It is hard to tell how often Dhosmont met with the police chief. Presumably he would occasionally ask her to come to his office. On at least one occasion, Dhosmont was too chatty during with her interview with the police chief. On October 25, Dhosmont wrote to Berryer: "I beg your Grace's indulgence and ask that you pardon me the errors which I committed during our last interview. I remember, your Grace, that I talked too much and I ask a thousand pardons of your Grace. . . . Never again will I go to dine at the café des Anglois on the day I am privileged enough to be in your presence; a glass of champagne loosened my tongue" (Archives de la Bastille, 120).

9. Gaston Capon is convinced that one of the Berryer's employees recopied Madame Dhosmont's reports (Gaston Capon, *Les maisons closes aux XVIIIe siècle* [Paris: Daragon Libraire, 1903], 55). I don't see any particular basis for this conclusion, especially since the Dhosmont documents are filled with spelling errors. Moreover, the comments written in the margins are in another hand. My guess—though it is only a guess—is that a scribe made the notations and presented them as a kind of "executive

summary" to Berryer. Did anyone else read Dhosmont's reports? Probably not the police inspectors Meusnier and Marais. The latter in particular is the subject of a number of critical, even angry remarks in Dhosmont's and Baudoin's journals. Both hated Marais and were delighted to malign him to his boss.

10. Apparently, when she failed to follow the guidelines, Berryer dressed Dhosmont down during their private interviews. "You see Sir," she inserts in the report of February 20, 1751, "that when I don't write down the exact amount of time that a client is here, it's because he stays less than an hour." In the same entry she reports on a conversation and then adds, "Whenever I hear such talk I do my best to determine who is involved and where they live, just as you have instructed."

11. What we don't know is Madame's Christian or married name. She never refers to herself by her first name nor does inspector Meusnier or Marais. Her autobiography occupies pages 124–30v in Archives de la Bastille 10,253.

12. On the origins of other bawds see Inspector Marais's reports, Bibliothèque nationale, Ms. français, 111.358. Also, Capon, *Les maisons closes au XVIIIe siècle.*

13. Madame Dhosmont never regretted the loss of a male companion. She told Berryer on many occasions that she felt lucky not to have a man around. Her friend Madame Fleurance certainly suffered from her connection to a reprobate who lived off her earnings. Most madams did have lovers who caused problems. Madame Baudoin, for example, had a husband who tried to steal from her and with whom she had such a colossal fight that they were dragged before the commissioner of the quarter. Madame Fleurance had a dissolute lover who drank, gambled, and sponged off his mistress (Archives de la Bastille).

14. On whore biographies see Kathryn Norberg, "The Libertine Whore: Prostitution from Margot to Juliette," in *The Invention of Pornography*, ed. Lynn Hunt (New York: Zone Books, 1991).

15. I probably need not remind the reader that "choice" has been a crucial element in feminist interpretations of prostitution. A reasoned and reasonable summary of the debate between sex radical and pro-sex feminists appears in Wendy Chapkis, *Live Sex Acts: Women Performing Erotic Labor* (London: Routledge, 1997), 11–61.

16. Only Carlier had a different career path: she had débuted as a camp follower in the north of France (Archives de la Bastille).

17. These details come from Gourdan's death inventory that was located by Erica Marie Bénabou (*Prostitution et police des moeurs*, 250).

18. "I have no one with me today," Madame Dhosmont remarked on November 12, 1750 (Archives de la Bastille).

19. See sex workers' testimony in Wendy Chapkis, *Live Sex Acts*, 119.

20. This figure might be a bit on the young side. Madame Dhosmont was more likely to report the ages and family situation of very young girls because she wanted to protect herself from the retaliation of their parents. If the police chief knew that she had not debauched the girls, then she had some hope of deflecting charges of corrupting youth.

21. Just how much of the prostitutes' wages third parties appropriated is very hard to determine. These figures are based on police records from the Chatelet and the Archives de la Prefecture de la Police and on literature, in particular on Restif's *Pornographe* and Fougeret de Montbrun's *Margot la Ravaudeuse.*

22. It was not unusual for the most common form of feminine employment—domestic service—to go unpaid. Employers only actually paid servants their wages when they left and then gave them only a portion of their wages.

23. There is no question that Madame Dhosmont's pensioners experienced prostitution differently from their boss. Invariably, they were of a much lower social standing and probably could neither read nor write. They lacked Madame Dhosmont's cultural resources as well as her business acumen. Wendy Chapkis has found that among sex workers today, class background determines the degree to which a woman enjoys or is deprived of autonomy in sex work (Chapkis, *Live Sex Acts*, 97–107).

24. Thanks to inspectors Meusnier and Marais, we have voluminous police reports detailing the lives of these women. The reports can be found in the Bibliothèque nationale, Ms. français and in the Archives de la Bastille.

25. Pimps did tend to be more common in the lowest echelons of the sex trade. We know that pimps or *souteneurs* regularly protected brothels less elegant than that of Madame Dhosmont by intimidating the neighbors and harassing the competition.

26. We may assume that Madame Dhosmont omitted the names of clients too humble to merit mention. Consequently, we have at best a very partial picture of her bordello's clientele.

27. "He has her use up half a broom on his body," continues Madame Dhosmont, "and he only gives her 6 *livres*. If he came to my house I'd make him pay in advance and I'd skin him to the point that he would remember it a long time" (Archives de la Bastille, 10 sept 1752).

28. Madame Dhosmont describes her pensioners in much the same way she talks about her domestics. Certainly she instrumentalizes both: they are means to an end. But she has none of the prurient interest in them that is so liberally displayed by inspectors Meusnier and Marais.

29. If the whore's voice was familiar to eighteenth-century readers, so too was the madam's Procuresses or *macquerelles* filled French literature from the early seventeenth through the eighteenth centuries. From *Francion* to the *101 Days of Sodom*, French literature is filled with chatty madams.

30. The inspectors were hated by all the madams, but Marais was more resented than his predecessor. Madame Baudoin in particular loathed Marais and did her best to malign him in letters to Berryer.

31. "Monsieur de la Fosse," she tells Berryer, "came today with a letter of change for 25,000 *livres* on which he wants to borrow at least 20 *louis*." Had Monsieur de la Fosse failed to return the 20 *louis* as agreed, Madame Dhosmont would have made a great deal of money. But her chronicle breaks off.

# References

Adler, Laure. 1990. *La vie quotidienne dans les maisons close.* Paris: (n.pub.).

Allan, William. 1979. *The Police of Paris 1718–1789.* Baton Rouge: Louisiana State University Press.

Archives de la Bastille.

Archives de la Police.

Benabou, Erica Marie. 1987. *La prostitution et la police des moeurs aux dix-huitième siècle.* Paris: Editions Perrin.

Capon, Gaston. 1905. *Casanova à Paris.* Paris: (n.pub.).

———. 1903. *Les maisons closes aux XVIIIe siècle.* Paris: Daragon Libraire.

Chapkis, Wendy. 1997. *Live Sex Acts: Women Performing Erotic Labor.* London: Routledge.

Cheek, Pamela. 1995. Prostitutes of "political institution." *Eighteenth Century Studies* 28: 193–221.

Corbin, Alain. 1984. *Les filles de noce.* Paris: Plon.

Darnton, Robert. 1984. A police inspector sorts his files: The anatomy of the republic of letters. In *The Great Cat Massacre and Other Episodes in French Cultural History.* New York: Basic Books.

Hufton, Olwen. 1996. *The Prospect Before Her: A History of Women in Western Europe.* New York: Random House.

Hunt, Lynn, ed. 1991. *The Invention of Pornography.* New York: Zone Books.

1987. *Les Buchers de Sodome.* Paris: Editions du Seuil.

# Throwaway Women and the Politics of Sexual Commerce in Golden Age Spain

## Mary Elizabeth Perry

Sex workers of the 1990s have deep cultural roots in history, sharing many of the same issues and concerns with countless women and men from the past. For centuries sex workers have lived within a politics of sexual commerce that exemplifies the old missionary position, with men on top and women on the bottom. In this system of power men dominate and women serve, held in their respective places by a gendered economy that offers far fewer opportunities for livelihoods to women than to men. Moreover, a sexual-religious double standard has sanctified this missionary position of dominant men and sub-servient women, condemning sexually active women on the one hand while winking at the sexual exploits of men. Although important political, eco-nomic, and social changes have taken place in history, sex workers of today, whether male or female, continue to work within the same politics of sexual commerce. My argument is that by looking at prostitutes in the past, we can become conscious of this power system and question its assumptions—two major steps toward breaking a centuries-long pattern of oppression.

I want to develop this argument by looking at Spain four hundred years ago, when this country enjoyed what is called its Golden Age of art, literature, and imperialism. Writings of the period exalted virginity and chastity over sexual pleasures, and they also encouraged men to look at female sexuality not as a luxury to be enjoyed, but as a danger to be mastered, so evident in paintings of the temptations of Saint Jerome[1] that invariably portrayed these temptations in female form. One alternative women could choose was to vow chastity as a nun, but not many were called to be saints, such as Teresa of Avila, who must be considered an exceptional woman. Marriage, idealized in many portrayals of the Holy Family, provided the only alternative to chastity for women and the only legitimate place for sexual relations, which were meant for reproductive purposes only. Exchanging sex for money repre-sented a sterile and perverse form of sexuality, acceptable for male buyers, but not for female sellers.[2] Here the women who engaged in sexual com-merce lived lives of vulnerability and degradation, discounted and discarded as used toilet tissue.

In this society of Golden Age Spain, in which the lowliest material objects were too valuable to simply discard, women and children became disposable, but not because men could get along without them. In fact, men's demands for sexual services even seemed to increase in this time, and growing cities and towns established legal brothels for them (Perry 1990, 53–63). In the words of one cleric of the period, who paraphrased Saint Augustine, "The brothel of the city is like the stable or latrine for the house. Because just as the city keeps itself clean by providing a separate place where filth and dung are gathered, etc., so neither less nor more, assuming the dissolution of the flesh, acts the brothel: where the filth and ugliness of the flesh are gathered like the garbage and dung of the city"(Farfan 1585, esp. 730).* Such brothels could function effectively as a necessary evil, serviced by women and children who lacked other options and flooded the market with potential, part-time, or practicing prostitutes. And, because males usually supervised the brothels in early modern Spain, they preserved that missionary position of men on top, women on the bottom.

Men and boys also worked as prostitutes in Golden Age Spain, although officials vigorously prosecuted them for the crime of sodomy. Between 1567 and 1616, seventy-one men were burned to death in Seville for anal intercourse or intercourse with an animal. Concerned with sins "against nature," officials believed homosexual behavior so dangerous that they isolated men accused of this crime from others in the Royal Prison of Seville. Historical records show far less concern with homosexual relations between women and no recognition of female prostitutes as lesbians. They also indicate that most cases of sodomy did not involve the exchange of money, although some men provided gifts and favors for male partners. During this period, male prostitutes were perceived to be filling a female role. A sheriff, for example, was accused of keeping boy pros-titutes for male clients in a house of games, and one case prosecuted a black man who procured clients for "handsome, painted young gallants."

Yet the story of prostitutes past, as the story of prostitutes present, most often is that of female prostitutes who sought male clients. These women per-formed sex work for at least some part of their livelihood. Some worked in legal brothels, subject to rules and inspections; profits from their work went to various respectable people, including a sheriff in Seville, a large charitable hospital, and the Cathedral Chapter, which had been willed the income from

---

*Here and in other titles and quotations from literature of the period, I have provided the translation; the spelling and punctuation in Spanish are from the original source.

the property used for the city's legal brothel. However, the majority of female prostitutes worked outside the law, finding clients in the streets, in bars and inns. In Seville clandestine prostitutes favored streets along the waterfront and even the steps of the cathedral. Pimps and family members took money from many of these women and sent them out to engage in occasional or full-time prostitution.

Both legal and illegal prostitutes lived lives of great vulnerability, but they cannot be dismissed as passive victims. In Golden Age Spain these throwaway women also found ways to survive; moreover, they developed power to resist a sexist and racist world. Often abused, sometimes murdered and publicly humiliated, they developed strategies to protect themselves. Particularly significant for us in the present time, I believe, are attempts by these women to shape their own identities and their own lives, and to form a protective community of women.

The 1563 case of Alonso Cubillo, an employee of the tribunal of the Inquisition in the city of Seville, reveals the politics of sexual commerce in this major port of Golden Age Spain, for he was accused of killing Catalina Nuñez, a Portuguese mulatto whom he called a prostitute, a title vigorously denied by her mother and the women who lived with her.[3] Fiercely defending her reputation, they attacked Cubillo's abuse of power and succeeded in getting the Supreme Council in Madrid to reverse his acquittal by the tribunal in Seville. Far more than a single exceptional example, this case opens a window into the confused identities and oppressive power relations that characterize sexual commerce not only in Golden Age Spain, but also in our present-day world.

According to the testimony of several witnesses in the Cubillo case, a group of women singing and playing songs with a young man came down a narrow street very late on a summer night and tarried not far from the window of Alonso Cubillo, secretary for the tribunal of the Inquisition in Seville. Irritated at this disruption in his sleep, Cubillo got up and went to the window, where he shouted at the group to be quiet. He went back to bed, but as the music and noise resumed, Cubillo returned to the window. This time he shouted at the merrymakers that they were "drunks," and, according to some of the witnesses, he threw a brick or stone at them through the open window. Suddenly a cry came from below as the missile struck one of the women, later identified as Catalina Nuñez, a Portuguese mulatto living in the neighborhood.

Probably nothing more would have come of this case, except that the wounded woman died after lingering for three weeks in the hospital, and her mother, Margarita Çalema, went before the Inquisition to plead for justice in this homicide. Tearfully, the mother told inquisitors that when she had tried to file a suit against Alonso Cubillo in the court of ordinary justice, the magistrate had told her she had to bring suit in the court of the Inquisition because Cubillo was a secretary of the Holy Office. Inquisitors now took over the investigation and called for testimony from Alonso Cubillo, the house-keeper who lived in his house, the mother and companions of the dead woman, and the surgeons and clerics who attended and buried her.

Cubillo vigorously defended himself. He was some forty years old, he told the inquisitors, and a secretary "of this Holy Office, a person of note and nobility, a God-fearing good Christian. . . ." In contrast, the people in the street who had interrupted his sleep were "public women of bad life" who earned money through selling their bodies to men. The victim, Catalina Nuñez, and the women who lived with her were all "public women of bad reputation," he asserted. He also used the term, "women in love publicly dishonest," and declared that with their "lovers and pimps" they had caused in his neighborhood "many scandals," fights, and stabbings. Because of this, he had tried to clear the streets of them and had provoked their animosity, especially that of one of the women called "la Pastora." On the night in question, Cubillo testified, he had gone to his window only once to ask the noisemakers to be quiet and let him sleep. Then he heard cries and the voice of la Pastora saying that the Secretary Alonso Cubillo had thrown a stone that had hit a woman. Cubillo thus took the offensive in suggesting that la Pastora, an immoral and disorderly prostitute, had fabricated the story that he, a respectable officer with the Inquisition, was responsible for the murder.

Moreover, Cubillo stated, the prostitutes and their lovers and pimps had already engaged in rock-throwing in their street fights, and probably one of them had thrown the stone that hit Catalina Nuñez on that July night. Besides, he could not possibly have been the one who hit the woman because he had no enmity against her nor any prior dealings with her. In addition, the distance from his bedroom window to the woman made it physically impossible for him to have thrown the stone far enough to hit her.

Testimony by other witnesses supported only parts of his story. Cubillo's housekeeper, Ynés Hernando, for example, corroborated his version that the people making noise in the street that summer night were prostitutes, or "women of love," a euphemism she used perhaps out of modesty or wanting to give the appearance of refinement. She knew the names of two of them: María (or Mari) Méndez and Rosario la Pastora. At the time, she said, Cubillo was in a bad mood, and he went to the window to tell them to shut up not once, but twice, the second time shouting at them that they were drunks and scoundrels. Nevertheless, she denied in this testimony that she had seen him throw anything; and she stated that even if he had thrown something, the window was too far from the wounded woman for Cubillo to have hit her.

Here we might note a subtext important to this testimony—that Ynés Hernando depended on Cubillo not only for a livelihood, but for the place where she lived. She carefully separated herself from the women in the street, whom she labeled as prostitutes, although with a polite term, "women of love." Note that all of the euphemisms used for prostitutes in this case came from witnesses who were not themselves prostitutes and thus represent identities imposed externally. However, actual prostitutes might have used for themselves the phrase "women of love" so that this euphemism, which was also used by Alonso Cubillo's housekeeper, resembled the assumed names that brothel prostitutes took to attract customers and shape their own identities.[4]

In contrast, friends and the mother of Catalina Nuñez vehemently denied that she was a prostitute. They said that she had been married and some said she had a lover who was a ship's pilot, while one said she was a widow. All testified that she was quiet and peaceful, "honest and enclosed and of good life and reputation," in her mother's words. Furthermore, Margarita Çalema denied that the women her daughter had lived with were prostitutes, although several witnesses had testified that these women made their living from selling their bodies to men and that they lived on the street where prostitutes lived. One of the women who had been with Catalina Nuñez on the fateful night said that she had lived with her in the house of Ana de Ribera who rented out beds—a major strategy of survival, both for the landlady and for women of no wealth who needed a place to live.

Beneath all this testimony lurked a significant contradiction. Witnesses defending the reputation of Catalina Nuñez had to emphasize her living within the enclosure prescribed for all respectable women in this society. Expected to remain indoors except for very essential forays into the neighborhood, they clearly would not go out on the streets at night to sing and play songs with friends. The fact that Catalina Nuñez had been singing and playing songs in the street late at night seemed to contradict the testimony about her good reputation.

In addition, a significant gap in the testimony further undermined the attempts of Margarita Çalema and the other women to defend the reputation of her daughter. Absent from any of the testimony is information that could have shown that Catalina Nuñez and her companions had livelihoods other than prostitution, an absence that is particularly noteworthy since most Inquisition and legal records identified individuals by their occupation or marital status, age, and place of origin. As unmarried or widowed women, they had to have a livelihood; but for those like Catalina Nuñez, sex, race, and national origin constituted three strikes against their finding a successful livelihood. In these cases, it is not unlikely that Catalina Nuñez and her friends engaged in at least casual or occasional prostitution.

Clearly present in the records is the assumption that only a legal connection with a man—either as his wife or as his widow—could establish a legitimate status for a woman. A single woman with a lover or recognized livelihood was less reputable, but clearly more acceptable than a declared prostitute. Moreover, beneath the testimony of the mother and friends of Catalina Nuñez who defended her moral reputation was an implicit belief that inquisitors were more likely to find Alonso Cubillo guilty of a crime he should pay for if they believed that Catalina had been a virtuous young woman than if they assumed that she and her companions had noisily invaded public space, violating the prescriptions that women should be silent and enclosed, obedient to the strictures of gendered space.[5]

We should note here that in their testimony none of the women with Catalina Nuñez directly accused Alonso Cubillo of throwing the stone or brick that killed her. However, Juan de Medina, the hospital administrator, testified that he had asked Catalina Nuñez before she died who had thrown the brick or stone, and she said it was the secretary of the Inquisition, whose name she did not know. This same witness said that some Portuguese women had brought Catalina Nuñez to the hospital and that one day Alonso Cubillo had gone to the hospital and told him that the wounded woman and others had been playing and singing "dirty and dishonest" songs in the street when a stone had been thrown and hit her.

Juan Gonzáles, the young man who had been playing and singing with the women, testified that he was twenty-two years old, worked as a bread-maker for ships, and lived with Marco Caño, the local sheriff. On the night in question, he and the women were playing songs and singing when a man came to the window and shouted, "Get away, scoundrels, you are drunk," but the women didn't want to leave. The man threw something and hit one of the women and made two wounds in her head. Juan Gonzáles then went to look for a cleric and for a barber to treat her. After a day or two, they took the woman to the hospital, and later he heard that she had died there.

Marco Caño, the sheriff with whom Juan Gonzáles lived, testified that he had heard Alonso Cubillo call the women "putas," a vulgar name for prostitutes. He also stated that Cubillo had thrown a rock that wounded the woman in the head. He identified the women involved as Mari Méndez, who lived in the neighborhood at the house of Ana de Ribera; la Pastora, who lived nearby on a little street; Blanca Hernández, who lived nearby in the house of Francisca Hernández; and the youth, Juan Gonzáles. In giving the only direct testimony that Alonso Cubillo had thrown the missile that killed Catalina Nuñez, Marco Caño and his young friend, Juan Gonzáles, demonstrated confidence in their ability to get a verdict against Cubillo and a firm resolve to bring him to justice. Perhaps they harbored old resentments against this Inquisition official who had trespassed on their territory when he had taken it upon himself to clear the neighborhood streets of the prostitutes and their pimps. Perhaps their testimony against Cubillo merely represents in a small way the larger power struggle between the Inquisition and secular law officials and the competition between officials seeking to control commerce on the streets.

Alonso Cubillo called five witnesses from his neighborhood who could not give testimony about the actual wounding or death of Catalina Nuñez but verified his version that she and her companions were prostitutes. They lived in "a neighborhood of public women who had pimps," where "many fights" took place, these witnesses said. One person declared that Juan González was the lover and pimp of the dead mestiza Catalina, but another witness said that he was the lover and pimp of Catalina Romera and she knew this "because he came to her street with his sword and buckler to guard his lover and each day he came with her and hit and slapped her and then they were lovers."

The role of Juan Gonzáles in the world of the women accused of being prostitutes deserves closer scrutiny. A young man, variously described as a breadmaker and a servant, Gonzáles had befriended the women in question. Obviously more than a would-be customer, the role that most city people assumed for young single men, Gonzáles represents a less acknowledged aspect of the connection between unmarried women and young men of the city. He may have simply befriended these women and enjoyed having fun with them. If the two witnesses were correct, however, he had become a pimp, determined to profit from the work of a prostitute and to hold her as his income-producing property. Prostitutes in this society may have escaped the oppression and brutality of a husband, but not that of the pimp. Men continued to hold the dominant position in sexual commerce, even when a prostitute could demand money for the services that wives were expected to give free, out of obedience.

For some two years the case of Alonso Cubillo continued as inquisitors interviewed witnesses and heard charges and responses from the accused and the plaintiff. Finally in September 1565 the Inquisition sent an official to Seville to try to resolve it, first actually viewing the house of Cubillo to verify whether it would have been possible for him to have thrown the stone or brick that struck Catalina Nuñez, and then consulting with inquisitors of the tribunal in Seville. Four days after his arrival, the tribunal reached a decision: "The said Alonso del Cubillo should be absolved of the charge and perpetual silence should be imposed on any party in opposition." Specifically, it placed Margarita Çalema under this order, prohibiting her from asking or demanding anything from Cubillo.

However, Margarita Çalema seemed not to hear the order of perpetual silence, for she obtained a royal provision that sent the case to Madrid in November 1565. Perhaps strengthened in her resolve by the testimony of the sheriff and her daughter's friends, she appealed the absolution of Cubillo. Declaring that she was "a poor widow and a miserable person," she nonetheless had the acumen, or perhaps some legal advice, to point out the legal irregularity that inquisitors in Seville had never let her see letters regarding this case that she should have seen. Three months later, inquisitors in Madrid overturned the decision of the tribunal in Seville and sentenced Cubillo to pay 60 ducats to Margarita Çalema plus costs of the entire case. Yet the case did not end here, for many petitions followed—most from Cubillo, who contested the decision from Madrid, and one from Margarita Çalema, who asked the Inquisition to order Cubillo to deposit four ducats on her behalf within three days.

Obviously, the case is not about the value of a young woman who was killed for singing in the streets. Nor is it about whether or not Catalina Nuñez was a prostitute. In fact, witnesses used so many euphemisms and assertions to identify Catalina Nuñez that her identity remains very much masked. She seems to have been one of those many nameless women who lived in a vast gray area between survival and transgressing sexual respectability, where the slightest change in fortune or the smallest misstep could push them into prostitution. These women shared a frightening vulnerability, not only to attacks on their reputation, but also to physical violence. We can honor these women as we gather together at this International Congress on Prostitution, especially their attempts to shape their own identities and lives, their moments of subverting an oppressive sexual order. We can celebrate the community of women that helped one another cope with vulnerability and, at the death of one of them, determined that her murderer should be brought to justice. Yet we must also remember the dark side of this world that still continues for sex workers, the world of women like Catalina Nuñez who sought to survive in the shadows of masked identities, careless murders, and sexual politics.

# Notes

1. For a thorough discussion of sexuality in early modern Spain, see Maria Helena Sánchez Ortega, *La Mujer y la sexualidad en el antiguo régimen: La perspectiva inquisitorial* (Madrid: Akal, 1992). Michel Foucault, *The Use of Pleasure*, vol. 2 of *The History of Sexuality*, trans. Robert Hurley (New York: Pantheon, 1985), esp. 22, 92, describes a change in attitude from a classical Greek ethos of sexual moderation, in which the male avoided self-indulgence that could enslave him, to a Christian ethos of self-renunciation.

2. For further discussion of the condemnation of sexual commerce, see Thomas Laqueur, *Making Sex: Body and Gender from the Greeks to Freud* (Cambridge, Mass., and London: Harvard University Press, 1990), 230–32.

3. This case is in the Archivo Histórico Nacional, *Inquisición*, legajo 2057, no. 12. Sociological theories of labeling may help to explain why the friends and mother of Catalina Nuñez so vigorously denied that she was a prostitute; see, for examples, Howard S. Becker, *Outsiders: Studies in the Sociology of Deviance* (New York and London: The Free Press, 1963); Kai T. Erikson, *Wayward Puritans: A Study of the Sociology of Deviance* (New York: John Wiley and Sons, 1966); Harold Garfinkel, "Conditions of Successful Degradation Ceremonies," *American Journal of Sociology* 61 (March 1956): 420–24; Walter R. Gove, ed., *The Labelling of Deviance: Evaluating a Perspective* (Beverly Hills, Calif.: Sage, 1980).

4. Mary Elizabeth Perry, "Deviant Insiders: Legalized Prostitution and a Consciousness of Women in Early Modern Seville," *Comparative Studies in Society and History* 27, no. 1 (January 1985): 146, discusses names given by brothel prostitutes in response to official inspectors. However, note that Jacques Rossiaud, *Medieval Prostitution*, trans. Lydia G. Cochrane (New York and Oxford: Basil Blackwell, 1988), 34–35, found that French brothels gave prostitutes a "nom de guerre" as they began to work in them.

5. For a discussion of these prescriptions, see Teresa S. Soufas, "Silence and Violence in the *Comedias*," in *Sex and Love in Early Modern Spain*, ed. Alain Saint-Saëns (New Orleans: University Press of the South, 1996), esp. 129. For disorderly women's intrusions into public space, see Mary Elizabeth Perry, "Marginadas y peligrosas: Las mujeres y la transformación de los ámbitos públicos en la época moderna," en *Mujeres y ciudadanía. La relación de las mujeres con los ámbitos públicos*, Preactas del II Coloquio Internacional de la Asociacion Española de Investigación Histórica de las Mujeres (Santiago de Compostela, 1994).

# References

Archivo Histórico Nacional. *Inquisición*, legajo 2057, no. 12.

Becker, Howard S. 1963. *Outsiders: Studies in the Sociology of Deviance*. New York and London: The Free Press.

Erikson, Kai T. 1966. *Wayward Puritans: A Study of the Sociology of Deviance*. New York: John Wiley and Sons.

Farfan, Francisco. 1585. *Tres libros contra de peccado de la simple fornicación: Donde se averigua, que la torpeza ente solteros es peccado mortal, segun ley divina, natural, y humana; y se responde a los engaños do los que dizen que no es peccado*. Salamanca: Herederos de Matthias Gast.

Foucault, Michel. 1985. *The Use of Pleasure*, vol. 2, *The History of Sexuality*, translated by Robert Hurley. New York: Pantheon.

Garfinkel, Harold. 1956. Conditions of successful degradation ceremonies. *American Journal of Sociology* 61: 420–24.

Gove, Walter R., ed. 1980. *The Labelling of Deviance: Evaluating a Perspective*. Beverly Hills, Calif.: Sage.

Laqueur, Thomas. 1990. *Making Sex: Body and Gender from the Greeks to Freud*. Cambridge, Mass., and London: Harvard University Press.

Perry, Mary Elizabeth. 1985. Deviant insiders: Legalized prostitution and a consciousness of women in early modern Seville. *Comparative Studies in Society and History* 27, no. 1 (January): 146.

———. 1990. *Gender and Disorder in Early Modern Seville*. Princeton, N.J.: Princeton University Press.

———. 1994. Marginadas y peligrosas: Las mujeres y la transformación de los ámbitos públicos en la época moderna. In *Mujeres y ciudadanía. La relación de las mujeres con los ámbitos públicos*, Preactas del II Coloquio Internacional de la Asociación Española de Investigación Histórica de las Mujeres. Santiago de Compostela.

Rossiaud, Jacques. 1988. *Medieval Prostitution*, translated by Lydia G. Cocharane. New York and Oxford: Basil Blackwell.

Sánchez Ortega, María Helena. 1992. *La Mujer y la sexualidad en el antiguo régimen: La perspectiva inquisitorial*. Madrid: Akal.

Soufas, Teresa S. 1996. Silence and violence in the *Comedias*. In *Sex and Love in Early Modern Spain*, edited by Alain Saint-Saëns. New Orleans: University Press of the South.

# SEX WORK AND PUBLIC POLICIES IN CHINA

## WAN YAN HAI

In a 1991 press release, the Chinese Ministry of Public Security reported that 200,000 sex workers had been arrested. In 1992 the number had increased by 20 percent, and it has continued to rise each year since. This, however, is the tip of the iceberg because most experts on the topic estimate the real number of sex workers and their clients is far higher than the number arrested, and some estimate that there are twenty times more than those reported.

In China, sexual work has been both ignored and targeted. For many years during the reign of Mao, there was an official denial of the existence of prostitution and the ruling party's political and ideological need even today is to maintain the denial of the existence of such activities. Every year there is a nationwide campaign against commercial sex work in China that involves police detention and media stigmatization. Recently, because Chinese society has become more commercial, capitalist, and corrupt, it may be that the law and action against sexual work is simply an exercise for the ruling party to sharpen its tools for use in the political, police, and ideological arenas, and in other areas where pressure can be applied. Still, every year, in the campaign against sexual work, political dissidents and marginal groups such as gays and lesbians are regularly arrested.

It also seems that the criminal cases against sex workers and sexual minorities in general are not just for political and ideological reasons, but economic ones, i.e., graft. Many police punish the sex workers and sexual minorities, pocketing the money they carry on them and requesting bribes not to arrest them again. Not only do the police condemn sex workers and minorities, but they also ignore crimes committed against these individuals by others. Every year, when the campaign against sex work or sexual promiscuity begins anew, the incidence of crimes against sex workers and sexual minorities also increases to ever-higher levels.

Interestingly, prior to 1996 there was no criminal law against commercial sex work in China if only because it was claimed not to exist. Still, sex workers have been sentenced to hard labor and re-education since 1991 under various other charges. The detainees were put to work and forced to undergo "socialist spiritual" education although, unfortunately, they were never taught any useful skills or given health education.

Inevitably, the incidence of STDs (sexually transmitted diseases) among sex workers is very high. According to the statistics of the Gunagzhou re-education center, the rate of STD infection among female sex workers who had been arrested was 83 percent in 1990. Like the incidence of drug use, HIV is now also spreading rapidly in China. In Kunming, the capital city of Yunnan Province, as late as 1994 condom use was less than 5 percent among those diagnosed as having STDs, multiple use of the same syringe was common, and females arrested for sexual activity and required to undergo re-education (mostly commercial sex workers) were also on drugs.

Acquired immune deficiency syndrome (AIDS) is becoming a serious problem for gay male commercial sex workers. Transgendered people are not common, but several of the known ones earn money through commercial sex because of the financial burden brought on by the expensive operation. In fact, gay male commercial sex work has become common in contemporary China, especially in the larger and more open cities. It is estimated that Beijing has several thousand gay male sex workers and the number is growing rapidly as many gays leave their villages and move to urban areas to escape family pressure, homophobic attitudes, and so on. Many turn to prostitution because they have been arrested and find it difficult to get other jobs. Those gays and lesbians who have managed to not yet be exposed work in fear of blackmail and of being robbed. No openly gay organization exists in China and even health groups working to deal with the growing crisis in STDs find themselves hassled by the authorities.

Government slogans continue to emphasize that sex workers, gays, lesbians, and others need to be eradicated in order to eliminate sexually transmitted diseases. There is a lack of psychological, social, legal, and even health services for commercial sex workers and participants in illicit sex activities until they are arrested. In jail the emphasis is on transforming them into "morally" healthy people, not on helping them come to terms with being gay or lesbian or providing alternative employment for the sex workers. The result is a growing underground of stigmatized individuals who seek out services from friendly physicians or, in many cases, understanding families.

In short, commercial sex work remains illegal in China. This, however, does not eliminate it, and the ideology is such that no community-based organization can play any role in providing health and social services for sex workers or participants. The social and health workers who do try to help face a massive challenge from the police, government, and the party.

# COMMUNITY HONOR/SEXUAL BOUNDARIES: A DISCURSIVE ANALYSIS OF *DEVADASI* CRIMINALIZATION IN MADRAS, INDIA, 1920–1947

JUDY WHITEHEAD

In the late nineteenth century, colonial ideology emphasized the moral and scientific inferiority of India's traditions. The position of Indian women and supposedly "barbaric" Hindu practices such as child marriage and the *devadasi* system became symbols of Britain's higher level of civilization and of its moral right to govern a subject population. Beginning about 1880, the indigenous intelligentsia reacted with a fervent nationalism that asserted the superior spirituality of its culture and, in particular, the spirituality of the uncolonized domestic abode and the mothers who resided therein. In this contest between colonial images of the superior education and "civilization" of British women and Indian nationalist images of the superior spirituality of Indian women, less "respectable" expressions of female sexuality, such as the courtesans and *devadasis,* were gradually marginalized and criminalized. The criminalization of the *devadasis* in the 1920s, 1930s, and 1940s was the result of the intersection of apparently competing discourses, imperialist nationalism and anticolonial nationalisms. These discourses shared similar premises regarding the regulation of female sexuality. "Normal" and "moral" expression of female sexuality was that contained in monogamous marriages and motherhood: the health of the "family" and of the "race" was partly dependent on the behavior of mothers, considered as caregivers to the nation. In the case study of the criminalization of the *devadasis* of the Madras Presidency between 1920 and 1940, I will discuss the similarities among several discourses: imperial medical condemnation of traditional religious practices, nationalist reformers who viewed the *devadasis* as simple prostitutes posing a hygienic risk to the nation, and Tamil nationalists who viewed the *devadasi* system as an insult to Sudra honor. What tied these nationalist discourses together was a single underlying premise: the morality/health/progress of the national com-

91

munity was dependent upon the sexual honor/cleanliness/normality of "its" women. Indeed, by the 1920s, reformers, colonial administrators, and nationalists drew implicit equations between national morality and community hygiene. Hence the supposedly scientific discourse of public health and the more "traditional" discourse of national honor and morality were frequently conflated, each becoming metaphors for the other. Fears about the spread of venereal disease through prostitution became a frequent symbol for anxiety about sexual transgressions of national boundaries and moral communities. In this convergence between middle-class colonial administrators' views, and those of (mainly) middle-class nationalists, the *devadasi* became equated with commercial prostitutes and viewed as an undesirable "alien" to be suppressed in the nation's march to modernity and enlightenment.

Kay Jordan (1989) has explained the criminalization of *devadasis* in the Madras Presidency as due to a growing sense of shame toward indigenous traditions that was imparted by Western colonial education and missionary activities among middle-class Indians. Yet this explanation is incomplete. It ignores the fact that by the 1920s, social reforms, such as *devadasi* abolition, were promoted by and seen as emerging from within the nationalist block itself. In relation to public health policy concerning venereal diseases and prostitution, most nationalist reformers argued that British commitment to a policy of non-interference with Indian beliefs and customs had led to a serious neglect of public health (Arnold 1993, 241). In fact, Jordan's own information, taken mostly from legislative records, shows that the colonial administration was far more reluctant to intervene in religious matters such as the *devadasi* institution than were nationalist legislators during this period. A simplistic colonial discourse perspective, such as that of Jordan, assumes that all hegemony and will to power resides in the domain of the colonizer and none emanates from the colonized themselves (Sarkar 1993, 1869–70). Yet by the later colonial period, during which time the actual criminalization of Madras *devadasis* occurred (1927–1947), Gandhi had forged a mass movement for India's independence and various electoral reforms enacted through pressure from the nationalist movement had partially devolved power to the Indian electorate. Increasingly, both colonizer and colonized were becoming aware that the question of India's independence was more a matter of time than of fact. In addition, by focusing on legislative records alone, Jordan ignores local discourses of gender and power, in particular the anti-Brahmin and Brahmin conflict in Tamil Nadu. This conflict provided a major backdrop for Madras politics in the late-colonial and postcolonial periods.

Colonial control of the sexual body politic was evident in the late nineteenth century in the enactment of the Contagious Diseases Act (1868–1888) and Cantonment Regulations. These laws provided for the inspection and regulation of Indian women even suspected of providing sexual services for British troops. In addition, regulated brothels were created for British troops in India and a number of courtesans were transferred to regimental brothels (Ballhatchet 1980). The nationalists of the 1880s strongly objected to the operation of the Contagious Diseases Act, seeing it as evidence of India's national shame and of the brutal exploitation of Indian women by British troops (Whitehead 1995). Yet by the early twentieth century, Western medicine and public health policies had gained increasing prestige among the nationalist intelligentsia due to successes in treating infectious diseases and they became an active aspect of indigenous rhetoric and social practice (Arnold 1993, 242). Although nationalists criticized many aspects of British and European culture and society, the basic terms through which the human body and the Indian body politic were to be understood, regulated, and controlled were unconsciously set by nationalist acceptance of the superiority of Western medicine. Increasingly throughout the early twentieth century, legislative debates concerning the role of sexuality, women, and motherhood were couched in scientific, medical arguments, rather than through the religious precepts of the *Darmashastras*.

Historically, *devadasis* arose out of the South Indian bardic tradition and consisted of groups of dancers and oral historians who became attached to specific courts and temples throughout southern and eastern India. The first scriptural mention of *devadasis* is found in an eleventh-century collection of stories, the *Kathasaritsagara*, and there are no known references to *devadasis* and temple dancing in the oldest books of dance theory, the *Natya Shastra* and the *Abinaya Darpana*. In inscriptions and textual evidence from the thirteenth century onward, the *devadasis* are referred to as "ever-auspicious" females who were to deal with the dangerous divine, especially in its feminine aspect of *shakti*. The status of *devadasis* varied throughout the subcontinent, being most closely connected to the courts and of highest status in Tamil Nadu and Orissa. Since the *devadasis* of Orissa managed to maintain their privileges throughout the colonial period (Marglin 1984), I will be focusing only on the *devadasis* of Tamil Nadu in this chapter.[1]

In ritual terms, the word *devadasi* was applied to that class of women who dedicated themselves to temple worship through ceremonies of marriage to deities. During the Vijayanagar period (1346–1565), the term was applied to all women devotees who donated money to temples, and not only to temple dancers (Orr 1996). *Devadasis* were considered ever-auspicious, or *nitya-samungali*, because they had been symbolically married to deities and could therefore never be widowed. No *devadasi* caste per se existed. Rather, there existed a *devadasi* way of life and professional ethic. The profession of *devadasis* was hereditary, but it did not confer the right to work without adequate qualification. These qualifications included a rigorous education and five to ten years of training in *Bharat Natyam* dance undertaken with a *guru*, or dance teacher. The teacher also came from the *devadasi* community but was invariably male. The caste term *Isai Vellala*, which many men from the *devadasi* community claimed as their own, only emerged in relation to the reform movement and the anti-Brahmin Self Respect organization to which many belonged (Anandhi 1991, 23). Following the dedication ceremony, the *devadasi* usually acquired a Brahmin patron who sponsored her dance performances and contributed to the financial upkeep of her household and orchestra. He also often became her lover.

The matricentric features of *devadasi* households and communities have been much remarked upon, and indeed roused missionaries' disgust in the nineteenth century. *Devadasis* were awarded land grants and heritable rights in revenue from temple lands, called *inam* grants. Women of the *devadasi* community were favored over men in inheritance matters, as daughters inherited the bulk of *devadasi* estates. *Devadasis* were also the only women allowed to adopt children under Hindu customary law. They had a great deal of choice over their sexual partners and patrons and also performed in the Thanjavur courts and at important domestic ceremonies of elite families, being considered a prestigious adjunct to domestic institutions, rather than their ravager (Srinivasen n.d., 183). They were also forbidden from exerting themselves in domestic labor.

The *devadasi* community was divided into two sections: the *periamelam* and the *cinnamelam*. The former consisted of offspring from marriages within the community, the latter were the offspring of the *devadasi* and her patron. The former produced the dance teachers and players in the large orchestra and were considered the pure section of the community, while the latter provided accompanists for the *devadasis'* dance and were considered the "mixed" or "impure" section of the *devadasi* community (Srinivasen n.d., 181). The *devadasis* were also stratified into various classes, a classification that arose during the hegemony of the Tanjore kingdom. At the top of the hierarchy were *rajadasis* (royal *dasis*), who performed various sacrifices for the king; next the *natana dasis* (dancing *dasis*), who were able to perform *Bharat Natyam* dance services for the deities in the temples, and finally *sannidhi dasis*, those who belonged to the shrine. Another class of *dasis*, the *Kamalambal paramparai*, were considered to belong to the "house of the consort" of the deity, and hence were of lower ritual status than the first three classes of *dasis*. It is probable that the lowest class of *dasis* practiced temple prostitution and did not have the same financial autonomy and status as the *natana dasis* and the *rajadasis* (Kersenboom-Story 1987, 184).

The relative legal and financial autonomy of *devadasis* placed them in an unusual and somewhat marginal position in early-twentieth-century South Asia. According to most schools of Brahminical Hinduism, women's sexuality, although auspicious and activating, had to be controlled through spatial restrictions and arranged marriages. In addition, intimate social contact between upper and lower classes and castes, especially sexual relations, was highly regulated in Brahminical Hinduism, upper castes equating caste endogamy with high status. Hence, the relative status of a family was judged partly by the fidelity of wives and their conduct as mothers, as upper-class women were viewed as symbolic gate keepers of their family's status or honor (Engels 1987, 425). The values of fidelity, chastity, and purity were especially marked among Brahmins, for whom even remarriage of widows was disallowed. Indeed, although maintaining a pure lifestyle, widows were considered exemplars of female inauspiciousness: the death of their husbands was viewed as a part of their *karmic* burden. The *devadasi*, through her symbolic marriage at puberty to a deity who could never die, was considered permanently auspicious and life-enhancing. She was to be present at those critical life-moments that required the balancing of the auspicious and inauspicious. She was also required to remove the accumulated destructive force of the evil eye that the god might contract during a procession by waving the pot-lamp in front of him (Kersenboom-Story 1987, xix).

For the English middle classes who formed the bulk of the colonial administration in the Victorian and post-Victorian eras, sanitary reforms, social hygiene, and purity movements were linked with evangelical values of progress, thrift, sobriety, respectability, and self-improvement (Davidoff 1988, 17–23). Middle-class British ideology also valued the chastity of daughters and fidelity of wives. However, this was justified through eugenics and social hygiene discourse. Extramarital sexuality, especially that of women, was dangerous because it could spread disease and degeneration throughout the body politic. In fact, the British intelligentsia was largely accepting of eugenicist views in the early part of the twentieth century. The British Eugenics Society and Social Hygiene Council examined the health of family lineages through the pedigree and promoted laws that denied the rights of alcoholics and the medically and morally unfit to marry (Mazumdar 1992). In the eugenicist paradigm, extramarital female sexuality was a sign of degeneracy of families, as well as being a physical danger to the health of communities and families. Tendencies to prostitution could be identified by heredity and by certain physiological markers of degeneration, e.g., a large second toe and a Darwin's ear (Gilman 1985). Hence both Brahminical Hinduism and eugenics philosophy attempted to control female sexuality, albeit in different ways, since psychological, rather than spatial restrictions, were the main means of controlling women in middle-class Britain. In addition, Hinduism at least provided a marginal yet auspicious space for a minority of women who were trained as classical dancers in the *devadasi* tradition. This space came under attack in the early twentieth century, as eugenics views became an important defining discourse of health policies among the nationalist intelligentsia in India.

Equations between the health of mothers and the future health of the "race" gained increasing prominence internationally from the early twentieth century onward, as eugenics movements from Britain, continental Europe, and North America articulated a supposed connection between national advancement and racial health (Whitehead 1996, 187–211). The development of Indian nationalism as an organized force dates from the first sitting of the Indian National Congress (INC) in Bombay in 1885. Despite lodging protests against the Contagious Diseases Act and Contonment Regulations in early sessions, between 1880 and 1910 both male and female leaders of the INC developed a construct model of the ideal female citizen whose role was primarily that of an educated mother and wife. Indeed, the mother was simultaneously the repository of ancient traditions, an icon of the nation, an embodiment of *shakti,* and the educated caregiver of future generations (Chakravarti 1990). The domestic sphere, symbolizing ancient traditions, thus became opposed to the outer world of politics and economics, a site where Indian middle-class men continued to experience subordination (Chatterjee 1990, 233–54; Sarkar 1987, 2011–15). The nationalist intelligentsia promoted female education that would improve the ability of women to be educated mothers, aware of domestic science and hygiene. In this process, less respectable expressions of female sexuality became devalued and marginalized, seen as a symbol of historical degeneration of a past great tradition.

Partly through the influence of the eugenics movement, the Western medical profession infiltrated social policy and legal debates concerning sexuality internationally in the first decades of the twentieth century. The Rockefeller Foundation, the major financier of tropical disease institutes after 1910, saw a close, causal connection between national progress, racial health, the health of mothers, and moral hygiene associated with monogamous familial sexuality. In fact, the health professionals of the Rockefeller Foundation believed that disease was a major cause of poverty, not vice versa (Farley 1991). After World War I, the League of Nations and the International Labour Office also adopted social hygiene policies and promoted hygienically educated motherhood as the goal for all emerging and developed nations. As a result of the dissemination of social hygiene models, the health of each nation became linked with the role of its mothers (Davin 1979).

Due to its enclave character in the nineteenth century, the influence of Western medicine on most people's lives in India was negligible before 1910 (Ramasubban 1988). However, by the second decade of the twentieth century, Western-trained physicians were offering real competition to *vaids* and *hakims,* indigenous doctors trained in humoral and herbal medical traditions, in major cities through the growth of dispensaries. At the level of legal debate and jurisprudence, their influence was much more profound as nationalist concerns about the health and progress of the nation promoted a medicalized view of both the human body and the social body. This is shown not only in debates about the *devadasis* in Madras, but also in most social reform issues relating to women during the 1920s and 1930s. These included raising the legal age of marriage, the reform of *purdah,* increased education for girls, concerns about tuberculosis, and the banning of mining work to women. The editorial in the first issue of the magazine of the first nationwide women's organization, *Stri-Dharma*, reflected the equations that were constantly being made between the state of the nation's health and the state of motherhood: "Women's health is important to national progress because women are the mothers of the nation, and if they are physically underdeveloped and sickly, then the whole nation will become weak and enfeebled" (1913, 2).

"Science," it was argued, "should be brought into the training of the strong, great race of the future children of India through its mothers (*Stri-Dharma* 1913, 2–3). In fact, throughout the 1920s *Stri-Dharma* continued to agitate against prostitution, seeing it as a social evil spreading potential disease to the body politic of "respectable society." A 1921 editorial in *Stri-Dharma* praised the Social Purity Committee of the Bombay Women's Council for strenuously agitating to remove the "Bombay Blot." "The increasingly immoral state of the city is becoming a menace to the health of even the purest women" (*Stri-Dharma* 1921, 18). Dr. Muthlakshmi Reddy, an editor of *Stri-Dharma* and president of the Women's India Association in the 1930s, argued that prostitution constituted a menace to children and that "mothers of the race could not tolerate places that were centres of moral and physical disease" (*Stri-Dharma* 1928, 1).

The 1920s were a highwater mark in legal reforms for women, marking the first period in which the necessity for changes in the position of women acquired nearly unanimous consent from various currents of the nationalist movement (All-India Women's Congress 1927–1936). Reformist pressure increased after the Montagu-Chelmsford reforms in 1919, which instituted a principle of dyarchy that enfranchised Indian-elected legislatures at the provincial level for an array of domestic matters. During this period, reformers and nationalists often criticized the colonial administration for inhibiting social reform and for its lack of concern with public health and social hygiene measures. As the family and the home were symbolized as the microcosm of the nation, the domestic roles of women as mothers were absorbed into various nationalist debates concerning the future progress of the Indian nation.

By 1920, most nationalist reformers accepted the unconscious distinctions between familial and nonfamilial sexuality embedded in Western medical discourse, as well as the oppositions between chaste and unchaste women that were, in turn, now linked to medicalized conceptions of normality and abnormality.[2] Even Gandhi idealized the chaste Sita as the role model for both male and female nationalists and expelled the Barisol prostitutes from participation in the Bengal Provincial Congress Committee. Clearly, for most nationalists and reformers of the 1920s, the respectable icon of the self-sacrificing mother figure excluded the *devadasis*, whose sexual relations with their patrons were increasingly interpreted as a recent degeneration from a pure past when they were supposedly chaste temple servants and dancers.

Given the prominence of the eugenics model in international and national health policies, it is perhaps not surprising that the leader of the anti-*devadasi* campaign in Madras was a prominent doctor. In fact, she was the first woman doctor to graduate from medical school in India, Dr. Muthulakshmi Reddy. Dr. Reddy was a prominent member of the Women's India Association, an editor of *Stri-Dharma*, a member of the British Social Hygiene Council, and finally the first female member of the Madras Legislative Council. Born into a Brahmin family of modest means in Pudukottah, she was sent to a boys' school, where she excelled in the sciences, passing among the top ten students in matriculation exams and finishing her intermediate schooling at Pudukottah Boy's College. Admitted to Medical College in Madras in 1907, she obtained her medical degree in 1912. In the next ten years, she set up her own obstetrics and gynecological practice, married another doctor, and completed postgraduate study in London in 1925 (Reddy 1964, 43). Although specializing in the treatment of cancer in London, she became active in the Child Welfare Movement there and joined the British Social Hygiene Council, of which she remained a member throughout her life. Her year in London persuaded her that lack of hygienic practices of Indian mothers and venereal diseases were among the most important medical dangers facing India and other emerging nations. Upon returning to Madras, she was elected the sole woman member to the Madras Legislative Council in the anti-Brahmin Justice Party Ministry headed by the Raja of Panagal. From this position, Dr. Reddy campaigned relentlessly against the *devadasi* institution until she resigned in 1931 to protest Gandhi's arrest. She introduced the law that was instrumental in spelling an end to the *devadasi* institution, the Madras Hindu Religious Endowments Act of 1929, which unlinked temple service from the granting of *inam* lands and revenue rights to the *devadasis*. In her medical practice and legislative career, Dr. Reddy was a major proponent of eugenicist views, by which the application of hereditarian principles to practices of sexuality, childbirth, and socialization was thought to increase national fitness and economic progress. In the legislative debates on the *devadasi* land grants, she criticized the *devadasi* system thus:

> It is beyond my comprehension how in a country which can boast of innumerable saints . . . irresponsibility in vice has been ignored and even encouraged (through the devadasi system) to the detriment of the health of the individual and of the future race. . . . Modern science has proven that continence is conducive to the health and well-being of the individual, family, and the future race, and that sexual immorality harms both the individual and the community. Venereal disease is responsible for fifty percent of child blindness and deafness, much insanity, and other diseases such as paralysis, liver and kidney disease and heart disease . . . and it is a racial poison capable of being transmitted to one's children, the second, or even the third generation. (Reddy 146–47)

In *Stri-Dharma*, Dr. Reddy further editorialized on the *devadasi* "problem," attempting to convince Indian feminists and social reformers that the institution was an example of backwardness, disease, and irrational tradition:

> I would advise my country people to shut the stable before the horse is stolen. Who does not realise that "prevention is better than cure?" Why then this nervousness on the part of our people to put an end once and for all to a practice that disfigures and defiles our sacred temples, that contaminates the youth of the country, a practice that brings ill-health, disruption, discontent into happy families and is thus a menace to family life and finally poisons the future race through venereal diseases. If we want to come up as a nation to command the self-respect of the world, I feel very strongly that all the social diseases must be cured, because to my knowledge India is the only country in the world that condemns a particular class of girls into prostitution. . . . What is still more deplorable is the prevalence of the popular belief that this iniquitous custom has the sanction of our holy religion—hence should not be interfered with. . . . Hindu Society . . . is neglecting a most dangerous disease and so deserves the serious attention of all healthy- minded citizens, of all earnest reformers, patriots, and statesmen. Only an . . . amendment of the Hindu Religious Endowments Act will save the future race from further mental, moral, and physical decay. (*Stri-Dharma* 1927, 103)

In Dr. Reddy's conception of the "nation," medical health and moral boundaries become conflated. The future of the nation and the health of the "race" were linked to sexual continence, motherhood, and the hygienic education of young girls and women. Although Dr. Reddy was more explicit in her social hygienic views than many others, most of the nationalist intelligentsia shared her views linking motherhood, female suffrage, increased female education, and national independence. The health of the nation was linked to the goal of *swaraj*, through self-governance over physical, moral, and spiritual aspects of life. Hence those aspects of Hinduism that extolled sexual continence and purity were praised, while those traditions that viewed female sexuality as potentially auspicious, if controlled, were critiqued and reformed. Dr. Annie Besant, the president of the Theosophical Society, leader of the Home Rule League, and first editor of *Stri-Dharma* (from 1917 to 1925), opined that the *devadasis* were originally virgin devotees attached to Hindu temples whose status had fallen in recent centuries due to invasions (Besant 1919). K. Gandhi, a cultural nationalist in many respects, viewed the abolition of *devadasis* as a positive step:

> The whole of enlightened public opinion that is vocal is against the retention of the system in any shape or form. The opinion of the parties concerned in the immoral traffic cannot count. . . . The Devadasi system is a blot upon those who countenance it. . . . I hope that Dr. Reddy will receive the hearty support of all lovers of purity in religious and general social life. (Reddy 113–14)

For most of the nationalist intelligentsia, it was only the revered mother role that was emphasized, while other roles for women were cast into shadow.

Another important political force in Madras politics in the late colonial period was the anti-Brahmin movement, which also condemned the *devadasi* institution, but for apparently different reasons. Anti-Brahmin activists in early twentieth-century Madras promoted the nationalist idea of a separate country, Dravida Nadu, which would encompass all non-Brahmin castes in the region, theoretically excluding South Indian Brahmins and all North Indians. The anti-Brahmin movement became an important political and intellectual force in the Madras Presidency at the turn of the century, and remained so throughout the twentieth century. The strength and persistence of the anti-Brahmin movement in Madras has been explained by the numerical, commercial, and landed predominance of non-Brahmin castes in Tamil Nadu, who were galled that this predominance was eroded by the professional gains made by Brahmins through colonial education. Anti-Brahminism acquired a mass appeal after the creation of the Self Respect Association in 1926, which was founded by Periyar, one of the most prolific and erudite leaders of anti-Brahmin reform organizations.

The grievances of the various anti-Brahmin movements centered around the dominant position accorded Brahmins in social hierarchy by Hindu scriptures, the pre-eminence of Brahmins in ritual practice, and the influential roles played by members of this caste in the public spheres created during colonial rule. Such leaders as Periyar and Annarudhi argued that "traditional" Brahmin status dominance enabled and reinforced their "modern" professional dominance. Through its various later transformations into the Dravida Munetra Kazzagam and the Annuradai Dravida Munetra Kazzagam, the anti-Brahmin movement emerged as the most important political force in late colonial and post-colonial Tamil politics. Non-Brahmin reforms were the central focus of the Justice Party, which predominated in the Madras Provincial Legislature between 1925 and 1936, the years during which the major anti-*devadasi* laws were enacted. Elements of the Justice Party merged with elements of the Self Respect Association to form the Dravida Munetra Kazzagham in 1947, which became one of the major political parties in Tamil Nadu in the post-Independence period.

Anti-Brahmin activists attacked almost all symbols of scriptural Brahminism in a series of inversion rituals that were meant to shock society into awareness about caste hierarchy. These included the denigration of Brahminic norms; abuse of Hindu deities, epics, and scriptures; and derision of the acts of godmen who claimed divine inspiration. The Self Respect movement that Peryiyar created in 1926 to raise the pride of backward castes promoted intercaste marriages, widow remarriages, and marriages of consent. These marriages were conducted without Brahmin priests and recitation of religious texts and did away with the ceremonial of *tali* tying. Some also took place at midnight, an inauspicious time in Brahminical astrology. Periyar also raised questions concerning the relationship between the monogamous family and norms of chastity prescribed for and enforced upon women. He viewed women and lower castes' lack of property as the cause of their ritually low and impure status (Anandhi 1991).

Periyar and other leaders of the anti-Brahmin movement articulated a notion of bounded Tamil community. However, this notion was constituted by a layered concept of community identity and "honor." At the center of this identity was the *sudras* of Tamil Nadu,[3] and in successive concentric circles around this center, Tamil Christians and Muslims, Tamil-speaking Scheduled Castes,[4] and other South Indian non-Brahmins. Groups clearly beyond the pale were Brahmins from Tamil Nadu and other parts of South India, as well as all North Indians; these groups were deemed "Aryans." Periyar called for a separate country in which the Dravidian as *sudra* would enjoy primacy, and Christians, Muslims, and Scheduled Castes would also find a place. As for the "Aryans," their ideological hold through Brahminism over the Dravidian Tamils was to be broken and, at times, he said that they should be expelled from South India.

Although Periyar viewed property as the basis of the caste system, and the nonproperty of women and lower castes as the reason for their subordination, he strongly opposed the *devadasi* system. Periyar and other leaders of the anti-Brahmin movement saw it as almost equivalent to prostitution. Women who were dedicated to temples and trained in classical dance and music were almost invariably from non-Brahmin castes. Their patrons, however, were usually Brahmins, and indeed a wealthy Brahmin patron was the desired ideal of most *devadasi* households. Periyar's disapproval of the *devadasis* was due to his view that it represented the prostitution and concubinage of *sudra* women for Brahmin men. He argued that Brahminical codes had treated non-Brahmin women as *dasis* (prostitutes) of gods. Periyar argued that the word *sudra* implied in the scriptures that someone was born out of wedlock, while *parayan*, or untouchable, carried no such connotation. This, he argued, showed that the *sudras* were more dishonored by Brahmins than were the untouchables, because they had mythically arisen from "dishonorable" unions between Brahmin men and non-Brahmin women. He saw the *devadasi* institution as an example of Brahminical dominance over *sudra* women, and therefore as a tradition that had to be reformed in the emergence of Dravida Nadu. Hence, while appearing to support the liberation of women, the ideology of the anti-Brahmin movement placed the control over women's sexuality securely within the boundaries of the *sudra* community.

A few former *devadasis,* apparently believing Periyar's feminist rhetoric, joined the Self Respect movement, becoming important activists for the anti-Brahmin cause. For example, Moovalur Ramamirtham Ammaiyar, who was born in 1883, brought up in a *devadasi* family in Thanjavur district and initiated as a *devadasi* at puberty, later left the community to join first the Congress Party in 1920 and then the Self Respect movement, after Periyar's break with Gandhi and the Indian National Congress in 1926. She acted as a relentless campaigner against what she viewed as women's sexual and domestic slavery, elaborating how Brahminical Hinduism and upper-caste men were legitimizing women's oppression. In a widely read Tamil novel that is thought to be autobiographical, she wrote "The women of the lower castes have been suppressed in all spheres. The legitimisation of the suppression given through the *shastras* is evident in the manner in which women have been assigned the role of religious prostitutes and concubines in the *devadasi* system" (Anandhi 1991).

Unfortunately Ammaiyar, who joined the Self Respect movement apparently out of its liberatory potential for women, lived to see intercaste marriages, free choice marriages, and the critique of female chastity and propriety jettisoned by the anti-Brahmin movement when it became a formal political party, the Dravida Munnetra Kazagham (DMK), in 1947, on the eve of India's independence. One of the first pieces of legislation of the newly independent DMK-led provincial government in 1947 was the Madras Devadasi (Prevention of Dedication) Bill, which made any performance of the *devadasi* dedication ceremony a penal offense.

Thus by the late 1920s, there were a number of converging discourses that linked together community identity with communal or national honor and articulated these with a conception of sexual boundaries that was tied to monogamous familial sexuality. Missionaries and Western medical doctors opposed commercial prostitution in both medical and moral terms. This condemnation converged with a modernist and eugenicist conception of the nation, most clearly articulated by Dr. Muthulakshmi Reddy and the Women's Indian Association.[5] In addition, the anti-Brahmin movement that played such an important part in the political arena of Madras and Tamil Nadu in the late colonial and post-colonial periods also opposed the devadasi institution on the basis of defending *sudra* honor.[6] Finally, men from the *devadasi* community, who occupied a subordinate position as musicians and accompanists to the *devadasis'* dance ceremonies, joined the Self Respect movement in large numbers. The aggressive anti-Brahminism and anti-ritualism of the Backward Classes Movement of the south provided the men of this group with a powerful ideology to fight for dominance both within the household and the wider society. Men of the *devadasi* community also gained from the denial of property rights to female *devadasi* members as they could now inherit the shares of land that had earlier been kept aside for their sisters (Srinivasen 193). Pressed from both above and below, the criminalization of *devadasis* was an almost foregone conclusion.

Actual laws criminalizing *devadasis* in Madras included a 1924 amendment to the Penal Code to make the dedication of girls under eighteen a crime, the 1929 Amendment to the Madras Hindu Religious Endowment Act, which disallowed *devadasis* from being renumerated in land and revenue-collecting rights on temple lands, and the 1947 Madras Devadasi (Prevention of Dedication) Bill. All these laws were introduced and passed in a Legislative Assembly dominated by either the Justice Party, the precursor to the Dravida Munnetra Kazagham, or by the DMK itself in 1947. The crucial bill spelling an end to the *devadasi* institution was the 1929 Amendment, which eliminated any financial incentive accruing to the devadasi institution, and was introduced by Dr. Reddy during her term as the Deputy President of the Legislative Council. The amendment detached the *inam* grants—both land and revenue rights—from the requirement of temple service (Jordan 1989, 276). Future and potential generations of dancers were therefore precluded from receiving any lands whatsoever. By the time the law preventing any dedication of women to temples was passed in 1947, most *devadasis* had stopped dancing and the institution was completely eroded.

The *devadasis* themselves provided a vigorous defense of the system during the 1927 Legislative Debates. They first differentiated themselves from commercialized prostitutes per se, objecting to reform efforts to equate the two systems. If some *devadasis* were practicing prostitution, then existing legislation against prostitution was in place to deal with it, they argued. Rather than focusing on their dance activities and traditions, they dealt almost exclusively with the religious and ritual side of their lives, emphasizing that the dedication ceremony was a means of making a lifelong commitment to God and the Hindu religion. The marriage of religiously inclined individuals to deities was found throughout devotional Tamil literature and they pointed out the importance of dance aesthetics to the worship of both Siva and Vishnu. They also argued that since their right to property would be eroded by the proposed legislation, their freedom of worship would be infringed upon (Government of Madras 1927).

However, the *devadasis* were not able to mount an effective challenge to the increasingly hegemonic discourse of Western medicine with its hygienic discourse that conflated public health with private morality, and which used apparently universalistic and scientific proof of the causal relation between prostitution and deviant sexuality and venereal disease. Neither were they able to effectively challenge the male members of their own community who viewed the *devadasi* institution as a mark of community dishonor and subservience to Brahmins, and who may also have been somewhat jealous of the *devadasis'* relatively greater fame and acclaim.[7] In addition, the Brahmins, who formed the community from which the patrons of *devadasis* were typically drawn, were too numerically, economically, and politically weak in Tamil Nadu to offer an effective challenge to the views of the anti-Brahmin movement. Although they had gained an early lead in the professions during the colonial period, they only constituted 3 percent of the population of Tamil Nadu, were concentrated in two major river valleys in the presidency, and had to share economic power with a variety of other non-Brahmin castes.

By the late 1940s, the *devadasi* institution was virtually dead, while their dance, Bharat Natyam, was unlinked from temple service and reborn in a more "respectable" form. The *devadasis* themselves fared quite badly. Although a few were able to marry wealthy patrons, and some were able to maintain themselves as dance teachers, the majority became increasingly impoverished and destitute.

What ties these various anti-*devadasi* discourses together is the idea that women's sexuality belongs to and is the property of the community, rather than to the individual who has the right to dispose of that sexuality. The public health model that idealized the role of motherhood repeated the distinction between respectable versus unrespectable sexuality that socially organized the class relationships of women through their sexual relationships to men. It tied the expression of female sexuality to an idealized mother figure, who was envisaged as the icon of tradition, the site of spiritual solace, and the modern mother of future generations. The anti-Brahmin movement, while articulating connections between propriety and property, caste and gender oppression, still viewed women's sexual choices as a matter of community honor and anti-Brahmin closure. Honor for women was thus aligned with the suppression of concubinage from within the *sudra* community. The notion that family and home were the microcosm of the nation imbued the domestic sphere in each community with the imagery of cultural defense against outsiders, and hence pulled the question of sexuality into a discourse concerning intra- and intercommunity boundaries. In all these discourses, it was the motherhood figure who typically became the metaphor of ideal femininity, an icon that signaled the respectability and power of the nationalist middle class through its symbolic and legal exclusion of the unchaste female.[8] Through the reform movement that suppressed the *devadasi* institution, as well as instituting other legal changes for middle-class women in India, the subcontinent's patriarchial structures were reconstituted in a new, modernized form.

# Notes

1. Tamil Nadu is the post-Independence term that applies to the region in southeast India around Madras. During the colonial period, it was referred to as the Madras Presidency.

2. This was very evident in debates concerning raising the age of marriage in the 1920s. See J. Whitehead, "Modernizing the Motherhood Archetype: Public Health Policies and the Age of Marriage (Sarda)Act of 1929," in *State, Sexuality and Social Reform*, ed. P. Uberoi (Delhi: Sage Publications, 1996).

3. The *sudras* were the fourth and lowest caste group in a ritual hierarchy, which placed Brahmins in the top ritual and status position. In Tamil Nadu, many economically and commercially successful castes were non-Brahmin, and after the British census operations starting in 1880, they were considered a part of the *sudra* class. There

was not a one-to-one correspondence between ritual status and economic predominance in either pre- or postcolonial India. In a number of regions, *sudra* castes may be economically predominant in terms of landownership and commercial success.

4. "Scheduled Castes" is the term the British government, and later the Independence government, applied to groups who were considered untouchables. Gandhi referred to them as "harijans," or children of god, a term which many of them find patronizing.

5. The similarities between a eugenicist conception of the pedigree and feudal conceptions of family honor has been often noted. Both seemed to have fulfilled the same functions, in that they regulated the sexual choices of women and defined respectable and healthy sexuality as that contained within monogamous marriages. See M. Foucault, *The History of Sexuality*, vol. 1 (New York: Penguin, 1980).

6. In the precolonial period, Brahmins constituted only about 3 percent of the Tamil population, much less than in northern India. The extent of their control over land was also less than in Kerala, Mahashtra, Uttar Pradesh, and Bihar and they were largely concentrated in two river valleys, the Kaveri and Tamiraparani. Even in these regions, they shared land control with other groups. For this reason, the anti-Brahmin movement in Tamil Nadu was able to mount a strong challenge to early colonial Brahmin predominance in Madras professions and politics, which the Brahmin community was never able to successfully counter. Indeed, the DMK and ADMK (Adi-Dravida Munnetra Kazagham) have successively formed most of post-Independence state governments in Tamil Nadu. See N. Subramanian, "Ethnicity, Populism, and Pluralist Democracy: Mobilization and Representation in South India," Ph.D. diss., 1995. Cambridge, Mass., MIT.

7. In fact, the most vociferous demands for *devadasi* reform from within the community came from the men from the periamelan or "pure" section.

8. See A. Parker, M. Russo, D. Sommer, and P. Yaeger, "Introduction," to *Nationalisms and Sexualities* (New York: Routledge, 1992), 1–32, for a discussion of this process of exclusion in many nationalist movements throughout the world.

# References

All-India Women's Congress. 1927–1936. *Annual Reports*. Delhi: AIWC Library.

Anandhi, S. 1991. Women's question in the Dravidian movement. *Social Scientist* 5–6: 23.

Arnold, D. 1993. *Colonizing the Body: State Medicine and Epidemic Disease in the Nineteenth Century*. Berkeley: University of California Press.

Ballhatchet, K. 1980. *Race, Sex and Class under the British Raj*. London: Weidenfeld and Nicholson.

Besant, A. 1919. *India: A Nation*. Adyar: Theosophical Publishing House.

Chakravarti, U. 1990. Whatever happened to the Vedic *Dasī?* In *Recasting Women: Essays in Indian Colonial History*, edited by K. Sangari and S. Vaid. New Brunswick, N.J.: Rutgers University Press, 27–87.

Chatterjee, P. 1990. The nationalist resolution of the women's question. In *Recasting Women: Essays in Indian Colonial History*, edited by K. Sangari and S. Vaid. New Brunswick, N.J.: Rutgers University Press, 233–54.

Davidoff, L. 1983. Class and gender in Victorian England. In *Sex and Class in Women's History*, edited by J. L. Newton, M. P. Ryan, and J. R. Walkowitz. London: Routledge and Kegan Paul.

Davin, A. 1979. Imperialism and motherhood. *History Workshop Journal* 1, no. 1.

Engels. D. 1987. The changing role of women in Bengal: 1890–1930. Ph.D. diss., London.

Farley, J. 1991. *Bilharzia: A History of Imperial Tropical Medicine*. Cambridge: Cambridge University Press.

Gilman, S. 1985. Black bodies, white bodies. In *Race, Writing and Difference*, by H. L. R. Gates. Chicago: University of Chicago Press.

Government of Madras, Law Department (General). 1927. *Proceedings*. December 20: G.C. 4079.

Jordan, K. 1989. From sacred servant to profane prostitute: A study of the changing legal status of the *devadasis*, 1857–1947. Ph.D. diss., Ames, University of Iowa.

Kersenboom-Story, S. C. 1987. *Nityasumangali: Devadasi Tradition in South India*. Delhi: Motilal Benarsidas.

Marglin, F. 1984. *Wives of the God King*. Delhi: Oxford University Press.

Mazumdar, P. 1992. *Eugenics, Human Genetics, and Human Failings: The Eugenics Society, Its Sources, and Its Critics in Britain*. London: Routledge and Kegan Paul.

Parker, A., M. Russo, D. Sommer, and P. Yaeger. 1992. Introduction. In *Nationalisms and Sexualities*. New York: Routledge, 1–32.

Ramasubban, R. 1988. Imperial health in British India, 1857–1900. In *Disease, Medicine, and Empire: Perspectives on Western Medicine and the Experience of Expansion*, edited by R. MacLeaod and M. Lewis. London: Routledge, 38–60.

Reddy, S. M. 1964. *Autobiography of Dr. (Mrs.) S. Muthulakshmi Reddy*. Mylapore: M. L. J. Press.

———. *My Experience as a Legislator.*

Sarkar, T. 1987. Nationalist iconography: Images of women in nineteenth century Bengali culture. *Economic and Political Weekly of India*, 21 November, 2011–15.

———. 1993. Rhetoric against age of consent: Resisting colonial reason and death of a child-wife. *Economic and Political Weekly of India*, 4 September, 1869–70.

Srinivasen, A. Reform or conformity? Temple "prostitution" and the community in Madras Presidency. In *Structures of Patriarchy*, edited by B. Aggarwal. London: Zed Press.

*Stri-Dharma.* 1913. 1, no. 1: 2.

*Stri-Dharma.* 1921. (November): 18.

*Stri-Dharma.* 1927. (May): 103.

*Stri-Dharma.* 1928. (November): 1.

Subramanian, N. 1995. Ethnicity, populism, and pluralist democracy: Mobilization and representation in South India. Ph.D. diss., Cambridge, Mass., MIT.

Whitehead, J. 1995. Bodies clean and unclean: Sanitary legislation, prostitution, and respectable femininity in colonial North India. *Gender and History* 5, no. 1.

———. 1996. Modernizing the motherhood archetype: Public health models and the Child Marriage Restraint Act of 1929. In *State, Sexuality and Social Reform*, edited by P. Uberoi. New Delhi and Newberry Park, Calif.: Sage.

# THE DISCARDED LEMON: KANT, PROSTITUTION, AND RESPECT FOR PERSONS

## TIMOTHY J. MADIGAN

To allow one's person for profit to be used by another for the satisfaction of sexual desire, to make of oneself an Object of demand, is to dispose over oneself as over a thing and to make of oneself a thing on which another satisfies his appetite, just as he satisfies his hunger upon a steak. But since the inclination is directed towards one's sex and not towards one's humanity, it is clear that one thus partially sacrifices one's humanity and thereby runs a moral risk. Human beings are, therefore, not entitled to offer themselves, for profit, as things for the use of others in the satisfaction of their sexual propensities.

—Immanuel Kant (1993, 254)

It would be hard to find a more complete condemnation of prostitution than that just quoted from the philosopher Immanuel Kant (1724–1804). For him, prostitution was the ultimate example of treating a human being as merely a means to an end and was despicable because it thereby placed a human being on the same footing as that of an animal. In this chapter, I will examine the reasons for Kant's view and attempt to show that it is nonetheless possible to give an argument along Kantian lines in *favor* of prostitution.

In his writings on sex and marriage, Kant provided a seemingly traditional defense of monogamy—the only sexual relation that is morally acceptable is that which occurs between a married man and woman. However, the *argument* he gave for this differs tremendously from the natural law tradition that had predominated in Western thought. For Kant, the foundation of ethics was "the Categorical Imperative": it is always wrong to treat another person as merely a means to an end, rather than as an end-in-itself (which is to say, one must show proper respect for other persons). This is a secularized version of the so-called Golden Rule, to treat others as one wishes to be treated. But what is it that constitutes a "person"? For Kant, it is the fact that persons alone possess rationality.

The ability to reason raises us above our passions and allows us to act autonomously. We are not mere creatures of instinct. In respecting others, we are acknowledging the fact that they are fellow reasoning creatures, fully responsible for their actions. Anything that goes against reason should be suspect, because it lowers our status and affects our moral worth.

What Kant feared most of all, as a disturber of reason, was sexuality. In his estimation, sexual urges are the desire to possess another person. But to fulfill such a desire is to place a human being on the same level with nonreasoning animals, which is an unacceptable degradation. Those who engage in sexual acts for the sake of pleasure "make of humanity an instrument for the satisfaction of their lusts and inclinations, and dishonor it by placing it on a level with animal nature. Sexuality, therefore, exposes mankind to the danger of equality with the beasts" (Kant 1993, 254). Because morality can only pertain to rational creatures, such a lowering of status is the worst sort of action one can take.

Kant was not noted for his turn of phrases—his style was usually a plodding one. But in writing about the dangers of giving in to sexual urges, he is positively eloquent: "Sexual love makes of the loved person an Object of appetite: as soon as that appetite has been stilled, the person is cast aside as one casts aside a lemon which has been sucked dry" (1993, 254).

Sexual desire, then, in and of itself, is degrading. It places us on the same level with beasts and thus lowers our moral status. To make a person an *object* of desire is wrong. "This is the only case in which a human being is designed by nature as the Object of another's enjoyment. Sexual desire is at the root of it: and that is why we are ashamed of it, and why all strict moralists, and those who had the pretensions to be regarded as saints, sought to suppress and extirpate it" (Kant 1993, 254). One *dishonors* other persons by focusing upon them as sex objects only. It is the supreme case of treating another as merely a means to an end, the end being sexual gratification. Thus, a human being is treated much like the discarded lemon that has been sucked dry.

Yet such desires are extremely powerful, and for most people—especially nonphilosophers—quite hard to control. What to do? Prostitution is impermissible not because of the harm it might cause to society (Kant was not a consequentialist), but because it treats a person as a commodity. Persons are not at their own disposal. They do not own themselves, because if they did, they would be a thing. "To let one's person out on hire and to surrender it to another for the satisfaction of his sexual desire in return for money is the depth of infamy" (Kant 1993, 255). One would thereby be acquiescing in the act of commodification.

For Kant, even mutual sexual satisfaction, rather than the selling of sexual services, would be morally impermissible because it still treats a person as a thing. It involves showing concern for only a part of the person, rather than one's personhood in its entirety. And it shows a lack of regard for the other individual's reasoning capabilities, as opposed to his or her sensual qualities.

The only morally acceptable route for sexual expression would be through legal matrimony. Only *marriage* allows for a moral exchange of sexual pleasure. "The sole condition on which we are free to make use of our sexual desires depends upon the right to dispose over the person as a whole—over the welfare and happiness and generally over all the circumstances of that person" (Kant 1993, 255).

How does marriage give one the right to use another? By also giving one's spouse the same right over *you*. Matrimony is an agreement between two persons in which they grant each other reciprocal rights—"each of them undertaking to surrender the whole of their person to the other with a complete right to disposal over it" (Kant 1993, 255). Or, as the old song says, "All of Me / Why Not Take All of Me?"

Marriage, in a sense, allows two individuals to mutually degrade each other, to treat each as the property of the other—to use each other. Although individuals are still placed on the level of nonrational creatures for a temporary time, it is permissible because it is done in the broader context of two rational agents freely engaging in a cooperative, lifelong contractual venture. Thus, while Kant's conclusion may be conservative—only sex within marriage is moral—the implications are quite radical. The purpose of marriage, he states, is not procreation. "The End of producing and educating children may be regarded as always the End of Nature in implanting mutual desire and inclination in the sexes; but it is not necessary for the rightfulness of marriage that those who marry should set this before themselves as the End of their Union" (1993, 256). The purpose of marriage is to allow the union of two persons of different sexes to have lifelong reciprocal possession of each other's sexual faculties. Husband and wife are on equal footing, in this regard. Sexual enjoyment is a right to be expected within the partnership.

Kant's deontological ethics, with its emphasis on rights and duties, has often been used to justify practices against which he himself had strongly argued. Would it be possible to develop a Kantian argument in *favor* of a contractual exchange in which one partner receives sexual gratification and the other some financial remuneration? I think that this can be done, if one no longer looks upon sexuality as *degrading* in and of itself. A similar argument has been made by philosopher Ann Garry in her seminal article "Pornography and Respect for Women." In it, she gives a Kantian defense of some types of pornography. Garry writes that "Although much current pornography does degrade women, I will argue that it is possible to have nondegrading, nonsexist pornography. However, this possibility rests on our making certain fundamental changes in our conception of sex and sex roles" (1993, 258). In other words, it is not the depiction of sexual acts, or the excitement such depictions cause, that are immoral, but rather certain *types* of depictions, namely, those which show individuals in degrading positions.

Garry agrees with Kant that objectification is morally unacceptable but raises interesting questions about what this means. The notion of "respect," she argues, is not the same for all people in our society—women are still often treated as less able to live autonomous existences, less able to function on their own. Because their status is so different, the loss of respect has greater repercussions for women in general. Pornography is often pernicious because it perpetuates images of the so-called fallen woman. Garry writes: "This fall is possible, I believe, because the traditional 'respect' that men have had for women is not genuine, whole-hearted respect for full-fledged human beings, but half-hearted respect for lesser beings, some of whom they feel the need to glorify and purify" (1993, 260).

This is an interesting observation, especially coming from a Kantian perspective: "losing respect" for men as a class is more difficult than losing respect for women. Therefore, it is not sexual desire per se that is objectionable, but the different standards that apply to men and women. Garry ends her article by speculating on possible types of acceptable pornography:

> Plots for nonsexist films could include women in traditionally male jobs (e.g., long-distance truckdriver) or in positions usually held in respect by pornography audiences. For example, a high-ranking female Army officer, treated with respect by men and women alike, could be shown not only in various sexual encounters with other people but also carrying out her job in a humane manner. Or perhaps the main character could be a female urologist. She could interact with nurses and other medical personnel, diagnose illnesses brilliantly, and treat patients with great sympathy as well as have sex with them. (1993, 264)

This article originally appeared in 1978. Since then, feminist filmmakers such as Candida Royalle and Annie Sprinkle have been producing just the sort of scenarios Garry is describing. Although Kant may have found such films unwatchable, Garry is arguing that by his own criteria he should *not* find them morally objectionable, provided they show true respect for autonomous agents. At the beginning of her essay, Garry states that she does not accept the assumption that sex is an evil to be controlled—an assumption that is at the heart of Kant's stricture against prostitution. She adds that "it seems preferable to try to change pornography instead of closing one's eyes in the hope that it will go away. For I suspect that pornography is here to stay" (1993, 264). A similar assertion can be made regarding prostitution.

If one accepts human sexuality as a natural and good aspect of life, rather than a degrading and evil aspect, it takes away much of the force of Kant's argument against prostitution. Rather than looking upon sexual desires as flaws that place us on the level with beasts, they can be seen as drives that unite us all. Whatever our station in life, the libido is common property.

Kant is opposed to treating humans as *merely* means to an end. But he does not hold that it is wrong in and of itself to satisfy human needs. For example, one can fulfill the role of being a food server, and thereby help to alleviate hunger. It *would* be morally unacceptable to treat a waiter as *merely* a serving thing. One should recognize his or her common humanity. But giving money to the waiter in recompense for services rendered involves two free agents mutually living up to their ends of an agreed-upon transaction. In a similar fashion, sex workers provide a valuable service in alleviating the sexual hunger of their clients. One might object to this if one accepts the argument was that *only* sex acts that lead to procreation are morally acceptable, but as was seen earlier, Kant did not hold to such a natural law line. Thus, if one uncouples Kant's repulsion about sexual acts from his overall contractual emphasis, a strong case can be made in favor of prostitution.

For what it is worth, Kant was a lifelong celibate whose knowledge of sexual fulfillment must have been primarily theoretical. Annette Baier emphasizes that "the great moral theorists in our tradition not only are all men, they are mostly men who had minimal adult dealings with (and so were then minimally influenced by) women" (Baier 1993, 362).

Just as Garry points out that much pornography is degrading, so undoubtedly is much prostitution. One can justly object to situations involving those who engage in such acts against their will, those who find the role they are playing demeaning, and those who may be harmed mentally or physically by it. All of this needs to be opposed. But a consistent Kantian can look upon providing sexual services as morally acceptable, provided no coercion is involved, and provided each participant fulfills his or her end of the bargain.

While Kant's lemon analogy seems to say a good deal about his own negative attitudes toward sexuality, his emphases on reciprocity and respect remain fruitful avenues to explore when looking at the morality of prostitution.

# References

1. Baier, Annette. 1993. Trust and anti-trust. In *Doing and Being: Selected Readings in Moral Philosophy*, edited by Joram Graf Haber. New York: Macmillan.
2. Garry, Ann. 1993. Pornography and respect for women. In *Morality and Moral Controversies*, edited by John Arthur. Englewood Cliffs, N.J.: Prentice-Hall.
3. Kant, Immanuel. 1993. The philosophy of law, translated by W. Hastie. In *Morality and moral controversies*, 3d. ed., edited by John Arthur. Englewood Cliffs, N.J.: Prentice-Hall.

# You've Come a Long Way, Baby, or How to Cure Sex Worker Burn-Out: Annie Sprinkle's Twelve-Step Program

### Annie Sprinkle

**Step 1.** Admit you're burned out. This sounds easy, but it is actually the hardest step. Our egos, as well as our income, are invested in feeling good about our work. It is not easy to admit that you are a mess. Try to see it as an opportunity to grow.

**Step 2.** Take plenty of breaks—vacation from your work and spend some time in nature. Get some sun, breathe fresh air, and smell the flowers. Boat rides are the best.

**Step 3.** Spend some time alone, doing something relaxing or meditative. A long walk alone or a candle-lit herbal bath can do wonders.

**Step 4.** Get in touch with your deep feelings and learn to express them.

**Step 5.** Get some therapy with a professional therapist. It really does help to put things into perspective.

**Step 6.** Get together a support group of other sex workers with whom you can have sympathetic, honest communication. The best cure of all is to share your feelings with people who have had similar experiences.

**Step 7.** Take good care of your body. Eat well, exercise, get body work. A good massage can do wonders for a worn-out whore or stripper.

**Step 8.** Get your mind off work. Take a class, go to a funny movie. Hang out with children or old people.

**Step 9.** If at all possible, do not have any sex for a while. Keep your clothes on for a change. I never thought I would ever say this, but it really does help to recharge your battery.

**Step 10.** Be willing to make less money. Clean out your little black book. Learn to say NO!

**Step 11.** Learn other skills that can create alternative sources of income so that when you need a break from sex work you will have one.

**Step 12.** If your sex work burn-out is chronic, get the hell out of the business. Sometimes getting out of the biz is really hard, but if there is a will, there is always a way.

# FORTY REASONS WHY
# WHORES ARE MY HEROINES

## ANNIE SPRINKLE

1. Whores have the ability to share their most private, sensitive body parts with total strangers.
2. Whores have access to places that other people do not.
3. Whores challenge sexual mores.
4. Whores are playful.
5. Whores are tough.
6. Whores have careers based on giving pleasure.
7. Whores are creative.
8. Whores are adventurous and dare to live dangerously.
9. Whores teach people how to be better lovers.
10. Whores are multicultural and multigendered.
11. Whores give excellent advice and help people with their personal problems.
12. Whores have fun.
13. Whores wear exciting clothes.
14. Whores have patience and tolerance for people that other people could never manage to put up with.
15. Whores make lonely people less lonely.
16. Whores are independent.
17. Whores teach people how to have safer sex.
18. Whores are a tradition.
19. Whores are hip.
20. Whores have a good sense of humor.
21. Whores relieve millions of people of unwanted stress and tension.
22. Whores heal.

23. Whores endure despite the fact that many people have prejudices against them.
24. Whores make good money.
25. Whores always have a job.
26. Whores are sexy and erotic.
27. Whores have special talents that other people do not have. Not everyone has what it take to be a whore.
28. Whores are interesting people with lots of exciting life stories.
29. Whores get laid a lot.
30. Whores help people explore their sexual desires.
31. Whores explore their own sexual desires.
32. Whores are not afraid of sex.
33. Whores hustle.
34. Whores sparkle.
35. Whores are entertaining.
36. Whores have the guts to wear very big wigs.
37. Whores are not ashamed to be naked.
38. Whores help the handicapped.
39. Whores make their own hours.
40. Whores are rebelling against the absurd, patriarchal, sex-negative laws affecting their profession and fighting for the legal right to receive financial compensation for their valuable work.

# 2

# CELEBRATED WHORES: THEIR STORIES OF LAW ENFORCEMENT AND THE MEDIA

## Introduction

Sex workers often capture the attention of the media. The media, however, although important to the success of many sex workers, are not particularly objective nor do they try to bring an understanding of the people involved. Eventually, after exploiting the sex workers as much as they can, they pass on to other things. Sometimes they do tremendous damage to the individual psyches of those they have used and discarded. Other individuals seem to thrive on the attention and continually try to keep their name before the public. This section includes the personal accounts of a number of women whom the media seized upon at some time in their careers. The session devoted to them at the conference was one of the most moving and exciting of any of the presentations. The presenters included Margo St. James, founder of COYOTE (Call Off Your Old Tired Ethics), who moved from social worker to champion of the rights of prostitutes, and continued on through Xaviera Hollander, who seized upon the publicity and became a name known to almost everyone. Unfortunately, not included in this book is the account of Sidney Biddle Barrows, the Mayflower Madam, who had a troublesome time until, after several personal crises, she seems to have gained a new life. People such as she seemed to be able to patch their lives together again, but others seemed to have suffered great financial and personal loss. Several served time in jail. Listed alphabetically, those whose personal accounts are included are Helen Buckingham, Dolores French, Xaviera Hollander, Cynthia Payne, Margo St. James, and Coral Velisek. We think their accounts provide an insight into the joys and perils of sex work not easily available from any other source.

117

# How It Was:
## Recollections by
## Well-Known Prostitutes and Madams
### Margo St. James, Helen Buckingham, Dolores French, Xaviera Hollander, Cynthia Payne, and Coral Velisek

## Margo St. James

I started COYOTE, an activist organization for prostitutes and their friends, in 1973. The Glide Memorial Church wanted to help the hookers, the ones who were still on the street, but they didn't want us to use *prostitute* in the title of our organization. I came up with COYOTE because it was like, you know, the Panthers, the Moose, the Elks, and all the rest of them. So why not get the hookers back into the animal kingdom? John Stevens, who's gone, gave us an acronym. He came up with CALL OFF YOUR OLD TIRED ETHICS. He was a brilliant songwriter, and I hope to use his pop opera soon in a musical about Margo. The sheriff said, "Hey, somebody from the victim's class has to speak up." So that's why, with my mother's and son's blessings, I went to the press. It caused me to get fired from my job, but now, here COYOTE is, a vibrant organization helping to sponsor the First International Conference on Prostitution.

## Margo St. James Introduces Helen Buckingham

One of the first people I met in Europe in 1975 was the woman who had started an organization much like COYOTE in Great Britain. They called it PUSSY. I ended up spending a day or two over there, of which I have fond memories. From this contact, the international prostitution movement began. In 1976, I moved on to Paris. And the movement continued to grow until we had the congresses in 1985 and 1986, and now here we are in 1998.

Here are the remarks of a leader in the movement, the wonderful Helen Buckingham of Great Britain.

# Helen Buckingham

Although the police like to think that the public are concerned with prostitution as a nuisance and as a form of exploitation, my own experience has been rather contrary to this. When prostitution began to evolve as a non-nuisance and a non-exploitive activity, the police attacked it on the grounds that it threatens class boundaries. In other words, it corrupts women who are further up the social scale. What they really mean by this, I discovered, is that there is no money for third parties in allowing women to be self-determining. Keeping prostitution illegal results in the exploitation of more vulnerable women, such as illegal immigrants, and through them, a persistent nuisance, to members of the public who feel too vulnerable to complain about it—mainly middle-class men with much to lose if their reputations were to be tainted by associations with prostitutes. And this little vice ring is run by the police themselves, who are busy kicking middle-class women out of five-star hotels. These women have their proper credentials, they're in their own country, they've got their rights. The police are harassing this kind of woman. They're actually forcing illegal immigrant women into vice rings and instructing them to make a persistent nuisance of themselves in order to force them back to the pimps. And this is really quite, quite apparent—or it was in London twenty years ago. And I mention it now because I don't think it was exclusive to London. It seems that under certain conditions—conditions prevailing at the time in London were that the IRA (Irish Republican Army) had put on a big terrorist campaign—the major hotels recruited personnel, security personnel, from the ranks of policemen and ex-policemen to keep undesirables out of their hotels. Alongside this security buildup, there was a sudden burst of laws concerning prostitutes. London had become the third major capital of the world in business. Arabs, Americans, Germans—everybody was meeting in London to do big oil deals.

A lot more madams appeared on the scene and so did something called the escort agency. Now, middle-class women discovered this situation and they liked it very much. I've worked with the escort agency, and we liked what we were given: a very small fee and an introduction to a well-heeled man. The agency had met the man and knew all about him. He paid a fee and we paid a fee just for that introduction, and off we would go to a hotel, where he would rent a room. If we ended up going out to dinner and having sex, that was nobody's business but our own, and we negotiated the fee. Everything was working splendidly. We were really operating in a very free way. We were not breaking the law by soliciting on the streets. Nobody was interfering with whether we had sex with clients. Nobody was on the take.

The security networks observed, of course, that a lot of money was being made through prostitution in these hotels at the time. And it seemed unfair to them that they weren't on the take here. It's very difficult to go up to a woman who's got a right to be around and tell her she's got to give him some money. Not only were we not very good at knowing whom we had to tip, but we always had to tip the right people. But tipping wasn't good enough for them. Little by little, the harassment started. First of all, they started tapping the main telephone systems, claiming they had a right to because they had to make sure that there were no IRA terrorists around. They intercepted the calls of a man to his favorite woman or to a new woman with whose credentials he was happy. That such interception was dangerous to international politics or company practices didn't concern the security people. So when we women appeared at the hotel, the security men would be waiting for us, accusing us of being on the hotel premises as trespassers. If we resisted that, they would start to manhandle us. Now, if the man heard the commotion and came out to the door to see what was happening, they would manhandle him, too. And if he got on his high horse and said, "I should not be treated like this. I'm paying big sums of money to stay in this hotel," he was then told that his government or his multinational company might like to know about his dalliance with prostitutes. Because this would be absolutely detrimental to such men's careers, he would then shut up.

Little by little, we began to notice, those of us who were still trying to filter through into the hotels, that there were a number of foreign women who were soliciting quite blatantly up and down the corridors, in the elevators, in the lobbies, all over the place. There were men behind them who seemed to be managers who would kind of give them a shove, pushing them into the bar to interrupt a group of men and force their company on them. Women were coming back out of bedroom doors with bundles of money and shoving this into their pants, quite blatantly, and were sitting there in the lobbies counting it. It was that conspicuous. Then luggage started being stolen from the hotel rooms. There was such anarchy around that stories got out. Then, of course, the press came in and went to the hotel publicity departments to find out what was going on. The press was very easily satisfied when it was told, "Yes, we're having a serious problem with prostitutes." But what the media did not say is that the IRA were sending undercover women in as prostitutes. That's how we got through the door, and then they were stealing trunks.

One peeress in the upper House of Parliament picked this gossip up and got very worried because men wouldn't be able to bring their wives to hotels anymore because of all these dreadful women around. But I had friend in the upper house whom I'd been campaigning with, and we commiserated about what was really happening. So she trotted along to one of these hotels and ordered herself coffee. This is a Buckingham woman, seventy years old with gray hair, a very dignified lady with a title. Security asked her to leave as an unescorted woman. She asked why she had to go since the sex discrimination act is on the books. What had she done wrong? They said that she was now a trespasser, and they had absolutely no reason to tell her why they didn't want her there. It made a good picture for them, because it looked as though they were completely impartial about this discrimination against unescorted women.

Then I teamed up with one of the women from the other side, a woman who had been lured into London under false pretenses, and found that she was part of the vice ring. I helped her get out, but first she did me one favor. She said, "I'm sitting quite good with the management. I will go back and find out a bit more about what's going on." This woman discovered a whole room full of dossiers on women, containing driving licenses, state identification, and all kinds of other personal identification. She waited for the man in charge of the office to come back, and she flirted around with him a bit and then said, "You've got a lot of women's mug shots and a lot of women's driver's licenses and things like that here. Tell me, do they like to give you these things? Why do you have this collection?" And he said, "No. Of course they don't. We have to take it off of them by force. These are prostitutes, and we have to keep them out."

The grapevine had already spread the rumor that a number of wives had been caught up in this ring, quite a number of women who were not, in fact, in the game at all. The ring wanted the women who could work. One member of the Arab royal family was caught, arrested, and mug-shotted. He was told he could not leave to catch his plane until he gave the name of the madam who had sent the girl to him. Now, the Arab refused to do it, but they also had the girl locked up in another room. In the end, she was worried about what would happen to him back in his country if he was besmirched with this sort of scandal, which can be very serious in some of the Arab countries, so she came forward and gave the name of the madam to get him, as well as herself, off the hook. It wasn't long before the madam was getting quite threatening phone calls. She was never quite able to identify whom they were coming from.

So this is actually what was going on twenty years ago. A lot of people were angry because the men never said a word, but I think what we have to understand is that the men have a lot to lose. It's up to the women to prepare the ground for public opinion to change sufficiently before all of these men who would dearly love to see the law change will come forward and share this public plea with us.

# Helen Buckingham Introduces Dolores French

I met Dolores French through Paul Krasner, the editor of the *Realist,* which was published at that time in New York. I was a *Realist* nun in the 1960s, and Paul said, "I have this friend from Atlanta who I think you need to meet." Sure enough, Dolores and I hit it off right away. She was a graphic artist. I painted around, had a few scholarships and all that, but I didn't want to go in that direction. Too much sitting around. So anyway, Dolores took the ball and ran. Now, working for prostitute rights has become a team effort; it has been ongoing, and it's getting bigger. We have to have a few more stadiums. Here we go.

# Dolores French

Thank you. All week, I've been remembering sitting on Helen Buckingham's floor at the first international congress, which was in her living room. I think there were eight people there. Priscilla Alexander was telling us how to spell "decriminalization." Now hundreds of people attend a conference on prostitution. I never, in my lifetime, expected the movement to grow to what it is now. It shows how the media have affected our lives, and the term "prostitute" catches the headlines. I think I'm the only person on this panel who claims to be working still, and I think I'm also, perhaps, the only person on this panel who has never been convicted. The reason that I wasn't convicted wasn't because I was so clever or my attorneys were so wonderful; it was because I honestly wasn't doing anything at the moment that I was arrested—that is a pretty rare thing!

This poor vice cop had been trying to arrest me for years. He thought that he could just arrest me and claim that I had solicited him, and so on. But I happened to have a tape recorder on me at the time, so I recorded our conversation. When we got to court, he stated that I was introduced to him as a "Lady of the Evening," and I had asked him what he was interested in and he said, "The usual." He took that to mean oral sex and sexual intercourse. But then I played the tape recording of what our real conversation was: I had understood that he was a dentist, and I talked with him about making some changes in the way dental offices operate, to make them more attractive for people to get their teeth taken care of regularly. One of the things that I pointed out to him, this dentist, was that people spend more money on their nails than they do on their teeth. Anyway, he proceeded to bust me and stated that I had solicited him. When they heard the tape recording of our real conversation, the judge was furious and the prosecutor was furious.

If I had actually been doing something, I would have handled the case very differently. I have been in the business now for twenty years. I am so tired of having to avoid being arrested all the time that sometimes I feel sort of crazed and just want to run into the street and call the media, tell them to show up, and just start randomly soliciting people, demanding that the police arrest me so that they could just get it over with. I want to just duke it out with them once and for all and get that straight.

When I first started working, one of the places I went to was San Juan. A friend of mine said, "You know, I think Xaviera Hollander worked there." And I said, "Really? Send me the book." Well, she sent me Xaviera's book. I started taking notes about everything because I had heard so much about how horrible prostitution is. I thought, "Well, I'll just take notes and then one of these days when I end up being a junkie on the street and I'm stabbed to death by some horrible john or something, there will be this chronological history of how I got this way." So from reading Xaviera's book and hearing stories about prostitution, I was influenced in my writing. I was not actually intending to write a book at all because, one, it doesn't pay very much and, two, I don't type.

Until after I got arrested. Yeah, it's an amazing experience to be suddenly in international headlines. It changes your life unbelievably. Then you have to do something about it. One of the things that happened is a publisher came up to me about writing a book. Before I got busted, I had made a choice to go on a television show. I was probably influenced because Andrew Young had put me on the mayor's task force for prostitution, but it was a very difficult choice because I was going on television not as a an ex-prostitute, but as a prostitute. I was the first person who had not been arrested who went on TV with my own identity saying, "Yes, I am still working." I want to quote a little section from my book about that choice I made:

I thought about how, in those fifties movies, there would be a public meeting to decide some critical issue, and there would be a show of hands, a crowd. They'd be silent. And then one brave person would not just raise their hand, but stand up. Slowly, one by one, the rest of the crowd would stand. That's [what I pictured when] I decided to do the Donahue Show. I told Darlene [Hayes, the show's producer], I would do it if she would pay me. And I said I wanted my real name used and I wanted to be on camera. It may be hard for people to now understand how a good thing it was back in 1982 to have working prostitutes on TV talking about their lives, and at the time I remember thinking, "This is going to be—this is going to lift the burden off everyone." I knew we'd be doing it for hundreds of thousands of women. I would be sitting on the camera proving that a prostitute does not necessarily wear hot pants or Tammy Faye mascara or have five-inch nails. I wanted to show them that someone can be mature, intelligent and pretty, and still say, "I'm proud to be a prostitute. I love the work. There are other things I could do. There are other things that I have done, but this is what I would rather do." I told Darlene, "Women in this business have had to live in the shadows for far too long, and I'm not going to be one of them."

We walked out and started the show.

Darlene warned me that this was going to change my life. I had no idea. And I'm working on a book, a coming-out book. It will be a collection of stories of women and men in the sex industry and their experiences with becoming public. Until now, there's been no book, no single book that has had a collection of stories about what it's like to come out and then what it's like to deal with the media. And it's really something.

# Dolores French Introduces Xaviera Hollander

When I heard I was going to be on a panel with Xaviera, I was just awestruck. I had never met Xaviera, and she was a mythical character in my mind. It was such a thrill—like being on the same panel with Wonder Woman. Xaviera was one of the first ladies to be out there and one of the women that I thought about often when I was out there having to deal a lot with the press and with the public.

# Xaviera Hollander

I'm so flattered by the praise of other ladies on this panel. The Internet has made it possible to be in touch with them. I know Margo suggested way, way back through an old boyfriend of mine that I get in touch with Katherine LaPlau. He said, "She has been talking with other activists on the Internet." I do believe that was only a year ago, and now I'm an e-mail junkie. I adore the group of people on WhoreNet I and WhoreNet II. I seem to be the humor provider. Sex and humor have to go together, although sometimes humor is a bit lacking in the heavy debates on the Internet. The articles I read from Canberra, Australia, and New Zealand impressed me with the hookers' loyalty and helpfulness to one another. When I read of someone being ill, other people chipped in and helped console the sick person. One such helper is a man I met yesterday, John Gefferklitz. He wrote on e-mail about the death of his mother. At that point, I was also involved with my failing, ailing mother, and we suddenly got this whole e-mail thread about how it is to deal with parents who are getting older and who are obviously going to be leaving us. So it's not just sex that binds us together. It's emotions, it's family. Even when there wasn't an Internet, they were there but we did not know it. I got arrested. I was alone. I had a boyfriend and that was it, and he took off one night. Still, I was a happy hooker and wrote my book about it.

The book came out in 1971 and was a nationwide paperback best seller. The cover was the only thing that was soft, and the book sold hard. I've written more than a dirty dozen since. In 1986, I wrote a new epilogue to *The Happy Hooker*. The book was being reissued fifteen years after it first appeared, and I was answering the question put to me: "How much has changed since then?" Before I spoke out and helped to blow the cobwebs off the closet door, sex, even in a matrimonial bed, was a matter of, if not actual shame, at least of embarrassment. Having children was a biological necessity, a religious duty almost. So having sex was something to be tolerated. God forbid it should be enjoyed by anybody. Even an upright and uptight man of the church used his most upright member. Lights off, clothes on was the order of the day, or rather the night. I have a little English rhyme, because I like poetry:

> The dean undressed with heavy breaths
> His lascivious wife to lie on.
> He thought it lewd to do it nude
> So he kept his old school tie on.

This speech is called "Cocks, Cuffs, and Cops." I know Norma Jean Almodovar, who wrote a book called *Cop to Call Girl*, so I borrow part of her title. I compare cops and prostitutes to physicians and disease. If some genius found a wonder drug tomorrow that would infallibly cure every disease, all those overpaid medical consultants—don't call them doctors, that sounds too cheap— would automatically become bums. Doctors need a disease in the same way cops need a crime. Just think for a minute what a sad world it would be if there were no kind, neighborly police to come around and make your life hell.

Now they say that sex is the second oldest activity, next to eating. Speaking from personal experience, I would guess that it might well be the first one: ask the average guy, "What do you want to do first, feed or fuck?" Okay, you probably know the answer. So sex is here to stay, and that means it must, in some form or other, be made a crime if we are to have a happy, potent, busy, busy, busy life. That's my understanding of the way these upholders of the law treated me during my time in the land of the free.

What am I saying, really? I paid for everything. Quite often, cops prefer that you're breaking some law, real or imaginary. Let me remind you that back in 1971, as the Happy Hooker, I was bringing a little life, love, and laughter into the lives of some quite prominent citizens, defenders of the nation's morals, and all that jazz, during the presidency of Richard Nixon. Remember him like this: the guy who brought lying, deceit, blackmail, and burglary into public life and then set up a national commission to rout out corruption. Nixon himself was eventually exposed and was no longer president. What a surprise. One of the victims was me. Why, little ole me? I looked younger in those days. Just possibly because one day, at my apartment, they intercepted all my telephone messages they found from the telephone company's account, including calls to the White House. They were running scared. They already had Watergate, which was eventually to wash away Nixon and his gang. They needed to ensure that there would not also be a Hookergate.

I shouldn't complain. In every country where prostitution is a crime, it's the girl who takes the rap. The john goes free. So if prostitution was not a crime in the States, running a house or call girl business was. I was a foreigner before that. I had written a whole library of books. Inevitably my apartment was bugged. When a friend swept my apartment for bugs, he found many planted by the commission to secure evidence about me. They even rigged up a hidden television camera in my bedroom on top of my mirror. As far as I know, the man who did it was not a paid voyeur. Now, mark this dilemma with which every worker in this industry could be faced. On the one hand, there's a puritan and prurient right, demanding that we reveal the identity of our clients or be subject to prosecution. On the other hand, the clients themselves need to protect their image as law-abiding citizens, threatening anything from economic blackmail to physical violence if we open our mouths.

This is just a another example of how it is always the girl and not the john who is the victim. My old response, when I was asked the names of my clients, was to tell the district attorney to go to hell. It was not because I was so fond of everyone whose name appears in that little black book, but there's such a thing as personal integrity. Cynics point out that there's not much future for a hooker or a madam who is regarded as a blabbermouth. Others prepared to point a finger at one man who, though not a client, was yet someone who enjoyed the freedom of the house. Bill Furst was a policeman who quite openly demanded a very high percentage plus his choice of free girls to protect him from risk. A more vicious, grasping bastard could hardly be found. And, of course, he was quite prepared to be paid off to turn us in.

So when I was confronted with the tapes, which had been recorded one night in my apartment, and challenged to identify the voices—a big deal, after all, if you cannot trust the government, whose word can be accepted?— I was promised immunity. But as soon as I said anything about Bill Furst, the government conveniently forget about me, and I was kicked out of the country as an undesirable. Moreover, they brought me back in 1971 to testify. I must admit, it was that broken promise of the government that I resented even more than the penalty for having exposed the crooked Mr. Cop. Just how crooked? You could judge for yourself. He was a double murderer who got away by being a police stool pigeon. However, his excesses were so blatant—like a private airplane for a policeman—that finally he had to go into hiding and cool off somewhere way out of New York before taking out a form of life insurance called plastic surgery. Of course, once outside the jurisdiction of the United States, one is free from prosecution.

Remember the boys who, like Bill Clinton, refused to be sent off to fight and die young? Many took their *touches* over the border into Canada, and so did I. But a security crusade is not confined to any one country. The Canadians could not nail me for running a bordello or call girl agency. Their attack was more subtle. My book *The Happy Hooker* had been published. Whatever its merit is, it was definitely a declaration of war against prudery and double standards, which is our plan in the sex business. I was challenged by them to say whether the contents were fact or fiction. Of course, there was no way that they could be thought of as flights of fantasy. If I admitted they were based on facts, I in effect became a self-confessed criminal. Criminal? Sure, there were such dangers as the poolside orgy in San Juan, of all places.

Anyway, I ended up working for *Penthouse* magazine. In each country, there's an unpublished list of little words that cannot be written. Like in America, I cannot use four-letter words like "cock," "cunt," "fuck," and "suck" —well, maybe "suck" I could say. But then I wrote for South Africa, and in South Africa I could use all those words, but not others I could use in America. And in South Africa, I could write about any weird subject, because they hadn't heard about such items.

In the meantime, I am living partly in Holland (Amsterdam) and partly in Spain. I'm working on a website, which hopefully someday will be finished if I get the right financial sponsors. I'm also working on marketing products in the cosmetics business. I hope within the next year to be back here with a vengeance and promote those. Why not a fragrance, for instance, called Xaviera? And we're aiming for the market that I would love to enter, a line of fashion, let's say, for voluptuous women. Why do we always have to go to dowdy shops and wear dowdy clothes? The ripe and mature woman (like me), who often has more money than most young ones, would like to have elegant clothes that look good. So when I'm in L.A. I've spent fortunes at a fancy shop called The Forgotten Woman.

# Xaviera Hollander Introduces Cynthia Payne

Cynthia Payne is a lovely lady who at first sight does not appear to be a naughty lady. I met her in Edinburgh where I was attending the Edinburgh Theater Festival because I like cultural things. She arranged for a wonderful spectacle there by having a one-woman show.

# Cynthia Payne

Welcome to an afternoon of innocent sin, because that's all we're gonna get today. In my thirties I was doing it. In my forties I was organizing it, and in my sixties, unfortunately, I can only talk about it. In the last twenty years an awful lot of things have happened to me that I never imagined. By 1979, I'd been raided by the police twice, convicted in court, sentenced to prison, and had two films and two books made about my life. In addition, I had managed to get on the front page of every national newspaper in Great Britain. In 1988, I decided to go in for elections—not erections—elections, to get our laws changed. And just to think, all this came about through a very harmless swinging Christmas party.

I did run a brothel where, at the same time, I used to give sex parties for middle-aged and elderly men who had lost their wives. We used to advertise in a contact magazine, and I'd put in an advertisement for afternoon parties for tired businessmen. You'd be surprised how tired these men were. We got thousands of letters. So that's how I got into it. We had barristers, lawyers, and peers of the realm. This was before 1980. We were very cheap, really. We charged only twenty-five pounds and that was for food, drink, and a lady of their own choice. They called me the Freddy Laker of sex in those days. And, like Freddy, I did go bust. We used to knock five pounds off for old-age patrons, and we used to charge half-price if they were past it. We let the disabled in free, but I couldn't have too many because they used to block the gangways up with their wheelchairs. Why I tell this story is that we had three or four men in wheelchairs at the party the night that I got raided. The press had been tipped off that Cynthia Payne was going to get raided again.

I did go to prison in 1980. Seven years later they raided me again. The press were outside. The front page of the newspaper said that after the raid one man sped off in a wheelchair with half the police assisting him down the house steps and another man rushed off with the aid of a walking stick. And a very portly young man complained about his smudged mascara. I have that newspaper cutting. I've had two big raids by the police—one in 1980 and one in 1987. At the trial in 1980, I pleaded guilty, because I was guilty. To be honest, I was nervous. I didn't really know anything about law, so I pleaded guilty and received a sentence of eighteen months in prison and 4,000 pounds in fines. Now, I had a wonderful press—they've never had problems with me, the police or the press really. I mean the police wanted me stopped, but I always blamed it onto somebody else. But due to the press, I got my sentence reduced from eighteen months to six, which I did in four.

I have had two or three convictions for brothel keeping. So, really, the English wanted to stop me once and for all. The funniest thing that's happened to me this last year is that, with my criminal record, the English government actually asked me to do jury service. I was thrilled to bits because the clerk said my name came up on the computer. One or two people in the court didn't realize I had been recently detained, so I didn't tell them. I went up and did my jury service. Not only did I do jury service, but I was even made foreman. When they found out that I was recently detained, they turned around and said very nicely, "We do not need you for a second week." I was embarrassing the government because the press would take more interest in me being on the jury than they would in the defendant. I was described as a comic figure, really, right from 1980.

The headlines, really, have never ceased. I've been in the headlines now for over fifteen years. I thought I would only be an overnight sensation, but thank God it did lead to my two films: *Wish You Were Here*, starring young Emily Lloyd, about my early life (which is 100 percent true) and *Personal Services* with Julie Walters about my sex parties. I enjoyed giving pleasure to men, especially men who live on their own, who don't have wives. It's all right if you've got plenty of money. You can go and get what you want. But most of the men that I had didn't have a lot of money. Therefore, really, my place was like a club, and I didn't feel it was a brothel in any way.

So, that's what I'm all about. One gentleman asked me if I've got any regrets. To be honest, the only regret that I've got was that I didn't charge a bigger entrance fee.

# Coral Velisek

One bright fall morning in 1992, a small university town in Florida's Panhandle awoke to this headline story in the *Tallahassee Democrat*: "Take an Uptown Tour of Prostitution in Tallahassee. Coral Velisek is in jail for running an escort service that took care of the city's top professional patrons," complete with pictures and all the details. The next thing I knew, the wire service had flashed the story all around the world and I was receiving phone calls from tabloids and talk shows as far away as England. In the United States, I appeared on Donahue, Geraldo, Maury Povich, *Current Affairs*, and *Hard Copy*.

But April Fools' Day 1992 was when I was busted, and it altered my life forever. I never meant to remain a prostitute. I never wanted to stay one for very long. I was only doing it on a short-term basis to cover a financial shortfall that I was having. It was just something to do to make a little money. But the State of Florida's prosecution of me assured that I would stay a prostitute. I was convicted and jailed on twenty-seven prostitution charges and seven felony prostitution charges, fined $3,000, and sentenced to one month in the Leon County Jail and four years' probation. I had no prior record before this arrest. I had never been in trouble for more than a speeding ticket.

When the state attorney's office had finished tallying points for criminal charges, they then seized my home, my car, and my checking and savings accounts under the RICO federal statutes. They then went on to attack my family, seizing $2,500 from my daughter's checking account, money she had earned waiting tables in a local restaurant. Before it was all over, fighting both the civil seizure and the criminal charges, I owed over $16,000 in attorney's fees.

Immediate repercussions included a loss of a straight job that I had at the time and a never-used teaching certificate that would have eventually got me a good job. This teaching certificate, the State of Florida has assured me, will never, ever be reinstated, whether I get into trouble again or not. I also underwent an IRS audit. They are not pretty.

The greatest impact personally was upon my family. All my daughters' friends knew what April and Summer's mother had been doing. April was waiting on tables the Sunday that this article appeared in the *Tallahassee Democrat*. As she took an order from a large group of people, she was listening to them discuss and comment upon her mother's crime. They never knew that they were talking about the mother of their waitress. The stigma attached to my children finally became so acute that I sent them to live in Orlando, a big city by Tallahassee standards, where it was a lot easier to be anonymous and fit in.

It's five years later now. I've worked an assortment of $7-an-hour jobs. Seven dollars an hour! And I've got a bachelor of science degree in math education. I get discouraged quite often. With a fine education and my initiative and my business sense, why can't I do better? It's a good question, and there's an answer. A little more than two weeks ago, I made it through to the final level of a job selection process. The office manager had been impressed with me, so impressed that I got the interview with the boss. The boss had interviewed me and hired me, pending a background check. Oops! I didn't know about that part. Can you imagine the impact of thirty-four charges of prostitution on a prospective employee trying to gain legitimate employment?

Tallahassee business owners still remember my name. They call for an interview, but all they really want to do is have a look-see at the woman who ran a classy escort service five years ago. They look kind of sly and finally get around to the fact that they know who you are, maybe even ask a few questions, but they never hire you.

And then there's the inevitable question on the employment application: Have you been convicted of a felony within the past seven years and, if so, what? I lie. I lie because saying yes means that I'll be disqualified from a selection process before I even get started.

A woman convicted of prostitution becomes an easy target for victimization. You know that, and I do too. I worked for a sole proprietor for over a year, and when I asked for a raise and a one-week paid vacation, which all the other employees of this business were entitled to after one year's consecutive employment, it was denied me. They knew I wouldn't quit. I had the cost of supervision and court fines to pay on top of keeping me and my family afloat.

I'm going to tell you about a law in the State of Florida. This Florida law requires an employer to have fifteen or more employees before an employee can file a sexual harassment suit. My boss showed up at my front door one day during the fall football season, a six-pack of beer in hand, and invited himself into my home. He knew that I was on probation. He knew that I owed money to the court. He knew I would not protest or quit my job. He knew that I would do as he asked, and I did.

I never meant to stay in the business, a working girl. But being prosecuted means that future repercussions of that one crime force a woman to stay a prostitute. Most of the time I'm happy, or at least content. Don't get me wrong about that. I'm a fighter. I fight to survive.

I was afraid to come here today to speak on this panel. I know personally what happens to activists, such as the ladies on this panel whom I admire, who dare to speak out for sex workers' rights. They usually end up paying, paying in ways that you people haven't got a clue about. And I've already paid more than I ever dreamed I would for my crime. I slept with a man, and I accepted money for it. Did I do something so terribly wrong that I deserve to have my home taken away from me? Did I do something so terribly wrong that I had to send my children to live far away from me? Did I do something so terribly wrong that I deserve to be forced to sleep with my boss just to keep my job? Stop this injustice! Decriminalize prostitution, please!

# 3

# THE JOHNS

## Introduction

Although a bibliography of studies and writings on prostitutes will fill several volumes, there are only a comparative handful of studies dealing with their patrons. Because prostitution at its simplest is an economic transaction with the prostitute selling her (or his) services to a buyer, and both elements have to exist to have prostitution, the neglect of the buyer, superficially at least, would tend to emphasize that buying of sexual services is a normative aspect of the male experience. Feminists would argue, probably rightfully, that the lack of attention is just another indication of the male-centered scholarship and studies of the past. It is not so much the feminist issue that has brought about an interest in the study of the patrons of sex workers, however, as the concern over sexually transmitted diseases, particularly AIDS. We probably know more about the clients of sex workers now than we ever did in the past, but a lot still remains unknown. This section is devoted to studies of johns in the United States by Elroy Sullivan and William Simon; in England by Rosie Campbell; in Canada by Chris Atchison, Laura Fraser, and John Lowman; and one of elderly male clients in Puerto Rico by Maria Del Carmen Santos Ortiz, J. L. Laó-Meléndez, and A. Torres-Sánchez. There is also a more personal account by Jim Korn on his successful encounters with sex workers and by Hugh Loebner on being a john.

The result of the studies is to challenge many of the stereotypes that have for so long appeared in accounts of prostitutes.

# THE CLIENT:
## A SOCIAL, PSYCHOLOGICAL, AND BEHAVIORAL LOOK AT THE UNSEEN PATRON OF PROSTITUTION

### ELROY SULLIVAN AND WILLIAM SIMON

Prostitution, like most other public and semi-public representations of the sexual, has often been viewed, and not without considerable justification, as a venue for expressions of male sexual drive. Consequently, most of the previous discourses on prostitution have "explained" the phenomenon with references to the nature and management of this desire. Most of these "explanations" share an assumption of an all-but-imperative drive that requires substantial efforts to be ignored or satiated. Among sociological "functionalists," such as Talcott Parsons (1960) or Kingsley Davis (1949), a major service of the prostitute was to provide a place for the effective discharge of excess drive, and to provide an outlet for that part of the drive that could not be realized within the marital relationship and in ways that need not be threatening to the marriage itself. Similar explanations, also following this essentially hydraulic model of accumulating pressures, suggest a providing of sexual outlets for those men who are not yet married, those separated from conventional living, socially inept men, and the socially unattractive.

A related line of "explanation" involves the utilization of prostitutes for specific sexual acts, such as oral sex, and suggests that attitudes of both the female and the male in an emotionally committed relationship may give rise to this alternative sexual venue. Female spouses may be unlikely or unwilling to perform these services, or the men themselves may be unable to effectively integrate the sentimental with the erotic. The very potency of these men may be challenged by suggestions of the sentimental and the maternal. This latter explanation was described by Freud (1953) as a curse of modern man: that which you love you will not be able to desire and that which you desire you will not be able to love. We can view these essentially psychodynamic explanations as being related to the prior explanations in that they share the con-

134

cept of the prostitute as serving society by protecting it from the potentially dangerous sex drive of the masculine gender. Indeed, these "explanations" can be found in both formal social theory and "folk" theory; a general acceptance that was clearly reflected in the ambivalence with which prostitution was treated: regulation without elimination. Prostitution was and remains criminalized in ways so as to affirm the privileged status of the marital bed without exposing it and the rest of society to the permanently threatening and disruptive character of male sexuality.

However, an examination of the data generated by Alfred Kinsey and his associates (Kinsey, Pomeroy, and Martin 1948; Gebhard and Johnson 1979) suggests that prostitutes were not a frequent form of sexual expression except for relatively small numbers of men, and for many of those only during limited periods in their lives. Most North American men had no or very little contact with prostitutes. The Kinsey data were broken down into three groups of males: white men with a college education, white men with less than a college education, and African-American men with a college education.[1] Only 21 percent, 26 percent, and 33 percent, respectively, of these three groups of men reported something other than rare or no experience with prostitutes. And this, it should be noted, occurred during periods in which women were under far greater pressure than is the case today to restrict their coital activity to serious courtship or marriage and when oral sex was viewed as perverse (see Gagnon and Simon 1987). Similarly, only 19 percent, 23 percent, and 30 percent, respectively, of the men reported having more than rare premarital contact with a prostitute, and even these occurrences tended to more typically represent incidental rather than extensive use. Much of this activity may have taken the form of "rituals" surrounding sexual initiation: 19 percent, 23 percent, and 6 percent of the men, respectively, reported that their initial coital act was with a prostitute. Lastly, the constraints of the marital bond were also managed without significant recourse to prostitutes as 94 percent, 88 percent, and 81 percent, respectively, reported no or relatively rare (1 to 5 events) experiences of extramarital sex with a prostitute.

Even though prostitution does not play a part in the sexual lives of most men, it is clear that fellation was a relatively rare event with 62 percent, 78 percent, and 86 percent of the men, respectively, in Kinsey's data reporting no or rare occasions of fellation in their first marriages, and that the prostitute, as it were, took up the slack in what was, if only because of its rarity, an act of hypereroticism. Fellation while with a prostitute was reported by 48 percent, 49 percent, and 37 percent of the men, respectively. Thus the prostitute as a source of perverse sexuality had considerable relevance to the men (roughly 1900 to 1945) described by the Kinsey research.

Many of these factors have lost much of their explanatory significance as much of the double standard restraining female involvement in premarital sex has diminished, leading, in turn, to a lowering of the age of first intercourse for both genders as well as an increased acceptance of premarital sex. Similarly, oral sex has generally become normative both as a precoital petting technique as well as a substitute for coitus itself. Thus, it is not surprising— risking the approximations inevitable in comparing two radically different research strategies—that the proportion of American men currently having some experience with a prostitute has declined. As will be seen, only 18 percent of those men aged eighteen to fifty-nine in 1993 reported having paid a woman for sex.

From some perspectives what might be surprising is that the use of a prostitute has not declined even more. By speculation, it is possible that the prostitute remains a substantial player in the sexual expression of many men because of an elevation of erotic interest in a social landscape that advertises the explicitly erotic to an unprecedented degree. It is even possible that within this more diffusely erotic context, expanded interest in commercializable sex that is not immediately genital, such as domination and humiliation—what else is suggested by toe sucking?—may have enlarged the use and activities of "sex workers."

Even more than the prostitute herself, the client has been considered in the most decontextualized of ways, as if both the client and the prostitute existed only in a fantasy-laden twilight zone of degraded eroticism—all the more exciting for that fact. Here, the term "decontextualized" can be applied in a double sense in that sex with a prostitute is isolated and marginalized, and that the client as well as the prostitute become distinct and detached from the lives of all others. This is true both for society at large and the social science community. A search through three major social science databases revealed only one paper examining the clients of prostitutes (Holzman and Pines 1982) in recent decades, and this research studied only thirty clients who were sampled in a somewhat haphazard way. The present chapter, drawn from the National Health and Social Life Survey (NHSLS), with people randomly sampled and questioned from all fifty states, seeks to correct this virtual void in the literature, if only by a slight degree, by being able to compare men who reported having "paid a woman for sex" with those who say they have not. Unfortunately, this most recent survey, which is likely to remain the benchmark research for the coming decade or more, provides us with no more information regarding male use of female prostitutes than the bare fact of reporting having paid a woman for sex at some point in their lives. The obvious questions such as "How often?" "At what age, both in terms of the prostitute and the client?" "What kind of woman?" and "What kind(s) of sex?" were not asked. Nonetheless, some preliminary ideas regarding the demographic, sexual, and attitudinal attributes of men who exhibit a predisposition to exchange money for sex can be suggested.

# Methods and Results

The NHSLS data were collected from 3,432 respondents between February and October 1992 via a multistage area probability sampling design. The design was applied to all adults between the ages of eighteen and fifty-nine living in the fifty states of the United States and Washington, D.C., with households as their residence. For the purposes of the present analysis, the 1,511 men who were surveyed were isolated and analyzed.

One of the "self-administered questionnaires" of the NHSLS asked the following question, allowing for yes or no responses: "Have you ever paid a woman to have sex?" Two hundred sixty-seven of the men in the survey, 17.7 percent, answered in the affirmative to this question. These men, as contrasted with 75.6 percent (1,143) men who responded in the negative, are the primary focus of this study.[2] This variable will subsequently be referred to as PaidWomanForSex.

This PaidWomanForSex variable will be compared with a number of other variables that one might think are related to prostitution, as well as a few variables revealing aspects of the sexual careers of the men in the NHSLS survey. The standard demographic variables will be examined along with many other variables rather directly related to the sexual. The number of sex partners and the number of marriages and cohabitation relationships will be pulled out and compared to the PaidWomanForSex variable, as well as a host of variables related to specific sexual behaviors, desires, and feelings.

There were two groups of men we felt might cause potential problems to the analysis: gay (or bisexual) men and men who had been in the military. Two questions in the survey were possibly capable of identifying gay men:

1. Would having sex with someone of the same sex be appealing?[3]
2. Have you had a male sex partner in the last five years?

If a man answered yes to either of these questions, he was considered gay. Identified in this way, 5.5 percent (83 out of 1,511) of the men in the survey were identified as gay or bisexual.[4]

Eleven of the eighty-three gay men (13 percent) had paid a woman for sex at some time in their lives as opposed to 256 of the 1,327 nongay men (19 percent). Via a $\chi^2$ analysis, it was determined that this difference was not statistically significant, p = .173. Given this information, it was determined that a gay (or bisexual) man was just as likely to have visited a prostitute as a "straight" man, and no further distinction was made between these two groups of men in the analysis.

The second group of men that were of concern, men who had served in the military (referred to as ServedInMilitary), were identified via a relatively straightforward question: "Not counting the reserves, are you currently serving full time in any branch of the armed services or have you served in the past?" The frequencies to the responses to this question were 27.1 percent (1,101) in the affirmative and 72.9 percent (409) in the negative. (One respondent did not answer.) In contrast to the gay men, these 409 men showed a markedly different pattern when compared to the PaidWoman-ForSex variable. Of those men who had served in the military, 35.9 percent (137 out of 382) had, at some time, paid a woman for sexual favors, where only 12.6 percent (130 out of 1,028) of those men who had not served in the military had paid for sex. The $\chi^2$ was significant, $p < .001$.

This is not particularly new information. It has been known for years that men in the military visit prostitutes more often than men in civilian life. However, this finding in the NHSLS dataset instructs the subsequent analysis in two ways. First, it informs us that we should be on the alert for other differences between men who have visited a prostitute and those who have not as part of this military experience effect. The ServedInMilitary may be the mediator variable (or the true explanatory variable) with respect to other variables related to PaidWomanForSex. The second thing to look for is possible interactions between the military and other variables with respect to their influences on whether or not men have paid for sex. The attributes of men who have paid for sex and not been in the military may be different in significant ways from those of men who have paid for sex and have been in the military. For these reasons, many of the other variables will be analyzed with the ServedInMilitary variable in the statistical model.

At this point, several other variables from the NHSLS dataset were compared to the PaidWomanForSex variable.[5] The first of these was the age of the respondent. For convenience, this variable was recoded into six groups (Age-Group). Tested with $\chi^2$, these variables illustrated a significant relationship, $p < .001$, with the relationship seen in figure 1. Logistic regression, with Paid-WomanForSex as the dependent variable (DV), was used to examine the effects of the ServedInMilitary variable (AgeGroup and ServedInMilitary were independent variables [IVs]). This analysis revealed that the AgeGroup effect was persistent and that there was no interaction, $p = .093$.

The effect of education was next to be examined. A $\chi^2$ analysis revealed that the two-variable effect between Education and PaidWomanForSex was not significant, $p = .485$. However, a logistic regression analysis, with Paid-WomanForSex as the DV and both Education and ServedInMilitary as IVs, revealed that there was an interaction, $p = .018$. Table 1 shows the percentage of those men who have visited a prostitute broken down for each of the Education and ServedInMilitary categories. The effect between Education and PaidWomanForSex appears to be U-shaped for nonmilitary men while it seems to form more of an inverted U for the military group. Vocation or trade school training is both the lowest and the highest.

## Figure 1:  Percentage PaidWomanForSex (Yes) by AgeGroup

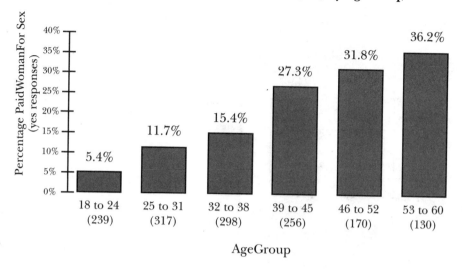

## Table 1: Percentages  PaidWomanForSex (Yes)
## by ServedInMilitary and Education

| ServedIn Military' | Percent Base Count | Education | | | | | | Row Total |
| --- | --- | --- | --- | --- | --- | --- | --- | --- |
| | | Less than Hi Sch | Finish Hi Sch | Vocation Trade Sc | Some College | Finish College | Advance Degree | |
| No | | 19% (168) | 11% (280) | 06% (54) | 10% (248) | 13% (182) | 16% (90) | 12% (1,022) |
| Yes | | 30% (33) | 33% (121) | 46% (26) | 44% (126) | 25% (48) | 23% (26) | 36% (380) |
| Column Total | | 21% (201) | 17% (401) | 19% (80) | 22% (374) | 15% (230) | 17% (116) | 19% (1,402) |

The race or ethnicity (RaceEthnicity) of the respondents is next on the agenda. The $\chi^2$ analysis for this variable revealed a significant relationship, p = .023. As evidenced by figure 2 it appears that white males have a somewhat lower probability of having visited a prostitute than African-American, Hispanic, or Asian men. None of the fourteen Native Americans in the study had paid a woman for sex; however, this count is somewhat low to make confident generalizations.

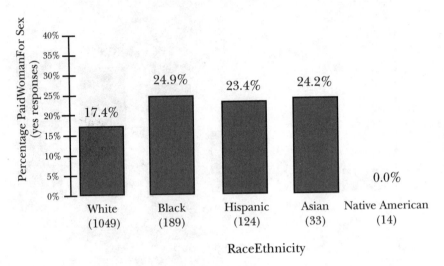

Figure 2: Percentage PaidWomanForSex by RaceEthnicity

Continuing with the use of logistic regression, it was found that an inter-action existed between ServedInMilitary and RaceEthnicity with respect to PaidWomanForSex, p = .040. Table 2 illustrates that the military appears to have a leveling-off effect with respect to different RaceEthnicities. The RaceEthnicity effect is augmented among the non-military men whereby it is all but removed for the military men.

Table 2: Percentages PaidWomanForSex (Yes) by Military and RaceEthnicity

| Military | Percent Base Count | RaceEthnicity | | | | | Row Total |
| | | White | Black | Hispanic | Asian | Native | |
| No | | 10% (755) | 20% (137) | 21% (99) | 24% (25) | 00% (12) | 13% (1,028) |
| Yes | | 37% (294) | 37% (52) | 32% (25) | 25% (8) | 00% (2) | 36% (381) |
| Column Total | | 17% (1,049) | 25% (189) | 23% (124) | 24% (33) | 00% (14) | 19% (1,409) |

Several other variables, as shown in table 3, were compared to PaidWom-anForSex that did not reveal significant relationships. Each of these variables was also tested for an interaction effect with ServedInMilitary, and none of the interaction effects were statistically significant.

**Table 3: Variables without Statistically Significant Relationships
to PaidWomanForSex (Yes)**

| Variable | p = value |
| --- | --- |
| Household Income | .140 |
| Political Preference | .353 |
| Religion Raised | .148 |
| Frequency of Religious Attendance | .140 |
| Current Religion | .129 |
| Raised in Rural or Urban Setting | .079 |
| Raised in Broken Home | .520 |

The $\chi^2$ test statistic was used in all cases for these variables.

It is now time to turn to some variables that are more directly related to sexuality and sexual behavior. The first of these is the number of sex partners the respondent has had since his eighteenth birthday (SexPartners). As one would expect, this was related to PaidWomanForSex, as seen in figure 3 ($\chi^2$ was significant, $p < .001$). There is a steady rise in the likelihood of a man having visited a prostitute the more sex partners he has had, and there is a rather dramatic 17 percent jump for men who have had more than ten partners. In many of the variables to come, it is not clear that PaidWomanForSex should continue as the DV. Therefore, hierarchical loglinear analyses (HLAs) are used to test for the ServedInMilitary mediator and interaction effects. The variable SexPartners, along with ServedInMilitary and PaidWoman-ForSex were placed in an HLA. The best-fitting model continued to show the SexPartners by PaidWomanForSex relationship, and it did not reveal a three-variable interaction.

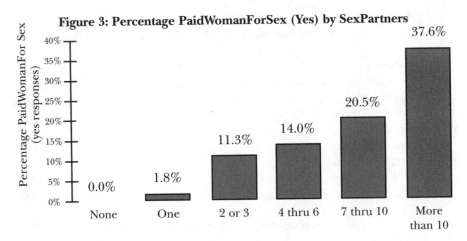

Figure 3: Percentage PaidWomanForSex (Yes) by SexPartners

The number of marriages or living-together (for at least thirty days) arrangements (Cohabs) the respondent had was examined next. As with Sex-Partners, and shown in figure 4, the relationship with PaidWomanForSex was statistically significant ($\chi^2$ revealed that p < .001). An HLA analysis revealed no ServedInMilitary mediator or three-variable effect.

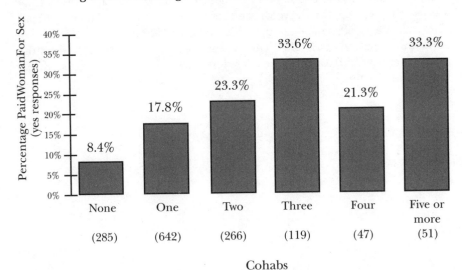

Figure 4.  Percentage PaidWomanForSex (Yes) by Cohabs

The present marital or cohabitation status (CohabStatus) of the respondents was examined. A $\chi^2$ revealed that the direct relationship between this variable and PaidWomanForSex was not significant, p = .361. However, an HLA analysis revealed that there was a three-variable relationship when ServedIn-Military was included. A logistic regression analysis, with PaidWomanForSex as the DV and CohabStatus and ServedInMilitary as IVs, confirmed this finding, p = .029. The percent of the men who had paid a woman for sex for each of the CohabStatus and ServedInMilitary categories is shown in table 4.

**Table 4: Percentages PaidWomanForSex (Yes)
by ServedInMilitary and CohabStatus**

|  |  | CohabStatus | | |
|---|---|---|---|---|
| ServedIn Military | Percent Base Count | No | Yes | Row Total |
| No | | 12% (503) | 14% (525) | 13% (1,028) |
| Yes | | 43% (129) | 32% (253) | 36% (382) |
| | Column Total | 18% (632) | 20% (778) | 19% (1,410) |

A variable referred to as EroticInterest was constructed from four of the questions in a fantasy section of the NHSLS:

1. Would you enjoy having sex with more than one person at the same time?

2. Would you enjoy seeing other people doing sexual things?

3. Would you enjoy having sex with someone you don't personally know?

4. Would you enjoy watching partner undress/strip?

Factor analysis revealed that one significant construct ran through these four questions. The EroticInterest variable represents a quartiled version of this factor. Figure 5 illustrates that this EroticInterest variable is positively related to PaidWomanForSex ($\chi^2$ was significant, p < .001). Through an HLA analysis, it was determined that the relationship between PaidWomanForSex and EroticInterest was persistent and that there was no three-variable interaction.

A variable referred to as SexAttitude was constructed in a similar fashion as the EroticInterest variable. This SexAttitude question was constructed from three question in the NHSLS questionnaire:

1. There's been a lot of discussion about the way morals and attitudes about sex are changing in this country. If a man and a woman have sex relations before marriage, do you think it is:

2. What if they are in their teens, say 14–16 years old? In that case, do you think sex relations before marriage are:

3. What is your opinion about a married person having sexual relations with someone other than the marriage partner—is it:

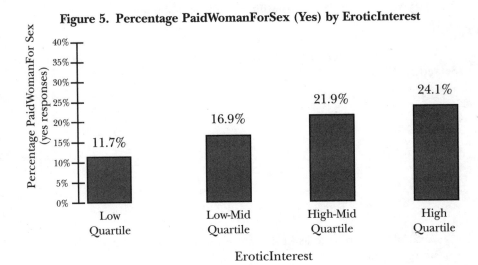

Figure 5. Percentage PaidWomanForSex (Yes) by EroticInterest

As with EroticInterest, factor analysis revealed one underlying construct ran through these three questions. The SexAttitude variable represents this construct. As opposed to the EroticInterest variable, a $\chi^2$ analysis revealed that there was no relationship between this SexAttitude variable and Paid-WomanForSex, p = .294. Furthermore, an HLA analysis failed to find any three-variable interaction with the inclusion of ServedInMilitary.

The frequency of masturbation during the last twelve months (Masturbation) was examined via a $\chi^2$ analysis with the results graphed in figure 6, p < .001. The primary difference is between the "Never" masturbate category and the "Once a year or more" category. After this initial jump, there is little difference among the PaidWomanForSex percentages and the other masturbation categories. An HLA, with the inclusion of ServedInMilitary, revealed that the PaidWomanForSex and Masturbation relationship was persistent and that there was no three-variable interaction.

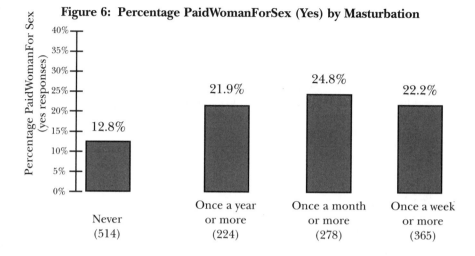

Figure 6: Percentage PaidWomanForSex (Yes) by Masturbation

In addition to the variables just analyzed, a handful of other variables were compared to PaidWomanForSex. Of the variables that had a significant relationship with PaidWomanForSex, none ceased to have the relationship when ServedInMilitary was controlled. In addition, none revealed a three-variable interaction with ServedInMilitary and PaidWomanForSex when analyzed via HLA.[6] A list of the variables and whether or not they revealed a significant relationship to PaidWomanForSex is provided in table 5. Some of these variables had simple yes/no responses and others had four-point or five-point Likert-style responses. In all cases, they were treated as categorical and tested with the $\chi^2$ statistic.

# Discussion

From an analysis of this data, there are seven overall findings that are particularly worthy of distinction: general variables that did not show a relationship with PaidWomanForSex, the effects of the military, the effects of age, the race/ethnicity effect, the education effect, the possibility that men who visit prostitutes are somewhat hypersexual, and the possible revelation that these men have socio-emotional problems. Each of these effects (or group of effects) will be discussed in turn.

## Table 5: Variables Related to the Sexual Compared to PaidWomanForSex (Yes)

| Variable | p-value |
| --- | --- |
| In the last 12 months did | |
| You go to club with nude or semi-nude dancers | .029 + |
| You buy any sexually explicit books or magazines | .012 + |
| You buy any vibrators or dildos for sexual purposes | .248 |
| You buy any other sex toys | .118 |
| You have anal intercourse | .468 |
| You receive a professional massage | .095 |
| You attend a nude public gathering | .887 |
| You have picture taken in the nude | .491 |
| You call any sex phone services | .154 |
| You buy/rent any X-rated videos | .021 + |
| Sex make you feel anxious/worried | .903 |
| Sex make you feel cared for | .396 |
| Sex make you feel guilty | .471 |
| Sex make you feel loved | .077 |
| Sex make you feel sad | .532 |
| Sex make you feel satisfied | .010 − |
| Sex make you feel scared | .495 |
| Sex make you feel thrilled | .071 |
| Sex make you feel wanted | .027 − |
| You feel emotionally satisfied in your relationship | .008 − |
| You feel physically satisfied in your relationship | .003 − |
| You have sex to make up after a fight | .134 |
| You have sex to express love | .020 − |
| You have sex because you wanted it | .381 |
| You have sex to get your partner pregnant | .060 |
| You have sex to relieve tension | .167 |
| You achieve orgasm often during sex | .416 |
| Your partner achieve orgasm often during sex | .434 |
| Hire a prostitute or pay for sex | .001 + |
| Would you find the following appealing: | |
| Anal intercourse | .461 |
| Partner stimulating your anus with finger | .002 + |
| You stimulating partner's anus with finger | .001 + |
| Using a dildo or vibrator | .027 + |
| Being forced to have sex | .212 |
| Forcing someone to have sex | .004 + |
| Performing oral sex on your partner | .220 |
| Having oral sex performed on you | .003 + |
| Does thinking about sex make you feel guilty | .225 |

The $\chi^2$ was the test statistic used in all cases for these variables.
+ Statistically significant at .05 and positively correlated with PaidWomanForSex.
− Statistically significant at .05 and negatively correlated with PaidWomanForSex.

## General Variables with No Significant Relationship to PaidWomanForSex

Somewhat surprisingly, several variables in the analysis revealed no significant differences when contrasting men who have visited a prostitute with those who have not. One of the most startling is the frequency of religious attendance. It appears that men who go to religious services on a regular basis are just as likely to have paid for sex than men who rarely or never attend services. The majority of religions place prohibitions on various sexual activities, including consorting with prostitutes. However, these canons have the two-pronged effect of prohibiting as well as bringing to the fore. The very act of making something off limits simultaneously brings it into consciousness and makes it an object of desire.

The household income of the men was not differentiating with respect to having visited a prostitute. One might think that the rates would be higher at both ends of the income brackets, with the poor being more familiar with where the prostitutes are and how to access them, and the rich being able to better afford these sexual treats. However, it appears that the likelihood of finding men who have visited prostitutes is relatively evenly spread across the income brackets. This reminds us that prostitutes, as is the case with most other professionals, do not work in a homogeneous world. There is a social hierarchy to prostitution, ranging from the streetwalker in the rundown side of town to the elegant call girl who will only visit the better hotels, with the women of escort services and massage parlors filling in the middle ground.

As shown in table 3, several other variables were compared to the Paid-WomanForSex variable that revealed no relationship. Those raised in rural or urban settings actually allowed a variety of responses such as on a farm, small town, suburb of large city, and in a large city, but the likelihood of men having paid for sex was relatively equal for all of these areas. As well, the likelihood of visiting a prostitute was not differentiated by having been raised in a broken home. The broken family has, of late, been the scapegoat for a plethora of social ills. However, men who were raised in a family setting consisting of something other than their biological parents are no more likely to seek out and give patronage to prostitutes. Whether or not the men were Republican or Democrat, irrespective of the religion in which they were raised or the religion with which they currently identified, the probability of finding men who visited prostitutes remains a relative constant.

It is striking that some of these variables, not so distantly removed from realms of the sexual, show no correlation with having paid for sex. One of the most striking is that measuring the attitudes of men toward sexuality and sexual behavior. Men who think sexual relations before marriage, teen sex, and extramarital sex are wrong are just as likely to have been to see a prostitute as those men who think these things are acceptable. Who are these men thinking about with respect to their attitudes? If they are thinking about themselves, they must be experiencing some degree of psychological dissonance. Is it more reasonable to suggest that they are thinking about their sons and daughters? It is possibly a reflection of the double message: "Just because I did it does not mean it is okay for you to do it." It is somewhat ironic that a generation that normalized premarital sex and brought us "free love" is now insisting that its children restrict their sexual endeavors.

## The Effect of the Military

As was shown in the analysis of the military men, having served in the military increases the chances that a man will have paid a woman for sex by about 23 percent. In the NHSLS dataset, the data are not available to determine the percentage of these "paid a woman for sex" experiences that happened exclusively while the men were enlisted. However, novelists, accounts of acts during military excursions, and common sense have long told us that the frequency of prostitution visitation is higher for military men than it is for civilians. The excursions after completing boot camp or on leave after a long tour are well known.

The argument can be made that the military is a total institution. It has a socializing effect that is capable of overriding such things as upbringing, race/ethnicity, and many other sociological and demographic factors. As an indicator of the strength of the military effect, the RaceEthnicity and Education variables can be examined (shown in table 1 and table 2). The probability of having visited a prostitute initially rises and then falls with respect to education when examining men who have been in the military, and it does virtually the opposite for men who have not. The RaceEthnicity variable illustrates the effect of the military even somewhat more dramatically. There is little difference across RaceEthnicities for men who were in the military while there are sizable differences for men who were not. The influence of the military introduces white, African-American, and Hispanic men to the prostitute experience in relatively equal proportions.

Interestingly, there was no case where the military experience revealed itself as a mediator to some other variable that was related to having paid for sex. This suggests that the military experience is quite strong but relatively well confined with respect to the clients of prostitutes. This is not to say that the military experience does not affect individuals. It is simply that the military experience is not the underlying cause of the correlation that other variables have to the PaidWomanForSex variable. These other variables represent independent relationships to and reasons for paying for sex.

The only other variable in the analyses that illustrated a three-variable interaction with PaidWomanForSex and ServedInMilitary was CohabStatus (whether or not the men were currently in a sexually cohabiting relationship). This variable that measured whether or not the men were currently in a cohabiting sexual relationship appeared to dampen the effect of the military on visiting prostitutes, whereas it had little effect on the nonmilitary men, as shown in table 4. The effect is not dramatic (an 11 percent decrease); however one might assume that some of the married (or cohabiting) men were married at the time they were in the military, and that they were more faithful to their wives (or girlfriends). It is worthy to note that even for those men who are currently in a cohabiting relationship, the military men still maintained substantially higher rates of visiting prostitutes, 32 percent compared to only 14 percent.

## The Age Effect

Figure 1 revealed that there was a sizable relationship between the age of a man and whether or not he had visited a prostitute. The rate was only slightly more than 1 in 20 for men age eighteen to twenty-four while it is more than 1 in 3 for men age fifty-three to sixty. Since the NHSLS survey was not a longitudinal study, the data are not available to determine whether this is a biological (or social) age phenomenon, or an effect having to do more with cohorts or generations. We know that the number of men with military experience has decreased in recent decades, but the military variable revealed no interaction effect with age. The likelihood of having visited a prostitute rises with age at about the same rate for those men who were in the military as it does for those men who were not. This age phenomenon is independent of the military effect.

A possible explanation, having more to do with cohorts rather than purely age, is that the women's movement washed over the American social landscape in recent decades. Many females who came into womanhood during and after the 1960s are more open to, if not more demanding of, the sexual than women of earlier years. In the early part of the century, it has been suggested that the prostitute served to provide an outlet for the excess sexual desire of men, but with the coming of the women's movement this desire is more readily and easily fulfilled through coital activity with spouses and other sexual partners. In using this as an explanation of the age effect, it must be noted that the essential, or hydraulic, model of male sexuality is still threatened. If the expression of sexuality among women is so easily changed through a social movement, why is it that the same could not happen to men, possibly in the reverse direction?

As opposed to a cohort effect, the biological—or, more to the point, the social—age of these men may serve as the better explanation. In the simplest of senses, the older a man is, the more lifetime opportunity he has had to consider visiting a prostitute. In a somewhat more complex vein, it is known that sexual interest in one's partner wanes with the length of the relationship. However, it is not at all clear that a corresponding waning of interest in the sexual per se accompanies this. With far less threat to the marital bonds than an affair with a co-worker or other female acquaintance, an occasional visit to the prostitute may be reaffirming to the sexual virility of many men. Unlike previous generations, the psychological need for a man to see himself as sexual, both in terms of duration and intensity, may exist as a social expectation—if not a mandate—for the contemporary male.

## The Race/Ethnicity Effect

The fact that the military overrides any racial or ethnic differences has already been discussed. However, both figure 2 and the nonmilitary men of table 2 illustrate that there is a race/ethnicity effect. If we focus on the non-military row of table 2, it can be seen that twice the proportion of African-American and Hispanic men have paid a woman for sex as have white men. The fact that these numbers can be changed so dramatically by a social phenomenon such as military service suggests that other social factors may be at play in producing the racial/ethnic differences among nonmilitary men. Even with equal rights and affirmative action laws, it is known that minority men are still a long way from achieving social, educational, and economic parity with American white men. This imbalance creates a situation in which the minority male has restricted opportunity to affirm himself as a man, both in terms of absolute expression and variety of expression. Expression of maleness in the realm of the sexual becomes the more singular avenue of self-masculine affirmation. In addition, the possibility of failure takes on a level of hypersignificance. The prostitute provides male affirmation in that interest in and performance of the sexual is demonstrated, and that the possibility of rejection by the female sexual partner is greatly reduced. One usually need not worry about being told "no" when with a prostitute.

## The Education Effect

The relationship between having paid a woman for sex and education was quite interesting. Analyzed directly, there was no correlation between the two variables. However, with the inclusion of military service, two opposite curvilinear relationships emerged. Focusing only on those men who have not been in the military, more education initially tends to cause decreases in the likelihood of prostitution visitation, bottoming out at trade school degrees, and then result in increases in prostitution patronage continuing through advanced degrees. The frequency of paying for sex is up at both ends of the continuum. Regarding the low end of education, it might be argued that these men live in environments where the prostitute is seen and available. These uneducated men know where to go to find her and engage her services. In addition, similar to the race/ethnicity effect, these men may have limited access to other expressions of maleness and the expression personal power.

The college-educated (and beyond) men may be exhibiting an increased interest in the forbidden areas of the sexual as an expression of personal freedom and prowess. It becomes more of an expression of "the challenge" or "the adventurous" as opposed to a need for maintaining a sense of self. Other research has demonstrated a rather strong relationship between erotic interest and education (Sullivan, in press). It may very well be the case that these educated men have allowed themselves to explore areas that appear less interesting or more threatening to men of more moderate educational attainment.

As opposed to these findings, the military tends to wash out and even reverse the entire education effect, as seen in table 1. The greatest discrepancy, the men with vocational or trade school training, may be the result of the educational opportunities afforded in the military. Trade school training is particularly available while serving in the military, and men who take advantage of this opportunity may be precisely the ones more dedicated to the overall military experience. If one allows for the high prostitution patronage scores among the "trade school" and "some college" military men, the differences in the scores are not terribly noticeable, once again illustrating the blanketing effect of the military. It should be noted that in no case do the non-military rates even approach the military ones for any of the education categories. Education, as with race/ethnicity, has the capacity to influence the likelihood that a man will visit a prostitute, but only if its influences are allowed to operate in an environment not dominated by much stronger social factors.

## The Question of Hypersexuality

The analyses make several suggestions of a hypersexuality among the men who have called upon a prostitute. These analyses report more lifetime sex partners and sexual cohabitation arrangements (marriages or "living together" arrangements) for prostitute visitors than for their male counterparts, as shown in figures 3 and 4. With respect to cohabitation arrangements, there is a 12 percent jump in the likelihood of prostitution visitation between men with four cohabitation experiences and those with five or more. A desire for the sexual is on the agenda and takes on a heightened significance for many of those men who visit prostitutes.

However, this notion of a hypersexuality cannot be taken as a singular reason for visits to prostitutes. Of those men with only two or three sex partners, 11 percent had taken in the prostitution experience. Masturbation frequency, another indicator of an inordinate interest in the sexual, is also related to prostitution visitation, as shown in figure 6, but almost 13 percent of those men who had never masturbated in the last year had paid a woman for sex. The constructed measure of erotic interest also showed a rather strong relationship with paying for sex, with over 24 percent of those men with high erotic interest scores having been to a prostitute, but almost 12 percent of those men with low erotic interest scores had indulged in the prostitute experience (see figure 5).

Continuing with this notion of hypersense of the sexual, table 5 reveals a cluster of other behaviors and desires that are positively related to paying for sex. These men are more likely to enjoy the services of nude or semi-nude clubs, to purchase sexually oriented publications and videos, and to have desires for sexual activities that may be considered deviant or adventurous, such as anal stimulation or the use of vibrator equipment. However, these behaviors and desires do not appear to run into areas that would be considered deviant in the extreme. Nude or semi-nude clubs as well as "sex shops" are found in virtually all major cities and are operated, for the most part, within the limits of the law. These men do not prefer nude gatherings, actual anal intercourse, or nude picture-taking sessions to a degree that is any different from men who do not visit prostitutes. Many prostitute patrons are clearly more interested in sexual variety and exploration in ways that other men are not. They are willing to explore their sexuality in terms of both thoughts and behaviors.

## The Possibility of Socio-Emotional Problems

In addition to interpreting a tendency toward the hypersexual, the reverse correlations in table 5, as well as the one positive correlation having to do with forcing someone to have sex, could be taken as a sign that those men who have seen a prostitute are more at risk for emotional problems. They are more likely to report feelings of emotional and physical dissatisfaction, they do not feel as wanted or satisfied with respect to the sex act, and they do not have sex as an expression of love. The data are not available to determine whether this is a reflection of the reality of these men or more a reflection of their perceived social worlds. But it is interesting to note that these men do not report lower frequencies of achieving orgasms for either themselves or their sexual partners.

With respect to the prostitute, it is difficult not to argue that she, at least to some degree, is fulfilling the social and psychological voids that are not being fulfilled in the other areas of the social lives of many of these men. The prostitute provides a social and psychological emollient while requiring little emotional competence or obligation in return.

## Concluding Remarks

Many variables have been compared with and contrasted to the act of having visited a prostitute at least one time in the sexual lives of the men in the NHSLS dataset. These comparisons and contrasts have been made, in many cases, without a great deal of integration to other related variables. However, this is not a grave concern if one recognizes that there are an abundance of "reasons" for paying for sex while there is a rather restricted number of "ways" that one might go about it. The purpose was not to identify the singular "explanation" of why men give patronage to prostitutes, but, instead, to open a discussion of the varied and complex "reasons" for the behavior.

It is clear that social factors surrounding the military provide rather strong encouragement for men to visit prostitutes. It may be that, in many instances, the likelihood of men paying for sex has more to do with situational factors than any psychological need or biological drive. One might speculate about other situations that may promote the use of prostitutes: the truck stop milieu, the image and expectations of the traveling salesman, the presumed favors expected of prospective purchasers at trade shows.

This activity is clearly not practiced by the majority of men in the contemporary United States culture, but it does occur with sufficient frequency to be a normal sexual experience for a large group of men who came of age in the latter part of the twentieth century. The overall probability of having visited a prostitute is 18 percent, with some segments of the population approaching 50 percent. This is not an activity with which we may all agree, but it is, as the saying goes, the oldest of professions, and there appears to be enough interested men to assure its continued survival. The fact that in no case, for the groups of men that were examined, does the incidence of visiting prostitutes exceed 50 percent does not suggest that prostitution is a minor part of the sexual milieu and lives of a great number men. For many, she may serve as more of a fantasy image than a real, accessible, or allowable participant in sexual life. One might ask, how many men are psychological, if not actual, clients of prostitutes in the terms of a privately fantasized tease or the creation of a desire?

# Notes

1. The frequencies and percentages for African-American men with less than a college education were removed from analysis in the Kinsey data because of problems related to sampling.

2. There were 101 men (6.7 percent) who did not respond to the question. They are dropped from all analyses involving the PaidWomenForSex variable.

3. This question allowed responses of very appealing, appealing, not appealing, and not at all appealing. Responses of very appealing or appealing were taken as an indicator of a gay man.

4. The first question used to identify gay men had 6 missing cases and the second question had 174 missing cases. These missing cases were assumed to be negative responses to the question. This assumption creates the possibility that some gay men were mistakenly treated as nongay men.

5. As the variables were coded in the original dataset, many were given categories of Refused, Don't Know, Unknown, and the like. In a great majority of the cases, there was no corresponding response on the original questionnaires. In an attempt to bring some order to these essentially missing values, all were recoded as missing data. For the variables of interest, in no case was the missing data percentage large enough to represent any substantial problems to the analysis.

6. Actually, the question regarding the appeal of receiving fellatio did reveal a three-variable relationship with the HLA, but the relationship did not hold up through a linear regression analysis with the receiving fellation variable as the DV, $p = .053$. Therefore, it was concluded that whatever three-variable effect was there was very weak at best.

# References

Davis, K. 1949. *Human Society*. New York: The Macmillan Company.

Freud, S. 1953. Three essays on sexuality. In *The Standard Edition of the Complete Psychological Works*. Vol. 7. London: Hogarth Press.

Gagnon, J. H., and W. Simon. 1987. The sexual scripting of oral genital contacts. *Archives of Sexual Behavior* 16: 1–25.

Gebhard, P. H., and A. B. Johnson. 1979. *The Kinsey data: Marginal tabulations of the 1938–1963 interviews conducted by the Institute of Sex Research*. Philadelphia: W. B. Saunders Company.

Holzman, H. R., and S. Pines. 1982. Buying sex: The phenomenology of being a john." *Deviant Behavior: An Interdisciplinary Journal* 4: 89–116.

Kinsey, A., W. B. Pomeroy, and C. E. Martin. 1948. *Sexual Behavior in the Human Male*. Philadelphia: W. B. Saunders Company.

Parsons, T. 1960. *Structure and Process in Modern Society*. New York: Free Press.

Sullivan, E. In press. *Demographic, behavioral and psychological correlates of erotic interest*.

# INVISIBLE MEN:
## MAKING VISIBLE MALE CLIENTS OF FEMALE PROSTITUTES IN MERSEYSIDE

### ROSIE CAMPBELL

## Introduction

Despite a limited number of recent pieces of research, there has been little research that has focused on men who pay for sex in the United Kingdom. The focus has tended to be on the women who sell sex. The men who create a demand for and pay for commercial sex have remained relatively invisible. This chapter summarizes some findings from a series of twenty-eight interviews with male clients of female prostitutes in Merseyside, which is located within the northwest region of the United Kingdom. I will briefly outline our methodology and summarize the sociodemographic characteristics of the respondents and the nature of their reported commercial sex involvement. I will outline the reasons they gave for paying for sex and some of the meanings they attached to their commercial sex involvement, making some links between these and dominant cultural constructions of heterosexual masculine sexuality. This chapter urges further research with men who pay for sex to enable a more comprehensive analysis of the socio-economic and cultural relations that sustain prostitution.

## Background

The research on which this chapter is based was part of a broader project that examined female street prostitution in inner-city Liverpool during 1995–1996 (Campbell, Coleman, and Torkington 1996).[1] The objective of the project was to examine the views and experiences of those affected by and involved in street prostitution. Utilizing a range of methodologies, researchers gave several groups the opportunity to identify the issues and problems related to street prostitution that were most salient to them. These groups included female street prostitutes, residents, men who pay for commercial sex, and representatives from police, health, and other statutory and voluntary agencies.

## Secrets and Lies: Researching Male Clients

As McKeganey has remarked, "There are enormous methodological difficulties associated with interviewing male clients" (1994, 290). Many of these are linked to the secretive and illicit nature of this group's involvement in commercial sex. This secrecy means that it is difficult to assess the proportion of the male population who pay for sex. Hence, one problem for researchers is establishing a meaningful sampling frame for men in this population; as a result they are unable to identify, with confidence, a "representative" sample. In a recent large-scale survey of sexual behavior and attitudes in Britain, Johnson et al. (1994) found that 6.8 percent of men in their sample reported that they had paid for sex at some point in their lives. A smaller proportion, 1.8 percent, reported that they had paid for sex during the last five years. It seems highly likely that respondents would underreport such illicit behavior. Although a minority, this underestimation is a significant minority.

The taboo related to buying and selling sex still persists, certainly in the United Kingdom. It has been identified as one key reason why so few men who pay for sex identify themselves publicly (McCleod 1982; Faugier and Cranfield 1995). Recent research confirms this secrecy among British men, suggesting that most men conceal their involvement in commercial sex from family and friends (McKeganey and Barnard 1996; McKeganey 1994; Faugier and Cranfield 1995).

No men in our research were completely "out" about their commercial sex involvement. A small number of men (five) had informed others, usually one close friend or family member. One man had confided in his mother, one his sister, one several close friends, another in his brother-in-law (who as a result went on a visit to see a prostitute), and one man had informed his partner. It's important to note that this group of men still stressed the importance of concealing their behavior from others.

The majority of men in this research chose not to tell any friends or family about their behavior. The three key reasons given were (1) fear of partner's reaction, (2) fear of being labeled as strange or sexually perverse, and (3) sense of shame. One man said, "I'd be scared of someone saying why does he go? They'd think I was weird and my girlfriend would not be too pleased at all." Another said, "I can't bear to think about the wife and daughters finding out—it would destroy them. I don't want to upset them like that, so I keep it very discreet."

This continued invisibility and analogous secrecy also demonstrate the inequitable, gendered, social, and economic power relations that facilitate the relative imbalance by which prostitutes become scrutinized by researchers, health educators, and the criminal justice system, while clients quietly carry on with their lives.

It has been easier to pay attention to the women who sell sex and label them as a category of "unrespectable," deviant women than pay attention to clients and examine the reasons why men pay for and create a market in commercial sex.

McCleod (1982) stressed that the invisibility of male clients and the focus on the women who sell sex have meant there is a limited understanding of prostitution because there has been limited exploration of men's motivations and "men's experiences of daily life" that partly sustain prostitution.

# Methods Used

Although one of the key problems researchers face, therefore, is making contact with and accessing this "hidden" population who engage in illicit, often secretive behavior that they are likely to want to conceal, this group has not proved impossible to contact. In recent years researchers have utilized several methods of contact and have begun to gather information about the sociodemographic characteristics and motivations of men who pay for sex (McCleod 1982; Faugier, Hayes, and Butterworth 1992; Day, Ward, and Perrotta 1993; McKeganey 1994, McKeganey and Barnard 1996).

Contact methods that have been used by researchers include, among others

- Approaching clients directly as they solicit women on the streets or in other settings where they contact prostitutes (Leonard 1990; Kinnell 1989)
- Contacting clients via police stations (Faugier, Hayes, and Butterworth 1992)
- Utilizing women working as prostitutes as researchers/observers to gather information about their clients (Kinnell 1989)
- The use of media to advertise a research interview phone line, to facilitate telephone interviews

In the United Kingdom several researchers have used the first method as part of their methodology for contacting men who pay for commercial sex.

Although not without difficulties and limitations, it has generally been found to be a relatively efficient and effective means of reaching this "hidden" population, particularly in terms of response rate and time.

Faugier and Cranfield noted that "The use of media (i.e., advertisements and telephone survey) appeared to be an effective method for talking to this hidden population" (1995, 30). We had only limited time for this component of the research and hence partly for pragmatic reasons decided to replicate this approach.

We placed an advertisement in the personal columns of the local daily newspaper (*Liverpool Echo*) for three evenings over a two-week period. The same advertisement was placed in a free weekly newspaper in the Merseyside area over the same period. Leaflets with the same advert were also placed in the Genito-Urinary Medicine (GUM) Clinic at the Royal Liverpool Hospital. The advertisement invited men who pay for sexual services with female prostitutes to take part in the research project and stressed the academic nature of the research. A temporary telephone line was set up for a two-week period. A semi-structured schedule was designed for interviewing male clients, which incorporated both closed and open questions, with scope for unstructured in-depth exploration of issues. Interviews on average lasted forty-five minutes. Similarly to McKeganey (1994) and Faugier and Cranfield (1995), we received few nuisance or silent phone calls. One of the problems we did encounter was that several interviews were terminated because the respondent was interrupted and could not continue the interview in privacy.

Given the secretive nature of commercial sex involvement, you may ask Why would any client take part in any research?

Respondents stressed two key reasons for participation. First, the telephone gave them a rare opportunity to discuss this aspect of their lives, an experience that was described as cathartic by several respondents, and, second, they liked the opportunity to contribute to research that may have a role in changing policy/law, etc. It seems telephone interviews provide researchers with a means of contacting male clients in which the clients feel their anonymity is not seriously jeopardized.

# Limitations

There are, of course, many limitations with the methodology used in this research. The respondents were clearly a self-selected sample, constituting only those who saw the advertisement and who then chose to make contact. There may be differences in attitude and behavior between those who wanted to cooperate with the research and those who did not. Also, our number of responses and hence sample size was limited. Responses could have been increased if further advertisements had been placed and the time period for research extended. Our research cannot claim to have examined a statistically reliable representative sample of male clients of prostitutes nor can its results be generalized to the larger "hidden" populations of male clients either in Merseyside or beyond. Yet this was not our aim. Our aims were to (1) carry out some exploratory research with clients in Merseyside, a group not previously accessed; (2) to enable male clients of female prostitutes to describe their commercial sex involvement from their own perspectives, to allow us to obtain an insight into what meanings they attach to their behavior and to elicit their views and attitudes toward prostitution and prostitutes; and (3) to provide some information about the behavior, motivations, and views of a small group of clients of prostitutes and attempt to locate these within the broader existing research on male clients.

## Sociodemographic Profile: "Ordinary" Men

Our respondents were drawn from a wide range of social backgrounds. This range concurs with existing research.

**Age.** Their ages ranged from eighteen to seventy-one with the majority (89 percent) between eighteen and forty-nine. Sixty-eight percent had first used the services of a prostitute between the ages of eighteen and twenty-nine.

**Ethnic origin.** In terms of ethnic origin all but one of the respondents described themselves as white British. Other researchers (McKeganey and Barnard 1996; Faugier and Cranfield 1995) report a broader ethnic spread.

**Employment Status.** Seventy-nine percent of our respondents were employed; of those who were not employed, five were unemployed, one was retired, and two were registered disabled. The respondents came from a wide range of occupational categories: professional, managerial, self-employed, white collar, skilled, and unskilled manual. Their occupations included laborer, businessman, electrician, city council worker, radiographer, and factory inspector.

**Residence.** The majority of respondents were from Liverpool (64 percent) or the surrounding Merseyside area; only one man resided outside the northwest. The majority regularly contacted women in the Liverpool or the wider Merseyside area. The majority of respondents were also involved in a steady long-term relationship (see table 1.)

### Table 1: Status of Respondents

| Status | Percentage of Respondents |
|---|---|
| Married or cohabiting | 54 |
| Steady non-cohabiting relationship | 14 |
| Single | 32 |

When male clients become visible, it is difficult to sustain the commonly held assumptions about this group that help to maintain invisibility and secrecy. In terms of their sociodemographic characteristics and broader lifestyles the existing research suggests that men who pay for sex are not necessarily socially inadequate or deviant men but "ordinary" men (McCleod 1982). Prostitutes reflecting on their clientele often refer to their ordinariness. This conflicts with dominant discourses that often constructed male clients as deviant, antisocial, oversexed individuals. As such, they can be easily compartmentalized from the broader population of "ordinary" men. The more "ordinary" the more challenging and disturbing. McKeganey noted that "the secret world of the client is sustained by the belief that the men who buy sex are never our father, brother, husband or boyfriend, but someone else, who we do not know and may not even wish to know." The indications of existing research are that men who pay for sex certainly could be our fathers or brothers. Hence for many people the "ordinariness" of men who pay for sex is an uncomfortable reality. A female resident of a street soliciting area of Liverpool commented in 1996: "One night I saw a man in a Ford Sierra drop a woman off, as he drove past I saw a baby seat in the back and I thought God he could be anybody." This "ordinariness" provides a useful way of understanding the behavior of men who pay for sex. Rather than approach male clients as a deviant social group, we should approach them as men whose behavior is shaped by dominant notions of masculinity and specifically masculine sexual expression and identity.

# Nature of Commercial Sex Involvement

The frequency for which the respondents reported paying for commercial sex varied (see table 2), as did the number of prostitutes whom they reported they had contacted during the previous twelve months (see table 3).

Table 2. Frequency of Commercial Sex Encounters

| Frequency of Commercial Sex Encounter | Percentage of Respondents (n = 28) |
|---|---|
| More than once per week | 14 |
| Once per week or fortnightly | 21 |
| Monthly | 22 |
| Less than monthly | 43 |

Table 3. Number of Prostitutes Contacted during Previous 12 Months

| Number of Prostitutes Contacted | Percentage of Respondents (n=28) |
|---|---|
| 1 | 18 |
| 2–19 | 36 |
| 20–39 | 15 |
| 40–59 | 8 |

# Sexual Services Purchased

The three most commonly purchased sexual services reported were vaginal intercourse, oral sex/fellatio, and masturbation. Only three respondents reported that they had paid for anal sex in their encounters with prostitutes during the previous twelve months. These findings concerning the types of services most frequently purchased reflect those from research in other cities (McKeganey and Barnard 1996). A small number of men reported that they had purchased other specialist services. Several researchers have noted the reported popularity of fellatio. Leonard (1990) argues this could be accounted for because fellatio is less risky, because it is quickly and easily done, and because it is one sexual act male clients report their partners won't do.

# Forms of Contact

The men in our sample contacted prostitutes in a range of ways. For most men, the primary place of contact with prostitutes was in saunas or massage parlors (see table 4).

## Table 4: Form of Contact

| Form of Contact | Number of Respondents (n = 28) |
|---|---|
| Saunas only | 12 |
| Streets and saunas | 5 |
| Street only | 5 |
| Escort agencies | 2 |
| Contact magazines/Personal columns | 4 |

When asked why they chose to contact women in particular settings, the respondents revealed that they perceived qualitative differences in the commercial sex encounter. Their preference for a particular setting seemed to depend on the type of experience wanted. The men who contacted women in saunas/massage parlors identified four key reasons why they chose this form of contact: safety, physical comfort, cleanliness/hygiene, and reduced possibility of being caught. Men commented: "It's within my locality and I feel safe there. It's very discreet and I've never felt a danger of being there." "It's warm, comfortable, clean, and more of a service." This emphasis on indoor establishments providing broader service was also mentioned by the respondents who went to an escort agency. They explained that, although it was more expensive, the woman spent more time with them and was more attentive.

Reasons given by men for contacting women on the street included lower cost, convenience, greater number of women from which to choose, and the thrill. Their comments included "I went to a sauna once, but I can get what I want cheaper on the streets" and "I enjoy the whole process of driving around seeing the girls and making a decision. The sex is often a letdown compared to the build up and the buzz."

Faugier, Hayes, and Butterworth (1992) also noted that some respondents in their study "expressed the need to experience risk to themselves as an important element of using prostitutes."

# Motivations

As other researchers have found when exploring with male clients why they paid for sex, we found the majority had more than one motivation. From their interviews with 143 clients McKeganey and Barnard (1996) identified five broad areas incorporating the reasons clients described for engaging in commercial sex: the capacity to purchase specific sexual acts, the wide number of different women that could be contacted, the ability to contact women with specific physical characteristics, the fact that contact with a prostitute was limited, and the element of thrill that was involved.

The key motivations revealed by men in this research encompass most of those identified by other researchers.

## Thrill/Excitement/Enjoyment

Among our respondents thrill or excitement was the most frequently mentioned motivation. Many men stated that they paid for sex because they enjoyed it, they found it sexually pleasurable and exciting. Some respondents said going with a prostitute was exciting because it fulfilled their sexual fantasy: "It's always something I'd thought about doing. I used to fantasize about going with prostitutes and masturbate thinking about that. So it's really exciting because it's something that has always turned me on." Some men described commercial sex as particularly exciting specifically because it was "taboo" and illicit: "It's so exciting partly because I shouldn't be doing it." Faugier and Cranfield (1995) suggest that the illicit nature of commercial sex is an integral part of its attraction for some clients who contacted women on the streets.

## Sexual Services Not Provided by Partner

The second most frequently mentioned reason for using prostitutes was to purchase sexual services that the men reported their partners would not perform: "I started going [to a prostitute] because I wasn't getting on with the wife. I enjoy the variety of women and sex. I can do things my wife won't do." "My wife's not interested in sex anymore, so that's why I go to prostitutes." Some men noted that their noncommercial female partners had explicitly indicated that they did not enjoy or did not want to engage in certain sexual acts. Indeed, some men explained that they had not openly discussed the matter with partners but assumed they would not enjoy or would refuse to be involved in certain sexual practices. For example, one man commented, "I just know she wouldn't be interested [in oral sex]. I know from things that have been on the telly and how she's reacted." Like this man, many men referred to oral sex as one sex act they could not experience with their partner. Many of these men expressed the view that their involvement in commercial sex supported rather than damaged their relationships with their wives or non-paid partners: "It keeps my marriage together. My wife won't try anything different so I go to prostitutes." Several researchers have noted that some men explain/rationalize their commercial sex involvement as either a solution to or a compensatory necessity in an unfulfilling sexual relationship with a spouse or steady partner (McCleod 1982). What many respondents shared was an ability to *compartmentalize* their relationships with their steady partners and their encounters with prostitutes. Many men stressed that their relationships with prostitutes involved purely sexual pleasure whereas relationships with other steady partners, although involving sexual relations, incorporated love, intimacy, and commitment. In these terms, their relationship with their wife/partner/girlfriend was not jeopardized and their behavior was not necessarily interpreted as a betrayal of their partner. As they saw it, the paid sexual encounter had no meaning once it was over. Linked to this, McCleod (1982) noted that clients often expressed the view that going to a prostitute was less of a betrayal than having an affair would be. This was the opinion of several men with partners in this research: "It could be worse, I could have affairs. I mean then I'd be really involved with the woman. With prostitutes it's just business, it's just the sex." Going to a prostitute was also seen as less of a risk. Sex with a nonprostitute woman on a casual basis allowed for the greater possibility of emotional involvement (particularly by the woman) and hence complications. So some men with partners saw prostitution as a way of having other sexual partners with less risk of exposure and potential hassle than a noncommercial affair. This is illustrated by the following comment: "It's casual sex with no complications, it's a business deal and that's that. I had an affair with a woman around from where I live. It got nasty when she told my girlfriend. This way there are no complications. I wouldn't have an affair again. It's too messy." McKeganey (1996) noted that: "Almost all the men shared the belief that the prostitutes existed in an entirely separate sphere of their lives from their relationships with their partners." Our transcripts revealed a similar separation.

## Loneliness/Inability to Form Sexual Relationships

Thirty-five percent of respondents mentioned loneliness or inability to form sexual relationships as a motivation for going to prostitutes. For example, one man reported that: "From twenty to twenty-five I was anorexic and very reclusive. There was no chance of forming a relationship. When I was twenty-eight I fell in love with a friend, but it didn't work out. I went to Amsterdam. It was strange at first going with a prostitute but now it seems normal. I know it's not a proper relationship with a prostitute but I wouldn't like one at the moment." One man linked his commercial sex encounters with what he perceived as his inability to attract women through other routes because of his disability: "I'm ugly, no women will go out with me. . . . It's because of my disability. So prostitutes are a sexual outlet for me." This man described himself as lonely, depressed, and sexually frustrated.

## Different Women

Some men reported that one of their motivations was being able to choose from a number of different women and having a variety of sexual partners: "I like

casual sex and I don't know why but I've always fantasized about going with different women. With a prostitute I can do that and pick a different woman all the
time. I like to drive around and find the woman who's the right one. The first
one I see is rarely the one." During interviews, several men also mentioned that
one attraction of paying for sex was the ability to be able to have sexual contact
with women who had particular physical characteristics: "There's some lovely
women. I like to choose women who've got big breasts and an attractive figure."

## Sexual Urge

Some men explicitly mentioned that they paid for sex to fulfill a sexual urge.
They described their sexual desire as an overwhelming urge that had to be
satisfied: "It's sexual frustration. That's why I go to prostitutes." The majority
of men interviewed shared a belief that their behavior was a reasonable,
normal expression of male sexuality. The following comment is indicative of
this view: "I think it's normal. Most men like to go with different women and
most would go to prostitutes if they could afford it and had the nerve."

## Convenience: Business

Many men expressed the view that sex with women who worked as prostitutes
was convenient—both practically and emotionally. Commercial sex was
described as practical convenience in the sense that it fitted in with their
schedules. One man, for example, explained that he could leave work, pick
up a woman on the street, have sex, then return home to his wife, adding just
over thirty minutes to his journey home from work.

Several men expressed the view that with a prostitute there was no need to
go through the rituals that would be required to pick up a woman in a pub or
club or initiate an affair with a work colleague. Several men mentioned their dislike of the dating rituals while explaining their commercial sex encounters. One
man said, "I've never liked going out drinking with groups of lads, clubbing it
looking for girls. I find it difficult and a hassle to go through all the chatting up
and all the trying to get off with them. This [commercial sex] is easier." Another
man commented, "I'd split from my fiancee and I didn't go out drinking or anything like that, and I didn't want to. I hate all that. Well I wanted sex so I went
to this massage parlor I'd seen advertised in the Sunday *Sport*. So it's convenient
and there's no questions asked, you just go in and pick someone up."

Several men commented that one of the reasons they paid for commercial sex was that it did not require any emotional commitment or involvement. In their research, Kinnell and Griffiths (1989) found the most
common reason given by both single men and men with partners was that
they wanted sex without emotional involvement. McKeganey and Barnard

(1996) also noted that men in their interviews "were attracted by the uninvolved nature" of commercial sex. One man commented: "I first went three years ago when I was thirty-eight. I wanted a change from my wife with no emotional ties." Another explained, "The women I see are very professional; It's very relaxed—we meet and talk before. It's not rushed. You pay for that better service with escort agencies. You know where you stand with the women. You know it's a business deal for them, and you both know that it's up front and there are no complications, no involvement."

Many men stressed the commercial/businesslike nature of the encounter as a positive element: "It's a business deal. It's straightforward. I'm paying for a service and I'm happy with the service I get." Davidson O'Connell points to the contractual nature of transactions between prostitutes in European countries and their clients. She stresses that the contractual nature is explicit to the client who "would no more expect a prostitute to cuddle or stroke him or act as his companion after sex than he would expect a plumber to after fixing a leaking pipe" (1995, 48). Yet she acknowledges contradictions in the expectations of some who want to buy sex as a commodity but are critical of the impersonal/business approach of prostitutes. Hoigard and Finstad reported a contradiction in the views of clients in their Oslo study. On the one hand the majority of men reported that they go to prostitutes because there was no commitment but they also wanted "warm girls, increased intimacy, and understanding" (1992, 95). This contradiction was evident among several respondents in our sample who expressed a preference for women who "didn't rush them," "were friendly," "set them at ease," and "didn't charge extra for everything." They were critical of "cut throat" prostitutes and those who were "cold" and "unfriendly." Yet some men still identified the commercial, noncommittal, contractual structure of the encounter as advantageous. O'Connell argues that "many punters want to buy sex as a commodity, but do not want the exchange to be simply a contractual one." Indeed some clients in our sample wanted to purchase a commodity but as customers felt they deserved exacting "customer service." This reflects one element of the ongoing dynamics of power and control that are constantly being contested in commercial sexual encounters. It also highlights one of several contradictory meanings men in our sample who paid for sex attached to their behavior.

# Buying Commercial Sex and Hegemonic Discourses of Male Sexuality

An analysis of the meanings men attached to their involvement in commercial sex should examine these in relation to, not in isolation from, broader cultural constructions of male heterosexual identity.

## Masculine Sexual Urge

It has been argued that male sexual desire is socially constructed as an expression of a powerful urge; within this discourse men are constructed as active, predatory sexual initiators. As noted, many of the men interviewed also constructed their sexual desire as something overwhelming and powerful. They shared a belief that their behavior was a reasonable, normal expression of male sexuality. It was "normal" for men to have several sexual partners, and the majority intended to continue their involvement in commercial sex. Those men who reported that they paid for sex because their partner wouldn't have sexual relations with them or wouldn't do specific things reasoned that it was normal and acceptable to "get it elsewhere," especially if their partner wasn't satisfying their sexual "needs" and "desires."

## Performance Pressure

As a result of this construction it is argued that sex is one area in which men feel pressured to prove their masculinity. As a result, they argue sex becomes surrounded by anxieties about performance and achievement. One man, who reported that he had spent considerable amounts of money on various treatments for impotency, explained that he went to a prostitute because of the sexual problems he was experiencing: "I'm impotent. The women are very good. There's one woman I see who's very patient." He explained that he was embarrassed by the difficulties he was experiencing and that he felt unable to deal with his inadequate sexual performance within a noncommercial sexual relationship. As a paying customer in a paid encounter, he felt pressures on him to perform were reduced. Yet it is important to note that the majority of respondents reported that they were comfortable with their sexual performance in noncommercial encounters.

## Intimacy/Sexuality

At a fundamental level the majority of men in our sample, whether single or involved with a noncommercial partner, made a clear distinction between sex and love/emotional involvement. As noted earlier, many men referred to the encounter as a "business"/contractual deal. The distinction between sex and emotional involvement/intimacy enabled many men with noncommercial partners to justify and rationalize their commercial sex involvement. According to some theorists, this dichotomous approach to sex and intimacy is not something confined to men who pay for commercial sex (Seidler 1992). According to Seidler, a powerful hegemonic discourse of masculinity is linked with control, strength, dominance, and rationality and not vulnerability, submission, and the expression of a wide range of emotions. He argues that to maintain their sense of masculinity, many men learn to think of sexuality in terms of conquest, control, and dominance. Therefore to maintain a particular masculine identity, men tend to separate sex and intimacy: "for many men sexuality often tends to be relatively isolated from intimacy and relationships. It is as if men control threats to our masculinity through this very separation."

Seidler argues that "getting off" with a woman is a way of affirming self esteem and masculine identity. At the root of this feeling, he argues, is a fear of vulnerability and rejection: "It is as if we want to deny the link between sexuality and vulnerability. As men we often have sex without vulnerability, for when we are vulnerable we fear that we can be rejected. This is not simply a matter of being rejected as individuals but of our own masculinity being brought into question." Therefore men attempt to sustain a sense of control in sexual relationships: "So it is that control becomes a crucial issue, because in controlling our partners we minimize the risk of rejection. . . . It is we who do, or order what is to be done to us. It is as if we have to maintain control of the sexual activity to protect ourselves." For many men in this research, commercial sex involves an encounter in which sex can be experienced with no intimacy or expectation of intimacy. Located as the customer, male clients in this research also felt that if they specify what service is to be provided, they control the encounter. Hence, in such encounters they can feel in control and securely masculine.

## Commodification/Objectification

No men questioned the notion of paying women for sexual services. This seemed to be universally accepted by the respondents, so much so that it was normalized. McCleod (1982) argued that "much of what men want from prostitution is a matter of self-centered gratification. The primacy accorded to men's sexual urges rules the day, as does the expectation that women will offer sex in return for donations of goods or money; though such phenomena extend through male/female sexual relations at large and are not confined to prostitution alone." Several men explicitly implied that paying for sex was really the bottom line dynamic in many noncommercial male-female relationships: "Why go through all the hassle of buying drinks for a woman, taking her out for a meal when you don't even know if you'll get anywhere? You might as well just pay a prostitute." In other words, for some men, even noncommercial relationships with women involved negotiation and exchange for sex. The sexual objectification of women working as prostitutes expressed as the commodification of sex was taken for granted by respondents.

Many feminist researchers and theorists have pointed to a mainstream culture that sexually objectifies women. Women become something a man possesses and this process is eroticized (Scully 1990). These researchers have argued that this impacts on male sexual identity and pleasure. Seidler (1989) argues that this objectification of the sexual partner complements the separation of intimacy from sexuality. If the sexual partner is an object, it is easier to reject feelings/concern for them and maintain greater emotional control. Hence, objectification of the sexual partner is a process not confined to the commercial sex encounter.

Yet respondents did make one important distinction between nonprostitute women and women working as prostitutes. One recurring theme among the men was their feeling that a woman working as a prostitute would be willing to do "anything." Although many men acknowledged that prostitutes had ordinary lives like other women and hence had a role beyond selling sex, they viewed women who worked as prostitutes as a special category of woman sexually. One man commented: "They're different from women you can meet in clubs. They're happy to do whatever you want." Another said, "You can get more out of them. They're more willing to do different things." McKeganey (1996) also commented on the view expressed by some men that you could "ask a prostitute to do anything" and that prostitutes were "no more than the sex they sold." He has argued that such attitudes could encourage violence against women. If prostitutes become mere sexual objects to be bought, then the potential to disregard their rights is heightened. The view expressed by some that men could ask for anything conflicts with statements of women who were very clear about what they would and wouldn't do. McKeganey and Barnard (1996) noted that encounters between prostitutes and clients involve dynamics of power and control and as such the potential for conflict.

## Concluding Comments

Our research suggests that the meanings and motivations of men who pay for sex in Merseyside are diverse. Understanding these motivations requires not that we approach these men as a product of a deviant sexuality, but that we locate their behavior in relation to wider cultural constructions of male sexuality. If there is some validity in Seidler's analysis, then men's separation of sex from intimacy attempts to maintain a sense of control over sexual encounters and the objectification of the sexual partner. Played out in the commercial sex encounter, these dynamics fit neatly with broader dynamics that are part of one powerful social construction of male sexual identity. Indeed they could be understood as extensions of components of male sexual identity present in many noncommercial sexual encounters. Therefore, I would suggest that the motivations of the men who pay for sex in this sample can be understood not as the product of a deviant sexuality but as the shaping of a persistently hegemonic discourse of male sexuality that impacts on male sexual identity.

However, I am not suggesting a reductionalist analysis of masculinity, male sexuality, and sexual motivations as uncomplicated monoliths. There are other discourses of masculinity. Male sexual experiences, expression, and identities are diverse, often contradictory and multistranded (Brod and Kaufmann, 1994; Morgan 1994). This was reflected in the varied and often contradictory meanings the men in this sample attached to their commercial sex involvement.

Methodologically, researchers are still developing creative ways of contacting and working with male clients. One area that needs to be further developed is collaborative work that involves sex workers and their clients more directly in the research process.

To develop a comprehensive understanding of prostitution, researchers and policymakers must pay further attention to the men who pay for sex. Making male clients visible raises new and challenging questions that must be explored if we are to come closer to mapping the socioeconomic and cultural conditions that shape prostitution.

# Note

1. This research was funded by Liverpool City Council, Liverpool City Challenge, and Liverpool City Centre Partnership.

# References

Barnard, M., N. McKeganey, and A. Leyland. 1993. Risk behaviours among male clients of female street prostitutes. *British Medical Journal* 307: 361–62.

Brittan, A. 1989. *Masculinity and Power.* Oxford: Blackwell.

Brod, H., and M. Kaufman, eds. 1994. *Theorizing Masculinities.* Beverly Hills, Calif.: Sage.

Day, S., and H. Ward 1990. The Praed Street project. In *AIDS, Drugs and Prostitution,* edited by M. Plant. London: Routledge.

Day, S., H. Ward, and L. Perrotta. 1993. Prostitution and HIV: Male partners of female prostitutes. *British Medical Journal* 307: 359–61.

Faugier, J., and S. Cranfield. 1995. Researching male clients of female prostitutes: The challenge for HIV prevention. *AIDS Care* 7: 1.

Faugier, J., C. Hayes, and C. Butterworth. 1992. *Drug Using Prostitutes: Their Health Care Needs and Their Clients.* Manchester: University of Manchester, Department of Nursing.

Graaf, R., et al. 1992. Prostitution and the spread of HIV. In *Safe Sex in Prostitution in the Netherlands.* Mr. A. de Graaf Institute, Westermarkt 4, 1016 DK Amsterdam.

Hearn, J. 1992. *Men in the Public Eye.* London: Routledge.

Hoigard, C., and L. Finstad. 1992. *Backstreets: Prostitution, Money and Love.* Cambridge: Polity.

Johnson, A., J. Wadsworth, K. Wellings, and J. Field. 1994. *Sexual Attitudes and Lifestyles.* Oxford: Blackwell.

Kinnell, H. 1989. Prostitutes, their clients, and risks of HIV infection in Birmingham. Occasional Paper, Birmingham Department of Public Health.

Kinnell, H., and R. K. Griffiths. 1989. Male clients of female prostitutes in Birmingham, England: A bridge for transmission of HIV? Central Birmingham Health Authority, Department of Public Health.

Leonard, T. 1990. Male clients of female street prostitutes: Unseen partners in sexual disease. *Medical Anthropology Quarterly* 4, no. 1: 41–55.

McCleod, E. 1982. *Women Working: Prostitution Now.* London: Croom Helm.

McKeganey, N. 1996. Sex in the shadowlands. *Guardian,* May 29.

———. 1994. Why do men buy sex and what are their assessments of the HIV-related risks when they do? *AIDS Care* 6, no. 3: 289–301.

McKeganey, N., and M. Barnard. 1996. *Sex Work on the Streets: Prostitutes and Their Clients.* Buckingham: Open University Press.

Morgan, D. 1992. *Discovering Men.* London: Routledge.

———. 1994. Theater of war: Combat the military and masculinities. In *Theorizing Masculinities,* edited by H. Brod and M. Kaufman. Beverly Hills, Calif.: Sage.

O'Connell, J. Davidson. 1995. British sex tourists in Thailand. In *(Hetero)Sexual Politics,* edited by M. Maynard and J. Purvis. London: Taylor & Francis.

Seidler, V. J. 1989. *Rediscovering Masculinity: Reason, Language and Sexuality.* New York: Routledge.

Seidler, V. J., ed. 1992. *Men, Sex and Relationships.* London: Routledge.

Scully, D. 1990. *Understanding Sexual Violence.* Cambridge: Polity.

# MEN WHO BUY SEX: PRELIMINARY FINDINGS OF AN EXPLORATORY STUDY

CHRIS ATCHISON, LAURA FRASER, AND JOHN LOWMAN

From a theoretical point of view, the client is central to the study of prostitution. Without him, there is no sex trade. Politically, the client is central because prostitution is held out to be the quintessential instance of the male sexualization, commodification, and exploitation of women. From the point of view of policymakers the client is central because he represents an obvious site of social intervention, be it in the name of protecting neighborhoods and preventing nuisance and/or preventing sexual exploitation of children and violence against women who prostitute. And yet we know very little about the client. To help fill this gap, the Province of British Columbia, Canada, funded a two-phase study of men who buy sex (and women sex buyers too, if we can contact any).[1] In this chapter we present the preliminary findings from this research.

## Two Phases of Research

The research comprises six components:

### Phase 1

- Review of the anglophone literature on the client and development of a questionnaire on "Sex and Sexuality in the 1990s, with a Focus on Men Who Buy Sex."
- A description of the content of court files of men charged in Vancouver, British Columbia, under Canadian Criminal Code section 213 (communicating in a public place for the purpose of buying sexual services).

- Continuation of previous descriptive analyses (see Lowman 1989; Lowman and Frasier 1996) of "bad date sheets" distributed in Vancouver.

## Phase 2

- Distribution via Internet of the questionnaire on "Sex and Sexuality" developed in Phase 1. The Internet survey requests responses from residents of Australia, Canada, England, New Zealand, Northern Ireland, the Republic of Ireland, Scotland, the United States, and Wales.
- Distribution of a version of the same survey for clients in British Columbia, Canada. (The two surveys are the same, except for sections on geographic sex purchasing patterns and prostitution law.)
- Interviews with clients in Canada.

The first phase of the study was completed in 1996 (Atchison 1996; Lowman, Atchison, and Frasier 1996). The second phase was completed in April 1997 (Atchison 1997; Lowman, Atchison, and Frasier 1997).

In this chapter we describe the extant literature on the client, and then present an overview of the court file study and some preliminary findings from the Internet questionnaire.

# Research on the Client in Britain, Europe, and the United States

## Psychiatry and Psychotherapy: Pathologizing the Buyer

Up until the past five or so years, there have been only a few studies of buyers of sex. One of the earliest systematic investigations of the client was by psychotherapist Edward Glover (1943). Like their female counterparts who sell sex, Glover argued, men who buy sex suffer a psychopathological condition, a regression to an infant stage of sexual development in which the child focuses its sexual desire on the parent of the opposite sex. The pathology occurs when adults subconsciously continue to separate "sacred" (emotional) and "profane" (erotic) love. Following Freud, Glover maintains that this separation first occurs when the infant's sexual attraction for the parent of the opposite sex is inhibited and idealized love or family love is encouraged. During normal development into sexual adulthood, sacred and profane love are reunited in a single object: the spouse. But for some people, the separation of sacred and erotic love continues subconsciously. In these cases of "regressive" sexuality, the adult cannot feel both sacred and erotic love for the same person. For the male in this situation, because he can only experience sacred love with his spouse, he turns to a prostitute for sexual fulfillment.

Another psychotherapist, Albert Ellis, also worked in a therapeutic setting with an unstated number of men. In order to develop a "cure" for the sex buyer's "deviant" behavior, he investigated the reasons men give for visiting prostitutes. He concluded that it is a man's irrational or neurotic attitudes about himself, sex, his wife, or the prostitute that drives him to buy sex. Ellis concluded that, by tailoring therapy to the specific source of the neurosis, the irrational drive to visit prostitutes could be cured (1959, 346).

Psychiatrists Gibbens and Silberman (1960) likewise suggested a link between psychological problems and the patronizing of prostitutes.

## Ethnography and Survey Research: Normalizing the Buyer

In their extensive studies of sexual behavior, Masters and Johnson (1970) confirmed that there is a pervasive belief that the client is psychologically defective and disturbed. In this respect, there may be some overlap between clinical and lay opinion. However, when researchers other than psychiatric professionals have interacted with the client, a different imagery emerges.

To date, the most extensive research on the buyer was by Winick (1962). He used a snowball sampling technique to interview 732 clients in five major American cities. The survey examined what function paid sex performs in the so-called personality economy of the client, and how he perceives himself and the sex seller. Winick concluded that "visiting a prostitute serves a wide variety of functions for the client" and that "any one visit is so complexly motivated that it is almost over-determined" (1962, 297). He concluded that the "emotional meanings and overtones" of the visit to a prostitute are more important than the desire for sex and that "conscious and unconscious elements seem to be present in the client's perceptions of himself and the prostitute." In contrast to its psychiatric predecessors, Winick's survey did not produce evidence of widespread psychological pathology or personal difficulty that explained a man's decision to buy sex.

In *The Lively Commerce* (1971), Winick and Kinsie suggest that at least three factors need to be taken into account in understanding the demand for sexual services:

1. Patterns of law enforcement may determine when and how frequently men visit prostitutes. In order to better understand the dynamics of prostitution, researchers would do well to examine the tactics that clients use to avoid detection by the law, their spouses, and the community at large.
2. Because the function of prostitution changes over time, researchers

should record and describe the changing reasons that men give for going to prostitutes.

3. Social-ecological considerations might be important in a man's decision to pay for sex. In order to understand the myriad of motivations for prostitution use, it is important to explore the social ecology of the client.

Winick and Kinsie note that the psychological dimensions of buyer motivation have been largely ignored by social scientists, and they contend that in order to get a more complete understanding of prostitution, the motivations and general psychology of the client ought to be explored.

In what he refers to as a "participant observer study," Diana (1985) presents data from interviews with 501 clients he met at truck stops, roadside lounges, brothels, and massage parlors over a twenty-five-year period in the United States. The sample included men of all ages, 70 percent of whom said they bought sex at least once a week. Roughly half the men were described as having white collar or business and professional occupations. Twenty percent of the men were single, 27 percent were separated or divorced, and 50 percent were married. Less than half (41 percent) of the married men said they were satisfied or very satisfied with the sexual aspect of their marriage. When it came to their attitudes to prostitutes, 57 percent of the men were "ambivalent" and 26 percent had "positive" attitudes (the remaining 16 percent had attitudes that Diana described as either "patronizing" or "contemptuous"). A majority of men claimed to experience "impotence" either chronically (11.4 percent) or occasionally (48.7 percent) when they were with prostitutes. The primary reasons clients gave for visiting prostitutes were "regular partner unavailable" (20.6 percent); "variety" (19.6 percent); sexual "experience otherwise unavailable" (13.4 percent); "curiosity" (9.6 percent); "chance" (9.2 percent); and "strong sex drive" (8.6 percent). Many of the men said that the greatest attraction of prostitution was the release from obligation that it afforded. In the case of married men, the attraction is

> the absence of risk of an emotionally intense love affair with a prostitute. There is less guilt and less of a feeling one has betrayed his marital commitment. Single men, too, may want no emotional involvements. As one client expressed it: "this woman wants nothing, asks nothing, needs nothing. I don't need to please her, or be concerned about whether she's enjoying it. I can do what I want, and please myself." (191)

Of course, if for men one of the main appeals of buying sex is that "provides temporary relief from the obligations inherent in involved sexual and emotional relationships" (191), one can only wonder what women do for such relief.

In a study of 183 massage parlor patrons, Simpson and Schill (1977) gathered information about respondents' biography; personality; sexual knowledge and experience; sexual permissiveness; reasons for buying sexual services; and physical, emotional, and sexual satisfaction with the sexual services they purchased. They suggest that personality, a man's opinion of women, and various dimensions of satisfaction all play a role in men's sex-buying practices. Most of the respondents were married, lower-middle class, white males, between the ages of eighteen and sixty-seven. Clients were no different from non-clients in terms of perceptions of women, degree of self esteem, feelings of belonging, or sexual appeal. Indeed, there was nothing particularly unusual about these men at all, other than their decision to buy sex at a massage parlor, although Simpson and Schill point out that their sample may not be representative of sex buyers in general.

In a similar vein, Armstrong (1978) concluded that there did not appear to be anything particularly distinctive or "problematic" about the massage parlor customers he studied. Holzman and Pines (1982) likewise suggest that when we talk to the johns themselves, we find a very different picture revealed from the one rendered by the sellers of sex, and that the "data obtained . . . do not seem to support the stereotypical image of the purchaser." The stereotypical "loser" image does not fit. Their phenomenological research explored the feelings and perceptions of men who buy sex, in an exploration of the buying experience through the eyes of the buyer. To accomplish this, thirty males were interviewed about "their experience of prostitution." They concluded that being a client is a "process" (a series of interrelated decisions and acts), as opposed to a role (one who exchanges sex for money). In order to understand the "process" of being a client, it is necessary to understand the client's intent, the pursuit of the encounter, the encounter itself, and the aftermath. It is through this process that clients structure the objective reality of their encounter with a prostitute (Holzman and Pines 1982, 112).

Eileen McLeod (1982), who conducted in-depth interviews with twenty clients in England, gives further reason to doubt conventional stereotypes of tricks:

> There are two influential explanations of why men go to prostitutes. First, men who do so are exceptionally isolated or a residual minority with particularly perverted sexual tastes, in the days of sexual liberation (Davis [1937]). A further explanation favoured by some feminists suggests that prostitution represents the macho desire for women as sex objects. (McIntosh 1979)

McLeod says that the picture obtained from prostitutes and their customers is substantially different and more subtle than these images in the literature. She concludes:

[First] prostitutes' clients cannot be dismissed as the perverted few. Secondly, going to prostitutes may reflect men's dominant social position in various ways. Their purchasing power sustains the market. Obtaining sexual relief through payment, whatever one thinks of the worth of the activity, is not unique to men but it is not proscribed for them to the degree that it is for women. Much of what men want from prostitutes is a matter of self-centered gratification. The primacy accorded to men's sexual urges rules the day.

From this perspective, prostitution is organized around the ability and proclivity of men to indulge in a self-centered sexuality, or what Gemme et al. characterized as a "brief uncomplicated sexual encounter" (1984, 134). As well as asking why some men buy sex, we also need to consider why more women don't.

From her research with sellers and buyers, McLeod reached the somewhat unconventional conclusion that "men too are victims of existing social structures" (59), in particular (1) the pressure created by the conventional male heterosexual role's emphasis on masculine prowess and dominance; and (2) the failure of the institution of marriage to cater to male sexual and emotional needs accompanied by the male fear of revealing this failure (90).

# A New Wave of Survey Research: Epidemiological Concerns

Over the past seven years in Britain and North America, a rather more concerted interest in the client has developed, and several fairly extensive client surveys involving from fifty to several hundred respondents have been published (e.g., Barnard et al. 1993; de Graaf 1995; Leonard 1990; Leonard, Freund and Platt 1989; McKeganey 1994; Pickering et al., 1992; Vanwesenbeeck et al. 1993a, 1993b). Although various disciplinary mandates have mobilized this research, one of the main stimuli for funding has been epidemiological. Concerns about HIV infection and AIDS has led to funding of general research on the sexual behavior of "high risk groups" (those groups of individuals who are sexually active with more than one partner and/or with intravenous drug users) such as the buyer of sex, in order to investigate the general risks they pose to themselves and others (Leonard 1990; de Graaf 1995; Vanwesenbeeck et al. 1994).

We draw from these studies substantively and methodologically, and we set out to emulate some of their methods for meeting interview subjects. Methods for contacting clients have included

1. distribution of questionnaires to clients by sex trade workers;
2. introduction of researchers to clients by sex trade workers—Thomas,

Plant, and Plant (1990) with fourteen interviewers contacted 209 clients this way; McLeod (1982) contacted thirty-three;

3. female researchers standing in known stroll areas have distributed surveys when approached by would-be clients—Leonard (1990) contacted fifty clients this way;
4. contacts with men treated for sexually transmitted diseases;
5. clients contacted through radio talk show (Gemme et al. 1984);
6. clients contacted through newspaper advertisements and interviewed in person or over the telephone—Vanwesenbeeck et al. (1993a) obtained ninety-one interviews this way, McKeganey (1994) obtained seventy.

The most extensive of these recent studies has been done in the Netherlands. The first study, reported in Vanwesenbeeck et al. (1993a) and de Graaf (1995), focused on epidemiological concerns. Vanwesenbeeck et al. reported on the results of a partially structured questionnaire/interview with ninety-one clients on the perceived costs and benefits of condom use in commercial sex transactions. The questionnaire/interviews also gathered information about a client's background, personality, interaction with commercial sex workers, how these factors relate to a client's decision whether or not to use condoms during commercial sex interactions, demographic data (age, marital status, education, and nationality), and sexual contact data (contacts, number and frequency of partners, sexual behavior, and condom use). The men were contacted by placing an advertisement in local newspapers and tabloids asking them to call and arrange a meeting with an interviewer. The results indicate that most clients use condoms. Those who don't use them tend to have a negative perception of commercial sex, commercial sex workers, and condoms, and have an "unrealistic" perception of personal risk due to a lack of knowledge about methods of infection (Vanwesenbeeck et al. 1993a, 90).

In addition, de Graaf used the research presented in Vanwesenbeeck et al. (1993a) to report on various epidemiological topics relating to commercial sex (all of which are reported in his 1995 monograph). In one study de Graaf examined how HIV is spread within commercial sex circles and then into the general population. Also, he investigated clients' experience of condom use in heterosexual commercial sex encounters in order to determine how effective condoms are in preventing the spread of HIV. He used structured interviews to determine the frequency with which condoms broke or slipped off during various sexual activities, and why they did so. This research indicated that condoms are frequently used by commercial sex workers with minimal failure and concluded that condoms provide good protection from disease for commercial sex workers, clients, and their noncommercial partners.

In a second study, a telephone survey, de Graaf (1995) examined commercial sex use, attitudes to commercial sex, motivation for purchasing sexual services, social support, and understanding and fear of disease. In this study, de Graaf interviewed 115 clients over the telephone about alcohol and drug use during commercial social contacts and their relation to contraceptive use. He collected general demographic data, and information about frequency of condom use, alcohol and drug use, and sexual behavior during commercial sex interactions. Clients were recruited through advertisements in bi-weekly magazines and newspapers, and by snowball sampling. This research indicates that alcohol and drug use is not common in many clients and commercial sex workers. Alcohol use does not appear to be related to unsafe commercial sexual activities, whereas drug use may lead to unsafe sexual practices (de Graaf 1995, 126). Drug use varies among different types of prostitutes.

These studies indicate that most clients in the Netherlands use condoms during paid sex encounters, but they tend not to use them when they are with noncommercial sex partners (de Graaf 1995, 75). Condoms are used least by "regular" clients (those visiting commercial sex partners more than twenty times a year), ethnic minorities, those with less than a high-school education, and those who frequent commercial sex partners at street and window venues (de Graaf 1995, 158).

Epidemiological issues have also been examined in three Scottish studies of the client. In the first study by Thomas, Plant, and Plant (1990), 209 clients were interviewed about their alcohol and drug use and its relation to HIV risk behavior. The study used a structured interview schedule to examine demographic characteristics; alcohol, tobacco, and drug use; sexual behavior; health care and AIDS-related attitudes, beliefs, and knowledge. Commercial sex workers assisted researchers to obtain a snowball sample of customers. The results indicate that alcohol and illicit drug use are common among clients; however, use of alcohol and drugs is not related to use/nonuse of condoms. Furthermore, there is little evidence that HIV is spread through commercial sex (Thomas, Plant, and Plant 1990, 268).

Barnard, McKeganey, and Leyland (1993) interviewed 143 clients on their condom use and sexual behavior preferences with commercial and noncommercial sexual partners in order to determine the possibility of HIV being spread both within and from the commercial to the noncommercial populations. They used short, structured questionnaires to measure amounts of commercial sex, demographic information, types of commercial sex, STD (sexually transmitted disease) history, and condom use with commercial and noncommercial partners. Clients were contacted in genitourinary clinics, from newspaper advertisements, and through "cold contact" (where the researcher is completely unknown to the individual subject) on the street. The majority of clients in the study were between twenty-one to sixty-three years of age, employed, married, and had no history of STDs. The most frequently requested service is vaginal intercourse, and condoms are frequently used for commercial sex contacts but not for noncommercial ones (Barnard, McKeganey, and Leyland 1993, 361).

McKeganey (1994) interviewed seventy clients over the telephone about their attitudes to and perceptions of their commercial sex contacts. One of the main objectives of this study was to determine the clients' HIV-related risk behavior and identify ways to reduce risk. The telephone interviews were semi-structured, with a standardized pre-coded section asking about demographics, visits to commercial sex partners, preferred sexual acts, condom use, and STD history, and an open-ended response section asking about reasons for contacting commercial sex partners, appeal of commercial sex, assessment of STD risk, and communication with other people about commercial sex behavior. The clients were contacted through an advertisement in a local newspaper. The results indicate that clients visit commercial sex partners for a variety of reasons; however, the main appeal of commercial sex lies in the commercial sex workers' "willingness to do anything for money" (McKeganey 1994, 229). Although many clients believed that commercial sex workers may be HIV-positive, few clients believed that they were at risk of infection.

Leonard (1990) interviewed both sellers and buyers. Self-report data obtained from commercial sex workers were validated by the accounts of fifty clients. The study focused on type of sexual activity purchased, condom use, frequency of commercial sex transactions, and clients' perceptions of risk of HIV infection. The study included pre-coded and open-ended questions covering demographic variables, patterns of commercial sex use, frequency of sex in other venues and locations, desirable characteristics of commercial sex partners, and a detailed record of the last commercial sexual encounter. The interviewer posed as a street prostitute and interviewed would-be sex buyers (a method that is risky and ethically questionable). The results suggest that clients are the main determiners of condom use because they hold the economic power in the relationship. Also, clients adjust their behavior (e.g., the way they select partners) in the hope of avoiding infection by HIV and other sexually transmitted diseases (Leonard 1990, 51).

Freund, Lee, and Leonard (1991) interviewed 101 clients about their sexual behavior in order to determine risk of HIV infection, and for the purpose of constructing a mathematical model to predict the spread of HIV. A short, open-ended questionnaire was used to gather information about the demographic characteristics of the client population, the nature of their activity with commercial sex partners, and sexual behavior during their last paid sexual encounter. The interviewer posed as a street prostitute and handed out questionnaires to would-be sex buyers. The clients interviewed had a well-established pattern of commercial sex use, most visited commercial sex partners on a monthly or more frequent basis, and had been paying for sex for an average of 5.3 years. Clients tended to visit the same commercial sex sellers or group of sellers. Clients reported using condoms in 53 percent of their commercial sex contacts, and 72 percent of the time when the services they paid for included vaginal sexual intercourse (Freund, Lee, and Leonard 1991, 587).

# Canadian Research on the Client

## Surveys of Clients

In Canada over the past fifteen years, well over a thousand interviews were conducted with the sellers of sexual services. During this same period there were just two client surveys which between them yielded only fifty respondents (Gemme et al. 1984; Lowman 1989). In Vancouver, seventeen clients were interviewed by two women who had been involved in the sex trade (Lowman 1989, appendix 10), but because of the small number of respondents, the results are impressionistic. In Montreal, Gemme apparently made his contacts by appearing on two radio talk shows to ask clients for interviews (Gemme et al. 1984). He obtained thirty-three interviews this way, but only a brief account of the findings of this survey is available (133–36), including information about age, income, and marital status, the frequency of sexual purchases, and the general reasons clients give for visiting prostitutes (the most frequent of which was for "a brief, uncomplicated sexual encounter") (134).

   Some other information is available about men charged under the communicating law (Lowman, 1989; Moyer and Carrington, 1989) which we will return to below when discussing the results of our Crown file survey.

## Sellers' Perceptions of Buyers

In the anglophone literature, there are numerous social surveys with prostitutes, many of which include questions about the behavior and characteristics of buyers. Until recently, these have constituted the main source of information on the buyer. Also, several studies on the client have used data gathered from sex trade workers to help corroborate information from interviews with buyers (e.g., de Graaf 1995; Pickering et al. 1992). Rather than providing an overview of this extensive literature, we briefly review the results of one Vancouver study (Lowman 1984), and the "Juvenile Prostitution Survey" reported by the Committee on Sexual Offences against Children and Youth (CSOACY 1984). When it comes to descriptions of sex buyers, the results of these two studies seem to be fairly typical of this genre, although the CSOACY's interpretation of some of this information is open to dispute.

As part of the 1984 Vancouver Field Survey of prostitution (Lowman 1984), forty-eight sex sellers (mostly street prostitutes) were interviewed about their experiences in the sex trade. The survey included questions about buyers' demographic characteristics, sexual preferences, and behavior during sexual interactions. Also, respondents were asked about their general feelings toward their "tricks." They suggest that most clients are between twenty and fifty years of age (mostly over forty) and that they come from a variety of income brackets (mostly "middle class") (Lowman 1984, 227). The average client of the street commercial sex worker generally purchases oral sex and sexual intercourse in roughly equal proportion. Many women who work in the street trade report having antagonistic relationships with at least some of their clients. Some women, particularly those who work for professional pimps, hold their "tricks" in very low regard. Nearly 60 percent of the prostitutes interviewed said that their clients were "mostly nice guys"; 42 percent said that "some" or "all" of their clients were "jerks."[2]

The Committee on Sexual Offences against Children and Youth interviewed 84 males and 145 females under the age of twenty about their background and general experience selling sexual services on the street. This survey included questions about the general demographic characteristics of tricks, their sexual preferences, and the nature of the respondents' interaction with them. Respondents reported that the overwhelming majority of clients are male, and the majority are thirty to forty-nine years of age, married, and "middle class" (CSOACY 1984, 1055). They apparently come from all walks of life. When it came to the motivation of sex buyers, respondents reported that many tricks had "sexually unfulfilling home lives or went to prostitutes in order to engage in a wider variety of sexual acts" (particularly oral sex) that they would not otherwise experience.

Young males suggested that one kind of trick is the "homosexual" man who has not managed to "come out of the closet." Prostitution is the only way they can experience a stigmatized sexual relationship. Many respondents, male and female alike, portrayed buyers as "socially inadequate" and "lonely." The committee concluded that most sellers

> regard their clients either with hostility or as being pathetic, contemptible or disgusting individuals. The tricks were often portrayed as being physically unattractive persons with whom the young prostitutes found it distasteful and unpleasant to engage in sexual acts. (CSOACY 1984, 1055)

Although there is no doubt that this characterization captures the opinions of many street prostitutes, it is much too one-sided. Indeed, the Badgley Committee's appropriation of its subjects' voices gives a better impression of the committee's opinion of clients than it does its subjects, at least some of whom did not project this very negative imagery. Also, it is important to remember that these surveys are mostly confined to the street prostitution trade. We have no idea what escorts and massage parlor workers think of their clients.

# Client Population Size Estimates: Some International Comparisons

We are aware of only one Canadian study that estimates the proportion of the adult male population who purchases sexual services. The study, one of a series done as background research for the Fraser Committee, examined Canadians' attitudes toward and perceptions of pornography and prostitution (Peat Marwick 1984, 5). In order to determine the extent to which respondents participated in "sexual bargaining activities," they were asked whether they had ever paid for sex or previously accepted money for sex. The survey found that 4 percent of male respondents (n = 989) admitted to having paid for sex one or more times, and that less than 1 percent of the survey respondents had accepted money in exchange for sex (the percentage of females is not given).

Studies in other countries vary widely in terms of the estimates they yield of the proportion of men who buy sex. Beginning with U.S. studies, Kinsey, Pomeroy, and Martin (1948) reported that 69 percent of U.S. men they questioned had sex with prostitutes at some time in their life (see also Winick 1962; Winick and Kinsie 1971, 185), while 15 to 20 percent visited a few times a year. In the 1970s Reinisch et al. found that 30 to 45 percent of U.S. men had visited a prostitute (de Graaf 1995, 14). Using data from the 1993 National Health and Social Life Survey, Sullivan and Simon (1997) found that 18 percent of males aged eighteen to fifty-nine in 1993 reported having "paid a woman to have sex" (note: male-male and male-transgender commercial transactions are excluded). They note that of men who had served in the military (n = 409), 36 percent had paid for sex, in contrast to men who had no military experience (n = 1,101), of whom only 13 percent had paid for sex. There is also a clear relationship between age and having paid for sex: the rate was just over one in twenty in the case of the eighteen-to-twenty-four-year age group, as compared to one in three of the men aged between fifty-three and sixty years.

Turning to other countries, several studies are available. One study in the Netherlands estimated that 21.6 percent of all men said that they had visited a prostitute at least once during their lifetime, and that 4 percent of heterosexual men surveyed in Amsterdam had visited a prostitute at least once in the previous year (de Graaf 1995, 15). Prieur and Taksdal (1989) estimated that 13 percent of Norwegian men had paid for sexual contact with a prostitute (cited in Finstad and Hoigard 1993, 209). Johnson, Wadsworth, and Elliott (1989) estimated that 3.6 percent of British men had been to a prostitute, although another British study (reported in de Graaf 1995, 15) indicated that this number could be as high as 6.4 percent, and that older married men were more likely to visit prostitutes than their younger, unmarried counterparts. A French study estimated that 3.3 percent of French men had paid for a prostitute in the previous five years (de Graaf 1995, 16). Melbye and Biggar (1992) estimated that 13.1 percent of men in Denmark had visited a prostitute. And the Select Committee of the Legislative Assembly upon Prostitution, Parliament of New South Wales (1986) estimated that anywhere from 7,000 to 9,600 clients visited the state's prostitutes in one day. The committee estimated that from 1,400 to 1,950 persons worked in brothels, escort services, and on the street at any given time.

These European estimates are much lower than Southeast Asian equivalents. Studies of Thai men produce the largest estimates of the proportion of men who buy sex. Nopkesorn, Mastro, and Sangkharomya (1993) estimated that roughly three quarters of northern Thai men had at least one sexual experience with a prostitute, and Celentano, Nelson, and Suprasert (1993) reported that 81.1 percent of a sample of northern Thai men (average age twenty-one years) had at least one sexual experience with a prostitute, while 69.5 percent had paid for sex at least once during the year prior to being surveyed. McCaghy and Hou (1993) estimated that 42 percent of the Taipei male population had during their lifetime visited a prostitute at least once, 82 percent of whom reported that they had visited a prostitute on more than one occasion.

Several estimates for African populations are provided by the research of the Global Programme on AIDS/World Health Organization, which estimated that the proportion of men using prostitutes during the year prior to being surveyed was 11 percent in the Ivory Coast, 10 percent in Lesotho, 8 percent in Togo, and 13 percent in Kenya (Carael et al. 1991).

# Explaining the Gender Structure of Prostitution

When it comes to the primary overarching gender structure of prostitution—male buyers, female sellers—two types of determinism have prevailed: biological and sociological.

At the heart of biological determinism is the idea that there is an essential difference between the sexes, a difference usually described in terms of the alleged contrasting "sex drives" of men and women. One version of this type of causation theory is the sociobiology of Burley and Symanski (1981), which purports to identify two biological and three sociological "preconditions" of prostitution. Ultimately, though, at the core of the explanation is a genetic imperative that selects men to be promiscuous and women to be monogamous, and without this fundamental and essential difference between the sexes, prostitution would not have the basic gender structure that it does.

Even in some attempts to construct a self-consciously sociological explanation of prostitution, the sociological structure is built on a biological foundation. Such is the case with Kingsley Davis's (1937) functionalist explanation of prostitution. For Davis, while the manifest function of prostitution is to provide sex for money, its latent, and much more important, function is to resolve a sexual double standard that requires women to be chaste prior to marriage and monogamous afterwards, but allows men to be promiscuous. Prostitution provides the resolution to the obvious contradiction in the sexual double standard: if women are supposed to be monogamous, then who are men supposed to be promiscuous with? The institution of prostitution is a principal method for resolving this contradiction and, in so doing, becomes a guardian of the family and the value-system that supports it. When it comes to why the double standard exists, Davis offers a hydraulic model of sexuality—because of their greater sex drive, men tend to be more promiscuous than women. When their desire for sex cannot be fulfilled, they need an outlet. In this rendition, prostitution becomes the safety valve for the male sex drive.

In challenging the biological assumptions underlying most of these theories of prostitution, Mary McIntosh (1979) struck at the heart of the matter when she posed the question: "Do male/female differences in sexual needs really exist, or are they related to a specific social ideology?" She concluded that there are at least three possible answers to this question: (1) "differences are socially scripted: if males and females act differently, it is because they are scripted to learn differently"; (2) "women's sexuality is suppressed by men in the interests of patriarchy . . . so their sexual expectations and opportunities are limited and they are prevented from realizing their full potential"; and (3) "differentiation of sexuality, along with other orientations, occurs in the history of each individual in an infancy in which mother and father play specific different parts."

Although there are many "feminisms," probably most feminists would agree that in Western (and many other) societies, prostitution is, among other things, a patriarchal social relation, the quintessential expression of male exploitation and commodification of women.[3] Where feminists differ is in how they explain the origins and meaning of patriarchy, and how they characterize sex work—from Barry's (1979) image of all prostitution as sexual slavery to Bell's postmodernist rejection of any such grand narrative in favor of a more complex analysis of power in which prostitution represents resistance as well as subjugation. For many feminists prostitution has no single transhistorical and transcultural meaning (e.g., Bell 1994; Shrage 1989).

# Explaining Which Men Buy Sex

Regardless of how we explain the gender structure of prostitution in Western countries, the fact remains that only some females (and even fewer males) sell sex for money, and only some males buy their services. In the Western literature, much of the theorizing at the individual level has focused on the female sex seller, with an eye to explaining the circumstances leading to her decision to prostitute. Until the arrival of modern feminism, much of this theory tried to establish that females who prostitute are *essentially different* from females who do not.

But in neither feminist theory nor in more traditional social science has much thought been given to why some men buy sex and others don't. In prefeminist social science, and in some radical feminism, the biological underpinnings of more general theories of prostitution and sexuality provide a commonsense answer as to which men pay for sex: they are the ones who do not have an outlet for their (uncontrollable) sexual impulses. But that is the only thing that differentiates them from other men, in comparison with whom they are *essentially the same*; i.e., they all experience (uncontrollable) sexual urges, almost as if "sexual urges" defined "maleness."

When we canvass the literature for the opinions of researchers and their subjects—including accounts of people who sell and men who buy sex—we find the following array of "explanations" of why particular men buy sex:

1. In the face of *personal deficiencies,* most notably physical or social "unattractiveness," various male "losers" have to buy sex because it is the only way to satisfy their sexual urges. In academic parlance, these are men with various "psychological problems" related to their "malaise."

2. A variation of (1) suggests that, because of happenstance, like the death of a partner, some men buy sexual services because they are "over the hill" and find it difficult to get sexual partners any other way.

3. Because of their work, some men lack opportunities to meet sexual partners or often spend long periods apart from their regular sexual partners. Buying sex is a quick and relatively inexpensive way to satisfy their urges (one can only wonder why their female partners don't satisfy their urges the same way).

4. Because their sexual partners refuse to indulge in certain sexual activities, some men buy sex to fulfill desires that would otherwise remain only fantasies.

5. Buyers are men who are not sexually satisfied by their mates or do not feel they have "enough" sex.

6. Prostitution provides men with temporary relief from male sex-role obligations.
7. Prostitution offers "weirdos" (pedophiles) access to girls and youths.
8. Prostitution represents a primitive stage of sexual development. Men who buy sex are psychopathologically maladjusted because they have subconsciously regressed to an infantile stage of sexual development in which the child focuses its sexual desire on the parent of the opposite sex. The consequence is that they cannot find erotic satisfaction through their spouse and turn to prostitutes instead (Glover 1943).
9. Repression of sexual experiences during infancy and childhood produces psychological problems (particularly a sense of shame) that translates into a desire to buy sex precisely because of the moral opprobrium that is associated with prostitution.
10. Prostitution provides males with the illusion that they are sexually successful.
11. Radical, leftist, and some liberal feminists put an entirely different spin on the commercial heterosexual sex transaction by analyzing it in terms of *power*. The purchase of sex is an expression of male power over women.

When it comes to young hustlers' accounts of why their clients purchase sexual services, three themes recur:

1. Men who buy sex from other males do so as a way of fulfilling a (homo)sexual desire that they otherwise repress. Buying sex from male prostitutes helps keep the customer sexually satisfied while remaining "in the closet."
2. "Chicken-hawks" (pedophiles) like to have sex with boys, and "boys town" (the male prostitution stroll) is one of the best places to find them.
3. Because of various personal deficiencies (such as physical or social "unattractiveness"), men who cannot attract regular male sex partners purchase them instead.

Analysis of prostitution by males is not inimical to feminism, of course, because feminist perspectives draw attention to the *exercise of power* that generally characterizes commercial sexual transactions in contemporary Western (and many other) societies. As with female sellers, males who sell sex do so to a mostly or exclusively male clientele. The transaction involves an economically privileged man buying sex from a relatively young male, many of whom are economically marginalized. In the case of street prostitution, the seller typically left the home of his parents at a relatively early age, and is relatively unskilled, undereducated, and thus likely eligible for only the lowest paid positions at the margins of the job market.

*Summary*

The various theories about which men buy sex can be distilled into six main propositions: (1) "physical unattractiveness" thwarts certain men's opportunity to satisfy their sex drive, so they buy sex from prostitutes; (2) "social unattractiveness" caused by psychological maladjustment thwarts certain men's opportunity to satisfy their sex drive, so they buy sex from prostitutes; (3) psychopathology rooted in early phases of sexual development causes some men to seek out prostitutes; (4) prostitution is a way for men to live up to cultural gender-role expectations; (5) prostitution is a way for men to avoid gender-role responsibilities; and (6) buying sex is one way that men express male power over women, particularly men who feel disempowered by women.

The first two propositions are linked to the more general explanation that attributes the gender structure of prostitution—male buyer, female seller—to the male "sex drive." The problem with such formulations is that empirical research on human sexuality does not show men to have more intense sexual desire than women. Indeed, the concept of a "sex drive" is misleading. It conjures up a hydraulic image of male sexuality. Some men may "think with their penis," as the barroom banter goes, but "sex drive" cannot be empirically generalized into a biological male imperative that explains prostitution. Rather, in Mary McIntosh's (1979) opinion, prostitution is a patriarchal social relation supported by the ideology of male sexual need.

Regardless of which explanation finds favor—biological, social, or biosociological—one thing is sure: as currently constituted, prostitution is a distinctly male way of expressing sexual desire, a male way of thinking about sex. But, depending on how it is conceptualized, it is not a ubiquitous male way of expressing sexual desire. Indeed, there is no single, essential male expression of sexuality.

# Method and Epistemology of the Exploratory Research

Although we doubt that the male sex buyer has any single "essential" nature that differentiates him from other men, the buyer is a distinct empirical object and subject of study insofar as he has directly paid money for sex. Because there is very little Canadian information about the buyer of sexual services, one of the main purposes of this exploratory research is to provide an empirical description of the men (and the women, if we can contact any) who buy sexual services. By resorting to the Internet as a means of contacting clients, we hope eventually to facilitate international comparisons as a way of situating the Canadian research.

In this chapter we do not discuss at length the general epistemological issues that characterize this (and all other) social research. But because we necessarily make epistemological choices in deciding what methods to use, it is worth briefly reflecting on the nature of those decisions. For epistemological purists with a firm conviction about what is "real," certain methods are ruled out automatically. That is not the case here. The approach we prefer to take is methodologically eclectic inasmuch as we take advantage of as many methods as possible. Although our methodological preference is for semi-structured taped interviews—preferably a series of interviews with the same men several months apart—few clients are willing to be taped. Our use of a self-administered questionnaire is not indicative of a preference for quantitative over qualitative methods, but of taking the best advantage of the opportunities that are currently available to collect information about men who buy sexual services. In other words, our approach is empirical but not empiricist.

The court file survey takes advantage of a relatively new information source to provide general information about the characteristics of men charged for "communicating." We were able to obtain data relating to cases that went to court between 1993 and 1995 (some of the charges were laid as early as 1991, but took many months to get to court). Data for charges laid in 1986 and 1987 (Lowman 1989, app. 3) are also available for comparative purposes.

The self-administered questionnaire includes questions about the "objective" characteristics of buyers (their gender, age, income, occupation, etc.), and their sexual behavior (age of first purchase, frequency of purchases, venues, preferences, etc.). By incorporating measures of various attitudes, and by being designed as a general survey on "Sex and Sexuality in the 1990s," not just client behavior, the questionnaire also attempts to ascertain if any subjective patterns distinguish people who purchase sexual services from those who do not. Although we do not set out in a hypothetico-deductive mode to test specific hypotheses, some of our decisions about what kinds of information to collect are based on speculation in the literature about what motivates men to buy sex.

One version of our self-administered questionnaire will be distributed over Internet, a communication medium that is only just starting to be utilized for social science research. The results of the Internet survey will be compared to the results of a similar questionnaire distributed in Vancouver (Lowman, Atchison, and Fraser 1997). The two surveys are the same, apart from the sections on geographical sex-purchasing patterns and respondents' knowledge of the law. In order to produce a control group of nonclients to compare to clients, the first half of the questionnaire was designed to be answered by male and female adults and concerns general sexual behavior and attitudes to sex and prostitution. The second half of the questionnaire focuses on client behavior. In advertising the Internet questionnaire, we invited any adult to respond, not just clients. Distribution of the British Columbia version of the questionnaire was targeted exclusively at clients.

Because of the limitations of questionnaire research we intend to supplement the data provided by the two surveys with more qualitative information from semi-structured interviews with up to twenty clients (Lowman, Atchison, and Fraser 1997). By using a more open format in the interviews we hope to avoid being overly constrained by previous research and remain skeptical of preconceived—perhaps even stereotypical—images of the client.

In the present chapter, we restrict our review to the results of the Crown file survey, and some of the preliminary findings of the first 392 Internet responses available at the time of writing (we anticipate ending up with roughly 540 respondents, including nearly 130 clients).

## A Profile of Men Charged with Communicating in Public for the Purpose of Purchasing Sexual Services

When the communicating law was enacted on December 20, 1985, it explicitly made the customer of the street prostitute liable to prosecution. Although enforcement of the law against customers and prostitutes has been inequitable in Vancouver (the charge rate for prostitutes has consistently been from two to three times the charge rate for customers), some 3,000 customers have been prosecuted. Our first description of customers comes from information obtained from court files on 440 of these cases from charges occurring between 1991 and 1995. We briefly compare this profile of men charged for communicating with the findings of an earlier study of 220 men in Vancouver who were charged with communicating (Lowman 1989, app. 3). The profile includes:

1. Information about the offense (date, time, number of accused, number of individuals in accused's vehicle, location, type of transportation used by accused, service request made, police operation, photograph of accused);

2. Information about the offender (age, marital status, area of residence, citizenship, ethnic origin, occupation, criminal record);

3. Information about court proceedings and case disposition (date of final court appearance, representation in court, plea, disposition, and sentence).

We examined 440 individual cases dating back to 1991 involving 434 accused persons (i.e., there were six repeat accused) in 416 separate incidents (nineteen incidents involved more than one accused). As a way to provide a context for interpreting the customer cases, we also examined one hundred prostitute cases disposed of in 1995 (we took the hundred most recent prostitute cases ordered by date in the biweekly reports of the Regional Crown Counsel office).

## Offense Characteristics

The majority of customers (83.9 percent) traveled alone. In forty-five incidents (10.3 percent), there were two men in a vehicle; in sixteen incidents (3.6 percent) there were three men; in eight cases (1.8 percent) there were four men; and in one case there were five. Most of the men charged were driving a car (67 percent); a van, truck, or RV (23.9 percent); or a bicycle (0.7 percent); only 8.2 percent of the men were on foot (the remaining 0.2 percent arrived by taxi).

Overall, the arrest locations demonstrate that most arrests are made in four of the seven main strolls in Vancouver that existed at various times from 1992 through 1995 (figure 1): the Victoria-Lakewood stroll bounded by Hastings and Triumph streets, on Vancouver's East Side (23.6 percent); the Quebec-Ontario stroll in Mount Pleasant (23.6 percent); the stroll along the Broadway strip in Mount Pleasant (23.2 percent); and, to a lesser extent, the Downtown East Side (15.7 percent). The stroll along First Avenue has largely been ignored by police, and very few arrests of customers have been made in the Richards-Seymour and Franklin strolls. These three areas have two common characteristics: they are all controlled by professional pimps, and they are mainly commercial land-use areas.

In order to provide a context for customer arrest patterns, a comparison was made between the sites in which 153 buyers and 100 sellers were arrested in 1995. The area with the highest proportion of charges against sellers in 1995 was Downtown East Side (34 percent); however, it accounted for only 0.7 percent of the men who were charged with offering to buy sexual services. The largest number of buyers (46.4 percent) was arrested along Broadway. An equivalent proportion of sellers (23 percent) and buyers (21 percent) were arrested in the Victoria-Lakewood stroll.

In only three of the four hundred cases were charges other than those relating to s.213 laid against customers at the time they were charged. There were two charges for resisting arrest and one for an indecent act (s.173, exposure—this man was naked when he approached the police decoy).

## Client Characteristics

The average age of buyers was thirty-four years. Of the men, 77.7 percent were less than forty-one years of age. The vast majority of accused were Canadian citizens (83.7 percent), and 10.4 percent were landed immigrants. Most of the men charged worked in blue-collar occupations, or in low- to middle-income professions. Of the accused buyers, 36.6 percent were employed in occupations such as manufacturing, trades and transportation/freight handling, natural resource-based occupations, or unskilled labor. Only 16 percent had occu-

Fig. 1. Vancouver Prostitution Strolls 1992–1995

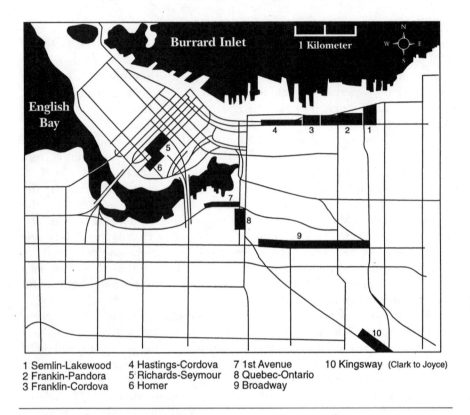

| | | | |
|---|---|---|---|
| 1 Semlin-Lakewood | 4 Hastings-Cordova | 7 1st Avenue | 10 Kingsway (Clark to Joyce) |
| 2 Franklin-Pandora | 5 Richards-Seymour | 8 Quebec-Ontario | |
| 3 Franklin-Cordova | 6 Homer | 9 Broadway | |

pations that fall into upper-income, "professional" categories—indeed, almost as many customers were unemployed or on welfare (13 percent).

Ethnic origin was recorded in the terminology used in police Informations to Crown. The majority of accused were Caucasian (52.9 percent), and 15.7 percent were of East Indian descent. Almost all of the other accused were of Asian descent—5.1 percent were Chinese, 4.4 percent were Vietnamese, and 2.3 percent were Japanese. A further 5.3 percent were reportedly of an unspecified Asian or Oriental origin. About 3 percent of the accused were Native Indian and less than 2 percent were black. In contrast, 73 percent of sellers were "Caucasian" and 18 percent were Native Indian.

Where marital status was recorded, 42 percent of the accused buyers were married or in a common law relationship; 43.4 percent were single. Of the accused buyers, 48.9 percent lived in Vancouver, another 44.2 percent coming from the surrounding municipalities or the Fraser Valley. Only 2 percent of the accused men came from outside British Columbia.

Of accused buyers, 24.2 percent were known to have criminal records; in contrast, over 75 percent of sellers had previous convictions. Of the forty-two sellers for whom criminal record information was available, 76 percent had five or more convictions (including 57 percent who had more than ten convictions). The main types of convictions of customers include property crimes, driving offenses, and assaults/threats; for sellers they were property offenses, failing to appear in court, communicating, drugs, and assaults/threats.

When compared to their 1986–1987 counterparts (Lowman 1989, app. 3) there is a somewhat larger proportion of men recorded as single in the 1992–1995 cases (44 percent as compared to 35 percent in 1986–87). Otherwise, the two populations are strikingly similar. They are much the same in terms of their age (a mean of thirty-five in 1986–1987 as compared to thirty-four in the 1990s group), their Blishen socioeconomic status (in both groups the mean is 38), and their "racial" composition (which is almost identical). Also, the geography of residence of the two groups of buyers is similar. In the case of men living in Vancouver, the geography of customers' residence (figures 3 and 4) is roughly the reverse image of the geography of average family income (figure 2). It is mainly men from lower socioeconomic groups who are being charged and convicted. This pattern is at least partly explained by communicating law enforcement patterns: because of the difficulties female police decoys experience, there is little enforcement against customers on the "high track" (the Richards-Seymour stroll), which is not only where the highest prices are commanded, but it is also closest to the West Side residential areas of the city where the higher socio-economic status men live (Lowman 1990).

## Disposition of Cases

About 74 percent of accused buyers retained the services of a lawyer or were represented by duty counsel; over 90 percent of sellers had legal representation. Of those cases in which the plea was recorded, approximately 77 percent pleaded guilty. Sixty-eight percent of the accused buyers were found guilty (as compared to 84 percent of sex sellers), 7.8 percent were acquitted, in 8 percent of cases there was a stay of proceedings, in 5 percent of cases the accused were diverted, and in 11 percent the charge was dismissed.

Of the seventy-six men who pleaded not guilty, only nine (12 percent) were found guilty. Of the remaining cases, thirty-four men were found not guilty, twenty-six charges were dismissed, five charges were stayed, and two persons were diverted.

Among customers who were found guilty, the majority were given absolute discharges (51.2 percent) or conditional discharges (36 percent). About 8.7 percent were fined, and 3.4 percent were given suspended sentences. Two men were sentenced to the jail time they had already served—in these rare instances the accused were held because of outstanding charges.

### Fig. 2. Average Family Income, 1985

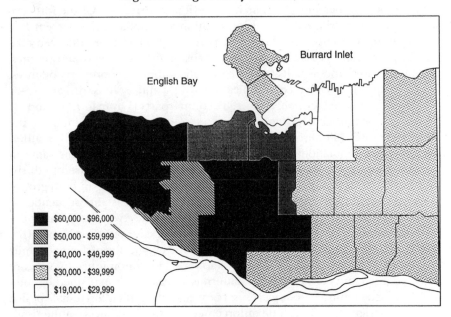

### Fig. 3. Vancouver Men Charged with Communicating
### for the Purpose of Purchasing Sexual Services (n = 91).
### January 1986–June 1987: % of Total Per Area of Residence

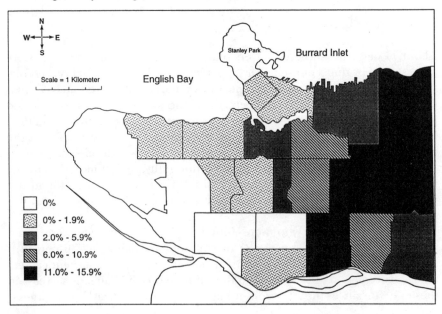

**Fig. 4. Vancouver Men Charged with Communicating
for the Purpose of Purchasing Sexual Services (n = 210).
1992–1995: % of Total Per Area of Residence**

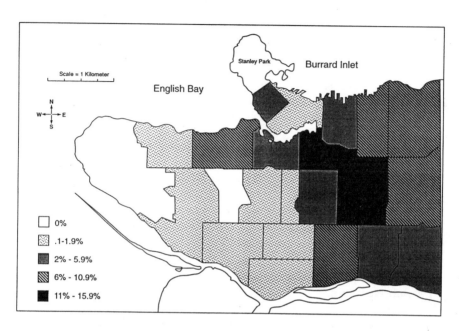

Among sellers, 34.6 percent were given discharges, over 29.4 percent were jailed (many of these were sentences that took into account time already served), and 32 percent were given suspended sentences. As with sentencing in 1986 and 1987 (Lowman 1990, 67–69) sellers are still relatively much more likely than buyers to end up with a criminal record for communicating (87 percent of the buyers were discharged, and thus end up with no criminal record for communicating, as compared to 35 percent of the sellers).

In the 297 cases in which buyers were found guilty, 109 (37 percent) were put on probation (including all ten persons who were given a suspended sentence, 98 of the 107 persons who were conditionally discharged, and one person who was fined). Of the seventy-eight cases involving sellers who were convicted, thirty-nine (50 percent) resulted in a probation order (including sixteen of the seventeen conditional discharges, twenty-one of the twenty-five suspended sentences, and in two of the cases where jail time had been served).

# Preliminary Findings from the Internet Survey

The questionnaire on "Sex and Sexuality in the 1990s" includes a general survey on sex and sexuality to be answered by all respondents, and a focused survey on client activity.

The general survey includes the following sections:

- Personal information: age, sex, occupation, religion, national/cultural/racial identity, income, education;
- Family information: number/ages/sex of children; number/sex of siblings, marital status of parents, age and circumstances of leaving home;
- First sexual experience: age, partner involved, nature of experience;
- Childhood sexual abuse: age, person involved, nature of experience;
- Attitudes to sex and sexuality;[4]
- Descriptions of self;[5]
- Relationship with spouse/regular sexual partner: length of relationship, partner's occupation, feelings about relationship, emotional and sexual satisfaction with partner;
- Behavior with sex partners: victimization by and of sex partners;
- Epidemiological issues;
- Substance use;
- Sexual activity: type of activity and number of partners;
- Attitudes toward and understanding of commercial sex: various attitude and perception scales about buyers and sellers of sex;
- Attitudes toward street prostitution;
- Attitudes toward men and women.[6]

At this point, persons who had never purchased sex finish the questionnaire.

## The Client Survey

The second part of the questionnaire focuses on buyer behavior. This part of the questionnaire was written in anticipation of a mostly male response and designed primarily to capture the male heterosexual commercial sex experience in Western countries. The questions on male buyer behavior are organized as follows:

- Frequency and type of sex purchases;
- Factors influencing the decision to buy sex;
- Duration of encounters;

- Substance use during commercial encounters;
- General reasons for buying sex;
- Satisfaction with sex sellers;
- Purchasing activity: where, what venues, what time of day and week;
- Sharing information about commercial sex;
- (Vancouver survey only) Areas of street prostitution: use of street prostitution in and around Vancouver;
- Crime victimization and safety issues: victimization experiences and precautions taken to avoid rip-offs and other problems;
- Characteristics of the most recent sexual encounter: venue, type of service, duration, substance use, satisfaction with, reasons for, and feelings after;
- First sexual encounter;
- Geographic purchasing patterns;
- Legal experiences: knowledge of law, history of arrest, effect of laws on purchasing activity.

The questionnaire has 162 questions comprising 960 variables. Although none of the results of the British Columbia survey are yet available (there will be about fifty respondents), we can report the preliminary findings of the Internet survey, which was first posted on November 9, 1996, and ran until March 31, 1997. In this chapter we report some of the general characteristics of the first 392 accepted responses (those that were available at the time of writing)[7] as a way of introducing this research (for further information see Atchison 1997; Lowman, Atchison, and Fraser 1997).

## The Respondents as a Whole

The 392 respondents include 301 men (77 percent), 87 women (22 percent) and 3 transgenders (0.8 percent). The remaining respondent did not answer the question on sex/gender. Overall, their ages ranged from eighteen to sixty-seven years, with a mean of twenty-nine. In the calculation of the percentages that follow, missing values are excluded; where there are a large number of missing values, the number of valid cases is provided. Of the respondents who answered the question on marital status (n = 367), 57 percent are single, 33 percent are married or live in a common-law relationship, and 9 percent are separated or divorced. The sample is dominated by respondents residing in the United States (77 percent), with the remainder living in Canada (13 percent), Australia and New Zealand (5 percent) and the British Isles (5 percent). Eighty-seven percent of the respondents are Caucasian. The majority of respondents are employed full-time (56 percent) or they are students (30 percent). When it comes to sexual orientation, 74 percent reported that they are heterosexual, 16 percent are bisexual, 9 percent are gay, and less than 0.5 percent are lesbian.

Overall, then, the sample is dominated by young adult, white males from the United States.

## Clients

The client sample (n = 86) is 95 percent male. There are two females and two transgendered persons. Both female respondents described themselves as bisexual, and in both cases the sexual activity with a female prostitute included a male partner as well (i.e., they were involved in a *ménage à trois* consisting of a prostitute interacting with a male and female couple). We do not yet have a single instance of a woman reporting that she had purchased sex from a man.

Eight percent of the clients had paid for sex only once in their lifetime. Another 33 percent reported between two and ten lifetime commercial sexual encounters, 32 percent reported between eleven and fifty lifetime sexual encounters, and 27 percent reported having purchased sexual services more than fifty times. Most of the clients had purchased sex in more than one venue: 55 percent had visited street prostitutes, 54 percent had visited escorts, 54 percent had purchased sex in massage parlors, 44 percent had met a prostitute in a bar or club, 26 percent in a hotel, 43 percent had contacted prostitutes through personal ads, and 44 percent had visited brothels.

## Comparing Clients with Men
## Who Have Not Purchased Sexual Services

Although we have not yet had a chance to compare various subgroups in the sample (e.g., men and women, clients and nonclients), some potentially important differences are evident in the comparisons we have completed. For example, the average age of clients is thirty-six years, while the average age of men who have never purchased sexual services is twenty-eight. One corollary of this age differential is that 45 percent of clients are married as compared to 27 percent of the other men, and 45 percent of clients have children as compared to 21 percent of the other men. Also, 74 percent of clients work full-time as compared to 49 percent of the nonclients, and only 12 percent of the clients are students as compared to 36 percent of the nonclient men. We have yet to control for the effect of age to ascertain if any of these differences are statistically significant.

At this point the only other comparison we have made concerns early sexual experience and sexual abuse.[8] There are two notable features of this comparison. First, clients tend to have become sexually experienced at an earlier age than nonclients. For example, of the men who have never purchased a sexual service, only 19 percent had sexual intercourse prior to the age of sixteen (which is roughly the same proportion as the women in the sample) as compared to 40 percent of the clients. Second, a larger proportion of clients report incidents of childhood sexual abuse than do the other men—of those who have never purchased sex, 9 percent report some form of childhood sexual abuse, as compared to 27 percent of the clients (the equivalent figure for the women in the sample is 28 percent).

## Conclusion

Needless to say, because we are still in the process of analyzing the information yielded by the client survey, it would be premature for us to draw too many conclusions at this point. Rather, the purpose of this paper has been to provide a progress report on our client research. The experience of presenting some of the preliminary findings from the Internet survey at the March 1997 conference sponsored by COYOTE and California State Northridge served to remind us just how suspicious many people are of research via the Internet. "How do you know if the respondents aren't just bullshitting?" one person asked. To us, this issue is troubling regardless of whether the research is conducted over the Internet or in some other way. For this reason, several devices are built into the questionnaire that enable us to ascertain the internal consistency of respondents' answers. We are very encouraged by the results. Also, we would note that the profile of respondents is very much what one would expect to be yielded by an Internet survey—the sample is dominated by young white males—which suggests that, at least when it comes to the age, race, and gender of respondents, they have provided accurate information. Moreover, by using different methods to contact clients in Vancouver, British Columbia—a sample also dominated by white males—we will be able to compare not just "objective" demographic indices, but also the much more subjective attitudinal measures that comprise much of the survey, and which may well produce some of the most interesting results. At that point we will be in a better position to move beyond description and reflect on speculation in the extant literature about the causes and meaning of client behavior.

## Notes

1. Funding was provided by the Ministry of the Attorney General.
2. Because those were multiple-response questions, there is some overlap in the responses—i.e., some of the responses said their clients were "mostly nice guys," but that some were "jerks."

3. One exception to this is the style of argument popular among certain prostitution rights advocates (some of whom would consider themselves "feminist") who insist that prostitution is a form of work, and that a woman should be "free" to sell sex if she so desires.

4. Attitudes toward sex and sexuality are gauged by questions about a respondent's opinions about the moral acceptability and appropriate legal status of twenty-five different types of sexual activities, ranging from premarital sex to snuff films. The sexual activities included in this measure were derived from an Internet questionnaire developed by Perry (1995).

5. Questions 45 and 46 are based on psychological scaling techniques that attempt to measure *self-concept*. The first set of questions asks respondents how they feel about themselves in various ways, whether they are able to express emotions, whether they feel they can do most things well, whether they are able to cope successfully with day-to-day problems, and so on. The second set of questions asks how respondents would compare themselves to other people in terms of their physical attractiveness, how likely they are to lose their temper, how easy they are to get along with, and so on.

6. Attitudes to men and women are gauged by asking respondents whether they agree or disagree with a set of thirty-two statements about men and women on topics ranging from level of competiveness to child care. These statements were derived from the 109-item Gender Attitude Inventory developed by Ashmore, Del Boca, and Bilder (1995).

7. Three cases were rejected because they were obviously not serious (in several answers one respondent claimed to have an "alien living in my arse," a second made a variety of utterly implausible claims, including having access to "A-bombs," and the third claimed to have had over 500 encounters with prostitutes over the past year). Roughly a dozen more cases were rejected because only a few questions had been completed. For further discussion of the criteria for excluding cases, see Atchison 1997 and Lowman, Atchison, and Fraser 1997.

8. Our definition of "sexual abuse" is based on offenses in the *Canadian Criminal Code* and reproduced in the questionnaire. *In the case of fourteen- to seventeen-year-olds, sexual abuse* includes interference, exploitation, incest, anal intercourse, corrupting a youth, procuring, pimping, sexual assault, and sexual touching by a person in a position of authority, trust, or a relationship of dependency. *Sexual abuse of person under fourteen years of age* includes interference, sexual touching, exploitation, incest, anal intercourse, bestiality in the presence of a child, corrupting a child, indecent acts, procuring, pimping, and sexual assault. In the case of persons aged twelve and thirteen, sexual touching is not an offense if it is consented to and the partner is within two years of age of the victim.

# References

Armstrong, E. 1978. Massage parlors and their customers. *Archives of Sexual Behaviour* 7: 117.

Ashmore, R. D., F. K. Del Boca, and S. Bilder. 1995. Construction and validation of the gender attitude inventory. A structured inventory to assess multiple dimensions of gender attitudes. *Sex Roles* 32(11/12): 753–85.

Atchison, C. 1997. Men who buy sex: A preliminary description based on the results from a survey of the internet using population. Master of Arts thesis, School of Criminology. Burnaby, British Columbia: Simon Fraser University.

———. 1996. Turning the trick: The development and partial implementation of a multi-dimensional research instrument designed for clients of sex sellers. Honours thesis. Burnaby, British Columbia: Simon Fraser University.

Barnard, M. A., N. P. McKeganey, and A. H. Leyland. 1993. Risk behaviours among male clients of female prostitutes. *British Medical Journal* 307: 361–62.

Barry, K. 1979. *Female Sexual Slavery*. New York: Avon Books.

Bell, S. 1994. *Reading, Writing, and Rewriting the Prostitute's Body*. Bloomington: Indiana University Press.

Burley, N., and R. Symanski 1981. Women without: An evolutionary and cross cultural perspective on prostitution. In *The Immoral Landscape: Female Prostitution in Western Societies*, by R. Symanski. Toronto: Butterworths.

Carael, M., J. Cleland, L. Adeokun, and Collaborating Investigators. 1991. Overview and selected findings of sexual behavior surveys. *AIDS* 5(supp.): S65–S74.

Celentano, D. D., K. E. Nelson, S. Suprasert. 1993. Behavioral and sociodemographic risks for frequent visits to commercial sex workers among Northern Thai men. *AIDS* 7: 1647–52.

Committee on Sexual Offenses Against Children and Youth (CSOACY). 1994. *Sexual Offences against Children*. Ottawa: Department of Supply and Services.

Davis, K. 1937. The sociology of prostitution. Reprinted from *American Sociological Review* 1937 in *The Sociology of Deviance*, edited by K. Stoddart. Richmond: Open Learning Institute, 1980: 232–49.

de Graaf, R. 1995. *Prostitutes and Their Clients: Sexual Networks and Determinants of Condom Use*. Den Haag: CIP-Gegevens Koninkijke Bibliotheek.

Diana, L. 1985. *The Prostitute and Her Clients: Your Pleasure Is Her Business*. Springfield, Ill.: Charles C. Thomas.

Ellis, A. 1959. Why married men visit prostitutes. *Sexology* 25: 344–47.

Finstad, L., and C. Hoigard. 1993. Norway. In *Prostitution: An International Handbook on Trends, Problems, and Policies*, edited by N. Davis. Westport, Conn.: Greenwood Press.

Freund, M., N. Lee, and T. Leonard. 1991. Sexual behavior of clients with street prostitutes in Camden, NJ. *Journal of Sex Research* 28 (4): 579–91.

Gemme, R., A. Murphy, M. Bourque, M. A. Nemeh, and N. Payment. 1984. A report on prostitution in Quebec. *Working Papers on Prostitution and Pornography, Report No. 11*. Ottawa: Department of Justice.

Gibbens, T. C. N., and M. Silberman. 1960. The clients of prostitutes. *British Journal of Venereal Disease* 36: 113.

Glover, E. 1943, 1957, 1969. *The Psychopathology of Prostitution*. London: Institute for the Study and Treatment of Delinquency.

Holzman, H., and S. Pines. 1982. Buying sex: The phenomenology of being a john. *Deviant Behaviour: An Interdisciplinary Journal* 4: 89–116.

Johnson, A. M., J. Wadsworth, and P. Elliott. 1989. A pilot study of sexual lifestyle in a random sample of the population in Great Britain. *AIDS* 3: 135–41.

Kinsey, A. C., W. B. Pomeroy, and C. E. Martin. 1948. *Sexual Behavior in the Human Male.* Philadelphia, London: Saunders.

Leonard, T. L. 1990. Male clients of female street prostitutes: Unseen partners in sexual disease transmission. *Medical Anthropology Quarterly* 4 (1): 41–55.

Leonard, T., M. Freund, and J. Platt. 1989. Behavior of clients of prostitutes. *American Journal of Public Health* 79 (7): 903.

Lowman. J. 1990. Notions of equality before the law; the experience of street prostitutes and their customers." *Journal of Human Justice.* 1 (2): 55–76.

———. 1989. *Street Prostitution: Assessing the Impact of the Law: Vancouver.* Ottawa: Department of Justice.

———. 1984. Vancouver field study of prostitution: Field notes. *Working Papers on Pornography and Prostitution, Report #8.* Ottawa: Department of Justice.

Lowman, J., C. Atchison, and L. Fraser. 1996. *Men Who Buy Sex, Phase 1.* A report prepared for the British Columbia Ministry of Attorney General.

———. 1997. *Men Who Buy Sex, Phase 2: The Client Survey.* A report prepared for the British Columbia Ministry of Attorney General.

Masters, W., and V. Johnson. 1970. *Human Sexual Inadequacy.* Boston: Little, Brown.

McCaghy, C. H., and C. Hou. 1993. Taiwan. In *Prostitution: An International Handbook on Trends, Problems, and Policies,* edited by N. Davis. Westport, Conn.: Greenwood Press.

McIntosh, M. 1979. The ideology of male sexual needs. In *Women, Sexuality and Social Control,* edited by C. Smart and B. Smart. London: Routledge and Kegan Paul.

McKeganey, N. 1994. Why do men buy sex and what are their assessments of HIV related risks when they do? *AIDS Care* 6 (3): 289–301.

McLeod, E. 1982. *Women Working: Prostitution Now.* London: Croom Helm.

Melbye, M., and R. J. Biggar. 1992. Interaction of persons at risk for AIDS and the general population in Denmark. *American Journal of Epidemiology* 135: 593–602.

Moyer, S., and P. J. Carrington. 1989. *Street Prostitution: Assessing the Impact of the Law, Toronto.* Ottawa: Department of Justice.

Nopkesorn, T., T. D. Mastro, S. Sangkharomya. 1993. HIV-1 infection in young men in Northern Thailand. *AIDS* 7: 1233–39.

Peat and Marwick Partners. 1984. Canadians' attitudes toward and perceptions of pornography and prostitution. *Working Papers on Pornography and Prostitution, Report #6,* Ottawa: Department of Justice.

Pickering, H., J. Todd, D. Dunn, J. Pepin, and A. Wilkins. 1992. Prostitutes and their clients: A Gambian survey. *Social Science and Medicine* 34 (1): 75–88.

Prieur, A., and A. Taksdal. 1989. *A Sette Pris Pa Kvinner. Menn Som Kjoper Sex.* Oslo: Pax Forlag.

Select Committee of the Legislative Assembly of New South Wales. 1986. Parliament of New South Wales. Sydney: Government Printer.

Shrage, L. 1989. Should Feminists oppose prostitution? *Ethics* 99: 347–61.

Simpson, M., and T. Schill. 1977. Patrons of massage parlors: Some facts and figures. *Archives of Sexual Behaviour* 6 (6): 521–25.

Special Committee on Pornography and Prostitution (Fraser Committee). 1985. *Pornography and Prostitution in Canada.* Ottawa: Department of Supply and Services.

Sullivan, E., and W. Simon. 1997. The client: A social, psychological, and behavioral look at the unseen patron of prostitution. Paper presented at the International Conference on Prostitution, California State University, Northridge. March.

Thomas, R. M., M. A. Plant, and M. L. Plant. 1990. Alcohol, AIDS risks, and sex industry clients: Results from a Scottish study. *Drug and Alcohol Dependence* 26: 265–69.

Vanwesenbeeck, I., R. de Graaf, G. van Zessen, C. J. Straver, and J. H. Visser. 1993. Condom use by prostitutes: Behaviour, factors and considerations. *Journal of Psychology and Human Sexuality* 6 (1): 69–91.

———. 1993. Protection styles of prostitutes' clients: Intentions, behaviour, and considerations in relation to AIDS." *Journal of Sex Education and Therapy* 19 (2): 79–92.

Vanwesenbeeck, I., G. van Zessen, R. de Graaf, and C. J. Straver. 1994. Contextual and interactional factors influencing condom use in heterosexual prostitution contacts. *Patient Education and Counseling* 24: 307–22.

Winick, C. 1962. Prostitutes' clients' perceptions of the prostitutes and of themselves. *International Journal of Social Psychiatry* 8 (4): 289–99.

Winick, C., and P. M. Kinsie. 1971. *The Lively Commerce: Prostitution in the United States.* Chicago: Quadrangle Books.

# My Sexual Encounters with Sex Workers: The Effects on a Consumer

## Jim Korn

My name is Jim Korn, I'm forty-nine years old, and I live in San Francisco. I'm also a consumer of sexual services, a client, a "john."

For at least twenty years, I knew where to find prostitutes and other sex workers, and I had enough money to pay for their services, but I stalled. I accepted the conventional notion that sex with a stranger for money would be a hollow, empty, unfulfilling experience. When I finally relented and tried it at age forty-five, I was at first confused, but then pleasantly surprised.

Now, I believe my interactions with sex workers have altered my own psychological, sexual, and spiritual nature. Indeed, I strongly feel those experiences have enhanced my enjoyment of life in general. I've been patronizing sex workers for about four years, and that includes both exotic dancers (strippers) and full-service prostitutes. I've actually spent more time and money with strippers than with prostitutes.

I come from a middle-class background, where my mother achieved a higher level of formal education than my father. She was a registered nurse, and he was a World War II veteran.

I received both physical and emotional abuse as a child. The physical mistreatment was mostly slapping and hitting, and the psychological abuse mainly took the form of negative messages about what I hadn't, wouldn't, and couldn't do. One such pronouncement was that I would never father children, and that's turned out to be true.

My first role models were my parents, and nearly all of my early physical contact with them took the form of violent punishment. I suspect that I most likely learned to associate physical contact with pain and shame. Years later, the intellectual side of me observed that physical intimacy could be used to express a much wider range of feelings and emotions, but a deeper layer of

204

my psyche needed to be reprogrammed. I've never been married, and I've never had a girlfriend or a lover, as most of us would use those terms. My aversion to physical intimacy assured this.

One landmark incident took place when I was twenty-six years old. At that time, I lived with a twenty-year-old female roommate who was very much my type. I shared a complex and satisfying intellectual exchange with her, but when the conversation turned to sex, I became nervous and quiet. One day the two of us were exchanging back rubs, and for an added flourish I bent down and kissed the back of her neck. Her response was to yelp with glee and approval, and she then suggested it might be high time that she go ahead and seduce me. My reaction to her proposition was to become absolutely still and silent, as if paralyzed in mind and body. The moment passed, and years later I realized that my frozen response had been my body's way of saying no. Now, thanks to my interactions with sex workers, I'm certain that I've doubled my options. Should I find myself in a negotiable situation, I'm confident that I can now express either yes or no, mentally and physically.

When I finally appeared on the doorstep of my first full-service sex worker, I was still a virgin in the popular sense of the word. My demeanor was somber and ceremonial, which led to a strange though not unpleasant experience. For one thing, my melancholy and ritualistic approach caused me to focus too much on genital intercourse, something I'd told myself for thirty years I'd never do. As a result of my fixation, I was unable to attain an erection, and I couldn't be properly deflowered, in spite of often-valiant efforts on the part of the first three full-service prostitutes I visited.

After some trial and error, I retreated to the sanctity of the peep shows and lap dance theaters. In these venues the eroticism was high, but I put much less pressure on myself to perform physically. Consciously or subconsciously, I realized that I'd have to savor this meal in smaller bites. Especially helpful was the peep show, where for the first time I masturbated and had an orgasm in the presence of another human being, separated from my playmate by a barrier I call the glass condom. On my very next peep show visit, both the dancer and I had orgasms, hers occurring first. For over a year afterward, I documented many peep show visits by maintaining a "hers and mine" orgasm scorecard, but counting orgasms was never the central issue. What was exhilarating for me was that I was finally becoming comfortable negotiating with another person for sex, a subject that I had been unable to talk about a few years earlier.

In the lap dance clubs I was able to practice the more peripheral aspects of sexuality, beginning with mere physical closeness. I gradually stopped placing genitals at the center and learned or perhaps relearned to eroticize the whole body, and finally the whole experience, from greeting and negotiation to the physical scene and parting. Positive feedback from dancers helped immensely. I often received compliments on my warmth and attentiveness, on my consideration and fairness. This praise from dancers was sometimes verbal, which may have been mostly show biz, and often physical, which I believe was mostly genuine. In any event, I came to believe that my behavior was more egalitarian than most other customers', and I no longer had any doubt that I was and am a feminist. I had established an internal positive feedback loop where I could sense that I was getting from each scene about what I had put into it.

The icing on this cake came just over a year ago, when I got into a conversation with Margo St. James about my experiences with sex workers. When I told her I'd lost my virginity to prostitutes, I meant that I'd finally become comfortable with what for me was a new kind of intimacy. My newfound skill and self-confidence transcend the act of bringing a particular two pieces of flesh together. I blurted out that with sex workers I'd learned how to have fun, to which Margo replied, "That's what it's all about." With sex workers as my teachers, guides, and coaches, I had developed a heightened sense of self-esteem and a new capacity for joy and playfulness that now spills over into all of the nonsexual areas of my life. I suppose I might have arrived at the same place through primal therapy or who knows what, but the path I took was most likely more enjoyable, and maybe even cheaper to boot.

I still hire sex workers, although my motivation is somewhat different now than it was four years ago. I was never very monogamous at heart, and I like having a variety of sexual partners. Adding money to the mix short-circuits the conventional courtship ritual and gives me access to partners I feel attracted to but who may not be attracted to me.

For me at least, it turns out that sex with a stranger can be quite intimate and hot, depending on the context and on the demeanor of the players. I agree with those who say that sometimes a higher level of eroticism can be achieved in a context where the emotional stakes are low. Especially in the early days of four years ago, it would have been very stressful for me to have done that kind of exploration with someone in whom I had a great emotional investment. I very likely would have died a virgin if I hadn't somehow gotten comfortable with physical intimacy, and sex workers enabled me to do that. At least for me, it's been a healing experience.

As a political person, I believe that decriminalization of prostitution is a pro-choice issue. Government has no moral authority to deny practitioners or their customers their sexual, personal, or economic freedom, just as it has no mandate to deny women access to abortion services. For me, the pro-choice position is that all adult consensual sex, including prostitution, should be decriminalized. Whether we're talking about abortion or sex work, the fundamental question is whether the individual or the government should decide what that individual may do with her or his own body. If anyone finds my choices to be immoral, that's fine, but when anyone uses the awesome power of the state to stop me from doing it my way, that's coercion, which is nonconsensual, and I say *that's* immoral. The government should stay out of the morality business where it can't produce a victim. Please note that neither I nor my service providers are complaining.

I fear that sex work may always be maligned because it's a melding of sex and commerce. The conservatives don't like it because it's sex, and the liberals don't like it because it's commerce. I wish they'd both get used to it.

# Sex Workers and the Elderly Male Client[*]

## M. C. Santos Ortíz, J. L. Laó-Meléndez, and A. Torres-Sánchez

Among the different elements that influence human sexual behavior, culture is of the utmost importance. Members of a society learn social behavior parameters and standards through the socialization process, which encompasses the whole of a person's activities, whether they are physical or mental, overt or hidden. Culture includes the norms, values, beliefs, and knowledge that serve as the guides for the society member's behavior. This shaping process begins at birth and is encouraged and maintained through a person's formal education, family, and religion and by the mass media, the law, and the human behavior and health professions.

One of the most important aspects of this process is learning the expression of sexuality. Culture shapes and channels sexual perception by providing guidance for viewing one's own self, one's own body, and one's sexuality, and also how to view one's own body and sexuality in relationship to others and their selves, bodies, and sexualities. Social control mechanisms are used to teach the individual to act, think, and believe according to preformed expectation and accepted parameters of sexual behavior.

In Puerto Rican society, as in many others, human sexuality is considered to be a private subject and often taboo, although subjects such as HIV/AIDS, abortion, and sexual harassment among others have forced us to discuss this issue in a more open manner. Considering that culture is of a dynamic and heterogeneous nature, even within one country, and that it is influenced by economic and political elements, the analysis proposed in this article is exploratory in its approach. We base the facts presented on a descriptive

*Funded by the Committee for Scientific Research Integration and Development, Dean for Academic Affairs, Medical Sciences Campus, University of Puerto Rico.

study of knowledge about HIV/AIDS, risk perception, and sexual practices among a group of elderly Puerto Rican adults and a group of sex workers who offer sexual services to elderly males. Results from an HIV Prevention Need Assessment made in Puerto Rico in 1996 by the Puerto Rico Health Department and Puerto Rico's Community Planning Group will be also discussed.

Traditionally, people have related sexual expression to the following parameters: heterosexuality, coitus (penis-vagina penetration), monogamy, and exclusion of children and old people as sexual beings. In Puerto Rico, as in many other countries, sexual relations are generally regarded as being something for the young, healthy, and attractive. People, particularly the young, still frequently see sexual activity as a wasting asset that has no interest to anyone of more than sixty years of age. To many people, the thought of an elderly couple engaging in sexual relations usually provokes discomfort or distaste. In our culture it is often very difficult to imagine parents or grandparents enjoying masturbation, oral sex, and intercourse on a regular basis.

Masters, Johnson, and Kolodny (1992) indicate that despite the cultural myths about sexuality and older people, the psychological need for intimacy, excitement and pleasure does not disappear in old age, and there is nothing in the biology of aging that automatically shuts down sexual function.

In part, our cultural negativism about sex and romance in older people is a reflection of an attitude called ageism, a prejudice against people because they are old. Some of these ideas consider older people as being rigid, boring, talkative, senile, old-fashioned in morality, lacking in skills, useless, and having little redeeming social value. Some authors suggest that ageism in relation to sexuality is the ultimate form of desexualization: "If you are getting old, you are finished" (Alexander and Allison 1995).

Widespread stereotypes, misconceptions, and jokes about old age and sexuality can powerfully and negatively affect older people's sexual experience. Let us analyze some of these ideas.

# Interest

One principal attitude concerning sexuality and the elderly is the assumption that as people get older, interest in sexual relations decreases. Older people who speak of enjoying sexuality may be viewed as sinful, exaggerating, or deviant, for example, the "dirty old man." Those who express caring and physical affection for one another may be infantilized, defined as "cute," and ridiculed by professionals, age peers, and family members. These people grew up in a period of restrictive guidelines regarding appropriate sexual behavior and taboos relating to other forms of sexual activities such as masturbation. Many of these attitudes may reflect a Victorian morality that views sex only as intercourse and intercourse only as appropriate for conception; sex for communication, intimacy, or pleasure is considered unnecessary and immoral.

The widely accepted attitude in our society that sexual interaction between older people is both socially unacceptable and physically harmful may have negative consequences for the older people themselves. Surrounded by those with such beliefs and fearing ridicule or censure, many older people may unnecessarily withdraw from all forms of sexual expression, thereby depriving themselves of the energy, vitality, and many other positive aspects inherent in sexuality, such as overall physical and mental well-being.

## Sexual Functioning

One of the most prevalent societal ideas is that age-related physiological changes detrimentally affect sexual functioning. Understanding the natural physiological alterations in sexual response associated with the aging process is an essential first step toward dispelling such myths.

Compared with age changes in other systems of the body, such as those in the eyes' focusing ability or the lungs' vital capacity, changes to sexual organs are minimal. Sexual function, judged by intercourse as well as by other activities, is maintained much better than most other functions.

According to Masters, Johnson, and Kolodny (1992), among the changes that occur in the male are a slower sexual response and a greater physical stimulation being required for erection. They cite:

1. The sexual response is generally slower and of diminished intensity.
2. During the excitement phase, greater physical stimulation and a longer time is required to produce erections.
3. The erection may be partial instead of full.
4. A longer period is required to reach climax and orgasm.
5. Decrease of volume and force of ejaculation.
6. Occasional lack of orgasm during the intercourse.
7. Increased length of time between orgasm and subsequent erections.

These authors conclude that although physiological changes occur with age, the capacity for both functioning and fulfillment does not disappear. The male's subjective level of pleasure derived from sexual activity does not change at all with age. They conclude that there are no known limits to sexual activity.

Impotence, the most common sexual disorder among older men, is influenced by both physiological (diseases, such as diabetes and vascular and prostate diseases; operations; use of drugs and alcohol) and psychological factors.

These negative ideas about aging and sexuality have contributed to the neglect or avoidance of health issues such as sexually transmitted diseases in this population.

Of all male AIDS cases reported to the Centers for Disease Control and Prevention, 11 percent have involved individuals fifty years of age or older, and 3 percent have been among persons over sixty (CDC 1996). In common with the general adult population, most of the AIDS cases are men. According to some authors (Whipple and Saura 1995), incidence of AIDS among older adults appears to be rising faster than in young age groups.

In Puerto Rico, most cases reported are also men. The distribution of cases among the sixty-years-and-older age group shows an increase pattern. In 1985, the incidence of male cases was 1.4 percent while in 1997 it had climbed to 5.3 percent (Puerto Rico Department of Health 1997).

When analyzing the mode of exposure, we found that the most prevalent type of reported risk factor for this sector of the population was related to sexual practices. In all the different age categories, sixty to sixty-nine, seventy to seventy-nine, eighty to eighty-nine, and ninety and older, heterosexual contact was the primary (63.2 percent) mode of transmission of HIV and homosexual and bisexual contact was the secondary (21.1 percent) mode of exposure (Puerto Rico Department of Health 1997).

Why is HIV so often overlooked in older people? In large part it is because clinicians do not consider them to be at risk. They may subscribe to society's stereotyping of older people as being sexually inactive and so they do not question their sexual histories. That same stereotyping also prevents older people, who may feel they are not supposed to engage in sexual activity, from telling health professionals and caregivers about their behavior or asking for information. Older gay men, who may have spent a lifetime hiding their sexual preference, may be specially reluctant to speak frankly. Intravenous drug (IV) use is another high-risk behavior that is wrongly assumed not to occur among older adults. In Puerto Rico 15.8 percent of males of sixty years and older cite IV use as the mode of HIV exposure. Many elderly patients who know that caregivers, family members, and friends will judge them do not disclose their HIV status or risk behaviors.

Some factors specific to older persons may increase their risk of becoming infected through sexual activities. Not all older people who are sexually active are in marriages or other long-standing monogamous relationships, and not all who have married have been active only with their spouses. Also, older people usually do not use condoms because pregnancy is no longer a concern and they do not see themselves as being at risk from sexually transmitted diseases. To obtain further information about this group, we conducted a study in the San Juan metropolitan area.

# Method

## Participants

A convenience (nonprobabilistic) sample of 160 persons of sixty years and older (sixty females and one hundred males) and sixty female sex workers were recruited. For this study, however, we shall only refer to data obtained from the elderly males and sex workers.

Elderly males were recruited in Multiple Service Centers in the San Juan metropolitan area. Sex workers were recruited through referral from a community-based organization that offers social and health services to elderly males. The criteria for entry into the study was having provided sexual services to elderly males (sixty years or older) within six months prior to the interview.

## Data Collection

After having obtained their informed consent, researchers collected information from each participant through a personal interview lasting from forty-five minutes to one hour. These interviews were conducted by experienced and trained health professionals or graduate students. Female sex workers and elderly females were questioned by female interviewers and elderly males by male interviewers. The structural interview included questions on knowledge of HIV/AIDS, risk perception and behavior, sexual practices, condom use, and health and sociodemographic characteristics.

Seven focus groups were also convened, four with elderly people (two all male, one all female, and one mixed) and the remaining three composed of sex workers. Both the interviews and the focus groups were held in community centers or organizations conveniently accessible to the participants.

Samples of food, hygiene products, and condoms were issued to all participants, and sex workers received $20 in recompense for attending the interviews and group activities.

# Results

## Elderly Males

The age range of the elderly male was sixty to ninety-three years, 37 percent being between sixty to seventy years, 35 percent between seventy-one to eighty years, 28 percent between eighty-one and ninety-three. Marital status enquiries revealed that 35 percent were married or living with a person and 65 percent were single, widowed, divorced, or separated. The majority reported a monthly income of $600 or less and cited Social Security and food stamps as their main source of income.

When asked about with whom they had sexual relations, 93 percent said women, 5 percent said other men, and 2 percent reported both. Seventy-two percent reported being very satisfied with their sexual relationships. Of the total, 68 percent referred to their spouse or girlfriend as their sexual partner, the remainder indicated sex workers, drug users, and casual partners whom they met in public places.

Thirty-nine percent reported having paid for or given drugs or gifts in exchange for sexual services during their lifetime and, of these, 50 percent reported having had sexual relations during the previous year. Of those who paid for sexual services during the previous year, 63 percent reported having had relations with a sex worker during the preceding month.

When asked about frequency of sexual relations, 61 percent of those who employed the services of sex workers reported a frequency of one or more instances per week.

When questioned about when they would seek sexual services, 34 percent stated that they would do so on any day, while 24 percent did so at the beginning of the month ("social security syndrome").

When asked why they paid for sexual favors, 47 percent indicated pleasure, 16 percent sexual necessity, and 11 percent the desire for a woman without having an established sexual partner.

It was revealed that the main point of contact between elderly males and sex workers was the street, but full details are given in table 1.

**Table 1: Contact Points between Elderly Males and Sex Workers**

| Location | Percentage |
|---|---|
| Street | 26 |
| Brothel | 18 |
| Sex worker's residence | 16 |
| Bars | 16 |
| Client's residence | 8 |
| Hotels | 5 |
| Others | 11 |

The majority (84 percent) paid for services in cash, but other items, such as clothes, drugs, and food were also exchanged for sexual favors. Prices paid ranged from $6 to $30.

Among the sexual practices most frequently requested by this group were penis-vagina penetration (66 percent), oral sex (18 percent), and sexual play

(8 percent). Fifty-eight percent reported never using condoms while only 21 percent used them on all occasions when having sexual relations with sex workers.

Attitude and behavior regarding preventive measures to avoid HIV infection was also examined in an HIV Prevention Need Assessment Study conducted by the Puerto Rico Department of Health in 1996. When asked about penis-vagina sexual relationships occurring during the preceding six months, 87.5 percent of men over sixty years of age reported engaging in them without the use of a condom.

Among all the different age groups interviewed in that study, the elderly males were the most reluctant to use condoms "because it diminishes sexual pleasure" (173).

## Sex Workers

The sociodemographic data of this group is presented in table 2. The age range varies from eighteen to forty-eight years, with 42 percent falling in the thirty-one- to forty-one-years-old bracket. Only 20 percent of the group were married or living with a person, 16 percent were separated, and the remainder were single, widowed or divorced. One-third (30 percent) had completed high school and 21 percent had undertaken university studies to undergraduate or graduate level. Seventy-four percent of the group had children, and although overall these ranged in number from one to ten children, 55 percent reported having only two or three.

The majority (96 percent) indicated sex work as their main source of income, while 4 percent reported being the owner of a "shooting gallery" or drug point. Other sources of income were food stamps, family, church, and alimony. When asked about monthly income, 56 percent reported receiving between $200 and $800 (see table 3).

Questions regarding the number of clients entertained per day understandably revealed the difference between "the good days and the bad days." A "good" day would provide between one and twenty clients, although 49 percent cited one to five as the norm. "Bad" days were variously defined as having zero to thirteen clients, with 45 percent quoting figures between zero and two. It was also revealed that clients in general favored the weekends for seeking sexual services (76 percent), whereas elderly males tended to do so on the days on which they received their Social Security checks.

Analysis was then made regarding the difference in practice when the sex workers had sexual relations with their partners as compared to similar instances with their clients. These data include their perceived degree of success in persuading the male to use a condom, actual condom use, source of condom supply, and degree of sexual satisfaction attained.

**Table 2: Sociodemographic Characteristics of Sex Workers**

| Variable | Percent |
|---|---|
| **Age (years)** | |
| 18–20 | 11 |
| 21–30 | 35 |
| 31–40 | 42 |
| 41–48 | 12 |
| **Marital Status** | |
| Married/Consensual union | 20 |
| Separated | 16 |
| Single | 31 |
| Divorced | 22 |
| Widow | 12 |
| **Education** | |
| Elementary | 14 |
| Junior high | 33 |
| High school | 30 |
| University | 16 |
| Graduate | 5 |
| Never in school | 2 |
| **Children** | |
| Yes | 74 |
| No | 26 |
| **Number of Children** | |
| One | 12 |
| Two | 33 |
| Three | 22 |
| Four | 14 |
| Five | 7 |
| Six | 3 |
| Seven | 3 |
| Eight | 3 |
| Ten | 3 |

### Table 3: Monthly Income of Sex Workers

| Income | Percent |
|---|---|
| $60 | 2 |
| $200–$400 | 21 |
| $500–$800 | 35 |
| $1,000–$1,500 | 20 |
| $2,000–$2,400 | 16 |
| $2,500–$2,800 | 4 |
| $5,000 | 2 |

Table 4 reveals that in cases where the sex worker was always the one to decide condom use, they insisted on doing so in 75 percent of instances with clients but in only 20 percent of instances with their partners.

### Table 4: Who Initiates Sexual Relations and Decides Type of Practices and Condom Use

| | Who initiates sexual relations? | Who decides sexual practice? | Who decides condom use? | |
|---|---|---|---|---|
| | % Partner | % Partner | % Partner | % General Client |
| Male always | 28 | 15 | 2 | 4 |
| Male mostly | 7 | 6 | 2 | 3 |
| Both | 49 | 64 | 33 | 9 |
| Female mostly | 7 | 6 | 2 | 9 |
| Female always | 2 | 7 | 20 | 75 |
| Nobody talks | 7 | 2 | 41 | – |

When studying the use of the condom in vaginal relations (see table 5), we find that 51 percent never used it with their partners, whereas 87 percent always used it with clients in general, and in 76 percent of instances with elderly clients. Only 11 percent reported never using them with this latter group.

### Table 5: Reported Condom Use in Penis-Vagina Relations

| | % Partner | % General Client | % Elderly Client* |
|---|---|---|---|
| Always | 39 | 87 | 76 |
| Mostly | 2 | 7 | 7 |
| Sometimes | 8 | – | 4 |
| Almost never | – | – | 2 |
| Never | 51 | 6 | 11 |

*Refers to condom use in general sexual relations, not specifically penis-vaginal.

Enquiries about who obtained the condoms and from where again revealed differences between partners and clients. Where the female was always the condom provider, she actually did so in 81 percent of instances with clients, but in only 34 percent of instances with her partner (table 6). The pharmacy was the preferred source for obtaining condoms for 39 percent of sex workers and 91 percent of elderly males (table 7).

**Table 6: Who Obtains the Condoms**

%

|  | Partner | Client |
|---|---|---|
| Male always | 6 | 4 |
| Both | 18 | 16 |
| Female always | 34 | 80 |
| Condom not used | 42 | – |

**Table 7: Sources of Condom Supply**

%

| Sources | Sex Workers | Elderly Males |
|---|---|---|
| Pharmacy | 39 | 91 |
| Kamaria (community-based organization) | 19 | – |
| Health clinic | 7 | 6 |
| Gasoline station | 5 | – |
| Food store | 4 | – |
| Physician | 2 | – |
| Other (friends, clients, etc.) | 24 | 3 |

Table 8 reveals the sex workers' perception of their degree of success in attaining an acceptable level of condom use by both their partners and their clients.

**Table 8: Perception of Degree of Success in Persuading Partner/Client to Use a Condom**

%

|  | Partner | General Client |
|---|---|---|
| High | 58 | 75 |
| Satisfactory | 7 | 9 |
| Average | 11 | 12 |
| Little | 4 | 4 |
| None | 20 | – |

The next aspect to be considered was the degree of sexual satisfaction enjoyed by the sex workers themselves and, as table 9 indicates, there were again differences between partner and client relationships. Seventy-six percent of sex workers reported being satisfied or very satisfied by their partners but only 30 percent obtained such a level of satisfaction with clients in general, this falling to 29 percent in case of elderly clients. The small difference between general and elderly clients is worthy of note.

### Table 9: Satisfaction Achieved in Sexual Relations

|  | With Partner | With General Client | With Elderly Client |
|---|---|---|---|
|  | % | % | % |
| Very satisfied | 36 | 12 | 7 |
| Satisfied | 40 | 18 | 22 |
| Average | 19 | 32 | 32 |
| Unsatisfied | 3 | 18 | 17 |
| Very unsatisfied | 2 | 20 | 22 |

When asked about the sexual capabilities of their elderly clients, 74 percent confirmed finding adequate sexual function, while 26 percent had experienced problems due to failure to achieve or maintain an erection.

In the focus groups, most sex workers expressed a preference for elderly as opposed to younger males due to the way in which the former treated them, i.e., by showing more kindness, respect, and consideration, and having less expectations. One interviewee stated that "when they see you in the street, they ask you if you have eaten, and they invite you to dinner or give you money, even if they don't do anything." Another advantage was "That they pay well for sexual services." Further quotes included, "They are more free with money"; "They pay more and are not mean"; "They are better off economically and if they don't have the cash, they go and get it." It was further stated that this older age group was cleaner and more careful with their health than younger clients. Also, they were much easier to please and "We have to do less work because they are easier to ejaculate."

The disadvantages of serving this elderly group were that they tended to talk and touch too much, "Like it was a loaf of bread. They love to touch here and there." It was also pointed out that on occasion, they became sexually excited but had difficulty in ejaculating, "becoming aggressive sometimes."

Among the sexual services most sought, masturbation was prominent 92 percent, followed by seeing the sex worker naked (89 percent), oral sex (75 percent), vaginal sex (74 percent), dancing for them (28 percent), and anal sex (21 percent). Other practices mentioned in the focus group were masochism (hitting or being hit), fetishism (use of stockings and clothes), touching or introducing the finger into the male anus, and participating in fantasies.

When asked in the focus groups why they thought these men solicited their sexual services, the women gave as the principal reason the lack of a sexual partner in the case of single men and widowers. In the case of married clients, the causes included refusal of the wife to have sex, loss of interest or desire on the part of the wife after giving birth, a change of routine, or reluctance on the part of the man to ask his wife to indulge in certain practices. One of the participants stated that "Even though they have an active sexual appetite, they respect the woman and dare not ask her to do things." In other cases, the wife was unable to provide satisfaction due to illness or incapacity, and as another participant put it, "Some elderly men say that the menopause makes women dry and they cannot have relations." When asked where they met their elderly clients, 93 percent said on the street and 7 percent by visiting the men's homes.

# Discussion

In the light of these investigations, we must eliminate the belief that elderly males are not active or interested in sexual activity. For those who do not have a regular sex partner, sex workers provide one of the opportunities to indulge in sexual activities and practices. For this reason, it is important that both groups identify sexual risk behaviors—for example lack of condom use—and be encouraged to use preventive measures when having sexual relations.

Designing and providing preventive intervention measures are important for both groups. Some aspects that may be included are education about condom accessibility (money is an important aspect in both groups and buying condoms in the pharmacy can be costly), sexually transmitted disease evaluation (information and testing for all such diseases, not only HIV), family planning, and rehabilitation programs for drug users.

A comprehensive approach must be employed when designing and developing human services for these groups, and guidance regarding living arrangements, employment, food, and medication should be integrated with the other services provided. In Puerto Rico, cultural values and norms ascribed to condom use by the males is one of the main barriers to the prevention of sexually transmitted diseases. Health and behavior professionals should take into consideration these aspects when designing intervention strategy both with the elderly population and with sex workers.

This study revealed that elderly clients established a more regular and personal relationship with sex workers than other clients in general. It must be recognized that these sex workers are possibly the only people who validate their elderly clients as sexual beings, and this may help them to feel more receptive and free to discuss safer sexual alternatives, such as condom use and other nonpenetrative practices. Sex workers can become a possible resource to provide clients and their peers with health promotion and education. We should remember that as in any other service, the better educated the client and provider, the better and more satisfying the experience for both parties. This reasoning should be used to encourage a more pro-active approach by sex workers in the education of their clients.

# References

Alexander, E. A., and A. L. Allison. 1995. Sexuality in older adults. In *Care of the Elderly: Clinical Aspects of Aging*, edited by W. Reichel. Baltimore: Williams & Wilkins.

Centers for Disease Control and Prevention. 1996. HIV/AIDS Surveillance Report. U.S. Department of Health and Human Services. Atlanta, Georgia. December: 8 (2).

Masters, W. H., V. E. Johnson, and R. C. Kolodny. 1992. *Human Sexuality*. New York: HarperCollins.

Puerto Rico Department of Health. 1997. HIV/AIDS Reporting System. Puerto Rico AIDS Surveillance Report, 28 August.

————. 1996. HIV Prevention Needs Assessment Puerto Rico, 1996. Complete Report. Puerto Rico Department of Health and Puerto Rico's Community Planning Group.

Whipple, B., and K. W. Saura. 1995. The overlooked epidemic: HIV in older adults. *American Journal of Nursing* 96 (2): 23–28.

# BEING A JOHN
## HUGH GENE LOEBNER


## Being a John Is Being Normal

I pay for sex because that is the only way I can get sex. I am not ashamed of paying for sex. I pay for food. I pay for clothing. I pay for shelter. Why should I not also pay for sex? Paying for sex does not diminish the pleasure I derive from it. I am proud that I can afford to pay for as much sex as I need. Indeed, I sometimes pay more than asked or expected.

I have ongoing relationships with two wonderful women. One I have been seeing for over two years, and the other for almost a year. My relationships with them are boringly mundane. In addition to engaging in sex, we frequently go out for dinner and engage in a variety of social activities. I consider them girlfriends, but I know that the only reason they have sex with me is because I pay them, and from time to time I pay for "one-night stands."

My paying for sex is nothing new. Prostitution *is* the oldest profession. Indeed, prostitution is observed in chimpanzees. A significant part of a chimp's diet is monkey meat. Let me quote an excerpt from the *New York Times*, June 27, 1995. It regards chimpanzees, monkey hunting, and chimpanzee sex workers:

> As early as the 1960s, Dr. Geza Teleki, an American primatologist, said after observing male chimpanzees swap meat for sex with females that nutrition was only one of several reasons chimpanzees ate flesh.
>
> Dr. Stanford builds on this finding, saying that male chimpanzees often hunt as a way to finance their sexual barter when traveling with sexually receptive females. And the more such receptive females are present, the more likely a group of chimpanzees will hunt.

Time after time, Dr. Stanford documented how male chimpanzees dangle a dead red colobus monkey in front of a sexually swollen female, sharing only after first mating. He said that human sexual relationships could have been just as material-based.

"When chimps arrive at a tree holding meat on the hoof, the male chimps seem to have an awareness that, 'Well if I get meat I will maybe get more copulations because the females will come running over once I get a carcass," Dr. Stanford said.

Female chimpanzees are sexually promiscuous, with or without meat, copulating with more than a dozen males each day. But Dr. Stanford believes the attraction of flesh, consumption of which is shown by Dr. McGrew to be linked to the survival of offspring, could give lower-ranking males a better chance at matings; or that it could be "the difference between getting lots of sex and getting lots and lots of sex."

I'm nothing but a successful chimpanzee with three hundred pieces of monkey meat.

# Being Out of the Closet

I am a self-admitted client of prostitutes. I proclaim this without shame or fear.

## Why I Came Out of the Closet

I sponsor the Loebner Prize, a contest in computer artificial intelligence. It is a Turing test, named after Alan Turing, the brilliant English mathematician who laid the foundations of computing theory. In 1950 he described a test for computer intelligence which now bears his name. In 1952 Alan Turing was arrested for homosexual behavior. In 1954 he committed suicide, presumably out of despair at the oppression against gays and his mistaken belief that it would be impossible to end that oppression. Thus, the life of one of our greatest geniuses, a man who was instrumental in winning World War II with his work in deciphering the German Enigma machine, the device that encoded the most secret Nazi war communications, was lost to sexual oppression.

When Rudolph Giuliani became mayor of New York, he instituted a crackdown on prostitutes and johns as part of a so-called quality of life program. Whose quality of life, I wonder? I live in New York City. My knowledge of Turing's martyrdom because of oppression of his sexual preferences gave me the courage to make public, in a letter published in the *New York Times*, my anger based on oppression of my sexual behavior—consorting with sex workers. I have never regretted my decision to write that letter.

# What Are the Consequences of My Candor?

## Benefits

One benefit of my candor has been the opportunity to appear on television and radio and in print. I have been on *20/20, Oprah, Geraldo, Maury Povich, Susan Powter, Charlie Perez, The O'Reilly Report,* the *Cochrane and Grace Show* on Court TV, and others whose names I cannot remember. I have been written up in *New York Newsday, Time Out New York, The Village Voice,* and the *Insider.* Others may not consider these as benefits, but you must remember that my telephone number is 1-500-EGO-TRIP.

A second benefit is an absolute lack of fear of arrest. This is not courage. It is that I cannot be shamed by an arrest.

## Penalties

One penalty for my candor is a certain reluctance of one of my sex worker friends to be seen with me in some social settings. Had I remained in the closet, the nature of our relationship would have been ambiguous, and she would be more willing to be seen with me in those settings.

Another potential downside is the possible impact of my notoriety on the Loebner Prize.

# What Are the Ethical Considerations of Paying for Sex?

## Prostitution Is Not "Exploitive"

Prostitution is no more exploitive than any other occupation. I pay sex workers more for a one-hour session than I pay the men I employ in my business for a week's work. *Who* is being exploited?

One of the sex workers I see has a boyfriend with whom she has sex for free. I have the same physical desires that her boyfriend has, yet I must pay. *Who* is being exploited?

## Prostitution Is Not "Degrading"

According to the *American Heritage Dictionary*, to degrade is (1) to reduce in grade, rank, or status; demote; or (2) to lower in dignity; dishonor or disgrace. Degradation is entirely a mental construct. If people consider prostitution as degrading then it is degrading, but *only* because it is defined to be so. There is nothing intrinsically degrading about prostitution.

Consider the prostitute. She (or he) is an object of sexual desire. The fact that her or his client is willing to pay money in exchange for sex is objective, quantifiable evidence of that sex appeal. Among the shortcomings of my existence is the fact that I am no longer an object of sexual desire for those whom I desire. I was never as sexually attractive as I would have wished.

Let us examine the notion that prostitution is "evil because it is the result of childhood sexual abuse." Some opponents of prostitution label it as evil because (they claim) people become prostitutes as a result of childhood sexual abuse. I do not think this is the case. But even if it were true, it would still be logical nonsense. The fact that an evil produces a consequence does not imply that the consequence is evil.

Consider wheelchair basketball games for paralyzed Vietnam war veterans. We all agree that having one's spinal cord destroyed in the Vietnam war is evil. The reason that paralyzed Vietnam veterans play wheelchair basketball is because they were paralyzed in Vietnam. That does not make wheelchair basketball evil.

# Being a John Means Being in Hell

We are oppressed, we sex workers, sex clients, and facilitators of commercial sex. We are arrested, fined, imprisoned; our cars and buildings are confiscated; our names and reputations are besmirched; we are outcasts and pariahs. Consider Robin Marie Head, currently in a Texas prison for the offense of "engaging in organized criminal activity." Her *criminal act* (as stated in the indictment) was that:

> on or about between the dates of June 15, 1992, and September 15, 1993, [she] did then and there unlawfully, with the intent to establish, maintain, and participate in a combination or in the profits of a combination consisting of three or more persons, did then and there knowingly own, control, supervise and manage a prostitution enterprise that used at least two prostitutes.

This is the relevant excerpt from the transcript of her sentencing:

> THE COURT: Robin Marie Head, on your plea of guilty and the evidence introduced herein, the Court finds you guilty of the offense of Engaging in Organized Criminal Activity and assesses your punishment at 10 years confinement in the Texas Department of Corrections. Do you have anything to say before sentence of the law is pronounced against you?

THE DEFENDANT: No, sir.

THE COURT: Having nothing to say, it is the order of the Court that you, Robin Marie Head, who has been adjudged guilty of the offense of Engaging in Organized Criminal Activity, and whose punishment has been assessed at 10 years confinement in the Texas Department of Corrections, be delivered by the Sheriff of Harris County, Texas, to the Director of the Texas Department of Corrections or anyone else legally authorized to accept such convicts, where you shall be confined for a period of 10 years, in accordance with the laws governing the Texas Department of Corrections.

That sentence, that injustice, that monstrous judicial malignancy was pronounced by Judge Michael T. McSpadden.

# Being a John Means Being a Social Activist

Gays and lesbians were once victims of oppression. They, too, suffered opprobrium for engaging, with other consenting adults, in sexual conduct that was declared "deviant." However, by standing up for their rights, by rioting at the Stonewall, by speaking, nay shouting out, they earned their freedom.

Now it is our turn.

We millions (for we are indeed millions) must show the world that we *shall* have our freedom. We must become visible.

The Manifesto of Sexual Freedom proclaims June 9 as End Sexual Oppression Day. It calls for all those who agree with the principles of the manifesto to demonstrate at noon in front of city halls across the nation.

Last year, on June 9, 1996, the first demonstrations were held. They will be held again this year and every year until we are free. I call upon you at this conference to join those of us who demonstrated last year in this year's demonstrations. The price is but one hour of your time. That hour is down payment on your freedom and freedom for those like Robin Head who are rotting in jail.

We *must* demonstrate. How can I motivate you? I have no carrot with which to entice you but our freedom. I carry no stick with which to compel you but our oppression. *Our* freedom is up to *us*.

# 4

# Rent Boys, Hustlers, and She-Males

## Introduction

In the last section we indicated that the patrons of female prostitutes had been more or less ignored, but this has also been the case of the male prostitute. Again this is hard to explain because male prostitution has as old a history as female prostitution. Traditionally, male prostitution is associated with homosexuality, but clients also include large numbers of men who identify themselves as heterosexuals, which only serves to emphasize that sexual labeling is not as simple as many would want it to be. There are four papers in this section. D. J. West, an English scholar who as a pioneer investigator of male prostitution, provides an overall view of male homosexual prostitution in England. Also from England is Michael P. Knox, who examines the negotiations of male sex workers and their clients in Liverpool. One aspect of male prostitution is what Dwight and Joan Dixon have called she-males, males who dress and act as women and who earn their living by selling their sexual services. Unlike the prostitutes who serve the gay community primarily, the she-males have significant number of customers who identify themselves as heterosexual.

Although male and female prostitutes share many of the same problems, there have not been very many comparative studies between the two. Jacqueline Boles and Kirk Elifson attempt to remedy this situation by pointing out how difficult it is not only to organize male prostitutes themselves, but also to get the kind of public support that COYOTE and some of the other female sex worker groups often have.

227

# MALE HOMOSEXUAL PROSTITUTION IN ENGLAND

## D. J. WEST

These comments are mainly based on a study of male prostitutes that the author conducted when chairman of the charity Streetwise Youth, an organization set up in West London to befriend young male street prostitutes (West 1993). The word "homosexual" is in the title because most male prostitution, at least at street level, is directed toward male customers for gay sex. The nature of the male homosexual sex trade and the workers engaged in it differ in some important respects from their female counterparts. Because heterosexuals are in the majority, female prostitutes are more numerous than males and they are more visible and more often written about. Female red-light districts and organized brothels are to be found functioning more or less openly in many parts of the world. The clients of prostitutes, both heterosexual and homosexual, are nearly all males, although this may be changing as women are allowed to assert equal rights. I have recently seen for the first time in the British press reference to the alleged prevalence of lesbian prostitution.

Male homosexual behavior is against the law of many countries and considered morally wrong by large sections of the population even in countries where it is not actually illegal. Although male homosexual prostitution is considered by many to be particularly reprehensible, it is a worldwide phenomenon and apparently always has been. In London, England, for example, there were gay resorts and brothels called Molly houses in the eighteenth century. The scandals of Oscar Wilde and his stable lads and the Cleveland Street gay brothel show the tradition continuing through the nineteenth century.

# Law

The law in England is peculiar in its approach to prostitution. It treats heterosexual and homosexual prostitution somewhat differently. In theory, it is no crime to sell or to buy sex; but to advertise the facility, or for a third party to profit from it, or anyone to facilitate or manage another person's prostitution activity is a crime. For example, a female prostitute's husband or live-in boyfriend is at risk of being prosecuted for the imprisonable offense of "living on immoral earnings." He doesn't have to depend on her earnings: so long as he gets some benefit from it he can be convicted. Prostitutes complain about this because they say it prevents them from having a family life for fear their partner will be imprisoned. They also fear for their children because, under the Children's Act, Social Services can remove children thought to be "exposed to moral danger."

People who benefit indirectly from prostitution, such as cabdrivers who regularly conduct foreign visitors from their hotels to a prostitute's flat, can also be charged under the immoral earnings provision. The owners or legal tenants of premises where a prostitute works can also be prosecuted if they knowingly allow the activity to go on there. Landlords who let premises—often at inflated rents—knowing what they will be used for can also be charged. If the prostitute operates from the same house or flat as one or more other prostitutes the premises count as a brothel, and managing or keeping a brothel is a crime. Businesses that provide covert sexual services on the premises under the guise of massage are defined as brothels. Owners or managers of sexual massage parlors are not infrequently subject to prosecution. During the period of my survey, one such massage parlor for homosexual men, situated in a wealthy residential quarter of West London and run by a Thai gentleman who provided customers with attractive young Orientals, was convicted and fined, but that did not put an end to the business.

Although these laws apply equally to homosexual and heterosexual prostitution, in practice some of them affect male and female workers differently. For example, the immoral earnings law affects women sex workers in particular, because they are much more likely than male prostitutes to have a male pimp or manager who takes part of their earnings in return for introductions, for protection from violence, or simply for being their regular lover. Male prostitutes, unless they are very young boys, generally act independently and have no pimp. Even if their earnings go toward the support of girlfriends they are seemingly not prosecuted, although sometimes the homosexual lovers of a male prostitute have been prosecuted for benefiting from immoral earnings.

Prostitutes who solicit prospective customers in public places by verbal propositions (or even by body language) commit an offense, but in this regard the law differs for males and females. Females must have had at least two previous recorded police cautions before they can be prosecuted for soliciting as a "common prostitute." They can be fined but not imprisoned on this charge, although many do end up in prison for nonpayment of the fine. A man cannot be charged as a common prostitute, but he can be charged with persistently importuning male persons for immoral purposes. Approaches to two different persons suffice to fulfill the criterion of "persistence" and the offense is imprisonable. Moreover, such solicitation does not need to be for prostitution; invitations to unpaid homosexual activity count as an "immoral purpose."

Prosecutions for importuning by males have decreased. They used to be more common when young policemen, out of uniform and dressed provocatively, would hang around gay cruising areas or male toilets waiting to be importuned. As a means of controlling male street prostitution it is not much used, partly, I think, because male street prostitutes stand out less blatantly than their female counterparts and partly because police prefer to use charges without a sexual label, which are less likely to be challenged. "Behavior liable to cause a breach of the peace" is one useful catchall. Local bylaws, such as loitering in railway stations without a ticket, can also be used. Highway obstruction was a favorite of the London police during my survey. The clients wanting sex who approach rent boys—the equivalent of American hustlers—are also, at least in theory, guilty of importuning, although in practice it is normally the rent boy who is prosecuted.

The clients of female prostitutes have appeared in the criminal law only recently. The Sexual Offenses Amendment Act 1985 made it an offense for a man persistently to solicit women on the street for purposes of obtaining sex for payment. The same act introduced the curious offense of "kerb crawling." It is an offense for a man to solicit women from a car while it is in the street, or to do so while near a car that he has just left. This law is directed against men who drive slowly round the streets where prostitutes operate, soliciting the women from the safety of their cars. Early in the history of this new offense, the Director of Public Prosecutions was obliged to resign after being cautioned for driving around the notorious streets beside London's Kings Cross Station—an area that has since been targeted by a local version of zero tolerance.

Since the age of consent in England is sixteen for heterosexual and lesbian acts, but eighteen for male homosexual activity, the sexual performance of male prostitutes aged sixteen or seventeen renders themselves and their clients liable to charges of gross indecency, which is an imprisonable offense, regardless of whether the sex was for payment. If anal intercourse occurs, the maximum sentence for an older partner to the transaction can be severe. Under Section 4 of the Sexual Offenses Act 1967, it is an offense to procure (that is to say, to introduce) one man to another so they can commit buggery, even though the couple who commit the act may not themselves be breaking the law.

# Pedophiles

One reason for the condemnation of male prostitution is its supposed links with pedophilia. The involvement of children in sexual acts has become the most demonized of crimes. Child prostitution is certainly to be deplored, but there is no evidence that young boys are at greater risk of being recruited to it than young girls. The female age of consent was fixed at sixteen in England a century ago as a result of so many parents selling girls as young as twelve or thirteen into prostitution. Boys were expected to bring home money by other means. Society seems to have been always less concerned with protecting young boys from sexual encounters; they are allowed more freedom to roam the streets and so runaway boys are less conspicuous. The opportunities for young boys to be befriended and then seduced by pedophiles, or to learn for themselves how to make money that way, undoubtedly exist, although probably not on the scale the sensationalist tabloid press in Britain would lead one to suppose. Most of the rent boys working from the streets in London are sixteen and over, that is to say beyond the legally permitted school-leaving age. However, in some Third World countries with a substantial impoverished underclass, it would seem that many hard-up parents are not too troubled if their children, while still in their early teens, are able to bring back money by selling sex.

In Muslim countries, where girls are strictly sequestered for fear of pregnancy and becoming unmarriageable, boys are more available. A recent television documentary shown on the BBC (British Broadcasting Company) about child prostitution in Sri Lanka showed young boys playing on the beaches and being offered as sex objects to rich male foreigners. The girls were nowhere in evidence. One might get the impression from such a spectacle that prostitution for pedophiles centers on boys, but where both boys and girls are available (as has traditionally been the case in Thailand, for example) the heterosexual prostitution trade also has its pedophile section.

# Advertisements

The days are long gone when female prostitutes used to advertise by offering "French Lessons," which customers were not expected to take literally. Models, masseurs, and escorts are the modern euphemisms. Exactly what laws would be broken by using plain English is unclear, since the common law of England surrounding indecency, public outrage, public nuisance, and the like is so all-embracing that the authorities would be hard put to choose which to apply. There was a celebrated prosecution of the publisher of a book entitled *The Ladies' Directory* under a common-law provision called Conspiracy to Corrupt

Public Morals. In recent times, the magazines in which adverts appear, the illustrations that sometimes accompany them, and the phraseology employed leave the customer in little doubt that the advertisements are for call girls. Notices also appear in some shop windows and, in London, telephone kiosks are favorite places for advertisements. British Telecom (BT) keeps removing them and threatens to disconnect the phone numbers, but the notices quickly reappear. Cellular telephones, which are not controlled by BT, are frequently used.

Under the euphemistic headings of masseurs or escorts, advertisements for male prostitutes appear quite blatantly in specialized newspapers of limited circulation, financed by ads and distributed free at gay bars and other gay venues. Since the so-called escorts often put "in/out" on their ads, meaning they are prepared to receive as well as to visit clients, it is obvious they are not really escorts. In some of these papers the advertisements include nude photographs and genital displays, which could scarcely be more explicit. Furthermore, a proportion of them includes offers of CP (corporal punishment), C&BT (genital torture), "bondage" and "playroom" or "dungeon," all designed for clients wanting sadomasochistic titillation. The postcard ads found in telephone boxes and elsewhere are all for female heterosexual prostitution.

# Street Workers

In London, there is a big difference between the street workers, known as rent boys, and the usually more mature sex workers who operate from their own accommodation, using telephones and advertising in the gay press as masseurs to attract clients. The street boys hang around certain well-known areas, such as the concourses of railway terminals. Many of them have no settled accommodation and are often dependent on finding a client in order to secure a bed for at least part of the night. They are generally young—late teens or early twenties. Many are delinquents on the run, wanted by the police for skipping bail or nonpayment of fines. Most come from broken or unhappy homes and a high proportion have spent much of their childhood under the care of the Social Services, from which they have either run away or been discharged without benefit of any settled home or work. For them, prostitution is a means of survival. Usually they have no legitimate income. Jobs for poorly educated young men are very scarce in England and there is no state benefit for those under eighteen. They are supposed to be living at home, supported by parents or in government training programs. The rent boys tend to be too undisciplined to fit into such schemes, or too unwilling to take part for the meager amount of money they provide.

The rent boys profess to despise their clients (whom they call punters), but most admit to being homosexual themselves, otherwise they would probably be surviving by the more usual means of theft, burglary, or drug dealing. Some do indulge in these activities as well, but prostitution is the main source of income for most of them. In spite of what they sometimes say about punters, rent boys are more open than most female street prostitutes to an amount of fraternizing with customers. To some extent this is forced upon them. Having no place of their own to take a client, they are ready to accompany him to his own place where, along with sex, there is likely to be drink—if not drugs—as well as talk and a possible invitation to call again or meet up in a gay bar in preparation for a repeat performance. In this way rent boys can acquire a few regular customers, some of whom become "sugar daddies," older men who help them out with money or even accommodation when they are desperate.

The habit of going back to the client's place opens up possibilities other than sex, such as theft, robbery, or threatening the client with scandal if he does not pay more than the agreed fee, but this does not happen too often. Other rent boys don't like it because it damages the trade. The rent boys in a particular locality tend to know each other, to congregate in the same all-night cafes, to help each other out, to know who steps out of line, and to warn their own clients against such a trouble-maker.

Rent boys are usually younger, stronger, and tougher than their clients, who are generally middle-aged men who run the risk of being beaten up, robbed, and occasionally murdered by criminals posing as prostitutes. Nevertheless, the rent boys also take risks. They can be plied with drink or drugs to the point where they neither know nor care what sort of sex takes place, so that any idea of precautions against AIDS or other sexually transmitted diseases is lost. Instead of the solitary client whom he has agreed to go home with, the rent boy may find several men waiting for his arrival who subject him to multiple rape or sadistic practices. A subsequent complaint to the police by an obvious male prostitute doesn't always receive a sympathetic reception.

Street work is a precarious and short-term career. Although some rent boys boast of being taken on expensive holidays by rich punters, most of their contacts are brief and distasteful efforts to satisfy the sexual demands of unattractive older men who can't find their own unpaid partners. The boys' own ability to attract customers diminishes rapidly with increasing age. Having no settled address and nowhere to bank money, and being hooked on drink, drugs, and homosexual nightlife, their earnings, though often far in excess of what they could get in unskilled work, are quickly spent. Since their earnings fluctuate and are unpredictable, the boys are often broke. Risk of AIDS apart, their lifestyle is unhealthy, meals are irregular, and ailments are neglected because they are not registered with any National Health Service doctor. In the course of the research a number of former rent boys we interviewed had become alcoholics and social derelicts. Others no doubt gravitated to straightforward crime as their sexual attractiveness diminished. The longer they remain dependent on prostitution, the harder it is to get back into the legitimate labor market.

## "Masseurs"—Call Boys

Call boys, advertising themselves as masseurs, are better organized and much better off than the street workers. Most were living in reasonable comfort and using part of their own accommodation to receive clients. They were officially in the self-employed business of massage, some being duly registered, accepting clients' fees by credit card, paying taxes, and even taking out mortgages. Virtually all were themselves homosexuals who had freely chosen this line of work rather than, like the street boys, being forced into it by circumstances. Unlike the street workers, they did not often come from socially deprived or problem families and their educational level was higher. Some of them had had experience in other employments, but found what they were now doing more profitable. Some were sex workers only during free time from other work. They tended to distance themselves from rent boys, looking upon street workers as feckless dropouts and delinquents. Many were devotees of gyms and keep-fit establishments and seemed able to remain attractive to clients to ages beyond that of the street workers. Those who specialized in sadomasochistic sex play—some well into middle age—had expensive collections of leather, slings, and other apparatus.

Being in better control of their lives and their clients, they were less exposed to risks. They were not going to be arrested for importuning. Since their first contact with a prospective new customer was by telephone, they did not need to give their address immediately, but decided on the basis of preliminary conversation whether to offer a service. As a further precaution against time wasters, before giving an exact address, they would usually indicate the area where the client was to come and ask him to ring again on arrival. As a check on the seriousness and stability of a new client, some masseurs would use a permanently switched-on answering machine instructing callers to leave their own number and expect a call back.

Although they generally socialized freely in the gay community, some of these workers kept their occupation undisclosed save to a few intimates. Some complained that the work interfered with their own personal sex life, either because they had had enough of sex after dealing with a succession of clients, or because their living arrangements were not suited to a live-in lover. Nevertheless, a few were sharing space with a partner who was offering the same service.

## Clients

Gay men have more reasons than to use prostitutes heterosexuals. It is still the case that many predominantly homosexual men are in unsatisfying heterosexual marriages that may have been contracted to keep up appearances. For them, a secret, paid sex session with no social commitment is less disruptive than a lover on the side. Sex for its own sake, as opposed to sex in the context of an ongoing relationship, is a prominent feature of male homosexuality in our society. Indeed, it used to be a tenet of gay liberation that homosexuals should not be bound by heterosexual ideals of monogamy and family. In a subculture that revolves around youthful attractiveness and values sex without commitment, the promiscuously inclined male can find it increasingly difficult to secure partners as he grows older. The paid sex trade therefore flourishes. More often than in the female prostitution scene, an initially impersonal contact between client and prostitute becomes an ongoing relationship of mutual dependency, material on the part of the rent boy, emotional on the part of his older patron.

## Sex Abuse

These days it is fashionable to attribute almost any problem to having experienced sex abuse in childhood. A minority of the street workers did recall having been coerced into homosexual activity when they were under fourteen, sometimes by outsiders, sometimes by household members or members of staff or fellow occupants of children's homes. None of them connected these experiences with either becoming homosexual or becoming prostitutes. Usually their abusive experiences were part of a wider context of childhood neglect or conflict-ridden parental homes.

## Conclusion

The most striking finding of the survey was the contrast between the socially deprived street workers who presented a multiplicity of personal and social problems—classic representatives of the image of prostitution for sheer survival—and the more independent and socially assured workers operating in private from stable accommodation. This was confirmation, if any were needed, of the fallacy of generalizing about the characteristics and motivations of sex workers.

## Reference

West, D.J., with B. DeVilliers. 1993. *Homosexual Prostitution*. Binghamton, N.Y.: Haworth Press.

# NEGOTIATIONS AND RELATIONSHIPS AMONG MALE SEX WORKERS AND CLIENTS IN LIVERPOOL, MERSEYSIDE, UNITED KINGDOM

## MICHAEL P. KNOX

This chapter is an exploration of some of the themes associated with negotiations and relationships among male sex workers and their clients. Kinsey et al. in the late 1940s defined males who engage in prostitution as those "who provide sexual favors for other males in exchange for money" (Kinsey et al. 1948, cited by Allen 1980, 1).

The definition requires expansion for the purposes of this chapter because the exchange of sexual favors can be for other rewards that may or not include money. The other rewards could be temporary accommodation, consumer goods and male affection, or care and attention.

Males involved in prostitution are commonly referred to as "rent boys," "hustlers" (in the American texts), "call men," and by a host of variations. However, the term "sex worker" is preferred as it is general, does not infer stereotyping, and is nonpejorative. The term also serves to link workers in the sex industry collectively, be they street workers or off-street workers, escorts, and masseurs (Barrett 1995).

Clients of male sex workers are referred to as those male adults who reward male workers financially or otherwise for engagement in sexual encounters with themselves. They are generally reported in the literature as being middle-aged married men who are covert in their homosexual behavior (Bennetto 1994; Bloor, McKeganey, and Barnard 1990; Cory and LeRoy 1963).

Male sex workers have not been studied or publicized as extensively as female sex workers, although it has been reported that there are probably equal numbers of male sex workers as there are female workers. However, the position of male sex work in society is more hidden from view than its female counterpart (Kinsey et al. 1948, cited by Allen 1980). A survey of the cumulative medical index for the ten-year period (1970–1980) indicated that only

236

10 percent of over one hundred papers published on prostitution related to males (Allen 1980). The studies conducted are generally limited to the street worker, research tending to fail to recognize the inherent diversity that characterizes the male sex work population (Weisberg 1985).

Prostitution does not rest comfortably in society. It is an emotionally charged subject that is stigmatized. In the context of male prostitution there is an added stigma toward homosexual activity and homosexual relationships between males of non-same generations. There is strong denial in society regarding the existence of male sex work, although the media does cover it, reporting on it in a scandalous and sensational manner.

# Literature Review

## Negotiations and Contracts

Within the literature there appear to be limited reports on how male sex workers conduct negotiations with clients. The classic studies of male prostitution conducted in the 1960s and 1970s are studies of young male prostitution: boy prostitution. Negotiations between workers and clients were reported as either being conducted by procurers of young male workers or by workers themselves who negotiated their sexual services with clients which were in accord with the prescribed norms of their subcultural peer groups.

The role of the procurer in the early studies was largely seen as the young worker's protector: a man who would negotiate the sexual services on behalf of the youth with an adult male. This form of prostitution was child exploitation and existed in many major cities of the world (Davidson 1970; Drew and Drake 1969; Lloyd 1979).

Within the early studies on male prostitution the majority of workers were reported to be heterosexual and their reasons for engagement in sex work were largely associated with financial hardship, involvement with risk-taking, and illicit behavior, which involved sex work (Ginsburg 1967; Harris 1973; Jersild 1956; Lloyd 1979; Reiss 1961). MacNamara's (1965) research study contrasted with the contemporary studies conducted at that time with regard to sexual orientation, citing that the majority of male sex workers in his research study identified as homosexual. What was reported in these early studies was how the heterosexual street workers negotiated their sexual services with clients. The street workers who operated within the peer subcultural groups adhered to the prescribed norms of their groups, especially with regard to the sexual activities engaged in with clients that helped to retain their heterosexuality and masculinity. Violating the prescribed group norms or developing an emotional relationship with their clients would question their heterosexuality and imply homosexuality. Moreover, the workers' group norms were understood by the clients and were largely respected.

What is then negotiated between worker and client is that the worker will for a given fee engage in those sexual activities that safeguard his perceived heterosexuality and masculinity. These early studies demonstrate how stigmatized homosexuality was within society at that time and this could account for the fact that the majority of sex workers identified themselves as heterosexual. However, recognition is also given to the fact that the majority of these workers were adolescent at time of interview, and a firm sexual preference may not have been established for these adolescent males. Moreover, a reluctance to discuss homosexuality within this period could account for it being denied by both researcher and subject (Boyer 1989).

However, other than a recognition of betrayal and ostracism from the peer group itself, what is not explored in these early studies is what happens when workers involve themselves in sexual activities that violate the prescribed norms. It is suggested that involvement in these "taboo" sexual activities created ambivalent feelings in workers with regard to their concerns of homosexuality. This in turn helps us to understand today why sexual negotiations among workers and clients are not totally explicit. Perhaps they are tentatively constructed because of the negative associations with homosexuality.

Thus, forging contracts and negotiations between workers and clients operates in the same manner as it does for men who have sex with men and who negotiate their sexual encounters in the public setting. This form of negotiation lies within the realm of nonverbal communication (Corzine and Kirkby 1977; Desroches 1989; Hoffman 1972; Humphreys 1970). "Cruising" is the general term applied when males negotiate sexual contact with other males, whether in the public park, public toilet, gay bar, street, or sauna. It is a subtle language spoken with gestures and actions (Lee 1978). Hoffman (1968) reports that a large part of "cruising" among men who have sex with men is done with the eyes by means of heavy stares of a prolonged nature and through the surveying of the other male's entire body. The silent cues and significations used among cruisers have to have a shared social meaning for any mutual interaction to develop (Delph 1978). A reasoning behind silences in these sexual encounters is thought to be attributed to the pervasiveness of the public nature of the settings. Silence safeguards the individuals' anonymity. Also, open verbal communication with reference to sexual overtures can be seen as dangerous in the public setting. (Delph 1978). Moreover, these silent forms of communication were largely developed at a time in society when sexual encounters between males were more taboo then they are at present. These forms of communication also exist for male sex workers and clients.

Soliciting occurs in the public setting when the sexual activities between men who have sex with men are negotiated for monetary gain or other reward. And it is recognized that money or the exchange of other rewards can take place within "cruising" and it is then, technically, prostitution.

The negotiations, rules of the game that are known among men who have sex with men in public settings, are deemed somewhat problematic in the context of male sex work. Although recognized as safeguarding anonymity and personal disclosures, etc., their implicit nature does not explicitly identify for the worker or client what sexual activities are being exchanged and for what reward.

The gay bar is a venue where men who engage in sex with other men make negotiations for sexual encounters (Achilles 1967; Cavan 1966; Myres et al. 1991; Stall 1988). Cavan (1966) reported that, other than alcoholic beverages, the commodity most frequently handled in the bar setting is probably sex, either on a commercial or noncommercial basis.

Alcohol use has been associated with the engagement in male homosexual behavior. (Myres et al. 1991; Stall 1988). Sexual negotiations under the influence of alcohol are facilitated by the relationship between alcohol consumption and disinhibition. Thus, alcohol reduces the individual's powers of reason and causes a loss of inhibitions through its pharmacological effect on the central nervous system and its anesthetizing of the higher cortical brain mechanisms that ordinarily control such activities as sexual behavior (Leigh 1990). However, it is also reported that the association between alcohol consumption and disinhibition is a cultural belief rather than a clinical action; the effects of alcohol disinhibition are regarded as socially learned behavior (Room 1983).

Male sex workers and their clients do negotiate sexual encounters in the bar setting (Plant et al. 1989; Rechy 1963, 1977; Westwood 1960). The reasons why workers and clients may conduct their negotiations within the bar may simply be because the bar setting is the only locale where workers and clients of the sex industry congregate. However, it is to be noted for some workers and clients in the sex industry the association between negotiating and engaging in sexual activity and alcohol use may be significant. The disinhibitory effects of alcohol, whether proven or culturally learned, cannot be dismissed in this context. Workers may use their alcohol drinking to assist their negotiating skills with clients; similarly clients may use alcohol to give them the confidence and courage to seek out paid homosexual relations that they may not do when they are sober. For the client or worker who seeks out covert homosexual experiences under the influence of alcohol, this behavior can be explored through the psychological principle of cognitive dissonance, i.e., when there is disparity between the individual's cognitions, thoughts, attitudes and beliefs and behavior that is incompatible with those cognitions (Festinger 1992; Miller 1980). Cognitive dissonance can be seen in this context with both workers and clients who have ambivalent feelings toward homosexual sexual activity exchanged for reward.

The co-mingling of alcohol drinking and negotiating sexual services among male sex workers and their clients has been reported in a Scottish study (Plant, Plant, and Morgan-Thomas 1990). The findings of the study reported that 67 percent of workers acknowledged alcohol drinking (at least sometimes) occurring during the course of their work with clients. This finding suggests that alcohol's disinhibitory effects assists those workers in forging negotiations with clients.

The impact of HIV and AIDS in the early 1980s brought about concern regarding how the sexually active population can adopt safer sexual practices to safeguard themselves from the risk of HIV. Although the early information on HIV brought about panic that the virus's spread would be brought about by those individuals in high-risk groups—principally gay men, prostitutes, and intravenous drug users—as more knowledge and understanding was brought about through HIV research, it began to be recognized in the context of "high-risk activity" as opposed to stigmatizing it among "high-risk groups" (Garfield 1994; King 1993).

The HIV research has implications for male sex work. It questions how workers and clients can protect themselves from HIV in their sexual contacts. The risk of HIV raises issues with regard to how workers and clients negotiate safer sexual practices when very little is known about their negotiations with each other. Also, the little that is known gives an indication that limited verbal communication exists between workers and clients anyway with regard to exchanging sexual practices for rewards.

Male sex workers do not appear to be a group targeted by health education campaigns that encourage the reduction of HIV risks (Barnard, Mc-Keganey, and Bloor 1990). That male sex workers, specifically street workers, lack sufficient HIV information has been reported by a HIV/AIDS worker in London, who found that there was considerable ignorance with regard to correct HIV information among male street workers in London (Gibson 1995).

Given the situation that if male sex workers have insufficient HIV information, does this not conflict with what has been reported on the substantial higher levels of HIV knowledge among gay men (Garfield 1994; King 1993)? However, what is recognized is that male sex workers have little identification within the gay community; generally workers regardless of their sexual orientation are not supported by gay men within the gay community (Fishe 1989, cited by Pheterson 1989; McMillan and Hunter 1992). Therefore, if related HIV information is targeted toward gay men in the gay community, it is not known whether workers have access to it. Moreover, this accessibility is not there for those workers who do not define themselves as gay and who have no contact with the gay scene.

Within female sex work there appears to be more organization with regard to how negotiations are conducted in relation to safer sex practice. (Barnard, McKeganey, and Bloor 1990). Community projects working with female workers have conducted skills training expressing the importance of effective negotiating skills on the street in order to safeguard themselves from HIV. Female workers have also been reported to work within their peer groups, exchanging information and knowledge that contribute toward their safety within the sex industry (Hanslope and Waite 1994). However, this is not replicated to the same level within male sex work, and male sex workers could learn from the women with regard to developing effective negotiating skills. What is emerging within the few community projects that work with the needs of male sex workers are training skills sessions that look at effective safer sex negotiation skills. Some community projects in London are pioneering this work. However, what has to happen before male workers can conduct effective negotiations with their clients is a recognition and acceptance of their sex work activities. This may prove problematic for those workers who may be uncomfortable with their involvement in sex work, for example, the heterosexual drug user who engages in sex work to support his drug use.

Moreover, as already discussed, the negotiation between street worker and client may be no more than a series of meaningful looks with no spoken words, which creates difficulty for the worker or client when it comes to negotiating safer sexual practices. Engagement in unsafe sexual practices among some male sex workers is also associated with receiving higher prices for unprotected sex (Morgan-Thomas et al. 1989).

Within escort work, negotiations between workers and clients are largely more direct. Workers negotiate their services and prices charged. It is a form of terms and conditions and as such it is a contract. The escort/masseur will make contact with clients largely through advertisements in the gay and local press. His services will be advertised discreetly. Negotiations between clients and worker will be conducted by telephone. They are generally discreet.

## Relationships

The classic studies have tended to purport that relationships between workers and clients are inherently exploitative and there is little emphasis that this assumption is seldom challenged. However, reference has been given to the fact that the early studies were undertaken in an era where society held stronger prejudices against prostitution and homosexual sexual activities than it does at present. These studies were also largely based on adolescent male prostitutes where it is recognized that there were imbalances of power in their relationships with adult clients and these relationships were appropriately recognized as exploitative. However, terming these relationships as exploitative appears to have served as the benchmark for interpreting present-day relationships between workers and clients, regardless of whether workers are of adult years.

It is recognized that relationships between workers and clients can be interpreted as exploitative in the context of abuse: a worker who has previously been abused (sexually and emotionally) in childhood may be continuing his abuse in his encounters with clients. Also, workers who are subject to adverse socioeconomic conditions, financial hardship, homelessness, etc., are in a vulnerable position in the sex industry, which may be open to exploitation by clients and procurers.

Within the literature the findings overwhelmingly report that a high proportion of workers come from unhappy, broken homes. Often their backgrounds are of neglect and abuse. They appear to have histories of runaway behavior. They have had poor, unsupportive relationships with their parents and siblings. Absent or present, hostile fathers or father figures are a common experience and their uncaring relationships in general have left them feeling emotionally deprived, little understood, and unwanted (Allen 1980; Coombs 1974; Cory and LeRoy 1963; Ginsburg 1967; Lloyd 1979; Weisberg 1985). Given the background of these workers, their position in life is suggestive of vulnerability and their engagement in sex work has been associated with their need to achieve power and positional importance. Attaining "power" through sex work has been interpreted as getting even with parental/authoritative figures, seeking revenge. Through their encounters with clients, workers may view their position as one of superiority, allowing them to vent hostility they may hold toward authority figures (Cory and LeRoy 1963; Ginsburg 1967; Janus, Scanlon, and Price 1984). Within this context it is acceptable to see that the client is open to being exploited by the worker, although the exploitation is brought about by the workers' unresolved experiences of abuse and neglect.

The worker who operates at a level whereby he wants to gain power over an authoritative figure may act out his role through his involvement with those clients who seek semipermanent relationships with workers. The clients who are generally older and wealthier than the workers will financially support them in return for sexual services and companionship. The worker referred to as a "kept boy"/"kept partner" may choose to take advantage of this position, accruing finances and enjoying a lifestyle he does not have to work for conventionally. Through exploiting this relationship the worker may perceive himself as powerful, achieving a degree of power over the client that may be associated with previous abuse.

The reverse of having positional importance—not being powerful, being powerless, and not in control—is also reported among male sex workers, especially when workers regard themselves as being externally controlled, viewing the responsibility for their actions as outside of their own domain (James 1982). This can be witnessed when workers start compromising between their original sexual activities with clients and become compliant to clients' further sexual demands because they require finances. This then places the worker in a powerless and more vulnerable position (Marlowe 1964).

Exploitation within commercial sex is evident when procurers are involved. "Procurer" in the context of male sex work is the general term to explain the activities of a man who has access to and facilitates contact between clients and workers. The procurer in male sex work does not exist to the same degree as he does in female sex work, largely due to the understanding that males are more able to protect themselves physically than females (Janus, Scanlon, and Price 1984). The procurer in male sex work operates within organized houses of male prostitution—"brothels"—and at street level, where he is there to coerce homeless runaways into the sex industry.

Procurers take advantage of homeless young runaways and try to coerce them into sex work. The following scenario is common: the homeless runaway makes for the city, arrives at a transport terminus; his vulnerability status is recognized and sought after by a procurer; he is easy prey and is subsequently introduced into sex work through various means. (Allen 1980; Kempe and Kempe 1984; Lloyd 1979; McMullen 1988). Moreover, emotional deprivation is a vulnerability factor for those homeless males who may translate this loss into a search for adult affection and attention on the streets (Allen 1980; Harris 1973; Kempe and Kempe 1984; Lloyd 1979). Therefore, on meeting a procurer the homeless runaway is perceived to be susceptible to the procurer's coercive nature and is taken in by false promises: the offer of care and attention.

With regard to the client being exploited, a man of advancing years and declining attractiveness who wants to have sex with a younger man may have limited opportunities for noncommercial sex (Bloor, McKeganey, and Barnard 1990; Cory and LeRoy 1963). Involving himself as a client in commercial sex places him in a position to be exploited by a younger worker because convention has it that to have sex with a younger male requires payment; as Winick and Kinsie (1971) reported, relationships between older and younger male homosexuals are undoubtedly suggestive of the older male paying for the sexual encounter. The young worker may use his youthfulness within the sex industry to exploit older clients. Clients can also be open to exploitation with regard to theft, assault, and coercion from workers with the likelihood of them not being reported to the police for such misdemeanors because of the effect it is likely to have on the client's private life (Donovan 1991).

Relationships between workers and clients can be interpreted as sexually abusive relationships when they are developed around issues of power, control, and coercion (Hunter 1990; Lew 1993; McMullen 1987). These relationships may not be readily understood as sexually abusive for participants in commercial sex who have been the victims of childhood sexual abuse. What has been cited in the literature on childhood sexual abuse reports that there are strong elements of denial for male victims in accepting their sexual abuse. Reasons associated with this denial center around their concerns and anxieties associated with sexual orientation and their confusion with regard to viewing themselves as victims, as their interpretation of being a victim is likely to be incongruous with their understanding of society's definition of masculinity and what it means to be male: to be able to defend and protect (Boyer 1989; Hunter 1990; Lew 1993). Workers and clients who were victims of childhood sexual abuse may continue their sexual abuse through their engagement in commercial sex as it is understood that there is a tendency for victims of childhood sexual abuse to involve themselves in abusive relationships in adulthood because they consider their adult (abusive) relationships as normal relationships (Hunter 1990; Lew 1993). Their relationships within commercial sex are termed sexually abusive when they are centered around issues of power, control, and coercion.

Moreover, the victim of childhood sexual abuse may understand sexual activity as something that is done to another instead of it being mutually reciprocal (Hunter 1990). When this form of sexual activity happens in commercial sex, it is not readily recognized as abuse, if it is abuse. In addition to what has already been said, sex workers who involve themselves in sexually abusive relationships with clients may view their rewards as enhancing their self-esteem in the short term, and it may also serve to camouflage the abusiveness of their encounters (Hunter 1990). This is applicable to whether workers were or were not victims of childhood sexual abuse.

Violence associated with male commercial sex has been reported in the literature, in the accounts of both workers and clients. Workers experiencing physical assault by clients has been reported by Bennetto (1994). Bloor, McKeganey, and Barnard (1990) in their study of young male sex workers in Glasgow reported that violence and intimidation was experienced by these workers. The reports included homophobic assaults by youth gangs, clients' refusal to pay for sexual services, workers being ejected from clients' cars in locations far from their homes, and coercion into non-negotiated sexual activities. Similar findings have been reported by Bennetto (1994). Clients' experience of violence is associated with their refusal to pay for negotiated sexual services, as reported in Janus, Scanlon, and Price's (1984) study of young male sex workers in Boston.

Interpersonal relationships have been reported to exist between workers and clients. Both workers and clients have commented on the positive relationships they have had with each other (Allen 1980). Clients have been referred to by the workers as caring, nurturing men who have befriended them, and their caring relationships have superseded their initial sexual encounters. Clients have also been looked upon as confidants and advisors in life issues (Allen 1980; Harris 1973; Lloyd 1979).

The home backgrounds of the majority of workers, backgrounds of neglect and abuse, account for workers having great difficulties in forging and sustaining interpersonal adult relationships (Burke 1991; McMullen 1987). An abused worker's involvement in an interpersonal relationship with a client may prove problematic. He may have ambivalence associated with an underlying desire for security and male affection, which was probably denied at home but which may now be obtained from a client. However, it is entwined with his antagonism toward the client. He is providing sex for reward and this serves to be a conflict for the worker (Allen 1980; Ginsburg 1967; Lloyd 1979). However, it is not to say that workers from neglectful and abusive backgrounds do not forge inter-personal relationships with clients.

Interpersonal relationships are generally sought out by those clients who are termed "sugar daddies." The "sugar daddies" generally identify those older, wealthier clients, who seek to establish interpersonal relationships with younger workers. These older men search for companionship, trust, and romance in these relationships (Allen 1980; Cory and LeRoy 1963). However, when there is an age differential between the partners these relationships are suggestive of abuse as there is an imbalance of power between the partners.

It cannot be overlooked that for some male workers in the sex industry there is an emotional involvement attached to the work they do that exists to a much greater extent than what happens in female sex work. This is recognized when some workers are prepared to offer a "sliding scale" of prices, so that the more personable, more attractive, and younger clients pay less than the relatively unattractive ones. Their concern about client appearance suggests that these workers have a degree of sensitivity and emotional involvement in their sexual encounters within sex work (Winick and Kinsie 1971).

## Methods

The data presented in this chapter have been obtained from semi-structured interview schedules from male subjects who have involvement or have previously had involvement with the male sex industry in Liverpool and Merseyside. Eleven interviews are commented upon within the chapter. They were secured in a thirteen-month period between November 1995 and December 1996. Six interviews were conducted with workers and five with clients. Seven of the interviews were taped, the remainder were handwritten during interview.

The method of recruitment aimed to target a cross-section of participants who were involved in the male sex industry in Merseyside. Subjects were recruited to the study through outreach and fieldwork observations, networks with local community projects, advertising, and through "snowball" sampling. Outreach and fieldwork observations were conducted in the locales where subjects were reported to meet and negotiate sexual contacts, principally around two city center gay bars and two city center public toilets. However, only one interview with a worker was secured through this method. Networking with local community projects in the areas of health and social welfare enlisted three interviews, two of which were with workers. Advertising in the local papers and regional gay press secured four interviews, three of which were with clients. The remaining three interviews, two of which were with workers, were obtained through a "snowballing technique" whereby subjects who had co-operated with the study introduced participants for interview.

Interviews were conducted at places of mutual agreement: at tables in city center cafes, within the university where the researcher is based, or at private addresses. One interview was conducted in a community project and one was conducted on the telephone. Interviews lasted between thirty and ninety minutes. Subjects were not financially rewarded for their interviews, although interview expenses were paid to one subject.

The semi-structured interview schedule elicited information with regard to family backgrounds, education and work experiences, personal relationships, sexual identity, early sexual experiences, initiation and engagement practices in commercial sex, motivation for operating in commercial sex, substance use, and other risk-taking practices. The semi-structured interviews obtained textual data, analyzed qualitatively, in terms of looking at "life histories" and "recurring themes." The interview schedule was developed in accordance with the aims and objectives of the research project. The interview format allowed for the use of open questions, with follow-up questions used to clarify specific points. To assure the validity of the interviews, wherever possible, the same questions were repeated and data compared with other information obtained within the interview or from other sources. However, much of the information was not amenable to validation from other sources.

The ethical considerations governing the study appeared in a research brief presented to subjects prior to the interview. The brief outlined the purpose and scope of the study together with information regarding the uses to which the interview material would be put, to namely, inclusion in research thesis and journal articles. At no time during the interviews were subjects expected to discuss anything they did not feel comfortable with and subjects were aware that they could terminate the interview at any time. Anonymity of the subjects has been safeguarded by the nonidentification of subjects' personal features or circumstances. Moreover, the tapes which were used for recorded interviews were erased once transcriptions were taken.

Six subjects were interviewed who had experiences of exchanging sexual services for rewards. At the time of interview two subjects reported that they no longer had involvement with male sex work. Their involvement ceased five and twenty-two years ago, respectively. Of the four subjects who reported having had recent experiences within male sex work in Merseyside, one subject indicated that his recent experiences were his last experiences of male sex work in Merseyside. The experiences of former workers are commented upon. Their experiences are related to those of current workers' experiences; for the purposes of this study all are included because the study is based on the individual's experience and not when this experience took place.

# Findings and Discussion

## Background Information—Workers

Six workers were interviewed. They ranged in ages from twenty-six years to thirty-eight years. The majority of workers (five) were aged between twenty-six and twenty-nine years.

All of the workers were born in Merseyside. The majority (five) had spent all of their childhood in Merseyside. The four subjects who reported recent experiences of male sex work live in Merseyside and three live in Liverpool. The two subjects who had former male sex work experiences live in locations in the northwest of England, within fifty miles of Merseyside. Two subjects reported that their commercial sex experiences were localized to Merseyside. Four subjects had reported having had experiences of selling sex in Merseyside and other English cities: Manchester, London, and Birmingham.

Five of the workers identified as gay, one as bisexual. One of the gay workers operates as a transvestite sex worker. The same worker had also reported commercial sex experiences as a male sex worker. The gay-identified workers reported that they were aware of their sexual attraction toward their same sex at a young age (nine to fourteen years).

All of the workers reported that they had come from home backgrounds where both parents were together, although three workers reported that at some time within their childhood/adolescence they had experiences of institutionalized care. Subjects came from families that ranged in sizes from two to eight siblings. Four of the workers were the youngest in the family, one was the oldest, and one was the second youngest in a family of five siblings. In general workers reported good relationships with their brothers and sisters. However, their relationships with parents were mixed. The majority (four) reported that they had good, caring, and supportive relationships with their mother, but relationships with their fathers were generally experienced as ones of contempt, their fathers being nonemotional and showing little or no interest in their lives. Only one worker reported a positive relationship with his father. Three of the workers indicated that their fathers had been physically abusive toward them in the family homes. Among the gay-identified workers, the majority (four) inferred that their relationships with their fathers were further strained by their fathers' growing awareness of their gay identity.

Alcohol misuse among parents in the family home was reported by half (three) of the workers.

The majority of the workers (five) left school at either fifteen or sixteen years, four with standard qualifications and one with no qualifications. One stayed on at school to undertake further qualifications until he was eighteen.

Truant behavior was a common feature of the workers' school experience. Five of the workers had experiences or had undergone training on practical courses such as catering, hairdressing, manual labor work, etc. At present three of the subjects who reported recent sex work experiences are employed or are undertaking educational courses. One is in receipt of state benefit.

Regarding the living arrangements of the subjects who reported recent sex work experiences (four), two lived alone and two lived within the parental home. One of the subjects was involved in a long-term gay relationship.

## Background Information—Clients

Five clients were interviewed, their ages ranging from thirty-five years to sixty years. One client was aged sixty, two clients were in their late fifties, and two were in their mid to late thirties.

Two of the clients were born and brought up in Merseyside. The remaining three clients moved to Merseyside twenty-two years ago, fifteen years ago, and one year ago, respectively. Four of the clients interviewed currently live in Merseyside.

Three of the clients identified as gay, two as bisexual. One of the gay-identified clients had formerly been married and fathered seven children. The two bisexual clients, both in their thirties, are married and have families. The three gay-identified clients are single and live alone. The bisexual clients live with their wives and children.

Two of the clients are in receipt of state benefit, two are employed full-time in manual occupations, and one client is in receipt of a personal pension.

The gay clients report having had approximately ten to thirty years' experience of commercial sex experiences with workers. The bisexual clients report having had four to five years' commercial sex experience.

## Negotiations—The Workers' Experience

Three of the workers reported having made contact with clients in areas reputed for gay cruising: mostly outside and within certain city center public toilets, within the city center's transport terminals, and within public parks located outside the city center. The negotiations that took place were largely nonverbal, involving body gestures and certain eye movements. One worker reported that the nonverbal cues he used in the cruising locales informed potential clients that he was willing to engage himself in commercial sex. He reported: "You sit or you stand in a way which basically says . . . you know what they want and you are available." This worker's experience supports the reported knowledge on nonverbal communication that exists between men who have sex with men (Corzine and Kirkby 1977; Hoffman 1972; Humphreys 1970).

Although open solicitations in general were not taking place in the cruising locales, the workers did indicate that they did receive payment for the majority of their street encounters with clients. This is most likely due to the fact that these locales were known for commercial sexual encounters among participants operating within the field. No set format of when payment was made to the worker was indicated by subjects, although, in general, it was inferred that payment took place after the sexual activity.

One worker who engaged in street work did report verbally soliciting clients. His initial method of solicitation was vocalizing his hardship to potential clients: "I'm skint and I need a few bob." This worker reported that most clients would respond financially, rewarding him for sexual activity.

All three workers who made contact with clients in cruising locales reported experiences of being verbally solicited by clients.

Workers generally reported conducting business in isolation in the cruising areas. Workers conducting business alongside each other as has been reported in the literature (Harris 1973; Reiss 1961) was not reported by the workers in Merseyside. A reason behind this was reported by one worker who understood the situation to be that workers who work alongside each other do not get business from the clients. It is suggested that perhaps clients do not engage in commercial sex negotiations with workers who operate alongside each other because of fear of having their identities recognized among the workers. They may also fear potential group assault. However, within the study it was recognized that workers did associate themselves with their peers in the cruising locales, although they did refrain from conducting business alongside them.

Three workers made contact with clients in gay bar settings. One of the workers who works as a transvestite sex worker and who has also worked as a male sex worker reported experiences of having made contact with clients in nongay as well as gay bars. Two of the bar workers reported that their contact with clients largely emerged through the use of nonverbal communication, principally eye contact followed by the offer of drinks and verbal compliments. The negotiations that emerged were generally implicit, both workers and their clients having an understanding that their sexual encounter was of a commercial sexual nature.

Workers who made contact with clients in the bar setting gave reference to the value of youth in forging gay sex contacts. Youth was interpreted as a commodity that is desired and subsequently rewarded by older men on the gay scene. This understanding appeared to assist those workers who operated within bars to engage in commercial sex with clients. Their negotiations were reported as more implicit and they were more covert about selling sex to clients. This method of negotiation served to protect workers when faced with those encounters where the negotiations were not so straightforward or were open to misinterpretation.

Two workers who operated within bars did report that negotiations were explicit on behalf of the clients. They reported that clients were direct with them in their negotiations for commercial sex.

With regard to negotiations taking place under the influence of alcohol, two of the three workers who operated within bars reported negotiating sex work with clients under the influence of alcohol. It is inferred that alcohol was used in these situations as a social lubricant that facilitated negotiation between both worker and client. Neither of the two workers had experiences of being compromised by clients into sexual acts under the influence of alcohol. Moreover, the two workers did not report engagement in unsafe sexual practices under the influence of alcohol.

Engagement in safer sex was practiced by those workers who reported recent commercial sex experiences, although discussion about safer sex was not indicated by those workers in their negotiations with clients.

Three workers had experiences with escort work. They were familiar with negotiating sexual services and payments with clients beforehand and payment was either made before or after engagement in sexual activity. Two workers appeared to be confident when it came to specifically negotiating certain sexual services and the various charges for these services with clients. Nevertheless, one worker who worked as a transvestite escort appeared confident in forging sexual contacts with clients but appeared to lack confidence when it came to negotiating payment for services, reporting that "she" was not assertive with specifying charges to clients and allowed them to financially reward "her" for what they thought the sexual activity was worth. Not explicitly charging clients was associated with this worker's understanding that "she" was somewhat old to be operating as a transvestite sex worker. "She" was in her late twenties. This worker reported that "she" was competing for clients in the sex industry with younger transvestite workers. Moreover, this worker expressed a social conscience toward charging clients, stating "Some of them haven't like got much money and they want a bit of company and a bit of companionship." Two of the workers who had experiences with escort work reported that their contacts with clients were through a third party. This was the only way in which one of these workers forged contact with clients. It was not known whether the assistance of the third party was renumerated by the client although the workers reported that they themselves did not pay the third party for their assistance.

Four workers within the study reported some form of peer induction with regard to negotiating worker and client sexual encounters. Two workers who had experiences of street work reported getting to know the work through their peers who operated at street level. One worker who operated within bars, got to know the "rules of the game" from a fellow worker: "Joe told me the rules . . . not to undercharge." Another worker who operated as an escort was introduced to escort work through his association with a female escort.

## Negotiations—The Clients' Experience

Three of the clients reported that they made contact with workers through advertisements in the local and national papers and the regional gay press. These workers advertised themselves as escorts and masseurs. Negotiations were conducted by telephone. The clients reported that workers negotiated with them their services and fees. These ranged from negotiating massages to various sexual services. Clients who had initially negotiated massages with workers experienced in sexual services. Two of the clients had experiences of re-negotiating sexual services and prices on meeting the workers.

One client had experiences of making contact with workers on the street. This client indicated that he could recognize male sex workers on the street. On engagement in conversation with street workers this client reported that they would verbally solicit him. His experience of negotiating contact with workers therefore differs from the workers' experiences whereby they report that their negotiations with clients are largely nonverbal.

One bisexual client, although not making contact with workers at street level, had experiences of personally engaging in impersonal sex with men who have sex with men in a public park outside the city center.

Two of the gay clients within the study reported experiences of making contact with workers through their acquaintances and friends who were of similar years to them, who were gay identified, and who shared similar interests in forging sexual contacts with younger workers. One of the clients, who usually established contact with workers through acquaintances and friends, reported an experience of being solicited by a worker in a venue not reputed for commercial sex contacts. Moreover, this client reported that he did not formally reward workers financially but he rewarded them "in kind": he bought dinners, provided temporary accommodation, and gave workers a lot of affection and care.

Only one client reported making contact with workers in the gay bar setting. His negotiations with workers developed through verbal dialogues. He did not conduct negotiations under the influence of alcohol but was unsure on whether the workers he negotiated services with negotiated under the influence of alcohol. In conversation the workers would inform him (the client) that they charged for sex. He would then ask the workers how much they charged for sexual services and if he agreed to the amount being charged the negotiation was accepted. This client also had experiences of negotiating lower charges with workers for their services if he could not afford the amount requested. In reference to negotiating lower prices with workers he added, "I try and pay them as little as possible." What was interpreted from this interview was that this client held an underlying resentment toward workers for paying them for sexual services, as highlighted in the preceding quotation, when the client somewhat disparagingly refers to workers as "them." It is possible that the reasoning behind this inferred resentment is that the client is in his late fifties and pursues sexual encounters with young men in their twenties. This supports findings from the literature (Winick and Kinsie 1971) and what has been reported in the other interviews: a recognition that younger males are rewarded for sexual encounters with older males on the gay scene. Negotiating lower prices with workers was also experienced by another client in his associations with escort workers.

Two gay clients within the study commented upon youth having particular desirability within gay society. They gave reference to the recognition that among older men who involved themselves in sexual encounters with younger males there were rewards for younger males having sexual involvement with older men. This supports Winick and Kinsie's (1971) findings with regard to relationships between older and younger men being suggestive of the older male paying for the sexual encounter. However, unlike the gay clients who expressed preferences for sexual encounters with younger workers, the bisexual clients did not indicate this preference. In fact one of the bisexual clients had reported having commercial sex experiences with a worker who was older than himself, and the other client having had commercial sex with a worker of similar years to himself. Yet again, unlike the gay clients the bisexual clients did not give any sign that youth held particular desirability within their sexual encounters with workers. Reasons behind this finding could be associated with the ages of the bisexual clients. They were younger than the gay clients by approximately twenty years and perhaps male youth does not hold the same desirability for bisexual clients as it appears to for gay clients. An interesting finding within one of the interviews with the bisexual clients is that one reported having had an experience of selling sex. This isolated experience was conducted under the influence of alcohol in a cruising area. The experience left the client feeling "quite powerful" and "confident." However, the client expressed no indication of wanting to repeat the experience.

With regard to preferred ages of workers only the gay clients reported the ages they looked for in workers. They ranged between late teenage years to early thirties.

## The Workers' Relationships with Clients

Workers within the study, whether they operated as street, bar, or escort workers, did not identify a specific type of client who could be termed representative of either being a street, bar, or escort client. The workers reported that there was a cross-section of clients who engage in commercial sex with male sex workers in Merseyside. In general the clients were reported within the age range of mid-twenties to fifties. They identified as heterosexual, bisexual, and gay. Some clients were married men. One worker who had experiences of street work reported that he had come into contact with clients who cross-dressed as women. All of the workers reported that at some time within their sex industry work they had experiences of having regular clients. Four workers reported experiences of having met clients who were in search of companionship alongside payment for sexual services.

Three workers had experiences of being a "kept partner." They were looked after and cared for by older clients. One of the workers commonly referred to these clients as "sugar daddies." The duration of these relationships between worker and client ranged from two months to a number of years. The role the client took in these relationships was generally that of provider, financially and emotionally. Two of these workers reported that they looked for a client to provide them with security and affection. Both of these workers formerly reported that within their parental homes they had felt neglected. One of the two workers indicated that the relationship he had with his father had some reference to why he forged relationships with older clients. He reported, "I've always wanted an older guy, because I started young (involvement in gay sex) you know, I saw it as some sort of security. . . . [It] made me feel right and secure you know, maybe I was clinging onto some sort of fatherly figure but didn't realize, because you know my dad was very rarely at home—he worked away a lot." What can be interpreted in this workers' experience is his vulnerability and need for adult male affection as he expresses feelings associated with abandonment attributed to the non-presence of his father in the home environment. Similarly, a worker who had experiences of street work reported that his motive for involvement in commercial sex was to have affection needs met. He reported: "I went out looking for love, understanding, and affection and I found the rent scene and somehow sort of thing, I needed the affection more than the money." This worker also reported relationship problems with his father. The relationship was devoid of affection and attention and was reported by the worker as physically abusive. It can be inferred that there is some association for this worker between his earlier experiences of not receiving affection and attention from his father and his search for adult male affection. However, what is interesting in this worker's experience of commercial sex is that he did not have experiences of being a "kept partner" whereby he would be looked after and cared for by an older client.

One worker within the study reported an experience of forging a long-term friendship with one of his clients. This relationship between himself and the client emerged from a rewarded sexual relationship to that of being a nurturing friendship. The client became an advisor and confidant to the worker.

Feelings of being exploited were reported by one worker in his associations with clients. This worker, who had involvement with clients in "providing" relationships, reported that through the course of time it became evident that he felt clients were only interested in him as a younger sexual partner. His youth was thus exploited.

Workers' involvements with procurers were not interpreted as exploitative, as has been reported in the literature (Allen 1980; Lloyd 1979). One worker who had experiences of street work reported having involvement with a procurer. This procurer would "pimp people out" for clients who would not contact workers themselves. He would arrange for the worker to meet the client at a certain meeting place. This worker, commenting upon his experience, reported that he was comfortably rewarded for his involvement by the client. The worker, however, did not know what financial transaction existed between the client and the procurer. This worker did not consider his encounter with a procurer as abusive. Similarly, one escort worker within the study who was introduced to male sex work through a female escort reported that all his contacts with clients were through this procurer. This worker did not report whether there was a financial transaction between the woman and his clients. Moreover, this worker's involvement with this procurer was not reported as unusual.

Violence was reported by four workers in their encounters with clients. One worker reported experiences of having been assaulted by clients after they had engaged in a sexual act with him. This worker reported that these clients would assault him because they felt uncomfortable about their engagements in commercial gay sex with a gay-identified male sex worker. These clients identified themselves as bisexual or heterosexual. One worker who operated as a transvestite worker reported being violently attacked by a client because of "her" refusal to engage in a particular sexual act. One worker had experienced being physically attacked by a client because he requested negotiated payment for sexual services. This worker also reported an experience of being held hostage by a client for three days. Two workers within the study had experiences of being forced into sexual acts against their will by clients.

One worker also reported that he came under attack from other older workers when he was street working. Due to his younger years he secured more contacts with clients than the older workers and this annoyed them.

With regard to receiving rewards other than money from clients, one street worker reported that when he was homeless he received accommodation and hospitality from some of the clients. Other workers within the study reported receiving various rewards from clients, which included being bought items of clothing, given gifts, and being taken out for meals in restaurants.

## The Clients' Relationships with Workers

All three of the gay-identified clients reported that they had been involved in interpersonal relationships with workers. One of these clients refrained from discussing his interpersonal relationship with a worker. The two clients who discussed their interpersonal relationships with workers reported having had experiences of workers living with them in their homes. These clients reported befriending workers and providing for them. Both clients reported that they understood themselves to be source of security for the workers. The live-in relationships they had with workers ranged from one week to two years. One of the clients reported that his motive for being involved with workers in "providing" relationships was always to help the worker. This client attempted to exude confidence in the young workers. In his involvement with "kept partners" this client received youthful company, a sexual relationship, and humor. Both of the clients reported experiences of being exploited by "kept partners," both clients reporting having been "conned" by workers.

The two gay clients who discussed their interpersonal relationships with workers reported that they forged long-term friendships with workers. The clients' long-term friendships with workers were borne out of their commercial sexual encounters with workers and were also developed through the parting of a live-in "providing" relationship. One of the clients who developed a long-term friendship with a worker with whom he formerly had an interpersonal relationship understood that he was important to this worker's livelihood. He reported, "I am the only really stable person in his life."

The two clients within the study who identified as bisexual reported that they had never forged interpersonal relationships with workers. Their involvements with workers remained at an impersonal level and were purely for sexual gratification. It is inferred that their associations with workers remained impersonal because they were married men and fathers to young children, and the clients thus wanted to protect their anonymity. Neither of the two bisexual clients reported ever having had an interpersonal relationship with another male, although one of the clients made reference to the desire of wanting to have the experience of having an interpersonal relationship with a man.

# Conclusion

This chapter has discussed some of the issues associated with negotiations and relationships between male sex workers and clients. Interviews were conducted with workers (six) and clients (five) of the male sex industry in Liverpool, Merseyside.

The findings from the study supported the literature (Allen 1980; Coombs 1974; Cory and LeRoy 1963; Ginsburg 1967; Lloyd 1979; Weisberg 1985) in relation to the home backgrounds of male sex workers who in the study reported nonemotional relationships with their fathers. Workers largely identified as gay, which contrasts with the earlier studies (Ginsburg 1967; Harris 1973; Jersild 1956; Lloyd 1979; Reiss 1961) where the majority reported a heterosexual identity. Similarly, clients in the study differed from what has been reported in the contemporary literature (Bennetto 1994; Bloor, McKeganey, and Barnard 1990; Cory and LeRoy 1963) in that three of the five clients identified as gay, whereas previous studies have found them to be mostly heterosexual and married.

An interesting finding is that two of the clients were younger men in their thirties who identified as bisexual; their association with male sex work inferred that this was a viable avenue for them to have same-sex relationships.

Four settings were reported in which negotiations took place: cruising locales, the gay bar setting, through escort advertisements, and contact through friends or acquaintances. The literature predominantly referred to the first two settings (Cavan 1966; Desroches 1989; Humphreys 1970; Plant et al. 1989; Rechy 1963, 1977; Westwood 1960).

While few studies have looked at the nature of negotiation between participants in male commercial sex, a number of authors (Corzine and Kirkby 1977; Delph 1978; Desroches 1989; Hoffman 1972; Humphreys 1970; Lee 1978) have noted nonverbal communications between men who have sex with men in noncommercial settings. Workers and clients within the study gave differing accounts of the role of verbal and nonverbal negotiation. Although workers largely reported nonverbal negotiations both in the cruising locales and bar settings, one client did describe verbal solicitation in the bar setting and on a street encounter.

Findings from the study partially support reports in the literature that associate alcohol consumption and sexual negotiation (Myres et al. 1991; Plant, Plant, and Morgan-Thomas 1990; Stall 1988). Workers within the bar setting reported the use of alcohol to facilitate their negotiation with clients.

Interpersonal (live-in) relationships grew out of commercial sex encounters. Both workers and clients who reported these experiences gave positive accounts of these relationships. They were reported as a source of security and affection. However, clients who were involved in these relationships had experiences of being exploited by workers. This supports the findings in the literature (Allen 1980; Harris 1973; Lloyd 1979).

Long-term friendships developed out of the interpersonal relationships between workers and clients. The clients fulfilled a role of confidant and advisor to these workers in the reported cases of this. Similar findings have been documented by Allen (1980), Lloyd (1979), and Harris (1973).

Youth was an issue commented on by those workers and clients who identified as gay. Both understood youth as a commodity that was rewarded by the older man in his sexual encounter with a younger male. This supports the findings of Winick and Kinsie (1971). An interesting finding within the study is that the bisexual subjects did not share these values. It was noted that one gay worker felt exploited as a result of his youth.

The majority of the workers within the study reported some experiences of violence from clients for varied reasons. This supports the research (Bennetto 1994; Bloor, McKeganey, and Barnard 1990). In contrast to what was reported by Allen (1980), Kempe and Kempe (1984), Lloyd (1979), and McMullen (1988), where a third party was involved in the role of procurer, neither workers nor clients reported this involvement in unfavorable terms.

Although beyond the scope of the present study, the relationship between location and mode of communication may merit further research while the connection between youth and exploitation in male commercial sex relationships may also be worthy of further investigation.

As witnessed in the study, a range of negotiations and relationships existed between workers and clients. Further areas of exploration will be documented in the forthcoming thesis.

# References

Achilles, N. 1967. The development of the homosexual bar as an institution. In *Sexual Deviance*, by J. Gagnon and W. Simon. New York: Harper and Row, 228–44.

Allen, D. M. 1980. Young male prostitutes: A psychological study. *Archives of Sexual Behavior* 9 (5): 399–426.

Barnard, M., N. McKeganey, and M. Bloor. 1990. A risky business. *Community Care* 5 (July): 26–27.

Barrett, D. 1995. Child prostitution. *Highlight: National Children's Bureau* (March).

Bennetto, J. 1994. One in three rent boys has HIV, says study. *The Independent on Sunday.* (23 January): 8.

Bloor, M., N. McKeganey, and M. Barnard. 1990. An ethnographic study of HIV-related risk practices among Glasgow rent boys and their clients; report of a pilot study. *AIDS Care* 2 (1): 17–24.

Boyer, D. 1989. Male prostitution and homosexual identity. *Journal of Homosexuality* (17): 151–84.

Burke, T. 1991. Streetwise on streetlife. *Young People Now* (31 November): 23–25.

Cavan, S. 1966. *Liquor License: An Ethnography of Bar Behavior.* Chicago: Aldine.

Coombs, N. R. 1974. Male prostitution: A psychosocial view of behavior. *American Journal of Osthopsychiatry.* 44 (5): 782–89.

Cory, D. W., and J. P. LeRoy. 1963. *The Homosexual and His Society—A View from Within.* New York: The Citadel Press.

Corzine, J., and R. Kirby. 1977. Cruising the truckers—Sexual encounters in a highway rest area. *Urban Life* 6 (2): 171–92.

Davidson, M. 1970. *Some Boys—A Homosexual Odyssey*. London: David Bruce & Watson.

Delph, E. W. 1978. *The Silent Community: Public Homosexual Encounters*. London: Sage Publications.

Desroches, F. J. 1989. Tearoom trade: A research update. *Qualitative Sociology* 13 (1): 39–61.

Donovan, K. 1991. *Hidden from View: An Exploration of the Little Known World of Young Male Prostitutes in Great Britain and Europe with Recommendations for an Effective Interagency Approach*. Birmingham: Home Office PRSU in association with the West Midlands Police.

Drew, D., and J. Drake. 1969. *Boys for Sale—A Sociological Study of Boy Prostitution*. New York: Brown Book Company.

Festinger, L. 1992. *Cognitive Dissonance*. San Francisco: W. H. Freeman and Company.

Garfield, S. 1994. *The End of Innocence: Britain in the Time of AIDS*. London: Faber and Faber.

Gibson, B. 1995. *Male Order: Life Stories from Boys Who Sell Sex*. London: Cassell.

Ginsburg, K. N. 1967. The "meat-rack": A study of the male homosexual prostitute. *American Journal of Psychotherapy* 21 (2): 170–85.

Hanslope, J., and M. Waite. 1994. Safer on the streets. *Heartlines* (March): 20–21.

Harris, M. 1973. *The Dilly Boys—Male Prostitution on Piccadilly*. London: Croom Helm.

Hoffman, M. 1972. The male prostitute. *Sexual Behavior* 2 (8): 6–21.

Humphreys, L. 1970. *Tearoom Trade: A Study of Homosexual Encounters in Public Places*. London: Duckworth & Co. Ltd.

Hunter, M. 1990. *Abused Boys—The Neglected Victims of Sexual Abuse*. Lexington, Mass.: Lexington Books.

James, J. 1982. *Entrance into Juvenile Male Prostitution*. Final Report prepared for the National Institute of Mental Health, Rockville. Seattle: Washington University.

Janus, M. D., B. Scanlon, and V. Price. 1984. Youth prostitution. In *Child Pornography and Sex Rings*, by A. W. Burgess. Lexington, Mass.: Lexington Books, 127–46.

Jersild, J. 1956. *Boy Prostitution*. Translated by Oscar Bojesen. Copenhagen: G. E. C. GAD.

Kempe, R. S., and C. H. Kempe. 1984. *Common Secret: Sexual Abuse of Children and Adolescents*. New York: W. H. Freeman and Company.

King, E. 1993. *Safety in Numbers*. London: Cassell.

Lee, J. A. 1978. *Getting Sex: A New Approach—More Fun, Less Guilt*. Ontario: Musson Book Co.

Leigh, B. C. 1990. The relationship of sex-related alcohol expectancies to alcohol consumption and sexual behaviour. *British Journal of Addiction* 5 (7): 919–28.

Lew, M. 1993. *Victims No Longer—A Guide for Men Recovering from Sexual Child Abuse*. London: Cedar.

Lloyd, R. 1979. *Playland—A Study of Human Exploitation*. London: Quartet Books. First published under the title *For Money or Love: Boy Prostitution in America*. New York: Vanguard Press Inc., 1976.

MacNamara, D. E. J. 1965. Male prostitution in American cities: A socioeconomic or pathological phenomenon? *American Journal of Orthopsychiatry* (35): 204.

Marlowe, K. 1964. The life of the homosexual prostitute. *Sexology* 31: 24–26.

McMillan, B., and A. Hunter. 1992. Men at work: Male sex work and HIV. *International Conference on AIDS* 8 (2). Abstract Number: PoD 5640.

McMullen, R. J. 1988. Boys involved in prostitution. *Youth and Policy* (23): 35–42.

———. 1987. Youth prostitution: A balance of power. *Journal of Adolescence* (10): 35–43.

Miller, W. R. 1980. *The Addictive Behaviours—Treatment of Alcoholism, Drug Abuse, Smoking and Obesity.* Oxford: Pergamon Press.

Morgan-Thomas, R., M. A. Plant, M. L. Plant, and D. I. Sales. 1989. Risks of AIDS among workers in the "Sex Industry": Some initial results from a Scottish study. *British Medical Journal* 299 (15 July): 148–49.

Myres, T., D. Locker, K. Orr, and E. Jackson. 1991. *Men's Survey 1990: A Toronto Venue-based Survey of Gay and Bisexual Men and Their Knowledge, Attitudes and Behaviour Related to HIV/AIDS.* Toronto: AIDS Committee of Toronto.

Pheterson, G. 1989. *A Vindication of the Rights of Whores.* Seattle: The Seal Press.

Plant, M. L., M. A. Plant, and R. Morgan-Thomas. 1990. Alcohol, AIDS risks and commercial sex: Some preliminary results from a Scottish study. *Drug and Alcohol Dependence* (5): 51–55.

Plant, M. L., M. A. Plant, D. F. Peck, and J. Setters. 1989. The sex industry, alcohol and illicit drugs: Implications for the spread of HIV infection. *British Journal of Addiction* (84): 53–59.

Rechy, J. 1963. *City of Night.* New York: Grove Press Inc.

———. 1977. *The Sexual Outlaw: A Documentary.* New York: Grove Press Inc.

Reiss, A. J. 1961. The social integration of queers and peers. *Social Problems* 9 (2): 102–20.

Room, R. 1983. Alcohol and disinhibition: Nature and meaning of the link. Proceedings of a Conference: California.

Stall, R. 1988. The prevention of HIV infection associated with drug and alcohol use during sexual activity. In *AIDS and Substance Abuse,* edited by L. Siegal. New York: Harrington Park Press.

Weisberg, D. K. 1985. *Children of the Night—A Study of Adolescent Prostitution.* Lexington, Mass.: Lexington Books.

Westwood, G. 1960. *A Minority.* London: Longmans, Green & Co.

Winick, C., and P. M. Kinsie. 1971. *The Living Commerce—Prostitution in the United States.* Chicago: Quadrangle Books.

# SHE-MALE PROSTITUTES: WHO ARE THEY, WHAT DO THEY DO, AND WHY DO THEY DO IT?

## DWIGHT DIXON AND JOAN K. DIXON

Sexologists insist on establishing labels—little boxes if you will—into which they lump people who seem to have various constellations of characteristics. Unfortunately, people don't come prepackaged in a finite number of boxes. We are beginning to realize more and more as time goes on that people who were previously being placed by sexologists into the same labeled box for purposes of therapy, etc., often have significant differences. That has proven to be quite true in the group of people said to be gender dysphoric (meaning someone who was born with an indeterminate sex, such as a hermaphrodite, or with the usual male or female chromosomal pattern but whose sociopsychological self-image is partially or totally inconsistent with that sex).

Evidence of gender-dysphoric people is found in most cultures around the world throughout history where sufficient historical record has been preserved (Williams 1986). Many, if not most, of those cultures were very accepting and tolerant of an individual who assumed the partial or complete identity of another sex, apparently different from that in which the person was born. We purposely use the term "another" sex instead of the term "opposite" sex because many of those cultures believed such a person actually to be of a third or even a fourth sex.

Before the arrival of the white man in the Americas most of the indigenous tribes actually considered such gender-dysphoric people (the great majority being males at birth) to be special products of the "great spirit" that controlled all things (Williams 1986). In those tribes these "special" people were usually accorded very high honor. They assumed commanding roles in a variety of important ceremonies, especially in those involving the spirit world. They were often involved in healing and tending to the sick and the old. It was a high honor and was considered great luck for a family or a tribe to have such a person in their midst.

Typically, these special men, which the European usually called a *berdache*, dressed as women, did women's work rather than hunt game and kill enemies with the men, and had sex exclusively with men (Williams 1986). They received many gifts from appreciative lovers and from other tribal members. They worked hard and well at their chosen tasks and were often one of the wealthiest members of their tribe. The arrival of the white man—bringing with him his superior weaponry along with his desire for stolen riches and his Judeo-Christian baggage of biblical intolerance of such "weird, ungodly, unspeakably "sinful" behavior—marked the beginning of a reign of terror against these "special" people that in various forms and degrees continues today (Williams 1986).

We won't go into the long and sordid history of how sexology got to where it is today in terms of understanding people with gender dysphoria. We'll simply point out that only relatively recently have most sexologists who work in the field of gender dysphoria begun to come to a new awareness of the many varieties and degrees in which this phenomenon manifests itself in the desires and behaviors of different individuals. Indeed, some sexologists, such as Walter Bockting (1996), Anne Bolin (1996), and Sandra Bem (1995), have for several years pointed out to their colleagues that the preferable view is to affirm various combinations of sex, gender, sociosexual role, and sexual orientation; and that these combinations may vary in a particular individual at different times.

This is a study of a group of people born male but who wish to have certain physical characteristics of a female. They do not wish to have their penis or testicles removed but have taken steps to attain a variety of female physical characteristics. Because their sex-object choice is males and they typically do not become erotically aroused by the cross-dressing itself, they would seem to fit within a category of she-males that John Money and Ray Blanchard have termed gynemimetics (Blanchard 1993). We refer to them simply as she-males, which to our ear is the more attractive descriptor.

From our vantage point of being fairly active observers of the alternative sexual scene in southern California and particularly in San Diego for several decades, we began to notice about five or six years ago an apparent increase in the prevalence of she-male prostitutes functioning somewhat publicly in that area. At about the same time a significant change in attitude began to take place within the gender community, as that broad spectrum of gender-dysphoric individuals is called. It became more acceptable and more common for a person not to feel compelled to have to seek or obtain sex reassignment surgery (SRS), which involves one's genitals, in order to live as a person of the desired other sex. An individual who previously may have lied about his true feelings in order to qualify for SRS and thus attain help in making the identity switch he really wanted, found he could get some effective help without having to go through the professionally imposed surgery routine, only to come out of it much worse off than when he went into it. The lid had been lifted off of the boxes labeled "preoperative" and "postoperative" transsexual. It had become possible, for example, to look like a woman to the general public; to dress, live, and work as a woman, but to retain one's male genitalia. Now one who wished to do so could begin to build a life as a she-male. What made this an option was the change of mind of some sexual-health care professionals and the enhanced knowledge by the gender community about female hormones and other female-appearance enhancers and their availability to that community outside of professional channels.

We were interested in finding out who is this relatively new type of sex worker, the she-male, who had recently become so obvious. Our study of this fascinating group of gender explorers is only the first step of many more which we hope to make in the future. A computer search of the recent literature revealed only a few studies of prostitute populations that seemed to include some she-males. Most were composed principally of more broadly defined transsexual/transvestite populations and concentrated primarily on issues of HIV concerns.

We studied seven she-males, all living in San Diego. To locate them and secure their cooperation we used several sources. A female sex-worker acquaintance of ours passed the word about our study to some she-male prostitutes whom she knew and vouched for us. That helped secure their cooperation when we contacted them. We answered ads in a sexually oriented local newspaper. Some of our initial interviewees recommended us to other potential interviewees. Securing participants was facilitated by our offer from the beginning to pay interviewees $100 for approximately an hour of their time and a $50 referral fee for each successful referral.

Their ages ranged from 25 to 53. Although each person met our criteria of a she-male, not one used that term to self-identify when given an open question about her gender. Answers were female, in-between, woman, special woman, female mostly, he/she, and just a person. Each had made a studied decision to become and to remain a she-male, although one subject revealed a lingering possibility of a future sex-change operation.

There was no particular pattern in the sex or gender of an identified "closest friend." Answers included gay male, she-male, female, and male. Asked whether she related better to males or females, five out of seven said she related better to males—one of the five also included transsexuals.

Among the attractive features cited about living as a she-male were: the exciting opportunities of all the sex and social action; the money; the softness of the female side, and the sexual release from the male genitals; it's more comfortable; likes being able to live as a female without the trauma of surgery; likes using cock as a female; it feels more natural; life is less hassle as a female than as a male; easiest way to live; feels better about self; and it eliminates the machismo and aggressiveness of life as a male.

The decision to live as a she-male was preceded by a much earlier incli-nation to dress as a female. Five of the seven she-males reported that some of their earliest childhood memories were of being strongly attracted to wearing female clothes and that they actually began wearing them while very young. All of the she-males were wearing female attire either full time or a large part of the time in their teen years. Each of them reported having had a series of unpleasant experiences while growing up as an unmasculine male. Most of them had been treated badly by their peers and by some or all of their family because of their obvious feminine appearance or inclinations.

In each case the first step these she-males took to begin changing their physiology to a more feminine appearance was to take some form of femi-nizing hormone. The earliest this was done was as a high school junior in one case. The latest was during one person's forties. Typically, they started with estrogen pills and then proceeded to a variety of injections. A few had used pills and injections simultaneously in various combinations. Presently four were using injections and three were taking Premarin pills. The hormones are usually acquired in Mexico. All of the interviewees self-prescribe and self-administer. They reveal a history of pure trial and error of what to take, how much to take, and when to start and stop. Some have had bad reactions, both emotionally and physically, to wrong dosing.

One of the considerations about finding the individually correct female-hormone intake is the effect on penis and testicle appearance and func-tioning. Again, this is done by trial and error. Although each she-male thus aided by estrogenic hormones and other means outwardly appeared typically female, each currently reported having a functioning penis. Some penises and testicles were said to have diminished in size. And some reported degrees of erectile difficulties and diminished ejaculate volume and frequency from pre-hormone-usage levels.

Other steps at physical change reported were a nose job; breast, chin, hip, cheek, buttock, and lip injections with liquid silicone; breast implants; and various amounts of electrolysis. Most of the silicone injections are done at some place other than a medical facility.

All but one of these she-males had long hair styled in an attractive, typi-cally female fashion. The one who did not was in a transition stage to full fem-inine appearance. Their body types ranged from delicate and very slim to stocky. One was close to six feet tall. The others were around 5′7″–5′9″. One was Venezuelan and Black, one was Black, and one was mixed Polynesian. The other were Caucasian and of probable Anglo-European descent. These she-males typically had what would normally be considered in our society an attractive female face, body structure, and skin texture. Their walk, posture, and gestures were those of a typical female. Even their voices carried a pleasant feminine tone throughout our phone and in-person contact with them. With their make-up and casual feminine-type attire, they certainly appear to be female. Our subjective overall ratings would describe them as ranging from very attractive to average for a female. We could easily believe a few of them when they said they had modeled and danced professionally as females.

The first sex with a partner for most of these subjects was with a male. However, four of the seven have experienced sex with a female. None preferred the latter. Only one or two would now perhaps have sex with a female for money. One had been married to a woman and has a grown son. And one had had marriages, of sorts, to two different men.

Their current professional sex activity differed from each other substantially. Some engaged only in active anal sex. Some combined that with performing as a dominatrix. Some performed oral sex at times. One only wished to receive oral sex. One seemed to "do it all," even posing at times as a biologic female. A few currently engaged at times in modeling, stripping, and massage for a fee. Several were vague about their activities. Most claimed condom use at all appropriate times with customers, but two admitted doing so only occasionally. Two did not use condoms with their regular sex partners.

Most worked out of their apartments. A few seemed to get contacts in bars. One got dominatrix business over the Internet. Their fees seemed to range widely depending upon the circumstances. Only one person, the transitioning one, had a substantial job and she was about to lose it because of the harassment she was getting at work. Several worked at times as a hairdresser. A couple of the she-males began homosexual hooking as a male while still a teen. Several were vague about that, but a couple of the subjects seemed to have begun their professional career as a she-male.

In each case, the principal members of the she-male's family knew of her new self-identity. In three of the cases the principal family members were very understanding and supportive. In one case, the deceased parents were not at all supportive. In three cases the family in varying degrees was not comfortable with the alternative identity. Yet, six of our seven interviewees seemed to be very comfortable with their identities and their dual-purpose bodies.

The common answer given by each of them when asked about their hopes and dreams for the future was to someday get a good, regular job. Three hoped to someday develop a permanent relationship with a loved one. One aspired to a better education. And one wished to acquire a child for herself and her husband through a surrogate mother.

Our impression of the she-males we interviewed is that they are people with a good heart who are earnestly trying to cope with a society that does not wish to provide a place for them. Their lives are made unduly and unnecessarily hard by the official insistence of our culture that there be only two sexes. Unlike the more enlightened societies of historical times that treasured and even revered people of combined or intermixed sex and gender attributes, the she-males of today are truly an oppressed people.

Unlike a postoperative transsexual who can legally acquire a new identity in her or his postsurgical sex, the she-male has no such opportunity. Left in the limbo of appearing to the outer world to be totally female but retaining the legal status of a male means sure disqualification from most avenues of meaningful, legal employment. The financial cost of all of the chemical, surgical, and other treatments she-males must undertake is an ongoing additional burden of great proportions.

The existence of an almost overwhelming amount of employment distress has been routinely mentioned in other studies of inter-sex individuals in this and other countries (MacFarlane 1984; Levine, Gruenewald, and Shaiova 1976). Most of the she-males we studied would probably not be working as a prostitute if adequate, normal job opportunities were open to them. They seemed to enjoy their work as a prostitute in varying degrees. It can be a great ego boost for a hunky man to turn on to them and pay them for sex—especially since the customer almost always knows of the she-male status. Yet, few of the she-males seemed to enjoy the actual sex for which they were being paid.

The ego boost, the qualified acceptance by the customer of who the she-male is, the money to be made by hooking, and the lack of adequate alternative employment opportunities seemed to be the controlling factors in their choice of work.

This is an extremely limited view of she-male prostitutes in the San Diego area. There are other segments of that population that we did not study. There is a sizable streetwalker segment and a segment that works principally out of bars and clubs. And there is a growing group of illegal immigrant she-males, mostly from Mexico and other Hispanic countries, who speak almost no English and often have done little to transition to look female. We heard from several sources that some of the latter are not above relieving their customers of valuables without their consent. Our interviewees were quite upset about the negative image that group casts on the whole she-male community.

Even though the she-male prostitutes in San Diego are a definite community of sorts, there is no identified support group of and for them. They are suffering from that lack as they are seriously suffering from the lack of adequate medical support in their efforts to balance their unique emotional and biological needs. In the final analysis, our society has left them to drift alone through a hostile world.

# References

Bem, S. L. 1995. Dismantling gender polarization and compulsory heterosexuality: Should we turn the volume down or up? *Journal of Gender Studies* 17: 55–67.

Blanchard, R. 1993. The she-male phenomenon and the concept of partial autogynephilia. *Journal of Sex and Marital Therapy* 19 (1): 69–76.

Bockting, W. O. 1996. *Transgender coming out: Gender revolution?* Paper presented at the annual meeting of the Society for the Scientific Study of Sexuality, Houston, Texas.

Bolin, A. 1996. *To transgender: Destabilizing genes, genitals and gender.* Paper presented at the annual meeting of the Society for the Scientific Study of Sexuality, Houston, Texas.

Levine, E. M., D. Gruenewald, and C. H. Shaiova. 1976. Behavioral differences and emotional conflict among male-to-female transsexuals. *Archives of Sexual Behavior* 5 (1): 81–86.

MacFarlane, D. F. 1984. Transsexual prostitution in New Zealand: Predominance of persons of Maori extraction. *Archives of Sexual Behavior* 13 (4): 301–309.

Williams, W. L. 1986. *The Spirit and the Flesh.* Boston: Beacon Press.

# OUT OF CASH:
## THE RISE AND DEMISE OF A
## MALE PROSTITUTES' RIGHTS ORGANIZATION

### JACQUELINE BOLES AND KIRK ELIFSON

In the 1960s the Civil Rights Movement began its challenge to the status quo. After its success in meeting at least some of its goals, i.e., passage of the Civil Rights Act of 1964, other identity groups began to engage in claims-making rhetoric and direct action to further their goals. While many of these identity groups consisted of people well within the mainstream, e.g., women, victims of sexual abuse, people with disabilities, others formed around those who hold stigmatized or devalued status.

Until recently the resource mobilization paradigm has dominated sociological research on social movement organizations (SMOs). Based on a rational actor model, this theoretical approach suggests that actors make assessments by weighing the costs and benefits of participating in these organizations (Buechler 1993). The organizations that are the most viable are those that have access to valued resources.

New mobilization theory focuses on movement ideology and culture in explaining movement success (Benford 1993; Valocchi 1996). One of the key tasks of an emerging social movement is to develop an ideology, i.e., "the ideas, beliefs, values, symbols, and meanings that motivate individual participation and give coherence to individual action" (Buechler 1993, 222) which can then be "framed." Framing involves the development of an interpretive scheme for directing the efforts of the organization. Framing identifies the victims and villains and suggests how injustices can be removed and wrongs righted (Snow and Benford 1992; Vallochi 1996). From this perspective the success of a SMO is based not only on the resources that it has, but also on the message, that is, the framing of the movement's ideology.

Most research on SMOs has focused on large-scale movements whose members are well within the mainstream (Freeman 1975; McAdam 1982).

267

Further, most of this research describes the outcome of the efforts of these movements to develop their ideology and framing strategies with scant attention given to the processes of negotiation that finally produced the finished product.

Gay and lesbian SMOs were certainly among the first sexual identity organizations to push for acceptance/tolerance within the larger society (D'Emilio 1992; Rechy 1995). Now a number of sexual identity groups including transgender, bisexual, and transvestite groups have formed organizations to put forth their claims to societal acceptance.

Sex workers, including exotic dancers, pornography film actors, and prostitutes, have formed organizations to articulate their claims to legitimacy. The only one of these organizations that has had any success is COYOTE (Call Off Your Old Tired Ethics), a prostitutes' rights organization. For sexual identity groups the formation of an ideology and framing that ideology so as to recruit members and gain at least some acceptance in the larger society is crucial. In this paper we describe the efforts of one sexual identity group, CASH (Coalition for Safer Hustling), a male prostitutes' rights organization, to develop and articulate an ideology. Our analysis of the failure of this organization will add to our understanding of the processes by which social movement ideologies are created and framed.

# Methods

The data for this paper come from two sources. The authors were active participants in CASH from its inception. We were present at the first organizing conference and also at the regional conference held the following year. Over the life of CASH we held many informal conversations with its members.

Second, we rely on official documents and newsletters distributed by the sponsoring organization. We have a complete set of CASH newsletters plus proceedings from national and regional conferences.

This is a case study of one organization. We trace the history of CASH in its efforts to develop an ideology that would function to recruit and retain members and legitimate the organization to the larger society.

### The Ideology and Framing Strategies of Prostitutes' Rights SMOs

In the 1970s a number of "deviance liberation" groups began to resist negative labeling and to demand equal rights.

Transvestites, transsexuals, paedophiles, sadomasochists, fetishists, bisexuals, prostitutes, and others—each group marked by specific sexual tastes or aptitudes, subdivided and demarcated often, into specific styles, morals, and communities, each with specific histories, of self expression—have all appeared on the world's stage to claim their space and "rights." (Weeks 1985, 187)

Many of these sexual identity groups borrowed from the early civil rights groups and co-opted their ideology (Boykin 1996). The gay and lesbian rights' movement has been in the forefront of sexual identity groups in their efforts to legitimate their special statuses. Supported by a relatively large number of well-to-do, educated, and politically influential advocates, gays and lesbians mounted increasingly successful campaigns to legitimate their sexual status (Seidman 1992). Gays support numerous national and local organizations that are diligent in protecting/extending their rights. For example, Jenness (1995) demonstrated how gay and lesbian SMOs were successful in getting violence against homosexuals defined as a social problem.

Prostitutes constitute another sexual identity group that sought to change their public perception. The prostitutes' rights movement in the United States began in San Francisco in 1973 when Margo St. James, a self-proclaimed ex-prostitute, founded COYOTE. The public proclamations of COYOTE have been well documented (Jenness 1993; Weitzer 1991); however, we know little about the internal discussions and negotiations that went on within COYOTE. What follows is a brief discussion of the ideology and framing strategies of COYOTE.

## COYOTE Organization

Until she left the organization, Margo St. James was the head of COYOTE. She had an advisory board but no formal organizational structure (Jenness 1993). Most of the advisory board members were not prostitutes, and perhaps only about 10 percent of the membership of COYOTE was or had been prostitutes (Jenness 1993). Anyone could become a member of COYOTE just by paying a membership fee. According to Jenness, artists, lawyers, judges, and other influential people joined the organization. St. James (personal communication) said that "For awhile it was quite the thing to be a member of COYOTE." Although St. James was head of COYOTE, there were no paid positions and no official duties. Those who chose to be active "did their own thing."

## COYOTE Ideology and Framing

The central goal of COYOTE was to "protect prostitutes from public designations of deviance, as well as from systems of legal and social control" (Jenness 1993, 314). To accomplish this COYOTE developed a few core tenets that they framed and disseminated. First, they argued that "a woman has the right to control her own body." This is part of the ideology of the women's movement and has been used particularly in regard to abortion issues. By appropriating that tenet and applying it to prostitution, COYOTE offered a legitimation for its push for the decriminalization of prostitution.

COYOTE's second major tenet was that prostitution is voluntarily chosen work; prostitutes became sex workers and, as such, were entitled to all the rights and protections of other service workers. Until the beginning of the AIDS pandemic, COYOTE's message was that female prostitutes are like other personal service workers; they do legitimate work and should be able to carry out their work activities without the interference of the police. Prostitution should be decriminalized and prostitutes/sex workers accorded the dignity and respect of other service workers.

By 1985 Americans were beginning to be concerned about AIDS, and many believed that prostitutes were significant transmitters of HIV into the heterosexual population. To counter this new threat to the legitimacy of prostitution, COYOTE began to change directions. The new co-directors, Gloria Lockert and Priscilla Alexander, became very active in AIDS education and prevention. They received grants from organizations like the Centers for Disease Control and Prevention (CDC) to educate prostitutes about HIV, and they wrote pamphlets and papers and made countless presentations showing that female prostitutes were not responsible for the spread of HIV.

In sum, over its history COYOTE's ideology included: (1) the argument that a woman should control her own body; (2) the redefinition of prostitution as voluntarily chosen service work; and (3) the view that female sex workers practice safer sex and should not be penalized by the spread of the HIV virus. Properly framed, this ideology allowed COYOTE to recruit and retain members who wanted to decriminalize prostitution, including some members of women's and civil rights SMOs, and public health workers and researchers who were impressed by the education and prevention efforts made by COYOTE and its affiliates.

## Male Prostitution and Male Prostitutes' Rights Organizations

Until recently, prostitution has been perceived as a primarily female activity, and most studies of prostitution actually considered only female workers. With the advent of AIDS there has been more scholarly as well as public interest in male prostitutes. As research on HIV seropositivity multiplied, so did the perception that male prostitutes were responsible for the transmission of the HIV virus into the heterosexual population:

> Because of their propensity toward risk-taking behaviors, including substance abuse, unsafe sexual behaviors, and prostitution, male prostitutes

likely serve as a recipient of infection, and as an important epidemiological bridge of transmission of HIV infection from high-risk populations (such as homosexual/bisexual males and intravenous substance users) to the general heterosexual population, their wives, partners and families. (Morse et al. 1991, 535)

Further, a number of research studies reported that male prostitutes, including transvestites, had higher rates of HIV seropositivity and were not as consistent condom users as female sex workers (Elifson et al. 1993; Boles and Elifson 1994). Consequently, male prostitutes became more visible and increasingly harassed by agents of social control.

Gay SMOs have never evidenced much interest in hustlers (male prostitutes), rather they focused on "degaying AIDS" (Rofes 1996). However, because of the increased visibility of hustlers and the assumed relationship between prostitution and the spread of HIV, one gay SMO decided to intervene.

## The Rise and Demise of CASH

The Gay Men's Health Crisis (GMHC) was founded in 1982 as a response to the AIDS pandemic and has taken the provision of services to those who are HIV positive as its major mission (Kayal 1993). In 1993 GMHC received a grant from the American Foundation for AIDS Research (AmFAR) to develop a network of individuals and organizations in the United States and Canada to:

> provide primary and secondary HIV prevention education to male sex workers. The network's purpose is to link these individuals and groups together to share information, coordinate activities, plan research and interventions, advocate for increased education and services for male sex workers, develop an action agenda to better address sex workers' needs, and affect policy and legislation related to the sex industry. (GMHC proceedings, 1993)

Thus was the Coalition for Safer Hustling (CASH) formed; it ceased to exist three short years later. In this section we review its organizational history and the ideological battles fought by its members to determine the "soul" of the coalition.

### The Organizing Conference

The first event in CASH's history was a national invitational conference held in San Francisco in October 1993. More than seventy-five people, including researchers, sex worker activists, and service providers attended. Shortly afterward, GMHC published a list of CASH members: sixty-six were affiliated with community-based organizations (CBOs), seventeen were researchers, twenty-six were public health workers, and twenty-three were sex worker advocates.

The conference opened with a plenary session, and then participants were divided into four facilitated regional work groups. The three plenary speakers were Kirk Elifson (a sociologist and HIV researcher), Cajetan Luna (a behavioral epidemiologist and director of the Joves Project), and Andrew Sorfleet (a sex worker). Kirk Elifson reviewed our and others' research on HIV/AIDS among male prostitutes. Luna addressed ethical issues involving sex workers and insisted that: (1) male sex workers are a discriminated minority within a discriminated minority; (2) the terms "prostitute" and "hustler" are pejorative; and (3) programs should be developed that will enable sex workers to leave prostitution.

In contrast Sorfleet discussed the approach of the Prostitute Safe Sex Project. He argued that prostitute work is a valid choice, and that outreach workers have no right to impose their values on sex workers:

> There's also an assumption in a lot of social service agencies that sex work isn't work. You hear terms like "survival sex." I think working at McDonald's is survival work. . . . My attitude is that any kid who's learned how to make fifty bucks in fifteen minutes should be commended for that kind of ingenuity. (Sorfleet 1993)

At the close of his presentation Sorfleet asked for a meeting of all sex workers so as to determine their agenda for the conference.

Each of the four regional caucuses (West, Midwest, Southeast, and Northeast) held a series of meetings to work on issues, plans, and goals. In general the caucuses agreed to: (1) try to recruit sex workers into CASH; (2) advocate for the decriminalization of prostitution; and (3) work to improve the delivery of services to sex workers.

During these discussions heated debates, largely between sex workers and service providers in the Northeast and West caucuses, arose. Under the leadership of sex workers from Toronto, the Northeast caucus took the strongest stand in advocating leadership by sex workers. They called for: (1) "representation and leadership of hustlers"; (2) "hustler ownership of the network"; (3) "promote leadership within the sex industry"; (4) development of a "whore exchange and whore social events"; and (5) development of "public service announcements for the general public about hustler population—to legitimate it" (Northeast Regional Reports 1993).

The sex workers' caucus went even further in demanding leadership by sex workers:

> The group decided that for the network to be effective, the workers must be in charge of decision making and policy. We would create a mission policy, a membership policy, and decide the direction of the network. (St. Blaise 1993)

At the end of the conference the resolution by the sex workers was put to a vote. There ensued a heated debate between the sex workers and the service providers who argued that it would be difficult to recruit and keep sex workers and that the conservative communities in which their agencies were located would not be responsive to sex workers' demands. With the addition of a number of sex workers from the San Francisco area who attended this meeting, the sex workers' resolution passed.

## Developments at CASH: 1994–95

In 1994 AmFAR renewed its grant to support CASH; however, AmFAR was critical of the amount of time and energy CASH devoted to "governance issues," and urged CASH to concentrate on HIV education and prevention. The GMHC began publishing a quarterly newsletter, as did several of the regional networks. The GMHC newsletter contained reports from each of the regions as well as interviews and reports, e.g., "Packing for a Call" (Minneaux 1994). In June CASH adopted a constitution that identified the threefold mission of the organization as "prevention, networking and advocacy" plus a set of "Principles and Beliefs" that included:

> to avoid AIDS male sex workers must take control of all aspects of their own lives . . . when people do sex work because of a lack of choice, it is the lack of choice that is the problem . . . to avoid AIDS sex workers must see their lives and their work as valuable . . . most of the problems sex workers experience . . . are not inherent in sex work but result from laws and attitudes that disregard the worth and rights of sex workers. . . . AIDS can only be stopped by encouraging people to voluntarily change their behavior . . . criminalizing sex work and consenting sexual activities are a barrier to AIDS prevention. . . . HIV+ people have the right to have safe sex with others, whether for free or for profit. HIV+ sex workers should not be blamed for their condition . . .

The most controversial part of the constitution involved the governance of the network: "There are three categories of members: voting members (individual sex workers), honorary voting members (individual former sex workers), and supporting members who may not vote." A steering committee consisting of two coordinators from each region would direct the network. Coordinators were to be elected by sex workers or former sex workers. Coordinators had to be either sex workers or former sex workers, and a female sex worker could substitute for a male if necessary.

Most CASH members were employees of CBOs or public health agencies, and they believed that this constitution was unworkable. They argued that sex workers would probably lead the coalition in such a radical direction that their CBOs might lose their funding, or they might lose their jobs. Members complained that they or their agencies were always threatened by the "Christian Right" so that they had to be cautious about drawing any unfavorable publicity (Manalansan and Kaplan 1994).

Through all this turmoil coalition-building continued. The CASH members brought new people, usually associated with CBOs, into the regional networks and met with other prostitutes' rights organizations like PONY (Prostitutes of New York), gay rights groups (ACT UP), and the influential San Francisco Task Force on Prostitution.

In November, Steven Humes, CASH's project director, resigned from GMHC. In his final column in the CASH newsletter, he said, "CASH must focus on HIV prevention strategies for male sex workers. . . . However, this kind of action is possible only if individual representatives and regions are communicating clearly and are in consensus about goals. This is painstaking work in which all voices must be heard, respected, and given a fair share in decision making."

In August a team from GMHC (Manalansan and Kaplan 1994) submitted an evaluation of CASH to AmFAR. They identified three major problems: lack of clarity of goals, the decision-making process, and communication. They also pointed to a lack of racial and sexual orientation diversity in CASH membership. Whether homosexual-identified white males can represent heterosexual-identified and minority sex workers was thought to be questionable.

## The Regional Conferences, 1994

Each region held a GMHC-funded conference in October. We attended the Southeast conference in New Orleans. Reports from the regional conferences indicated that all were having difficulty recruiting sex workers. Because they could not recruit any sex workers, the Midwest coalition voted to form a new organization, SPEAR (Service Providers, Educators, and Researchers), though they continued their affiliation with CASH and GMHC. The Southeast network also criticized the constitution but would continue to work within CASH's structure. The caucus developed a statement of purpose: "We are the Southern coalition of service providers and researchers promoting harm reduction and HIV education among male sex workers through the direct input of the clients we serve."

The West coalition agreed to consider "all voices equal" in decision making but did establish a sex worker advisory council. No one at the Northeast caucus voiced any opposition to the constitution nor did they see it as an obstacle to effective participation.

Beyond their concern over governance, all the caucuses were critical of their own and GMHC's activities. The CASH members felt that GMHC had not shown enough leadership in helping them develop a workable agenda that would include concrete, attainable objectives. They were also critical of their own networks for failing to develop action plans and realize some concrete objectives: "People need results in a form they can show to their co-workers and other sex workers. The region is frustrated with the lack of tangible accomplishments to show for the last year" (St. Blaise, Sept., 1994).

## The Beginning of the End, 1994–95

After the regional conferences, the network coordinators met at GMHC headquarters and developed a new constitution that was sent out for ratification. This constitution gave an equal vote to all members. The steering committee also developed an agenda for the coming year: (1) identify possible funding agencies and put together a package to be distributed to these agencies; (2) work on procedures to establish CASH as the national voice representing sex workers; and (3) include female sex workers.

In May CASH published a position paper that described the mission and purpose of the organization. By distributing it to various news agencies CASH hoped to become the "national voice on HIV prevention and other issues related to male and transgender sex workers."

The funding organization AmFAR did not renew its grant to GMHC; so CASH was without funding. GMHC agreed to continue publishing the CASH newsletter, but the steering committee was supposed to seek new funding. Members of the steering committee debated whether or not to try to find funding and carry on the organization. Those who worked for CBOs said that fundraising efforts, i.e., grant writing, should be undertaken under the auspices of their organizations. Further, most believed that there was little commitment to CASH among their regional memberships. Joe Wright, steering committee member from the Southeast, said:

> It just wasn't there. We all realized that there was not a commitment from the regions. If I'm going to write a grant, it's going to be for _____ [CBO employer]. We did network, and I learned a lot from others—what they were doing—problems they had. But basically we [the steering committee] just felt that we couldn't give CASH any more time.

# Discussion and Conclusions

The prostitutes' rights organization COYOTE is over twenty-five years old; it has several branches, a number of affiliates, and a world-wide reputation. Although organizations with competing ideologies, e.g., Women Held in Systems of Oppression (WHISPER), have dissolved, COYOTE continues to represent the public face of prostitution to the larger society. It has co-sponsored several international conferences on prostitution, and some of its members have given presentations at international conferences dealing with AIDS and other communicable diseases. Why has COYOTE managed to sustain itself as a viable organization and CASH did not?

Over its history COYOTE had few financial resources, and, though it formed coalitions with other SMOs, e.g., the National Organization for Women, these organizations' resources were never at COYOTE's disposal. The strength of COYOTE has been in its message, clearly articulated by Margo St. James: prostitution should be decriminalized because it is legitimate work performed by people who should have the right to control the use of their own bodies.

According to traditional resource mobilization theory, financial and organizational resources are crucial to the success of an SMO (Buechler 1993); however, new directions in social movement research suggest that the movement's ideology is crucial in explaining the success of some and the failure of others (Benford 1993; Buechler 1993; Valocchi 1996).

Initially, COYOTE had practically no dependable source of funds, and its existence was always precarious. Nor was it directed by a woman with a background in organizational management; its accountants and lawyers were generally volunteers. What COYOTE did have was a message and a messenger who could articulate it. Until she left the organization Margo St. James was COYOTE; she articulated the message and communicated it to the public. Under its straightforward banner, COYOTE recruited a small core of dedicated members and a larger group of sympathizers including academics, judges, and even police officials. Over the years other well-known prostitutes, e.g., Xaveria Hollander, Dolores French, always referred to St. James as the founding mother of prostitutes' rights and adhered to the ideology of the prostitutes' rights movement as articulated by St. James. French (1988, 136), the founder of Hooking Is Real Employment, said:

> The women who approached me had a simple political creed: that a woman has a right to sell sexual services just as much as she has a right to sell her brains to a law firm when she works as a lawyer. . . . Therefore, they wanted prostitution decriminalized . . . they wanted to assert prostitutes' rightful place within the women's movement; and they wanted to provide an outreach program, to help other prostitutes.

The history of CASH differs dramatically from that of COYOTE. Initially, CASH certainly had more financial and organizational resources than COYOTE; it had a substantial budget and a strong, successful CBO to provide structure and direction. However, those were not enough.

There are three primary reasons for the failure of CASH to survive. First and foremost, a deep and perhaps unbridgeable divide separated the service providers and the sex workers. The service providers, who were numerically in the majority, viewed the coalition as a resource to aid them in providing services for male prostitutes in their communities. The sex workers wanted an advocacy organization controlled by themselves. Only a few sex workers from Toronto had a model about how a prostitute-directed organization would work, and that model was not shared with the membership. Because of the chasm between these two groups, CASH was never able to articulate an ideology that it could communicate to the general public.

Second, no one person or core group "owned" the organization. Members of the steering committee were elected from their regional coalitions, and almost all were employees of CBOs or public health departments where their primary loyalties lay. At the initial conference GMHC publically disavowed "ownership" of the network and thereafter played only a supporting role. The few active sex worker advocates were more committed to CASH than any other members, but the organizational structure made it impossible for one or a few of them to take the reins of the organization. No one person's job, identity, or career was tied to the success or failure of CASH.

Finally, CASH utterly failed in its goal of becoming a spokesperson for male and transgender prostitutes. Even though CASH distributed a position paper, there is no record of anyone from the media requesting an interview. The reasons for this failure are probably rooted, in part, in the media's timidity about dealing with male and transgender prostitution; however, the lack of a clearly articulated message, properly framed, and an articulate spokesperson are also important factors.

In this case study we have described the birth and death of one CBO, detailing the ideological struggle between members of the organization. We argue that the fundamental cause of the failure of CASH, in contrast to COYOTE, was its inability to develop an ideology behind which all the members could rally and which could be articulated to the mass media and to the general public.

Any SMO may experience difficulty articulating its message and getting it heard by the public, but deviance liberation groups are particularly disadvantaged. To overcome this the stigmatized group must develop and articulate a message that will draw adherents and create at least sympathetic tolerance from the general public. In this study we have documented the failure of one SMO to develop such an ideology.

# References

Benford, R. 1993. "You can be the hundredth member": Collective action frames and vocabularies of motive within the nuclear disarmament movement. *Sociological Quarterly* 34: 195–216.

Boles, J., and K. Elifson. 1994. Sexual identity and HIV: The male prostitute. *Journal of Sex Research* 31: 139–46.

Boykin, K. 1996. *One More River to Cross: Black and Gay in America.* New York: Doubleday.

Buechler, S. 1993. Beyond resource mobilization: Emerging trends in social movement theory. *Sociological Quarterly* 34: 217–35.

D'Emilio, J. 1992. *Making Trouble: Essays on Gay History, Politics, and the University.* New York: Routledge.

Elifson, K., J. Boles, M. Sweat, W. Darrow, E. Posey, and W. Elsea. 1993. Male transvestite prostitutes and HIV risk. *American Journal of Public Health* 83: 260–62.

Freeman, J. 1975. *The Politics of Women's Liberation.* New York: McKay.

French, D. 1988. *Working: My Life as a Prostitute.* New York: E. P. Dutton.

Jenness, V. 1993. *Making It Work: The Prostitutes' Rights Movement in Perspective.* Hawthorne, N.Y.: Aldine De Gruyter.

———. 1995. Social movement growth: domain expansion, and framing processes: The gay/lesbian movement and violence against gays and lesbians as a social problem. *Social Problems* 42: 145–70.

Kayal, P. 1993. *Bearing Witness: Gay Men's Health Crisis and the Politics of AIDS.* Boulder: Westview Press.

Manalansan, M., and J. Kaplan. 1994. *An Evaluation of the Coalition Advocating Safer Hustling.* New York: Dept. of Evaluation Research, Gay Men's Health Crisis.

McAdam, D. 1982. *Political Process and the Development of Black Insurgency.* Chicago: University of Chicago Press.

Minneaux, S. 1994. Packing for a call. *CASH Newsletter* 1 (2): 8–9.

Morse, E., P. Simon, R. Osofsky, P. Belson, and R. Gaumer, 1991. The male street prostitute: A vector for transmission of HIV infection into the heterosexual world. *Social Science and Medicine* 32: 535–39.

Rechy, J. 1995. The outlaw sensibility in the arts: From drag and leather to prose; the mythology of Stonewall and a defense of stereotypes. Presented at Queer Frontiers Conference, University of Southern California, March.

Rofes, E. 1996. *Reviving the Tribe: Regenerating Gay Men's Sexuality and Culture in the Ongoing Epidemic.* New York: Hawthorne Press.

Seidman, S. 1992. *Embattled Eros: Sexual Politics and Ethics in Contemporary America.* New York: Routledge.

Snow, D., and R. Benford, 1992. Master frames and cycles of protest. In *Frontiers in Social Movement Theory,* edited by McClung and Mueller. New Haven: Yale University Press.

St. Blaise, V. 1994. Report on Sex Worker's Caucus. *GMHC Hustler Network Conference Proceedings.* San Francisco: n.p.

Sorfleet, A. 1993. HIV/AIDS and hustler activities. *GMHC Hustler Network Conference Proceedings.* San Francisco: n.p.

Valocchi, S. 1996. The emergence of the integrationist ideology in the civil rights movement. *Social Problems* 43: 116–30.

Weeks, J. 1985. *Sexuality and Its Discontents: Meanings, Myths and Modern Sexualities,* Boston: Routledge and Kegan Paul.

Weitzer, R. 1991. Prostitutes' rights in the United States: The failure of a movement. *Sociological Quarterly* 32: 23–41.

# 5

# PROSTITUTION ON THE AMERICAN FRONTIER AND THE CURRENT SCENE

## Introduction

Prostitution was an established institution in most of the American West, even in Salt Lake City, the heart of Mormon Zion. Although hundreds and thousands of families moved west, the family units were outnumbered by the men, sometimes by as much as 20 or 30 to 1. The men sought their recreation and pleasure in the saloons, dance halls, and special houses of prostitution. Many of the women who found employment on the frontier were themselves looking for a better life, but opportunities for unmarried women on the frontier were limited, and many ended up in what might be called the sex industry.

Mostly their lives remain unrecorded, but photographs of many have survived, and Renée Blake, who coordinated the art exhibit at ICOP (International Conference on Prostitution), persuaded Timothy Gordon of Missoula, Montana, to exhibit photographs from his collection, some of which we have included here. Also included is a series of photographs collected by The Margo St. James Task Force on Prostitution of COYOTE to give a somewhat different slant on the topic.

Perhaps the best way to introduce the topic is to have Renée speak for herself in two of her brief poems and in her story of Jolette.

# POEMS AND A PERSONAL PERSPECTIVE

## COMPILED BY RENÉE BLAKE

### VINYL FLESH

You say I am like vinyl flesh, bendable to you and yours . . .
Tainted money, rented time, borrowed feelings of sublime,
a lended smile at the drop of a dime . . . all of this should never be a crime!
You say you understand this just fine—so why do you look
at me like I was grime? Who are you to say we are all alike,
that everyone of us has been made from the same design!
I am vinyl flesh to you because I want to be—I too have
desires but I choose not to see the empty bodies that lie
here for me.
I am unreachable for you and a thousand more, 'cause they're
not what I want anymore. I will find my true bleeding flesh again and cry no
more for my still living soul . . . encore,
encore for this divine goal because beyond that there can be nothing more
. . .

### CYNICAL INNOCENCE

To all who found not respite after they've bled,
this is an ode to those of us who fled the pleasures of momentary lust and
had those feelings of post-mortem
coitus dread.
Her virginity is dead, the malevolent erection imbedded its head in a velvet
of red . . .

And so she waits until the constant thrusting sledge
is no more a threat.

She lies wide-eyed on the bed—awaiting the promised
caresses, the warm zephyr of his breath—
what she wants is not met.
She feels cobwebbed by his clutch and un-embraced by his touch.
Trapped by all this temporal activity, half-human, half-foreign
. but most bereft of depth . . .

Her first expectant triumph is not recept,
all that's left is a decorum of the past,
chapters taking form in the storm yet to be born.

It is so mundane, she only awaits the final test
so she can get some rest.
Her heart thumps to a rhythm of a thrusting
she doesn't know yet how to keep. Her arms and legs seem
like lead and she's still not wet. Is that what they call the
"grateful dead"?

As future denizens of promiscuity,
some of us learn to use our bodies as gratuity for the
affinity we crave
but don't have the courage to claim.
Tell us, why does all this have to be such pain?

### JOLETTE—HER BIO AND VIEWS BUT NOT HER REAL NAME

Jolette is a twenty-year veteran of sex work and is recently happily retired—although not so happily impoverished. During her career she worked in a handful of cities, mostly in the U.S., but also in Europe while traveling abroad. She has been arrested twice.

I have always been pretty careful about confiding the true nature of my nightly work to anyone. Very early on I became dismayed when even friends reacted to my status as a prostitute with stereotypical and inaccurate assumptions. I long ago decided not to tell anyone about my sex work until I trusted that they already accepted and knew me as a person. Otherwise they could just never get past the prostitution stigma. And these were people who were not close minded in most respects.

There was one area, however, where this social dilemma was an asset. When dating "regular" men in the conventional manner, I found that by revealing my secret prostituting self I was provided the perfect escape from a relationship I no longer desired. Uncomfortable with outrightly rejecting an unwanted suitor, it seemed easier to gently present my revelation and allow the course of events to unfold the way I knew they would. The script rarely changed. First came my gentle presentation of the big revelation—softly confiding, "I'm a call girl." This was immediately followed by any one of a few different types of stunned expressions hastily suppressed by the arrival of regained composure. Next my soon-to-be-ex would utter the words,

"Okay, well, I'm not a judgmental person." With a nice amount of relief in my voice I'd then reply, "Oh good, great," and then sit back to give it a few days. Somewhere around the predicted time slot, the phone would ring and there I was, just like clockwork, patiently listening to my male friend's uncomfortable explanation of withdrawal. I'd confirm our termination with a very nice voice, saying, "It's okay. I understand."

I was much more nervous about revealing my secret career with men I was truly interested in. During the couple of decades that I worked as a call girl, I was involved in three major relationships—not at the same time—and happily, none of them fit the above script. These men had questions but seemed quite able to transcend society's conventions.

I find the laws against prostitution to be nothing more than the old double standard between men and women, endlessly reinforced by a barrage of covert and overt means—always striving to undermine the power of choice for a woman. There are times the issue of sex work is a million miles from my mind and then I'll hear or read something derogatory about prostitution and suddenly I'm jolted as I remember once again the vehemence and opposition in this society against prostitutes—and they hardly know us.

Jolette is currently active in the rescue and care of abused and abandoned animals, which she says is "somewhat similar to my old careers except I like dogs better even though the money is less." Other life experiences include working on fishing boats in Alaska, driving a taxi in Honolulu, being a soldier in the U.S. Army, working as a teacher's aide, a nurse's aide, a medical transcriber and lots more. She is currently working as a freelance writer and is a mom.

# Prostitutes on the American Frontier: A Pictorial Perspective

## Timothy Gordon

Many wide-eyed, unsuspecting gals who wanted to find adventure, a better life from home, or just seek employment, came west to booming mining towns like Helena, Bodie, Jerome, Dodge, or Virginia City, looking for happier life escaping the squalor of a big city or the hard, back-breaking work in a rural area, just to find that most jobs for women in teaching, banking, seamstress work, child caring, or store keeping were already filled by the older resident ladies. Consequently, the only work available for single women who just arrived, perhaps escaping their husbands or abusive fathers to this harsh world of single men (most often outnumbering the females about 20 or 30 to 1) in the wild West . . . ended up in saloons, "Boarding Houses," or brothels.

They became dance-hall girls, "Hurdy-Gurdy" dancers, and, where provision of female companionship was at great demand, they even rented out their bodies parttime for money or other needed commodities . . . from gold nuggets to food, wine, opium, or even chickens.

The living conditions were so hard on these women that even if they survived the long stagecoach rides through the waterless deserts coming out west to some of the rugged mining towns, a lot of them perished from diseases, rapes, mental breakdowns, or suicides after a few years of brutish treatment by these hardened men and the rough environment they lived in.

But the special women who did survive contributed to upholding the morale and humor of these very lonely and affection-starved men, who often had not been close to any female for years, much less touch one. The West would have never expanded so rapidly if it was not for their wonderful high spirits and help during such trying times.

**Fig. 1. (Top)** Many girls worked in theater, burlesque, or modeling by day and as "Hurdy Gurdy" dancers or saloon "entertainers" by night. (Photos pictured in figures 1-10 are courtesy of the Timothy Gordon Collection, Missoula, Montana.)

**Fig. 2. (Left)** A lot of attractive working girls were sought out by amateur photographers because they tended to pose more seductively and unabashedly than their more prim and proper counterparts.

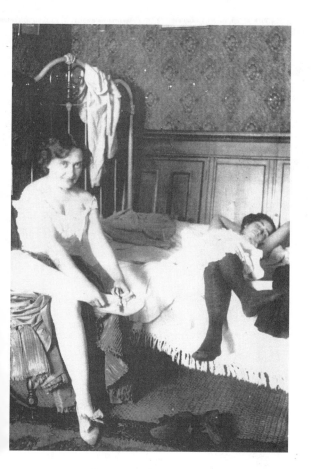

*Fig. 3. (Left)* Resting "in between takes" with a friend . . .

*Fig. 4. (Below)* A typical brothel in Saltese, Montana.

*Fig. 5.* An aging but still feisty-looking saloon prostitute of the Old West.

*Fig. 6.* As evidenced here, beauty was not always a prerequisite for the career of prostitute.

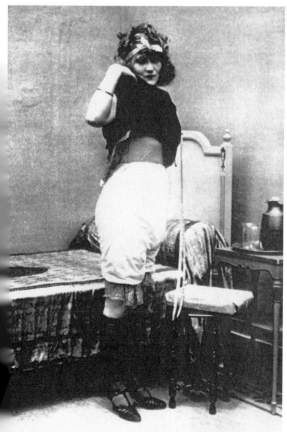

*Fig. 7. (Top)* Occasional playfulness and the use of alcohol or opium were popular "anesthetics" that quelled the very harsh conditions the "ladies of the night" had to endure in the 1800s.

*Fig. 8. (Left)* Provocative "new arrivals" from Europe were in frequent competition with the local girls.

Fig. 9. "The Duke," a business manager at Chicago Joe's in Helena, Montana.

Fig. 10. This Butte, Montana, prostitute poses in the only available artistic prop, some wrinkled bed linen.

# POSTERS FROM THE MARGO ST. JAMES TASK FORCE ON PROSTITUTION

## MARGO ST. JAMES

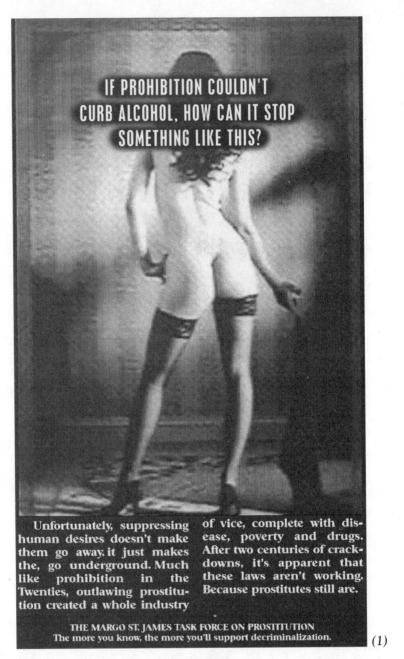

**IF PROHIBITION COULDN'T CURB ALCOHOL, HOW CAN IT STOP SOMETHING LIKE THIS?**

Unfortunately, suppressing human desires doesn't make them go away. it just makes the, go underground. Much like prohibition in the Twenties, outlawing prostitution created a whole industry of vice, complete with disease, poverty and drugs. After two centuries of crackdowns, it's apparent that these laws aren't working. Because prostitutes still are.

THE MARGO ST. JAMES TASK FORCE ON PROSTITUTION
The more you know, the more you'll support decriminalization.

(1)

Figs. 1–3. The 1997 International Sex Worker Art Exhibit: These posters were created in 1995 by Gerard Vaglio and Neville de Souza for Margo St. James, founder of COYOTE (Call Off Your Old Tired Ethics), for the San Francisco Prostitution Task Force. The models for the photos are members and supporters of COYOTE. The complete set of seven posters was on display at the 1997 International Conference on Prostitution.

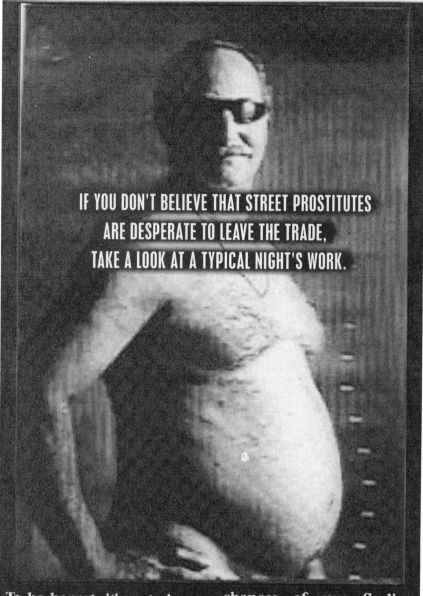

IF YOU DON'T BELIEVE THAT STREET PROSTITUTES ARE DESPERATE TO LEAVE THE TRADE, TAKE A LOOK AT A TYPICAL NIGHT'S WORK.

To be honest, it's not always like this. Often it's worse. So why can't the typical street prostitute just do something else for a living? Because our legal system won't let her. A police record ruins her chances of ever finding another job. A hefty fine just forces her right back on the street to come up with the money. Laws like these benefit nobody. Except for a few irresistible men.

THE MARGO ST. JAMES TASK FORCE ON PROSTITUTION
The more you know, the more you'll support decriminalization.

(2)

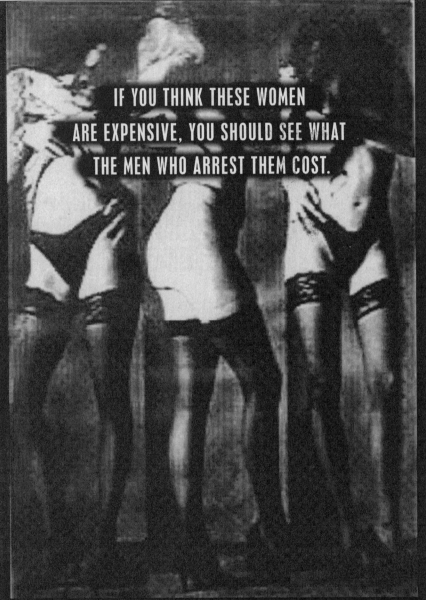

**IF YOU THINK THESE WOMEN ARE EXPENSIVE, YOU SHOULD SEE WHAT THE MEN WHO ARREST THEM COST.**

The City of San Francisco employs 12 vice squad officers who do nothing but arrest street prostitutes. Their salaries aside, it cost well over $5 million to process the 4900 cases they added to our already backed-up court system last year. So yes, we do think you'll find these women rather expensive. Because under the current laws, you're the one who ends up paying for them.

**THE MARGO ST. JAMES TASK FORCE ON PROSTITUTION**
The more you know, the more you'll support decriminalization.

# 6

# FEMINIST PERSPECTIVES

## Introduction

As should be evident from the articles so far in this book, much of the past study and writing about prostitution was from the male point of view. Unfortunately, most men did not realize the narrowness of their own perspective. A much needed corrective came when women themselves began writing and researching the topic. Some inkling of different viewpoints on the topic appeared early in the twentieth century, but again, unfortunately, prostitution was a subject that most women avoided for fear of compromising their own status in society. This has all changed in the last part of the twentieth century, and women have begun to investigate prostitution and sex workers generally in significant numbers. The articles in this section indicate some of the different ways in which women have approached the subject. The feminist approach is not a monolithic approach and as Judith Bradford, Sarah Bromberg, Marti Hohmann, Wendy McElroy, and Sibyl Schwarzenbach demonstrate, there are many different ways of looking at the issues. It should be added that men too can have a feminist approach to the issue, and some have attempted to do so, including the male co-editors of this volume. Still, when it comes down to it, it really took the women scholars and researchers to reinterpret the topic in ways quite different from what had been done in the past. Read on.

# FEMINIST ISSUES IN PROSTITUTION

## SARAH BROMBERG

## Preface

Feminist issues are divided into two distinct sections. The first section concerns itself with analyzing the moral sense of the words feminists use to describe prostitution, while in the second section there is more emphasis on the political sense of the words. While portions of this section may appear more speculative, they are firmly grounded in reasoned ethical theory.

In spite of their tendency to misrepresent and exaggerate the meaning of words such as "degradation" and "rape," radical feminists make a philosophical case for the idea that men's aggressive sexual nature is not biological but rather culturally engendered and therefore capable of being modified. Many men believe their sexual inclinations are inherited traits, and therefore a birthright. This belief serves to perpetuate the myth of their natural dominance. Radical feminists promote the idea that changing men's attitude towards women to a more enlightened one is an important goal for all feminists. Their argument that male attitudes can be changed enjoys some credibility as a result of biological studies that show that all human behaviors are not necessarily inherited, that many behaviors potentially arise as a function of human cultures.

With the exception of existentialist feminism, the other four feminisms discussed rely all too often on stereotypical notions of the personal lives of prostitutes by focusing too much attention on one socioeconomic group at the expense of examining the wide diversity of experiences, values, and beliefs of prostitutes. In an effort to shed some light on prostitution, nine categories of prostitution are discussed.

Basic to this writing is the idea that a climate of immorality is everywhere evident in the society, and obviously not only in the lives of prostitutes. This pervasive cultural climate of immorality (cheating, lying, manipulating, and exploiting others to serve one's own ends) contributes to the oppressions that feminists condemn. The common belief that the manipulation of people in pursuit of one's ends is an acceptable behavior reinforces and perpetuates a myth that such behavior is right. The problem is that once such a belief becomes embedded in the society, more forceful forms of exploitation can arise. Thus, it is reasonable to posit the idea that a multiplicity of influences leads to the oppression of women, not simply the aggressive impulses of men.

# Radical Feminism, Prostitution, and Morality

From the beginning, prostitutes and radical feminists have appeared to be at odds with each other. Laurie Shrage makes a case for the radical feminist perspective when she says "female prostitution oppresses women, not because some women who participate in it 'suffer in the eyes of society' but because its organized practice testifies to and perpetuates socially hegemonic beliefs which oppress all women in many domains of their lives" (in Stuart 1995, 74). Such views of radical feminists are seemingly well thought out and difficult to dismiss. However, if some of their arguments are analyzed in the context of classical and contemporary ethics, they begin to take on a different light and lose their integral character. Even though the argument that prostitution corrupts women appeals to logic, it is a position driven by highly charged emotions that ultimately corrupt its logic. The position further deteriorates, as exemplified in the first two chapters of *The Prostitution of Sexuality*, because it oververbalizes[1] the issue and overemphasizes statistical information in an attempt to paint a real-world view of prostitution. Gail Pheterson, in her book *The Prostitution Prism* (1996), touches on other research abuses and the misuse of statistics to define what a prostitute is. This is perhaps the greatest failing of the radical feminists who have built a theory of social right and wrong on a stereotypical notion of what constitutes a prostitute. Statistics about a person or group of persons obviously are not the actual person or group. In relation to this, linguist S. I. Hayakawa reminds us in *Language in Thought and Action* (1978) that "the word is not the thing," that "the habitual confusion of symbols with things symbolized, whether on the part of individuals or societies, is a perennial human problem" (24).[2]

Radical feminist Kathleen Barry, in *The Prostitution of Sexuality* (1995), envisions prostitution as connected to a darkened world of sex, abuse, and violence. But to others more connected to the world of sex work, common sense and ordinary experience show that the world of prostitution is not a grim and humorless world of only pain, suffering, and abuse. Some of what Barry has to say is relevant and has elements of truth to it, but there are other important aspects of prostitution that are positive and life-affirming. Barry's book largely paints prostitution in the light of a violent, thankless, and grim occupation that degrades not only the prostitutes themselves but the whole feminine gender as well. It is her statistical analysis of many facts that seems to guide her conclusions rather than a deep understanding of or intimacy with the world of sex work. The way prostitutes are analyzed—in some instances—objectifies, dehumanizes, and strips them of any personality, like so many flies pinned to a board for an entomologist to study. She reduces prostitutes in moral stature by objectifying them in the same way she charges that men objectify and reduce women.

Radical feminism does not view prostitution as a victimless crime, but as a situation where men have reduced women to an image of being mere sexual objects (Pheterson 1996, 30–36).[3] This allows men to oppress and coerce women unconscionably in order to satisfy their own fantasies through prostitution. Political and economic power seems unfairly divided in the world to these feminists. Men are in the position of dominance, demanding and getting what they want. "According to the radical feminist view, men are socialized to have sexual desires and to feel entitled to have those desires met, whereas women are socialized to meet those desires and to internalize accepted definitions of femininity and sexual objectification" (Freeman 1996, 194).

From the radical feminists' standpoint, the issue of prostitution is an extension of the power politics that govern social intercourse between men and women. They assert the inherent immorality of prostitution by defining its wrongness in terms of its corrupting influence on the dignity of all women. They also seize the higher ground in a battle between men and women, using prostitutes as pawns in a struggle to assert their worldview. In the heat of this battle, the idea of prostitution is oversimplified and subsequently molded into a form that fits well into the political views of the radical feminist. Oversimplifying an issue frequently produces a logical outcome that can support just about any political position. Prostitution is an enormously diverse and complex issue. Lumping virtually all prostitutes into one general category will yield an inaccurate and insensitive view of their lives.

In constructing theories about prostitutes and prostitution, radical feminists would do well to take into account the diversity of reasons why people enter the profession. They also need to take into account the corrupting effect of any deviant behavior as it makes an impact on society. Moral degeneration of any sort affects people both individually and collectively. It could be argued that prostitution, while it undoubtedly degrades women to some extent, is not necessarily as degrading as many other forms of degeneracy.

There is not just one, but at least nine, categories of description into which prostitute women appear to fall.[4] First, there are women who inadvertently fall into poverty and turn to prostitution but have the emotional fiber to withstand the hardships of the profession until they can find something else to do. Second, there are women born poor into families with a long history of poverty and a lack of education. Third, a woman may be abducted against her will for no reasons of defect in her character and be forced into prostitution. Fourth, a woman might voluntarily enter the profession because of defects in her moral character that allow her to fall into association with violent and exploitative social predators, who, like her, do not wish to follow the rules of any legal or moral system. She associates with people in an intimate way, well beyond the protection of the police or the assistance of social agencies that can effectively assist her in fighting off abuse. She underestimates her intelligence and skills and ends up being pimped or trafficked as a prostitute. As illustrated in a subsequent chapter, there is a relationship between working within the social value system(s) and abuse. Thus, it can be said there is potentially a cost for deviating too far from social values.[5] This is where Kathleen Barry's statement that "most women would leave if they could" (Weisberg, 1996, 248) is most relevant to the issue of prostitution. Fifth, a woman may have been "distanced" and demoralized by a fiercely competitive childhood in which she was unable to compete successfully for sufficient attention from parents, teachers, or employers for her to find acceptance and develop direction.[6] Many prostitutes who have their rational faculties intact are able to resist the intimidations of pimps and avoid a considerable amount of abuse. Sixth, low intelligence and physical and mental problems may lead a woman to find a viable way to be part of a productive society through prostitution. Some of these women might be so unpredictable or incorrigible that they would not make "good women" for pimps. They would be difficult people to get close enough to for exploitation by a pimp trying to establish a relationship by way of feigned intimacy. Some, on the other hand, are perhaps easily guided by the more intelligent pimp. Such women might feel protected by a pimp in spite of low-level abuse that might be considered acceptable by the standards of their experience. Seventh, some women perhaps find that they take to prostitution naturally like "fish take to water."[7] This category may include prostitutes whose mothers or relatives were prostitutes through several generations. Such women often know what they are doing and are confident that they can handle most of the dangers. Knowing how to derive value and meaning from what they do, they overcome hardship, obstacles, and abuse. Eighth, the smallest category, attractive women who are very smart. These women recognize an opportunity to make an extraordinarily high income as prostitutes. They place themselves out of danger with wealthy, influential, and intelligent men who can afford a premium price for sexual service. Finally, ninth, some people are irrepressible personalities who seek the challenge of the most dangerous of undertakings. This category includes artists, poets, writers, and political activists of many descriptions who are of adventurous spirit, testing the limits of their society. These are intelligent members of the high culture of prostitution that promotes the profession on a higher spiritual and intellectual plane than other categories.[8] They, with their many supporters in mainstream society, often see prostitution in a different light than that of oppression, abuse, and despair. They are on the cutting edge of change for prostitutes and are its main moralizing force, gradually evoking openness in the hearts and minds of ordinary people.

Most of the violence and abuse radical feminists talk about falls into the first four categories. Abuse in the sixth category, that of physical and mental problems, is a special consideration of its own. The women of the first four categories at greatest risk are those lacking moral fiber, who, with an outlaw attitude, try to tackle the world on their own terms only to be outsmarted by cunning social predators. Their lives perhaps look grim and bleak, but they often voluntarily lead themselves into danger. An analogy could be made comparing prostitution with mountain climbing. It appears easy to do, but in the end it is an occupation fraught with hazards that only the best and the brightest appear to overcome. This inherent danger is mirrored in the moral device of stigma. Stigma of certain descriptions serves to warn unwary people of the inherent dangers of any entry into a particular area of social life. In this instance, it serves not so much to pronounce on morality but to dissuade people from climbing mountains they are unskilled at climbing. The many fine points of stigma are too involved to discuss here but are dealt with in subsequent writings.

Radical feminists do not generally subscribe to this broader view of prostitution as outlined in the above nine categories. It seems almost imperative for such individuals to find a link between pimps as oppressors and a generalized theory of male dominance that views men as perpetuating their power by being oppressors. By narrowing their view of prostitution, radical feminists make a point. Moreover, by reducing social dynamics to sexual oppression as the central focus of male-female relationships, radical feminism attempts to make an end run around conventional and classical ethical views of right and wrong. Constructing a theory for the restriction of the rights of prostitutes in terms of oppression, not morality, is simply another creatively conceived method of rejecting prostitution as a valid way of life.

The focus of Barry's writing, which can in some senses be seen as representative of radical feminists, appears to be a heroic intervention on behalf of prostitutes and women in general to save them from violence and degradation. The extensive abuse that Barry cites can be viewed as a statement on the condition of human civilization in which it is clear that humans are not nearly as moral as they believe themselves to be. She cites numerous instances where violence perpetrated by pimps is the rule rather than the exception in prostitution.[9] Violence and abuse are about immorality. Political dialogue constructed in terms of oppression is a second-order attempt to solve a first-order problem better resolved in conventional moral terms. Contemporary and classical ethics have built, over centuries of ethical discourse, a fairly stable foundation (or foundations) from which to evaluate self-serving and exploitative behaviors. On the other hand, the social theory of Barry, which assigns the cardinal value of moral discernment to be sexual oppression, does not have a substantial foundation on which to build and integrate well into other areas of credible thinking. Theory that is held to be superior is generally theory that integrates well into a broad spectrum of human experience, scientific fact, and other theoretical views. Theory that is narrowly subjective usually has a limited scope of application. In my view Barry's assessment of the moral nature of prostitution falls into this limited category.

There are other reasons for being skeptical of her strong case against prostitution. First is the hasty way in which she develops her ideas, and second is the way in which she holds out a pitiful view of the prostitute's life without distinguishing a wide spectrum of experiences relating to prostitution. She frequently moves from premise to conclusion with great rapidity and employs strong, emotionally laden language to assert the authority of a premise. This kind of reasoning guides one down a selected pathway rather than conveying an understanding of the situation. Appeal, however subtle, to the wretchedness, despair, and abuse of prostitutes can support a theoretical position only so far. Quite a few of Barry's ideas are presented well, but the constant hammering away at oppression eventually paints a portrait of wretchedness and despair afflicting prostitute women without any counterbalancing concepts. Observations that might include enjoyment of prostitution in repartee with clients, or experience that might show pimps in a different light, are totally absent from her work.

If *The Prostitution of Sexuality* does in fact inspire a sense of pathos for women to make a point, it commits an informal fallacy of logic[10] because the issue becomes clouded with emotions that prevent an objective analysis of the situation. Observing poverty is almost always a situation that evokes emotions. Mixing poverty and prostitution together as one thing may give prostitution a different emotional appeal than if it were analyzed on its own. In an over-populated world, there may simply be situations that leave no other choices to women. The pain and suffering they experience might perhaps be realized with any choice they might make. Many probably enjoy what they do. In spite of the seemingly tragic aura of some of their lives, many prostitutes might be more accurately described as being friendly, warm, and sensitive human beings; not as women whose greatest value is to be pawns in a game of political chess for the empowerment of one political group over another. If the primary cause of predatory practices and trafficking is a function of over-population, educational deficiency, feudal social policy, or fierce social competition for attention at school, wealth, and jobs, the fact that prostitution thrives and subsequently degrades women is beside the point. Feminists are likely blaming the wrong people for the existence of a degradation that is a part of a vicious cycle of degradation that has its sources elsewhere.

The corruption of conscience is endemic to human life without regard to gender. Possessing power demonstrably exacerbates the misuse of it no matter who possesses it. Whether men or women were in the dominant position, the situation might not be much different. The heart of the issue is not to be found in vivid descriptions of oppressions and wrongdoing by this party or that, but rather in the wider context of morality itself. Barry, as well as many other feminist writers, cites a seemingly endless list of human rights violations. Such violations are not new to people dedicated to attempting to lead the "moral life" and commonly experiencing a world in which "morality is always a struggle." Where there is unfairness, there is often immorality at work. Morality attempts to bring reason and fairness to an unreasoning world, but it is a difficult struggle. Ethicists have endured consciousness of many forms of unfairness for centuries, but this is a brand-new form of injustice to some feminists.

Prostitution should not always bear the brunt of condemnation for abuse or inspiring abuse. The sheer folly of getting involved with people so obviously unscrupulous has to be noted as a contribution to scenarios of abuse. The mean and complex balances of power, greed, dominance, and dependency between prostitutes and pimps give rise to abusive interactions, a subject surprisingly undiscussed in Barry's work. In contrast, Priscilla Alexander's essays in *Sex Work* (Delacoste and Alexander 1987) show more awareness of the larger world of prostitution. She utilizes more restraint than Barry does in the matter of leaping from premise to conclusion or in oververbalizing ideas.

## Moral Considerations

Radical feminism is linked to morality because feminists assert that prostitution is "wrong." The field of ethics is a formal discipline in which rightness and wrongness are analyzed, and this is where the matter of prostitution should be analyzed and discussed. In the case of both the radical feminist and the conventional morality, prostitution is deemed inappropriate behavior. However, the moral nature of prostitution does not traditionally derive from the belief that it degrades other women. The nearest analog in ethics to the degradation that feminists identify is the view that certain behaviors are generative and others degenerative and that the latter therefore should be discouraged and avoided.

Shifting the ethical center of sexual morality, from contemporary and classical ethical theory toward a new morality in which moral right and wrong is ultimately a function of male domination, would not logically hold. If male domination becomes the underpinning of morality, all systems of moral theory then must be explicable in consistent terms with this new moral centering in which male domination and the thirst for sexual power are central. Marxism seems to have this same theoretical weakness as it attempts to explain the human system in terms of economic considerations. Activists are often slow to realize the limitations of this theoretical approach. They persist in the belief that this approach is a viable explanation of human action. Good theory can be defined as made up of propositions that integrate best in the widest spectrum of theory, observation, and human experience. Narrow theory focusing on special interests may have minimal applicability to other reasoning systems. Describing human action in terms of exploitation and oppression is useful but it has limitations. Biological explanations yield far more consistent and interesting ideas of underlying forces that govern human behavior.

As previously mentioned, the fact that prostitution is considered morally wrong derives in part from moral sentiments that view certain behaviors as degenerative and others as generative. Persons involved in prostitution must look critically at what they are doing in terms of generative or degenerative behavior. If prostitution is causing a degeneration of values and attitudes, moral concern might be valid. If it is a positive circumstance leading to personal growth, as a general rule, other people ought to focus their attentions on other aspects of potentially degenerative behavior in society. For instance, the consumption of wine at social gatherings seems fairly generative up to a certain point. When consumption becomes frequent and obsessive it can inspire a series of degenerative changes in behavior that can totally alter the person. Alcohol addiction radically changes a person's behavior. For some people the consumption of alcohol is a degenerative activity.

If prostitution is not regulated, degenerative behaviors can evolve. Prostitutes want rights and the freedom to practice their trade. But there must be a recognition that problems can arise from this sort of activity. Making prostitution a truly professional occupation will help keep prostitutes on a generative course of personal evolution. To the extent that prostitutes are willing to regulate themselves, as other professionals do, society might be inclined to a greater acceptance of sex workers. This potential relationship is later explored in a theory of social assimilation.

There is an underlying assumption in conventional morality that involvement in prostitution will "necessarily" have degenerative effects on a person, leading her to other criminal activities. This is untrue and is a strong point in favor of prostitutes. Even given their exposure to the criminal environment that the street and drugs present, it cannot be demonstrated that they descend into deeper and deeper forms of crime.[11] Prostitution is not a profound condition of degeneracy and in many instances it may be a self-regarding expression of people surviving in the best way given their skills and opportunities. Society to some extent has overlooked any semblance of a moral aspect of prostitution. The corrupting effects of involvement in prostitution differ from involvement in lying, cheating, and stealing. If anything, prostitution is actually a mild form of degeneracy. True degeneracy feeds on itself. Lying begets an enthusiasm for lying and whets the appetites of the devious to make fools of naive people. Lying "feels good" particularly when it makes a person feel superior and enriches him or her as well. This close relationship between an act of lying and the immediate gratification of feeling power can pull a person deeper and deeper into certain kinds of activities. The driving force in many forms of prostitution is probably closer to survival rather than to an activity to enhance one's ego. Moral degeneration, in the normal sense, seems to be held in check by some other influence. The explanation for prostitutes' lack of complicity in a wide array of crimes would make an interesting study.

# Theoretical View of the Degrading Nature of Prostitution

Radical feminism opposes prostitution ostensibly because it degrades all women. There are at least three approaches to viewing degradation. First, when radical feminists talk about degradation, they are discussing it in terms of an activity that affirms and sustains the male power dynamic, which in turn dominates and oppresses nonprostitute women as well. Second, feminists are sometimes speaking of degradation in Marxist terms where "Prostitution, like wage labor, degrades the actor" (Weisberg 1996, 192). Third, if a woman behaves in a manner that fits the stereotype of what men commonly perceive as a whore, she is degraded by that association. Certain actions and style of dress lead people to certain other expectations about what that person is saying about him or herself. The idea of degradation, therefore, derives from not being fully aware of how one is perceived in the world by association with certain behaviors.

In the first instance, the idea of sexual empowerment asserts the notion that the value of equality between the sexes is the cardinal value in a hierarchy of values that guide human evolution and human behavior. But competing with this view is the likely fact that survival of the individual, and the species as a whole, is the cardinal value in a hierarchy of values that profoundly affect human behavior and determine the context of morality. As the human species has evolved, raw survival is no longer the primary issue. At this point, in order for civilization to grow and remain secure it must theoretically acknowledge both genders as equals. Without this recognition, society will be deprived of an essential social spirit and fair play sufficient for the evolution of a better world. The survival of a culture can also be viewed in terms of a function of harmony producing the greatest social gains and economic efficiency. But oppression as an issue does not replace the fundamental importance of survival as the cardinal value that ultimately determines the evolution or extinction of humankind.

In the second instance, there is a Marxist perspective that tends to seep into feminist thinking, promoting the idea that even ordinary wage labor is degrading. In Barry's writing it is unclear how much of her conceptualization is grounded in Marxism. The application of Marxism to political process never demonstrated itself as a viable approach to the governance of people, so why apply it to prostitution in this case?

Third, prostitutes and their clients also have a worldview about the degrading nature of prostitution. Exploiting sexuality is not uncommon, and it is not always men who are exploitative. Men could probably cite numerous instances of exploitation by women who have used their sexual prowess to exploit them for favors, money, or promotions. In a very abstract way, it could be said, the power of human sexuality—which is the source of its perpetuation—is the power of the species, and in this light anyone caught in its power can be vulnerable to making immature and unwise judgments that result in the corruption of the conscience. Barry's arguments focus only on sexual power operating at the social level, not at the genetic or biological level of action. If the cause of what she observes is biological or genetic, how can she hope to resolve the issue without addressing principles of biology?[12] If Theodosius Dobzhansky is correct, culture is an "instrument [biological] adaption" (1962, 20). Biological survival is a systemic process that appears to extend itself into the governing principles of societies it ultimately creates. The precise reasons why men oppress or appear to oppress, therefore, likely address higher considerations of adaptation and survival found in biology.

## Figurative, Not Actual, Degradation

Barry's discussions of degradation may proceed more from an idea in the mind than from realities of human behavior. Prostitution, in her view, is a form of moral corruption because it degrades women. A person who is a prostitute is generally viewed as a person of low social stature. Society encourages certain forms of behavior and discourages other forms through stigmatization. In a sense, the discouraging of the selling of sex reflects a value citing some behaviors as better than others. If a woman conducts herself in a way that goes against commonly held values, there is a cost. The costs will vary depending on mitigating factors defining an individual's personality. The cost for prostitutes is that they are relegated to a lower social status. Defining right and wrong in terms of how the society will view a person's status is a powerful motivating factor that naturally guides many away from activities not sanctioned by society. Because each individual case is different, and some prostitutes come from impoverished backgrounds, the power of the stigma to degrade them varies. While social image may be important to more culturally "refined" women, it may be less important to poor women, despite the elements of civility that can be potentially corrupted in either case.

Philosopher Robert Nozick sees values emerging in society as a function of that society's organic unity. Value is not simply some cold, mechanistic prescription set down by a bureaucratic government, it is the product of shared "valuable characteristics" of each person that ultimately created the notion of morality (1981, 470). When a woman or a man of mainstream character abides by most of the values of society, they benefit by a certain level of society's responsiveness to their needs. Accommodating the cultural values benefits people by providing them with the means of networking resources and ideas with other people to get what they want more effectively. When there is conformity to certain held values, everyone in the social pool benefits and no person is degraded. In the higher value system, prostitution is already given to be an activity that runs counter to important cultural values. As long as a woman does not appear to be complicit in prostitution, no one questions her integrity. Her integrity is a reflection of how closely she holds to the predominant value system. When she slips and begins running counter to these values, her integrity suffers, and she is degraded in the eyes of her community. She is no longer predictable as before and so is pushed more and more to the fringes of the mainstream value system.

Most human beings exploit their sexuality to some degree or another. Individuals have self-regarding obligations, within certain logical constraints, to promote their own interests and build safe and secure futures. It is not uncommon or immoral to any significant degree for a person to try to garner attention or extract simple favors by using his or her sexuality. There is, however, a line reached when exploiting one's sexuality in exchange for the favors it produces crosses over into the domain of activity that would be more accurately defined as prostitution. This is exploitative sex, a form of emotional violence against another person because he or she is led to false expectations by the enticement of sex. A prostitute may entice, but will usually be straightforward about what is expected in return. Prostitution in this sense bears a sense of virtuousness because it is not involved in exploitative mind games that can harm another person emotionally.

If a woman benefits by adhering to high cultural values, she is expected in return to uphold those values wherever and whenever she can. If she crosses the line and begins to act like a prostitute, men may begin to deem her one. Although she would vigorously deny being a prostitute, her actions might suggest that she is behaving in a way that fits the objectified view of a woman as a prostitute. Many men would perhaps not be inclined to look at a woman in a degrading way if she were in keeping with the held cultural values.[13] Values discourage prostitution and even the appearance of prostitution. If a woman behaves in a way that discernibly fits the pattern of a prostitute, men perhaps take the perception to be true and in some instances follow through with aggressive harassment to establish a relationship with an obviously sexually available female. If she is doing nothing approaching sexual indiscretion, not giving off objectively definable cues suggesting availability, there is no way that a woman can be degraded by the fact that some people do practice prostitution.

Pornography and prostitution establish a stereotype for what constitutes a sexually receptive situation. The means by which the stereotype is established is by way of objectifying sexually available women and transforming the results into an erotic presentation of the female for male enjoyment. When you objectify a situation or behavior you break it down into discernible parts. These parts describe the smallest details of what defines a pornographic situation or what defines a prostitute. If none of the behaviors of an ordinary woman fit any of these descriptions, there is no possible way the presence of prostitution should be able to harm her dignity. A woman behaving in a reasonable and conservative way, being careful not to elicit any ambiguous cues in her actions, is often described as a virtuous woman.[14] Her integrity and dignity are a function of adhering to held social values. The argument that all women are degraded by prostitution, therefore, is a somewhat overstated assumption of the deleterious effects of sex work on the dignity of all women.

The idea of virtue can be extended to men as well. Sexual knowledge provides one with a degree of personal power that can be used for good or bad ends. Using sex as a tool of exploitation invariably institutes a game state in which both men and women lose an element of their former purity. Barry tends to emphasize the misuse of this power at the hands of men, but common sense and ordinary experience suggest women can be exploitative as well. A fierce game between sexual players, each seeking to maximize his or her gains over the other, can easily lead to the moral degradation of both. In this perspective the idea of prostitutes degrading women is an issue that extends to what nonprostitute men and women do in their private sexual lives.

# Liberal Feminism

In liberal feminism, prostitution is conceived of in the contractarian sense of being a private business transaction. Radical feminists, on the other hand, view a prostitute as a human being who has been reduced to a piece of merchandise. The liberal contends that a woman is free to enter into contracts. However, the radical feminist does not believe that a prostitute's desire to enter into such a "contract" is done of her own free will. The radical feminist usually sees prostitution as an exploitative relationship in which the customer is interested only in the prostitute's services and not her personally. But the liberal responds to this by pointing out that when one seeks out a professional such as a doctor, lawyer, plumber, or mechanic, one is not centrally concerned with the person doing the professional work—only his or her services (Weisberg, 1996, 211).[15]

Since variations in educational level and experience will define how much freedom a person has to make his or her own decisions, the radical feminist argument that prostitutes are victims is overstated. The Marxist feminist response to the liberal position is that prostitution represents a corruption of wage labor and is therefore degrading and oppressive. But Carol Pateman in *The Sexual Contract* (1992) goes to some length to show that the prostitute is not really a wage laborer but rather an independent contractor who has it within her means to start or stop a transaction. Her contract is with a male customer and not an employer (202). In this respect, the liberal position's defense of the contractual work agreement makes sense.

Liberal feminists believe that personal "rights" should predominate over concerns for the social good. This political view goes back to the early feminism of John Stuart Mill, who believed that government should stay out of the private affairs of its citizens (Weisberg, 1996, 189). The oppression liberal feminists identify involves the injustices fostered by gender roles that favor men over women. The liberal feminist wants to free women from oppressive gender roles. This focus bears a similarity to the existentialist position that seeks equality of rights and freedoms between women and men. But just because liberal feminists tend to see the choice of prostitution as an inherent political right does not necessarily mean that they all approve of prostitution in a moral sense.

While the liberal feminists' view may be "supportive," there are, within the ranks of prostitutes themselves, people who object strongly to the ideals of the liberals. Their ideas tend to value the radical feminist position, not the liberal feminist one. To women in WHISPER (Women Hurt in Systems of Prostitution), harsh experiences in prostitution separate them from liberals. Members of WHISPER are commonly in contact with women who have been terrorized, traumatized, bruised, and beaten in prostitution. This experience leads women to conclude that the liberal position is wrong because it accepts a social system in which women can be exploited and harmed. And there is little doubt that WHISPER does see the harm that has been done.

The two prostitute organizations WHISPER and COYOTE (Call Off Your Old Tired Ethics) hold widely divergent views on the issue of harm and degradation attributable to their profession. Some of the divergence in experience can be explained in terms of the nine categories of prostitution referred to earlier. In these categories the danger to the individual prostitute varies widely between the first four categories and the last five. Women in WHISPER may not have the same background or political skills as those in COYOTE. In both cases, prostitutes are led by their experiences to believe that prostitution is either very dangerous and degrading or relatively safe. One would not claim that WHISPER members have not experienced prostitution the way they describe it, nor would one deny that members of COYOTE have experienced prostitution the way they describe it. The organization WHISPER is generally more involved with the experiences of women of color and very poor white women, many of whom have had fewer educational advantages than COYOTE women. In addition, many of WHISPER's members may have additional hurdles to overcome that are rarely encountered in COYOTE. For those with limited political skills, inspiring spirited cooperation from advocacy agencies that only marginally understand their lives or their culture is a major hurdle (Jackson and Scott 1996, 70). It takes considerable political skill and organization to succeed in obtaining advocacy. The liberal position does not include any safety net for prostitutes who might experience difficulties in prostitution that that same liberal policy toward prostitutes engenders. Liberals sometimes seem to want to "get off the hook" of responsibility for what prostitution does to some women by claiming that they do not promote prostitution but merely view it as an inherent right of choice.

Prostitution is described by WHISPER in such terms as "disgusting, abusive, and like rape" (Leidholdt and Raymond 1990, 68), sentiments that seem quite the opposite of those expressed in COYOTE. The organization WHISPER probably represents a much broader view of prostitution, finding its analog among prostitutes in underdeveloped countries where educational levels are lowest and advocacy agencies are few. But COYOTE is a necessary ally for all prostitutes. Although members may not have experienced the same harshness and brutality in prostitution that members of WHISPER have, it is within the power of their more politically influential members to gradually influence change in the world toward improving the quality of life of all prostitutes. At the same time, the liberal approach has the capacity to encompass the arguments of WHISPER. Given enough time to understand the complexities of all forms and "levels" of prostitution, they are in a good position to work toward realistic solutions to the problems involved.

# Existentialist Feminism

Existentialist feminism derives from the school of thought of Simone de Beauvoir. In her worldview, the woman is not always powerless and does not always need to be dependent in a male-female relationship. Prostitution allows women an avenue of escape from dependency on men in a way that does not leave them victims, but empowered women (Weisberg 1996, 191). Equality of rights and freedom between the sexes is desirable. However, if they are not forthcoming, prostitution can provide the woman with the kind of liberty that is immediate, affirming, and temporally rewarding. De Beauvoir appears to exalt all women as possessing the capacity to realize their innate power in the sense of the feminine warrior spirit. In the existentialist view, the power of a competent woman over a man is not an illusion. A man may think he is in charge of a situation by virtue of his power to degrade and subdue a woman, but with a woman of competence and spirit this "power" is not incontrovertible. In Carol Pateman's words directed toward the role of a woman as a prostitute, "The man may think he 'has' her, but his sexual possession is an illusion; it is she who has him . . . she will not be 'taken,' since she is being paid." The spirit of entrepreneurship prevails here instead of the darker concerns of Marxism, which views employment as exploitative and oppressive. To her the prostitute is not the fallen and oppressed victim, rather the "quintessential liberated woman." While believing that women are oppressed by an inequality between the sexes, she also believes there is an escape by economic means.[16] So on the one hand a prostitute is viewed as an oppressed woman, and on the other, a liberated one by way of a successful economic strategy for her own survival.

# Socialist Feminism

Socialist feminism appears to adopt some of the same tenets of Marxism, but instead of focusing on economic determinism as the primary source of oppression, the socialist feminist sees the oppression as having psychological and social roots (Tong 1989, 211). They share a genuine concern for women that transcends politics. Their focus is on people, not profits. To the socialist feminist, the prostitute is a victim of the corruption of a society that accompanies class distinctions. The oppression of class in a materialistic society degrades people by categorizing them in a particular class and objectifying them so that they are merely parts of a mechanism that can be replaced by other parts of the same description. In both the socialist feminist and Marxist feminist perspectives prostitution is discouraged, but neither school of thought seeks a legal remedy for its elimination. They believe that the cause of prostitution is in the structuring of society, and that is where the solution will reside.

## Marxist Feminism

Marxist feminism arises out of the doctrines of Karl Marx, whose theory is centered less on the material aspects of life than on the more broadly defined social ones. Simone Weil in *Oppression and Liberty* (1973) describes Marxism as being a theory quite incomplete insofar as its application is concerned, yet very relevant in describing the mechanisms of economic growth. Central to Marxism is the idea of the *divisions of labor,* which are familiarly evident in the capitalist system. Marxist feminists base their arguments of moral right and wrong in reference to the corruption of wage labor that is in itself an expression of class distinctions.[17] "Wage earning is a form of oppression, that the workers are inevitably enslaved under a system of production where, deprived of knowledge and skill, they are reduced practically to nothing" (Weil 1955, 161). Following this doctrine, Marxists are opposed to any social or political action that perpetuates the enslavement and oppression of members of the work force. Prostitution is a form of labor and therefore has been specifically noted as falling under the designation of a corruption of wage labor. Marx himself asserted that "prostitution is only a specific expression of the general prostitution of the laborer" (Pateman 1992, 201). Prostitution, therefore, can be seen as standing as a symbol of all that is wrong with world policies in society. Prostitutes may feel that they are free, but looking at the larger economic picture in Marxist terms, they are in reality oppressed workers reinforcing and perpetuating an exploitative capitalistic scheme. However, Pateman in *The Sexual Contract* sees prostitutes otherwise, pointing out that they are not wage laborers, but rather independent contractors. In her thinking, "The objection that the prostitute is harmed or degraded by her trade misunderstands the nature of what is traded. The body and the self of the prostitute are not offered in the market; she can contract out use of her services without detriment to herself" (Pateman 1992, 191). Moreover, philosopher Robert Nozick believes that peoples' rights predominate over concerns for what harm may come to them. He believes that a person has the right to sell himself or herself into slavery if that is his or her decision.

What appears to have gone unnoticed in Marxism, Marxist feminism, and radical feminism is that there is the perception that in the capitalist system there is a stripping away of the spiritual qualities of life as a person is reduced to being a mere cog in a machine.[18] There is a tendency in some feminist writings to discuss the relationship between feminism and prostitution in much the same terms, thus stripping away the transcendent and spiritual qualities of prostitutes and leaving only a mechanistic view of prostitutes within prostitution.

## Radical Feminism

To radical feminists, women's oppression is the most fundamental form of oppression (Tong 1989, 71). It is the model for all other kinds of oppression. A prostitute, in their view, does not act out of free choice but is a victim of coercion in both its most subtle and direct forms. Because oppression is so entrenched in people's thinking, changes in the structuring of society alone are not sufficient to overcome it. The attitudes of men must be changed and a state of equality made manifest in the power dynamic between men and women. As in the case of the socialist feminist and the Marxist feminist perspectives, once equality has been achieved and the structuring of society corrected, prostitution as we know it will play a diminished role in society—if one at all.

Liberal feminism and radical feminism contrast sharply in certain of their fundamental views. Liberal feminist thinking is a more reasoned, intellectual perspective than the radical feminist position, which has both emotional and political centering in its logical expressions. It has been said of the radical feminists that their tactics and their philosophy are inseparable.[19] This is understandable, because their focus is on widespread cultural awakening rather than on scholarly debate (Whelehan 1995, 86). Their political vibrancy comes in part from the fact that (1) they are saying something relevant and true about men that can almost universally be appreciated by women, and (2) their logical standards are predicated on politics rather than precise theory and thus they become the be-all and end-all for a diversity of people. Although their central logic may be "unrefined" compared to the scholarly approach, it could ultimately command the widest base of political support given certain changes. Radical feminists tend to muddle their ideas, producing concepts that do not make finer distinctions of reality.[20] The oppression of women by men is assumed to be of the same intensity among all men, yet obviously, as Imelda Whelehan has pointed out, "Men have different degrees of access to [the] mechanisms of oppression" (1995, 80). The distinction between rape and prostitution is obscure; its logic is tied to an abstract theory of degradation distant from representing the actual sense of the word "degradation." Radical feminism focuses on men as oppressors, yet says little about the possibility of the woman being an oppressor of other women or of men.[21]

Radical feminists do not view prostitution as a harmless private transaction. On the contrary, they believe that it reinforces and perpetuates the objectification, subordination, and exploitation of women.[22] They see men as universally believing myths regarding their own sexuality. Two myths are (1) that men need more sex than women, and (2) that they are genetically the stronger sex and therefore should be dominant in relationships with women. Feminist writer Alison M. Jagger describes the radical feminist view as one in which "almost every man/woman encounter has sexual overtones and typically is designed to reinforce the sexual dominance of men." To the feminist, a man's belief that he has no choice other than to respond to his sexual urges creates a self-validating tautology of belief predicated on the notion that his aggressive behaviors are linked to his inherited traits. The feminist sees otherwise, viewing the source of men's sexuality as deriving in part from the culture and not exclusively from biology. According to this line of thinking, prostitution and pornography as factors in male experience only exacerbate his self-serving belief in the primacy of his sexuality. His role as the "dominant" sex is reinforced in his mind as something very real, when in fact it is not. In this sense, influences such as prostitution and pornography can be viewed as degrading to all women, as acceptance of these events reinforces and perpetuates a cruel fantasy of women as weak and submissive. In *Application of Feminist Legal Theory to Women's Lives*, D. Kelly Weisberg describes this process in the following way: "According to the radical feminist view, men are socialized to have sexual desires and to feel entitled to have those desires met, whereas women are socialized to meet those desires and to internalize accepted definitions of femininity and sexual objectification" (1996, 194). As men cling to the idea that their sexuality is an absolute expression of their need and dominance, they prevent women from effecting new attitudes, self-realizations, and behaviors.

As discussed earlier, when radical feminists speak of "degradation," they inappropriately apply the term in ethical statements setting forth right or wrong behavior. What they mainly are talking about is degradation in a social sense and not a moral sense, although they allude to their ideas as morally sound. In a social sense they seem to see degradation as existing over a broad spectrum of society in which everything that men do, from opening doors for women to sexual assault, reinforces their view of men as "dominating." Discussion, in a social sense, could do well without framing everything in terms of degradation, Such rhetoric obscures their more important premise that specifically addresses the male power dynamic that reinforces and perpetuates itself by ignoring certain biological and cultural facts.

In spite of the fact that radical feminists tend to overemphasize or globalize concepts such as degradation, they appear to more than compensate for it by making several assertions that have high credibility. One of these assertions is that human sexuality derives essentially from culture and not from biology. This idea is reasonable and consistent with contemporary biological theories that emphasize the role of culture rather than genetics in viewing the evolution of human societies. For example, zoologist Theodosius

Dobzhansky would recognize the radical feminist assertion framed in biological and genetic terms. He views culture as an instrument of human adaptation that is virtually inseparable from biology (1962; Weisberg 1996, 20).[23] Dobzhansky separates biological and cultural theories into three categories: ectogenic, autogenic, and biological (1962, 15). One interesting thing he brings up is a biological belief called eugenics that was popular in the early part of this century. Eugenics asserts the strategic role of heredity in determining one's class and dominant status in society. He goes on to explain that with the rise of Hitlerism this idea was carried to tragic excess, as expressed by the statement, "The belief in the influence of heredity overreached itself when it was used—as it still is all too often—to justify the continued domination of some particular caste or group" (13). Surprisingly, this sounds somewhat like the ideological beliefs of some men who view their role in society to be one of dominance over women. Dobzhansky, however, does not take one side or the other in the dispute between cultural and biological factors as determinants of behavior. To him the various viewpoints represent credible realities that interact with the environment, creating a cybernetic state in which "there exists a feedback between biological and cultural processes" (18) to maintain the organic system's equilibrium. Thus, there is a certain degree of support for the radical feminist view that people are not necessarily responding to biological forces that are exclusive of cultural influences.

In the same way that biological knowledge can expand the ground of support for the arguments of feminists, so too can the study of ethics. The exploitation and oppression of human beings is considered to be an immoral act. Once women's oppression is framed in moral terms, it becomes easier to understand that there are other moral influences that can cause and exacerbate oppression. For example, if a man is forced by career interests to manipulate and pressure clients into making decisions that benefit his company, he soon develops habits in which lying and manipulation become part of the job. When he comes home he brings with him habits that can prove detrimental to his marriage. In this light, one must weigh the corrupting effects of prostitution on the degradation of women's lives against many other powerful influences such as the lying and manipulation just mentioned. A climate of immorality is evident everywhere in society, not just in the lives and actions of prostitutes. In a cultural climate where manipulation, half-truths, lying, and cheating are commonplace, people begin to believe that such practices are acceptable. Once they are established as acceptable, more virulent forms of manipulation and exploitation surface, leading to greater forms of social oppression. In this respect, a broader analysis of the radical feminist arguments about the degrading effects of prostitution must be made within an ethical context.[24]

One place to begin examining the ethical aspect of prostitution is the effect it can have on the tranquility of a woman's home life.[25] This is the balance point in the argument between the radical feminists and prostitutes since "love's delicate balance" is at risk in a marriage if prostitution is easily accessible (through mainstream publications and by broadcasts where most men would see advertisements for prostitutes), flagrant, predatory, or medically unsafe. Marriage is a highly regarded social institution that has for centuries inspired moral beliefs that encourage and protect it. Relationships which maintain a fine social balance are treasures in all civilizations because they inspire other relationships and contribute to a positive, cooperative, and stable social environment.

It is important to recognize that where struggles in a home exist there are at least three factors at work. There is the woman's experience, the man's experience, and illusions in the minds of both that create stress in the heat of conflict. Marriages can be stressful for reasons that emerge not only from the partners themselves but also as a result of influences from outside the marriage. In this respect it has long been a moral view that one should select a mate very carefully. If a woman is attracted to the superficial qualities of a man she may soon discover things about him she does not like. If she is looking for a "trophy" man to show off to the world, or one who can give her status and wealth, then she may be buying trouble later on when her mate's aggressive, domineering nature reveals itself. Under normal stress, things a woman did not initially notice about her husband can be exaggerated out of proportion in her mind. Ethical analysis is needed in feminist discussions of domination because ethics is a more carefully constructed matrix of ideas that provides a more comprehensive description of reasonable human behavior.

There are also nonmoral influences that must be incorporated into any theory of oppression. Even though two people may on the surface appear to be a good match, the methods by which they communicate can play an important role in how their marriage breaks down or is reaffirmed. Although people may think they know how to communicate, many are very poor at it in relationships. If the method of communication is by way of emotional pressure and manipulation, things can get out of hand when pressures from outside the home make a person irritable and testy.[26] If emotions get out of hand, and manipulation becomes the basis of communication, a woman can begin to see love's loss working its way into her life as simple and effective communication is obstructed by deceit. The loss a woman feels for the love and cooperation of her husband should not be transferred unreasonably to prostitution. The presence of prostitution in society can be a contributing factor to love's loss, but prostitution should not be used as an "out" for marital unhappiness. A man's need for a prostitute may be only a symptom and not a cause of marital conflict.

If one is to talk about the functional or moral impropriety of prostitution in relationships then it is appropriate to bring up the issues of good and evil. Thomas Aquinas, who viewed natural law as the source of morality, viewed "right actions" to be those that tend toward the good and away from evil. If love's delicate balance is at risk, there is certainly a threat of moral degradation of the marriage. Thus, if prostitution intrudes upon love's delicate relationships, such an intrusion in terms of natural law could be considered an evil. But, as indicated before, the potentially destructive influence of prostitution is minor compared to the many other forces at work in the shaping or testing of a marriage.

Moral degradation is a slow process. It grows out of practices that people learn while trying to survive and get ahead in the world. When competitions become fierce, some people discover the benefits of reducing those around them to mere objects. Once others are reduced to objects, the morally degraded person feels less pain and guilt in exploiting people. Lying becomes easier and its benefits fruitful. This callous way of looking at the world can also work its way into a marriage and transform it from a relationship based on cooperative love to one of exploitation. Once the marriage has been reduced to a convenience, the husband may seek more exciting experiences outside the home.

Where there is conflict there may be the desire to escape. The search for more exotic places and experiences can arise from conflict or from boredom. One motive married men may have for seeking out a prostitute is to experience exotic sex. In this role, the prostitute can be seen as a married woman's natural competitor.[27] Again, the man's desire to seek out the exotic in a prostitute-client relationship is only symptomatic of a marriage that has already lost its allure.

Radicals believe that when equality is achieved between the sexes there will be no prostitution. This is probably true in the sense that if harmony prevailed among all couples, seeking outside sex might not be considered, or would be understood if it did occur. But many moralists have noticed there is not a lot of love in a world that is preoccupied with pleasures and material things. Christian moralists have stressed time and again the importance of love prevailing in a relationship. A loving relationship is far more effective at thwarting oppressive conditions than one that is based on convenience. The presence of prostitution, therefore, only mirrors the immoral nature of the contemporary society.

From the beginning, radical feminists have shown a weak understanding of the nature of prostitution and of the personal lives of prostitutes themselves. A prostitute is not necessarily a homewrecker in the way nonprostitute women in extramarital affairs might be considered. The intimate nature of the prostitute-client relationship is much more complex than it first appears. Whether women are affluent call girls or street girls with few resources, clients sometimes find prostitutes' company comforting and therapeutic. At times, the only thing a client is looking for is simple warmth and human contact, even though he might initially define that need as sex. Time spent with a person who listens can be comforting and emotionally beneficial to one person in the same way that seeking out a professional psychologist might be reassuring to another. The belief that the prostitute-client relationship is always mercenary, cold, and mechanical simply is not true. Men experienced with prostitutes have sometimes found that showing their humanity and concern for the prostitute sometimes makes the potentially awkward encounter more enjoyable for both.

A prostitute can therefore be viewed either as a genuine threat to the peace and tranquillity of a loving relationship or conversely as an ally in that relationship, smoothing out unresolved tensions and misunderstandings. This sometimes therapeutic relationship does not threaten the marriage in the same way an extramarital affair does.

As prostitution becomes more highly regarded as a profession, its benefits will be more broadly understood and appreciated. Feminists should take more care in forming beliefs about prostitutes. Information and reflection on prostitution, then, has the potential for a humane, affirmative approach to this myth-laden institution.

# Summary

In summary, the active, logical component that degrades women here is not to be found in the word "prostitution." The logical component that degrades is to be found in individual actions that go against strongly held cultural values. In other words, prostitution does not degrade people; people degrade themselves by falling into objectifiably discernible patterns of behavior. The word "prostitution" implies the more passive component, while the "going against values" is the more active component. In general, prostitution is a result of an action or description of an action that alters a person's social standing with regard to cultural values. When the idea of degradation is extended to pornography, there is an implied degradation of the civility of men to control their impulses rather than a degradation of women in general. Although this would seem applicable to the presence of prostitutes in society, the issues are quite different. There are counterbalancing forces in prostitution that can limit destructive effects on the civility of men that may not be evident with pornography.

Radical feminists' views on prostitution are thoughtful but not always delineated well enough to firm up a credible social theory that prostitution is wrong because it degrades women. The argument that prostitution is degrading is a view that is part of a larger ethical view of human behavior that finds some actions generative and others degenerative.[28] There are many other competing degenerative behaviors to be considered in the larger picture of human affairs. Radical feminists have contributions to make to the discussion of prostitution, but their frequent narrowness of perspective, presented as global truth, leaves much to be desired in examining prostitution as a complex issue.

The goal of feminism can be seen as an attempt to improve the quality of women's lives by promoting a world in which they can thrive equally with men. Feminists have explored many facets of the problem and have come to divergent opinions on how to achieve such a goal. It is difficult to understand why some feminists feel that the presence of prostitutes in society is so threatening. What they want, and what most of us want, is a better world and a society that is morally, socially, and intellectually viable.

Prostitutes have been singled out and scorned for thousands of years. It seems almost to be a wired-in reaction of religion and politics to attack the weakest and most disenfranchised as symbols of the problems of society. Our society is a fiercely competitive one in which unfairness and exploitation are rife, thrusting some to the bottom, where their only avenue to survival is to become prostitutes. Upon finding an occupation in which they finally can view themselves as successful competitors, prostitutes are often attacked by feminists as perpetrators of the degradation of all women. It is amazing how creative societies are at coming up with new varieties of the same old complaints that view prostitutes with scorn. But having already endured centuries of exploitation, abuse, murder, and slavery for what they do, there is not much prostitutes have to worry about from feminists. The intentions of feminists are essentially benign. They make a compelling argument that the problem of oppression by men is every woman's problem. In this respect it is incumbent upon prostitutes to become aware of the problems that women are trying to work out with men. If prostitutes show some interest in the issues of feminism, feminists may become more familiar with prostitutes' lives in such a way that there may be a mutually beneficial influence in understanding the issue of prostitution.

# Notes

1. S. I. Hayakawa 1978, 251: Oververbalization: "If our intentional orientations are serious, therefore, we can manufacture verbally a whole system of values . . . out of connotations informative and affective. That is to say, once the term is given, we can, by proceeding from connotation to connotation, keep going indefinitely" (251).

2. Also see the section on the process of abstracting "leaping a huge chasm: from the dynamic process . . . to a relatively static idea . . ." (Pheterson 1996, 154).

3. Freeman says: "Radical feminists say that prostitution is not a harmless, 'private' transaction but a powerful means of creating, reinforcing, and perpetuating the objectification of women through sexuality" (242).

4. Prostitutes are generally described in these writings as being women. They are by far the largest group by gender of all prostitutes. Men and transgenders, of course, are also prostitutes, but the focus here is on women. Some of these nine categories can also be applied to men and transgenders.

5. By flaunting society's values and behaving immorally, a person believes he or she is getting away with something, but is not. They become less valuable people. See Nozick 1981, 409.

6. Barry 1995, 30: "Distancing can also be thought of as the result of the abuse caring people experience as they withdraw from a society that takes their kindness as a sign of weakness. Distancing may also result because every time a person gets socially intimate he or she has no defenses to keep from being exploited by that closeness."

7. Terri Goodsen coined the phrase in reference to her relationship to prostitution and reasons why she felt some women became prostitutes.

8. Women in the eighth category are described as smart and those in the ninth intelligent. "Smart" denotes purely optimizing strategies at work in thinking that is self-serving, while "intelligence" implies to some degree altruistic and non-optimific thinking. The former are in it for the money, because that is where the money is substantial compared with any other career they might choose. The intelligent women are in it for the money but on a higher level of social integration that includes helping other prostitutes and helping each other overcome political and social obstacles.

9. In one study that appears representative of her view of the pervasiveness of violence, 63 percent of women said they were horribly beaten by their pimps (Barry 1995, 202). Another study by feminist Catharine MacKinnon in *The Problems of Pornography,* says that only 7.8 percent of all women have not been sexually assaulted. The pervasiveness of violence and pimping needs to be examined more closely with better research methods (58).

10. The pathetic fallacy is an informal fallacy in philosophy. If an argument appeals to pity it is considered fallacious. There is a subtle, not exaggerated, sense of this in Barry's descriptions.

11. Call girls, in my opinion, show less of an affinity for involvement in drugs than street girls, while street girls (84 percent–100 percent) have at one time or another used heroin. (See Delacoste and Alexander 1987, 202: "life is so hard and painful that it is understandable why they descend deeper into drugs.") Despite the use of drugs, they are not cons, and do not inordinately get involved in an increasing array of scams.

12. In *The Prostitution of Sexuality,* Morris Berman is credited with pointing out "that cultural history is embedded in our bodies" (346). This likely is a reference to genetics, thus the entire problem of oppression is likely to be governed by factors existing on a larger scale.

13. Values in the broad category include marriage, having children, honestly working for a living, and so forth. There is an array of other values more narrowly delineated. Virtue and chastity are values associated with sexual activity. When a person begins to experience sexuality, the inherent power of sexuality to entice, manipulate, and play with other people's emotions becomes evident. There is so much power implied in sexuality that the immature usage of it is inevitable. Thus, the lack of chasteness also can imply the game-state that arises when a person cannot deal adequately with the power of sexuality. Sex in this condition degrades, from its higher

purpose for mating, having a family, or raising the spirits of humanity by imbuing courtship with a sense of romance, into self-serving expressions of ego-fulfillment.

14. In this respect, a prostitute being conservative with men in her private but not professional life could be considered a sexually virtuous woman given conformity to other virtuous characteristics. Although this appears contradictory, one must remember that the idea of temple prostitution was never construed as a desecration of spirit. Virtue is given an "extensional" characteristic here that gives it first-order qualities (the absence of a game-state) over the more "intentionally" defined words 'virtue," "purity," and "chastity," which are not as specific. This is important to note if the argument is to object to women being objectified on such a high pedestal of virtue. Virtue knows no gender. What applies to women applies to men equally.

15. The relationship between the public and professionals is that both treat each other for their own ends. The client needs sex and the prostitute needs money. Experienced men and experienced prostitutes sometimes share a rapport that goes unnoticed by any research.

16. Simone de Beauvoir "believed that one of the keys to a woman's liberation is economic, a point she emphasized in her discussion of the independent woman." Tong 1989, 211.

17. Class distinctions are what Marx objects to in his complex theory of economic determinism. But without such divisions of labor, productivity would be low and the quality of life diminished, except perhaps in small island nations in warm climates where the struggles of day to day survival might be less than in the colder regions. "Among all the forms of social organization which history has to show, there are very few which appear to be really free from oppression; and those few are not very well known. All of them correspond to extremely low level of production, so low that the division of labor is pretty well unknown, except between the sexes, and each family produces little more than its own requirements." Weil 1955, 61–62.

18. In *Oppression and Liberty*, Weil, speaking of Marx, writes in *Capital*, "In the factory there exists a mechanism independent of the workers, which incorporates them as living cogs. . . . The separation of the spiritual forces that play a part in production from manual labor" (41).

19. "Radical feminist writings are consciously deemed inseparable from group tactics, rather than as a discrete contribution to an abstract philosophical position." Whelehan 1995, 73.

20. "Radicals appear to pride themselves on being notoriously difficult to define, and this is in part an effect of their commitment to denying that one voice can speak for the many." Whelehan 1995, 70. Remaining obscure also has the added advantage of wearing down one's opponents as the logic is intentionally diffuse and difficult to understand. Some radical feminists are difficult to understand because they use specific words inappropriately. The degrading and oppressive nature of rape is not the same as willingly entering into a contract to have sex with someone for money. Theoretically they make a case that it is, but it is a weak one.

21. Women are also exploiters of other women. Human passions and greeds are not endemic to one sex or the other. If a woman of questionable morality wants something badly enough she is likely to exploit any easy source that can satisfy her desire, whether it is a man or a woman.

22. "Prostitution is not a harmless 'private' transaction but a powerful means of creating, reinforcing, and perpetuating the objectification of women through sexuality." Weisberg 1996, 242.

23. "Genetic or social change may also result from interplay between an organism or a culture on the one hand and the environment on the other." Dobzhansky 1962, 15. "Culture is, however, an important instrument of adaptation which is vastly more efficient than the biological processes that led to its inception and advancement." Ibid., 20.

24. Once the word "degrading" is used properly in a moral context it has more meaning and relevance to feminist arguments.

25. According to Whelehan (1995), the home is the crucial site of a woman's oppression (80).

26. Men also exploit other men in mean and insensitive ways. The competitions can be fierce and underhanded, leaving a man returning to the home sensitized to the slightest annoyance. Emotions that would not ordinarily get out of hand in the home may have been inspired by conflicts with other men in the workplace.

27. If conditions in society unfairly thrust some people to the bottom where their only recourse to survive is to sell themselves, then the malefactions of society produce prostitutes who turn out to be extremely successful competitors with married women in gaining the attention and resources of men. The exploitation and greed that cause some types of prostitution are a reflection of a general climate of immorality that prevails in the world, causing people in all walks of life to exploit one another. Some humans simply cannot compete, nor are they perhaps aware of the intensity of civil strife that ultimately determines a person's rank and occupation in society. Some women will always have a predilection for sexual activity for hire. Those who do so for political and economic reasons will continue to do so until the moral climate of the society improves, granting every citizen a full and fair chance to compete for jobs and educational opportunities. The radical feminist feels threatened by the prostitute for ostensibly political reasons. But the fact remains, the prostitute is willing to do what so many married women may be unable to, and that is perform exotic sex.

28. The concept of personal and social degradation is an extremely complex subject. Degenerative behavior requires closer consideration than it is given here and is better described in a larger writing. While lending some consideration to the radical feminists' position, in any analysis of social degradation one must also take into account the degrading effect of dividing men against women for the benefit of some political viewpoint. Degradation can be immediate or a slowly evolving process. It can be viewed as a personal problem or a social one. For example, on a personal level, a virtuous woman is not degraded by the presence of immoral women. If anything, the circumstance complements the virtuous woman because those around her behave in a less sophisticated way. She can be afflicted in a variable way by the presence of immorality in her life, but not degraded. On a social level, it could be said that while the presence of any degrading actions is undesirable, its effects address men and women equally by keeping civilization operating on a lower evolutionary plane.

# References

Barry, Kathleen. 1995. *The Prostitution of Sexuality*. New York and London: New York University Press.

Delacoste, B. Frederique, and Priscilla Alexander, eds. 1987. *Sex Work*. Cleis Press.

Dobzhansky, Theodosius. 1962. *Mankind Evolving*. New Haven and London: Yale University Press.

Dwyer, Susan. 1995. *The Problems of Pornography*. Belmont, Calif.: Wadsworth Publishing Company.

Freeman, Jody. *Applications of Feminist Legal Theory to Women's Lives: Sex, Violence and Reproduction*, ed. D. Kelly Weisberg. Philadelphia: Temple University Press, 1996.

Hayakawa, S. I. 1978. *Language in Thought and Action*. 4th ed. New York: Harcourt Brace Jovanovich.

Jackson, Stevi, and Sue Scott, eds. 1996. *Feminism and Sexuality: A Reader*. New York: Columbia University Press.

Leidholdt, Dorchen, and Janice G. Raymond, eds. 1990. *The Sexual Liberals and the Attack on Feminism*. New York and London: Teachers College Press.

Nozick, Robert. 1981. *Philosophical Explanations*. Cambridge, Mass.: Belknap Harvard.

Pateman, Carole. 1992. *The Sexual Contract*. Stanford, Calif.: Stanford University Press.

Pheterson, Gail. 1996. *The Prostitution Prism*. Amsterdam: Amsterdam University Press.

Russell, Letty M., and J. Shannon Clarkson, eds. 1996. *Dictionary of Feminist Theologies*. Louisville, Ky.: Westminster John Knox Press.

Stuart, Robert M., ed. 1995. *Philosophical Perspectives on Sex and Love*. New York and Oxford: Oxford University Press.

Tong, Rosemarie. 1989. *Feminist Thought: A Comprehensive Introduction*. Boulder and San Francisco: Westview Press.

Weil, Simone. 1955. *Oppression and Liberty*. Amherst: University of Massachusetts Press.

———. 1973. *Oppression and Liberty*. Amherst: University of Massachusetts Press.

Weisberg, D. Kelly, ed. 1996. *Applications of Feminist Legal Theory to Women's Lives: Sex, Violence, Work, and Reproduction*. Philadelphia: Temple University Press.

Whelehan, Imelda. 1995. *Modern Feminist Thought: From Second Wave to "Post-Feminism."* Washington Square, N.Y.: New York University Press.

## Feminist Positions on Prostitution

| Type of Feminism | Source of Women's Oppression | Coercive Effects of Prostitution | Solution to the Social Presence of Prostitution | Role of the Woman as a Prostitute | Degrading Effects | Position on Decriminalization | Prostitution Should Be Eradicated |
|---|---|---|---|---|---|---|---|
| **Radical** | Sexual and procreational practices. Men are socialized to have sexual desires while women are socialized to be submissive. Source of oppression cultural not biological, therefore changing attitudes is desirable. | Prostitution is equated to be on the level of rape. Prostitution is slavery. All women are affected by the coercive, exploitative, and oppressive inclinations of men towards women. Coercion has cultural derivations rather than biological ones. | Eradicate male oppression. Change attitudes and promote social change towards greater equality between the sexes. If prostitution is to be illegal the client should be equally pursued by the law. | The prostitute is a victim of a system of male oppression. Prostitution is not a harmless private transaction. It affects all women. | Prostitution is degrading to the prostitute and to women in general. Prostitution is equated to be on the level of rape. | Against Decriminalization will not solve the problem. Changing men's attitudes and fostering social equality are more important. | Yes Eradicate inequality between the sexes by discouraging any actions that degrade all women. |
| **Socialist** | Social and psychological sources including sexual and procreative practices. Changing social and economic structures desirable to eradicate oppression. | Women are coerced into degrading roles by the construction of social class systems. Without the presence of capitalism, women would choose other roles. | Seeks non-legal remedies such as changing the social structurings. When exploitative economic systems such as capitalism disappear, so will prostitution. | The prostitute is a victim of the system. | Prostitution is a corruption of the capitalist system. | Against It is more important to change the social structurings that cause prostitution in the first place. Socialists do not seek a legal remedy to prostitution. | Yes Eradicate exploitative economic systems such as capitalism. Focus on human needs in a more caring way. |
| **Marxist** | Class distinctions, corruption of wage labor, and capitalism. | The coercion is economic in its source. Wage labor is involuntary servitude and the subordination of the dignity of human beings, exacerbated by the definition of social and occupational classes. | Seeks non-legal remedies. When exploitative economic systems such as capitalism disappear, so will prostitution. | The prostitute is a victim of the economic system. | Prostitution is degrading of the dignity of humans caught in involuntary servitude to a system that unconscionably exploits people. | Against It is more important to attack the underlying cause of prostitution by eliminating capitalism. Marxists do not seek a legal remedy to prostitution. | Yes Eradicate systems like capitalism and prostitution will disappear. |
| **Existentialist** | Inequality of social freedoms. Improving individual liberties and rights is desirable. | Women are not coerced into prostitution. Prostitution can be a liberating and empowering experience. Where there is little freedom or few choices, prostitution is a good option. Biological differences important. | Encourages actions that liberate women as free human beings. Greater level of equality between the sexes is desirable. | The competent woman has a choice to be an entrepreneur and find methods to support herself. | Women of all descriptions and occupations possess extraordinary powers to overcome adversity. Prostitution is not degrading, rather it is empowering to women. | For | No |
| **Liberal Unconditional Freedoms** | Inequality of social freedoms. The need for education and reason to prevail as a solution. Improve society by promoting equal treatment between the sexes. | Prostitution derives from a natural biological urge. The prostitute contracts out her labor as is her right. That choice can be seen as an ordinary business decision. | Conditions for prostitutes can be improved through education and in seeking greater equality between the sexes. | The prostitute is an entrepreneur contracting out her labor as is her right. As with any business her ability to thwart danger is dependent upon her awareness of the world. | Prostitution is a business. In all businesses there are degrading aspects that must be overcome. | For | No Prostitution is a civil right. |
| **Liberal Freedoms With Moral Constraints** | Inequality of social freedoms. The need for education and reason to prevail as a solution. Improve society by promoting equal treatment between the sexes. | In theory the liberal might object to the undue effect of cultural persuasion on uneducated women interfering in her search for autonomy; thus being a coercive influence in her decision making. | These liberals question the possibility that a prostitute can make an informed choice, given certain levels of educational and cultural awareness. | The prostitute is an entrepreneur with the right to contract out her services. Prostitution has problems associated with it and should be encouraged. | Education, reason, and equality between the sexes could improve the conditions of prostitution. Liberals hint there are probably better choices a woman could make. | Qualified | No Prostitution is a civil right but should not be encouraged. |

Primary source material: D. Kelly Weisberg, *Applications of Feminist Legal Theory to Women's Lives*; secondary sources, Imelda Whelehan, *Modern Feminist Thought*; Alison M. Jagger in *The Philosophy of Sex*; and Rosemarie Tong in *Feminist Thought*

# WHORE STORIES: PROSTITUTION AND SEX-POSITIVE FEMINISM

## MARTI HOHMANN

In 1996, when *Ms.* magazine featured a special issue, "Hot Unscripted Sex," on the "rediscovery" of "feminist" sexuality, its editors did not feature writers or artists whose work involves S/M (sadomasochism). (Humorists said this accounted for the title: S/M sex is always "scripted" sex.) Even *Ms.*'s defensive posture was not enough for anti-porn feminists. Letters published in the subsequent issue decried their writers' disbelief that *Ms.* would stoop to "objectifying" women and to "pimping and pandering." Others commented that pornography had no place in a "healthy" female sexuality (Letters 4-6). The newcomer "alternative" to *Ms.*, the periodical *On the Issues*, also responded vituperatively, publishing an essay by Sheila Jeffreys deriding *Ms.* and accusing female eroticists of "false consciousness" and "collaboration" with the enemy.

Such charges are nothing new. After Susan Faludi published an article on male pornographic film stars in *The New Yorker*, an outraged reader accused her of collaboration with "pimp" and "one-man chamber of commerce" to the sex industry Bill Margold, and questioned not only how she could believe that male stars are "put upon" but also why Faludi did not write about women in the first place ("Pith" 1996, 12). It apparently did not occur to this writer that interviewing Margold might be considered responsible field work, nor did she allow it the scholar's province to choose her subject. Because it was Faludi's point that male porn stars' experiences are infrequently documented, it seems clear that the author of *Backlash* was excoriated not for her inattention to women's issues, but for treason.

In another exchange, Leanne Katz, the executive director of the National Coalition Against Censorship, and Andrea Dworkin, the author of numerous books and essays reiterating her position against pornography, battled over the

322

First Amendment (Katz and Dworkin 1996, 10–11). Dworkin's closing salvo is brutal:

> From the way the sister [Katz] conducts herself, I can only assume she's sick of hearing about collusion and collaboration with pimps because, in her professional life as a lobbyist for the interests of pornographers, she does it. (11)

To research and write about prostitution and pornography in the 1990s still entails identifying the enemy, then calling her names. Thus Wendy Chapkis, a veteran of more than a decade of such rhetoric, finds it "both unnerving and exhilarating" to know that sex-positive and anti-porn feminists will be scrutinizing her new book, *Live Sex Acts: Women Performing Erotic Labor,* "reinterpreting the findings, each according to their own strategic needs" (8).

What is the relationship of prostitution to feminism? Of feminism to pornography? These issues are still so central to the articulation of female subjectivity that they call for immediate and protracted answers, for testifying and theorizing. But they are only two questions, and of a limited range: why can't feminists let go of them? Perhaps because we wouldn't recognize the feminist subject in the absence of the prostitute and her literary counterpart, pornography. This is why Betty Dodson calls for a reclamation of the word "whore" at the same time as she draws varieties of female labia; this is why an erotic dancer, "feeling objectified by the fact that customers seemed to be looking only at her genitals," decides to write "her name across her stomach so customers would be forced to consider her as 'more than a pussy'" (as cited in Dudash 102). The prostitute has long been a writer; she is also (and some would argue, has long been) a feminist, asking the narrative of subjectivity to serve political ends.

Even at their most acrimonious, the sex wars have served feminism well. They are the place where two important (if fallacious) political identities were consolidated: the academic, intellectual "good girl," and the bad, practical, "real world" whore. Both women needed each other. The "good girl" feminist did not become a theorist until she discovered the "bad girl" prostitute, and she learned to tell her own story only after she had told the whore's. Likewise, in an alliance dating to Maimie Pinzer and Frances Howe, the prostitute became a writer only after the feminist activist encouraged her to pen autobiography and women's history: Later, the prostitute became a novelist when she tried her hand at pornography (witness the careers of Xaviera Hollander, Ulla, Brigitte Lahaie, and Jeanne Cordelier).

Let us examine one moment in the history of these alliances. As Jill Nagle points out in *Whores and Other Feminists,* "as early as 1970 in the United States, prostitute and non-prostitute feminists gathered in public, argued, formed friendships and alliances, and appeared in print side-by-side" (3). Though

Nagle is right to suggest that these relations worsened during the 1980s, they seem to have been long contested. In an early introduction to *The Prostitution Papers*, one of the first feminist texts on prostitution featuring the contributions of prostitutes, Kate Millett describes another first: a feminist academic conference on prostitution held in December 1971. To everyone's surprise, prostitutes attended the conference, but they were increasingly disturbed by the papers and presentations they heard. By the second day, as Millett reports, they

> . . . . came on like gangbusters. They had a great deal to say about the presumption of straight women who fancied they could debate, decide or even discuss what was their situation and not ours. The first thing they could tell us . . . was that we were judgmental, meddlesome and ignorant (32).

During a panel unfortunately entitled "The Elimination of Prostitution," panelists invited angry prostitutes (who were not eager to see their livelihood done away with) to join them on stage; even this did not stop long lines from forming at the twin microphones designated for those with questions or comments. The panel continued well beyond its agreed-upon end-time. As Millett states:

> After hours of heated and fuzzy argument, we had drawn lines, stated positions, denounced each other—or rather the prostitutes denounced the movement, some of whose members would occasionally stop defending themselves long enough to listen or vie with each other for approval from the prostitutes, who were enthralled to find themselves the center of attention in a group of women they were free, even encouraged, to insult. An S&M trip (33).

Millett's fortuitous turn-of-phrase ("S&M trip") reflects how quickly the academic conference became metaphorically sexualized. The mere presence of the prostitute body was enough, it seems, to turn an intellectual event into a sex party.

After several hours of dispute, Millett records, "things rapidly degenerated into chaos" (35). Finally, "dialogue grows impossible. The hope of it noisily evaporates in screaming" (37). In the end, the truth (or what seemed like the truth in 1971) comes out:

> The accusation, so long buried in liberal goodwill or radical rhetoric— "You're selling it; I could, too, but I won't"—was finally heard. Said out loud at last. The rejection and disapproval which the prostitutes have sensed from the beginning and, with the unerring instinct of the unconscious, have directed all their energy toward exposing, is now present before us, a palpable force in the air. The prostitutes are justified at last. There is fighting

now in earnest. Someone is struck, the act obscene, irreparable. Attempts at reconciliation are futile. Order and direction are out of the question in what is now an encounter group of more than five hundred people. The afternoon lies in shambles. (38)

The physical violence aside, I would not call a panel discussion drawing more than five hundred people, lasting for more than five hours, and prompting protracted, passionate interaction a "shambles." What interests me, though, is how Millett, positioned as an intermediary between the two groups, perceives the prostitute, to whom she is ostensibly sympathetic. In some instances she is particularly astute, not bothering, like other commentators, to cloak feelings like jealousy and loneliness in scholarly discourse:

The specter of sexual freedom, the real issue, was palpable in the room. Who knows most about sex? Who gets more? What is most? Who is cool? Money is fun. What's pride? What's prudery? Everyone was deeply ambivalent about everyone else. (33–34).

Through these admirably direct (and still pertinent) questions, Millett illustrates how the prostitutes' and the feminists' ambivalence about each other rapidly translates into a shared ambivalence over language. A never-ending panel like this one, unfolding in increasing hostility and frustration, betrays its participants' fear that mere language will not be able to convey their thoughts and feelings.

Words were not enough that day. Positions had to be restated, re-pitched, and as a last resort, re-performed, with the body becoming more implicated as the utterance failed. Language, whether framed as "rhetoric," "sophistry," or "reality," filled that school auditorium in 1971, and the heated discussion between prostitutes and feminists ended only because a blow was struck. How else may one explain Millett's increasing concern with the performative? As she notes, "the adventitious element of personality makes its appearance" in the person of "a formidable actress whose grandiose neuroticism, however paradigmatic of the personal disorientation of an Uptown call girl, rendered her completely impervious to logic of any kind" (37). That this speaker "took umbrage at everybody and everything" only partially explains Millett's rage (37). "Grandiose neuroticism"? "The personal disorientation of an Uptown call girl"? What does Millett mean? Are these "movement"-inspired phrases? If so, it is no wonder that the prostitutes were angry. As Millett continues, she does not cease to pathologize:

She ruled the occasion through an impressive hysteria which was equally effective upon her own contingent (of prostitutes)—increasingly silent, increasingly easy to manipulate—as it was upon her audience, cowed by her proclamation of authenticity. (37)

Things worsen when Millet turns to physical description:

A strange, nervous woman with strange hair dyed some unlikely color of gray, glamorous in a series of necklaces, ferocious in accusation, a Jesuit in argument, she grew and blossomed upon the stage, crowding out all other personalities in her euphoria of power. Mystic, an avatar, a force filling the banal ugliness of a school auditorium, she became The Prostitute, papal in her authority. (37)

Doubly "strange," nervous and hysterical, suspiciously "glamorous," a power-hungry egomaniac who knows how to stage her speeches, The Prostitute one-ups the feminist in authenticity and integrity. Though a "Jesuit in argument," her other strengths are anti-rhetorical and irrational: she is mystical, godlike, an ever-expanding force, an actress, a witch. Though talented in equivocation, she is first and foremost a plain speaker: whereas the feminist manipulates language (via "rhetoric" or "sophistry"), the prostitute tells the truth, or appears to do so. As Millett explains, for the prostitute,

The women on the panel and in the audience are not, in her . . . literal sense, prostitutes at all. They are straights. Their marriages are not the same as her prostitution. She is not flattered by being labeled a slave. Even the prestigious title of "most oppressed" has so little effect it could be rebutted with bravado—"We make more money than you chicks!" (36)

Feminism lies, deceives, and condescends to the prostitute in its equation of marriage with prostitution; the prostitute reminds the feminist of the very real material goods (corporeal and monetary) underlying the exchange of sex for money. Indeed, Millett comes to appreciate the prostitute's gift for literal-mindedness:

These women . . . did know where it was at, did know what they were talking about, had experienced it; and I didn't and hadn't—and now . . . they were going to drop all their defenses and finally tell me. If I could learn to shut up. So I did. (6–7)

Millett's description of the strange, hysterical whore at the conference is more than one feminist's interesting, if skewed, portrait of another woman, for as Millett explains, telling the prostitute's story made her a writer; indeed, made her a feminist. At the time of the composition of *The Prostitution Papers*, she had just published *Sexual Politics*, her doctoral dissertation, and was looking for a publisher for a novel, *Flying*. As she notes in the 1973 edition of *The Prostitution Papers*:

Reading over my earlier (1971) introduction, I find, rather to my surprise, that the first pages constitute a little essay on style. . . . Whence all this digression into literary aesthetics? What does that have to do with prostitution? Reading on, of course, I remembered how *The Prostitution Papers* had been my own turning point—the missing link that got me from the doctoral thesis prose of *Sexual Politics* to the freedom of *Flying*. (4)

Prostitution evidently demands that at least one feminist meditate on the meaning of style. Moreover, it is what turned Millett into a "real" writer:

> I no longer clung to that bleak pretense of objectivity routinely required of Ph.D. candidates. Ponderous sentences were whittled away to a natural length. Even to the sentence fragments in which we Americans actually think and speak. My language had to reflect the experience itself: colloquial, excited, immediate. . . . I began to write the way I talk and feel. In short, I was beginning to write. (26)

Millett acknowledges that "*The Prostitution Papers* was something of a watershed" in her development as a writer, a transformation she calls "agonizing" (27).

What were the elements of this transformation? One is named, the other implied. First, writing about prostitution apparently demanded simplicity of style, an unusual degree of identification with and empathy for one's subject, and a desire to "tell it like it is." Prostitute narrative has long argued for its essential "truthfulness": as Ruth Barnes notes, of *Pleasure Was My Business*: "This isn't a polite book. It isn't a fancy book either. But every word is true" (7). For Millett, working with prostitutes entailed learning to pay attention; indeed, altogether ceding her power as storyteller. Millett fondly remembers listening through the night to "the prostitutes M and J" as they "sat up all night 'laying it on me' while the coffee boiled over or the tape recorder stopped or ran out of thread" (1). Firmly convinced that her subjects should tell their own stories, she took pains to transcribe and (minimally) edit these recordings. Millett undertook this task because until then, the whore biography had consisted of "sociological statistics or *Playboy* glamorization, or pornographic hype" (30). What Nina Hartley posited in the mid-1980s was especially true in 1971: "many words had been written about sex workers, but few had been written by them" (57). The first edition of *The Prostitution Papers* thus appears in a four-column layout, juxtaposing the prostitutes' monologues with Millett's own (and another feminist's). This format gave equal weight to the prostitutes' work, instead of bracketing it or otherwise using it as evidence to buttress an academic narrative.

Millett's attraction for plain-speaking and the straightforward presentation of voices had its counterpart in contemporary sociology (Studs Terkel), anthropology (*Nisa*), sexology (Nancy Friday), and other disciplines, not to mention in the culture at large ("rapping" and consciousness-raising). But, as this last example indicates, it came to have particular resonance for feminism. As Millett explains:

> The shift from academic analysis in *Sexual Politics* to the record of life put down in real speech in *Flying* is significant. That it occurred through *The Prostitution Papers* is also significant. Because it's a process, an evolution, in which I have not been alone. (7)

Subsequent publications of the period capturing authentic prostitute voices include *Take Back the Night: Women on Pornography* and *Against Sadomasochism: A Radical Feminist Anthology*. Sociological reconnaissance eventually helped second-wave feminists arrive at what Millet calls the "Core," or "the final discovery of woman's condition: our physical enslavement, i.e., our entrapment in prostitution, our capture in rape, our imprisonment under beatings and domestic violence" (2). In other words, feminists learned to speak an essential "truth" about female existence by framing the prostitute's story (as they heard it): the whore (auto)biography helped construct the second-wave feminist subject.

If *The Prostitution Papers* turned Millett into a writer, it also made her a pornographer, and this is the second crucial element of her transformation into a "real" writer. As she explains, trying to account for her failure to mention *Flying* in her first introduction to the *Papers*:

> I never mention *Flying* . . . though I had already written it, already spent two years polishing and revising it. Of course it hadn't been printed yet. But the reason I never mention it is that I was quite sure it would never be printed. The publisher who contracted for it took one long horrified look at the scenes of eroticism between women and refused it. *Flying* was interdict. When it did finally see the light of print it caused astonishing outbursts of critical abuse, vituperation and anathema. It was an outrageous book; yet I was still bewildered by the degree of outrage, the Culture Police reflex in critics, the outlandish accusation of pornography even in *Ms.* magazine. *Flying* put me "beyond the pale," made me an outlaw. (5–6)

If the prostitute made Millett a writer and a pornographer, what did pornography and feminism do for the prostitute? She too took up her pen. After publication of *The Prostitution Papers*, Ruth Rosen's influential historical analysis, *The Lost Sisterhood: Prostitution in America, 1900–1918*, represented prostitution as one "choice" among others for women in Storyville, New Orleans; presses like Seal Press and Cleis Press solicited writing from prostitutes (and the publication of the prostitute anthology *Sex Work: Writings by Women in the Sex Industry* launched Cleis into erotica); the Women's Press published *Lyn*, and Viking translated Jeanne Cordelier's *The Life: Memoirs of a French Hooker*; and an unprecedented number of whore autobiographies, including *Madeleine* and *The Maimie Papers,* followed. Sex workers have been a powerful force in erotica's renaissance, not to mention in the production of twentieth-century autobiography in general. This is perhaps because, as Annie Sprinkle quips in "Forty Reasons Why Whores Are My Heroes," "whores are interesting people with lots of exciting life stories" (*XXXOOO* vol. I). In *Whore Carnival,* Veronica Vera notes that many prostitutes number among the new sex experts: they certainly number among the new pornographers (58).

It goes without saying that all prostitutes do not support or write pornography. Vicky Funari notes: "I'm still furious that I have to deal with the existence of pornography, that a portion of my energy has to go to thinking about this banal imagery" (27). A sex-positive analysis of prostitution by Belinda Cooper appears side-by-side in *Women's Rights Law Reporter* with an advertisement for Everywoman's *Pornography and Sexual Violence: Evidence of the Links* (119). Sydney Biddle Barrows rejected her first publishing offer for the manuscript that would become *Mayflower Madam* when it became clear "that the book they had in mind for me was far more salacious than the one I was planning—or able—to write" (1986, 281). Pauline Tabor decries "the out-and-out crude pornography that's flooding our nation today . . . adding new sickness to the already sick minds who delight in this sort of garbage" (1971, 236). Moreover, prostitutes' lives are not axiomatically pornographic; indeed, many are not, and as with Sally Stanford's and Nell Kimball's autobiographies, they often deploy their narrator's prudishness as a rhetorical trope. In *Moll Flanders* (Defoe 1973), for example, Moll stops narrating precisely when the story verges toward the pornographic: "Here he began to be a little freer with me than he had promis'd; and I by little and little yielded to every thing, so that in a Word, he did what he pleas'd with me; I need say no more" (176). Later she notes that "what pass'd between us" is a "Subject . . . not so proper for a Woman to write" (182). Readers appreciate it, apparently, when a woman who has seen and done it all retains a sense of propriety and a taste for refined language. Likewise, Linda Lovelace, calling herself a "cleanliness nut," closes *Ordeal* with a vacuum cleaner in hand, reminding the reader that Chuck Traynor once said of her: "She was better at housework and cooking than sex. She was a lousy lover. When I first dated her, she was so shy it shocked her to be seen in the nude with a man" (253, 249). As Michael Perkins notes,

> Most memoirs by hookers are disappointing. They're either so discreet both politically and sexually—like Polly Adler's *A House Is Not a Home,* or more recently, *Mayflower Madam*—that an inattentive reader might think he was reading about the business of futures trading rather than selling sex, or they're grim confessionals by reformed trollops. (414)

But other whore biographies are decidedly pornographic, and feminism seems to have helped effect this change: Xaviera Hollander's *The Happy*

*Hooker*, Barbara's *Confessions of a Part-Time Call Girl*, Cicciolina's *Confessions*, and Sylvia Bourdon's *L'amour est une fΩte*. Although literary history has long recognized the possibility of pornography in works like Daniel Defoe's *Roxana*, John Cleland's *Fanny Hill*, and Cora Pearl's *Memoirs*, nineteenth-century efforts to rehabilitate the fallen woman served to make her aubiographical narratives respectable as well. With a few exceptions, this tendency persisted until this century's so-called sexual revolution: *Madeleine, The Lady of the House, A House Is Not a Home, Dirty Helen*, and *Pleasure Was My Business* are sanitized (or at best, "salty") retellings, trading upon the potential for sex but not delivering any. *The Oakland Tribune* thus praises Polly Adler for delivering her life story with "surprisingly good taste." Of course there were political reasons for this reticence: Modernist texts could be subject to prosecution under extant obscenity law for theme alone, and the struggle in the Supreme Court for the liberation of language persisted well into the 1960s.

Xaviera Hollander must be credited with "remembering" the whore biography's pornographic potential in *The Happy Hooker*. Sex workers like Nina Hartley have long recognized *The Happy Hooker* as a formative political text: "The latter book taught me that an intelligent, sexual woman could choose a job in the sex industry and not be a victim, but instead emerge even stronger and more self-confident, with a feeling, even, of self-actualization" (143). However, Hollander's literary achievement is also impressive, as she not only reinvented whore pornography, but emancipated herself from autobiography to pornographic fiction in the more than fifteen works that followed *The Happy Hooker*. Although sequels like *Happily Hooked* retain the autobiographical frame (the female protagonist is named "Xaviera Hollander"), the Lucinda series (*Lucinda, My Lovely; Lucinda: Hot Nights on Xanthos; Erotic Enterprises, Inc.*) is frankly fictional. Dolores French's first madam advises her to read *The Happy Hooker* when she begins turning tricks: "She told me that a lot of it was trash, but that some of it was very accurate: how Xaviera had set up her own business, how she looked at the job, how she enjoyed the work." (26). She evidently also gleaned a lesson on style, as *Working*, her autobiography, marshals pornography to propel the narrative forward; witness, for example, a scene in which the narrator has sex with a generously endowed mental defective à la *Fanny Hill* (64–65).

Although it is still true that many prostitute autobiographies are not pornographic, other sex workers have recently experimented with sexually explicit stories. Carol Queen's short story, "The Best Whore in Hillsboro," tells the story of a foursome between Pamela and Tom, a suburban couple, and Kitty and Corinna, two prostitutes they have hired. Corinna is rather jaded and tired of her profession; Kitty worries that she too will grow disenchanted. The two couples hit it off and, when they convene to the bedroom, discover that they are more than compatible. During a breather, Kitty engages in "dirty talk" to increase Tom's excitement: "Put it in Corinna's cunt . . . right over Pamela's mouth, Tom, that's right, let her lick your balls while you fuck Corinna" (Queen 1996, 238–39). Increasingly impressed with Pamela's sexual performance, Kitty is thrilled when the suburban housewife also belies a talent for spinning smut: "This woman is good. She is fucking him so slowly and with such focus, eyes locked on his, whispering to him, that Kitty wouldn't be surprised if he started to whimper" (240). As it turns out, Pamela worked as a prostitute before her marriage, which accounts for her linguistic (and sexual) proficiency. Her narrative ends when she reveals this aspect of her history:

> "He drank my piss, baby, he drank it right out of me." She's riding Tom like a galloping polo pony. His eyes are standing out of his head, drinking her in, totally keyed in to this story he's obviously heard many times. "And he paid me for it, too, honey, a thousand bucks for it, a thousand bucks so he could drink my hot piss . . ."
>
> "Uhhhhnnn!" Tom is shooting, lifting Pamela up off the bed with the strength of his thrusts. (241)

Some may argue that Pamela is hardly Scheherezade, but within the context of the story, it does not matter: Tom has an orgasm because Pamela serves up the whore biography, and Kitty is so excited by the prospect that she asks for more love-making from Corinna. By the story's end, Kitty has "a faraway look in her eyes," not only because she has just had an orgasm, but also because she has realized "there's going to be life after whoring" (243). By this she means that "she'll be an ex-whore someday who whispers salacious tales to her lovers" (243).

It is dangerous to read fiction biographically, but Queen's contributor's note invites it, as she says she "writes stories that are often not untrue" (1996, 247). Moreover, she notes: "Since all characters but Kitty are composites and some of the things they do together are made up, any resemblance to persons living or dead is not surprising, but any exact description is a miracle" (247). Naturally Queen spoofs the disclaimer legally required by all works of fiction published in the United States, but she also plays with the boundary between fiction and autobiography. If Kitty is not a composite, perhaps she is based on Queen, and her trajectory has been precisely from autobiography to political commentary to fiction (she is now writing a novel). If (as I argue elsewhere) the contemporary anti-porn feminist used pornography to write her own story of exploitation and abuse, then the sex-positive feminist used feminism to contextualize her pornographic explorations. But where would they be without Pamela and Kitty? Where would they be without the prostitute? In 1997, as in 1970, pornography helped both groups stage autobiography as everyone else's story.

# References

Adler, Polly. 1955. *A House Is Not a Home*. New York: Popular Library.

Alexander, Priscilla. 1987. Why this book? In *Sex Work*, edited by F. Delacoste and P. Alexander. 14–19. Pittsburgh: Cleis Press.

Barnes, Ruth. 1961. *Pleasure Was My Business*. As told to Robert S. Tralins. New York: Lyle Stuart.

Barrows, Sydney Biddle. 1986. *Mayflower Madam*. With William Novak. London: Macdonald.

Chapkis, Wendy. 1997. *Live Sex Acts: Women Performing Erotic Labor*. New York: Routledge.

Cooper, Belinda. 1989. Prostitution: A feminist analysis. *Women's Rights Law Reporter* 11 (2): 99–119.

Defoe, Daniel. 1973. *Moll Flanders*. New York: Norton.

Delacoste, Frédérique, and Priscilla Alexander, eds. 1987. *Sex Work: Writings by Women in the Sex Industry*. Pittsburgh: Cleis Press.

Dudash, Tawnya. 1997. Peepshow feminism. In *Whores and Other Feminists*, edited by Jill Nagel. 98–118. New York: Routledge.

French, Dolores. 1990. *Working*. London: Victor Gollancz,.

Funari, Vicky. 1997. Naked, naughty, nasty: Peep show reflections. In *Whores and Other Feminists*, edited by Jill Nagle. 19–35. New York: Routledge.

Hartley, Nina.1987. Confessions of a feminist porno star. In *Whores and Other Feminists*, edited by Jill Nagle. 142–144. New York: Routledge.

———. In the flesh: A pornography star's journey. In *Whores and Other Feminists*, edited by Jill Nagle. 57–65. New York: Routledge.

Jeffreys, Sheila. 1996. How orgasm politics has hijacked the women's movement. *On the Issues* 2 (Spring): 18ff.

Katz, Leanne, and Andrea Dworkin. 1996. Whose bill of rights? Exchange of letters. *On the Issues* 2 (Spring): 10–11.

Letters. 1996. *Ms.* 6 (5): 4–6.

Lovelace, Linda. 1980. *Ordeal*. With Mike McGrady. Secaucus, N.J.: Citadel Press.

Millett, Kate. 1973. *The Prostitution Papers*. New York:Ballantine.

Nagle, Jill, ed. 1997. *Whores and other feminists*. New York: Routledge.

Perkins, Michael. 1994. *The good parts*. 339–41. New York: Richard Kasak.

Pith & Vinegar. 1996. *On the Issues* 2 (Spring): 12–13.

Prostitutes. *Social Text* (Winter 1993). Ed. Anne M. McClintock. 135–42.

Queen, Carol. 1996. The best whore in Hillsboro. In *Herotica 4*, edited by M. Sheiner. 234–43, 247. New York: Plume.

Sheiner, Marcy, ed. 1996. *Herotica 4*. New York: Plume

Sprinkle, Annie. 1997. "Forty reasons why whores are my heroes." In *XXXOOO: Love and Kisses from Annie Sprinkle*. New York: Gates of Heck.

Tabor, Pauline. 1971. *Pauline's*. Greenwich, Conn.: Fawcett Crest.

Vera, Veronica. 1995. *Whore Carnival*. Edited by Shannon Bell. 53–68. New York: Autonomedia.

Where do we stand on porn? 1994. *Ms.* 4 (4): 32–42.

# Prostitutes, Anti-Pro Feminists and the Economic Associates of Whores

## Wendy McElroy

A troubling situation has been haunting the issue of prostitution, and that is the growing antagonism between the prostitutes' rights movement, as expressed through organizations such as COYOTE, and those contemporary feminists who are anti-prostitution, which is a major focus of contemporary feminism. The conflict arises because most feminists maintain that their theories and policies help prostitutes, who are women victimized by male culture. The majority of prostitute activists, on the other hand, consider themselves to be sexually liberated women who are being harmed by the feminist theories and policies that claim to protect them.

The radical feminist Andrea Dworkin (1992) captures the anti-prostitute view of whoredom well: "The only analogy I can think of concerning prostitution is that it is more like gang rape than it is like anything else. . . . The gang rape is punctuated by a money exchange. That's all. That's the only difference."

Philosopher Laurie Shrage (1989) explains to prostitutes who consider themselves to be liberated that they are being duped by the patriarchal system: "Because of the cultural context in which prostitution operates, it epitomizes and perpetuates pernicious patriarchal beliefs and values and therefore is both damaging to the women who sell sex and, as an organized social practice, to all women in our society." At a feminist conference in 1987, a representative of CORP (Canadian Organization for the Rights of Prostitutes) related the impact that the anti-prostitution attitude was having on whores: "They find it necessary to interpret prostitutes' experience of their lives and then feed it back to the prostitutes to tell them what's really happening, whereas they wouldn't dare be so condescending or patronizing with any other group of women. Why is that?" (Bell 1987) Peggy Miller of CORP was more direct: "You're a bunch of fucking madonnas!" (Bell 1987)

The purpose of this chapter is to investigate the conflict between prostitute activists and anti-prostitution feminists in one area—namely, the treatment of the economic associates of whores,[1] particularly men. Most people might assume that this conflict, and others, is the natural state of affairs between willing prostitutes, who sell themselves sexually to men, and most feminists, who decry the sexual exploitation of women by men. This assumption is wrong. Prominent spokeswomen in the 1960s, such as Ti Atkinson, referred to prostitutes as the paradigm of a liberated woman. And a brief history of the prostitutes' rights movement illustrates that cooperation, and not conflict, characterized the early years.

# The Early Prostitutes' Rights Movement and Feminism

The prostitutes' rights movement first appeared through the organization known as COYOTE, an acronym for "Call Off Your Old Tired Ethics." In early 1973, COYOTE emerged in San Francisco from an earlier group named WHO; Whores, Housewives, and Others. The "Others" referred to were "lesbians"—a word no one even whispered aloud at that political juncture. The willingness of prostitutes to embrace the cause of lesbian rights was one of their early and strongest links with many feminists of that time.

The founder of COYOTE, Margo St. James, became convinced that a prostitute-based group was necessary because the feminist movement would not take the issue of prostitution seriously until whores themselves spoke out. Earlier, the lesbian community had reached a similar conclusion about the need to speak out for themselves. The mid-1970s were a propitious time for prostitute rights. The 1960s had created sympathy for decriminalizing victimless crimes. The abortion crusade had embedded the principle "a woman's body, a woman's right" into American society. The Gay Rights Movement in San Francisco had highlighted police abuse of sexual minorities.

Originally COYOTE limited itself to providing services to prostitutes in San Francisco, but a national prostitutes' rights movement soon began to coalesce around the local San Francisco model. By the end of 1974, COYOTE boasted a membership of over ten thousand, and three COYOTE affiliates had emerged: Associated Seattle Prostitutes, Prostitutes of New York (PONY), and Seattle Prostitutes against Rigid Rules over Women (SPARROW).

The feminist movement reacted with applause. In 1973, for example, the National Organization for Women (NOW) endorsed the decriminalization of prostitution, and this is still the "official" policy—at least, on paper.[2] Ms. magazine lauded both the efforts and the personality of Margo St. James. As late as 1979, prostitutes and mainstream feminists were actively cooperating. For example, COYOTE aligned with NOW in what was called a "Kiss and Tell campaign" to further the ERA effort. A 1979 issue of *COYOTE Howls*, the organization's newsletter, declared:

> COYOTE has called on all prostitutes to join the international "Kiss and Tell" campaign to convince legislators that it is in their best interest to support . . . issues of importance to women. The organizers of the campaign are urging that the names of legislators who have consistently voted against those issues, yet are regular patrons of prostitutes, be turned over to feminist organizations for their use. (1)

In the mid-1980s, the prostitutes' rights movement was decisively killed by an unexpected assassin: the AIDS virus. In the understandable social backlash that surrounded AIDS, prostitution came to be seen as a source of contagion every bit as virulent as IV (intravenous) needle use. Around this time, mainstream feminism also turned against the prostitutes' rights movement and began publicly to excoriate prostitution as a form of patriarchal abuse of women. In 1985, Margo St. James left the United States to live in France. She cited the sexually conservative swing in the American feminist movement as one of her motives in leaving.

# A New Image of the Prostitute

In 1985, with the decline of the prostitutes' rights movement in America, the image of the liberated whore declined as well. A new image took over almost entirely: The whore was viewed as a pathetic victim of male oppression, a victim of patriarchy, and prostitution inherently became an act of violence against women. To recall Dworkin's words, "prostitution is . . . more like gang rape than it is anything else." Feminists view prostitution as rape or gang rape. The whore is, by definition, a sexually abused and exploited woman. She is a victim whether or not she declares herself to be a willing partner to prostitution, and whether or not—in the presence of other reasonable options—she pursues paid sex. Her belief that she has consented is merely a delusion.

A great deal of feminist research has been conducted, seemingly with the goal of establishing this image of the whore. Some of the research is valuable, but—at least in terms of its value in forming any general policy on prostitution—the research is deeply flawed. This is because the sampling is almost always drawn from the streetwalking segment of the prostitute community, and usually from the further subcategory of streetwalkers who are in prison, who seek treatment for drug problems, or who otherwise enter programs to get off the street. In other words, these samples self-select for the women who are most likely to have been victimized by prostitution and most likely to want out of the profession. Moreover, the women seeking treatment or leniency in prison are likely to give an authority figure—the researcher—whatever answer they believe he or she wishes.

There is another reason that the studies on streetwalkers are inadequate in terms of forming general policy on prostitution. The National Task Force on Prostitution estimates that, of the entire female prostitute community in America, only 5 to 20 percent are streetwalkers. The percentage spread depends on the size of the city. Eighty to ninety-five percent of prostitutes work either incall or outcall. But because streetwalkers are the most visible of all prostitutes—in terms of public awareness, arrest records, and social work programs—they are incorrectly perceived as being "the paradigm of a prostitute." In reality, they form the smallest portion of the community, and they are *by far* the portion in which the problems associated with prostitution are most likely to occur: drug addiction, violence, police abuse, and disease.

The anti-prostitute feminists Melissa Farley and Norma Hotaling have conducted an interesting study of streetwalkers[4] from street areas of San Francisco, particularly the strolls frequented by homeless, drug-using prostitutes or particularly young whores. These whores are easy targets for violence: They are not necessarily representative even of the streetwalking community. Yet this study has been used by antiprostitution groups to present a portrait not simply of the most vulnerable of streetwalkers, but of "the prostitute."[5]

Farley and Hotaling entered into their research to test the hypothesis that streetwalkers suffered from post-traumatic syndrome and compared the psychological states of whores to those of hostages and torture victims. From a sample of 130 prostitutes, which included some male and transgendered ones, Farley and Hotaling arrived at disturbing statistics. Eighty-two percent reported having been physically assaulted since entering prostitution. Seventy-five percent stated that they had had or did have a drug problem; and 88 percent wanted to leave prostitution.

In 1995, I conducted an intensive study of forty-one female members of COYOTE. Thirty-four of the respondents were, or had been, prostitutes. Seventy-one percent of the women reported having experienced no violence over the years of sex work: 29 percent had experienced violence, more often from the police or a co-worker than from a client. One prostitute responded, "If you are on the street and you are dealing with someone who can remain anonymous, it is more likely that people you will encounter will be violent." None of the women stated, or evidenced, a drug problem. Seventeen percent of the women wished to leave sex work, with 24 percent not being sure.[6]

Needless to say, there is discrepancy between my results and those of such researchers as Farley and Hotaling. The difference grows deeper as I speak of the articulate, politically aware whores with whom I deal daily and as anti-prostitution feminists report the heartbreaking stories of ex-prostitutes who have been damaged on the streets. These are women such as those involved in the organization WHISPER, Women Hurt in Systems of Prostitution Engaged in Revolt.

I don't dispute the stories of damaged ex-prostitutes. My point is not that Farley and Hotaling are wrong and I am right. They surveyed the lowest rung of prostitution (streetwalkers in notoriously bad strolls), where abuse is rampant, while I dealt with the upper rung (call girls), where abuse is uncommon. The phenomenon of feminists researching different segments of the prostitute community can easily devolve into a circus of confrontation with each side claiming to have "better whores."

I am not saying this. What I am saying is that truth is usually more complicated than any one perspective can capture. Prostitution is not a monolith. Each woman experiences the profession in a different manner. Nothing can be gained by having different groups of feminists or prostitutes—all of whom are probably telling the truth of their own experiences—attempting to discredit each other.

The day-to-day realities of a streetwalker cannot be extended to say anything that is necessarily, or even probably, true of the daily routine of a woman in a massage parlor or of an exclusive call girl or of a stripper who hooks on the side. About the only political interest all women in prostitution seem to share is that—whatever their circumstances—it is better for prostitution to be decriminalized.

This brings us more directly to the policies most feminists now advocate against the economic associates of whores, and that prostitute activists decry.

## Decriminalization versus Legalization

Traditionally, society has legally approached the "problem" of prostitution in three general ways: suppression or *abolition*; regulation or *legalization*; and, tolerance, or *decriminalization*.

The meaning of abolition is fairly clear.

"Legalization" refers to some form of state-controlled prostitution, for example, the creation of red-light districts. It almost always includes a government record of who is a prostitute—information that is commonly used for other government purposes. For example, some countries in Europe indicate whether someone is a prostitute on her passport, and other countries automatically refuse her entry on that basis.

Decriminalization is the opposite of legalization. It refers to the elimination of all laws against prostitution, including laws against those who associate with whores: i.e., madams, pimps, and johns.

With startling consistency, the prostitutes' rights movement calls for the decriminalization of all aspects of prostitution. You will sometimes hear anti-prostitution feminists describe their position as "decriminalization with the goal of abolition." But, in using the term "decriminalization," each side means something very different. Prostitute activists mean that all aspects of prostitution must be legally tolerated. Anti-prostitution feminists mean that the police should not arrest the prostitutes, only the men (the pimps and johns) and the women who act as pimps (madams).

With the support of such feminists there has been a sea change in how many police departments in North America legally address the nitty-gritty of streetwalking. Namely, they are now arresting the men. In discussions with the vice cops who were invited speakers at the International Congress on Prostitution, all but one of them said that arrests now ran about fifty-fifty for prostitutes and for johns. This is opposed to something like 2 percent for the men in the past. Some police departments go even further, like the Edmonton Police Services in Canada that declared 1992 the Year of the John and concentrated on charging clients.

When I speak of cooperation between anti-prostitution feminists and vice cops I am referring specifically to the Schools for Johns, a phenomenon that seems to be sweeping North America, city by city. It began in San Francisco, when Norma Hotaling teamed up with the vice department to formulate new policy on prostitution.[7] Instead of ignoring johns as they normally did, police arrested them and gave first-time johns an option: They could erase the arrest from their records by paying a fee and by attending a one-day seminar during which they would be lectured, usually by feminists and damaged ex-prostitutes, on the turpitude of their ways. Some cities, like Chicago, have added the touch of publishing the names and addresses of men so arrested in major newspapers.

The dozens of prostitutes I've spoken with are appalled by this development. One of their arguments is that the School for Johns is making the streets less safe for prostitutes. The force of such laws will not determine, and historically never has determined, how many women will turn to the streets. But, prostitute activists argue, the laws *will* discourage a certain class of men from seeking out streetwalkers. Men who are married, with respectable careers and a reputation to protect, will not risk being publicly exposed as a john. On the other hand, men who are criminally inclined toward prostitutes will not be discouraged by the prospect of a police fine. Thus, police/feminist policy keeps peaceful johns off the streets and leaves women to compete more vigorously for johns and screen less rigorously those who approach them. Is it any wonder that violence against streetwalkers is rising in many North American cities?

Arresting the economic associates of prostitutes represents a farther step toward state control, rather than a step toward decriminalization. Arresting the men on whom they rely to make a living is a direct attack upon the women who "chose" prostitution as a profession.

# In Defense of Pimps

The prostitutes I've spoken with believe that the current feminist stress on targeting "the men" is harming "the women." Because the most reviled men in prostitution are the pimps, I want to argue against current anti-pimping laws under the assumption that, if I call these measures into question, doubt will be cast on all other laws against the men.

I want to begin by presenting an e-mail exchange—a discussion that occurred between myself and three female prostitutes—on the subject of pimps and madams. The first woman wrote:

> I would like the movement [prostitutes' rights] to be *less* oriented toward social work and *more* about giving people the skills (and other things they need) to be professionally successful. Key to this is supporting madams and business owners instead of trashing them (whether subtly or directly). Because in order to succeed and have staying power a prostitute eventually has to become more entrepreneurial. [Emphasis in the original.]

The second prostitute chirped in electronically:

> I think madams are a great asset to the industry—they're women who usually have first-hand experience, and tend to be thorough when it comes to protecting their underlings. I have a bit of a problem with pimps, though . . . especially men whose only experience in the biz is from the demand side.

The third whore voiced a dissenting opinion:

> What is the big fuss about pimps? . . . If you are talking about people who (but for a penis) might be called madams, I don't see a problem. I might prefer to work with another lady but that's a personality thing. When I was younger, I worked for an agency that was owned by two guys and one woman. They were all about the same—sometimes nice, sometimes annoying, like anyone else in the world.

It is interesting to note that the discussion of pimps does not even touch upon the issue of violence. It dwells entirely upon economics, and that is because the definition of pimp is an economic one. As the Canadian ex-prostitute Alexandra Highcrest commented in her book *At Home on the Stroll*, "In simple legal terms a pimp is someone who lives off the earnings of a prostitute. Such a broad definition can include many people most of us don't think of when we hear that word. Children live off the earnings of prostitute mothers; husbands, lovers, siblings, perhaps even parents, can all meet the basic requirements for being classified as pimps by the courts" (1977, 121).

Such laws do not punish people for beating, raping, or stealing from a whore. They do not define a pimp as a man who kidnaps a woman and coerces her onto the streets. Such laws refer to financial arrangements and target those who receive money from or give money to whores. So, it becomes illegal for a prostitute to form the economic associations that most women take for granted.

The public widely perceives anti-pimping laws as protecting prostitutes from abusive men. Kathleen Barry not only agrees, but also extends the definition of pimping to include anyone who promotes the commodification of women, including pornographers. But if mere economic arrangements with men were damaging the women who are streetwalkers, you would expect the prostitutes' rights movement to support measures against them. Instead, the community adamantly opposes anti-pimping laws.

In a 1995 COYOTE press release, the veteran prostitute activist Carol Leigh—"the Scarlot Harlot"—offered insight into sex workers' reasoning when she pleaded on behalf of her husband:

> You want to make laws against the pimps? Make sure that you make the distinction between forced prostitution, and those who want to be in prostitution by choice. Go after those who actually abuse us. Just as in marriage, some husbands are abusive of women. Not all husbands are that way. Don't take away my husband because he's really, really good to me. But if you want to help women, go after those people who actually abuse us, but be very, very careful how you word legislation that goes after those who you think exploit and abuse us, because those laws ultimately get used against us.

How do allegedly protective laws get used against whores? For example, in both the United States and Europe, it is common practice for the police to use anti-pimping laws to ignore a whore's right to privacy. In pursuit of pimps, the police may break into the home of a known whore, rifle through or confiscate her possessions, and harass anyone they find on the premises. The fear of such laws being used in reprisal makes many prostitutes reluctant to speak out or to become involved in community affairs. In turn, this makes them more alienated and less likely to break out of prostitution.

Anti-pimping laws also act as a barriers to those prostitutes who wish to marry and get out of the business in that manner. The husband, even of an *ex*-whore, becomes automatically vulnerable to charges of pimping. This is true even of husbands who do not live primarily off their wives' whoring, but who share household expenses with her.

But what of the husbands or lovers who are fully dependent on profits from prostitution? Are they not parasites, living off the sexual wages of their wives? Whores are quick to point out that other women have the right to support their husbands and lovers. No one passes laws forbidding waitresses, lawyers, feminists, or secretaries from having dependent men in their lives. Why are whores the only women legally singled out in this manner?

Yet pimps continue to be excoriated, with no reference to whether or not they are abusive. There are two main reasons for this. First, pimps—and not madams—are associated with streetwalking, which is the most violence-prone and stigmatized form of prostitution. Second, pimps—as men—have been systematically portrayed as exploiters and oppressors by modern feminism. As Kathleen Barry explains in *Female Sexual Slavery*:

> Together, pimping and procuring are perhaps the most ruthless displays of male power and sexual dominance.... Procuring is a strategy, a tactic for acquiring women and turning them into prostitution; pimping keeps them there. Procuring today involves "convincing" a woman to be a prostitute through cunning, fraud, and/or physical force, taking her against her will or knowledge and putting her into prostitution. (1981, 73)

How can this image of the pimp be reconciled with the following observation by a whore who chooses to remain anonymous:

> Many of the men who get described ... as "pimps" are boyfriends, lovers, license-plate-number takers and managers. Many girls seek out pimps and even love their "man." A girl has a right ... even if she is a bit dumb and is being taken. And the venom of the law is another way to get at prostitutes— by busting their lovers. If a bank teller's husband beats her, he is charged with assault, not with being a bank teller's husband.

The best explanation of the schism between these two portraits of the pimp is that pimping, like prostitution, is not a monolithic institution. Some pimps are husbands and friends who offer protection and partnership. But, especially on the street level of prostitution, other pimps are kidnappers, batterers, and rapists who deserve to be taken to a back alley where feminism can be more graphically explained to them. But such criminals are not generally the ones being prosecuted by the law and the court system. Barry reports talking to a street prostitute who had been raped and kidnapped by pimps, and another who had been slashed by a razor the night before. Barry mentions in passing that the women "didn't consider reporting [the assaults] to the police" (1981, 73). Barry details many horrifying cases of women being abused by pimps, but she never seems to dwell upon why the streetwalkers do not seek protection from the police. It is because regular women are protected by laws that prosecute rapists and kidnappers, but the law routinely ignores assaults against whores. Even worse, prostitutes are persecuted and physically abused by a legal system that protects other women. The police become just another layer of abuse.

# Conclusion

The foregoing has been a political analysis of the deepening schism between prostitute activists and anti-prostitution feminists, groups that should be natural allies rather than enemies. The poem that follows is meant to provide a window onto the emotional impact of the ongoing conflict.

Written by Norma Jean Almodovar, director of COYOTE Los Angeles, the poem has a specific history. In her capacity as one of the organizers of the 1997 International Congress on Prostitution, Norma Jean coordinated an exhibit of Whore Art.* One of the most distressing encounters she experienced was with a politically correct female academic who insisted that prostitutes could not use the term "whore" to describe themselves. The poem was written to explain why the prostitutes' rights movement prefers the word "whore." It also captures the emotional distress that women are inflicting upon each other over the issue of prostitution.

### THE "WHORE" WORD

I am a woman . . . and if I get out of line, you call me a whore
And if I have a good time, you call me a whore
And if I speak my mind—you call me a whore.
You throw the word at me when I stand on my own
You use the word often to hold me down.
You ever remind me that whores are the worst—
the outcasts, pariahs, without any worth.

"You're just a whore!" you repeat like a mantra—
Like a shot of cold water to dampen my joy.
"You're just a whore—so what do you know?
and what do I care of whatever you think!"
"You're a whore," is a dagger you drive through my heart
as you pound into my psyche that name.
You equate everything that I ever thought good—
with that word
which you spit out like venom—to show me how awful I am.
But I ask you, please tell me, just what is a whore?
A whore says what she thinks and she thinks for herself . . .
She's independent and feisty—so what? is there more?
Why does it frighten you so to know I've a mind of my own
and don't need your permission to live or to love or to be?
And what if I tell you
I don't care if you call me a whore . . .
What will you call me now?

*Some pieces from this display are included in Section 5 of this book.

# Notes

1. "Whore" is the term preferred by most prostitute activists. Please see poem "The 'Whore' Word" at the conclusion of this paper for an explanation why.

2. In reality, many of the most important offices in the highly centralized organization are held by anti-prostitution, antipornography feminists such as Tammy Bruce.

3. In its HIV/AIDS Surveillance Report 5, no. 30 (1993), the CDC found that of 202,655 males diagnosed with AIDS since 1981, only 123 cited sex with a female prostitute as their only risk factors.

4. Presented at the NGO Forum, Fourth-World Conference on Women, Beijing, September 4, 1995.

5. I also had questions about the study's methodology. For example, Farley and Hotaling entered with certain assumptions, including "Prostitution is almost always a continuation of abuse which began much earlier, usually at home." Using this assumption, they often interpreted or dismissed data from subjects, rather than simply record responses. For example, the study comments, "Several subjects commented that they didn't want to think about their pasts when responding to the questions about childhood . . . it was probably too painful to review childhood abuse."

Nor did they accept the subjects' own assessment of whether they had been abused. They called such subjects "profoundly confused." The study reports on one woman: "When asked why she answered 'no' to the question regarding childhood sexual abuse, one woman whose history was known to one of the interviewers, said: 'Because there was no force, and besides I didn't even know what it was then—I didn't know it was sex.'" The researchers concluded "Denial may be affecting these subjects' ability or willingness to report their trauma history."

6. For a more extensive report on this study, see Wendy McElroy, *XXX: A Woman's Right to Pornography* (New York: St. Martin's, 1995), Appendix.

7. The Prostitutes' Rights Movement was particularly outraged by this feminist cooperation because of the deep history of hostility displayed by the San Francisco vice police. For example, in the early days of AIDS awareness, Cal Pep—the California Prostitutes Education Project—sent workers into the San Francisco "stroll districts" where street prostitutes worked and distributed condoms, spermicides, bleach, and educational materials, as well as talked to the prostitutes about safe sex practices. Meanwhile, San Francisco Police Department members confiscated the condoms and used them as evidence of prostitution in court. Because of police policy, the street-walkers would throw the distributed condoms away.

# References

Alexander, Priscilla. 1991. Prostitutes are being scapegoated for heterosexual AIDS. In *Sex Work: Writings by Women in the Sex Industry,* edited by Frederique Delacosta and Priscilla Alexander. Pittsburgh: Cleis Press.

Barry, Kathleen. 1981. *Female Sexual Slavery.* New York: Avon.

**Prostitution**

Bell, Laurie, ed. 1987. *Good girls, bad girls: Sex trade workers and feminists face to face.*
     Toronto: The Women's Press.
*COYOTE Howls,* 1979. (Newsletter of Call Off Your Tired Old Ethics.)
COYOTE Press Release, October 1995. Los Angeles.
Dworkin, Andrea. 1992. Prostitution and male supremacy. Speech delivered at "Pros-
     titution: From academia to activism," a symposium sponsored by the *Michigan
     Journal of Gender and Law* at the University of Michigan Law School, October 31.
Highcrest, Alexandra. 1997. *At Home on the Stroll: My Twenty Years as a Prostitute in
     Canada.* Toronto: Knopf.
McElroy, Wendy. 1995. *XXX: A woman's right to pornography.* New York: St. Martin's.
Shrage, Laurie. 1989. Should feminists oppose prostitution? *Ethics* 99: 347–61.

# ON OWNING THE BODY

## SIBYL SCHWARZENBACH

In the debate surrounding the complex issue of prostitution, much unclarity exists regarding the form of the relationship we have to our own physical bodies. On the one hand, many who defend the decriminalization of prostitution treat our relation to our bodies as one of simple private ownership; the prostitute's body is her private property and she should be allowed to do with it what she will—including sell her sexual services for money. On the other hand, many object to our conceiving our relationship to our bodies in this way. My body is not just another physical object or tool among others (like a hammer or a car); my body is *me,* they argue, and they often oppose decriminalization on the grounds that it resembles a form of slavery. In fact, I believe this refusal to treat our bodies as just another commodity is at the heart of much of the resistance to the decriminalization of prostitution. Many feminists, including the well-known social theorist Carole Pateman, have argued, for instance, that the prostitute in having to sell her body actually sells her very "self" in the prostitute-client relation.[1] But if this is the case, if the activity in question does entail the sale of bodies and selves, arguing for decriminalization would be akin to defending slavery. How could we *not* be opposed?

My aim in the following is to present a third way out of this dilemma. I will argue that our relationship to our bodies is *not* the simple one of owning private property or a commodity as many defenders of decriminalization believe, and yet we still must allow a right to engage in sex for sale. How is this possible? What conception of the person is presupposed in this position? I here hope that a careful philosophical analysis might leave the ivory tower of academia and make itself useful by removing one serious obstacle to the future decriminalization of prostitution.[2]

345

# Property in the Person

What does it mean for us to have "property in our persons" and bodies? Nearly all adults today are granted certain rights in their own bodies and over their own actions; we are considered free and independent persons with a responsibility for our own actions. This may seem an obvious and natural state of affairs, but this fact is already the result of a long historical process. The slave by definition was not granted legal rights in his or her body and actions (both belonged to his master), and the bodies and actions of women throughout history were frequently under the legal control and ownership of a male (typically the father or husband). So first we must clarify what it means to have legal property in one's own person.

If one looks to the tradition of Western philosophy and law, as well as to everyday speech and usage, I believe one can discover the operation of two different conceptions of ownership and property. The first conception is the one more familiar to us all and I will call it the "private property" model. As originally set forth by John Locke, this form of property entails a number of characteristics. First, private property is typically something I obtain by my own efforts or an act of will; it is something I have "mixed my labor with," for instance, or for which I have contracted with another. If I own something in this private form it entails, secondly, that I can use, manage, and enjoy the property *exclusively* as I will (provided, of course, I do not harm others or infringe on their similar property rights). But the full-fledged or "mature" conception of private property entails something further; it entails, third, the right to *alienate* (sell) the thing and even *destroy* it if I should so wish.[3] In purchasing an automobile, for example, I cannot only use it as I will (provided I do not harm others), but I even have the right to destroy it (disassemble it, say, and sell it for scrap). Now some, namely, the philosopher Robert Nozick, actually seem to think that this commodified form of ownership is the form in which we possess our own bodies. Nozick advocates the right of the individual to suicide, self-sale into slavery, and presumably even to self-mutilation. But the vast majority of modern Western thinkers, as well as common sense, appear to disagree; they believe both our body and our personality are inalienable.

I now introduce a second, less well recognized (but equally fundamental) form of property that I shall call property *qua* gift. Unlike private property, the genuine gift is typically an unearned value that is "bestowed" upon us by another (a donor) for our benefit (in contrast, say, to a bribe), and our individual will here plays a far less active role. As one author has noted, the authentic gift (unlike private property or the commodity) tends to be far more than a simple transfer of value. A genuine gift brings into being a new moral relation between persons; it is a reality laden with subtle but very real "oughts." For instance, have I not violated the spirit of a gift when, say, on receiving a rare edition of the works of Kant from an old professor of mine, I turn the books over to a recycling plant? On this gift-model, "owning" comes closer to being a form of guardian- or *stewardship* and the intentions of the giver are relevant. In Locke's thought our life, limb, natural freedom, and equal political jurisdiction are original gifts granted us all by God in the state of nature. We did not "earn" such values; they were freely and generously given. Nor, Locke goes on, can we do with such property what we will; we can neither injure nor destroy our life and limb, because ultimately both belong to God, whose "servants" we are.

I wish to suggest that Locke's intuition regarding the fundamental stewardship of our bodies is very much alive today even if the surrounding theological justification has been dropped. That is, in nearly all modern societies, I may not cut off my hand and sell it, nor may I alienate myself (or my life) to another (as in slavery). Our bodies and limbs are not treated as simply another commodity that can be disposed of at will, but as a far more fundamental *ground* of our existence. My point is that we *still today* continue to treat our bodies and lives as, in large part, "gifts"—not as private property, but as objects of our stewardship. We did not, after all, create these original values; they were granted us at birth. So too—if we cannot agree on a theological description— my freedom to direct my life and limb may be viewed as a "gift" from the rational community at large; I was born free (and not a slave), acknowledged and recognized by others as an American at birth (or by naturalization), with a certain set of rights, duties, and so forth. Finally, the notion of our lives as primarily a "stewardship" of our bodies accounts for why many think we may have a right to suicide at the age of seventy, but that something is terribly wrong when teenagers do it. The teenager, it can be argued, has not been around long enough to fully appropriate and make life his or her own "private" possession.

My claim is that when most people speak today of our "owning" our bodies, they in fact have *both* these concepts confusedly in mind. I wish to claim further that *true self-possession* of one's life, limb, and actions entails the capacity to consider them under *both* property descriptions. That is, as I grow older, my early stewardship of my body and acts (although normally never abandoned) does become more fully "mine," as it were. But this is not to say that we ever condone treating our bodies and lives as private property, as mere alienable and destructible things.

## The Sale of Labor-Power

Again, an issue for those who defend decriminalization—if we do not believe our bodies are mere things to be disposed of at will—is to show how it is that

I can alienate an aspect of my most concrete self (my physical body for use, say, for half an hour) and yet not at the same time be alienating *myself*. In some sense, after all, my body is also "me." At this point it is important to look more closely at the notion of wage-labor (and the sale of labor-power), a notion that was first carefully analyzed by the philosopher Hegel in his *Philosophy of Right*. Hegel's analysis of wage-labor remains one of the most careful and trenchant ever performed.

In unison with the whole of the modern tradition, Hegel argues that our "substantial personalities" are not for sale; we are each but the first steward of them. Under "substantial personality" Hegel includes our life and limb (our bodies) as well as our reason, freedom of will, ethical life, and religion. We may presume that he would also include our sexuality. The fact that this core of our substantive personality is not for sale, Hegel claims, is already universally recognized in our modern system of rational law (which forbids slavery). However, in his careful account of personality, Hegel stresses a *dual aspect*; he distinguishes between the concrete empirical self, on the one hand, and the self as rational agency able to "abstract" or "distance" itself from any *particular* state of mind or action, on the other. Hegel writes,

> Single products of my particular physical and mental skill, and of my power to act, I can alienate to someone else and can give him the use of my abilities for a restricted period, because *on the strength of this restriction,* my abilities acquire an external relation to the [totality] of my being. (Emphasis added.)

That is, the human personality is distinguished precisely by its capacity for "expression" (*Entausserung*), by its ability to "distance itself" from particular products, actions, or aspects of its physical being. Hegel here points to a capacity that underlies not only our political personalities but even much of everyday human life; we all have the ability to obtain critical distance regarding many aspects of our own particular selves, actions, or products. Hegel cites examples of art works, lectures, but also sermons and even prayers (aspects of our substantive religious personalities) that may be distanced or relinquished to the will of another. Definite restrictions, however, always apply; by alienating (a) *too wide a range of one's abilities,* or (b) *too much of one's time,* moral personality, self, and our ultimate stewardship are clearly violated.

Allow me to illustrate this important point by way of an example that quite closely parallels, I believe, the case of prostitution. Assume I am a dancer and my body is clearly *not separable* from the dance I perform. Those who come to see me dance, therefore, are interested—not in some product separable from my body—but in *my body itself.* If I have freely decided to dance for a wage, however, we do not (today) consider it a transgression of moral personality that I do so. My autonomy has not been infringed because others make visual use (as it were) of my body's activities temporarily; it has been my decision to make public and for hire certain particular expressions of my physical being for a restricted period of time. If, however, there are no limits on the time I must dance (if I must dance nonstop all evening, for example), or if I must relinquish the wider range of my abilities (such as my reason or my religion), my personality will clearly be violated.

# The Case of Sexuality

I believe in the end there is no relevant *legal* difference between the case of the dancer and that of (at least a version of) what I shall call "sound prostitution." First, let me distinguish clear cases of "unsound" prostitution. If the prostitute is underaged, if she is tricked or forced (in any reasonable sense of the term) into the profession, if she must perform sex nonstop for hours (or all day, etc.), if she must, in doing so, alienate a wider range of her substantive abilities (such as her reason or her personal morality), if her life or limb are at risk in any way and so on, then moral personality is clearly being infringed upon. But if, on the other hand, a mature woman decides when and where to offer a particular expression of her being (use of her body for a stipulated period of time) to a particular man (or woman) for touch, if the surroundings are safe and healthful, if she always retains the right not to have to perform any act that is distasteful to her, etc., why—we are obliged to ask—should moral personality be violated? The woman has in no way relinquished her general stewardship but only treated various circumscribed expressions of herself as alienable property. She has in no way sold "her body"—in the sense of private property—to another even temporarily; she has only granted limited use.

A natural response here is that sexuality is surely of a different order from most other forms of wage-labor such as dancing or acting on stage. I agree, but it is not so easy to get at what this different order is. In the case of the dancer, one might argue that "visual touch" by strangers is surely far less intimate and distasteful than "physical touch" by a strange man, especially "physical sexual touch." Many women, at the *mere thought* of being in the prostitute's position, experience sensations of horror, humiliation, or disgust. But can these sensations (or responses) *at the mere thought* of another's being touched be sufficient grounds for rendering that other activity illegal? It seems they cannot for a number of reasons.

Most importantly, as was even argued in the 1979 Report of the (British) Committee on Obscenity and Film Censorship, "[i]f one accepted, as a basis for coercing one person's actions, the fact that others would be upset even by the thought of [his] performing those actions, one would be denying any substantive liberty at all." Nearly any action—under special circumstances and at certain times—can be upsetting to someone. So too, many activities cause near universal experiences of disgust, at least at first—the internal organs spewing forth from the butcher's knife, the cold touch of the cadaver to the undertaker's hand, the corpse's putrid smell, etc.—but these activities are not (and certainly not for that reason) illegitimate. (It goes without saying that no one should be forced to have to perform them.) And here it is of critical importance to stress that sexual responses are hardly uniform across particular women. Many, perhaps most, women are repulsed and humiliated by (even the thought of) the physical touch of a strange man, but others obviously mind it far less (and this will depend in part on each's cultural and sexual history).[4] The surrounding background conditions (the degree of choice or coercion, the level of health and safety, etc.) are here of foremost importance.

Similarly, just as responses among individual women vary significantly, so does the delineation of acceptable moral and social behavior between cultures. Western women, for example, freely expose their faces in public (and frequently their whole bodies, say, on a nude beach), but a traditional Arab woman will experience shock, embarrassment, and severe humiliation if only her veil happens to slip from her face.[5] It is important to remember that our own culture—but a short time ago—forbade women entry into the acting profession, and dancing on a theatrical stage not only spelled social ruination, but also prompted public outcries of "whore!"[6]

I wish to make it clear that I am not saying that there is not a fine line between selling one's abilities and selling one's self; I believe there is. What I am arguing is that this line is not a natural or a physical one, but a delicately constructed social and cultural identity. Moreover, I am suggesting that where the line is drawn at present in the United States (unlike many European countries)—where all forms of commercial sex among consenting adults are illegal (excluding, of course, certain parts of Nevada), and yet working as a butcher or body guard, in a dark factory day in and out, or at many other highly distasteful, dangerous, or unhealthy activities is not—begins to crumble under careful scrutiny. Further, I am suggesting that from a legal standpoint, there begins to be good justification for claiming that the activity of mature women (or men) who decide at some point in their life to sell their sexual services, limited in time, and who retain the right not to perform any act distasteful to them (as well as the right to interrupt the whole process at will), such mature persons should not be stigmatized and forbidden to do so, however much one's personal morality may rebel. For what is at issue here touches on one of the most fundamental individual rights of all: a person's right to direct his or her own life and limb as he or she thinks fit.[7] Remember, this is a precious right that is only just beginning to obtain for women. Finally, as I have tried to show, the prostitute in sound prostitution strictly speaking no more sells "her body"—as a physical entity and in the sense of private property—than the dancer for hire does. In both cases the individual remains the ultimate steward of his or her physical being and each relinquishes only particular, restricted expressions of him or herself for limited periods of time. This fact alone is enough to distinguish sound prostitution from slavery, from the practice where bodies and selves are literally being "bought and sold."

# Notes

1. See Carole Pateman's *The Sexual Contract* (1988), especially chapter 7, entitled "What's Wrong with Prostitution?"

2. See my "Contractarians and Feminists Debate Prostitution," *New York University Review of Law and Social Change* 18, no. 1 (1990–91) for the more extensive argument for decriminalization.

3. See A. M. Honore, "Ownership" in *Oxford Essays in Jurisprudence* 113 (1961), ed. A. Guest.

4. This point does not mean to overlook the fact that the sexual history of many prostitutes is often one of sexual molestation, incest, and child abuse—a state of affairs that must be battled on its own grounds. Nonetheless, this unpleasant fact notwithstanding, it still remains the case that prostitutes frequently have a different relationship to their own bodies than many of the rest of us do, and surely women in different times, places, and culture have.

5. For discussions regarding the veil (or chador), largely limited to Muslim women of the urban upper and middle classes, see the collection of essays in *Women in the Muslim World*, ed. by L. Beck and N. Keddie (Cambridge, Mass.: Harvard University Press, 1978).

6. For a discussion of the Victorian stance on the actress as "Fallen Woman" and where the use of the phrase "public woman" was still used interchangeably for performer and prostitute, see N. Auerbach's *Women and the Demon* (Cambridge, Mass.: Harvard University Press, 1982), 182.

7. See Locke's *Second Treatise*, para. 22.

# 7

# DOING RESEARCH WITH SEX WORKERS

## Introduction

Research on any kind of sexual topic poses potential problems. Alfred Kinsey, the dominant figure in sex research in the last part of the twentieth century, held there was a tendency for people to lie in responding to sexual questions, some exaggerating, while others attempted to cover up what they were doing, with all kinds of variations in between. Kinsey felt he solved this question by doing oral interviews and developing a coding method by which contradictions could quickly be ferreted out. He asked the same question in many different ways, and any inconsistencies had to be resolved before he was satisfied the interviewer was telling the truth. The kind of interviews Kinsey did, however, are very labor intensive, and many researchers have tried to find shortcuts or alternatives. But if the researcher encounters problems with gathering data from the ordinary person, the difficulties with sex workers are much greater. For many sex workers time is money, and the question immediately arises whether one pays for an interview or not and how much. Getting access to sex workers is in itself a problem. Many are suspicious of academics or others labeled as researchers. Often the language used is different from the one they are used to. The list of problems could be extended, but the point of this section with contributions by Wendy Rickard, Seymour Craig, Jacqueline Lewis, Amy Flowers, Priscilla Pyett and Deborah Warr is to explore new ways of getting answers to old questions.

# TALKING LIVED REALITY:
# USING ORAL HISTORY TO RECORD A
# MORE BALANCED HISTORY OF SEX WORK
## WENDY RICKARD

"Morally biased, sensationalized and lop-sided." This is the phrase that Roberta Perkins used in 1993 to describe the way that the history of prostitution tends to be recorded. Like many others before and since, she pointed to the domination of media presentations, police and court records and other official documents as the key conventional resources available to social historians (60–63). Perkins turned to oral history as a tool for documenting a more balanced history of prostitutes working in Sydney, Australia. Jan Jordan used a similar approach a few years earlier in New Zealand (1991). On a broader level, feminists, like social historians, have been attracted to oral history as a way of recovering the voices of suppressed groups of women, and a body of very exciting work has emerged since the late 1970s exploring the theoretical, methodological, and practical issues that arise when women utilize oral history as a tool of feminist scholarship.[1]

Using extracts from a set of life-story interviews currently being recorded with women working as prostitutes in London, United Kingdom, this chapter aims to arouse interest in the range of material the women have provided and to describe the process of using oral history as a research technique with a resulting archival product.[2] Although offering vast possibilities for analytic debate, because the project is still in progress, this chapter concentrates on presenting a thematic montage of women's voices, as a demonstration of oral history in the making, and highlighting the different and complex interactions involved in creating a dialogue through which women talk about their lived reality.

As a process account, it should first be mentioned that the women interviewed for this project initially came to me through word of mouth, while I was working as a maid in a flat in West London. By day, I worked as an academic in AIDS research, and while working in the flat was in part stimulated by my academic interests, for the most part it was a way to spend time with some women friends who worked as prostitutes and maids. They were interested in a national oral history project I was undertaking to record and preserve the life histories of people with HIV and AIDS and pressed me to consider the same approach specifically with women working as prostitutes. It was their suggestion that a national oral history of prostitution might serve to give more depth to ongoing contemporary debates, and using imagery drawn from *Star Trek*, they marvelled at how wonderful it might be if people in the future could understand history from the actual words and phrases of women who lived the life.

## Challenging Rhetoric

The British Library National Sound Archive agreed to fund one pilot interview and this is a short extract from the first interview recorded for the collection in September 1995. After talking for about an hour and a half about her family background and her youth, Lauren, who was born in 1965, describes how she first entered prostitution.

> I used to be . . . I used to work as an assistant photographer, uhm, for a well-known newspaper which I'm not gonna mention, and I knew a lot of the page three girls really well and a lot of them are really actually high class escort girls. I mean, when they're not doing pictures, they make money through just being . . . going around on someone's arm all night . . . and I got friendly with these girls and they used to take me out to Stringfellows . . . and . . . you know . . . they'd got a Cartier watch just for going out to dinner with an Arab and stuff like that and I thought "Oh that sounds easy," do ya know what I mean . . . and then one day this girl rang me up saying they're short of a girl . . . you know. I know the score; I've been out with them and seen what's going on—"would I get involved?" And I just said yeah. . . . And the first experience was really nice 'cos it was a young Arab prince and he was only about two years older so it was like, really good looking. It wasn't like doing anything like that . . . and that's how I got involved in this business, originally.

I highlight this particular extract to illustrate initial responses to the tapes. People were openly fascinated by the project. Yet too many asked one brief question about how Lauren "got into" prostitution and then dismissed the tapes as unrepresentative, particularly in relation to the perceived violence and degradation of sex work. The reaction from people who have actually listened to these early tapes beyond this short extract, is, needless to say, quite different.

As I met more women working as prostitutes, I started interviewing them, often in their homes or on quieter days while they were working in flats. Later, I went to work on a prostitutes' health outreach project and began actively to recruit among women working the streets and flats of South London.

This description of process is unremarkable, in that many women begin their research in this way. The more interesting part of this particular story is the connection with the British Library. In collaboration with them, as mentioned above, I had recently set up a new archive of oral history material documenting the AIDS pandemic, and this project was featured prominently in their promotional literature. However, the work with prostitutes, while being commissioned and catalogued in the archive, was notably listed under "miscellaneous." It is with subtlety that this is to be challenged in such national institutions in the United Kingdom. Progress has been made in getting prostitutes' voices into the library and individuals within the organization have been enthusiastic and supportive, yet there is still some way to go in gaining explicit acknowledgment for the collection at the institutional level.

# The Unexpected Insight—Health Issues

One theme explored in each interview is women's health issues in relation to their whole lives and particularly in relation to prostitution. From an initial focus on this topic, the next extract demonstrates an unexpected insight gained through the process of interviewing Lauren about health issues affecting her work.

> I've had to call an ambulance one day on this guy who I thought was having an heart attack. He suffered from angina, I found (out) in the end. And I gave him . . . he told me to get these pills for him out of his jacket. I gave him one . . . , but I still phoned an ambulance, just to be on the safe side.
>
> He was about ninety. It was a bit too much for him.
>
> *Q: And did you follow it up and find out what happened to him after that?*
>
> No, I didn't. But he actually called me a few weeks later and said, you know, thanks. 'Cos I had to tell the . . .: it was hard explaining to the ambulance men and everything.
>
> *Q: What did you tell them?*
>
> I said to him that I found this guy on the steps downstairs. He couldn't breathe so I brought him upstairs to my apartment, because he's obviously got family. And if he had died, you know, the family are gonna want to know

what happened and where and so I covered his tracks for him, you know. 'Cos at the end of the day, in this business even men that you think are the ideal husbands still come along.

This account offers some additional insight into the human interactions of sex work. It also illustrates how Lauren's narrative included unsolicited humorous stories as a recurring device for conveying symbolic messages about the caring side of prostitution.

## Giving Something Back to the Women

Author Paul Thompson said: "Oral history gives history back to the people in their own words. And in giving a past, it also helps them towards a future of their own making" (1978). It would be naive to state that the process of recording their life histories changed women's lives immediately, and it will be interesting to unpack further their self-evaluations about the experience of being interviewed. At the most basic level, largely due to the stigma attached to working as prostitutes, several women reported that they find it necessary in daily life to compartmentalize their existence, keeping secrets and never sharing much of their acquired wisdom. Some women reported that the life-story interview offered an opportunity to thread together disparate aspects of their lives, even where the process of reminiscence was, at times, harrowing and upsetting. There is a clear suggestion from the increasing number of biographical and autobiographical accounts now being published that prostitutes place significant importance in "going on record." Yet, without an approach like oral history, this option is only available to a small minority of articulate women who successfully achieve publishing deals. These aspects and others are clearly reflected in Amanda's evaluation of the interview process that, as becomes plain from the account, was also influenced by the fact that she is living with an AIDS diagnosis.

> I have never really looked at it from birth right up to now and all the sort of interconnecting things that happened, and looked back on family and that. I know certainly, since I just started doing it and started to think about it, I've made connections in my own mind like certain traits that my father had that I see in myself, or the men I have chosen, the partners, there's certain connections, uhm. It's quite hard to actually verbalize, but it's been a very positive thing to do. One thing that makes it very worthwhile, for me, er is, I mean . . . OK a worker said to me "look would you mind if we used a certain part of the tapes for education purposes." Great, but on a personal note, the fact that I can . . . it's like a living legacy, being able to leave something for my kids and family to look at. That's very important, especially when you feel

you are going to die young and you haven't got maybe a lot of time to just go into all of that. Or it mightn't be appropriate. Or when you feel able to you might not be well enough. It just is really great to get a chance to do that.

And also to show what it was really like, because . . . The written word, you know, and news reports—you're not going to get as accurate a thing as listening to people just talking about it. Actually, like I mean . . . Normal, I hate that word, but I'm a fairly normal, average person and that's what I've tried to stress. And I think you get that from these kind of interviews. Interview with Amanda, born 1961, recorded by Wendy Rickard, February 1996.

Amanda also draws an interesting parallel between written and oral sources of historical evidence. Most women who have worked as prostitutes assert and recognize that their profession is not "normal" in a conventional sense, but the oral record captures aspects of ordinary, day-to-day lived reality in a way that is difficult to convey in any written record. The silences, pauses, laughter, and velocity of speech are as telling as the actual words. By its very nature, the written record is often published only if it can capture a wide audience to make publication worthwhile and lucrative. At present, oral history recordings occupy a different, less commercial conceptual space and so can convey a realistic representation of what women in the sex industry consider to be "normal" in the latter part of the twentieth century.

All the women interviewed so far for the British prostitution archive have agreed that they want their accounts to gain prominence through formal archiving, and a procedure has been established to record the women's clearance and deposit instructions for the resulting life-story tapes. Most have given open access if under anonymous names, and two have restricted public access to the tapes for a period of up to thirty years.

# Health Promotion

As Amanda mentioned, one planned use of some of the material collected for this project is to inform health promotion debates in community settings in the United Kingdom and to develop educational resources. Again, this will be a collaborative exercise, with all those who have contributed tapes being given opportunities to shape the educational products. Tape recorded accounts lend themselves well to the required anonymity that many prostitutes wish to preserve while helping others to learn from their experience. One of the interviewees, Maria, who was born in 1959 and with whom I spoke in October 1995, was simply keen to exhort other women to make use of the support projects that are currently available to women working as prostitutes in some areas of London.

In the beginning, I was very proud. I didn't want to go to these places. I am used to that. In Spain, we don't have anything of that and my program in drugs was that you do everything yourself and you don't get anything and you do everything with effort and I felt guilty if I received any help. So for years I was working and I didn't want any help at all. I was working twelve hours, but now I see that once you need it, well, rely on them because it helps you. It's just, otherwise I will have half the time, I'm sure of it.

Maria's account portrays how she has come to depend on the support offered by these health projects and, perhaps, this account acts as a timely reminder to those who fund and administer such projects in the United Kingdom. First they should consider more seriously the long-term funding of projects because prostitutes' health and welfare needs are very real, and it is well recognized that they are often not well cared for in mainstream services. Second, they should think about the potential for community development approaches[3] and issues of empowerment so that service "dependence" is not engendered to devastating effect should they decide to cut the funding in response to political whim. These issues illustrate the essentially political nature of oral history.

# Conclusions

An individual life is the actual vehicle of historical experience. Evidence in every life story can only be fully understood as part of the whole life, but to make generalization possible, we must wrench the evidence on each issue from a whole series of lives, reassembling it to view it from a new angle. When this collection is further developed, it will offer a valuable, contextualized record of living interchange for present and future analysis. I hope that the extracts included here have provided some illustration of the process of starting formally to archive the oral history of prostitution in the United Kingdom, which alongside other more traditional sources contributes to the recording and depositing of a more balanced history.

My deepest thanks go to the women, and now men, who continue to be interviewed for the project, to individuals in the British Library National Sound Archive for their support, and to the University of East London for making it possible to bring the women's testimonies to the conference.

# Notes

1. See for example, Sherna Berger Gluck and Daphne Patai, eds., *Women's Words: The Feminist Practice of Oral History* (New York and London: Routledge, 1991).

2. Several of the women chose to record the interviews using their "working" names; others have been changed for anonymity respecting the tape deposit instructions of the women.

3. See for example, B. K. Tones and S. Tilford, *Health Education: Effectiveness, Efficiency, Equity* (London: Chapman and Hall, 1994).

# References

Gluck, Sherna Berger, and Daphne Patai, eds. 1991. *Women's Words: The Feminist Practice of Oral History.* New York and London: Routledge.

Jordan, Jan. 1991. *Working Girls: Women in the New Zealand Sex Industry Talk to Jan Jordan.* Auckland.

Perkins, Roberta. 1993. Talking deviance history: Sydney sex workers of the past. *Oral History Association of Australia Journal* 15: 60–63.

Thompson, Paul. 1978. *The Voice of the Past: Oral History.* Oxford and New York: Oxford University Press.

Tones, B. K., and S. Tilford. 1994. *Health Education: Effectiveness, Efficiency, Equity.* London: Chapman and Hall.

# STUDYING MYSELF/STUDYING OTHERS: ONE (PROFESSIONAL) BOY'S ADVENTURES STUDYING SEX WORK

## CRAIG SEYMOUR

There's an old Redd Foxx joke in which a man and a woman are talking at a bar. The man, who is down on his luck, says to the woman, "If the furniture business don't get no better, I'm gonna lose my ass." The woman then turns to the man and says, "Well, if the ass business don't get no better, I'm gonna lose my furniture."

I open with this joke because it suggests how sex work, the sale of sexual services, is, in many ways, equivalent to other forms of work. For many, sex work is simply a way to make a living, a way, as the woman states in the joke, to keep one's furniture.

For over five years, I have used ethnographic methods of participant observation and interviewing to study male sex workers. My focus has been male strippers, or "dancers" as they are commonly called, at the many gay male strip clubs in Washington, D.C. These clubs provide an especially fertile and interesting research location because they are somewhat of a national anomaly. Until recently, the male strippers danced completely nude (with the exception of white socks on their feet for tips); and customers were allowed to stroke, rub, and fondle the dancers. This was an unusual practice because the clubs also served alcohol. In many jurisdictions (and currently in Washington, D.C.), clubs that serve alcohol are not allowed to feature nude dancers. Unlike the dancers in D.C., dancers in these clubs must wear either G-strings or garments that completely cover their genitals and their butts.[1]

My research into gay strip clubs began as an extension of my role as an avid and enthusiastic "regular." I first went to a gay male strip bar in the summer of 1990 to see my favorite porn star, Joey Stefano, perform. I had never been to anyplace like it so I had no idea what to expect. I was a little scared because, for me, a twenty-something gay man whose acculturation into gay culture came at the height of society's AIDS hysteria, places like strip bars, bath houses, and leather bars signified danger. For this reason, I was surprised at how comfortable I felt the first time I walked into one of the strip clubs.

On top of the bars—entirely naked—were the strippers, bathed in an embellishing red light. Like dreams, they glowed; and I was instantly enthralled.

Watching a special dancer at the club, I often thought of the scene from that '80s teen-sex movie *Risky Business,* where the main character, a suburban teenaged boy played by Tom Cruise, dances by himself in his underwear around his parents' living room. I remember watching him play "air guitar" and thinking how similar his hand and body movements were to the basic gestures of any good male masturbatory repertoire. I liked seeing such a private moment represented; and I felt similarly about watching the strippers dance at the club.

Of course, I also liked touching the dancers. Being posteriorly inclined, I often asked a dancer to turn around so that I could feel his ass better. Most of the times I have been obliged. Sometimes, however, I left the club—dollars exhausted—without ever knowing how it feels to touch that certain dancer in that certain place that is like no other.

I felt an immense appreciation of the boys that did let me explore their certain place. I have also left the club wondering how that dancer felt about me touching him. Did I communicate to him—beyond the dollar bill—how important he was to me? Did he know how profoundly more humanizing it was to explore him, a real boy, as opposed to those pretty, yet ultimately flat and cold, images of boys on the pages of a magazine or to the surface of a TV screen? I wanted him to know that my appreciation of his services went far beyond the dollar carefully folded and placed in his sock or the firm pat on the ass I always gave a dancer before he moved away on the bar.

I was a customer at the bars long before I started studying them. When I began my study, I primarily interviewed strippers about their work experiences. Although I was a customer at the bars, I was generally able to develop a good rapport with dancers because, in many ways, I had more in common with them than I did with other customers. I was much closer in age to the strippers than I was to the majority of other customers. I was also a student like many of the dancers; and I worked out and tried to stay in shape like many dancers.

These similarities affected not only my relationships with dancers, but also my relationships with customers. Other customers frequently mistook me for a dancer. They would ask me if I was dancing "that night" or if I was a dancer in general. On one occasion, an older man stuffed a dollar in my coat pocket and attempted to fondle me through my jeans.

Over time, I developed far more affinities with dancers than with customers. Through interviews and hundreds of hours of participant observation, I developed friendships with many dancers. These relationships soon began to influence my research methods directly, as friends would increasingly ask me why I simply didn't stop asking questions about stripping and try it for myself. At first, I would evade the question or vaguely imply that "it wasn't for me." But over time this became a pejorative distinction, as if I implicitly thought I was "too good" to strip for money.

This was one of the moments when I realized how much a part of the subculture I was becoming. It was clear that I was beginning to appropriate some of its values over the values of the dominant culture when the question of why I wouldn't try stripping became much more important to me than the question of why I would. So I started stripping.

Becoming a part of the culture one studies has long been a major facet of ethnographic research. It is often thought that one is better able to understand a culture by becoming part of it. In fact, some argue that participant observation is one of the most effective ways to study a subject as personal and intimate as sexual behavior. Ralph Bolton suggests that sex researchers "give priority" to participant-observation research in studying sexual behavior, because "sex is generally private and not available for observation except through participation" (1992, 130; 132).

Although I agree with Bolton that studies of sexual behavior that employ participant observation can be especially enlightening, I would never suggest that the only way one can study sexual behaviors or sexual subcultures is by participating in them. I believe that each researcher must decide which is the best way for him or her to study a particular subject; and, for many reasons, becoming a dancer made the most sense for me within the context in which I was working.

Becoming a sex worker who also studies sex work raised some interesting identity issues for me: Am I a researcher doing sex work or a sex worker doing research? The answer to this question is much more complex than it may appear on the surface. It is not simply a matter of how I "really" feel. Who I am changes significantly depending on the context in which I am speaking, whether I am, for instance, justifying my research methods to my dissertation committee or explaining my decision to my boyfriend, my family, my friends, or whether I am talking to customers or other dancers at the clubs.

It is often assumed that in all of these stories there is one "true" explanation of why I choose to be a stripper. The truth, however, is much more complicated than any one story would suggest. Another researcher/stripper has articulated this complication as follows: "Things become muddled when I try to explain why I am willing to disrobe in front of strange men in the name of research. What is it about me that I am able to do this when others in my culture find the concept untenable." (Ronai 1992, 107)

Asking these questions raised another set of theoretical and methodological concerns for me as well. For instance, I feel that it is essential that researchers who employ participant observation be rigorous about critically interrogating their position with respect to those they study. Therefore, in most of my work, I include many of the very personal reasons why I made the choice to do sex work. However, I also feel that sex work researchers, in general, must begin to move away from continually asking how it is that a person is able to do sex work. This, in my opinion, only perpetuates the stigma associated with sex work. Instead, researchers should begin to ask: What is it about our society that it hypocritically stigmatizes and pathologizes commercial sex while it reifies most other commercial exchanges? This, I feel, is more productive than continued studies that ask what it is about particular individuals that enables them to do sex work. Therefore, the focus of my research is on the work that my fellow dancers and I actually do and the oppressive factors that sometimes make doing that work very difficult.

One of the factors that most negatively affects strippers is the social stigma associated with sex work and the legal regulations and persecution that result from this stigma. It is a factor that most distinguishes sex work from other forms of work. In order to better the working conditions of strippers, this stigma must be interrogated. We can begin to interrogate many of the assumptions on which much of the social stigma of sex work is based by comparing it to other forms of work. In this way, my participant observation experiences as a stripper have been very instructive, particularly in comparison with my other work experiences.

In addition to being a sex worker, in recent years I have also been a graduate teaching assistant. One of the most revealing aspects of doing both of these jobs is what I have learned about each job by doing the other. The similarities between both jobs have been particularly revealing. In fact, these similarities challenge many of the assumptions upon which the social stigmatization of sex work is based.

Sex work, for instance, is often stigmatized for being exploitative. My work experiences, however, suggest that being a graduate teaching assistant in the academy is as exploitative as stripping. In fact, the exploitative labor situation of being a graduate teaching assistant facilitated me becoming a stripper. Teaching assistants are hired for nine months, leaving three months out of the year when we have to pick up work wherever we can. This is an oppressive situation that other university workers (dining hall and custodial workers at Yale, for instance) have successfully fought against (Wilhelm 1996, 14).

Being a graduate teaching assistant is also exploitative because teaching assistants are expected to do more than the job title suggests. We are called "teaching assistants," yet at the University of Maryland and at other universities, many of us design and teach our own courses. Similarly, strippers at the gay strip clubs are primarily called "dancers," yet it is openly acknowledged that we are clearly more than that and are clearly expected to be more than that.

These similarities are far more than semantic, however. The academy and the strip clubs depend on the labor of graduate teaching assistants and strippers, respectively; yet, in both cases, teaching assistants and strippers are implicitly and explicitly defined as nonessential workers. Graduate teaching assistants are not considered faculty or staff; and this status directly affects our pay, the benefits that we receive, and the demands that we can make on the academic institution. In the same way, strippers are defined as "independent contractors," a designation that restricts the rights of strippers to get health care benefits, worker's compensation, sick days, and other common work benefits.

Another charge often used to stigmatize sex work is that of objectification. Again, I would argue that I am as objectified in my role as a teacher as I am as a stripper. In both cases, my identity becomes synonymous with the function of my work. The difference is that imparting knowledge for money is more socially acceptable than inciting desire for money.

In his article, "On Fieldwork," Erving Goffman writes that one of the goals of field work is to try to "subject yourself" to the "life circumstances" of your subjects, which means that although you can, in fact, leave the setting at any time, "you act as if you can't and try to accept all of the desirable and undesirable things that are a feature of their life" (Klienman and Copp, 1993, 27). Goffman's description characterizes my experiences as a stripper studying the culture of gay male striptease in D.C. As stated earlier, stripping was my only job for much of the time that I stripped. I received no assistance or support from school or from any other funding sources. I was dependent upon the money that I made from stripping for all of my basic necessities like housing, food, clothes, and, of course, as the joke says, furniture. Because of this, I was as financially dependent upon the money I made stripping as other dancers were.

My financial dependence on dancing made me as concerned as my fellow dancers when we arrived at work one day and saw a sign in our dressing room that read:

Attention all dancers: You are not to be touched, fondled, fingered, or stroked in any shape, form, or fashion. This applies to both customers and yourselves. Your cooperation is both expected and appreciated. Thank you, the management.

These new rules were in response to a "show cause" notice brought against the club by the D.C. Alcohol Beverage Control Board. In such cases, a club or bar must "show cause" why their liquor licenses should not be revoked. The specific charges against the club were that the club allowed strippers to "perform" and "simulate" masturbation and also allowed customers to "fondle" the strippers' genitals "in an erotic manner." All of these charges were true, of course. In fact, they were the very reasons why the customers came to the club and the very ways that we made money as dancers.

In a few months, the board suspended the bar's liquor license and forbade the bar to continue having nude dancing. After a few unsuccessful nights of having strippers dance around in their underwear, the bar closed indefinitely, leaving more than fifty dancers out of work, and hundreds of regular customers without what was, for many of them, a primary sexual outlet.

The actions of the Alcohol Beverage Control Board significantly changed the focus of my research. In my early work on the gay strip clubs, I argued what I now call a "gay cultural defense" of the strip clubs. My argument was that the stripping at the clubs affirms homosexual desire within a public space, thereby symbolically resisting the social and sexual hierarchy that privileges heterosexuality over homosexuality. The stripping at the clubs, as Richard Dyer has argued of gay male pornography, "turns the definition of homosexual desire on its head, (proclaiming) good is bad, sick is healthy" (1990, 291).

This "gay cultural defense" argument is pervasive throughout many discussions of gay male sex work. There is a tendency among researchers and theorists to separate gay sex work from other forms of sex work.

The proceedings of the "show cause" hearing at which the bar's license was suspended revealed to me the inadequacy of the gay cultural defense of the strip clubs that I had argued earlier. At the proceedings, the chairman of the Alcohol Control Board stated:

> This board does not believe that social and cultural activities have anything to do with violations of the law. . . .There is no community for whom Erica Jong's *Fear of Flying* "zipless fuck" book—pardon my characterization or quote from that book—is different. It doesn't matter what your sexual ideation is. Anonymous sex is a tragic occurrence for all individuals . . . your establishment made a violation through its entertainers.

These words of the chairman and the subsequent actions of the board make it quite clear that, despite the many gay cultural critics, including myself, who make impassioned cultural defenses of gay commercial sex practices, they are of little help in defending these practices against repressive state regulation. The scope of the gay cultural defense is far too limited.

The only way to effect political change on the repressive regulation of commercial sexual practices is by encouraging coalitions of people across genders and sexualities. It is not enough to defend only gay male, commercial sexual practices. Where once I was interested in defending gay striptease as a distinct gay cultural practice, I am now most interested in the way that members of the gay male striptease community in Washington, D.C., can be seen as part of a larger social group encompassing all the individuals—gay or straight, male or female—who work in or support the sex industry.

The only way that we can address the continuum of oppressive commercial sex laws, which range from the regulations of Alcohol Beverage Control Boards to the criminalization of prostitution, is by forming such broad coalitions.

Forming such coalitions can help the ass business get better, not just to protect the furniture of the woman at the bar, but to protect the rights of us all.

# Note .

1. Dancers sometimes "get around" these laws by wearing G-strings and occasionally "flashing" well-paying customers. Dancers who must, literally, cover their butts sometimes wear tuxedo jackets with nothing on underneath, enabling their butts to be fully covered technically, yet still be seen through the flaps of the jacket.

# References

Bolton, Ralph. 1992. Mapping terra incognita: Sex research for AIDS prevention—An urgent agenda for the 1990s. In *The Time of AIDS: Social Analysis, Theory, and Method*, edited by Gilbert Herdt and Shirley Lindenbaum. Newbury Park: Sage.

Dyer, Richard. 1990. Coming to terms. In *Out there: Marginalization and contemporary cultures*, edited by Russell Ferguson, Martha Gever, Trinh T. Minh-ha, and Cornel West. 289–98. Cambridge: The MIT Press, 1990.

Kleinman, Sheryl, and Martha A. Copp. 1993. *Emotions and Fieldwork*. Newbury Park: Sage.

Ronai, Carole Rambo. 1992. The reflexive self through narrative: A night in the life of an exotic dancer/researcher. In *Investigating Subjectivity: Research on Lived Experience*, edited by Carolyn Ellis and Michael G. Flaherty. Newbury Park: Sage.

Wilhelm, John. 1996. A short history of unionization at Yale. *Social Text* 49 (Winter): 13–20.

# RESEARCHING WITH SEX WORKERS: A PRIVILEGE AND A CHALLENGE

PRISCILLA M. PYETT

## My Position in the Research Process

I am an academic sociologist, a feminist, and a health researcher with a community focus. Whenever possible I like to carry out research that is community-driven, by which I mean the research has arisen out of community needs, the research process is one of consultation and collaboration, and the research findings are relevant to the community it serves.

I have been working collaboratively with sex workers and with the Prostitutes' Collective of Victoria (PCV) for about four years and have just begun my fourth research project with them. We have used very different methodologies and the process of collaboration has been very different for each of these projects, two of which have been completed and two are still under way. An important factor in the collaborative process has been the role played by the community liaison officer (CLO) at the university research center where I work. The Centre for the Study of Sexually Transmissible Diseases has a commitment to fostering a relationship of cooperation and interaction with the community it serves. We have two CLOs who organize community consultations and disseminate research findings to the community through nonacademic channels. Anne Mitchell was our first CLO and brought to the center a wealth of experience that had earned her the respect and trust of many community groups, including the PCV. Anne has been an invaluable member of my research team and plays a significant role in mediating · between my position as an academic researcher and members of community groups. Although I have a particular training and an obligation to meet the specific requirements of funding bodies and the university, representatives of the sex industry often have their own research agenda and ways of working that may be quite different from mine.

As a feminist I am interested in women's lives, women's experiences, and women's health. I would be naive to think that the sort of research that I conduct could have a significant impact on policies or laws or change the social and economic opportunities for women. But I do hope that it might contribute to changing community attitudes, and that it will at least challenge some of the myths and stereotypes that are commonly associated with sex workers. I think it is especially useful to point to the variety of women's experiences, to demonstrate that sex workers are a heterogenous group with many different issues and different circumstances affecting them, both as sex workers and in their private lives.

Because I am employed in a research center that has a health focus, indeed a focus on STD (sexually transmitted disease), I can obtain funding for public health issues, but because other social issues impact on sex workers' lives, I have tried to maintain a broader research focus. We have tried to take account of the different circumstances of sex workers in different parts of the industry: we have explored aspects of women's private lives and family background; their relationships with lovers, friends, and family members; difficulties they have with child care; losing custody of children; drug issues; and some of the difficulties of getting out of sex work.

Although public concern in Australia in recent years has focused on the possibility of HIV-infected sex workers spreading the disease to the heterosexual community, our concern has been for the women (and men) who work in the sex industry and the risks posed to their health and safety by inappropriate legislation and police action and by clients who threaten and coerce workers or who demand unsafe sex.

# Processes of Research

## The Survey

The first study was initiated by the PCV, who asked the Centre for the Study of STDs to conduct a large-scale survey of sex workers in Victoria. With a great deal of voluntary help from the PCV we succeeded in obtaining valid responses from about 350 sex workers—the very large majority being women. The findings and limitations of this survey have been reported previously (Pyett, Haste, and Snow 1996a, 1996b). In this paper I want to focus on some of the key features of the collaborative process.

Principal amongst the reasons for the success of the project were the enthusiasm and commitment of the sex worker representatives who collaborated with us. Between six and ten women were involved at different times. We might ask why? what was in it for them? I believe it was a chance to have their side of the story presented. Collaboration with university researchers could give the study respectability and legitimacy. We negotiated meeting times and places to suit the sex workers and we provided lunches during our working sessions. Our hospitality offered an opportunity for the sharing of meals as equals, in a university setting that could otherwise be quite intimidating. Our professor/director often greeted the women or chatted with them in the corridor and frequently expressed envy at being left out of the lunches! The women felt welcome and the lunches were characterized by a great deal of good humor as we worked.

Issues to be researched were raised by the sex worker representatives and by myself or the CLO. The survey method was chosen because the sex worker representatives wanted to obtain data on large numbers, to provide a statistical profile of sex workers for the health minister. They hoped to dispel some of the public's anxieties about levels of unsafe sex in the sex industry. Because the PCV regularly visits brothels to talk with workers and to conduct safe sex workshops, they offered to take questionnaires with them and ask women to fill them in while they waited. The questionnaire was developed over several lunchtime working sessions with the sex worker representatives. From these women I learned to use appropriate language, to ask relevant questions, and to treat particular issues with sensitivity. On the other hand, I warned them that we had a responsibility to publish findings even if they were detrimental to the sex industry—if, for instance, we found high levels of drug use or that HIV-positive sex workers were working.

Over a six-month period, representatives of the PCV administered the questionnaire in 64 brothels and reported a high response rate among all workers who were approached. They were thus able to access the target population, which we would not have been able to do on our own. After we had analyzed the data, we held more lunches to check our interpretation of the findings with our sex worker colleagues. We prepared a report to the community written in plain language. This provided the PCV with the answers to all the questions on the survey, which they could make use of however they wished. We involved the PCV in talking with journalists before releasing the report to the media. We enlisted the support of a sympathetic journalist who promised not to sensationalize the report.

At the conclusion of this project we felt we had established an effective collaborative research relationship and had been able to report a good news story—high levels of knowledge about STDs and HIV among sex workers and almost 100 percent condom use with clients. We also surprised the media and the public with the "normality" of so many sex workers—the number of sex workers who were married or living with boyfriends, who were mothers with dependent children, or who were currently engaged in various types of study.

## The Qualitative Study

The second project arose out of the findings from the survey and the limitations of that method. Most of the women who responded to the survey were working in legal brothels, and we found ourselves asking whether there were others who had not been included and who might be more at risk. We felt that we needed a different approach to reach women who might be vulnerable to a number of health and safety risks and less able to use condoms at all times. We obtained funding from the National Health and Medical Research Council of Australia to conduct a qualitative study using in-depth individual interviews with women working on the streets and in the illegal sector of the industry, women who were very young and inexperienced, women who were homeless or without stable accommodation, and women who might be drug-dependent.

Staff and volunteers from the PCV were invited to join the research team. We established a critical reference group (CRG) composed of women who had been sex workers or outreach workers in the field. This time we were able to pay all these women for the time they spent at our lunchtime meetings, as well as for attending training sessions, for conducting the interviews, and for assisting with the interpretation of findings. We also paid the participants a sum approximating what they might earn in the time it took to conduct the interview (AUS$50). Some interviews were conducted in local cafes, some at the PCV, and some at welfare agencies that supported the project.

Lunchtime working sessions again provided a convivial setting and promoted open dialogue between the CRG and other members of the research team. Together we determined which women might be vulnerable and how they might be recruited for interviews. We worked through the issues that could and should be raised in the interviews and formulated an interview schedule using open-ended questions with a number of key prompts to assist the interviewers. A considerable amount of time was devoted to the needs of participants in the research process and how these could be met.

Semi-formal training sessions were conducted to teach interviewing techniques, research ethics, and protocol and to provide practice with tape recorders. The women in the CRG were quick to learn and keen to get on with the real thing—the interviews. After each woman had conducted a pilot interview, the study proceeded swiftly. Our training and trust were thoroughly rewarded by the quality of the 24 interviews that were conducted and by the generosity of the interviewers, who invariably gave the participants the additional AUS$10 we had allowed for spending on coffee and cigarettes. Findings from the qualitative analysis were presented to the CRG for discussion. A draft of the community report requesting written feedback was circulated to all members of the CRG and to the welfare agencies who had been involved. Collaboration thus continued throughout the reporting process.

We were able to attract considerable media attention by having two high-profile women launch the community report (Professor Marcia Neave, a very well-known senior academic, and Maryanne Phoenix, the union representative for the sex industry in Victoria). There has been a steady demand for this report and the findings have also been reported in several community newsletters. We used the findings to highlight the dangers associated with the illegality of street work in Victoria and the consequent reluctance of women to report violence to the police. We also drew attention to men's continued failure to take responsibility for condom use and safe sex practices in commercial sex transactions.

## The Outreach Study

The third study is in progress at the moment, and we are pleased to be giving something back to the community in the form of money, employment, and outreach support to sex workers. We have provided the salary for an outreach worker to the PCV. Half of her time is dedicated solely to outreach, the other half to research. Outreach workers usually collect statistics on the workers they see and talk to, and on various other issues including the number of needles, syringes, and condoms they hand out. The statistics and observations recorded by the outreach worker will be collated and analyzed in order to develop a profile of the local street worker community. We are interested in finding out how many workers work regularly or intermittently, how many are new workers, and how many seem particularly vulnerable or seriously drug-affected.

## The Client Phone-In

A fourth study with a significant and timely change of focus is now in its planning stages. This time we want to survey the clients, and we plan to advertise a 1-800 phone line through a range of venues and media outlets. We hope to entice men who have paid for sex with women to phone in and be prepared to talk about it. The Safe House Project Worker for the PCV is one of the four chief investigators on this project and a fifth of her salary will be paid to the PCV to compensate for the time she will put into this project. In this way we are recognizing with money and status Jocelyn Snow's expertise on matters relating to the sex industry as well as her experience in collaborating with us on the first three research projects. This study is a collaboration between two research centers as well as the PCV and we also have an advisory group that includes two sex workers. This will be a very challenging project and there are many problems that need to be solved before we get under way. One question is relevant to the topic of this paper: What community should we be collaborating with? Should we have client representatives on our advisory group? Should we be collaborating with brothel owners and sex industry entrepreneurs? Or is our community still the sex worker community?

## Privileges and Challenges

Because sex workers work outside or on the margins of society, they have good reasons not to trust people who represent the status quo—like researchers from universities (Jackson, Highcrest, and Coates 1992). I am therefore very much indebted to the number of sex workers who have trusted me. Many have worked with me for no money. They have demonstrated energy and commitment to teaching myself and others about the sex industry. We have shared a lot of fun and laughter—sometimes at the clients' expense but often at mine, at my naivete and the narrowness of my experience. I have learned a great deal about women who work in the sex industry and a great deal about researching within a marginalized community.

My sex worker colleagues have also challenged me in many ways. It has been a challenge for all of us to collaborate and to work in partnership when we come from different worlds and have different world views. I have learned that feminism is not always popular with women in the sex industry, but just as I have learned that there are many different kinds of sex workers, I hope the women who have worked with me appreciate that there are different kinds of feminists.

I suspect that my sex worker colleagues have found me difficult and even obstructive at times, and I have certainly not always found it easy to carry out research as I was taught to do. I have found sex workers difficult to train as researchers—not because they were unwilling or unable to learn but because they were so keen to get on with the research that we had to speed things up for them! We had a real sense of having to work fast—not to lose their enthusiasm and commitment—at the same time needing to ensure the validity and ethics of the research process. I think the slowness of academic research is one of the things they have probably found most frustrating in working with me: the lengthy procedures required by funding bodies, the time that elapses between an idea and starting on the research, the trouble we sometimes have with ethics committees, and so on. It has been a challenge to me to see the academic world through the eyes of women whose knowledge and experiences may have been very different from mine. Sometimes the clash of values and expectations have made it seem that the research would never be carried out.

Halfway into our second project, one of the women suddenly raised a lot of questions: Why are we doing this research? What's wrong with sex work? Why are women at risk? Why are they different from other women? I had to justify my concerns for the health of women in sex work before we could go on. In the middle of developing our interview schedule we met with another problem. Members of the CRG were united in their opinion that it would be inappropriate to ask sex workers about their health, because this was too personal. We could ask about anal sex and all sorts of details of services to clients but their own health was a private matter and questions might offend. Because the project was funded specifically to examine the health of sex workers, it was essential that we reach a compromise solution. Eventually it was agreed that a sensitively worded open question would enable the interviewee to choose the extent to which she was prepared to talk about her personal health.

Because of the terrific vitality and sense of purpose that the women from the sex industry have brought to the research process, and because I have had the good fortune to have a very highly respected and trusted CLO and the support of sensitive and committed research assistants, we have managed to overcome all the obstacles that have come our way so far!

# Value of Collaboration in Health Research

Some of the advantages of collaborative research are that it is inclusive, develops trust, achieves good response rates, and increases the likelihood of honest answers, or at least allows us to check the honesty of answers with our collaborators. I think it is particularly important that researchers collaborate with marginalized groups who have good reason not to trust, who have experienced exploitation, and who have few opportunities to have their perspective seen or heard: it is one way of bringing them in from the margins.

Finally, I think researchers have a responsibility to give something back to the communities we research—not only by sharing our findings and validating their experiences, but also, through collaboration, by increasing the skills and the confidence of people with whom we are researching. Academic research, slow as it is, can give credibility to what we call "findings" that are often things people in the sex work community have known about for a long time. With the stamp of a university research center on the study, we can attract media attention and public notice to issues that are important to public health or to sex workers. I hope that with our research we are helping to change public attitudes to sex workers by challenging the myths and stereotypes usually represented in the public arena. In the longer term, we would like to see our research used to support arguments for the decriminalization of all prostitution and the better protection of the occupational health and safety of all sex workers in Victoria.

# Acknowledgments

None of this research would have taken place without the initiative and support of the Prostitutes' Collective of Victoria and the individual women with whom I have been privileged to work—in particular, the Safe House Project Workers, Jocelyn Snow and Alison Arnot-Bradshaw, but also the Outreach Workers—Leonie Tehan and Julie Futol, and their program manager, Maria McMahon. I am also indebted to the Community Liaison Officer at the Centre for the Study of Sexually Transmissible Diseases, Anne Mitchell, for her continuing support and commitment to collaborative research; and to Deborah Warr and Benjamin Haste for their sensitivity and the high quality of their research assistance. Funding for the research described in this paper was provided by the Victorian Health Promotion Foundation and the Public Health Research and Development Committee of the National Health and Medical Research Council of Australia. The client phone-in is being conducted in collaboration with the Macfarlane Burnet Centre for Medical Research.

# References

Jackson, L., A. Highcrest, and R. A. Coates. 1992. Varied potential risks of HIV infection among prostitutes. *Soc. Sci. Med.* 35: 281–86.

Pyett, P. M., B. R. Haste, and J. Snow. 1996a. Risk practices for HIV infection and other STDs amongst female prostitutes working in legalized brothels. *AIDS Care* 8 (1): 85–94.

———. 1996b. Who works in the sex industry? A profile of female prostitutes in Victoria. *Aust. J. Public Health* 20 (3): 431–33.

# LAP DANCING:
## PERSONAL AND LEGAL IMPLICATIONS
## FOR EXOTIC DANCERS

### JACQUELINE LEWIS

Based on the literature on exotic dancing, field observations at strip clubs, and interviews with exotic dancers, there appears to be a variety of characteristics of the strip club environment: (1) the existence of table and lap dancing; (2) the availability of booths, VIP or champagne rooms for private dances; (3) physical contact/lack of barriers between performers and customers; (4) complete nudity; and (5) the consumption of alcohol on club premises. Although in most strip clubs it is not uncommon to find several of these characteristics occurring together, Ontario clubs are fairly unique in that all five characteristics can be found in most clubs. The clustering of these characteristics and activities in one location is significant because together they create an environment of permissibility. Such an environment alters customer expectations, the dynamics of interaction between the dancer and customer, and health and safety risks for dancers, including both emotional and physical health.

One form of exotic dance, the lap dance, is the most controversial of all strip club activities. Lap dancing raises questions about the boundaries between exotic dancing and other forms of sex work. Depending on the nature of the physical contact that occurs between dancer and customer, fear of STD transmission and concern for the health and safety of dancers have been raised. Such concerns are heightened in those instances where the women feel physical contact was unwanted or forced upon them either by club requirements or individual customers. This paper focuses on lap dancing, specifically, the personal and legal implications for dancers that have emerged out of both the lap dancing phenomenon and the subsequent ban on such performances in Ontario.

# Methodology

This paper is based on data from field observations inside strip clubs and interviews with exotic dancers and other club staff designed to address issues tied to the work and careers of exotic dancers. Observations were conducted at clubs in several cities in southern Ontario. Observational data were collected primarily to supplement interview data and assist us in describing the work environment of exotic dancers including physical setting, contacts between those present in the club (employees and clients), and the atmosphere of different clubs.

Thirty semi-structured, in-depth interviews were conducted with female exotic dancers, club staff, and key informants. Interviews with dancers explored each woman's history and anticipated future in the occupation, a description of her work and the various forms of interaction she engages in with clients, use of drugs and alcohol, current sexual practices, perception of risk for HIV and other STDs associated with dancing, sexual health-maintaining strategies, factors influencing risk and ability to maintain sexual health, and the presence and/or possibility of a community among exotic dancers. Interviews with other club employees were designed to tap their experiences in, and impressions of, club-related activities.

# Typology of Exotic Dancing

The striptease is a performance designed to titillate customers at a distance, to please through illusion and fantasy. Throughout the history of stripping in Ontario, Canada, one of the basic club rules has been no, or very limited, physical contact between dancers and customers within the club setting. If physical contact occurs, it is usually in the form of a friendly touch or embrace, as dancers greet customers while circulating in the club prior to their performances.

In most clubs, dancers are expected to engage in two forms of performance dance during their shifts: the stage show and the table dance. During the stage show dancers perform a striptease in front of the entire bar. The stage show is important from the perspective of both the club and the dancer. Men who cannot afford to pay dancers for private attention, or who are too cheap to do so, may still be attracted to the bar to consume alcohol and watch the show. Although dancers may wish to please management by drawing customers in to drink, for the dancer herself, the stage show is a time when she can attract the attention of customers who may then request a striptease of a more private nature, a table dance.

For a fee, dancers will perform table dances for customers. While table dancing, dancers perform directly in front of particular customers, usually while standing on a small platform/table. The level of privacy of these dances depends upon the amount of money the men are willing to spend. In most clubs, table dances can take place on the main floor of the club (and are therefore visible to others) for $5 per song, or they can take place in more private locations in the clubs, referred to as VIP Lounges or Champagne Rooms, for between $10 and $20 per song. The more private the location, the more money customers are charged and the more money dancers can expect to earn.[1]

Regardless of the location of the dances, the "no touch rule" was supposed to be in force. Adherence to this rule, however, gradually waned over time and eventually disappeared with the introduction of lap dancing. As the following two dancers noted:

> When I first started to dance, you could just stand on the box and dance. You didn't have to do anything. You didn't have to go anywhere near them [the men] and you made, um, you know, over two hundred usually every night. . . . But every year, everybody got closer cause the money was good—and they stopped worrying, you know, they weren't so picky about the rules and stuff so people get closer and closer. . . . It got to the point where . . . everybody was just out of control and I just quit for a while.

> Before lap dancing . . . people had a lot of misconceptions. People thought . . . things were going on in the strip clubs, but they weren't. Nothing was going on. It was just a show, it was a fantasy. If a man even touched a dancer's hair he could get thrown out.

Lap dancing varies from city to city in southern Ontario. Dancers are usually paid between ten and twenty dollars for a lap dance. Some dancers, however, talked about how they could earn more, anywhere from fifty to two hundred and fifty dollars per dance, depending upon the services they were willing to provide.

A typical lap dance involves the woman performing for her male customers while wearing little or no clothing and seated on the customer's lap or between his legs, often in private or semi-private locations in the clubs. When explaining what lap dancing involves one woman said:

> The men know that the basic lap dance is the dancer grinding her genitals against his and the man knows he can expect to get off.

In some clubs dancers sit directly on the men's laps during lap dances; in others the dancer is limited to sitting between the man's legs with her tailbone pressed up against the man's penis. Regardless of their positioning, during a dance the women move/gyrate their bodies to the music in order to arouse the men. Although the typical lap dancing scenario doesn't involve direct skin to skin sexual contact, some dancers talked about how they, or other dancers they knew, allowed some customers to touch their genitals or provided sexual services to the men in the form of masturbation or oral sex, usually in the VIP Lounges or Champagne Rooms. Sexual intercourse was also reported (masturbation and oral sex were much more common) as well as instances of sexual assault. Reports by dancers and other club staff of finding used condoms on the floor, under seat cushions, etc., provide further evidence that sexual activities were occurring in the clubs.

## Regulating Lap Dancing

The initial fervor over lap dancing in Ontario began in February 1994 after Judge Hachborn of the Ontario Court, Provincial Division, in the case of *R. v. Mara*, ruled that lap dancing was not indecent and did not violate community standards of tolerance ([1994] O.J. No. 264 (QL)). The ruling was in response to the 1991 charges laid against the owner and manager of Cheaters, a Toronto strip club, for allowing indecent performances (lap dances) to occur in their club, contrary to section 167(1) of the *Criminal Code of Canada* (R.S.C., 1985, c. C-46, s. 167(1)).[2]

Hachborn's decision had a significant impact on the lap dancing phenomenon and the lives of exotic dancers. In ruling that lap dancing was not indecent behavior, Hachborn essentially gave strip club owners and managers the green light to eliminate the "no touch rule" and offer lap dancing to their customers. As club owners and managers began capitalizing on this new moneymaking enterprise, lap dancing spread to clubs across Ontario (Van Alphen 1995, C3; Harvey 1995, 22). The elimination of the "no touch rule" opened the floodgates on what was permissible in strip clubs. In their interviews, the women talked about the consequences of this change.

> It's amazing when you take away the simple no touch rule . . . it's amazing what it actually leads to.

> Once one person does it, it's expected of you. Or if someone goes a little further with the lap dance than the next person, then the guys are going to start expecting it. So, when touch comes in then it just all gets out of control.

With the Hachborn decision, not only were lap dancing, touching, and sexual acts in the strip club considered acceptable, club owners, managers, and customers began to demand such services be performed by dancers. During interviews, dancers talked about feeling pressured to participate in lap dancing, especially in the clubs in the Toronto region. In some clubs, women reported being threatened with job loss if they didn't lap dance. For example, Katherine Goldberg, one of the founding members of the Association of Burlesque Entertainers,[3] was fired from her job, blackballed from dancing at clubs in Toronto, and had her life threatened for refusing to engage in lap dancing and trying to organize other dancers to do the same. In an interview with Katherine Goldberg, she talked about how she was fired and made an example of by the club owners where she worked:

> I think they used me as an example because they usually switch over girls. They don't like the same girls for a long time, but they kept me because I was very popular with the customers, and everybody knew this. So, when they fired me I heard that all the girls were just quiet. No more talking about anything.

Since monetary need is the primary reason given by dancers for entering dancing, threats of job loss can be a stressful and frightening prospect. Such concerns were paramount for those women who lacked an education, because few employment opportunities that pay this kind of money exist for women without an education.

Although Hachborn's decision, in the case of *R.* v. *Mara*, was appealed by the Crown to the Ontario Court of Appeal, where it was eventually overturned ([1996], 27 O.R. 643), there was a time lag of two years (February 10, 1994, to February 9, 1996) between the Hachborn ruling and that of the Ontario Court of Appeal. In the interim, dancers and other members of the public pressured government officials to legislate against lap dancing as a community health and safety risk. In response, municipal governments began introducing bylaws to regulate strip club activities.[4] These bylaws required the re-establishment of the "no touch rule" in the clubs and, in some jurisdictions, the removal of private enclosures within the clubs (VIP and Champagne Rooms), imposing hefty fines on violators (Brazao 1995, A7; Funston 1995, A6; Queen 1995, 3; Small and Swainson 1995, A3).

The ban on lap dancing, introduced through municipal bylaws and the overturning of the Hachborn decision by the Ontario Court of Appeal, was, however, ineffective in eradicating lap dancing. In some jurisdictions where we did participant observation and interviews, lap dancing and private booths totally disappeared for a while but re-emerged, sometimes with a new name (couch dancing, chair dancing, taboo dancing) or with a new type of dancer (e.g., women from Thailand or the Philippines, where dancing usually involves prostitution); in others it remained unaffected by the laws.

> After the ban on lap dancing they took the signs off [advertising the availability of lap dancing] and put Taboo Dancing, which is just as bad. But they

put all the signs inside. They don't advertise lap dancing on the outside but they say taboo dancing. And so, they're doing it upstairs somewhere and they're still doing it [referring to lap dancing].

They have like chair dancing now. . . . And what the girl does is they practically spread their legs apart and play with themselves. It's because, ok, we have the bylaw that says no touching and stuff. But now the girls, like, before when they were table dancing, you weren't allowed to really bend over and spread your cheeks or you weren't allowed to lift up your leg and . . . you know. There's certain rules to table dancing. You're not allowed to lean on the guys. But now after the lap dancing ban they are doing things that they never did before.

Despite the 1995 Ontario Court of Appeal's decision and existence of municipal bylaws banning lap dancing in Ontario, dancers and club staff reported during their interviews that lap dancing was still going on in some clubs. On March 12, 1997, when the Supreme Court of Canada upheld the decision of the Ontario Court of Appeal in *R. v. Mara*, the expectation was that lap dancing would be eliminated once and for all in Ontario ([1997] S.C.J. No. 29 (QL)). The Supreme Court ruled that lap dancing is indecent because it exceeds the community standards of tolerance in contemporary Canadian society and therefore is prohibited by s. 167(1) of the *Criminal Code*. According to the ruling, lap dancing is conduct that is harmful because "it degrades and dehumanizes women, it desensitizes sexuality, it is incompatible with the dignity and equality of each human being, and it predisposes persons to act in an antisocial manner" (*R. v. Mara*, [1997] S.C.J. No. 29 (QL)). In making its decision, in the case of *R. v. Mara*, the Supreme Court was, however, limited to addressing the issue contained in the original charge, specifically, whether lap dancing in a public place is an indecent act. As a result, left unaddressed was whether lap dancing in private booths in strip clubs is also indecent. The possible broad interpretation of the Supreme Court's ruling makes possible the continuation of lap dancing in strip clubs, as long as it doesn't occur in public—on the main floor of the bar. Although there is the potential for this type of interpretation, municipalities still have the power to regulate lap dancing through the implementation and enforcement of bylaws designed to control such activities (*Ontario Adult Entertainment Bar Assn.* v. *Metropolitan Toronto [Municipality]* [1996], 27 O.R. [3d] 643.).

# Impact of Lap Dancing on Dancers' Lives

Regardless of whether it continues to exist or not, dancers talked about how lap dancing has changed dancing forever. Even though lap dancing has been banned in Ontario, it has changed exotic dancing in a variety of ways. It has altered public perceptions of dancing—now dancing and prostitution are synonymous in the public eye. It has also changed customer's expectations, decreased earning potential for women who only want to dance, altered the way dancers view themselves and their job, and increased police surveillance in the clubs. These changes have both personal and legal implications for dancers.

Based on interviews with dancers, it appears that in general most believe that banning lap dancing was a good thing. In their interviews, the women talked about the various implications this form of dance had, and still has, on their job and their lives. In terms of their jobs, they talked about how lap dancing has destroyed the artistic value of dancing and has taken away some of the enjoyment they got out of their profession.

> I used to really enjoy dancing. Getting up there with all the focus on you. We put on good shows and kept the audience's attention. But not since lap dancing.

> When we were dancing on a box, we felt like goddesses. We felt like stars, untouchable. And then they started . . . when you sat on their laps, it's like, you just . . . felt so little, so small and vulnerable.

> I used to like it when it was table dancing, when there was no touching. But you don't see any happy faces anymore. Back when it was table dancing I used to have these fantasies about being really sexual in my real world. But now I can't do that. The touching really depresses me. (Bhabra 1995, 52)

Typically, dancers attribute changes in how they feel about dancing to the experience of being touched during lap dancing and the continual requests or attempts by customers for sexual contact with the dancers, despite the ban on such activities in the clubs. One woman talked about how lap dancing made her feel about going to work:

> It's like a spoiled kid who started kicking and screaming, I want to go home. I don't want to come here. Don't make me go here. I was having sort of a breakdown. And many times I would turn the cab around and go home. Like it just . . . it was like hell for me. It was . . . I'm going to be tortured. I'm going to be assaulted, I just know it.

Other women spoke of feeling assaulted by customers while working, sometimes on a daily basis:

> It was like, a cow, as if you're mechanical, like, they just assumed that they could do things and when you bend over they could poke their fingers up you and . . . They just did things. Like, poked you, injured you and, and things like that. And it was like every single night that you worked since lap dancing, you would have a few pokes. Some dancers, you could actually see

them fighting off a customer. . . . And some girls they were always pushing away their [the men's] hands and watching their backs. . . . And some of them [customers] even took out their penis. And you'd tell them to put it back, you know, like "don't do that." . . . Some of them try to hold your hand and make you touch their, you know, private parts.

I was almost raped. And after that I felt sick about myself. Like I went into a booth with a customer who pulled out his penis. I didn't even know this because he was a dark man. And I had no idea. And I was totally naked. I was over top of him dancing, and he pulled me down really fast. I just happed to look and there it was and that's a no no. You don't pull your cock out when you're in a bar. You know, and he did it and he was like, "fuck me" and all this stuff. I'm like "No. You know, that's not what I'm here for. I'm not a prostitute." He's like, "I don't give a fuck." And you know, I almost got raped. . . . After that night I felt like really low self-esteem. You know, I was really scared. I didn't want my fiancé to touch me. I was just petrified, you know? And I wouldn't go back there any more.

I had this guy who . . . he was trying to do more than I ever wanted to do and he got forceful with me. He grabbed my arms and grabbed my legs, left bruises and threw me down on the couch.

According to the women interviewed, the experience of lap dancing and the assaults that came along with it had two major effects on their lives. The first effect was on their sense of self:

When you go home, you look into the mirror. . . . You just couldn't look in it any more you seemed so ugly. And you couldn't even wash the dirt off. . . . I used to wear this long dress and if I was naked, you know how many times their semen came on my leg or my body parts? 'Cause they would ejaculate through their pants.

I felt like a prostitute afterwards.

And then the last thing I guess that made me change was the fact that I wanted to kill somebody. I wanted to kill the person who was like, when I was sitting there and I was just like, I was swearing, like my teeth were clenched. It was like I wanted to . . . you know, strike this person. I was so close to wanting to . . . you know, you pig . . . and just beat him up or something. That was the sort of feeling I got. And that's what scared me.

In the beginning it [lap dancing] bothered me. I felt dirty. It was disgusting.

Lap dancing removed the barrier/distance between the dancer and the customer/audience that many dancers felt was necessary in order preserve their self-image as entertainers. As exotic dancing shifted from striptease performances to sexual acts, some dancers found it difficult to retain a valued identity. Others found they could no longer avoid identifying as sex workers and over time began to view themselves as prostitutes and to engage in prostitution outside the club.

The experience of lap dancing therefore impacted on some dancers' lives by making it easier for them to move into prostitution. Some women reported that once the physical barrier was removed it was just easier to have sex for money with the men:

> And most of the girls now are all sleeping with the customers because it's a lot easier, now they're gonna get caught in the Champagne Rooms. So, we'll just take the customer outside of the bar, and go to a hotel.

> I never used to be a working girl [meaning prostitute]. Just in the last six months [since lap dancing], and it is so easy. You become very cold to it.

> The bad clubs are like a whore house. A walk-in whore house. I started in these clubs and that was lap dancing. It bothered me at the beginning, but you do become numb. . . . And once you become accustomed to it, it's a habit almost. And you just do it anyway.

> I think we've evolved. We've gone from strippers to escorts.

> Lap dancing became prostitution. It was, like, that's plain and simple. You know, and it was like an epidemic. It went through, like Toronto, like ninety and Niagara Falls and it was so easy to do after a while, to let the guys touch you. And it got to the point they were touching from the waist down. A lot of real escorts were coming into the bar then, so we had to compete with them. So, I said, well, if they're doing it, we've got to do it too.

In discussing the transition from exotic dancer to prostitute, a number of women who chose to engage in escort work expressed the belief that they never would have made the transition had it not been for the experience of lap dancing.

Although dancers tend to support the ban on lap dancing, they talked about the legal and financial implications the ban has had on their lives. Prior to lap dancing and the subsequent ban, it was acceptable for dancers to touch the men casually while they were dancing. They now, however, risk having steep fines imposed on them (up to $25,000) and having their licenses revoked if they touch a customer.[5] In Toronto, five exotic dancers were charged after the City of Toronto adopted a no-touch bylaw for strip clubs in August 1995 (Brazao 1995, A7). In their interviews, the women talked about how the law has gone too far:

The only thing that is bad is that there is no contact whatsoever. If I'm naked, even if I touch a customer's knees, even if I touch his lap. Like, I'm a touchy kind of woman when I'm talking. Like, friendly, I touch friendly his shoulder, his hand, his lap, his arms or something like this. I don't touch sexual parts. I just love to touch and I risk being charged when I do so. For that they are too severe, too severe.

Now the government is after us about lap dancing and everything, so it's no contact any more. So when we touch a customer a little bit, like this [she touches my knee], the government is after us. Because, it's five thousand dollars if you get busted. Can you imagine? Just because I touch a customer's knees. Plus you have to go to court and as soon as you get busted they take your license back so you can't work.

I think they carried it too far [the ban on lap dancing]. They don't even allow the causal contact any more.

Some bylaws are so stringent that dancers can now be charged for touching customers in a nonsexual manner, even if they were just reaching out to restore their balance to avoid falling off the box during a table dance. Not only do dancers report incidents of women being charged for casual touching, but there are also reports of women being charged for allowing the men to touch them.

Most of the lap dancing charges that have been laid have been against dancers rather than customers. As with prostitution, enforcement efforts are targeting the supply side, rather than the demand side, of the industry and therefore typically targeting women (Belknap 1996, 66; Boritch 1997, 110–13; Lowman 1992, 65–66; Schur 1984, 225; Shaver 1993, 154–55; Shaver 1996, 214–16). What is particularly interesting about the lap dancing bylaws that are used to charge dancers, compared to those used to regulate prostitution, is that in some municipalities customers are immune from prosecution (Brazao 1995, A7; Queen 1995, 3; Swainson 1995, A1). In making laws that result in dancers being subject to charges and customers immune from them, even in cases where the dancer either casually touched customers or the customer's touch was of a forced or coerced nature, these municipalities have made it more difficult for dancers to do their jobs and have essentially given men permission to continue to harass the women, to push for sexual services inside strip clubs, without repercussions for their actions. Case in point is the experience of Tracy Lynn Laird. On March 22, 1995, Tracy Lynn Laird, a single mother and dancer at the house of Lancaster I, in Toronto, was convicted of assault in Etobicoke Provincial Court. The charges stemmed from an incident in which Ms. Laird cut a customer with a glass, when he complained she wasn't allowing touching and fingered her without her permission (Bhabra 1995, 50). The variety of charges that have been laid against dancers suggests that they are in a no-win situation. If the women touch the men or let the men touch them they can be charged. They can also be charged when men touch them against their will or if they defend themselves from such assaults.

Since all the women interviewed identified financial need as the primary motivation for dancing, hefty fines, taking away licenses, and criminal charges can have serious, detrimental effects on these women's lives. Ironically, most women who engaged in lap dancing reported that they only did so in order to keep their jobs—jobs they needed to support themselves and their children:

> If you weren't a lap dancer then you were out, you know?

> Some girls felt obligated to do it . . . just for the money. If you need to feed your kids, what are you going to do?

In addition to lap dancing having financial implications for dancers in terms of fines and concerns for their licenses, it has also had an implication on the money that can now be earned dancing. Dancers and other club staff reported during their interviews that business in the clubs has dropped off since the lap dancing ban, decreasing club revenues and the earning potential for club staff. As a result, in response to the question "How do you feel about the decision to ban lap dancing?" the women typically provided answers such as

> I like it and I don't like it. I like it because they can't touch you and you know what I mean. You don't have to grind on them. But I don't like it because those were twenty dollar dances and guys buy more lap dances than anything else. And you made so much more money when lap dancing was around.

> Now it's a little quiet for everybody because when there used to be lap dancing, you got a little more close to the customers . . . so the customer was getting more attention. So now that we dance more like five feet away from them they are not as generous. Give a candy to a little child and take the candy back. What's it gonna do? It's gonna start to cry, that's what it's gonna do.

Some women pointed to the experience of lap dancing, and the change in earning potential resulting from the lap dancing ban, as the primary reasons they began to engage in prostitution.

> The lap dancing was done. And it was, well, shit. What's an easier way? Cause now, like the bars are dead. Every bar is dead. OK, how do we get this money back? Cause we were making fifteen hundred dollars a day.

# Conclusion

The decision of the Supreme Court of Canada in the case of *R. v. Mara* ([1997] S.C.J. No. 29 (QL)), is worded in a manner that suggests that the ruling was designed to protect female exotic dancers and other women from degradation and exploitation and was arrived at at least partially in response to the pleas from exotic dancers for help in regulating lap dancing.[6] However, since the Supreme Court was limited to addressing the issue of whether lap dancing in a public place is an indecent act, and its decision has been interpreted as only pertaining to lap dancing that occurs in public areas of strip clubs, control of lap dancing in other more private locations in the clubs falls to the municipalities. The problem with relying on the municipalities to regulate lap dancing is that some municipalities have implemented and applied lap dancing bylaws in a discriminatory manner. Bylaws that specify that customers are immune from charges are a good example of sex discrimination in the implementation of law. Even in those municipalities where the bylaws have been implemented in a gender-neutral fashion, and customers can therefore be charged, there has been a tendency for a gender-biased application of the law, similar to those regulating prostitution, resulting in the majority of the charges being laid against the dancers.

Not only have municipal bylaws been implemented and applied in a discriminatory fashion, but criminal charges tied to violation experiences of dancers are also being applied in a manner that suggests that the police and the courts value male victimization experiences more than females'. Similar to prostitutes, exotic dancers are not taken seriously by police and other agents of the criminal justice system when it comes to experiences of sexual assault. The case of Tracy Lynn Laird is a perfect illustration of this tendency and helps to explain the fear among dancers of being charged with assault should they take steps to protect themselves while working in the clubs.

Both the introduction and subsequent banning of lap dancing in Ontario has had physical, emotional, and financial implications for exotic dancers in the region. The coercion and violation that dancers have experienced while lap dancing have impacted on how they feel about their jobs and themselves, which in turn has affected their relationships and their lives. Although many dancers were supportive of introducing laws to control lap dancing, the reduction in earning potential from exotic dancing and the discriminatory implementation and application of such regulatory devices have exacerbated, rather than reduced, the impact of the lap dancing phenomenon on these women. The discrimination in implementing and applying lap dancing bylaws in various municipalities implies that it is female exotic dancers who are to "blame" for lap dancing, not the male owners, managers, and customers who demand such services be performed. As a result, little consideration is given to the actual implications of lap dancing and its control on the lives of exotic dancers.

# Acknowledgments

I would like to acknowledge the invaluable contribution of Jennifer Zubick, my research assistant, to this paper. Her law school training provided her with the skills to find and interpret the relevant legal documents on lap dancing and provide me with the proper citation style. I would also like to thank all the women who took time away from their lives to speak with me. This study was funded by the *National Health Research Development Program/AIDS Education Prevention Unit*, Ottawa, Canada.

# Notes

1. The primary source of income for dancers is customers' tips. Although dancers in Ontario often have the option of working for the club on salary for a minimal wage (e.g., thirty to fifty dollars per shift), many prefer to work freelance since it enables them to set their own hours. Freelance dancers, however, are required to pay the club for the "privilege" of dancing there, usually between $10 and $20 per day, and are therefore even more dependent on customers' tips.

2. Section 167(1) of the *Criminal Code of Canada* states: "Every one commits an offence who, being the lessee, manager, agent or person in charge of a theatre, presents or gives or allows to be presented or given therein an immoral, indecent or obscene performance, entertainment or representation."

3. The Association for Burlesque Entertainers was formed primarily in response to the Hachborn decision. According to an association press release, issued on May 11, 1995, fighting to have lap dancing banned from strip clubs was a top priority for the association.

4. Toronto was the first municipality to institute a lap dancing bylaw. The authority of the City of Toronto to create such a bylaw was challenged and upheld in the Ontario Divisional Court in the case of the *Ontario Adult Entertainment Bar Association* v. *The Municipality of Metropolitan Toronto* on October 30, 1995 ([1996], 27 O.R. [3d] 643).

5. Numerous municipalities in Ontario have bylaws requiring all exotic dancers to be licensed.

6. The Supreme Court ruled that lap dancing is conduct that is harmful because "it degrades and dehumanizes women, it desensitizes sexuality, it is incompatible with the dignity and equality of each human being, and it predisposes persons to act in an antisocial manner."

# References

Bhabra, H. S. 1995. Ten dollars a dance. *Toronto Life*. May, 50–53.

Belknap, Joanne. 1996. *The Invisible Woman: Gender, Crime and Justice*. Belmont, Calif.: Wadsworth Publishing Company.

Boritch, Helen. 1997. *Fallen Women: Female Crime and Criminal Justice in Canada*. Toronto: Nelson Publishing.

Brazao, D. 1995. Lap dancers charged under no-touching law. *Toronto Star*, September 13, A7.

*Criminal Code of Canada*. 1985. R.S.C., c. C-46, s. 167(1).

Funston, M. 1995. Mississauga bans lap dancing—but clubs, dancers protest. *Toronto Star*, September 14, A6.

Harvey, I. 1995. Dirty dancing killing our fun. *The Saturday Sun*, March 4, 22.

Lowman, John. 1992. Street prostitution. In *Deviance: Conformity and Control in Canadian Society*, edited by Vincent Sacco. 49–94. Scarborough, Ont.: Prentice-Hall, Canada.

*Ontario Adult Entertainment Bar Association* v. *The Municipality of Metropolitan Toronto* on Oct. 30, 1995 (1996), 27 O.R. (3d) 643.

Queen, L. 1995. York outlaws dirty dancing: Lap dancer urges council to permit "wholesome" profession. *The Liberal*, September 17, 3.

*R.* v. *Mara*, [1994], O.J. No. 264 (QL).

*R.* v. *Mara*, [1996], 27 O.R. (3d) 643.

*R.* v. *Mara*, [1997], S.C.J. No. 29 (QL).

Schur, Edwin M. 1984. *Labeling Women Deviant: Gender, Stigma and Social Control*. New York: Random House.

Shaver, Frances M. 1996. The regulation of prostitution: Setting the morality trap. In *Social control in Canada: Issues in the social construction of deviance*, edited by Bernard Schissel and Linda Mahood. 201–226. Toronto: Oxford University Press.

———— 1993. Prostitution: A female crime? In *In Conflict with the Law: Women and the Canadian Justice System*, edited by Ellen Adelberg and Claudia Currie. 153–73. Vancouver, B.C.: Press Gang.

Small, P., and G. Swainson. 1995. City attacks lap dance sleaze. *Toronto Star*, August 16, A3.

Swainson, G. 1995. Metro bans lap dancing. *Toronto Star*, August 18, A1, A16.

Van Alphen, T. 1995. Stripper protests lap dancing. *Toronto Star*, May 22, C1, C3.

# RESEARCH FROM WITHIN:
## PARTICIPANT OBSERVATION
## IN THE PHONE-SEX WORKPLACE

### AMY FLOWERS

If there is anyone more contemptible than an academic-turned-whore, it is a whore-turned-academic. The whore-turned-researcher faces the distrust and discomfort of colleagues and clients alike. Any researcher's objectivity can be sacrificed when she "goes native" and becomes one of her own subjects. The native who goes academic, likewise, is something of a traitor, no longer trustworthy with the intimate secrets of the group.

The researcher who participates in the sex work trade faces a similar loss of trust within the academic community. In addition to the obvious questions of objectivity, the academic who comes out as a sex worker also faces the challenge of being openly sexual in an environment that cherishes chaste cerebral thought. Academics are notoriously naïve to street life. The researcher who participates in sex work brings a gritty, carnal reality to the sheltered halls of academia. Grit is not welcome on tidy marble floors.

The risk of bridging the sex work and academic communities is a loss in reputation and trustworthiness in each community. The application of stigma and trivialization serves the latent function of minimizing such bridges. If the terms of exposure are unreasonable, none but the exhibitionistic will offer themselves for examination.

I did participant observation of the phone-sex workplace while doing research on the interaction between phone-sex operators and their clients. I used this data in my Ph.D. dissertation without shame or embarrassment. Perhaps naively, I thought that phone sex was not real sex, that having merely talked about sex would not bring on the kind of criticism or shock from the academic community that might accompany an admission of one actually having had sex.

I was wrong, and in the end I lost my data. Committee members advised that in order to get past university watchdogs dressed as ethicists, it was best for me to hide my own participation. Along the way I encountered a few jokes and comments that ranged from equivocal to lewd. I earned a reputation, later shaken I think, for academic un-seriousness, sexuality where sexuality ought to be unseen, and even for self-exploitation.

Sex work, as a research topic, is dense with the very obstacles that a diversity of methods is designed to traverse. The phone-sex industry, and the pornography industry of which it is part, is an insulated culture, which exists within a society that is largely hostile to it. These circumstances make participation a prerequisite for observation. Yet personal experience is perceived through the distortion of prior experience. Thus, the researcher must consult the perceptions of other participants. The others also work, and often live, in the creation of myth and fantasy, subjecting the researcher to the obstacles of manipulation and deceit.

Choosing one interpretation over another, placing focus and belief where best suited, the researcher carves out a maze of research actions: steps forward and back, turns, junctures, and deadends. The decision-making that is necessary to navigate such an environment requires certitude and decisiveness of the researcher; yet these qualities themselves generate new mine fields of ethical and practical bias.

The richness of human interaction obligates those who study it to apply a methodology that respects the depth and richness of the interactions they observe. Any empirical study, with the inferred interaction between researcher and subject, is an exercise in reciprocity. Many of the gender, race, class, age, and other biases imbedded in the history of social science research have been the result of the often-deliberate ignorance of the researcher concerning his (sic) funding sources, career interests, and personal history.

One of the feminist contributions to science has been the idea that epistemology, politics, practice, and the fruits of science are interrelated. In light of this awareness feminist research now emphasizes, rather than denies, the life experience that guides the researcher's choice of topic, methodology, and subsequently, data analysis. Such reflexivity is meant to reveal the conditions of research that always exist but are hidden by more traditional methods. Through standpoint thus exposed, the reader is enabled to reach her own informed conclusions concerning the accuracy and insight of the study at hand.

Scientific inquiry requires both detachment and involvement. The choice of a topic is itself a coming out. When a researcher does extensive work on any topic, a personal interest is often assumed. Nondisclosure of involvement is no solution in the academic environment where one is what one studies. Even without participation, the sex-researcher is naughtily sexual, and subject to censure on those grounds alone.

My experience as a sex worker taught me to be especially skeptical of the polarity arguments, the idea that the sex industry is either good or bad, choice or exploitation, glamour or degradation. The whore researcher who agendizes her research may understate the desperation that prompts many workers to perform acts that are repugnant or dangerous. Eating another person's feces, for example, is a rare and truly acquired taste. Although it may be argued that the dislike of such matter is the acquired mannerism, that argument I find to be naively privileged and removed from the empirical ramifications of the act. Such acts are often accompanied by profound psychological dysfunction, and the acts, as well as the solicitors, are intensely distasteful to those who perform them for reasons other than desire. To label such actions as "preference" ignores the conflict and complexity from which such desire emerges.

In obtaining a job as a phone-sex operator, I did not intend to deceive anyone. I did not intend to write about my experience in the form of a dissertation for the first two months out of four in which I worked as an operator. In fact, although I took notes akin to field notes, it was for an entirely different purpose: they were meant as a personal journal and a basis for writing fictional short stories based on the interactions I had with some of the more imaginative callers. As my intentions changed, I could have begun again. I could have gone to the phone-sex management, explained my new objective, and hoped to continue working and observing under these new conditions.

Pornographic businesses, known for their illegal activities, are not likely to accept a researcher hanging around, and I had already witnessed a variety of illegal activities. My experience with the particular management style was that they were downright oppressive toward workers. They insisted on a great deal of control over the personal interaction and conversation between workers on such matters as salary comparison, tardiness, and insolence toward supervisors. Since I had no intention to organize workers or report illegal practices, I did not wish to give management reason to think that I might.

My position as a privileged, white, middle-class, educated, noncommitted worker is obvious from my speech, appearance, and demeanor, and I made no pretense of hiding them within the phone-sex workplace. In reality, there was no need to announce that I was a graduate student, and the announcement itself would have been self-aggrandizing. Describing myself as a Ph.D. candidate would have been seen as putting on airs.

Additionally, I avoided using my position as an educated, marginal worker to explain other workers' experiences to them, to mediate or counsel, or to develop more effective training methods for the phone-sex industry.

I did, when asked, reveal to coworkers that I was concurrently a graduate student. This information was generally not well received. It put distance where there had been camaraderie. They usually confessed, in a tone of inferiority, that they were not very "good at school." I often responded with stories of harassment and agony, which seemed to increase their comfort level greatly. In general, when talking to any working-class acquaintance, I especially avoid the initials "USC," because of their class implications. The phone-sex workplace was no different.

The benefits of these modest "deceptions" were monumental. I gained entry, not only to the setting, but also to the substance of the material by working as a phone-sex operator. I was neither completely an observer nor was I completely a participant. Far from being problematic, this situation was ideal for the purpose of exploration. Moreover, recent ethnographic research has shown the dichotomy of participant/observer to be misleading. All participants observe, and all observers participate.

It was never my intention to study the callers, and it would have severely jeopardized my job, and hence, my access. This sort of utilitarian defense has been criticized as mere convenience, an inadequate justification for deception. There are possibilities and impossibilities, however, and one must discriminate between them. Esoteric concerns such as the protection of the anonymous from the unknown ought not be used to prohibit research that is useful. As important as it is for research to do no harm to its subjects, it is as important to disallow discomfort and social taboo from dictating the content or findings of research.

I weighed the benefits of this research against other relevant variables, such as possibilities for harm, which were slight; the value of the resulting research, which was potentially good; and the potential for harm or offense, which was small. I believe that the data I had collected during my tenure as a sex worker are valuable to academics and workers alike, and that my own personal risk of exposure in producing this document is equal to, if not greater than, the risk to which I have exposed my subjects.

In the phone-sex workplace, real names are unspoken and unknown. I honored confidentiality of pseudonyms, because, during the observation phase of the research, I was working in a setting and within a process that was not tied to any particular individual. I knew nothing about the other workers' identities outside the workplace. Workers did not have to trust my ethical judgments, because my knowledge of them was limited. I made no attempt to identify details about where they lived or grew up, never asked their real names, where else they might work, the occupation of a spouse, or any detail that might later be used in identification. Within this study I assigned pseudonyms for the working pseudonyms of the people I worked with.

Ethical decisions have meaning only within the context in which they are made. I admit that the decisions I made were retrospective and self-justifying; they were made in a microclimate of suppression and censorship. Other researchers, were they candid, might admit to an ethic that is similarly retrospective, but as the trend in social science moves to protect everyone from everything, and thus avoid all potential lawsuits, disagreements, and controversies, this honest admission becomes increasingly unlikely.

Researchers suggest that an honor system of professional ethics requires an "act of faith." For "if you believe," they counsel, "that in the long run truth makes men freer and more autonomous, then you are willing to run the risk that some people will use the facts you turn up and the interpretations you make to fight a rear guard action. If you don't believe this, if you believe instead that truth may or may not free men depending on the situation, even in the long run, then perhaps it is better to avoid these kinds of research subjects."

I do believe that forthright inquiry is liberating, and using my own history of sex work serves as my act of faith in that belief. I believe that I have as much to risk by my association with phone sex as any coworker risked by discussing, namelessly, her or his life with me. My right to ask questions of them comes from my willingness to subject myself to them, to answer anything they might ask of me, and to reveal, in this work, all that is relevant in my own participation.

By working with callers, I developed a vocabulary of the industry that I could not have gotten on my own in the pornography shops, bookstores, and libraries. The incentive of my phone-sex conversations provided focus in areas I might have otherwise bypassed. For example, I might have unthinkingly avoided close examination of the defecation and excrement markets, instead assuming that the excreter was demonstrating power over the excretee. In so doing, I would have failed to recognize the significance of its market share of the industry, and I also would have missed the motivations evident in the accompanying story lines: even excretory fantasies are ultimately about purity and innocence, desire and acceptance. I had not availed myself of the details of this class of fantasy until pressed, and consequently I risked losing sight of the depth and meaning of the themes inherent in this odd collection of intimate social interactions.

Contrary to its purpose, signing the confidentiality agreement was often more a source of tension than an inducement to participate. Occasionally the offer of the form served to officiate my position as researcher, for better or worse. This occasion was the only time I ever asked for a last name. If an interviewee was hesitant I offered that she may sign a pseudonym, although I believe there were only two operators who chose to do so. I recorded the interviews, had them transcribed professionally, verbatim, then I recorded over each tape, eventually destroying all of the original voices. Other than the confidentiality agreements, there is no remaining record of the identities of my research respondents.

The reciprocity of the research interaction was fundamental to the data collection in all phases, from unobtrusive analysis of pornographic materials to participant observation. My experience as participant observer substantially altered subjects' perception of my relative power. Many referred expressly to the *simpatico* they felt with me. They felt that I would be nonjudgmental and assumed that I had felt comparable emotions, wrestled with similar circumstances. Remarks commonly made, like "I know you've been there," and "you can understand this, Amy" revealed the need of the subjects to know that through personal experience I would understand their reaction and be nonjudgmental in my reaction. This was fundamental to my ability to get the essence of their stories. The details of the story often included sexual degradation they had experienced, brutality they themselves had inflicted on persons judged weak, and the guilt that ultimately resulted. I do not believe they would have been so bold as to deliberate these activities aloud if they had not known that I had also been a phone-sex worker and experienced similar phenomena.

The purpose of an ethnography is to elucidate the meanings that are used by participants in an interaction. The particular interaction at hand, the process of a phone-sex call, is especially difficult for a researcher to interpret because its meaning is so different for each of the participants: caller, operator, and researcher. Bestiality, for example, conveys an alluring promise of gratification to the caller who requests it, while it conveys an automated series of landmarks to the operator who recognizes the call for a particular script, and again for our poor researcher, bestiality conveys quite another culture-laden, politically loaded set of meanings.

The tension that exists between the research and sex work communities makes a hostile, warlike environment for those who choose to cross the lines of research and practice. Ethnographic, participative description offers a map for navigating the minefields in each territory, a guide for translators and tourists alike who seek to understand the ways of another, not-so-alien world.

# Using Qualitative Methods to Study the Hidden World of Offstreet Prostitution in Los Angeles County

## Janet Lever and David E. Kanouse

## Introduction and Study Background

Female prostitutes are widely believed to play a potentially important role in the epidemiology of sexually transmitted diseases (STDs), including HIV, both because of the sexual activity involved in their work and because some female prostitutes inject drugs or have sex with men who do (Darrow 1984; Darrow et al. 1990; Miller, Turner, and Moses 1990). The number of women involved in prostitution, the number of their client contacts, and their risk behaviors are all important to understand the epidemiology of HIV and other STDs. Nevertheless, little of what is known about any of these variables has been derived from careful scientific study.

Most studies of prostitutes rely on samples of convenience, typically recruiting in jails, sexually transmitted disease (STD) clinics, and methadone maintenance programs (Cohen et al. 1988; Khabbaz et al. 1990; Gellert et al. 1993; Astemborski 1994). A few studies also include outreach recruitment of respondents in areas known for street prostitution (Cohen et al. 1988; Khabbaz et al. 1990; Tabet et al. 1992). Sampling female commercial street workers (FCSWs) found in all those places overrepresents women who solicit clients on the street and underrepresents women who solicit clients in off-street locales or via advertisement or referrals, and reveals nothing about the size of any subpopulations. One authority—then a codirector of the National Task Force on Prostitution—estimated that in the United States there are five to ten FCSWs in the hidden prostitution workforce for every woman visibly working on the streets (Alexander 1987).

The Los Angeles Women's Health Risk Study (LAWHRS) is the first study of its kind to attempt to draw a probability sample of the prostitute population in a single major metropolitan area. As part of this study, we sought to draw a probability sample of offstreet prostitutes who work out of indoor locations associated with prostitution. This involved three stages: (1) using informants and documentary sources to construct list-based sampling frames of women and venues; (2) drawing probability samples from these lists; and (3) contacting and interviewing sampled women. We successfully compiled the information necessary to define sample frames, but it proved impossible to achieve adequate response rates in contacting and interviewing sampled women, largely because our access to those working in private places was restricted. Nevertheless, the qualitative methods we applied in developing sample frames revealed much about the size and demographic composition of the hidden workforce and the distribution of FCSWs by location of solicitation.

We categorized the FCSW population by how women find clients. Street prostitutes rely on direct contact with clients, who can see them in outdoor public places like streets, parking lots, and alleys. There are several ways offstreet prostitutes find clients, and different methods are required to study the various parts of this complex market. Elsewhere we will discuss those who solicit via advertisement or referral; this research note describes what we were able to learn about offstreet FCSWs who find clients by being available in locations associated with prostitution. We focus here on the various types of indoor locations within Los Angeles County that serve as a base of operations for offstreet prostitutes. Our objectives include: (1) describing the various sources of qualitative data that can be used to learn about the social organization of hidden prostitution and (2) seeking convergence of information gathered from different sources to arrive at estimates of the size and demographic composition of the FCSW population that solicits through known locations.

# Sources of Data Collection

Workers typically deny using legitimate businesses to meet men willing to exchange money for sexual services, so conventional strategies to approach and study subjects do not succeed. For ethical reasons, we could not gather data by posing as clients or workers in the participant observation tradition of data collection. Classic ethnography was also impossible, given the scale of the study and time and financial restrictions. With literally thousands of bars, clubs, hotels, massage parlors, and other pseudohealth salons scattered throughout the 4,000 square miles of the county, dozens of nonparticipant observers would need months to "hang out" in each setting to establish rapport and get past all the denial of eligibility to participate in our study. Furthermore, the enormous ethnic diversity of Los Angeles County would necessitate finding and training observers from at least a dozen racial/ethnic backgrounds, making conventional fieldwork an even more daunting challenge than in more homogenous regions. Instead of conventional fieldwork, we relied on various sources to identify the characteristics and estimate the size of the offstreet market. Those sources can be clustered into three categories: government agencies, directories and written materials, and ethnographic informants.

# Government Agencies

Various city, county, state, and federal government agencies either monitor prostitution activity or regulate the physical location in which it occurs as part of their explicit mission or as a byproduct of other organizational goals. In addition to the obvious sources—namely law enforcement and public health agencies—there are other public sector agencies with a "need to know" about the settings with possible prostitution activity. Table 1 displays the range of these agencies and the scopes of their jurisdictions, and specifies the relationship between offstreet prostitution and their organizational goals.

The general goals of law enforcement agencies require that they react to residents' and business owners' complaints about the impact of prostitution on neighborhoods and that they proactively arrest persons selling or buying prostitutes' services. Health services agencies seek to protect the public health, including curbing the spread of STDs, while the goal of the Alcoholic Beverage Control is to enforce state codes for premises with liquor permits. Information gathered by each division of these bureaucracies is not necessarily shared with other divisions; therefore, our requests for information had to be made at every precinct, station, and district-level office. The undercover investigation work of the State Labor Board and Immigration and Naturalization Services (INS) is less obvious than that of the other agencies. Many prostitutes work as "bar girls," "hostesses," and technicians in bars, clubs, and unlicensed massage parlors. When they are illegal entrants to the country or not recognized as formal employees, establishment owners are in violation of labor and/or immigration codes.

# Directories and Written Materials

The fifteen regional *yellow pages directories* are readily available sources of information. We made data entries of business names, addresses, and phone numbers of all listings under the headings "Massage" and "Escort," then cross-referenced to eliminate multiple counting of businesses that advertise in more than one directory. Many entries were for escort services or out-call

**Table 1. Government Agencies with a "Need to Know" about Prostitution**

| TYPE OF AGENCY | SCOPE OF JURISDICTION | RELATED ORGANIZATIONAL GOALS |
| --- | --- | --- |
| **Law Enforcement** | | |
| Los Angeles Police Department (LAPD) | Administrative (Ad) Vice Commission Investigation Division (CID) | Citywide policing of large operations that cross precinct lines |
| | | Monitor massage parlors for violations of reporting regulations and for illegal behaviors on premises |
| | Special Asian Task Force | Liaison to Asian community and businesses |
| | 18 precincts | Criminal activity within precinct lines |
| | 37 independent municipalities within county borders | Police criminal activities within their borders |
| Detective Bureaus | Headquarters | Parallel to LAPD Ad Vice; also subcontracted by some independent municipalities |
| County Sheriff's Departments | 17 sheriff's stations | Parallel to LAPD precincts |
| City Attorney's Offices | Citywide | Investigate and prosecute crimes |
| District Attorney's Offices | Countywide | Investigate and prosecute crimes |
| **Tax Collection** | | |
| City Clerk | Citywide | Maintains records of permits for tax collection with markers for adult entertainment businesses |
| County Tax Collector | Countywide | Same as city clerk |
| **Health and Protective Services** | | |
| L.A. County Health Department | 23 districts | Operate STD clinics (serve both prostitutes and their male clients); outreach to find FCSWs known or suspected of spreading STDs |
| Independent Municipal Health Departments | Three, countywide | Same as above |
| Naval Station STD Clinic | Long Beach | Service navy personnel with STDs |
| Alcoholic Beverage Control (ABC) | State-operated 5 districts in L.A. County | Undercover investigation to monitor regulations re minors, "bar girls," sale of narcotics, and prostitution on premises of licensed establishments |
| State Labor Board | Statewide | Enforcement of state labor codes (e.g., failure to pay workers' compensation taxes for "bar girls" and "hostesses") |
| Immigration and Naturalization Services (INS) | Federal jurisdiction | Trafficking in "illegal immigrants," forged documents; undocumented workers, including "bar girls" |

massage (masseuse travels to client); findings based on those entries will be discussed in a subsequent paper about advertising solicitations. The ones used here are confined to on-premise massage services, because the client need only know about the location and not necessarily the name of the prostitute or service. Our analysis of yellow pages listings was especially useful in a huge metropolitan area because Los Angeles Police Department records are kept only for those sites within Los Angeles proper. With more lax enforcement in the county and independent municipalities, many sensual massage businesses are located outside city lines.

*Advertisements in the sex tabloids* served to supplement city records of adult-entertainment establishments featuring nudity because they included businesses both in- and outside of city lines. Some advertisements also served to verify the sensual, rather than therapeutic, services of featured massage parlors. Although we were not able to get translations for all of the local foreign-language newspapers, we were told that some unlicensed massage parlors, especially those that were operated surreptitiously in residential areas, advertise only in Chinese or Korean papers to restrict clientele and minimize general public awareness. If other researchers concentrate on a single or few ethnic groups, legitimate foreign-language newspapers could provide useful information.

The number and location of hotels was established by promotional materials provided by the *Los Angeles Convention and Visitors Bureau*. We made use of expert informants—primarily law enforcement—to learn which hotels were likely to have prostitutes soliciting in public places like cocktail lounges. Then we used field workers to interview employees and make observations in hotel lobbies and lounges.

A valuable source that is now available, but was not at the time of our study, is the *World Wide Web*. The World Sex Guide can be found at http://www.paranoia.com/faq/prostitution. Once at the site, the visitor can select country, state, and city to consume or exchange information about several types of sex for sale. For this study we periodically check entries under Long Beach, Los Angeles, Pasadena, and Pomona—all within Los Angeles County. The communiques appear to be written by male clients rather than by female prostitutes attempting to attract clientele. The anonymous writers describe where precisely they found "street action" in a particular locale on a particular date, as well as user tips about how to avoid police decoys. For indoor locations, writers tell how they were able to get past fronts of "legitimacy" in massage and accupressure parlors that they name, and they also offer first names and descriptions of the technicians who are willing to offer illicit services (and prices) as well as those who lure and tease the client but who do not trade sex for money. Writers share information on other types of locations, such as places that advertise "Japanese girls, nude dancing" or "modeling studio" in legitimate press that they describe either as "ripoffs" or genuine.

# Ethnographic Informants

The remaining sources of data are various types of ethnographic informants. *Participant informants* are those directly involved in the business of buying or selling prostitution services; examples include current and ex- "madams," prostitutes, and their male clients. We call *"supporting cast" informants* those whose work facilitates, or places them in a position to be knowledgeable about, prostitution. Examples include current and ex–hotel employees (especially doormen, concierges, and those who investigate or record guests' accusations of on-premise robbery or other crimes), an Asian tour agency owner, and a sex tabloid employee who collected fees directly from advertisers who were often prostitutes, pimps, or madams.

Also included are *"expert" informants:* These were academic researchers who study the sex industry; for example, there was a filmmaker who established rapport for his short documentary on a downtown taxidance club, a historian of prostitution, and sociologists who published articles and a dissertation based on their participant observation (two as clients, one as hostess) of the hostess dance clubs.

Our own *field investigators* were trained to identify themselves as study research assistants; they included one white female and three white males who investigated hotels, massage parlors, or went on "ride-alongs" with divisional vice officers, and one Korean male who tried to investigate Asian clubs, hotels, and massage parlors.

# Methods of Data Collection

Methods of data collection included interviews, archival retrieval, and ethnographic field work, but as described below, the bulk of the data came from interview and archival materials. Most data were collected between July 1989 and December 1991; where significant change in location activity seemed likely, updated information was solicited in 1996.

## Interviews

Most of the data from government agencies was gathered through repeated in-person and telephone interviews by Janet Lever with personnel at various ranks identified as the best informed on the subject of prostitution. During the early stage of defining our sample frames for the study of street prostitution, the field supervisor and her research assistants interviewed dozens of precinct and other law enforcement officers and health department workers;

material in their notes that referred to offstreet prostitution was also used in this analysis. Lever was able to conduct interviews herself with personnel in the ABC, State Labor Board, INS, and city and district attorneys' offices.

Once data collection on the street began, our interviewers asked all 1,024 FCSW respondents to name any offstreet location they worked in themselves or knew of. Other informants included persons directly involved in prostitution, such as massage parlor managers or FCSWs, and those more peripherally involved, such as a downtown hotel employee who received complaints about theft allegedly committed by prostitutes, hotel desk clerks, sex tabloid employees, and many others. Interviews with key informants were conducted often over the course of the study.

## Archival Research

Important data were obtained from government agencies in the form of written reports and records. Most important were the reports kept by LAPD Commission Investigation Division (CID) after each routine or "sting" investigation of massage parlor premises, including full descriptions of sex acts observed or incriminating evidence collected (e.g., canisters of condoms); these extensive reports were kept by CID to be used in revocation-of-license hearings. The CID also made available the monthly reports from each parlor which required the names of all massage technicians. We could count ethnically identifiable surnames on those reports to use as indicative of informants' description of city massage workers. Because CID covered only city parlors classified as adult-entertainment locations, we used information provided by the sheriff's vice division and searched the yellow pages of fifteen regional phone directories to identify other massage locations.

The Alcoholic Beverage Control (ABC) gave us access to written information on the number of licensed establishments within their five jurisdictions. Because adult-entertainment clubs that feature nudity cannot serve alcohol, records at the City Clerk's office and the County Tax Collectors were used to supplement ABC records to determine the number of adult-entertainment bars and clubs within city and county borders.

## Ethnographic Field Work

Our attempts to learn about the social organization of offstreet prostitution by nonparticipant observation and on-premise interviews of employees met with limited success, because most gatekeepers denied knowledge of prostitution activity. Attempts were made by experienced ethnographers, but none was sufficiently successful to justify further expenditures for this method of data collection. Some useful data were gathered through observations. For example, one observer counted how many single women were present at an Asian nightclub during repeated visits to help us calculate our estimates of women offering "hostess" services. Another observer made sufficient visits to strategically located hotels (e.g., near the airport and downtown convention center) to confirm the information offered by the police that, as a result of their enforcement, these were not numerically important venues for offstreet prostitution at the time of our study.

## Results

Table 2 shows the sources of data available for each type of location studied. Each type can be studied with data from multiple sources, which makes it possible to examine the consistency of data from different sources and seek convergence. This helped us both to develop quantitative estimates and to assess how much confidence to place in those estimates. In most locations, authorities and informants were in reasonable agreement regarding the proportion of women on premises who were likely to offer sexual services. For example, low and high estimates of the proportion of women present in "cantinas"—bars that cater to Mexican and Central American immigrants—who might be FCSWs ranged from 20 percent to 75 percent. But most police and health officials were comfortable with the midrange estimate that roughly 50 percent of women in cantinas only hustle drinks while 50 percent also sell sexual favors, on or off premises.

Only in the case of taxidancers did the law enforcement officials' estimates differ dramatically from those of expert informants and participant informants; the police believed nearly all taxidancers are involved in at least occasional prostitution, whereas informants felt that only about 20 percent are involved. The researchers and student filmmaker agreed with the taxidance informants' estimates, so we used their 20 percent figure in our estimates. In all other locations, consensus was easily established.

Sometimes precise figures were not available, so we used data that were available to draw inferences. For example, the monthly technician reports submitted to the CID for city massage parlors were used to estimate an average number of workers per shift so we could calculate estimates of workers for the county and independent city parlors (derived from yellow pages entries) where counterpart records were not available to us.

Table 3 provides an overview of our best estimates of the size and racial/ethnic composition of offstreet prostitute population in each location, as well as total numbers for each racial/ethnic group and for the population as a whole. Street prostitution is more homogeneous and is dominated by African-American women who made up seven in ten women in our random sample (another 17 percent were white, 9 percent Hispanic, 4 percent mixed, and less than 1 percent Asian). In contrast, as Table 3 clearly shows, there is

## Table 2

### Multiple Sources of Information about Offstreet Prostitutes

| Strata | Sources |
|---|---|
| Massage parlor workers (on premises) | Sheriff, Vice Division |
| | Commission Investigation Division, LAPD |
| | Asian Task Force |
| | City clerk tax and permit system |
| | Yellow Pages listings and records from our field workers |
| | Informant owner/manager |
| Hotels—Class A | LA Convention and Visitors Bureau membership list (City and County) (~200) |
| | District Attorney's office |
| | LAPD Administrative and Divisional Vice |
| | Municipalities' Detective Bureaus |
| | Sheriff, Vice Division |
| | Ethnographic informants (including former and current hotel employees and field workers) |
| Clubs/adult cabaret | Alcoholic Beverage Control |
| a. Karaoke and other Asian clubs | County Tax Collector |
| b. Gambling clubs | City and District attorneys |
| c. Nude shows | City zoning and building and safety |
| d. Discos in hotels | State Labor Board |
| | LAPD Asian Task Force and Vice |
| | Sheriff, Vice Division |
| | Ethnographic consultants |
| Bars | Alcoholic Beverage Control |
| a. Cantinas (for new Hispanic immigrants) | State Labor Board |
| b. Neighborhood bars | INS |
| | LAPD Divisional Vice |
| | Municipalities' Detective Bureaus |
| | Sheriff, Vice |
| | STD field investigators |
| | Informants (researchers) |
| Brothels | LAPD and Sheriff, Administrative Vice |
| | Informants (including madams) |
| Hostess Dance Halls (Taxidance) | Alcoholic Beverage Control |
| | LAPD, Divisional Vice |
| | Ethnographic consultants |

**Table 3**

**Number of Women Involved in Offstreet Prostitution in
Los Angeles County in 1991 (by Race/Ethnicity)**

| Mode or Locale of Solicitation | White/Non-Hispanic | African-American | Hispanic-American | Hispanic Immigrant | Asian | Total |
|---|---|---|---|---|---|---|
| Massage Parlors | 25 | | 10 | | 325 | 360 |
| Hotels | 70 | 30 | | | | 100 |
| Adult Cabarets | 200 | 25 | 25 | | | 250 |
| Asian Nightclubs | | | | | 1,225 | 1,225 |
| Cantinas | | | | 1,600 | | 1,600 |
| Brothels and other private places | | 30 | | | 270 | 300 |
| Taxidance Halls | 25 | 5 | | 150 | 5 | 185 |
| Total | 320 | 90 | 35 | 1,750 | 1,825 | 4,020 |

a high degree of racial/ethnic segmentation across types of indoor locations where prostitution occurs. Racial/ethnic groups that are largely absent from the public world of prostitution are present in the hidden part of the market.

# Conclusion

The portion of the offstreet prostitution market in which clients and prostitutes meet in known locations is hidden by cloaks of legitimacy that allow participants to deny illegal activities. Given sufficient resources, traditional fieldwork methods might succeed in getting past the "fronts" in order to establish the actual numbers of FCSWs among all women found on such premises. However, in a large, multicultural metropolis like Los Angeles County, such fieldwork techniques would be prohibitively expensive. Instead of concluding that such hidden locations cannot be studied, we investigated what sources of information might be tapped.

We found numerous sources of useful information about the hidden offstreet prostitution market in Los Angeles County. Even though segments of the market operate in very different ways, all come under the scrutiny of government agencies for varying reasons, and agency officials were extremely cooperative in sharing with us what they knew and how they knew it. Data from other sources—most notably the yellow pages directories and more recently user-groups on the World Wide Web—are a valuable supplement to official public records. Informants of all types also provided essential information. Although field observation was only marginally successful, field notes were used to calculate numbers of prostitutes working out of less-regulated locations, like hotels and nightclubs. Convergence of data from different sources was helpful in deriving consensus-based estimates of the size and composition of each segment of the prostitution market.

After surveying that part of the offstreet market for prostitution in Los Angeles that occurs in locations known to have FCSWs available, we have concluded that approximately 4,000 women were involved in this part of the market at the time of our fieldwork.

# References

Alexander, Priscilla. 1987. Prostitution: A difficult issue for feminists. In *Sex Work: Writings by Women in the Sex Industry,* Frederique Delacoste and Priscilla Alexander, eds. Pittsburgh: Cleis Press, 184–214.

Astemborski, J., D. Vlahov, D. Warren, L. Solomon, and K. E. Nelson. 1994. The trading of sex for drugs or money and HIV seropositivity among female intravenous drug users. *American Journal of Public Health* 64: 382–87.

Cohen, Judith, Priscilla Alexander, and Constance Wofsky. 1988. Prostitutes and AIDS: Public policy issues. *AIDS & Public Policy Journal* 3:17–22.

Darrow, William W. 1984. Prostitution and sexually transmitted diseases. In *Sexually Transmitted Disease,* K. K. Holmes, P. A. Mardh, P. E. Sparling, and P. J. Wiesner, eds. New York: McGraw-Hill, 109–115.

Darrow, W. W., D. A. Deppe, C. A. Schable, S. C. Hadler, S. A. Larsen, et al. 1990. Prostitution, intravenous drug use, and HIV-1 infection in the United States. In *AIDS, Drugs, and Prostitution,* M. A. Plant, ed. London and New York: Routledge, 18–41.

Gellert, G. A., R. M. Maxwell, K. V. Higgins, T. Pendergast, and N. Wilker. 1993. HIV infection in the women's jail, Orange County, California, 1985 through 1991. *American Journal of Public Health* 83: 1454–56.

Kanouse, D. K., N. Duan, S. H. Berry, S. Carson, and J. Lever. (under editorial review). Drawing a probability sample of female street prostitutes in Los Angeles County.

Khabbaz, R. F., W. W. Darrow, T. M. Hartley, J. Witte, J. B. Cohen, et al. 1990. Seroprevalence and risk factors for HTLV-1/II infection among female prostitutes in the United States. *Journal of the American Medical Association* 263: 60–64.

Miller, H. G., C. F. Turner, and L. E. Moses. 1990. *AIDS: The second decade.* Washington, D.C.: National Academy Press.

Tabet, S. R., D. L. Palmer, W. H. Wiese, R. E. Voorhees, and D. R. Pathak. 1992. Seroprevalence of HIV-1 and hepatitis B and C in prostitutes in Albuquerque, New Mexico. *American Journal of Public Health* 82: 1151–54.

# 8

# AGENCIES AND THEIR PROGRAMS

## Introduction

Sex workers have numerous problems that are not necessarily unique to their occupation: health problems, child care problems, lack of education, even self-image problems. Is it possible to help them and yet not condemn, try to convert, or arrest them? Many groups have tried and many have failed for one reason or another, but the agencies discussed in this section have had some success. Sarah Crosby details her experiences in England with the Manchester Action on Street Health group. Kimberly-Anne Ford from Montreal, Canada, emphasizes the importance of examining prostitution as a human service occupation. Lisa Anne Moore from San Francisco looks at ways to communicate more effectively with sex workers, while Shane A. Petzer and Gordon M. Isaacs examine a South African program, SWEAT (The Sex Worker Education and Advocacy Taskforce), with which they have been associated. Quite clearly dealing with the problems of the prostitute and sex worker is not easy.

# HEALTH CARE PROVISION FOR PROSTITUTE WOMEN: A HOLISTIC APPROACH

### SARAH CROSBY

This chapter will describe the approach adopted by Manchester Action on Street Health (MASH), a nongovernment organization providing an innovative sexual-health service for street prostitutes in the city of Manchester in northwest England.

Although MASH provides a service for both female and male street prostitutes and has recently begun operating a satellite service for women working in saunas and massage parlors, this paper will focus primarily on community-based responses to street working women prostitutes.

The chapter will provide a brief overview of the street prostitution scene in Manchester and go on to examine the wider social context in which street prostitution exists in the United Kingdom's major urban centers. This paper will also highlight the impact of drug use on this particular prostitution scene and discuss some of the implications that patterns of drug use have for service provision for female prostitutes.

The remainder of the paper will focus on the work of Manchester Action on Street Health—a fully integrated harm-reduction service for prostitutes. It will be argued that a holistic approach offering a range of facilities is the most effective means of addressing the health care needs of this client group. The paper will focus on MASH to illustrate how such a multidisciplinary approach can be developed without compromising service accessibility to a traditionally "hard-to-reach" group of prostitutes and will discuss the cooperation between major health trusts and MASH that has facilitated the development of a multidisciplinary service.

# Overview of Street Prostitution in Manchester

## Prostitution Scene in Manchester

Manchester, a major city in the northwest of England, is a diverse and cosmopolitan city with a population of approximately 432,640, although the surrounding conurbation of Greater Manchester has a population of around 3 million. In common with many other British cities, Manchester has a long-established and well-developed sex industry which comprises both "street" and "indoor" prostitution. In terms of overall numbers, approximately 300 women regularly work across the various "red-light" districts in Greater Manchester. In the United Kingdom we can identify a fairly rigid hierarchy among women involved in different forms of prostitution with little movement between the various strata. The city center is the main "beat" in Manchester and this area is unusual in the United Kingdom in that both women and men prostitutes work in the same vicinity. In recent years this area, also known as the "Gay Village," has also been the focal point for considerable public and private investment with numerous cafe bars, clubs, and restaurants emerging.

## Reasons for Prostitution

Poverty is a major factor that brings significant proportion of women into involvement in street prostitution within the United Kingdom. Research among prostitute women in Manchester (Faugier et al. 1992) found that most of the women resorted to prostitution out of despair and against a backdrop of a lack of alternative employment opportunities and social deprivation. Those women involved in prostitution were often single parents, living in poor-quality, rented accommodation and a significant number of them had been in the care of the local authority (Faugier et al. 1992; Faugier and Sargeant 1996). Within this context there are increasing numbers of young girls working as prostitutes. Recent changes to the benefit system mean that young people who leave home or have come out of local authority care do not have access to statutory benefits, and many end up "on the streets" with no legitimate means of income (Lee and O'Brien 1995). Recent government statistics show that the number of girls under 16 who have been cautioned for soliciting more than doubled between 1990 and 1995 (Thompson 1995). Statistics from a recent survey of 50 MASH clients showed that over half (57.1 percent) of the women had started work as a prostitute before the age of 20 (Crosby 1997).

## Composition of Client Group

The MASH client group mainly comprises prostitute women (80 percent), of whom approximately 78 percent are drug users. A further 15 percent of the client group are male partners of the women, generally also drug injectors, who access the MASH needle-exchange scheme. The remaining 5 percent of the client group comprises men and boys working as "rent-boys."

## Drug Use

These women's involvement in prostitution cannot be examined without reference to their drug use. Research confirms that women who work as street prostitutes are more likely to use drugs than those in off-street locations (McKeganey and Barnard 1992; Philpot, Harcourt, and Edwards 1989). Research also highlights that drug-using women work more frequently and for longer hours than their non-drug-using counterparts (McKeganey and Barnard 1992). The experience of MASH would support this evidence. As highlighted previously, over 78 percent of the female prostitutes MASH has contact with are injecting drug users and this is comparable to statistics for drug use among street-working prostitutes in other large cities in the United Kingdom, notably Glasgow (Carr et al. 1996).

Most of the women are working to support their drug habit, usually costing between £100–£300 per day. In the survey referred to previously, nearly 30 percent (29.7 percent) needed more than £500 a week to fund their drug use (Crosby 1997). Although the level and type of drug use can vary, it can generally be characterized as poly-drug use. Heroin is usually the primary drug of use with high levels of alcohol use and increasing levels of crack cocaine. A recent study of crack users in Manchester found that 64 percent of women in the sample were using prostitution to finance their crack use, despite having no history of prostitution prior to the commencement of their crack use (Bottomley, Smith, and Wibberley 1995). What is also apparent is that prostitution can often lead to a rapid escalation in drug use that, in turn, can necessitate a woman working longer hours and more frequently in order to make sufficient money to fund her habit. It has been highlighted that many street prostitutes have partners who are also drug users. In Manchester, over two-thirds (67.7 percent) of prostitute women who had a sexual partner stated that the partner was also a drug user, and it was apparent that their sex work income often finances both "habits" (Crosby 1997).

# The MASH Service

MASH was established in 1991 at a time when there was considerable public concern about HIV and AIDS with a number of alarmist media reports focusing on prostitutes, branding them "a reservoir of infection for HIV."[1] Using the opportunity to counteract this type of sensationalist media reporting, and taking care not to further stigmatize an already marginalized group, MASH aimed to provide a targeted service to a section of the population who, as a consequence of their sexual activity and drug-using behavior, were at potentially increased risk of HIV infection. Although MASH, like a number of other outreach-style projects for sex workers across the United Kingdom, was established under the auspices of HIV prevention, the service has expanded over the years to adopt a more holistic model of health care. The MASH service operates three evenings a week (Tuesday, Wednesday, and Thursday 8:30 P.M.–1:00 A.M.) from a purpose-built trailer that is located in the city's main "red-light" beat. The nighttime outreach service is staffed by a fulltime outreach worker and a team comprising a combination of unpaid volunteers and staff seconded from a range of relevant statutory services. The specific services offered includes:

- Harm reduction advice and information
- Condoms, lubricants, and spermicidal creams
- Needle exchange
- Nursing input for minor injuries treatment, first aid, and health advice
- Primary health care, including genito-urinary medicine [GUM] service
- Input from a specialist drug liaison midwife
- Input from specialist drug workers, including on-site assessments for drug treatment
- A male sexual health service for male prostitutes and the male partners of female prostitutes
- Referrals to appropriate agencies and organizations
- Staff who can undertake an advocacy role on behalf of clients
- Somewhere to have a break from work

# Outreach as a Model of Practice

Since the late 1980s, "outreach" has been used extensively as a method to make contact with "hard-to-reach" groups, most notably drug users and prostitutes (Casey et al. 1995). Outreach was recognized as a key component of strategies to improve the health of prostitutes and drug users and to reduce the risk of HIV transmission (ACMD 1993). However, within this general framework a variety of interventions have been employed, some with a greater degree of success than others. The particular approach that an agency may employ depends on a number of factors, including the local character of prostitution, geographical location, the level of resources available, local policing policy in relation to prostitution, and the avenues that exist for interagency collaboration.

The work of MASH can be defined as "detached outreach." In contrast to many statutory health services that are building-based and available during "office hours," MASH seeks to make contact with its potential client group at a geographical location and at a time that is convenient to them. Since its inception, MASH has operated late at night in the center of the "red-light" district and, in this respect, service delivery is clearly compatible with the lifestyle of the client group it seeks to attract, namely, chaotic, poly-drug-using prostitute women. Female and male prostitutes and drug users are able to use all aspects of the service on a walk-in, no-appointment basis. MASH offers a full range of services and equipment that are made available at a "one-stop" facility, without any of the perceived barriers sometimes inherent to statutory health care services.

# Holistic Health Care Service

Studies clearly show that women sex workers, and particularly those women using drugs, experience high rates of infection from sexually transmitted diseases (STDs) and face an increased risk of HIV infection (Plant 1990; McKegany and Barnard 1992; Darrow 1984). However, evidence from some of the most notable research (Faugier et al. 1992) also underlines that drug-using women prostitutes often have a range of other significant health care problems, which may typically include:

- Drug-related infections, e.g., hepatitis B and C and septicemia.
- In relation to drug use, a major health risk is drug overdosing.
- Abscesses, thrombosed veins, skin infections (through poor injecting technique).
- Amenorrhoea.
- Multiple unplanned pregnancies.
- Malnutrition and poor dental hygiene.
- Chest and skin infections, tuberculosis.
- Injuries from physical/sexual violence.

However, these multiple health care needs can sometimes be overlooked by health professionals focusing largely on STDs and, in particular, HIV. For the majority of street-working women, sexual and general health matters are a low priority. Issues relating to violence associated with their work, child care difficulties, housing, and financial problems are of far more pressing and immediate concern (Hartnoll and Power 1989; Jacquet 1992; Cameron et al. 1993; Synn-Stern 1992).

What is also apparent is that among drug-using street prostitutes there seems to be a much greater acceptance of poor health, injury, and harm—which are more often than not regarded as "part and parcel" of their lives. In this context it is not uncommon for health problems to be ignored until the situation has reached crisis point.

The Manchester Action on Street Health has attempted to address this problem by providing a range of health services that are more attractive and accessible to a group who have traditionally had little or no contact with mainstream health provision. As Reid (1995) states, the "social marginalization" of prostitutes is a key factor influencing their low take-up of health care services. Other reasons why prostitute women are failing to access mainstream health services include:

- Fear of admitting to illicit drug use
- Chaotic lifestyles of these women
- Lack of knowledge of services that are available
- Fear of losing care and custody of their children
- Inadequate confidentiality, the length of time spent waiting
- Perception of a hostile and dismissive attitude from health personnel
  (Casey et al. 1995; Faugier and Cranfield 1993)

The holistic health care service MASH provides is purposely delivered within a nonmedicalized context. The nonjudgmental and informal environment generated at MASH contrasts sharply with many of the clients' experience of statutory services. The service MASH has developed is culturally attuned to the lifestyle of its client group, but one that also recognizes the diversity of this client group in terms of race, gender, and sexuality.

Therefore, a project that was originally started in response to an immediate need in terms of HIV prevention has expanded to meet the multifaceted health care needs of its client group. These examples illustrate the way in which the MASH service has evolved over the last six years in response to these identified needs:

1. Men at MASH is a new element of the core MASH service targeted to respond to the sexual and wider health needs of prostitute men and the male partners of prostitute women. There is an increasing recognition that interventions to respond to the sexual health needs of prostitute women are inherently limited if they fail to correspondingly address those same

needs of the women's sexual partners. This is not intended to demonize the partners of female prostitutes, but to further "normalize" and "popularize" safer sex practices and harm reduction techniques. Evidence from both North America and Europe suggests that prostitutes may be *more* at risk of HIV infection within the context of their private sexual lives than in terms of their work as prostitutes (Day 1988; Grates et al. 1994; Rosenberg and Weiner 1988; Ward et al. 1993). There are numerous and complex reasons for the low levels of condom use among female prostitutes in their private sexual relationships (Jackson and Highcrest 1996). Although there are no simplistic remedies to this problem, it is apparent that MASH is better placed than many statutory agencies to address these sorts of sensitive and problematic issues because of the established levels of contact and trust it often has with both female prostitutes and their partners.

2. As highlighted earlier, prostitute women using MASH often have a range of general health care concerns, such as respiratory infections, asthma, and skin infections, and are not generally in contact with mainstream health services. The general practitioner–led primary health care sessions have been developed out of this recognized need for a broader health care that is easily accessible on a no-appointment basis. Since this service has been operating, it is not uncommon for clients to present to the doctor with one particular medical complaint and then, during the course of the consultation and after having established a level of trust, raise other health problems which might otherwise have remained neglected. As highlighted earlier, this pattern is symptomatic of the general lack of contact that the client group has with mainstream health services.

3. Although research points to high levels of condoms use among prostitute women in relation to commercial sexual activities, it also highlights substantial condom failure in this context. As previously highlighted, there is a low level of condom use among prostitutes in their private sexual relationships, and furthermore, the use of other forms of contraception is also low (McCullagh 1996; Faugier 1996). The evidence, therefore, suggests the importance of encouraging the use of additional forms of family planning. In recognition of this, MASH has made available and actively promoted a range of contraception (including emergency contraception) as part of its broader primary health service. Furthermore, in the experience of MASH, it is not uncommon for some prostitute women who become pregnant to have a passive approach to their pregnancy and significant numbers of the women do not access ante-natal services. A specialist drug liaison midwife has therefore been appointed on secondment from a local statutory service to work with female clients using MASH. The midwife can provide pregnancy testing, emergency contraception, referrals for terminations, basic ante-natal check-ups, and ongoing followup and support.

These examples are intended to highlight how MASH has attempted to introduce new initiatives into its core service without losing sight of its basic principles or its low-threshold approach. The model that has emerged is one that could best be described as a "multi-tier" service. Manchester Action on Street Health is able to offer interventions at a variety of levels dependent upon the needs of the individual. The various aspects of the service provide and require a different level of intensity and can range from the provision of condoms and safer sex advice through to a medical consultation and followup appointments. An individual can make contact with MASH anonymously and without prior appointment at any of these stages of service delivery.

# Collaborative Approaches

During the course of its development MASH has been aware that any targeted provision for prostitutes can potentially have the effect of further perpetuating the marginalization and alienation faced by this particular group. As Faugier and Sargeant state, this may occur when specialist projects, such as MASH, have the effect of *"reassuring mainstream health care workers that the problems posed by prostitution are now effectively taken care of"* (1996, 14). The MASH organization has therefore proactively forged links with statutory health providers in an attempt to prevent them from abdicating their responsibilities in relation to prostitutes. In contrast to an isolationist approach that can potentially reinforce barriers between the two sectors, MASH encourages its clients to use mainstream provision, in particular hospitals, general practitioners, and community drug clinics. However, recognizing the practical and other limitations that may prevent women from using statutory provision, MASH has negotiated with various National Health Service (NHS) trusts to have mainstream medical and related staff seconded to work on the street-based outreach project. In addition to nursing and medical staff, this principle also extends to mainstream staff from drug agencies and a specialist drug liaison midwife from the local maternity hospital. Such a multidisciplinary and multisector approach provides users of the service with a range of skills and expertise, encouraging a broad approach to health care provision.

These secondments represent a mutually beneficial and cost-effective means of providing high-quality specialist staff to ensure a more comprehensive health care service. From the perspective of health service managers, these secondments offer a valuable opportunity for their staff to work in an environment with which their formal employment would not normally bring them into contact. These secondments also mean that statutory providers have a major role to play in MASH and have a stake in ensuring the service continues to develop successfully. Furthermore, they see the value of these collaborative approaches in bringing direct and cost-effective health care benefits to a vulnerable section of the population.

## Conclusion

Although this particular model of working has proved highly successful for MASH, it is important to recognize the importance of the local social and political context that created the environment for the project's inception and continued development.

As mentioned earlier, prostitution is historically well established in particular areas of the city of Manchester. However, the last decade has witnessed a period of considerable urban regeneration in parts of Manchester with previously derelict industrial areas being developed into new business and residential complexes. The local authority (the institution of local government that, in this case, is Manchester City Council) is keen to attract economic investment into the city, which is actively being promoted as a "twenty-four hour" entertainment center of international significance. Therefore, the local authority, under pressure from a variety of sources, including businesses, residents, and the police, are keen to discourage street prostitution from these newly developing business and residential areas. Like other local authorities in cities across the United Kingdom, Manchester City Council has become more involved in both the regulation of prostitution and in generating preventative strategies, such as the introduction of traffic management schemes to disrupt the street prostitution trade by breaking kerb-crawlers' "circuits."

However, Manchester City Council also recognizes that prostitute women, as a marginalized group of the community, have unmet needs. In particular, the council acknowledges its responsibilities to these women in respect of community safety and public health. Accordingly MASH has been fortunate that the local authority has been supportive of the project since its inception, and they are clearly attempting to find a solution to these conflicting pressures that will not be detrimental to prostitute women's health and safety.

Other agencies have shown a similarly supportive attitude toward the work of MASH. In particular, the local and regional health authorities have recognized the value of primary health care interventions for people, such as prostitutes, who may not be accessing any other health provision. Similar collaboration has also been possible with the police who, at a national level, are primarily concerned with the regulation and control of prostitution, not its elimination. They are more interested in those criminal activities occurring on the periphery of the prostitution scene, i.e., robbery and drug dealing. Accordingly, in Manchester, the police are much less likely to arrest prostitutes in certain areas of the city, and within this framework MASH has been able to build up a good relationship with the police at all levels of the hierarchy. The police will refer women they have cautioned or arrested to MASH, and we have worked closely with them in encouraging women who have suffered sexual or violent assault to report the incident formally to an appropriate agency.

For policymakers it is clearly difficult to balance the concerns of the different groups involved. The pressure on local authorities to respond to the demands of local residents and/or businesses could mean that they solely enforce measures in relation to prostitution, while ignoring the needs of prostitute women themselves. However, if local authorities and other agencies are serious about addressing the problems and issues surrounding prostitution, *"their starting point has to be practical rather than moralistic"* and they need to recognize that a pragmatic strategy can result in very real benefits for both prostitute women and the surrounding community (Campbell et al. 1996, 6). The need to establish forms of interagency cooperation appropriate to the local situation is essential, and such collaboration must recognize that the problems involved require not just a coercive approach, but a wider and flexible response (Benson and Matthews 1996), and ultimately one ". . . *which considers the interests of all groups and doesn't simply replicate the social marginalization of prostitutes"* (Campbell et al. 1996).

# Note

1. *The Sunday Times,* London, 21 June 1987; *Daily Record,* Glasgow, 16 March 1988; *The Times,* London, 18 March 1988.

# References

Advisory Council on the Misuse of Drugs (ACMD). 1993. *AIDS and Drug Misuse Update.* HMSO, London.

Benson, C., and R. Matthews. 1996. *Report of the Parliamentary Group on Prostitution.* Middlesex University, Middlesex.

Bottomley, Smith, and Wibberley. 1995. Not so cracked: Peer education among crack users. *Druglink* (May/June). London: ISDD.

Cameron, S., W. Peacock, and G. Trotter. 1993. Reaching out. *Nursing Times* 89 (7): 34–36.

Campbell, R., S. Coleman, and P. Torkington. 1996. *Street Prostitution in Inner City Liverpool.* Liverpool: Abercrombie Prostitution Project, Liverpool Hope University College.

Casey, M., S. Day, H. Ward, and A. Ziersch. 1995. *Sexual Health Services for Prostitutes in the UK.* London: EUROPAP UK.

Carr, S., D. J. Goldberg, L. Elliott, S. Green, C. Mackie, and L. Gruer. 1996. A primary health care service for Glasgow street sex workers—6 years experience of the "Drop-in Centre," 1989–1994. *AIDS Care* 8 (4): 489–97.

Crosby, S. 1997. Unpublished M.Sc. diss., in progress.

Darrow, W. W. 1984. Prostitution and sexually transmitted diseases. In *Sexually Transmitted Diseases*, edited by K. K. Holmes et al. New York: McGraw Hill.

Day, S., H. Ward, and J. W. R. Harris. 1988. Prostitute women and public health. *British Medical Journal* 297: 1585.

Faugier, J. 1996. Prostitutes and unwanted pregnancies. Reducing Teenage Pregnancy Symposium: Translating Research into Practice, 8 November 1996, University of Central Lancashire, Preston.

Faugier, J., and M. Sargeant. 1996. Positive awareness: Health professionals response to child prostitution. In *Child Prostitution in Britain: Dilemmas & Practical Responses*, edited by D. Barrett. The Children's Society, Luton: University of Luton.

Faugier, J., and S. Cranfield. 1993. *Making the Connection: Health Care Needs of Drug Using Prostitutes*. Department of Nursing, Manchester: Manchester University.

Faugier J., C. Hayes, and C. A. Butterworth. 1992. *Drug Using Prostitutes, Their Health Care Needs, and Their Clients*. Department of Nursing, Manchester: University of Manchester.

Grates, S., S. Gedros, and C. Hankins. 1994. Factors mitigating against partner condom use among women sex workers visiting Montreal's needle exchange. *Canadian Journal of Infectious Diseases* 5 (D): 37D.

Hartnoll, R., and R. Power. 1989. Why most of Britain's drug users are not looking for help. *Druglink* 4 (2): 8–9.

Jackson, L., and A. Highcrest. 1996. Female prostitutes in North America: What are their risks of HIV infection? In *AIDS as a Gender Issue*, edited by L. Sherr, C. Hankins, and I. Bennet.

Jacquet, C. 1992. Help on the street. *Nursing Times* 88: 24–26.

Lee, M., and R. O'Brien. 1995. *The Game's Up: Redefining Child Prostitution*. London: The Children's Society.

McCullagh, J. 1996. Female prostitution in Merseyside, Reducing Teenage Pregnancy Symposium: Translating Research into Practice, 8 November 1996, Preston: University of Central Lancashire.

McKeganey, N., and M. Barnard. 1992. *AIDS, Drugs and Sexual Risk—Lives in the Balance*. Open University Press, Milton Keynes.

MASH. 1994. *Results from a Survey of 58 Service Users*. Internal Report, Manchester Action on Street Health, MASH.

Philpot, C. R., C. L. Harcourt, and J. M. Edwards. 1989. Drug use by prostitutes in Sydney. *British Journal of Addiction* 84: 499–505.

Plant, M. 1990. Sex work, alcohol, drugs and AIDS. In *AIDS, Drugs and Prostitution*, edited by M. Plant. London: Tavistock/Routledge.

Reid, T. 1995. A street-wise approach. *Nursing Times* 91 (33): 24–26.

Rosenberg, M., and J. Weiner. 1988. Prostitutes and AIDS: A health department priority? *American Journal of Public Health* 78 (4): 418–23.

Scrambler, G., and A. Scrambler. 1995. *Health issues for sex workers in London: Report produced for King Edward's Hospital Fund for London*. London: UCL Medical School.

Synn-Stern, L. 1992. Self-injecting education for street level sex workers. In *The Reduction of Drug-Related Harm,* edited by P. A. O'Hare et al. London: Tavistock/Routledge.

Thompson, A. 1995. Abuse by another name. *Community Care,* October 19–25: 16–18.

Ward, H., S. Day, J. Mezzone, L. Dunlop, C. Donnegan, S. Farrar, L. Whitaker, J. R. W. Harris, and D. L. Miller, 1993. Prostitution and the risk of HIV: Female prostitutes in London. *British Medical Journal* 307: 356–58.

# Evaluating Prostitution as a Human Service Occupation

### Kimberly-Anne Ford

## Why Compare Sex Work to Hospital Work?

> Certain services, or the use-values, resulting from certain forms of activity are
> embodied in commodities; others, on the contrary, leave no tangible result
> existing apart from the persons themselves who perform them; in other
> words, their result is not a vendible commodity. For example, the service a
> singer renders me satisfies my aesthetic need; but what I enjoy exists only in
> an activity inseparable from the singer himself, and as soon as his labor, the
> singing, is at an end, my enjoyment too is at an end. I enjoy the activity
> itself—its reverberation on my ear. (Marx 1867, 395)

Much has been written on what distinguishes prostitutes from other
human service workers; my research identifies the ways in which prostitution
is similar to other service occupations, more specifically to hospital work.
Marx described service work as "a form of activity embodied in a commodity."
From this definition of service work, the waitress who serves coffee, the nurse
who gives a vaccine, and the prostitute who provides sexual services are all
performing activities that we, the consumers, purchase as commodities. Prostitution is only rarely viewed from this perspective in academic literature.

Although it is often referred to as the world's oldest profession, few
researchers have taken the perspective of evaluating prostitution as work. Most
academic articles on prostitution focused on the deviant nature of the sex trade,
the feminist debate surrounding prostitution, the legal/criminal aspect of the
sex industry. Research I am doing in conjunction with Dr. Fran Shaver explores
these areas, as well as evaluating job satisfaction and job stress within sex work.

At a Toronto conference on sex work in 1985, it was reported that:

[sex] workers did not want others to speak authoritatively about their lives; they resented the assumptions that their work was necessarily demeaning and never freely chosen. Instead, they defended their right to be prostitutes, and the value, dignity and liberty of their work, which many of them take to be a profession. Prostitutes reject support that requires them to leave prostitution; they object to being treated as the symbols of oppression and demand recognition as workers. (Cited in Overall 1992, 705)

Prostitutes are beginning to demand respect as workers.[2] They wish to conduct their work in a safe environment, free from the stigma held against them by many people in their society.

The research project reported here compares sex workers to a matched sample of hospital aides and orderlies and evaluates similarities and differences in their working conditions. In many ways, sex work is similar to hospital work. For example, each type of worker must relate to the client or patient on an intimate level. Both workers have direct contact with the client/patients' physical body. They both experience similar occupational health hazards from spending numerous hours in a standing position.[3]

A satiric discussion on the similarities between sex workers and social workers (Appendix) was found on Carol Leigh's web page;[4] it provides an interesting social commentary that argues the same premise as this research project explores: namely, that sex work can be compared to other forms of human service work.

One important distinction between hospital work and sex work remains noteworthy: hospital workers are respected for what they do, while sex workers are stigmatized.[5] A comparison between the experiences of sex workers and hospital workers promotes the view of evaluating prostitution as a job and attempts to legitimize sex work as work. Furthermore, learning the "realities" of prostitution, from the viewpoint of the sex worker, increases our understanding of sex work. This is necessary when formulating prostitution policies. A broader understanding of the realities of sex work could alleviate some of the social stigma against sex workers.

To evaluate the similarities and differences in the working conditions of sex workers and hospital workers, I analyzed interview data in the summer of 1993 gathered by a Concordia University research team headed by Dr. Fran Shaver. The research team attempted to interview all sex workers working in particular geographical areas of Montreal, often referred to as "the main," through a snowball sampling technique. The sample of Montreal street prostitutes was then "matched" with a sample of hospital workers from Montreal's St-Luc Hospital. When possible, the matching of subjects was done on the basis of gender, marital status, number of years on the job, and time of shifts worked (evening versus day shifts). The total sample consists of 20 female sex workers and 26 male sex workers, paired with 20 female hospital workers and 26 male hospital workers.

# Moving beyond the Question of Choice

Feminist articles on prostitution usually emphasize sexual equality and free choice. For example, Jolin (1994) defines the "sexual equality first" faction of the feminist debate as "women who stress emancipation from male sexual oppression"; in this case the prostitute is viewed as a victim of male sexual domination. On the other hand, the "free choice first" group stress freedom of choice and views the prostitute as a worker (Jolin 1994, 75). Traditionally, opposing viewpoints are divided into those who view the prostitute as one who "chooses" or one who "is forced into" prostitution. When discussing major life decisions, it is often difficult to identify true choices because our decisions are often made within circumstances that we did not chose. Current discourse on prostitution has moved beyond the dichotomy of choice versus nonchoice. For example, Overall (1992) remarks that women might not "choose" to work in a canning factory, a restaurant, a supermarket, or in the cleaning industry (715–16).

## Exploring Pre-Work Circumstances

Moving beyond the discourse of choice, the circumstances surrounding the decision to enter into sex work versus those surrounding the decision to enter into hospital work were examined. It was found that female sex workers were most likely to have entered their line of service work after having run away from home, or for other (unspecified) reasons. Approximately half of all hospital workers of both genders, and male sex workers, identified "unemployment" as the main factor initiating the decision to begin their line of work. Table 1 shows the different reasons listed as motivations to begin working in each type of service work.

Regarding resources applicable to the job market, hospital workers and sex workers differed. For example, the majority of male and female sex workers have not completed high school, while all hospital workers have completed high school, and most have some college education or higher. A difference in the age at which each sample of workers began working in their respective jobs was also found: sex workers started their job around the age of 18, while hospital workers were, on average, 28 at the start of their job. Such a significant difference in age and educational attainment leads to the belief that prostitutes enter their line of work with fewer alternatives than do hospital workers, because they possess fewer marketable resources. Table 2 and Table 3 illustrate the different educational levels attained by workers, and different age at the start of each service occupation.

**Table 1. Various Motivations to Begin Each Line of Service Work**

| | Females | | Males | |
|---|---|---|---|---|
| | Prostitutes | Orderlies | Prostitutes | Orderlies |
| Ran Away from Home | 6 | 1 | 3 | 0 |
| Kicked Out of Home | 1 | 0 | 1 | 0 |
| Worked Elsewhere | 2 | 3 | 2 | 4 |
| Unemployed/Welfare | 5 | 10 | 10 | 13 |
| Left Abusive Home | 0 | 0 | 1 | 0 |
| Other | 6 | 6 | 6 | 6 |
| Total Frequencies | 20 | 20 | 23 | 23 |
| (Missing observations=6) | | | | |

## Deviant Beings, Deviant Industry

Many authors identify aspects of the sex trade that are deemed by them as "morally repugnant"(Pateman 1983; Shrage 1989; Overall 1992; Jolin 1994). For example, it is often argued that women become prostitutes as a continuation of a sexually deviant lifestyle (James and Davis 1982). Women who participate in the sex trade are commonly viewed as unchaste (Pheterson 1996). What is often described as morally disturbing about prostitution is that the women involved are selling their bodies. Pateman (1983) explains that "Sexual services and labor power are connected to the body, the body is connected to the sense of self. Hence, a prostitute sells herself" (563). Whether a sex worker sells himself or simply provides services can be debated extensively. However, if we adopt the view that all labor power that is connected to the body should be condemned, are we not thereby damning athletes, for example, for selling themselves? Sex workers employ many techniques to separate the services that they provide through their work from their own sexual sense of self. For example, Newmeyer (1995)[6] demonstrates how male sex workers can maintain a heterosexual identity despite the fact that they are hired to perform sex acts on men.

## Exploring the Deviance of Sex Workers

The data on personal relationships and sexual identity revealed similarities in the dispersion of sexual orientation among workers. Most females sampled stated that they were heterosexual, while a similar proportion of males in

### Table 2. Average Age in Years at the Start of Employment

|                   | Females | Males |
|-------------------|---------|-------|
| Sex Workers       | 18.5    | 17    |
| Hospital Workers  | 26.8    | 27.5  |
| Total Frequencies | 40      | 46    |

### Table 3. Educational Attainment of Service Workers Sampled

|                     | Females | | Males | |
|---------------------|------------|-----------|------------|-----------|
|                     | Prostitutes | Orderlies | Prostitute | Orderlies |
| <High School        | 12 | 0 | 21 | 0 |
| High School         | 6  | 6 | 4  | 7 |
| Some College        | 2  | 5 | 1  | 5 |
| College Complete    | 0  | 2 | 0  | 6 |
| Some University     | 0  | 3 | 0  | 2 |
| University Complete | 0  | 4 | 0  | 6 |
| Total Frequencies   | 20 | 20 | 26 | 26 |

both occupation groups responded that they were homosexual. A substantial proportion of male sex workers identify themselves as bisexual. The proportion of those involved in intimate personal relationships among both sample groups was similar. These findings call into question the common view that prostitutes are "sexually deviant" beings. Table 4 shows the dispersion of sexual orientation among both types of workers, and table 5 illustrates involvement in personal relationships.

Of the four subcategories of workers, findings indicate that male sex workers were most likely to consume a variety of all categories of drugs and alcohol on a regular basis. Female sex workers expressed a limited use of drugs; some (approximately 35 percent) admitted to using pot/hash at least once or twice per month, and only one female sex worker said that she used cocaine. Of all the hospital workers sampled, 11 percent of males admitted to using pot/hash. Drug and alcohol use is depicted in table 6 and table 7.

**Table 4. Sexual Orientation of Male and Female Service Workers Sampled**

|  | Females | | Males | |
|---|---|---|---|---|
|  | Prostitutes | Orderlies | Prostitutes | Orderlies |
| Heterosexual | 96% | 96% | 30.8% | 73.3% |
| Bisexual | 4% | 0 | 50% | 0 |
| Lesbian | 0 | 4% | 0 | 0 |
| Homosexual | 0 | 0 | 19.2% | 23.3% |
| Total Frequencies | 20 | 20 | 26 | 26 |

**Table 5. Involvement in Personal Relationships of Workers Sampled**

|  | Females | | Males | |
|---|---|---|---|---|
|  | Prostitutes | Orderlies | Prostitutes | Orderlies |
| Have a Boyfriend | 61.1% | 44.4% | 4.2% | 6.7% |
| Have a Girlfriend | 0 | 0 | 20.8% | 26% |
| Have Neither Boyfriend nor Girlfriend | 38.9% | 55.6% | 75% | 66.7% |
| Total Frequencies | 20 | 20 | 26 | 26 |

# Job Stress

## Symptoms of Stress

When subjects from each work setting were asked about their perceived stress level, there were no statistically significant differences found between the sex workers' and the hospital workers' responses; most respondents within both subject groups perceive their work as "somewhat stressful" and/or "not very stressful." In an effort to measure physical experiences of stress, an index of ten stress-related [SRI} physical symptoms, including back pain, upset stomach, cramps, headache, sore feet, shortness of breath, difficulty sleeping, diarrhea/constipation, fatigue/weakness, difficulty concentrating, was constructed. Interestingly, no difference was found between sex workers' and hospital workers' physical symptoms of stress; 70 percent of workers from each

**Table 6. Frequency of Alcohol Consumption
by Each Type of Worker Sampled**

|  | Females | | Males | |
|  | Prostitutes | Orderlies | Prostitutes | Orderlies |
|---|---|---|---|---|
| 1-2 times per month or less | 10 (50%) | 14 (70%) | 6 (23%) | 12 (46%) |
| 1 per week or more | 10 (50%) | 6 (30%) | 20 (77%) | 14 (54%) |
| Total Frequencies | 20 | 20 | 26 | 26 |

**Table7. Monthly Drug Use of Workers Sampled**

|  | Females | | Males | |
|  | Prostitutes | Orderlies | Prostitutes | Orderlies |
|---|---|---|---|---|
| Pot/Hash | 7 (35%) | 0 | 19 (73%) | 3 (11%) |
| Crack | 0 | 0 | 4 (15%) | 0 |
| Cocaine | 1 (5%) | 0 | 16 (62%) | 0 |
| Acid/LSD | 0 | 0 | 4 (15%) | 0 |
| Others | 0 | 0 | 3 (12%) | 0 |
| Total Frequencies | 20 | 20 | 26 | 26 |

subject group scored over 8 on the SRI index, indicating that the majority of both types of workers experience at least 8 of the ten stress symptoms more than once per month. This evidence suggests that the sex workers experience the same level of work-related stress as the hospital workers sampled.

## Experiences of Violence

Violence was found to be a stressful aspect of both types of service work under examination; however, the type of violence experienced in each work setting differed. Sexual violence was found to be more prominent in sex work: it was determined that sex workers were sexually harassed approximately ten times more per month than the hospital workers sampled. The data regarding sexual assault were negligible: only one female sex worker reported that she had been raped over the year prior to the interview. Occurrences of physical violence were higher in hospital work than in sex work: it was found that hos-

**Table 8. Average Number of Violent Experiences
per Month in Each Type of Work**

|  | Males | | Females | |
|---|---|---|---|---|
|  | Prostitutes | Orderlies | Prostitutes | Orderlies |
| Insults, Threats, Being Yelled at | 6.27 | 10.08 | 29.3 | 6.55 |
| Sexual Harassment | 4.88 | 0.50 | 6.90 | 0.55 |
| Physical Assault | 0.81 | 4.54 | 4.10 | 4.90 |
| Robbery | 1.35 | .08 | .25 | 0.10 |
| Sexual Assault | 0.39 | 0.00 | 0.15 | 0.00 |

pital workers were twice as likely to be physically assaulted by their patients than sex workers were by their clients. Table 8 shows the average number of violent experiences within each category of service work.

## Criminal Aspect of Sex Work

The criminal aspect of the sex trade has severe repercussions on the lives of sex workers. In Canada, the exchange of sexual services for money or other goods is not illegal; however, many of the activities surrounding sex work are: for example, keeping a "common bawdy-house," transporting a person to a bawdy house, procuring, living on the avails of prostitution, and communicating in a public place for the purpose of prostitution. These laws restrict the manner in which sex workers can conduct their business; they endanger the lives of sex workers,[7] and impinge upon their private lives.[7, 8] Because of the severe legal implications of operating a bawdy house and living on the avails of prostitution (pimping), many sex workers chose to work on the streets, alone. Often, they must service their customers in cars, because they cannot bring them anywhere that could be considered a bawdy house. The communicating laws limit the amount of negotiation time in which a sex worker can "deal" with a client. Hasty decisions to do dates in cars or other unsafe areas increase the danger to sex workers.[9] Thus, it is very difficult for Canadian sex workers to conduct their business safely and free from the risk of arrest.

Because the legal aspect is a circumstance that is particular to sex work, questions regarding criminal arrest were asked only of the sex workers in the sample. It was found that approximately 75 percent of sex workers interviewed had been arrested in the twelve months prior to the interview; for 60 percent of female and 40 percent of male sex workers, the charge against them was prostitution-related (communicating, soliciting). Moreover, the majority of sex workers (62.5 percent of females and 47.1 percent of males) cited "police harassment" as another dangerous or stressful aspect of their work. Hence, the threat of arrest and the criminal aspect of the trade are particularly stressful parts of sex work.

# Job Satisfaction

The Canadian advisory committee on the Status of Women (1984) states that "Prostitution is a commercial enterprise, and evidence strongly suggests that the women who engage in it do so primarily, and often exclusively for economic gain." (as cited in Overall 1992, 709). The economic subordination of women involved in sex work is often cited as a criticism against the sex trade. However, most workers in various work settings do so for economic reasons. "Money" was cited as the primary motive to begin working for the majority of hospital workers and sex workers alike.

When workers were asked what they like about their job, over 60 percent of sex workers surveyed strongly agree that their pay is good, compared to less then 10 percent of hospital workers. It was found that female sex workers earn higher income levels than other workers sampled; the majority of female sex workers sampled earn over $50,000 (Can$) per year. Personal income of workers is illustrated in table 9. Interestingly, female sex workers were also most likely to state that they have savings in the bank (73.1 percent of sex workers surveyed responded that they have savings, compared to 23.1 percent of male sex workers, 48 percent of female hospital orderlies, and 37.9 percent of male hospital workers). Of workers surveyed, female sex workers have on average $15,892 of savings in the bank. When one in four women live below the poverty line,[10] such as is in the current Canadian situation, prostitution, for women, may be a means to an end. As Catherine MacKinnon (1987) points out: "Aside from modeling, hooking is the only job for which women as a group are paid more then men" (24).

Personal control over working conditions is identified as a key element of satisfaction among human service workers.[11] Differences regarding the working conditions of hospital workers and sex workers indicate that in many ways, sex workers have more control over their work then do hospital workers. Sex workers are more likely to agree that they have freedom to decide how to work, and they have more freedom to refuse potential customers. Most of the sex workers interviewed (over 85 percent of males and females) have refused a potential date, compared to less than half of all hospital workers who have refused to care for a patient. Furthermore, the number of clients or patients

### Table 9. Yearly Personal Income of Workers Sampled

|  | Males | | Females | |
|---|---|---|---|---|
|  | Prostitutes | Orderlies | Prostitutes | Orderlies |
| Less than $15,000* | 3 | 1 | 0 | 4 |
| Between $15,000–$20,000 | 5 | 7 | 1 | 6 |
| Between $20,000–$50,000 | 9 | 17 | 4 | 10 |
| Over $50,000 | 9 | 0 | 15 | 0 |
| Total Frequencies | 26 | 25 | 20 | 20 |

*Note: Amounts are in Canadian dollars.

### Table 10. Average Number of Clients/Patients Refused in One Month

|  | Males | Females |
|---|---|---|
| Sex Workers | 5.65 | 23.00 |
| Hospital Workers | .81 | .30 |

refused is significantly different between sample groups: hospital workers had refused an average of one patient in the month prior to the interview, while male sex workers had refused an average of six dates, and female sex workers refused an average of twenty-two dates. The average number of clients/patients refused in the month prior to the interview is depicted in table 10. In regard to the issue of personal control, all hospital workers work for someone other than themselves, but the majority of sex workers (70 percent of females and 96 percent of males in the sample) are self-employed and thus have more freedom to decide how to conduct their work.

## Expressions of Work Dis/Affection

One might assume that sex workers enjoy a substantial amount of satisfaction from their work, due to the high level of personal control they have over their working conditions and greater levels of income. However, sex workers express more dissatisfaction with their work. When asked "How well do you like your work?" most prostitutes responded that they dislike their work or expressed neutral feelings of work affection (over 75 percent of male and female sex workers); most hospital workers replied that they like their work (70 percent). Half of all sex workers rate their work as important, compared to 70 percent of hospital workers who rate their work as important.

# Conclusions

This research project presents the work experiences of sex workers and hospital workers sampled in an effort to promote the recognition of sex workers as workers. It also argues the case that sex work can be compared to other, more legitimate forms of service work. Charles Taylor (1994), an important contemporary social theorist on identity formation and identity politics, spoke of the importance of recognition. To quote Taylor:

> The thesis is that our identity is partly shaped by recognition or its absence, often by the misrecognition of others, and so a person or group of people can suffer real damage or real distortion if the people or society around them mirror back to them a confining or demeaning or contemptible picture of themselves. Nonrecognition or misrecognition can inflict harm, can be a form of oppression, imprisoning someone in a false, distorted, and reduced mode of being. (25)

Taylor here explains the effects of the social stigma held against sex workers. Assuming that someone is sexually deviant, a drug addict, a victim, or morally unsound simply because of their occupation as a sex worker is a form of oppression; furthermore, it is often unfounded by their lived experiences.

This brings us full circle back to the reasons why research pertaining to the actual lived experience of prostitutes is needed. People in society have made value judgments about prostitutes without acknowledging the realities of those who work in the sex industry. Often these "myths" are perpetuated despite the fact that they may not be related to the actual situations of prostitutes. My study was conducted for the purpose of clearing up some of these myths, by presenting the experiences of street prostitutes in Montreal. More importantly, this study implies the necessity of further research into the lived experiences of those who work in the sex trade.

# Appendix

*The two resolutions below provide some interesting social commentary. The first is from the National Association of Social Workers (1994) regarding sex workers. The second is from the National Association of Sex Workers regarding social workers.*

## National Association of Social Workers' Resolution on Prostitution and Commercial Sex

• WHEREAS, The National Association of Social Workers (NASW) is dedicated to the concepts of self-determination, development of full potential, and highest possible quality of life for all people, as well as the elimination of coercion and violence towards others; and

• WHEREAS, Most individuals in prostitution are recruited before the age of 16 and often well under the age of 12; and

• WHEREAS, Persons in the prostitution industry and their patrons constitute a very high-risk group for HIV infection; and

• WHEREAS, Individuals in prostitution frequently have a background of family sexual abuse; and

• WHEREAS, Persons used in prostitution suffer a high rate of sexual dysfunction and disease; and

• WHEREAS, The rate of depression, anxiety disorder, dissociative disorder, suicide attempts, and suicide is very high among individuals in prostitution; and

• WHEREAS, Drugs and alcohol are commonly used to numb the physical, emotional, and psychological pain concomitant with prostitution; and

• WHEREAS, Those in prostitution are victimized by crime at an immensely higher rate than other population groups; and

• WHEREAS, The conditions that create and perpetuate prostitution, including poverty, racism, classism, homophobia, sexism, sexual abuse, bigotry, and despair, often force people into prostitution; and

• WHEREAS, The prostitution of women, children, and gay men is estimated to net traffickers at least $14 billion a year; therefore be it

• RESOLVED, That NASW develop a public policy statement on prostitution to be presented to the 1996 Delegate Assembly.

• RESOLVED, That, in developing the policy statement, NASW make full use of resources available in the organization.

## National Association of Sex Workers' Resolution on Social Workers

### Pathologizing Prostitutes: A Satire Response

- WHEREAS, The National Association of Sex Workers (NASW) is dedicated to the concepts of self-determination, development of full potential, and highest possible quality of life for all people, as well as the elimination of coercion and violence towards others; and

- WHEREAS, Most individuals in social work are recruited at a vulnerable time in their academic careers; and

- WHEREAS, Persons in the social work industry constitute a very high-risk group for pathologizing people and abusing their power with clients; and

- WHEREAS, Individuals in social work frequently have a background of mental, and sometimes physical, abuse; and

- WHEREAS, Persons used in social work suffer a high rate of sexual dysfunction and mental disorder; and

- WHEREAS, The rate of careerism, failed marriages, abusive personality disorder, abuse of children, self-righteousness, reductive reasoning, racism, sexism, classism and moralism-disguised-as-concern is very high among individuals in social work; and

- WHEREAS, Food, drugs, cigarettes and alcohol are commonly used to numb the physical, emotional, and psychological pain concomitant with social work; and

- WHEREAS, Those in social work are victimized by low salaries, and a classist, sexist and racist hierarchy that determines promotions, at an immensely higher rate than other population groups; and

- WHEREAS, The conditions that create and perpetuate social work, including poverty, racism, classism, homophobia, sexism, sexual abuse, bigotry, and despair, often force people into social work; and

- WHEREAS, Social work as practiced on women, children, and gay men is estimated to net middle class bureaucrats and their flunkies at least $14 billion a year; therefore, be it

- RESOLVED, That NASW develop a public policy statement on social workers to be presented to the 1996 Delegate Assembly.

- RESOLVED, That, in developing the policy statement, NASW make full use of resources available in the organization.

# Notes

1. I'd like to thank Dr. Fran Shaver for agreeing to supervise this project. Many of the ideas developed in this research report were inspired by discussions with Dr. Shaver. The interview data examined was gathered by a Concordia University research team headed by Dr. Shaver in Montreal 1993. For a detailed description of the research program, see Shaver 1992 SSHRC, 1992B *Sex Work As Service Work: Program Integration.*

2. This was evident at the 1996 Montreal conference on sex work "When Sex Works" in which a number of sex workers spoke about prostitution and gave their opinions on the sex trade.

3. For a complete view of occupational health and safety issues of sex workers, see Shaver (1997).

4. The National Association of Sex Workers' Resolution on Social Workers (1995), taken from Carol Leigh (The Scarlet Harlot's) web page.

5. For a discussion on the "whore stigma," please see Pheterson (1996).

6. Presented at the 1995 Montreal Inter-University Sociology Colloquia.

7. For a complete discussion on prostitution laws in Canada, see Lowman (1995), chap. 10.

8. For a cross-cultural discussion on repercussions of the legal system on the lives of sex workers, see Pheterson (1996).

9. These ideas were expressed by Dr. John Lowman (a criminologist from U.B.C.—University of British Columbia) and Kara Gillis (a member of CORP—Canadian Organization on the Rights of Prostitutes—and a Toronto sex worker) in a panel on legal reform in Canada, at a Montreal international conference on prostitution "When Sex Works," 1996.

10. Synnott (1996).

11. See Brauss (1992) and Orpen (1994).

# References

Brauss, P. 1992. What workers want. *American Demographics* 14: 135–41.

Canadian Criminal Code. 1985. *Revised Statutes* (1985): C-46–C-54.

Ericsson, L. O. 1980. Charges against prostitution: An attempt at a philosophical assessment. *Ethics* 90 (3): 335–66.

James, J., and N. Davis. 1982. Contingencies in female sexual role deviance: The case of prostitution. *Human Organization* 41 (winter): 345–49.

Jolin, A. 1994. On the backs of working prostitutes: Feminist theory and prostitution policy. *Crime and Delinquency* 40 (1): 69–83.

Lowman, J. 1995. Prostitution in Canada. *Canadian Criminology*. N.p.: Harcourt, Brace Canada.

MacKinnon, C. 1987. *Feminism Unmodified: Discourses on Life and Law.* Cambridge: Harvard University Press.

Marx, K. 1867; reprint 1977. The economics. *Karl Marx Selected Writings,* edited by David McLellan. N.p.: Oxford University Press.

Newmeyer, T. 1995. Maintaining masculinity and heterosexuality: Identity management and the male prostitute. *Les Actes Du Colloque,* University Laval.

Orpen, C. 1994. Interactive effects of work motivation and personal control on employee job performance and job satisfaction. *Journal of Social Psychology* 134: 855–56.

Overall, C. 1992. What's wrong with prostitution? Evaluating sex work. *Signs* 17 (4): 705–24.

Pateman, C. 1983. Defending prostitution: Charges against Ericsson. *Ethics* 93: 561–65.

Pheterson, G. 1996. *The Prostitution Prism.* N.p.: Amsterdam University Press.

Shaver, F. M. 1997. "Occupational Health and Safety on the Dark Side of the Service Industry: Findings and Policy Implications." Paper presented at the International Conference on Prostitution: An Interface of Cultural, Legal and Social Issues, Van Nuys, California, March, 1997.

Shrage, L. 1989. Should feminists oppose prostitution? *Ethics* 99 (Jan.): 347–61.

Synnott, A. 1996. *Social Problems.*

Taylor, C. 1994. The politics of recognition. In *Multiculturalism,* edited by Amy Gutmann. Princeton, N.J.: Princeton University Press.

# THE VARIABILITY OF SAFER SEX MESSAGES: WHAT DO THE CENTERS FOR DISEASE CONTROL, SEX MANUALS, AND SEX WORKERS DO WHEN THEY PRODUCE SAFER SEX?

LISA JEAN MOORE

## The Slippery Slope of Risk Reduction and Safer Sex

After more than a decade of analyzing the multiple facets of AIDS, many scholars have critically examined the various forces that socially construct our perceptions of the AIDS epidemic (Abramson 1992; Aggleton 1993; Altman 1993; Berridge 1992; Juengst and Koenig 1989; Watney 1994). Primarily concerned with how knowledge about AIDS is produced and represented to audiences, Treichler (1988, 229) implores researchers to interrogate the sites that produce "facts" about AIDS:

> How and why is knowledge about AIDS being produced in the way that it is? Who is contributing to the process of knowledge production? To whom and by whom is this knowledge disseminated? What are the practical and material consequences of any new interpretation? Who benefits? Who loses? On what grounds are facts and truth being claimed?

With these insightful sociological guidelines in mind, in this essay I examine production of knowledge about safer sex prevention practices dispensed by the Centers for Disease Control's (CDC) public service announcements, sex manuals, and sex workers. I explore the production, dissemination, and consequences of safer sex messages. This essay illustrates and interprets some of the contested meanings of safer sex as represented within these different sites.

In order to flesh out a more sophisticated understanding of representations and knowledges about safer sex, I discuss three sites of production. First,

I situate and critically interpret some of the Centers for Disease Control's safer sex AIDS/HIV prevention materials. Second, I analyze sex manuals published in the past decade, exposing the stakes of each manual and interpreting how they represent, and thus construct, safer sex. I use the methods of content and discourse analysis to analyze data produced by the first two sites. Third, based on my interviews with sex workers, I explore their descriptions of actual practices with varying degrees of safety. My purpose is both to demonstrate the range of variation in definitions of safer sex and to show how safer sex is more than a mere list of practices. Safer sex discourse and practices are situated within broader, sometimes unacknowledged, agendas of the authors, individuals, or communities that create them.

Researching safer sex as a cultural artifact and a discourse enables the use of certain social theories of discourse, particularly the work of Michel Foucault. Foucault, through his genealogical analyses,[1] examined the historical context from which knowledge emerges in order to ascertain what social conditions make knowledge possible. Foucault repudiates much of the Enlightenment thinking regarding the singular Truth of science and progress and alternately reflexively evaluates scientifically and legally constructed "truths." The video, printed manuals, and interview text (narratives) are mutually constitutive of safer sex and produce substantially different and similar discourses of safer sex. This production of discourse (or knowledge) is intimately linked to existing social relationships of power and existing strategies to create subjects or audiences in highly predetermined ways.

Before moving on, it is necessary to clarify differences among these groups. Although on a broad level the goals of each of these sites of safer sex representation are similar (to limit the rate of transmission of HIV and other STDs between sexual partners), the ideologies undergirding each of the group's strategies are quite different. For example, these sex workers, whether based on capitalistic business sense or political and moral conviction, share an ideology of sex as a positive, consensual, recreational activity. Crudely stated, the more successful they are at popularizing and eroticizing safer sex, the easier and more lucrative their jobs will be (Moore 1997a). In contrast, sex manuals have different ideological frameworks depending upon their intended audiences. Safer sex can either be an essay in a book, woven throughout the entire discussion, or occasionally mentioned as something worthy of concern. In even sharper contrast, the CDC, although acknowledging certain sexual activities of the American public, generally promotes a conservative message of abstinence, monogamy, or condom use. Of the three groups, the CDC is in the unique position of answering to an organized, institutional political hierarchy that periodically changes—the federal administration. To obtain funding from the federal government, the CDC must make messages palatable to the agenda of the elected party as well as the opposing party and the American public(s) in general (Silverman 1992).

Furthermore, the target audience of each of these three groups is different in composition and size. These different levels can be seen as on a continuum of global to local scope. However, knowledge produced about safer sex is assumed neither to trickle down nor to trickle up. Rather, there is traffic between and among all groups as they adopt and appropriate each other's knowledges for different purposes. Credit for these appropriations is often lopsided. Sex workers acknowledge the influence of the CDC and sex manuals. At least two of the sex manuals acknowledge the skillful safer sex practices of sex workers although most refer to the CDC. None of my data from the CDC cites the work of sex workers or sex manuals as being instrumental in constructing knowledge about safer sex. Although it is not uncommon for an institutional source to refuse crediting collaborated knowledge, it is noteworthy that the CDC does not discuss the diversity of sources creating the discourse of safer sex. By not acknowledging the safer sex experiences of sex workers and other sexual communities as crucial to current safer sex standards, the CDC creates knowledge from "nowhere" and does not legitimate the very critical work of actual sexual peoples.

Obviously, the CDC has much greater potential to reach out to the United States public(s) (Fraser 1989, 167). The use of television to air public service announcements (PSAs) and bulk mailings enable the CDC to contact large numbers of people. In contrast, because most sex manuals must be purchased, they have a readership limited by literacy, social class, accessibility, interest, geography, and so on. Finally, sex workers are perhaps the most limited source for the general population due in part to expense and illegality. However, the fact that their audience is in some sense a captive group leads to speculation about possibly high rates of successful education.

This essay investigates the production of safer sex by three types of authorities. Taking each site in turn, I sociologically interpret the meanings, strategies, and potential consequences of this production. This knowledge production process is not a one-way accomplishment. It is a dynamic process laden with unspoken agendas and unanticipated resistance. The CDC, sex manuals, and sex workers each construct themselves as representatives of safer sex. They transmit knowledge to particular groups of people. In addition to setting forth guidelines and advice about safer sex, in the consumption of these messages, audiences are also created. In their enactment of writing about and practicing safer sex, the producers make assumptions about their target audience's social class, including education level, sexual interests, and geographic locations by using linguistic registers (for example, words used can be medical terms or slang for body parts, i.e., penis or cock) and body techniques.

# The Centers for Disease Control

Born in 1947, the Communicable Disease Center was initially organized to fight malaria, which threatened training militias in the United States South. The organization changed its name to the Center for Disease Control in 1970 to "reflect responsibilities for noncommunicable disease problems" (MMWR 1992, 1). The growth of the CDC closely followed the prevalence of particular infectious conditions throughout the past five decades. The success of the agency in managing and containing these diseases, more or less, determines its stability and reputation. Etheridge's (1992) account suggests that the CDC had tremendous difficulties throughout the early 1980s in convincing government and health organizations like the Federal Drug Administration, blood banks, the Hemophilia Foundation, and the media to take AIDS seriously. Amid massive organizational denial, cuts in government funding through the Reagan administration, and social apathy regarding those infected with the condition, the CDC attempted to piece together the mysterious puzzle of AIDS in order to create a plan of action for containing the epidemic. Throughout the early 1980s, the CDC worked to establish the routes of transmission of HIV infection, including sexual activity with an infected person involving exchange of body fluids, blood, and semen—particularly anal, vaginal intercourse, blood transfusions with HIV-infected blood, sharing of intravenous needles with an infected person, and infected mother to fetus. The laudatory final sentences of Etheridge's (1992, 340) book indicate a belief in the tenacity of the CDC in such an adverse environment: "The action proposed by CDC during these years did not often find ready acceptance. By linking AIDS to a particular lifestyle, epidemiologists acted as a lightning rod for critics, but they also performed the task that historically has been theirs. They pointed out a means of prevention." In contrast, many others claim that the agency has not responded quickly, adequately, or forcefully enough since the beginning of the epidemic (e.g., Bull 1993). Don Francis (1992, 1447), a former retrovirologist with the CDC, has called the CDC's response to HIV "public health malpractice."[2]

Now called the Centers for Disease Control and Prevention, the CDC is in accordance with the Preventive Health Amendments of 1992 (MMWR 1992). Rosenberg and colleagues (1992) outline the major underlying assumptions of the CDC's prevention efforts. These include the belief that a knowledgeable and informed public is the necessary foundation to building a prevention program but is not sufficient to prevent the spread of HIV.[3] Changing behaviors requires more than mere information. One way to achieve a more consistent behavior change is to include community-based organizations as part of the prevention team, thus building trust between the social group and the prevention organization. The CDC has attempted to do this by funneling money to different players in the AIDS prevention game, including public health departments and community-based organizations.[4]

The history of CDC interventions specifically aimed at HIV/AIDS reveals a delayed reaction to distributing prevention materials to the American public. By most estimations, including the CDC's own, the epidemic hit in 1981 (Rosenberg et al. 1992). The first groups to respond were community and voluntary organizations in cities like San Francisco and New York. In 1984, the Centers for Disease Control became the foremost government producer and distributor of information about AIDS through the $10 million earmarked for AIDS education intervention. However, although the CDC was the premier governmental agency in prevention, education, and surveillance, it was not until June 1988 that an informational brochure developed through the efforts of twelve different focus groups with people from different genders, races and ethnicities, social classes, and sexualities was sent to 107 million homes in America. This document highlighted six areas: transmission, condom use, testing, casual contact, children, and blood supply. Although this publication, entitled *Understanding AIDS*, was widely distributed, it was estimated to be read by only half of those who received it (Silverman 1992).

# Public Service Announcements—Abstinence Makes the Heart (Consistently and Correctly) Grow Fonder

One wing of the 1990s CDC campaign for prevention is named "America Responds to AIDS" (ARTA). In this decade, official knowledge about safer sex and risk reduction is produced through ARTA. In October 1993, the CDC launched the Prevention Marketing Initiative (PMI) with the goal "to prevent the sexual transmission of HIV and other Sexually Transmitted Disease among young people 25 years old and younger" (Centers for Disease Control 1993). As part of this campaign, the CDC funded the development of twelve public service announcements, nine to be aired on network television and three on radio programs. While this is just one arena in which the CDC produces knowledge about safer sex, this campaign and its constituent segments represent the most explicit and "most direct" public discussion of safer sex[5] the CDC has engaged in to date. The constraints of time and political pressure,[6] in part, set the conditions under which these PSAs can be created. Additionally, even though the airing of PSAs is left up to the discretion of the local network programmers,[7] it is likely that these messages will reach populations more broadly than other published CDC information that must be requested. In other words, because of broad distribution to all network programmers, these messages about safer sex have the potential for wide public consumption (unlike knowledge developed by sex manuals and sex workers). According to the CDC's own promotional materials, these PSAs were tested both qualitatively and quantitatively. An 18–25-year-old audience equally distributed by gender and geographic location with particular sensitivity to African Americans, Hispanics, economically disadvantaged groups, and men who have sex with men viewed these segments and offered evaluations. These twelve messages have various titles including *Automatic, Turned Down, For a Free Brochure,* and *Peer Educator.*

There is an obvious two-pronged AIDS prevention approach in these PSAs: abstinence and condom use. The condom message, or mantra as it becomes after multiple viewings of these PSAs, always includes the need to use condoms *consistently* and *correctly.* These terms are not defined within the confines of 15-30 seconds. For example, these PSAs often end with "A latex condom, used consistently and correctly, prevents the spread of HIV, the virus that causes AIDS, and may save your life." The definitions of these words are, however, only included in the accompanying PMI materials that the CDC mails out in response to specific requests for the PMI:

> *Consistently* = "using a condom from start to finish with every act of intercourse."

> *Correct use* = Includes the need to use new condom each act, put condom on the erect penis before penetration, know how to put condom on, manage condom breakage, hold on to base of condom during withdrawal, use water-based lubes, store condoms in cool, dry place.

It is obviously problematic that these words are not defined as part of the PSAs. It is difficult to interpret what "consistently" and "correctly" mean, particularly if one already believes he or she is using a condom correctly. It is also important, although not surprising, to note that the PSA does not discuss what practices the latex condom must be used for: anal sex, oral sex, penis-vagina sex, and sex with sex toys; however it appears solely to assume penis-vagina intercourse. No other latex devices are mentioned. The absence of specificity of these two aspects of safer sex, practices and devices, is evident throughout these PSAs.

Taken together, what do these PSAs tell us about safer sex? The two options created by the CDC, condom use and abstinence, are constructed as mutually exclusive choices. Because each message focuses on only one option, safer sex choices are an either/or operation. Either you engage in sexual relations with a partner and use a latex condom consistently and correctly or you wait until it is the right time to have sex. These PSAs imply that individuals will intuitively know when it is "right" to have sexual relations. Moreover, at that point it does not appear to be necessary to use condoms.

Even though there are institutional sanctions against explicit discussions of sexuality, such as prohibitions against network programmers airing the PSAs, these CDC ads may make things more confusing for viewers.

# Sex Manuals: Beyond the Joy of Sex

For over a decade, sex manuals have incorporated safer sex advice and guidance to reduce the risk of sexually transmitted diseases, including AIDS. One important and to date unexamined source that provides knowledge about AIDS and safer sex practices are sex manuals. These manuals are recruitment books persuading particular readers to become practitioners of a particular constellation of activities. These sex manuals, as an interactive event, purport to offer certain individuals a means of self-education and thus construct an ideal reader or user.

The analysis that follows is based on my interpretation of eight manuals. I have examined sex manuals published within the past decade, 1985–1995. This time period was selected in order to give writers an adequate amount of time to tailor their discussion to include at least a cursory acknowledgment of safer sex practices. Selection of the manuals was based on the following criteria:[8]

- English language publication;
- Published within the 1985–1995 decade;
- Published with the specific intent to be a sex manual (books of erotica were excluded);
- Must be primarily concerned with activities that are penetrative (such as intercourse) and/or involve the exchange of bodily fluids (oral sex);
- Priced under $20.

## How to Get Under Our Skin

If we assume that most individuals who purchase and read sex manuals are looking for vital information about the transmission of HIV, then the knowledge produced about safer sex is consequential. An individual may turn to a sex manual to understand if a particular practice is risky or can be done in an alternate, "safer" way. This individual, however, gets much more from a sex manual than a list of risks associated with practices. Specifically, I explore three interrelated themes that emerged throughout my analysis of sex manuals: (1) the construction of safer sex as a right and a responsibility, (2) the construction of safer sex as a part of a regimen of disciplining the body or duty to be healthy, and (3) the use of safer sex as a platform to influence political consciousness.

## How to Get Under the Covers

**Sex Manual:** *Sapphistry: The Book of Lesbian Sexuality*
**Author—Author's Identification:** Pat Califia (1988/1993)—Writer, long-time community activist
**Intended Audience:** Lesbians
**Definition of Safer Sex:** Adopting methods that prevent any transmission of bodily fluids between you and sexual partners. Practices for performing safer sex include using rubber or vinyl gloves, using jar-contained water-based lubricants with latex devices, cleaning sex toys after each use, using dental dams for oral/genital or oral/anal contact, using condoms with spermicide for sex with men, and covering leather toys with latex.

**Sex Manual:** *Anal Pleasure and Health: A Guide for Men and Women*
**Author—Author's Identification:** Jack Morin (1981/1986)—Psychotherapist
**Intended Audience:** Anyone interested in practicing anal erotic activities
**Definition of Safer Sex:** Safe sex is "a source of freedom" (1986, 223). Safe sex is "Sexual activities that involve only skin-to-skin contact, without the exchange of any body fluids, making it virtually impossible for the AIDS virus to be transmitted" (1986, 223).

**Sex Manual:** *How to Persuade Your Lover to Use a Condom . . . and Why You Should*
**Author—Author's Identification:** Patti Breitman, Kim Knutson, and Paul Reed (1987)—A health editor, a psychologist, and a social anthropologist
**Intended Audience:** People who use condoms during sexual relations, especially recently divorced people, long-term single women, and gay men.
**Definition of Safer Sex:** Safe sex is "sex without risk of infection, sex that does not involve the exchange of bodily fluids. It is sex that is protected with condoms or sex that does not require condoms to be safe, such as massage, mutual masturbation, dry kissing (no tongues) caressing and fantasy" (1987, 40).

**Sex Manual:** *Making It: A Woman's Guide to Sex in the Age of AIDS*
**Author—Author's Identification:** Cindy Patton and Janis Kelly (1987)—Activists and policymakers
**Intended Audience:** Aimed at "women—heterosexual, bisexual, lesbian, rich, poor, single, married, of color or white" (1987, 5).
**Definition of Safer Sex:** "Safer sex is a new way of looking at our health. Safer sex starts with each one of us—individually and as part of a group effort—doing it, talking about it, trading advice with friends. Decisions about safer sex and drug use are not about doctors and tests; they are about each of us choosing to respect ourselves" (1987, 5).

**Sex Manual:** *The Complete Guide to Safer Sex*
**Author—Author's Identification:** Written by the senior faculty at the Institute for the Advanced Study of Human Sexuality (McIlvenna 1992)—Sexologists
**Intended Audience:** "Everyone." Both individuals and institutions: churches, schools, social service agencies, the military, the media, law enforcement personnel, the Justice Department.
**Definition of Safer Sex:** Safe sex is defined in the admonitions, "Do not exchange body fluids . . . don't share body fluids, and use barrier protection every time there is anal, vaginal or oral penetration in sex" (1992, 53–77). Embracing safer sex as a *new way of life* is reiterated throughout the manual.

**Sex Manual:** *Lesbians Talk (Safer) Sex*
**Author—Author's Identification:** Sue O'Sullivan and Pratibha Parmar (1992)—Self-help health educator and writer and a theorist, writer, and film-maker
**Intended Audience:** "Lesbians are not all women who have never had sex with men, or never will; who have never injected drugs, or never will; who have never been raped, or never will be; who had no blood transfusions before 1985; who had never self-inseminated with sperm from an untested donor. There is no single, pure definition of what a *real* lesbian is, let alone what real *lesbian* sex is" (1992, 11).
**Definition of Safer Sex:** "Safer sex is not about do's and don'ts. It is about much more than just latex. It is foremost about making our own informed decisions and assessing our own risks, taking into account all that is risky about sex. We know how to do these. We do this all the time about a myriad of sexual issues. Safer sex is about figuring out our own and our partners' histories, being honest with ourselves, and remembering that sometimes people lie to get sex. It is about making decisions about behaviors, and/or using latex barriers, based on knowledge. And safer sex is mostly talking. Practicing safer sex can push us to negotiate and communicate more clearly. It reminds us that we do have choices about our sexuality and that our sexuality is ours for our health and enjoyment" (1992, 32).

**Sex Manual:** *Safer Sex: The Guide to Gay Sex Safely*
**Author—Author's Identification:** Peter Tatchell (1994)—Author and gay activist
**Intended Audience:** Gay men. Men who have sex with men.
**Definition of Safer Sex:** Safer sex is "pro-sex. Real sex. Sexy sex. Raunchy without risk, it's about having sex in ways that are satisfying and safe . . . safer sex is simply a different, risk-free way of experiencing sexual pleasure. What safer sex involves is redirecting our sexual desire, not denying or diminishing it. To avoid the danger of HIV, we need to make some adjustments in our erotic techniques . . . safer sex is a sexual revolution . . . safer sex expands our

erotic horizons and spices our sexual experiences with new delights" (1994, 13–14).

**Sex Manual:** *The Good Vibrations Guide to Sex*
**Author—Author's Identification:** Cathy Winks and Anne Semans (1994)—Workers for 8 years at Good Vibrations, a 17-year-old "worker owned vibrator store" and an international "sex business"
**Intended Audience:** Everyone
**Definition of Safer Sex:** "Safer sex is the term used to describe sexual activities which do not involve the exchange of bodily fluids, the most common method of transmitting the AIDS virus" (1994, 216).

# Safer Sex as an Individual Right

First, if one were to read the eight manuals surveyed in this analysis, she or he would see safer sex illustrated in familiar metaphors. According to these manuals, safer sex can be conceptualized as a responsibility, a "source of freedom" (Morin 1981/1986), a health issue (Patton and Kelly 1987), "a birthright" (Winks and Semans 1994), a "sexual revolution" (Tatchell 1994), "an acquired taste" (Winks and Semans 1994), a communication system (O'Sullivan and Parmar 1992; McIlvenna 1992) and, most overwhelmingly, as an individual right. This liberal rights discourse arises directly from the manuals focus on a particular sexual identity or sexual variation. These are manuals that intend to reach a sexual minority group (lesbians, gay men) or a group of individuals who participate in a particular sexual practice that may be considered outside of the mainstream (s/m, anal sex). Sexual rights discourse establishes certain sexual activities as worthy of sexual exploration and potential sources of freedom from repression. In at least six of the manuals, there is a discussion of sexuality as a right. Granted the words *sexuality* and *right* can and do mean many different things within each manual. But for my purposes, within the manuals, "a right" is generally used to mean freedom to make sexual decisions and explore eroticism in a mutually consensual situation without interference from outside forces aimed at regulating behavior. Implicit in the rights discourse is an understanding of negotiating power relationships between people, like sexual partners, and larger social forces, like the state. In other words, in lesbian and gay sex manuals, sexuality that is nonheterosexual is established as a right even though certain repressive state apparatuses may condemn such behavior. It is within this framing of sexual identity as a right that rights concerning safer sex are also introduced.

In sex manuals, rights do not come without responsibilities. Or to paraphrase *How to Persuade Your Lover to Use a Condom* (Breitman et al. 1987), "good sex is your right" (3) "but it is not without responsibilities" (11). At the same time that a theme of a rights discourse operates in a majority of sex manuals' depictions of safer sex, two very different themes of responsibility emerge that seem to split the sample: manuals that encourage safer sex through an entire system of body discipline, and manuals that promote the development of political awareness through discussions of safer sex. In many ways, a rights discourse, with its component parts, personal empowerment and individual responsibility, lays necessary foundations for manuals to encourage personal responsibility.

# The Duty to Be Healthy

Sexually transmitted diseases and reproduction have already placed human sexuality within the realms of health and illness and medicine. There was a prior discourse about sexual health within which to situate safer sex and HIV concerns. Most sex manuals include a discussion of other sexually transmitted conditions including advice on how to manage transmission and how to recognize the symptoms. However, discussion of safer sex often takes the STD discussion a step farther. Within at least four of these manuals, safer sex is a component in the total overhaul of a current lifestyle questing for the perfect body. Here are two examples of safer sex discussions couched in a regimen of corporeal renovation. Both authors identify as health care providers.

From Jack Morin, psychotherapist:

> It is very important you do everything you can to maximize your health and, therefore, your capacity to fight disease. Give more attention than ever to your diet. Make sure you are getting adequate sleep. Consider ways of reducing all forms of stress. Find at least one form of relaxation that you enjoy and practice it every day. Take an honest look at your patterns of use for all drugs. Consider conducting this test: stop using all recreational drugs for two months. If you cannot do this, or you experience strong discomfort, this is a sign of dependence, or perhaps addiction. Seek professional help. . . . Think about your psychological health. . . . If you decide to make any health-promotion changes in your life, be patient with yourself. Over-zealous attempts to change too much, too quickly cause more stress. (1986, 225–26)

From the sexologists' group of the Institute for the Advanced Study of Human Sexuality:

> [U]se the AIDS crisis as the impetus to create an overall health improvement plan—a holistic approach to health, life and happiness. Defeat the AIDS epidemic by becoming healthier than ever before. There are many ways to

enhance our natural defenses against AIDS such as exercise, nutrition, stress
reduction and adequate sleep. (McIlvenna 1992, 50)

Of course, most would admit that having a healthy immune system and
feeling physically well would be a helpful defense mechanism for battling
potential sexual infections. However, aligning safer sex with health promotion discourse and personal empowerment/responsibility for health status
has particular consequences for how we view health, illness, and personal
accountability versus social preservation.

Health, in these accounts, is an individual, individualized, and individu-
alizing goal, a duty, an obligation, and a responsibility that can be achieved
through following recommendations of health promotion campaigns (Crawford 1985). Safer sex as part of a campaign is an integral part of body discipline; these campaigns are aimed at disciplining the body to refrain from particularly unsavory pastimes (such as drug abuse, unsafe sex) and to engage in
particularly virtuous activities (such as exercise, safer sex). Crawford (1985)
has noted, in rationalized, Western, industrialized societies, health is a balance between release and self-control. Health is an achievement of societal
expectations encouraging particular types of bodies to be manufactured for
contemporary capitalist cultures.[9]

Why is it of interest that safer sex manual writers are aligning their advice
with health promotion campaigns? In linking safer sex with entire regimens of
health achievement, these prevention messages establish yet another criterion
for determining health and wellness. They position safer sex as an entirely
individually motivated possibility, neglecting to recognize the social power
relations that may disable or severely impede an individual from achieving
health or safer sex. This assumption establishes a criterion from which to evaluate and separate those who are healthy, moral, and virtuous from those who
deserve what happens to them because they did not heed the warnings and
practice safer sex, get enough sleep, reduce stress, and eat correctly.

## Safer Sex as Political Discourse

On one hand, sex manuals present the reader with a call to transform the body
into a temple of "health" advocated by the psychotherapist and sexologist
authors. On the other hand, authors of manuals from groups traditionally
oppressed in society (lesbians, gays, and women) advocate different forms of
personal responsibility within/through their safer sex messages. The third
theme that emerged from sex manuals' representations of safer sex is the
linking of political messages to messages about safer sex. Within these manuals,
educating audiences about the dos and don'ts of safer sex is also an opportu-

nity to participate in consciousness raising. These examples range in their particular causes but use similar tropes to reach readers. Messages range from taking a stand against AIDS discrimination, engaging in public service for AIDS organizations and supporting the rights of a particular sexual orientation.

From Pat Califia, speaking to a lesbian audience:

> There is another disease that is every bit as dangerous as AIDS, and that is AIDS phobia. . . . The struggle against AIDS discrimination, demands for better treatment for people with AIDS, and obtaining funding for educating the public about AIDS prevention have to become part of the lesbian agenda. (1988, 185–86)

From Tatchell, speaking to gay and bisexual men:

> You can help change the world. Begin with your own life. Come out. Stand up for queer rights. Practice safer sex. Love people with AIDS. Support the lesbian and gay community. Encourage your friends to do likewise. Together, we can defeat AIDS and homophobia. (1994, 9)

This is but a mere sampling of the political messages expressed in the pages of these sex manuals. They all brim with political slogans aimed at expanding consciousness to considering safer sex in a broader societal context.

Although seemingly a noble gesture, this call to arms to unite all in a struggle of liberation also carries a political responsibility that can have pernicious side effects, similar to the effects of body discipline. In making safer sex part of community struggles, the responsibility of having safer sex and expressing certain political views changes the individual's accountability from the self to the social. With this overwhelming responsibility to an often-disenfranchised community, an individual's feelings and practices about safer sex take on added significance. This association of safer sex with "political correctness" may lead people to remain silent about the difficulties in maintaining safer sex and the possibilities of engaging in unsafe activities. As Odets (1995, 4, emphasis added), a psychotherapist working with gay men, states in his review of AIDS education efforts of community-based organizations:

> From the beginning, we have promoted safe sex as a moral responsibility for the gay man and treated any unsafe sex as *moral transgressions against the gay community*. Like the lie about community standards of behavior, the most profound effect of this moralizing has been to keep unprotected sex and feelings about it unconscious. Moral authority makes ambivalence or confusion about the issues or the occasional practice of unprotected sex a forbidden topic and prevents men from consciously thinking about their sexual feelings, desires and behaviors.

Society, as a whole, is implicated in both instances of safer sex being invoked as a responsibility. Within these manuals, individuals are simultaneously accountable on the microsociological level for their own health and on the macrosociological level for their communities and society more broadly. Ideally, in the cost-benefit analysis of practicing safer sex, sex manuals and public service announcements would like to encourage individuals to be risk managers. Self-surveillance would be the ultimate victory of these recruitment documents. Individuals would attain their sexual rights, conceptualize safer sex as a component of the quest for the healthy body, and organize their political priorities in recommended ways.

While I do not mean to suggest that being responsible for the self in sexual situations is a necessarily nefarious goal of these manuals, it is important to recognize the limits of individual responsibility. Given the access to the necessary resources (including education, tools, and information), it is legitimate to recommend that individuals be responsible for their actions. However, what appears to be occurring in many of these manuals is the linking of individual responsibilities of safer sex with multiple other responsibilities. There is an overwhelming encroachment on the individual to be attentive to the self, sexual partners, local communities, and the state. Are we creating neurotic individuals unsure of what safer sex actually really entails? It has become a monumental and complex series of messages and practices. Simultaneously we may be creating grounds to discriminate against people because they have not been responsible for themselves. In not acknowledging the *social* nature of the *production and access* to knowledge about safer sex, and thus suggesting it is equally within each individual's grasp to understand and adopt safer sex, individuals can be deemed noncompliant, problematic, and solely accountable for their health status. To summarize, sex manuals construct safer sex in dialogue with localized audiences. Safer sex is explicitly presented as an individual right, albeit for a diverse number of individuals. Manuals approach safer sex with more frankness and graphic discussion of sexual activities; readers can learn how to apply, use, store, and maintain latex devices. Many authors are also invested in agendas of political liberation for various groups of sexual minorities. In aligning safer sex with responsibilities to political goals or duties to be healthy and physically fit, safer sex becomes much more than abstaining from sex or using a condom consistently and correctly.

# Sex Workers[10]

## *Sexual Ambassadors*

> I mean absolutely prostitutes, like me, play a significant role in educating straight men about safe sex.—Angela, 28-year-old prostitute

I'm very angry about the fact that people keep talking about safe sex educators and safe sex control of the sex workers because we're not the problem, if anything we're one small population where there is a solution going on. There are a lot of people, doctors and health educators included, who don't have a clue and could learn a lot from us. That's true. And see when you're talking to a health educator, they don't have hands-on experience. The tips they give you, they're not things you're going to go home and do, you know? I mean you want to learn it from somebody who actually knows how to have fun doing it. And actually the doctors would like to learn it from those of us who know how to have fun too, and I just wish that people could actually know that, you know. Yeah, I'm so tired of that myth. Excuse me, but if you doctors do know anything about safe sex most of them learned it from us. So please, stop trying to save us. Come learn from us, let us educate you.—Michelle, 35-year-old prostitute

I now turn to the production of knowledge as a hands-on experience in which sex workers are *practitioners* of safer sex. The knowledge they produce about safer sex is different from the previous two sites because *sex workers actually produce knowledge in action and interaction.* The knowledge they produce is transmitted in the sexual encounter with clients. Additionally, as sex workers rely on different sources to shore up their own knowledge base about safer sex by requesting that scientific work be conducted on the transmission rates with particular fluids, sex workers also invent their own ways to embody the concrete practices that are producing health and competency through safer sex.

Sex work communities are key sites where experiential knowledge about AIDS has proved invaluable. Prostitutes and professional dominants have capitalized on their embodied knowledge and developed sophisticated strategies to manufacture and distribute information to others. This distribution has occurred at multiple social levels. For instance, institutionally CAL-PEP (California Prevention Education Project), an organization founded by prostitutes and ex-prostitutes, provides health care, prevention, and risk reduction information for "at risk" African American populations in San Francisco and Alameda County.[11] Another level at which sex workers develop and distribute information about safer sex is based on individual contact, through the sexual work they do.

Knowledge about safer sex[12] is not produced in a vacuum. Most frequently these sex workers learned about safer sex from three places: other workers, the media, (including sex manuals and alternative magazines like *On Our Backs*), and safer sex training. For instance, Gina recalls, "I learned about it from reading books about sex and working with more experienced women in the brothels." Billy explains, "The media. It was basically a fact of life when I was growing up and becoming sexual." Honing one's knowledge, skills, and practices about safer sex are continual and active education experiences. Anne, like many informants, considers herself still to be learning about the many aspects of safer sex. She has learned about it "in college, from a lesbian crowd I hung out with, from friends in the porn industry, other workers. It is really an ongoing learning process." Sex workers also avail themselves of institutional resources to verify the safety of particular sexual practices as part of a continual updating of information to integrate into their work. For example, when concerned about a particular sex activity with human urine, Hadley "called the CDC about piss play and they say it is safe to take it into your mouth. They just started saying that recently though, very recently." Hadley periodically checks in with the CDC, scrolling through her list of questionable practices. This may appear as a trickle-down knowledge transmission. The sex worker calls the CDC to verify her practices. However, Hadley claims and I concur that her "check-ins" with the CDC encourages the institution to conduct research to meet the needs of the public.

As sex workers continuously update and refine their knowledge base and in turn their practices, definitions of safer sex take on a fluid and changeable quality. Safer sex with a baseline definition as "no exchange of body fluids" is reiterated in all the interviews. However, one need only look a little further to see the multiplicity and nuances of the definition and differences in what safer sex signifies to sex workers. Strategies to contain body fluids are variable and require sex workers to develop flexibility in their work management (Martin 1994). Broadly, sex workers explain safer sex in two different ways. I label these the *metaphorical* (in which safer sex is likened to other activities or agendas) and the *practical* (in which safer sex is a series of activities performed in sexual encounters).

# The Metaphors of Safer Sex:
# The Healthy Professional

Although sex manuals advocate safer sex as one component of body discipline—a quest for the healthy body—sex workers conceptualize safer sex as a means of maintaining health. Sex workers, in anticipating client interest in their bodies, develop strategies to present their own bodies to meet clients' ideals, which include a manifestation of "health" as freedom from disease.

Furthermore, the sex workers I studied have chosen to develop safer sex as a body of knowledge. This claim enables them to appropriate a certain level of occupational prestige (Turner 1987). Professionalization, as theorized by Freidson (1986), encompasses three key tactics: establishing licensure, producing and applying specialized knowledge, and creating a code of ethics/conduct particular to the profession. Of these, it is the production and application of specialized knowledge that sex workers most closely link to their own conceptualizations of professionalism. Safer sex then becomes an explicit strategy of professionalization. If one is adept at the skills required to master safer sex, it can add to the professional presentation of self in a sexual encounter. When asked how her use of latex in different sexual acts makes her feel, Felicia replies, "How do I feel whenever I wear latex? I feel whenever I do my gloves or whatever, I feel knowledgeable and I feel professional. I feel like I'm a real—it's like the chance that sex workers are sex educators and I really believe that's true. And I feel like that every time I do it, because you know I could put on a condom like with my mouth, and my partners are like whoa! They're just amazed by that." There is an extension of knowing how to use a technology, developing routines and procedures for practicing safer sex and becoming and being recognized as a professional. Brad sees himself as a representative of a larger safer sex culture and a professionalized group when explaining his professional identity.

> How do I see myself when I am using latex? Well for people who aren't urbanites, my customers, who might be there one hour, I see myself as an emissary. That I get the opportunity to educate these people, that when they look back—you know, when they think about all the exchanges from the second I arrived at their hotel room, they can recall every instance in their mind, that at this point Brad put on a condom, it's a great feeling. That I'm an ambassador.

Brad is an ambassador from somewhere. It is in his conceptualization that we witness the construction of a professionalized group; Brad comes from a particular community of people or community of knowledge. In symbolizing himself as an emissary, Brad outlines the particular activities that encompass this job, including "the opportunity to educate" with his specialized knowledge.

Fiona has actually made a business out of the knowledge production process and education of safer sex practices. This represents the clearest example of someone actually teaching or professing about safer sex as an expert.

> I now advertise myself as a sexy older woman to teach, and I still charge a lot of money because it is illegal and my copy reads something like—the first ad I was writing like this the headline was "essential skill" and then it said "fun, nonjudgmental fun, hands on guidance to the ins and outs of women's sexuality by beautiful sexy older woman." And it's going over great. I am amazed, absolutely amazed. . . . So safer sex education would come into what I do with them. And what I do is different for each client. But it incorporates a geographic tour of women's bodies and there's lots of bits that they don't know about and what works and doesn't.

This advertising strategy has brought two types of clients to Fiona: young men who want to learn about sex, often virgins, and older men. For the latter, the "last time they were single the rules were very different, so I might be showing them that latex can be fun. And not to be intimidated by condoms."

In situations where the safer sex education is not an explicit part of the sexual encounter, the professional sex worker must master safer sex in a way that portrays a convincing (sometimes spontaneous-like) performance to the client. While discussing the actual work of maintaining a safer sex encounter, Michelle likens her profession to that of contemporary health care workers: both have standards to manage body fluids. However, her profession is constrained in specific ways:

> Because my cleanliness standards are so strict I know it gets on some people's nerves. Cleaning up this pre-ejaculate, it takes a certain amount of planning and time and carefulness to make sure that you are practicing all this safe sex when you're working with somebody who doesn't—who wants to think they're having a spontaneous romantic moment. And it's not like you've got a partner who's thoroughly educated. You're dealing with somebody who doesn't know shit and you're trying to educate them and have a spontaneous moment with them at the same time. It's hard work. And sometimes I can tell that I'm not getting the cooperation I want and I'm getting a little bit uptight, and they're starting to feel like—one of my clients calls it the "hazardous waste material." I mean going to see my dentist becomes—I feel like a hazardous waste material myself. First he had some new goggles, well then he got a shield, you know, and next I expect him to come in just like—you know, a space suit next time. It's so funny. But that's what we're having to do. See the medical profession has the luxury of looking like they're in this space suit. I can't look like I'm in a space suit. I have got to look like I'm being very intimate and everything, and yet really I am trying to have my own little space suit going on here.

Using safer sex is part of taking care of the body and is part of a valuable skill similar to other work skills. These metaphorical constructions can serve to legitimate the work they do by stating it is, in one instance, producing health and, in another, a specialized skill of a professional group of people.

## The Practice of Safer Sex: Containing the Hazardous Waste Material

As illustrated in the previous quote, the actual practices of safer sex in the moment become orchestrated acts that require many considerations. But the professional must also keep the ambiance authentic and sexy, managing their body fluids in a way that is safe and unintrusive. Sex workers must *reconcile* the seemingly dichotomous constructions of safe and sexual into a convincing performance. Michelle explains how she must appear to be relaxed in an effortless experience with her client when in actuality there is a lot of work required to engage in the sexual encounter. In these interactions, being sexual means being available for physical experimentation, as in being naked or scarcely dressed. Being safe means being able to protect oneself and others against antigens.

My informants were eloquent in articulating their safer sex practices. Two informants represent the extremes of the range. Hadley explains, "my party line is rubbers for fucking, rubbers for sucking, dental dams, barriers every time fluids are exchanged. I don't do anything without a barrier. Privately, I kiss, but in my professional life, I don't." This is in contrast with Natasha's practice of using condoms only for intercourse, both anal and vaginal: "I have always felt comfortable performing fellatio without rubbers and as long as a woman is not on her period I feel comfortable having cunnilingus without latex." Gina, carving out her own niche within her own standards of safety, believes safer sex enables her access to her own project of transforming eroticism. Within the confines of safer sex, Gina works to "create an alternate erotic experience that doesn't just rely on genital pleasure, you know, make them see that there is more about being erotic and sexual than just exchanging body fluids. I feel like I can do that and I am good at it."

As noted earlier, oral sex is the arena where the most diversity of safety standards exists. Sex workers craft very different strategies and practices for engaging in oral sex with their clientele, particularly oral sex with women as the recipient: cunnilingus. Reasons cited for the diversity of strategies are "the CDC says it is ok," the collective experiences assembled through talking to other workers, the belief that "the risk is minimal to me," and the lack of research about transmission of the virus through cunnilingus. For instance, Olivia discusses the unknown risk factor in describing her practices: "Well, there are some things that I am really sure about, like intercourse of any kind, but other things seem to be really undecided, like oral sex with women." Michelle has the same standards as Olivia around intercourse and oral sex on men (only practiced with latex condom). But Michelle engages in cunnilingus without latex barriers. She defines safer sex as

> no exchange of body fluids, that means no contact with anything that comes out of a dick, I am talking about pre-cum too. But, as far as we know there's a higher concentration of the HIV virus in semen and less in vaginal fluid. But, as far as I know, oral sex is still not considered safe sex. So some of them would choose not to do it [cunnilingus] and others will do it anyway. A lot of my clients go down on me [without a barrier] and I don't know if it's peculiar to me or what. If I can get them eating pussy for a little while, to me it's also less dangerous to my health.

# The Transmission of Knowledge: Creating the "Whore-Educated" Guy

Just as knowledge about safer sex is in the process of being produced and reformulated by these sex workers, it is also transmitted through their sexual encounters with clients. Some evidence of this transmission of knowledge or education of clients is the claim by many of my informants that clients come to them already knowing particular standards of practice. These are described as "whore-educated" or "prostitute-educated" guys.[13] These men are memorable to sex workers and stand out as enjoyable, relaxed, and "hassle-free" sessions. But how do these men become "whore-educated" guys besides responding to Fiona's advertisement for the explicit purposes of learning safer sex practices? Sex workers discuss the need to tailor their safer sex information to each situation and interaction. Not all sexual encounters are considered appropriate or worthy of educational energy. There are typical client resistance statements. "They got a whole litany of cute little lines you know, 'condom, schmondom,' 'I never use a condom,' 'I can't feel anything,' 'it's like fucking with a raincoat on.'"

Some strategies include sex workers constructing themselves as possibly infected, a high-risk partner. A common scare tactic that several sex workers like Brad use is "you know like when they say, 'oh you don't have to use that.' I say, 'yes, I do. I have to use this. You don't know my sexual history, but you are sleeping with every person I ever slept with.'" Most informants have prepared comebacks for the reluctant client. These prepared comebacks are used to diffuse a type of reluctance that sex workers feel is more of a challenge. Sometimes clients try to test the limits of sex workers' safer sex boundaries, a game of wills. Sex workers, experienced at this game, use the prepared and ready-made statements in an almost requisite conversation with this type of client. Then their work can proceed without further incident. These ready-made strategies enable sex workers to engage in their work safely and to attend quickly to safer sex considerations.

Alternately, a sex worker may take an opportunity to actually educate clients. In the remaining section, I discuss the ways sex workers successfully integrate safer sex into their practices using body techniques. The following illustrates Anne's decision to invest in educating a client about safer sex.

Anne: *I don't put it on right away because quite frankly if I can get away with just doing a hand job instead of having intercourse I would prefer that and I don't bother using a glove when giving a hand job. I check my hands first to make sure I don't have any open cuts, you know. I don't have a problem with them coming on me. As long as I don't have a cut there's no way it could enter my blood stream obviously. So no, I don't put it on right away. If it's looking like—you kind of have to really sort of read where they're coming from, because you can overly communicate, which I think some-times my partner does to the point where it becomes really unerotic for them, extremely unerotic.*

Lisa: *How do you avoid that?*

Anne: *She becomes very clinical, sometimes she'll talk about how we're sex radicals and how you didn't know you were getting involved with sex radicals. Sometimes she'll talk about how we like to watch fags together and their dicks become flaccid. But it depends a lot upon how quickly I can tell if they're going to come. There's some people who come quickly and who don't say "whoa, slow down," and there are other people who say, "whoa, slow down" and that probably means that they either don't want to come right away or they don't want to come like that, meaning they would rather come through intercourse. So you kind of just have to be able to really read what's going on. And for people who aren't coming from other kinds of stimulation then it's pretty obvious that the condom is necessary. Then I would ask them, would you like us to put a condom on? And virtually everybody knows what that means, that means okay, we're talking about oral sex or intercourse right now. But the other day I actually had a client who—I said would you like for me to put on a condom now, and he said no, actually I prefer not to, and I said, okay, so then he doesn't want to do that, that's fine, you know, but then he said at one point, can I go inside of you, and I said, well defi-nitely not without a condom.*

Lisa: *How did he respond to that?*

Anne: *He said, "Oh, okay, I was hoping not." And I said, "Really, you know." So I put it on him but I didn't want to go into a whole clinical discussion and talk about AIDS at that point, but I did afterwards with him. What ended up happening is he didn't stay hard with a condom on. So he said to me, "Okay, I guess I would prefer a hand job then." After I said to him, "I have some things that I can tell you about this, you know, education," I taught him a way to get over that would be to masturbate with a condom on.*

Lisa: *Do you think he appreciated that or is it just like, okay, this is some crazy woman telling me. . . .*

Anne: *No, he gave me a $40 tip and I don't think it was just because he thought I was attractive. I gave him some other information, too, and I think he realized where I was coming from. I was obviously educated.*

Simultaneously, Anne reveals ever-present simultaneous agendas to make her work easier and safer. She has a self-interested strategy in trying to do a hand job for greater ease and safety. There are certain sex work acts that she likes better than others, in this case giving hand jobs. In this story, it becomes apparent that Anne has a specific practice of introducing condoms to signify a particular sex act. She indicates that there is a preferred way and time to talk about safer sex in sexual interactions; she gives me examples of the wrong and the right way of educating. The timing is important to actually transmit infor-mation to a client while at the same time not disrupting the sexual exchange.

Safer sex can be effectively and successfully used when physical or corporeal integration is achieved. Sex workers describe how they use their bodies and the bodies of their clients to increase the comfort level around a new technique of doing things. Sex workers have constructed new body techniques involving the use of particular latex tools (Moore 1997b). There seems to be some level of awkwardness and adjustment time to actually integrate these techniques successfully. Success is the actual use of safer sex practices, according to a sex worker's definition, in a sexual interaction where the sexual transaction goes without incident. Success occurs mostly when there is not an awkward, clumsy, obvious, or difficult thing to perform. When safer sex practices become habitual enactments, it makes the self/body feel more dexterous and fluent in the technology. The more proficiently these techniques can be used, the more able they are to be integrated smoothly into a sexual setting. As Olivia states, "I pride myself on how I put on a condom. I put it in my mouth, I begin a massage putting the condom on so it's like a lot of the times they don't even know it is on, it just feels so good so it incorporates the latex as a part of a very pleasurable experience."

Quincy discusses her own realization about her "prowess" with latex and how it enables her to use latex more confidently and hence successfully during her sessions,

> And actually I haven't ever made this connection before. But there's a prowess thing with that, too. It's like with gloves that don't fit, using a barrier for oral sex I feel more clumsy. I feel less like I know what I'm doing and I feel less that it's very likely that I'm going to do a good job, which affects my morale about being in a sexual situation in the first place. So that's, I think that's one of the really big difficulties with oral sex barriers in the first place, particularly with oral sex with women. I don't have that experience so much with women. I don't notice my feeling of prowess and I think that's because with women you're so clear what they are, and I don't have to like aim proficiently to do what I want to be doing here.

Sex workers also discuss creating a physical reaction to the use of latex through close associations of latex to pleasurable acts. Quincy discusses her use of latex devices with clients:

> They at least get a taste of that Pavlovian strategy. It's really the way it is: The bell rings, the dog salivates, the condom goes on, the guy knows it's time to fuck. And I think that that's a really potent part of education. I try to do it with gloves too. I like to snap my gloves because it is exciting to me and they hear it and hopefully it will be exciting to them too.

Snapping of gloves as a strategy to alert clients to upcoming sexual activities is discussed in several interviews as a means to create a sensation association.

Hearing a glove, seeing a condom will hopefully encourage pleasant associations with what's to come, what is expected.

# Conclusions

## *Fluid Knowledge Production: Linkages across Different Sites*

The AIDS pandemic has had and continues to have a devastating impact on our world. With no cure in sight, behavior modification has become the primary (some might say the only) method to curb the continued transmission of HIV. Originating in marginalized sexual communities, safer sex was a collection of practices that allowed communities and individuals to remain sexual despite the conservative right-wing messages of abstinence and heterosexual monogamy. In the popularization of these safer sex practices through public service announcements, sex manuals, and sex workers' practices, there continues to be a transformation from the original, grassroots and word-of-mouth activities to a series of competing doctrines on practices, philosophies, and liabilities.

Currently safer sex messages and their applications are produced in everyday life to promote health and wellness. While the construction of safer sex messages is highly consequential for how we understand the concepts of health and illness, social and political responsibility, and individual rights, it also has the potential to become another form of discipline of the body (like dieting and exercise). Living though the epidemic, we are told and often shown that we must vigilantly protect our body's orifices from secretions and fluid exchanges. Building on the work of Foucault, in particular his formulation of biopower, Linda Singer (1993, 117) posits that the epidemic actually "provides an occasion and a rationale for multiplying points of intervention into the lives of bodies and populations." I have reviewed only a few sources of potential prevention intervention into daily life. In these sites the practices of safer sex can be associated with messages of individual and social accountability and/or integrated into a fun, playful sexual experience. It is crucial to testify and document these transformations, for as Foucault (1981) states, out of resistance comes new forms of discipline and new mechanisms to dominate. In the case of sex manuals, in particular, we see the alignment of safer sex with existing constructions of healthiness and virtue that have the potential to perpetuate social inequity.

If knowledge about safer sex is not viewed as connected to ideologies and agendas of these actors, we can lose site of the stakes in producing the messages and practices. In other words, safer sex is produced in a world that already exists with power differentials. Certain types of safer sex messages and knowledges support these power arrangements, certain messages attempt to dismantle them, leaving new ones in their place. Although different actors with different agendas produce safer sex, some of the resulting messages are similar. For example, all rely on constructing the individual as potentially ultimately capable of doing safer sex. It is up to each individual person. But something is certainly missing in this construction. By relying on the construction of the individual as a flexible risk manager, the individual is often taken out of the social context. These sex workers reside in particular communities that enable them great control and latitude to produce and perform safer sex. We do not all reside in places where control and information are so readily available.

Specifically, sex workers, probably a less accessible source of information about safer sex to a large audience, present the actual embodiment of safer sex within the work that they do. Safer sex is indeed part of a regimen of health awareness within sex work. At the same time, safer sex has been appropriated as a specialized knowledge toward goals of professionalization. Sex workers advertise their aptitude and expertise, develop different strategies to incorporate safer sex within the sexual session, and teach clients to become whore-educated guys. This safer sex in action, attested by these sex workers' accounts, encompasses a broad range of variation in activities. Safer sex is presented as an ongoing performance that varies from client to client. It is an enactment, which is situated within specific conditions of immediate environments and not related to an absolutist message.

What are some of the effects of these three sites of knowledge production about safer sex and our society in general? Despite their differences in presentation, method, and messages, these sites are mutually constitutive forces in creating knowledge of safer sex. Audiences have the potential of taking in information from all of these sources. The boundaries between these knowledge producers are porous, therefore audiences can develop their own cumulative and sometimes contradictory conceptualizations of safer sex. In this vein, safer sex has become a complex system of information, produced by different sources with different agendas and available for consumption on television, the radio, through books and printed materials, and interactions with others. Taken together, these sources of knowledge production may filter into broader transformations in thinking about health and the human body in the time of epidemic. These messages, the proliferation of safer sex concepts, point to changes in how we view ourselves within contemporary arrangements of sexuality.

# Notes

1. "Genealogy as the analysis of historical descent rejects the uninterrupted continuities and stable forms which have been a feature of traditional history in order to reveal the complexity, fragility and contingency surrounding historical events. . . . There is no hidden meaning or foundation beneath things, merely more layers of interpretation which through accretion have achieved the form of truth, self-evidence, and necessity and which in turn, it is the task of genealogy to breach" (Smart 1985, 57; 59).

2. Francis was depicted in Randy Shilts's book, *And the Band Played On* (1987), as a vanguard scientist. The book chronicles Francis's constant struggles within the CDC for more funds to research the transmission and prevention of AIDS. Shilts indicates that Francis left the CDC in 1985, frustrated and disenchanted by the failing financial support for research, politicking of certain scientific personalities, and lack of vision of the CDC.

3. This concept has been documented in many studies; for instance, research conducted on the sexual knowledge and sexual practices of lesbians and bisexual women (at both high and low risk) propose that although this group is highly educated about the risk of unprotected sexual practices, they are very unlikely to practice safer sex techniques (Einhorn 1994).

4. Take for example, the 3-year self-worth AIDS awareness campaign spearheaded by the San Francisco AIDS Foundation. Both the CDC and private business support funded this project. It is targeted toward young, stigmatized people who may have developed a blasé attitude about their health due to a lack of positive images with which they can identify (Armstrong 1995).

5. Information on the production of these public service announcements and their unique content was obtained through an informal interview with Mr. Laporte, an employee of Ogilvy, Adams and Reinhart, the advertising agency responsible for the development, design, production and marketing of PSAs. Throughout the past eight years, the ad agency has twice won the competitive bid (expiring in 1996) to produce these PSAs. The agency has produced between 40–45 PSAs through the collaborative efforts of CDC staff, subcontractors, medical personnel, and "a whole cadre of consultants, including local, public and community based organizations and state health departments."

6. Prevention messages regarding safer sex, sexually transmitted diseases, teen pregnancy, and other sexual conditions have long been accused of encouraging youth to be sexually active. Proponents of this view believe that youth may actually be inspired by messages about condom use to engage in sexual acts they would otherwise not attempt. These groups wield considerable power, which the CDC and its contracted advertising agencies must attend to in their production decisions (interview data).

7. According to Mr. Laporte, there has been no dispute over the quality of these productions, yet the reception of the PSAs has been "hot and cold." Certain PSAs do not air in the "Bible Belt." It is because of this reason that the ad agency has designed a "range of options" both in terms of time (15-/30-/60-second spots) and message (abstinence or condom use).

8. In order to determine the universe of sex manuals, I sampled from the Online Books in Print Service. For the decade 1985–1995 using a key word search "sex education," the breakdown by year is: 1985–33; 1986–38; 1987–36; 1988–59; 1989–98; 1990–110; 1991–104; 1992–115; 1993–128; 1994–146; 1995–92. "Sex education" included but was not limited to sex manuals. Other books captured by this search included books about education psychology on teaching about sex, pregnancy, and conception; sexual politics; and sociological studies of gender differences. Sampling for the key words "safer or safe sex" and the decade captured eighteen listings; four of these listings were books that I intensely analyzed. This sampling method also included a library search at the University of California's Online WorldCat System. This database is a listing of all the monographs in the world. When searching under the title or key words of "sex manuals" for the decade, roughly one hundred titles were captured. However, upon further examination, most of these manuals were teacher aids on sex.

9. Ruth Greenblatt, a prominent physician at UCSF, stated in a recent lecture that the greatest cost of AIDS/HIV is the loss in worker productivity or years of potential life lost (lecture data).

10. My experience with sex workers includes conducting twenty-seven semi-structured interviews with nineteen self-identified sex workers. I used modified grounded theory methods of data collection and analysis (Strauss and Corbin 1990). Conducting this research in the San Francisco Bay area has enabled me to access a diversity community of research subjects and colleagues. San Francisco, rich in racial, ethnic, and sexual diversity and home to a large gay and lesbian community, provides fertile ground for both collecting data and interpreting issues in human sexuality. These informants, seventeen women and two men, worked primarily through "in call" (in-home prostitution) or "out call" (worker- and client-agreed site). None were street prostitutes. They were all over eighteen years of age with a median age in their late thirties. The major requirements for inclusion in my interview sample was the sex worker's self-acknowledged consensual engagement in sexual activities that involved controlling the exchange of body fluids. These sex workers are career sex workers and are not drug dependent. They work on a freelance and relatively autonomous basis. Most are also actively involved in community-based organizations for health education, sex worker rights, or feminist concerns, and I have worked with some of them in such contexts as volunteering on sex information lines and political organizing. Their age, clientele, price ranges, and work sites all enable them to negotiate greater power and control in the sex work situation. Moreover, the conditions of this type of sex work establish an environment where safer sex practices are produced and shown to others, such as clients. These sex workers are also eloquent in explaining their own transformations of their professional selves encountered through practicing a sexual trade in the time of AIDS/HIV.

11. Forty percent of the target population is prostitutes. Obtaining state, federal, and private foundation money, CAL-PEP's annual budget is $700,000. CAL-PEP is an exemplar of the ironies arising in times of fiscal crises of the state (O'Connor 1973). In Altman's (1993, 5) estimation the state often finds itself in contradictory positions: "governments have adopted policies which have in effect legitimized unpopular and sometimes illegal behavior in interests of public health." One probable reason the

paternalistic, late capitalistic state funds CAL-PEP is because it is less expensive to legitimate the existence of prostitutes (although technically illegal) than to "let them get" or spread AIDS, leading to a reliance on an already overburdened healthcare system. Thus the state is admitting that the experiential knowledge of prostitutes is perhaps more effective at reaching sex workers than it (the state) is. Additionally, these strategies maintain patriarchy in that it is primarily male clients who are "protected" by educating female and male sex workers to use these safer sex techniques.

12. In this section, when referring to safer sex, I specifically discuss safer sex as it relates to HIV/AIDS transmission prevention. Other sexual concerns such as pregnancy and STDs—such as crabs, hepatitis B, genital warts, herpes, were brought up occasionally by workers but overwhelmingly most indicated that they began to incorporate safer sex for the explicit purposes of managing HIV.

13. During a conversation about the infrequency of resistance to using condoms in her sessions, Olivia states, "I mean I would think that the people who pay me $200 an hour have experienced the culture and are comfortable with what goes on."

# References

Abramson, Pinkerton. 1992. Is risky sex rational? *Journal of Sex Research* 29, no. 4.

Aggleton, Peter, Peter Davies, and Graham Hart, eds. 1993. *AIDS: Facing the Second Decade*. New York: Falmer Press.

Altman, Dennis. 1993. Expertise, legitimacy and the centrality of community. In *AIDS: Facing the Second Decade*, edited by Peter Aggleton, Peter Davies, and Graham Hart. New York: Falmer Press.

Armstrong, David. 1995. Savings lives. *San Francisco Examiner*, March 10, a25–a26.

Aronson, Naomi. 1984. Science as a claims-making activity: Implications for social problems research. In *Studies in the Sociology of Social Problems*, edited by J. Schneider and J. Kitsuse. Greenwich, Conn.: Ablex Publishing Corp.

Berridge, Virginia. 1992. AIDS: History and contemporary history. In *The Time of AIDS: Social Analysis, Theory and Method*, edited by G. Herdt and S. Lindenbaum. Newbury Park, Calif.: Sage.

Blumer, Herbert. 1969. *Symbolic Interactionism: Perspective and Method*. Englewood Cliffs, N.J.: Prentice Hall.

Breitman, Patti, Kim Knutson, and Paul Reed. 1987. *How to Persuade Your Lover to Use a Condom . . . And Why You Should*. Rocklin, Calif.: Prima Publishing.

Bull, Chris. 1993. Love at first sight. *The Advocate* 640: 34–37.

Califia, Pat. 1988/1993. *Sapphistry: The Book of Lesbian Sexuality*. Tallahassee: The Naiad Press.

Centers for Disease Control, Department of Health and Human Services and Public Health Service. 1993. It's your move, prevent AIDS: Packet to introduce the PMI. Department of Health and Human Services.

Crawford, Robert. 1985. A cultural account of "health": Control, release and the social body. In *Issues in the Political Economy of Health Care*, edited by J. McKinlay. London: Tavistock.

Edgley, Charles, and Dennis Brissett. 1990. Health Nazis and the cult of the perfect body: Some polemical observations. *Symbolic Interaction* 13 (2): 257–79.

# 462    Prostitution

Einhorn, Lena, and Michael Polgar. 1994. HIV risk behavior among lesbians and bisexual women. *AIDS Education and Prevention* 6 (6): 514–23.

Etheridge, Elizabeth. 1992. *Sentinel for Health: A History of the Centers for Disease Control.* Berkeley: University of California.

Foucault, Michel. 1981. The order of discourse. In *Untying the Text,* edited by R. Young. Boston: Routledge.

Francis, Donald. 1992. Toward a comprehensive HIV prevention program for the CDC and the nation. *JAMA* 268 (11): 1444–47.

Fraser, Nancy. 1989. *Unruly Practices: Power, Discourse and Gender in Contemporary Social Theory.* Minneapolis: University of Minnesota.

Freidson, Eliot. 1986. Professional dominance and the ordering of health services: Some consequences. In *The Sociology of Health and Illness,* edited by P. A. R. K. Conrad. New York: St. Martin's Press.

Juengst, Eric, and Barbara Koenig. 1989. *The Meaning of AIDS: Implications for Medical Science, Clinical Practice and Public Health Policy.* New York: Praeger.

Martin, Emily. 1994. *Flexible Bodies: Tracking Immunity in American Culture from the Days of Polio to the Age of AIDS.* Boston: Beacon Press.

McIlvenna, Ted, ed. 1992. *The Complete Guide to Safer Sex.* Fort Lee, N.J.: Barricade Books.

MMWR. 1992. CDC: The nation's prevention agency. *MMWR* 41 (44): 1.

Moore, Lisa Jean. 1997a. "I was just learning the ropes": Becoming a practitioner of safer sex. *Applied Behavioral Science Review* 4 (1).

Moore, Lisa Jean. 1997b "It's like you use pots and pans to cook. It's the tools.": The technologies of safer sex. *Science, Technology and Human Values* 22 (4).

Morin, Jack. 1981/1986. *Anal Pleasure and Health: A Guide for Men and Women.* San Francisco: Yes Press.

Odets, Walt. 1995. The fatal mistake of AIDS education. *SF Bay Times,* May 4, 1–7.

O'Connor, James. 1973. *The Fiscal Crisis of the State.* New York: St. Martin's Press.

O'Sullivan, Sue, and Pratibha Parmar. 1992. *Lesbians Talk (Safer) Sex.* London: Scarlet Press.

Patton, Cindy, and Janis Kelly. 1987. *Making It: A Woman's Guide to Sex in the Age of AIDS.* Ithaca, N.Y.: Firebrand Books.

Rosenberg, Mark, et al. 1992. The role of behavioral sciences and health education in HIV prevention: Experience at the US Centers for Disease Control. In *AIDS: Prevention Through Education, A World View,* edited by J. Sepulveda, Harvey Fineberg, Jonathan Mann. New York: Oxford University Press.

Scheper-Hughes, Nancy. 1994. AIDS and the social body. *Social Science and Medicine* 397.

Shilts, Randy. 1987. *And the Band Played On.* New York: St. Martin's Press.

Silverman, Mervyn. 1992. AIDS Education and Politics. In *AIDS: Prevention Through Education, A World View,* edited by J. Sepulveda, Harvey Fineberg, Jonathan Mann. New York: Oxford University Press.

Singer, Linda. 1993. *Erotic Welfare.* New York: Routledge.

Smart, Barry. 1985. *Michel Foucault.* New York: Routledge.

Strauss, Anselm, and Juliet Corbin. 1990. *Basics of Qualitative Research: Grounded Theory Procedures and Techniques.* Newbury Park, Calif.: Sage.

Tatchell, Peter. 1994. *Safer Sex: The Guide to Gay Sex Safety.*

Treichler, Paula. 1988. AIDS, homophobia, and biomedical discourse: An epidemic of signification. In *AIDS: Cultural Analysis, Cultural Activism,* edited by D. Crimp. Cambridge: MIT Press.

Turner, Bryan. 1987. *Medical Power and Social Knowledge.* Beverly Hills, Calif.: Sage.

Watney, Simon. 1994. *Practices of Freedom: Selected Writings on HIV/AIDS.* Durham, N.C.: Duke University Press.

Winks, Cathy, and Anne Semans. 1994. *The Good Vibrations Guide to Sex.* Pittsburgh, Penn.: Cleis Press.

# 9

# THE STRUGGLE OVER LEGAL ISSUES

## Introduction

This section presents a potpourri of issues. Richard Green looks at prostitution from an international perspective and examines the new laws that have appeared to deal with what is popularly called "sexual tourism." His article raises many questions concerning how the various societies will be able to enact international law to deal with the issue and the question of exploitation of third world countries. Robert Gemme presents the case of sexual pluralism. Yoneda Masumi examines the prostitution prevention law in Japan and the movement for abolitionism. Ignasi Pons and Victoria Serra write about the legal situation in Spain.

Helen Buckingham, who appears elsewhere in this book, questions whether prohibitionist law is very effective. Eliott Shaw takes the Jane Roe II case into the area of privacy and personal rights. Another legal brief by David A. J. Richards, due to its length, is found in appendix A. It examines the American tradition of the "rights of the individual."

# THE SEXUAL TOURIST AND INTERNATIONAL LAW

### RICHARD GREEN

## Background

Although child prostitution has been well known in nations for generations, it has recently attracted unprecedented interest. Reasons for this heightened concern are several. There has been an explosion of interest in adult-child sexuality, termed child sex abuse. There is great concern over child pornography. Cheaper world travel and computer-transmitted information have provided access and materials allowing persons of moderate financial means to travel abroad in search of the exotic. Some of these travelers engage in sexual activity with persons of an age younger than permitted or available in their home country. These are "sex tourists."

The reported scope of the problem of sex tourism was highlighted in the August 31, 1996, issue of *The Economist*. A conference in Stockholm learned that more than one million children, 90 percent girls, are added annually to the rolls of child prostitutes. Allegedly, child prostitutes are visited by ten million to twelve million men a week. Further, one-third of child prostitutes in Asia are said to be HIV positive.

The reported extent of the problem is also provided by child protection agencies. In Thailand estimates of the number of prostitute children range up to 800,000. Children are allegedly purchased or abducted from Burma, Laos, and China. The Philippine government calculated that the number of its child prostitutes is 60,000. Taiwan's child prostitute population is estimated at 70,000. In Sri Lanka the estimates range from 10,000 to 15,000, most of whom are boys. Reportedly there are at least 200,000 prostitute children in China, another 400,000 in India, and another 500,000 in Brazil (*Times*

[London] February 29, 1996, International Labor Organization). Efforts to stop sex tourism activity have invoked an esoteric legal strategy. It is "extraterritorial jurisdiction."

In this report I address some of the rationales behind sex tourism laws, some examples of recent laws, their legal basis, and some of the moral and legal questions they raise.

# Extraterritorial Jurisdiction

In exercising extraterritorial jurisdiction a country extends its legal authority to enforce a law for an act occurring outside its national territory. One justification for extraterritorial laws given by *The Economist* is the inadequacy of "poor-country law." As examples, the article cites a low age of consent and notes that commercial sex with girls may be outlawed, but not sex with boys. Another concern is the apparent lack of concern for law enforcement in the host country.

Four legal bases are typically given for extraterritorial jurisdiction:

1.  Effects doctrine—if the act abroad has or is intended to have substantial effects within its home territory
2.  Nationality principle—as an exception in common law, a state may exercise jurisdiction over a national for a crime committed abroad. The principle is derived from the concept of state sovereignty under which nationals are entitled to their state's protection even while outside its territorial boundaries. These individuals then have a corresponding obligation of allegiance to international laws when outside the state of which they are citizens.[1]
3.  Protective principle—if the act threatens the security of the home state
4.  Universality—acts of universal concern such as piracy, slave trade, hijacking, genocide, and some acts of terrorism (see *Restatement [Third] of the Foreign Relations Law of the United States,* Section 403 [c], [1987]).

# Some National Laws to Control Sex Tourism

## Australia

Australia in 1994 passed an amendment to the Crimes Act (Child Sex Tourism) in which one section warns that an Australian must not, while outside Australia, engage in sexual intercourse with a person who is under age sixteen. The penalty is imprisonment for up to seventeen years. A person contravenes another section of the act by committing an act of indecency on a person under sixteen. This is an act of a sexual nature that is "so unbecoming or offensive that it amounts to gross breach of ordinary contemporary standards of decency and propriety in the Australian community." Imprisonment for that is twelve years.

The 1997 case of the former Australian ambassador to Cambodia has the most information on attempted enforcement of the new law. It illustrates problems in obtaining evidence for prosecution and conviction.

Child witnesses, reportedly poverty-stricken, were paid a $5-a-day allowance. The defense argued that the money was an incentive to give false testimony (*Sydney Morning Herald,* November 6, 1996). The principal witness against the ambassador gave inconsistent testimony under extensive two-day cross-examination. Had the charges been laid in New South Wales instead of Canberra the youths would not have faced cross-examination (*Sydney Morning Herald,* November 17, 1996). The ambassador was acquitted. Some observers saw the case as demonstrating the near impossibility of obtaining convictions on testimony from foreign children facing language and cultural difficulties (*Sydney Morning Herald,* November 16, 1996).

## Germany

The German sex tourism law was introduced in 1993. A German resident is prosecutable for a sex act occurring in another country upon the German's return home. The law provides up to ten years' imprisonment for any German engaging in sexual activity with a person under fourteen, irrespective of where the act occurs. It does not matter whether the age of consent in the host country is under fourteen.

The German Ministry of Foreign Affairs has ordered its embassies in the Philippines, Thailand, Sri Lanka, and Brazil to inform German prosecutors of incidents involving sex crimes by German nationals in those countries. One result of the German sex tourism law is that travel agencies have removed sex tours from their catalogues.

## United Kingdom

In the United Kingdom, the proposed Sex Offenders Bill states that a sexual act done by a person in a country outside the United Kingdom which constituted an offense under the law enforced in that foreign country and which would constitute a sexual offense had it been done in the United Kingdom shall constitute an offense in the United Kingdom.

Offenses include rape, indecent assault, sodomy, and unlawful intercourse with a person under sixteen. What makes the proposed sex offenders bill in the United Kingdom distinct from those in Germany and Australia is that it takes into consideration whether the act was illegal in the host country. It must be.

Under the proposed bill, travel agents organizing sex tours could be prosecuted for incitement to commit sexual offenses.

## Sweden

Under Swedish law, sexual intercourse with a person under fifteen carries a term of four years in prison. This statute, combined with Sweden's extraterritorial jurisdiction ( a person who has committed a crime outside the realm shall be tried according to Swedish law and in a Swedish court), would cover the sex tourist. For the Swedish courts to have jurisdiction the act must be criminal both in Sweden and in the host country, thus requiring double criminality, as does the law in the United Kingdom. Sweden would have no competence to prosecute a Swedish national in a country where child prostitution is legal or where the age of consent is lower than in Sweden.

Sweden initiated prosecution of a sixty-six-year-old Swedish national whom Thai police took into custody in 1993 for sexual crimes against children. He was found in bed naked with a fourteen-year-old Thai boy. Thai authorities confiscated the Swede's passport and released him on bail. He then went to the Swedish embassy and obtained another passport. He then obtained an exit visa from Thai authorities and returned to Sweden. As a Swedish citizen, the man did have a constitutional right to receive a replacement passport even if accused of a crime in another country. On the other hand, Thai authorities claim a breakdown in communication regarding the exit visa so that the man was not known to be on bail when they issued him a new one.

## United States

In the United States extraterritorial criminal laws have been upheld in other areas of misconduct. For example, Panamanian leader Manual Noriega was convicted in the United States of racketeering, conspiracy, and cocaine smuggling, acts occurring in Panama but arguably extending into the United States.

An example of extraterritorial jurisdiction by the United States where local law is not involved concerns bribery of foreign business executives. In Asia this is reported as commonplace. Authorities look the other way. Between April 1994 and May 1995 United States firms reportedly lost 45 billion dollars to foreign companies that pay bribes ( *Wall Street Journal,* May 6, 1996). United States law penalizes such conduct whether in the United States or abroad (Foreign Corrupt Practices Act). United States businessmen attempting to level the playing field with their Japanese counterparts find themselves at a distinct disadvantage. They are threatened with United States prosecution.

The United States has a sex tourism law. It is part of the 1994 crime bill and was signed into law by President Clinton on September 13, 1994. The 1994 Child Sexual Abuse Prevention Act (18 USC section 2423 (b)) is an expansion of the Mann Act (the early-twentieth-century White Slave Traffic Act) ch.395,36 Stat 825(1910). It covers those who travel outside, or conspire to travel outside, the United States to engage in sexual activities with minors that would have been illegal in the United States. A minor for this statute is a person under eighteen. Imprisonment is ten years for the first offense.

The law contains no double criminality requirement. The sex act need not be illegal in the host country.

The United States law does not require actual sexual contact, only "intent" to engage in such acts; thus no victim is necessary. Under this provision of the law, persons who sign up for a sex tour, even if they do not engage in an illegal sexual act, can be prosecuted. Imprisonment for intent is possible for up to ten years. However, intent to travel for the purpose of engaging in sex with a minor could be difficult to prove where tourists travel independently or where businessmen have other legitimate reasons for their travel.

## Japan

Japan, with its large population of sex tourists, has not introduced legislation targeted at sex tourism.

## United Nations

The United Nations Convention on the Rights of Children, adopted in 1989, prohibits the exploitation of children in prostitution and in illegal sexual practices. The UN Working Group on contemporary forms of slavery reported that not only are prostitute children treated as sexual objects, resulting in a loss of dignity, but they are also subjected to physical harm, illness, and inhumane treatment, including beatings and torture. Under the United Nations pact sexual exploitation of children would constitute a crime against humanity, placing it in the same category as war crimes, willful killing, torture, and genocide.

## Council of Europe

In 1988 the Council of Europe recognized the problem of child prostitution and recommended that European countries consider establishing extraterritorial jurisdiction.

## Discussion

Poverty is seen as the major cause of the business of child prostitution. Some children's parents are misled by offers of work for their children. They do not realize the kind of work the children are getting into. Contrary to their belief, they will not be employed as maids or waitresses. However, reports also indicate that some parents know full well the fate of their children and agree to obtain modern comforts and luxury items that are available from their fee in payment for their child.

Another factor promoting child prostitution is that law enforcement is very poor. In a Philippine study of one hundred child prostitutes, 10 percent had a policeman as a pimp.

Several legal issues are generated by these extraterritorial laws. An evidentiary hurdle, as described in the recent prosecution of the former Australian ambassador to Cambodia, is one example. When the child witness is far removed from the place of trial, a video link for child testimony may be permitted in Australia. Under United States law this would compromise the literal meaning of the right to confront one's accuser, the Sixth Amendment to the Constitution. However the United States Supreme Court has already limited that right in trials involving allegations of child sex abuse when requiring a child to testify in the presence of the defendant is deemed harmful to the child.

Are other legal recourses available instead of a sex tourism law? Extradition treaties would appear to be an answer. The alleged violator would be returned by the home country to the host nation. Evidentiary problems of prosecution witnesses would be managed here by accessing direct testimony. However, court procedures in the host country may not afford the same protection to a defendant as is assured in the home country. The response to that asks whether an individual who violates a local law should be prepared for local justice. A possibility to remedy this inequity, though perhaps difficult to agree upon, would be for the host country to modify its court procedures in cases involving foreign nationals. Another problem with a trial in the host country is that a defendant's witness, if not resident in the host country, would have to travel, perhaps at substantial expense.

An argument against sex tourism laws is overreaching paternalism by first-world nations. A response to this concern is that many host countries do not prosecute abrogations of their law regarding child prostitution. Reasons include police corruption, reliance on foreign visitors for the host nation economy, and insufficient concern for the welfare of child prostitutes. In turn, if the host nation has minimal concern with regard to the sex acts, so as to ignore them legally, or criminalize them on paper but ignore them nonetheless, on what ground should another country take up the moral mantle of righting the wrong?

An argument continuing this dialogue is that the home country is also jeopardized by the actions of its citizens on foreign soil and therefore has the right to assert jurisdiction. The argument goes that a pedophile's acts abroad reinforce pedophilia in that individual so as to increase the likelihood of pedophilic acts upon returning home. Perhaps it permits renewed acting on impulses that had previously been confined to fantasy. There is an absence of data addressing these concerns. However, there may be an analogy to the use of child pornography. The often-cited inverse relation between the availability of child pornography in Denmark and reported acts of pedophilia in that country (Kutchinsky 1973) argues for an outlet that satisfies the illegal craving. If analogous, then periodic opportunities for experiencing underage sexual experiences abroad should reduce the need for such acts at home. Of course, this response does not answer the concern of the host country with respect to the best interests of its pediatric population.

The Australian, German, and American laws pose legal and ethical issues regarding the age of consent to engage in sexual acts. Consider the tourist who travels to the Netherlands or Spain, where the age of consent is below sixteen. The sex act on holiday was legal in the host jurisdiction, but the tourist is threatened with prison upon returning home. Arguably, if the sex act was consensual and legal, it would be difficult to mount an effective prosecution case, particularly if the child "victim" refused to testify. But could other witnesses provide sufficient evidence?

The inequity of the age-of-consent laws was pointed out by NAMBLA (North American Man-Boy Love Association). It protested that it would be a crime under the new United States law to travel to Canada and have sexual relations with a fifteen-year-old partner, an act not previously criminal because the national age of consent in Canada is fourteen. On the other hand, the Honorable Jim Ramstead wrote to the United States Congress on March 18, 1994, "some countries have a lower age of consent for minors or lax laws for enforcement against prostitution. But sex with children is harmful and immoral, regardless of the local laws."

And of course, there is the perennial legal concern: Is this a slippery slope? What if an Islamic nation seeks to prosecute a national upon return home for drinking a couple pints of beer in a British pub?

Finally what is the effect on a child of being a prostitute? Although there is a flood of psychiatric papers reporting consequences of sexual contacts by children with adults, these are usually reports of incestual abuse or sexual contact between nonparents and children who are not prostitutes. Although a few child prostitutes have been interviewed by journalists and child welfare agencies and have described the horrific consequences of their sex-for-pay experiences, these anecdotal reports are no substitute for detailed information from representative samples. A control group is necessary: children from the same deprived backgrounds who are not child prostitutes.

# Conclusion

Along with the relatively recent (re)discovery of child sex abuse, the very recent global anxiety over child prostitution generally and sex tourism specifically is extraordinary. In but a very few years, governmental entities, nongovernmental organizations, and international bodies have joined the chase for the sex tourist. The very term "sex tourist" is only just emerging into sophisticated vocabulary.

How successful will these efforts be? Sex tourism is big business. Like prostitution generally and pornography generally, child prostitution and child pornography are unlikely to go away. Laws are relatively easy to pass, but the social and psychological conditions promoting these activities are far slower to change, if at all, than the law. Lust is here to stay. Pedophilia is here to stay. Poverty is here to stay. We have learned from prostitution and pornography that impotence has more than a genital meaning.

It is probably naïve to seriously consider that sex tourism laws will vanquish the sex tourist, any more than prostitution laws eliminated prostitutes or pornography laws erased erotic film imagery. Ultimately, the well-meaning goals of those seeking to protect children from sexual victimization may be equally elusive.

# Note

1. The Ninth Circuit Court of Appeals applied the nationality principle in *United States* v. *Thomas* 893 F.2 1066 (1990), where a man crossed the border into Mexico with a thirteen-year-old girl and photographed his sexual acts with her. The court held the defendant guilty on the ground that congressional intent to apply the criminal statute on pornography extraterritorially could be inferred from the nature of the crime and from other legislative efforts to eliminate child pornography.

# Reference

Kutchinsky. 1973. *Journal of Social Issues* 29: 163.

# LEGAL AND SEXOLOGICAL ASPECTS OF ADULT STREET PROSTITUTION: A CASE FOR SEXUAL PLURALISM

## ROBERT GEMME

Ira Reiss, in his book *An End to Shame,* asked that social scientists move away from their traditional neutrality and seek creative ways of resolving sexual problems instead of limiting themselves to describing them with a "value free" approach. He suggested that sexual pluralism, i.e., giving people the freedom to choose their personal lifestyles in a context of honesty, equality, and responsibility, should be the ideological guideline for proposed solutions (1990). This paper is an illustration of this.

From 1984 to 1992 I was asked to evaluate the prostitution scene in Montreal and the effects of a new street prostitution law (Gemme et al. 1984; Gemme, Payment, and Malenfant 1989; Gemme and Payment 1990; Gemme and Saint-Pierre 1992). In 1990 the Research-Action Center of Sexo-criminology, Brussels University, asked for my sexological perspective on prostitution (Gemme 1992). The following is a mixture of both requests.

The first part describes the legal context of street prostitution in Montreal and the second part proposes a solution based on sexological facts and perspective. It stipulates that if we want prostitution to be considered as any other trade, decriminalization, regulation, or legalization are not enough. A societal attitude in favor of sexual pluralism, valuing sex as such, is necessary. Otherwise the social context surrounding prostitution will still be negative even in a neutral legal context. Arrests, fines, imprisonment would disappear but negative effects of stigmatization would not. Prostitute and clients would not respect each other more, and those police officers who do not respect prostitutes now would not respect them more after decriminalization.

# Methodology

The legal aspects presented here are based on the findings of our studies of street prostitution conducted for the Canadian government. In these studies 291 persons were interviewed: 114 male and female prostitutes, 39 clients, 74 enforcement officers, 9 Crown prosecutors, 5 defense lawyers, 11 judges, 26 social and medical workers, 10 other citizens or merchants' representatives, and 3 pimps. We also analyzed a random sample of 270 police and court files (175 prostitutes, 95 clients). Finally, we proceeded to 38 street counts of prostitutes. The sexological aspects are based on the abovementioned studies and a sexological perspective developed over twenty-five years as professor at the Department of Sexology, University of Quebec at Montreal.

## Legal Aspects of Street Prostitution in Montreal

We must first point out that prostitution is not illegal in Canada. This is clearly illustrated by a court decision concerning implementation of municipal regulation 333–2b of the city of Montreal. The regulation stipulated that "Every person loitering at night in the streets, lanes, fields, yards or other places in the city and who cannot satisfactorily account for his presence or refuses to do so shall be subject to the penalty hereinafter proclaimed."

The court ruled that a prostitute does not loiter; her stroll has a goal, that is, to find clients in order to prostitute herself, an act that is in itself not illegal. Nevertheless, almost all activities that permit one to practice prostitution are illegal (solicitation, to deliver service to many in the same place, to operate or to find oneself in a bawdy house, to transport toward this place, to initiate into prostitution, or to live from prostitution of others).

In 1985 the solicitation infraction had been modified in order to facilitate its implementation.

### Law C-49

The law modifying the Criminal Code was proclaimed December 20, 1985, following the adoption of bill C-49. This law aimed directly at the problem of public solicitation with the purpose of prostitution. In its adoption, the Parliament abrogated section 195.1 (public solicitation) of the Criminal Code and replaced it with a new article aimed at controlling the phenomenon of public solicitation in a more efficient manner. Section 213.1 states:

Every person who in a public place or in any place open to public view:

   a. stops or attempts to stop any motor vehicle,

b. impedes the free flow of pedestrian or vehicular traffic or ingress to or egress from premises adjacent to that place, or

c. stops or attempts to stop any person or in any manner communicates or attempts to communicate with any person

for the purpose of engaging in prostitution or of obtaining the sexual services of a prostitute is guilty of an offense punishable on summary conviction.

In this section, "public place" includes "any place to which the public have access by right or by invitation, express or implied, and any motor vehicle located in a public place or in any place open to public view."

This article is more restrictive than the old law in that it (*a*) declares automobiles as a "public place," (*b*) concerns the client as well as the prostitute, (*c*) criminalizes the sole fact of communicating for purpose of prostitution (with or without harassment). Paragraph c provides the basis for nearly all arrests.

This modification facilitated application of the law in that it was no longer necessary to organize a surveillance in order to catch prostitute and client "red-handed." It was sufficient to prove communication mentioning at least the rate which is requested or offered. This element of proof is easily obtained by resorting to having policemen or policewomen play the role of the prostitute or the client and waiting for the incriminating communication.

However, from the first arrests in January 1986, lawyers organized two types of defense by contesting either the legality of using police decoys or the constitutionality of the law. Both were unsuccessful and in 1990 the Supreme Court of Canada decided that nuisances caused by prostitution were serious enough to justify restrictions to the freedom of speech guaranteed in the Canadian Charter of Rights.

## Evaluation of C-49

Law C-49 had three major goals: significantly decreasing street prostitution, facilitating the application of the law, and equal prosecution of prostitutes and clients.

## IMPACT OF THE LAW ON PREVALENCE OF ADULT STREET PROSTITUTION

Because there were no baseline street counts of prostitutes before 1986, it was difficult to compare prevalence before and after the new law. We had to rely on official police reports or police interviews that we compare with our 1987, 1990, and 1992 street counts.

*Prevalence in Traditional Heterosexual and Homosexual Strolls.* According to police information, in 1987 there was a decrease of 30 percent–50 percent in prostitutes after implementation of the law, especially during daytime. An official tactic report mentioned that in 1985 there were between 75 and 100 prostitutes at peak hours on peak nights; whereas the estimate was 50 in 1987. This confirmed our 1987 street counts in which an average of 40 prostitutes were counted, thus confirming a significant decrease in those traditional strolls. Average counts remained the same from 1987 to 1992.

*Geographical and Modal Displacement.* Our own observation and those of the police indicated that implementation of the law resulted in geographical displacements, therefore maintaining prevalence at almost the same level as in 1985. Since 1986, sentencing policy included fines plus systematic area restrictions (i.e., prohibition for one year from being found in traditional strolls). This created five or six new secondary strolls of 3 to 20 prostitutes and sometimes major problems in residential areas.

Concerning modal displacement (a shift from one form of prostitution to another), change could be noticed in newspaper classified advertisements. Table 1 shows a 151 percent increase between 1985 and 1997 and that thirty-five individuals advertised their services in 1997 compared to one in 1992 and none in 1985, suggesting that maybe some street prostitutes are also offering sexual services off street.

The ineffectiveness of the law in eradicating street prostitution might be explained by the low fines (averaging $480 in 1987) and the low probability of being arrested (1.8 times per prostitute arrested in a ten-month period during 1987, totaling $869 in fines).

*Clients.* There are indications that police arrests and court procedures deterred certain clients although this is difficult to substantiate with exact figures. It is almost impossible to make street counts of clients because of their relative invisibility compared to prostitutes. However, according to the prostitutes, it now takes them a longer time to get clients. This is also confirmed by the police, who also take longer to arrest the same number of clients in a blitz. Table 2 shows the variation in clients' arrests from 1986 to 1995. Statistics indicate an almost annual increase from 1986 to 1990 corresponding to intense police activities in the years immediately following implementation of the law. The declining rate from 1991 to 1995 is explained by the decrease in police activity against street prostitution. Proxenitism and "bawdy house" (particularly bars offering clients the possibility to touch the dancers and masturbate) became the priority.

Table 1. Classified Advertisements for Prostitution in the
*Journal de Montreal* 1985, 1992, 1997

| Year | | Ads | Increase |
|------|------|-----|----------|
| | | n | % |
| 1985 | | 49 | |
| 1992 | | 63 | 29 |
| | individual | 1 | |
| 1997 | | 123 | 151 |
| | individual | 35 | |

Low fines (averaging $300) and low arrest probability may explain continued clients' activities.

## IMPACT OF THE LAW ON ITS APPLICATION

In Montreal, the law is enforced on a regular basis. All evidences show that the application of the law is relatively unproblematic.

*Simplicity of Evidentiary Requirement.* Under the new law, prosecution does not require proof of any nuisance, but only proof that communication for the purpose of prostitution with mention of rates took place.

*Easiness of Arrest Procedures.* Since a higher court confirmed the legality of a contract between a client or prostitute with a decoy (undercover agent posing as prostitute or client), most of the arrests used that strategy. Because the new definition of public place includes a motor vehicle, arrests can be made even when the offer, request, or price discussion happens in a vehicle. Even with few officers enforcing the prostitution law (approximately twenty including only two female officers), the number of arrests averaged 2,020 a year since 1986 with a peak in 1990 that was over 67 percent greater than 1986 (table 3).

*Rate of Conviction.* Almost 100 percent of arrests lead to prosecution, and table 4 shows that in our random sample of files, the rate of conviction of prostitutes and clients is 95 percent.

**Table 2. Street Client Arrests in Montreal from 1985 to 1995**

| Year | Number |
|------|--------|
| 1985* | 0 |
| 1986 | 454 |
| 1987 | 925 |
| 1988 | 919 |
| 1989 | 935 |
| 1990 | 1104 |
| 1991 | 758 |
| 1992 | 848 |
| 1993 | 684 |
| 1994 | 493 |
| 1995 | 720 |

* Under former solicitation law

## IMPACT ON EQUAL APPLICATION OF THE LAW TO PROSTITUTES AND CLIENTS

In Montreal, the police department always had an objective of achieving an arrest ratio of one prostitute for one client, even though they admit some difficulties in doing so. There are few female officers, and even fewer interested in posing as a prostitute, so enforcement relies mostly on two female decoys. Nevertheless, despite media complaints of discrimination against prostitutes, efforts were made to achieve more equal prosecution. Table 5 shows that the prostitute/client ratio decreased from 1:0 in 1985 to 1.2:1 in 1995.

However, when considering only heterosexual prostitution, table 6 shows that although the average ratio for 1986–1995 is 1.3, for the first time, more clients than female prostitutes were arrested in 1995.

Decreasing the ratio to 1:1 with the same number of enforcement agents means less time spent on prosecuting prostitutes who are considered to be the major cause of nuisances.

This attempt to achieve equal application of the law applies almost exclusively to clients of female prostitutes; almost no clients of male prostitutes are arrested. Male police officers do not like to pose as prostitutes to entrap a client.

**Table 3. Arrests of Street Prostitutes and Clients in Montreal from 1986 to 1995**

| Year | Prostitute | Client | Total |
|------|-----------|--------|-------|
| 1986 | 1167 | 454 | 1621 |
| 1987 | 1406 | 929 | 2335 |
| 1988 | 1501 | 919 | 2420 |
| 1989 | 1367 | 935 | 2302 |
| 1990 | 1606 | 1104 | 2710 |
| 1991 | 1192 | 758 | 1950 |
| 1992 | 1439 | 848 | 2287 |
| 1993 | 1023 | 684 | 1707 |
| 1994 | 811 | 493 | 1304 |
| 1995 | 848 | 720 | 1568 |
| Total | 12 360 | 7 844 | 20 204 |

## Conclusions on the Legal Aspects

After many years of application of law C-49, we conclude that

- the goal of significantly decreasing street prostitution was not achieved because fines and prison sentences have no deterring effects;
- the law greatly facilitated prosecuting and convicting prostitutes and clients;
- the law is still applied inequally. First, more prostitutes are being prosecuted than clients. Second, many more heterosexual clients are being prosecuted than homosexual clients.

# Sexological Aspects of Adult Street Prostitution and Prostitution Control

In most cities, some advocates of abolitionism, criminalization, decriminalization, and/or legalization of prostitution express explicitly or implicitly that prostitution is either a despicable evil or, at best, an uncontrollable necessary evil. Based on the adverse consequences of those negative attitudes, I suggest a sexological approach to prostitution that respects sexological findings related to repression, demand, and supply; this view expresses a positive sexual attitude towards prostitution and considers it as a trade to be regulated as

**Table 4. Final Plea of Prostitutes and Clients in Montreal in 1987 (n = 191)**

| Final plea | Prostitutes | | Clients | | Total | |
|---|---|---|---|---|---|---|
| | n | % | n | % | n | % |
| Guilty | 107 | 97.3 | 74 | 91.4 | 181 | 94.8 |
| Not guilty | 3 | 2.7 | 7 | 8.6 | 10 | 5.2 |
| Total | 110 | 100 | 81 | 100 | 191 | 100 |

**Table 5. Prostitutes (M-F)/Client Arrest Ratio in Montreal (1985–1995)**

| Year | Prostitutes (M-F) | Clients | Ratio |
|---|---|---|---|
| 1985 | 1189 | 0 | 1:0 |
| 1986 | 1167 | 454 | 2.6:1 |
| 1987 | 1406 | 929 | 1.5:1 |
| 1988 | 1501 | 919 | 1.6:1 |
| 1989 | 1367 | 935 | 1.5:1 |
| 1990 | 1606 | 1104 | 1.5:1 |
| 1991 | 1192 | 758 | 1.6:1 |
| 1992 | 1439 | 848 | 1.7:1 |
| 1993 | 1023 | 684 | 1.5:1 |
| 1994 | 811 | 493 | 1.7:1 |
| 1995 | 848 | 720 | 1.2:1 |
| Total | 12 360 | 7 844 | 1.6:1 |

**Table 6. Prostitute/Client Arrest Ratio for Heterosexual Prostitution in Montreal (1986–1995)**

| Year | Prostitutes | Clients | Ratio |
|---|---|---|---|
| 1986 | 852 | 454 | 1.9:1 |
| 1987 | 1028 | 929 | 1.1:1 |
| 1988 | 1162 | 919 | 1.3:1 |
| 1989 | 992 | 935 | 1.1:1 |
| 1990 | 1429 | 1104 | 1.3:1 |
| 1991 | 1030 | 758 | 1.4:1 |
| 1992 | 1280 | 848 | 1.5:1 |
| 1993 | 819 | 684 | 1.2:1 |
| 1994 | 686 | 493 | 1.4:1 |
| 1995 | 705 | 720 | .9:1 |
| Total | 9983 | 7844 | 1.3:1 |

such. Decriminalization, yes; regulations, some; but all in a context of sexual pluralism of which honesty, equality, and responsibility are integral parts.

## Sexological Aspects of Canadian Law and Its Enforcement

One major characteristic of the Canadian law is its ambiguity. Exchanging sex for money is not illegal but all related activities are, including offering or requesting the service.

This law also reflects a cultural erotophobia in which sex associated with pleasure, but not with love, affection, and/or reproductive intent, is considered as evil and degrading, particularly when money is involved.

By criminalizing the acts of prostitution, the law contributes to maintenance of a negative and discrediting context for this activity and thus encourages stigmatization of the participants and particularly of the prostitutes.

This attitude reinforces the negative self-image that many prostitutes already have, an image often caused by childhood sexual abuse. No wonder that no prostitute interviewed would recommend the trade to his/her children. Moreover, this low self- and trade-esteem is associated with alcohol and drug addiction, and it explains poor quality service, imprudence towards strange and potentially violent clients, sexually explicit acts in public, and risk-taking behavior regarding STD and AIDS.

This stigmatization leads clients to the conviction that they are paying for a "bitch," rather than for services offered on a trade basis by a worthy sex worker. Indeed they may use this perception to justify the violence that some of them use against prostitutes. Finally, the discrediting of paid sexual services contributes to maintaining contact between persons who have a negative image of themselves and of the trade, and who consequently contribute to the nuisances and major problems associated with prostitution (public indecency, theft, violence, rape, etc.).

For instance, repression in Montreal led to a geographic displacement of prostitution. When judges imposed area restrictions on prostitutes in 1986, it caused a displacement of indecent acts from commercial areas to residential ones. New groups of citizens became disturbed by those indecent acts, sexual provocations, verbal obscenities, fellatio in sight of children, condoms found in schoolyards, etc.

Finally, even though in Montreal there were 20,204 street prostitution-related arrests from 1986 to 1995 (12,360 prostitutes and 7,844 clients), the number of prostitutes did not dramatically decrease. Low fines and low arrest probability do not seem to deter clients with sexual urges. Since judges need to have a justifiable rationale in sentencing sexual offenses, it is most unlikely that sentencing policy could be made more severe for a victimless offense. So repression will continue to be ineffective and demand for sexual services will still exist.

## Sexological Aspects of Demand

We have already mentioned that some clients have a negative perception of the prostitutes and use violence against them. We also found that their motivation for paid sexual services included the desire for quick sexual gratification, without attachment and at minimal cost; curiosity; sexual timidity and lack of heterosocial skills; marital sexual dissatisfaction; lack of a partner; a desire for atypical services.

We also found that anonymity is essential. This is why motor vehicles are the preferred locations for sexual services. The risk of being identified is low since the major prostitution strolls are located in high-traffic commercial areas.

## Sexological Aspects of Supply

Our interviews with prostitutes in Montreal indicated that the most typical sexual service was fellatio with condom, thus preventing risk of STDs. Time of execution was short (averaging twelve minutes), with no or few preliminaries. Quality of the interaction could be considered poor. Because 12.5 percent of apparently female prostitutes were male transvestites and transsexuals, some of clients' violence could be explained. Moreover, 85 percent of the services are performed in cars parked along the streets or in public parking lots, creating potentially harmful effects to other citizens (including children) such as public exposure of sexual activity or hygiene problems related to discarded condoms or tissues with semen. Finally, the offer of sexual services was made mostly to car drivers, thus creating a traffic circulation problem.

Our data revealed that 44 percent of prostitutes had been sexually abused and 33 percent had been raped prior to prostitution activities. No wonder then that in a culture where sex is linked with love and tenderness, prostitutes who have been initiated to sex in a context of abuse, violence, and exploitation have a negative perception of sexuality. The negative perception they also have of their male abusers explains the contempt and disgust many of them feel toward their clients and hence the poor quality of their interaction with them. Again it is not surprising that adolescents who have exchanged sex for gifts or money in a context of abuse subsequently find themselves engaged in prostitution. It is quite understandable that some of them, in need of affection, will easily fall into the arms of a pimp. Many prostitutes also have low self-esteem and are alcohol- or drug-addicted, thus explaining poor quality service, clients' dissatisfaction, and prostitutes' victimization through violence and thefts. Finally, our studies showed that 35 percent of prostitutes had suffered physical abuse and that 30 percent had been raped an average of four times while prostituting, thus reflecting the clients' negative perception of the prostitutes.

## Sexological Perspective of Prostitution Control

Legal intervention in Canada or elsewhere does not take into account the sexological findings mentioned above and does not consider in a positive way that sexual needs/desires exist that cannot be satisfied by other than a commercial exchange. A negative perspective on prostitution exists even when adult participants are consenting and when there is no violence, exploitation, degradation, or use of children. Despite laws and sanctions, people will always have sexual needs that can only be satisfied by a commercial exchange because it is doubtful that the state will ever provide free services to those with such desires. Sexual satisfaction is not commonly considered a human right.

I would like to present here a liberal perspective that takes into account our sexological findings and considers that association of sex solely with pleasure, even if money is involved, is an acceptable alternative to association of sex with love, affection, or reproduction. Tolerance for sexual diversity should also apply to prostitution. This approach, although hardly acceptable to most cultures, is nevertheless in my mind the only possible solution when considering the adverse consequences of other approaches.

## A Liberal Sexological Approach to Sexuality and the Demand for Prostitution

*This sexological approach states that*

a. there are no supernatural nor suprahuman sexual values. On the contrary, values are of social or personal origin;

b. sex for pleasure is as valuable as sex for love, affection, or reproductive intent, even when money is involved, if participants are consenting and enlightened persons and if there is no violence, exploitation, degradation, or use of children;

c. for most people, sexual health implies that sexual needs are satisfied;

d. for most people sexual satisfaction implies preference for human interaction;

e. there will always be a sexual demand related to curiosity, atypical needs, or erotic incompatibility in couples;

f. the client is not a despicable person;

g. the law should not manage moral aspects of prostitution. This responsibility should be left to individual religious beliefs or personal consciences;

h. sex education should begin at an early age and should ultimately help individuals to communicate about their sexual needs, preferences, and fantasies. It should also teach that erotic compatibility is an important criterion in mate selection. Finally it would present prostitutes as worthy persons;

i.   it is necessary to insure anonymity of the demand for sexual services.

In that view, a humanistic and scientific sex education based on a positive approach to sexuality and prostitution would, on the one hand, help to reduce unintegrated and undesirable demand for prostitution and, on the other hand, promote a positive attitude when acceptable demand exists. The client would not seek satisfaction of a "low instinct" from a "bitch," but a sexually legitimate service from a worthy sex worker. The effects would be to reduce violence and thefts and to raise self-esteem of clients.

## Scientific Sexological Approach of Supply

The quality of services should be improved to reduce the dissatisfaction that is one factor leading to violence. Education of prostitutes about honesty, erotic skills, and sexual values could solve part of this problem. This sexological approach also implies the acknowledgment that this service should be delivered by prostitutes who consider themselves as worthy persons and their work valuable.

*This acknowledgment implies that*

a.   prostitution is not an evil act in itself and the prostitute not a despicable person;

b.   sex education should aim to prevent child sexual abuse and prevent adolescents who have been sexually abused from turning to an unintegrated prostitution;

c.   sex education should be based on autonomy and self-respect to prevent future prostitutes from submitting to a coercive or exploitive pimp;

d.   sex education should promote responsible decisionmaking. Prostitution would thus be presented as a type of work as acceptable as other types of services when performed in a context of free will, honesty, equality, and responsibility without violence, exploitation, degradation, or use of children. Advantages, disadvantages, and precautions to be taken would be presented in a scientific way. Prostitution would become a trade freely chosen with full knowledge of the possible disadvantages.

## Scientific Sexological Approach of Control and Management

To take into account the abovementioned sexological characteristics, a sexological approach of control and management would imply that:

a.  sexual repression should apply only to the harmful effects associated with prostitution and not to prostitution itself, therefore allowing control agents to be more efficient and imaginative in controlling its harmful effects (coercive or abusive proxenetism, traffic problems, public indecency, etc.);

b.  a zoning policy that concentrates prostitution activities in nonresidential areas while insuring the safety and anonymity of demand for prostitution;

c.  increased surveillance using foot patrols to insure safety at work;

d.  regulations applying to other trades apply to prostitution (unemployment insurance, work schedule, security at work, taxation, etc.);

e.  noncoercive or nonabusive pimps should be considered as any other business manager and controlled as such;

f.  we develop outreach programs to help prostitutes quit the trade if they feel prostitution is auto-destructive.

# Conclusion

I am fully aware that the liberal sexological and scientific approach to prostitution presented here may bring opposition because of underlying moral concerns. But one is facing two choices: the traditional restrictive approach that carries with it the harmful effects of harassment, arrest, incarceration of people who don't deserve it, stigmatization, violence, substance addictions, etc.; or this scientific, positive sexological approach that, I believe, can help reduce many of these problems. This proposition may seem unrealistic or scandalous. I believe, however, that the cultural process of thought that might lead to acceptance of this approach would be similar to the one that led to changed perspectives about oral-genital sex. Culturally unacceptable twenty-five years ago, termed a perversion, gross indecency, and an act against nature, oral-genital sex is now considered an acceptable erotic variation and is even promoted. I believe that a culture's moral perspective on such matters can change under the influence of scientific thought and the social commitment of the scientific community. This could happen if social scientists practice what Reiss called social therapy, i.e., consider that the patient is the society and that social scientists are seeking to find ways to help it control its sexual problems (1990). In the case of prostitution the destigmatization process will take a long time, but if we don't begin the social therapy now, it will take longer.

# References

Gemme, R. 1992. Perspective sexologique de la prostitution. In *La prostitution: Quarante ans après la convention de New York*. 55–74. Bruxelles: Bruylant.

Gemme, R., A. Murphy, M. R. Nemeh, and N. Payment. 1984. A report on prostitution in Québec. Ottawa: Department of Supply and Services.

Gemme, R., and N. Payment. 1990. Complementary evaluation of Law C-49. Unpublished. Ottawa: Department of Justice 10 p.

Gemme, R., N. Payment, and L. Malenfant. 1989. *Street Prostitution: Assessing the Impact of the Law*. Montreal: Ministry of Supply and Services, Canada.

Gemme, R., and R. Saint-Pierre. 1992. Complementary evaluation of Law C-49. Unpublished. Ottawa: Department of Justice.

Reiss, I. L. 1990. *An End to Shame: Shaping Our Next Sexual Revolution*. Amherst, N.Y.: Prometheus Books.

# The Prostitution Prevention Law in Japan and a Movement of Abolitionist Feminists for Amendment of the Law

## Masumi Yoneda

Japan enacted the Prostitution Prevention Law (PPL) in 1956 and it has been in effect since 1958. It was the first time prostitution had been prohibited in Japanese history, but in the forty years since it passed the law has proven to be ineffective. Currently there are proposals for amending the law and considerable discussion on the issue in Japan. This chapter represents my own position.

I hold that laws on prostitution should not be measured as an ethical or moral problem in sexuality but rather judged by how such a law affects women's rights. In particular, it is important to look at the rights of sex workers because they are the most vulnerable to sexual violence. In Japan, the term "sex worker" is not yet widely accepted, but as I use the term it means women who engage in sex industries of their own free will. Although sex workers are not limited to the practice of prostitution, I limit the discussion to prostitution because the PPL covers only prostitution. Moreover, sex workers are not only female but male as well, and I want to focus on the females.

Although prostitution technically cannot be regarded as a profession in Japan because it is illegal, there are many hard-working prostitutes. Their working conditions cannot be protected by the law, and their rights are violated by clients, pimps, police, the general populace, and the courts. I believe that PPL should be abolished because it only contributes to the violation of sex workers' rights as human beings. I hope to work with the feminists to enact a new law that punishes all forms of sexual violence against every woman, not just prostitutes.

# The Prostitution Prevention Law in Japan

The reasons for the original enactment of the PPL was to enable Japan to ratify the 1949 Convention for the Suppression of Traffic in Persons and of the Exploitation of the Prostitution of Others. In 1958, two years after Japan enacted the PPL, the country ratified the 1949 convention. Prior to this law, prostitution was legalized in specific "red-light areas." The brothels were compelled to close down in 1958 but even though they closed their doors, they continued in business under other legal guises, particularly as massage parlors, and other businesses in what the Japanese call the "ejaculation industry."

The PPL comprises four parts: general (articles 1 to 4), penal punishment (5 to 16), rehabilitation (17 to 33), and counseling (34 to 40). The aim of the law was not to punish prostitutes but to prevent prostitution; to this end punishment is directed at those promoting prostitution and the law promotes counseling and rehabilitation help for those involved in prostitution. The impetus for both the Japanese law and the international convention was the belief that prostitution violated the dignity of the individual person involved and posed a threat to public order. There was no attempt to distinguish between volunteer prostitutes and enforced prostitution.

Japanese law, however, differs from the 1949 convention in some ways. The convention does not define prostitution nor the traffic in women and it consistently regarded prostitutes as victims. Moreover, it did not require that prostitution itself be made illegal. The PPL defines prostitution as a means of sexual intercourse with unspecified persons for remuneration or under contract to get remuneration. This narrow definition fails to deal with any sexual services not involving intercourse, and it was this failure that led to the "ejaculation industry." Moreover, although the PPL criminalizes prostitution, it does not punish prostitutes or their customers except under certain conditions. It does, however, regard prostitutes as problem women who threaten public order; hence, they need to be protected. They can also be arrested for violating article 5, which prevents sex workers from publicly soliciting. Solicitation in private, however, is allowed.

Those advocates of abolition in Japan have always argued that the reason for enacting the PPL was to rescue victims from the control of pimps and other exploiters. This argument did not necessarily correspond with the reality in Japan because many sex workers were organized in unions to oppose the PPL. The newsletters and other materials published by such groups tend to document that not all Japanese prostitutes regarded themselves as victims. Moreover, the temporary alliance of the abolitionists and prohibitionists made for a confusing and uncertain law that seems mainly to be utilized rather selectively, according to the political clout of those involved. For example, recently many prostitutes who were not citizens of Japan were arrested under article 5 and deported to their countries of origin because the immigration law stipulates that any person directly or indirectly engaging in prostitution can be deported.

# Prostitution Case Law

The first case I want to examine is the Ikebukuro case. She worked out of a hotel where her clients awaited her. In 1987, she was serving a sadistically inclined client who threatened to kill her if she did not perform certain acts. She was unable to escape from him, the two fought, and she killed him with his own knife. For this she was prosecuted for murder, although she claimed self-defense. The court ruled that although she had acted in self-defense, she had overreacted, and sentenced her to three years in prison. On appeal, the Tokyo High Court reversed the decision in the first trial and sentenced her to two years with an additional three-year suspended sentence.

The High Court reported that the client had repeatedly battered her and threatened her with his knife for an hour before she killed him. She had her hands and feet tied with a rope and was compelled to commit "indecent acts" while under such confinement. To escape her confinement she promised him that she would do what he wanted in return for a fee. Thus, while she technically consented, I hold that the greater crime was the violation of her integrity and physical freedom.

The second case, that of Ichihara, dealt with traffic in women from Thailand. Her recruiter had told her that if she came to Japan she could work in a bar and engage in sexual intercourse but only if she wanted to do so with a client. He said that on arriving in Japan she would owe 3,500,000 yen (about $35,000) to the manager of the bar, but that this could easily be paid back in three to four months. She went to the Chiba area near Tokyo at the end of 1993 and soon found that the working conditions were far different than those described to her. She was in effect imprisoned in the bar and forced to serve as a prostitute. She managed to escape and moved to the Nagoya area where she worked for a different bar. She did well until the manager of the first bar traced her down and took her back in January 1994, raped her, and forced her to remain in prostitution. In February 1994, she killed a Thai woman who acted as her guard and stole her purse in order to escape. She was quickly arrested and prosecuted for murder and theft. The court sentenced her to four years in prison and refused to suspend any imprisonment for her because she had entered Japan illegally with a forged passport and had in effect consented to practice prostitution.

# Analysis

In the Ikebukuro case, the court distinguished prostitutes from women in general and did not afford them equal protection under the law. There were two reasons for this: first, the PPL made prostitution illegal and looked upon the "profession" as similar to the occupation of thieves. If a thief fell from a roof of a house he was robbing, if he was injured, he could not be compensated because he was in an illegal profession. On the other hand, if a carpenter fell from the roof of a house while he was working, he could be compensated. In short, as long as prostitution is illegal, prostitutes cannot be protected under the law without considerable discrimination being exercised. The second reason for the court decision is the lack of understanding of what kind of a profession sex work is. The court could not distinguish sex work from sexual slavery. Sex work is based on a contract with a client and if clients require unanticipated sexual services, the requirement goes beyond the contract and the contract should be renegotiated. If clients force prostitutes to go beyond the original negotiation, then it is rape. In the Ikebukuro case, the court simply ignored that she was raped while being held in confinement by her client.

The Ichihara case emphasized the importance of distinguishing free from forced prostitution. She consented to engage in sexual intercourse on the condition she could choose a client. Prostitution in Nagoya was of her own free will but that in Chiba was against her will. Interestingly, the court ignored that she was a victim of the traffic in women and children, something that Japanese laws were designed to prevent, and which would have made her an innocent victim.

Although many foreign women are involved in prostitution, and a disproportionate number are illegal immigrants from Thailand, they are the persons accused in courts and not those who talked them into coming to Japan. They may well have come to Japan knowing that they might be paid to engage in sexual intercourse, but they were at least told that they would have a choice in their customers.

# Conclusion and Some Questions to Feminists Who Support Abolitionism: My Opinions

Currently most Japanese feminists are attempting to amend the PPL from an abolitionist perspective. They propose to abolish article 5 and replace it with a new article punishing the customer. Other punishments would be provided for those who benefit from prostitution. The feminists in Japan are not unanimous on deleting article 3, which bans prostitution itself without punishment. Many hold that the human body is not and should not be a consumer product, which is the stand of the International Abolitionist Federation. This, however, can be interpreted as removing state regulation and exploitation, but not in prohibiting the freedom of a woman to engage in commercial sex work if she so desires. I believe, in fact, this is what the International Abolitionist Federation can be interpreted to mean.

The IAF, however, sometimes has a distorted view. The members argue that recent studies have shown that the majority of prostitutes (about 90 percent) have been subjected to incest or other forms of sexual abuse as children. When this psychological burden is added to the grinding poverty in which large segments of the world population lives, and the growing consumer orientation of many societies, the IAF holds that prostitution can never be a free choice on the part of the majority who practice it. They are simply victims. Nowhere in the writings of the IAF do I find that they have considered the opinions of sex workers, and although abolitionists are strongly opposed to treating prostitutes as criminals, they often regard them as sick persons.

The aim of abolitionism is a laudable one: to create a situation where no one finds it necessary to prostitute herself/himself against her/his will. But the abolitionists do not recognize that large numbers of free-choice prostitutes exist. For them prostitutes are victims of forced prostitution, but the abolitionists use force in such a wide sense that it sometimes becomes meaningless. Moreover, sex workers have their own will to make money and if they do it by prostitution then abolitionists should recognize this.

If they did we would work together for improving working conditions for women workers, including sex workers. Abolitionism is based on the assumption that one cannot be happy while working as a sex worker. The recent attempts of prostitutes to assert themselves and to proclaim themselves as sex workers indicate the efforts of such workers to gain respect and to reclaim their rights. We need to expand our activities throughout Japan and throughout the rest of the world.

Unfortunately, as long as women are themselves divided into two categories, prostitutes and others, we will discriminate against sex workers in our own minds and fail to ensure the rights of all women. Sex workers have their own will and ability to decide on their own lifestyle.

We should distinguish sex activity resulting from one's own will from sex activity against one's will. The problem is similar to the general problem of violence against women. How can we claim rape between spouses exists without making this distinction? To recognize sex work and respect their lifestyle is the first step to ensure sex workers' human rights. Perhaps the difficulty lies with the fact that the term *prostitution* is misleading because it encompasses both free choice prostitution and forced prostitution. Forced prostitution is a form of rape and it should be punished as a felony. Voluntary prostitution is something else altogether, and we should work to enact new laws to punish and prevent sexual violence against every woman, including sex workers.

# FEMALE PROSTITUTION IN SPAIN: NEITHER CRIMINALS NOR VICTIMS

IGNASI PONS AND VICTORIA SERRA

Our purpose in this chapter is to show the objective and technical difficulties of the criminalization of prostitution and prostitutes, and how the law itself creates a crime or an offense. To do this we will first analyze the Spanish Criminal Code of 1995, which devotes a section to prostitution although it says little about it. We will then report some data from research on the life and work conditions of prostitutes in the Asturias region in the north of Spain illustrating the victimization of prostitutes (Pons 1992).

## Does the State Dictate Law That It Does Not Want to Execute?

This is the seeming paradox that troubles the existence of prostitution in Spain. Before the reform of the Criminal Code in 1995, prostitution was considered in two legal texts: (1) the "Law of Dangerousness and Social Rehabilitation" of 1970 condemned prostitutes while (2) the then-existing Criminal Code did not condemn the prostitute but did condemn nearly all of her working environment. To explain: the law of 1970 considered pimps and procurers and all those who usually practice prostitution socially dangerous. The law proposed measures to deal with this danger, such as confinement of prostitutes in establishments for re-education, prohibition of their residence in areas and territories stipulated by a judge, and prohibiting them from visiting certain public places or entertainments without submitting to the surveillance of inspectors.

This law, however, was hardly ever applied to prostitutes. In fact, the Department of Interior itself informed several police stations that prostitutes were not to be prosecuted. The public prosecutor also gave similar instructions to all district attorneys. In effect, when the reform to the previous Criminal Code was made, there was a contradiction between legal texts and as a result the law of 1970 was not enforced even if it was not formally repealed.

The earlier Criminal Code, as was the case in the majority of European laws, included the absurdity of permitting prostitution as such while at the same time containing some articles making the practice of prostitution impossible. Condemned were pimping, the hiring out of a third party, and everything that could facilitate prostitution. As a consequence, if the law had been effectively enforced, the prostitutes would not have been able to have a place to contact and engage any client or to have a room in which to work. At the same time, the definition of what constituted a pimp was so loosely drawn that it could have prevented the prostitute from having a more or less stable companion, even if he did not force her to engage in prostitution in any way. In practice, the code did not support a systematic persecution, even if the existence of this law permitted chance counts or indictments by some police official or judge who did not take notice of the tacit agreement to not apply the law.

When the Criminal Code was reformed in 1995, everything that was not being prosecuted in practice was omitted, including the articles referring to pimping and the hiring out of a third party. At the same time, a significant semantic change appeared. What remained as prostitution offenses were mainly references to child prostitution, although coercion and abuse were placed under "offenses against sexual freedom." By such actions, the moral considerations so long associated with prostitution disappeared, and the law in fact showed a protective intention. Still, some authors argue that there is an underlying concept that prostitution is "a lower form of sexuality" and as a consequence, it can be considered as violating sexual freedom (cited in Silva 1995).

In these terms, there are two realities. First, the previous situation, where the state itself doesn't want to carry out its own laws on prostitutes and/or prostitution and its environment. Second, the present situation, a combination of a Criminal Code that substantially reduces the offenses related to prostitution, with the ones that still exist referring to coercion, authority abuse, and child prostitution. The latter could remain without the need for a specific reference to prostitution in aspects that already exist, taking into account coactions and coercions, authority abuse, the practice of child prostitution, economic exploitation and theft, and finally, the articles making reference to the protection of sexual freedom. According to these facts, the question of "why" this happens arises; why in situations where there is no application, is there an interest in the emergence of prostitution in the Criminal Code?

Without doubt it is inconsistent to call prostitution an offense, because it is contractual, voluntary, and is a free transaction between adult people. It is, in effect, an "offense without victims," and intervention in such activities is contrary to any juridical doctrine. Yet some argue it is in the interest of the state to give to some juridical texts the symbolic function of moral testimony.

Thus the discourse becomes a set of idealizations that pretend to keep the functional family within an institutional monogamy, reinforcing the sufficiency of such a unit in an atmosphere of loving mysticism and sexual fulfillment. At the real level there is an interest in the existence of adultery and prostitution, but both are always kept more or less hidden. The assumption of this fiction is that they offer a safety valve for the continuation of the institution. The ability of the state to in effect decriminalize prostitution, yet not legitimatize prostitution, manages to maintain the stigma attached to it. Thus, the prostitute becomes the antithesis of the decent, honest, good, and clean woman. Prostitution can thus be considered as an instrument for social control of feminine behavior. When a woman transgresses the unofficial sexual codes or behaves in a way that disturbs the "right of property," i.e., male control, she can be put down as a prostitute and feel the weight of the stigma. But such a label does not only arise from an external menace. It is internalized by the woman herself and hangs above her like Damocles's sword to the point that she departs from her rational convictions and her moral reasoning when some of her sexual behaviors are socially condemned. As a consequence she tends to repress her legitimate desires, in an aprioristic manner, or she feels her guilt, a posteriori, fueled by her own self-definition of being a prostitute. In any case, state intervention in this matter is, as Paulina Silva argues, an invasion of the law in a particular "sensitive area to privacy" (1995, 10).

# The Law as Producer of Delinquency and Definer of Offenses

Once the law identifies a behavior and includes it in a list of prohibitions or subsequent sanctions, it creates the offense and defines delinquent behavior that had previously been nonexistent. The answer to the question why any behavior is an offense is "because the law says so" (Shaver 1996). This results in a mobilization of law enforcement and society to persecute, to judge, and to apply sanctions against the behavior.

Prostitution offers a clear case of how the artificial creation of an offense has a multiplying effect on creating or increasing other offenses and crimes. As a justification for the fight against prostitution, it is usually argued that it attracts other offenders and delinquents, such as women traffickers, pimps, street marauders, and so on. These dangers, however, are normally produced when prostitution is made illegal, criminalized, and concentrated in ghettos in certain areas. A more likely hypothesis might be that the existence of such a large number of collateral delinquents and the higher proportion and seriousness of offenses closely related to prostitution normally occur in countries where the laws on prostitution are the most restrictive and its persecution more systematic and severe. In any case, it would be interesting and worthwhile to do a comparative study of this hypothesis, in effect disputing the statement that prohibition or regulations are necessary to solve and/or avoid other social and personal problems. In our view such prohibitions create and/or increase the number and seriousness of problems, not only among prostitutes but also in society as a whole.

# Victimization: Masterpiece and Profit of the Redeemers

A complement of the condemnatory attitude, or perhaps a strategic alternative to disguise the condemnation, is a discourse on victimization and commiseration. Persecution and attempts to suppress prostitution are expressed in terms of redemption. To achieve such redemption, the data are often subverted; the special difficulties of some individuals are accepted as general descriptions; and conditions that prostitutes have in common with many others, including large groups of other women, such as being of advanced age, immigrant, lacking education, etc., are all attributed to the fact that they are prostitutes. We try to answer this generalized kind of description through a field study that took place in 1991 in Asturias. We compare our findings with some of those reported by Dr. Frances Shaver in September 1996, in Montreal.

In general, quantitative study uses questionnaires that are done using partial samples referring exclusively to street prostitution, where it is possible to find the most dramatic situations. Qualitative studies are also used, which are based on life stories and in-depth interviews with prostitutes in tragic situations. There is usually a discourse on prostitution and prostitutes in general that comes from the information derived from both limited types of studies. The result, throughout much of the literature, is a quantitative overestimation and a qualitative caricature, in which poverty, the low cultural background, moral inconsistency, dependence on a pimp, and psychic pathology are underlined.[1] These particular approaches, however, are unnecessary because sociology is gifted with theoretical and methodological instruments to study prostitution in a variety of different ways. In our view, a better perspective would be to look at prostitution by studying it under the sociology of labor, or the sociology of the profession, or the sociological areas that study the institutionalization of sexual and affective relations.

In our research on the life conditions of prostitutes in Asturias, we turned to a theoretical and methodological frame that could be applied to the study of any social collective. Several discussion groups distributed questionnaires to a statistically significant sample (311 surveys) of the total prostitutes in the Asturian region. The samples represented different workplaces: 67 from urban areas, 167 from urban-industrial neighborhoods, 34 from rural-fishing areas, and 43 from the mining areas. Prostitutes were interviewed in different workplaces: 83 percent in their work setting; 10 percent in bars and cafeterias, 3.8 percent at home, 1.2 percent in agencies serving prostitutes, and 1.3 percent in other places.

As in the study presented by Dr. Shaver, street prostitutes were a minority (6.5 percent of the total in Asturias). This is an important point to emphasize since street prostitution is frequently used as source for describing and characterizing prostitution and prostitutes in general. The skewing of data from such sources is evident in our own study because the street prostitutes worked in the most unfavorable conditions, had lower incomes, were generally older, had a lack of contractual possibilities and little choice in choosing clients, served a greater number of clients, and were more likely to be addicted to drugs.

There is also a coincidence with Shaver's study. Both studies find that, in relation to the educational level, no significant differences appear within the general feminine population. At the same time, both show that general discourse exaggerates the importance of pimping. According to Shaver's study, 62 percent of prostitutes work by themselves in Vancouver; 50 percent in Toronto; and 69 percent in Montreal. These data are extracted from the Justice Department, so there is a supposed reference to a legal definition of a pimp, which is more than debatable from a sociological point of view: they are considered people who live with a prostitute and cannot justify other sources of income. A more adjusted definition should refer to whoever coasts a woman into the practice of prostitution and/or, under coaction, also makes a material or economic profit. If these conditions do not come to the surface, some questions should be asked: whether the prostitute is free or not to do what she wants with her money, whether it is as legitimate if a man is kept by a woman as it is for a woman to be kept by a man. Thus if we applied the same criteria and, because of its irrelevance, ignored the origin (source) of the incomes, how many woman should be defined as pimps? If the Canadian study had been able to detect the presence or absence of these coactions, it would have probably concluded, as did the study in Asturias, that the number of prostitutes dependent on pimps is very limited.

Both studies show that the dominant speech exaggerates the implication of drugs in this matter, and instead of talking about prostitutes who take drugs, what should be noted is the drug addicts who practice prostitution. In Asturias only 7 percent of habitual hard-drug users were found among prostitutes.[2]

Prostitutes, however, have problems, some of them different from other women. Child care was one of the problems frequently encountered. Some 54 percent of the children do not live with their mothers but with grandparents or other relatives, are cared for by a private nanny, or are in some institutional setting (see table 1.) Prostitute mothers do not visit their children very often. Many of the prostitutes can be classed as immigrants from the Third World (22 percent), and a significant percentage of these live in the worst conditions; here pimping is most prevalent. The problem, however, is not due to prostitution or even to the immigrant herself, but to the existence of a very rigid and inflexible immigration law that places the majority of such women in a situation in which the law, if it does not regard them as illegal, more or less ignores their problems, making them easy prey for predators and extortionists.

Apart from these problems, this brief summary on the victimization of prostitutes has forced us to question why there is so much exaggeration and caricature of prostitution. The camouflage of condemnation and the emphasis on dramatic and morbid narrations create a situation that encourages misinformation about prostitution.

The "political" sector victimizes prostitutes by nominally conforming to pressure groups from certain locales, prohibiting prostitutes from soliciting in the busiest areas or in close proximity to residential areas. For example, the City Council of Barcelona shifted street prostitution from the traditional Chinatown near "Las Ramblas,"[3] the historic and commercial center of the city. During the Olympic games, prostitutes were removed out of the proximity of hotels where the Olympic committee members were lodged. Simultaneously, in these hotels prostitution by females and males of high standing was practiced.

Although there is considerable publicity in the mass media about the banning of prostitution or even of policies of rehabilitation, the policies are in fact little more than symbolic action to emphasize that the authorities are making efforts to reduce the social scourge and trying to "save" the women. But the prostitutes entering into any rehabilitative program are usually few in number. The majority are more than forty years old, and therefore unable to practice very successfully as prostitutes. In a sense, then there is no real state intervention into prostitution, only a media effort to say there is.

In the economic markets and private institutions, public and private professionals (psychologists, social workers, educators, sociologists, anthropologists) operate as experts. They continue to say the same things and their dealing with problematic situations has its own continuity. There is also a "spiritual market" of soul dealers and "heaven plot speculators" who try to save the prostitutes from their sins. They justify their activity as attempting to improve the moral, economic, and fiscal psyche of society, and add to the victimizing discourse.

**Table 1. With Whom Do Prostitutes' Children Live?**

| With whom | % |
| --- | --- |
| Mother | 46 |
| Grandparents | 30 |
| Other relatives | 12 |
| Paid nannies | 3.1 |
| Intern in a college | 3.4 |
| Public institution | 4.8 |
| Private institution | 0.7 |
| TOTAL | 100 |

# Neither Criminals nor Victims

We hold that the criminal problems of prostitution are essentially the result of the law itself. In most countries the law focuses on prostitutes but exempts clients, a continuation of the double standard. Most of the petty crime associated with prostitution is a consequence of its illegal status and is not necessarily due to prostitution. No matter how severe the laws against prostitution have been, it has found ways to survive, perhaps because society needs groups of women to stigmatize. The only solution to prostitution, if it is a problem, is to legitimize it by a "deconstruction of the immoral aspects attributed to prostitution" (Cardinal 1993).

Victimization corresponds to a discourse, frequently with a hidden interest, based on partial and slanted studies that present the most dramatic features of prostitution or exaggerate the effect of the problems of prostitution. If prostitutes are victims in any way, it is due to their suffering from a social stigma put on them by society.

# Notes

1. A study published by the Institute of Women in the Spanish Department of Culture goes so far as to state that the majority of prostitutes suffer psychiatric pathologies and then adds that these pathologies can be either a cause of prostitution or a result of it. (Fundacion Solidarida Democratica, *La prostitucion de las mujeres* [Madrid: Instituto de la Mujer, Ministerio de Cultura, 1988]).

2. In spite of this finding, a newspaper report of this study headlined its report "Prostitution in Asturias: Drugs as an Occupational Problem."

3. Las Ramblas is one of the tourist centers in Barcelona. There is a large passage for public walking, and people visit and sit on benches to drink coffee.

# References

Cardinal, Christine. 1993. Prostitution e rue et legislation. *Rev. Can. Soc. & Anth.* 30 (2): 168.

Pons, I. 1992. *Condiciones de vida de las prostitutas en Asturias.* N.p.: Publicasiones del Principad-Oveido.

Shaver, F. M. 1996. Traditional data distort our view of (street) prostitution. Montreal: International Conference on Prostitution and Other Sex Work.

Silva, P. 1995. *Prostitution y Dereche Penal.* Master's thesis, Universidad Autonma de Barcelona.

# Appendix A

## COMMERCIAL SEX IN THE AMERICAN STRUGGLE FOR THE RIGHTS OF THE PERSON

### DAVID A. J. RICHARDS

Many American constitutional scholars and citizens have argued, as I have for some twenty years, that a basic American right of intimate life should encompass the protection of contraception use, access to abortion services, and consensual adult homosexual relations; but few have extended the conception, as I also have, to include a right to commercial sex.[1] My interest today is not to repeat an argument I have elsewhere made defending this scope of the background right of intimate life, as an argument of principle, but to explore and criticize what I take to be the main grounds on which the extension of the argument to commercial sex has been and continues to be resisted. My aim is thus to clarify how bad these arguments are, how necessary it is in contemporary circumstances critically to evaluate and resist the political force they have historically had in American political life, and thus to support, as based on a compelling argument of constitutional principle, the argument currently made in pending American cases to extend the constitutionally protected right of intimate life to embrace commercial sexual services.[2] My diagnosis of the problem rests on a historical interpretation of the reactionary role I believe that the demonizing of commercial sex has uncritically played in the longstanding American struggle for fuller recognition of basic constitutional rights under law and critically to address what I believe to be the unjust and indeed quite sexist force that such demonization continues to enjoy. I begin with the basic right to intimate life and its interpretive history (as part of the American struggle for human rights) and then, on the basis of that history, address what I take to be today the unjust pattern of resistance to a principled public understanding of the proper scope of the basic right to intimate life.

# Interpretive History

The struggle for recognition of one's human rights under public law is central to the progressive narrative of American constitutionalism. American public law may thus plausibly be understood as the procedural and substantive framework of principle to which Americans over the generations have appealed in their struggles for recognition of their basic human rights of conscience, speech, and intimate life as well as their rights of equal dignity against slavery, racism, sexism, homophobia, and the like.[3] The basic human right of intimate life has played an important part in these struggles both as a basic human right in its own terms and as an aspect of the claims of equal dignity often made against structural injustices like racism, sexism, and the like. In its own terms, the right to intimate life identifies basic claims of moral autonomy in intimate personal life, centering on the place of intimate sexual thoughts, feelings, and associations in human life, and calling for a heavy burden of secular justification for any state abridgment of this right (of the sort associated by John Stuart Mill with his requirement of harm to others as a requirement of the legitimacy of state action in a liberal constitutional democracy like that in Great Britain or the United States).[4] The fundamentality of this right (among basic human rights) is shown by the crucial place deprivation of this basic right plays among the structural injustices we associate in America with the constitutionally condemned evils of racism, sexism, and the like. American antiracist abolitionists in the antebellum period thus objected not only to the race-based slavery that persisted in the American South but to the persistent patterns of racist subjugation (both in the North and South) that explained and indeed largely rationalized American tolerance of slavery. Such racism crucially dehumanized African Americans from their status as equal bearers of human rights, and no abridgment of basic human rights was more fundamental to this dehumanization than abridgment of the basic human right of intimate life. African Americans held in slavery were thus deprived of central aspects of the basic right to intimate life, including rights of marriage and control of offspring; it was thus a not uncommon experience of slave life that family members (one's mother or father or grandparents or siblings or spouse or children, etc.) could be sold away without any available objection grounded in law; correlatively antimiscegenation laws forbade marriage between the races throughout the North as well as the South. In the minds of antiracist abolitionists (like Lydia Maria Child), such deprivation of central aspects of the basic human right of intimate life (acknowledged as basic rights of all other Americans) crucially constructed the unjust status of African Americans as subhuman.[5] The effect was that the intimate life of African Americans was treated on a par with marketable cattle or other income-producing animals, available for unlimited propagation to increase marketable capital as well as for unlimited salability. The construction of American racism depended, of course, on deprivation as well of other basic rights (including conscience, speech, bodily integrity, free labor, and the like), but, as the antiracist abolitionists clearly understood, no deprivation of basic rights was more fundamental to the irrationalist sexual mythology at the core of American racism than abridgment of the right to intimate life. Abridgment of such a fundamental right was not only a rights-based justice in its own terms, but, in virtue of the fundamentality of the right to our conception of reasonable moral personality, its abridgment was often part of larger structural injustices (like racism and sexism) that effectively dehumanized whole classes of persons from their legitimate status as bearers of human rights and equal members of our moral, political, and constitutional community.[6]

The American struggle for human rights under constitutional law has come a long way over two centuries both in recognizing the right to intimate life as a basic constitutional right (the constitutional right to privacy) and in condemning the expression through public law of structural injustices (like racism and sexism) supported, in part, by historical traditions that abridged this basic right.[7] But the close study of that struggle suggests that progress has often been retarded not only by the failure to recognize such basic rights at all but also by unprincipled conceptions of the scope of such rights rationalized in terms that often reinforce larger patterns of structural injustice. Thus, the dominant understanding of the Reconstruction amendments, at the time of their ratification, interpreted them as condemning many (though not all) racist practices of the era, but as not condemning, on common grounds of principle, sexist practices. Such a truncated understanding of the structural injustices condemned by a principled understanding of the amendments not only reinforced sexism, but also left uncritically unexamined some of the deeper structures of American racism (resting, as they do, on a racialized conception of gender). In consequence, outraged feminists of the period (including Elizabeth Cady Stanton) urged a comparably truncated conception of the relevant constitutional principles that condemned sexist but not racist practices, thus leaving uncritically unexamined the deeper structures of American sexism (resting on a racialized conception of woman's sphere).[8]

Stanton's myopia on this issue reflects a much larger problem in American feminism, one that Stanton herself acknowledged and combatted in her later years against the increasingly conservative trajectory of American suffrage feminists.[9] The narrative of American feminism illustrates this problem in three natural stages: first, its repudiation of its ideological leader (Mary Wollstonecraft); second, its war on free love; and third, its war on commercial sex. Each stage illustrates aspects of a phenomenon pervasive in the struggle for human rights: the tendency of an unjustly entrenched orthodoxy to cut off debate precisely in those areas where such debate is often most reasonably needed. I call this phenomenon the paradox of intolerance: the tendency of an irrationalist orthodoxy, precisely when it is subjected to reasonable doubt, to subjugate and silence minorities that often most reasonably subject the orthodoxy to the debate and discussion it needs.[10] Such ideological scapegoating has been, I shall argue, central to the repression of sexual minorities in the United States (including advocates of basic rights of sexual autonomy, both noncommercial and commercial). I more fully investigate this phenomenon below in three stages.

## The Wollstonecraft Repudiation

No feminist in the Anglo-American tradition more powerfully made the case for rights-based feminism, as an issue central to the ambitions of rights-based republicanism in Britain, the United States, and France in the late eighteenth century than Mary Wollstonecraft. Wollstonecraft's companion political essays (A Vindication of the Rights of Men [1790] and A Vindication of the Rights of Woman [1792])[11,12] were provoked by Burke's attack on the rights-based republican constitutionalism of her teacher, Richard Price, in particular, Price's defense of what he took to be the rights-based principles of the French Revolution.[13] Wollstonecraft's longer and more substantial second essay took the argument for toleration that the earlier essay applied only to women incidentally and focussed the argument, as it had never been before, on the condition of women. Wollstonecraft built upon the expansive interpretation of the Lockean argument for toleration in Richard Price's works,[14] including protection of all conscientious opinions (religious or irreligious) except when they supported overt acts of secular harm.[15] Price had condemned not only established churches,[16] but inadequately representative constitutions (like those of Great Britain) that, contrary to the argument for toleration, unreasonably entrenched the political authority of "[s]lavish governments and slavish hierarchies."[17] The startling originality of Wollstonecraft's second essay is the way in which she subverted the traditional appeal to natural subordination as applied to women and, in so doing, powerfully deployed all the terms of criticism Price had already mustered in service of his attacks on established churches and unrepresentative constitutions. The moral core of Wollstonecraft's argument was, as one would expect in such an elaboration of Price's interpretation of the argument for toleration, an appeal for respect for the inalienable right to conscience of women so that "freedom strengthen[s] her reason till she comprehend her duty, and see in what manner it is connected with her real good."[18] Of the basic issues of conscience, "[w]ho made man the exclusive judge, if woman partake with him the gift of reason?"[19] Is not this "[a]bsolute, uncontroverted authority [of men over the religious lives of women] a direct and exclusive appropriation of reason?"[20] From the perspective of the argument for toleration, nothing could be more dehumanizing than abridgment of the right to conscience. Wollstonecraft made her case for "the rights of woman" on this basis, which was, in the terms she adapted forcefully from Price, slavery. Women, by virtue of their moral subjugation to men's appropriation of reason, "may be convenient slaves, but slavery will have its constant effect degrading the master and the abject dependent."[21] Condemnation of the subjection of woman as slavery pervades the second essay.[22] Wollstonecraft quite remarkably identified and explored, on grounds of the argument for toleration, not only the injustice of the subjection of women, but also the underlying cultural evil of giving unreasonable political weight to "the privileges of rank and sex" in place of "the privileges of humanity."[23] The evil, which we today call sexism, was, for Wollstonecraft, "subversive of the birth-right of man, the right of acting according to the direction of his own reason."[24] Being fundamentally unreasonable, sexism was described by Wollstonecraft as resting on prejudice, indeed making both men and women "all their lives the slaves of prejudices."[25] Wollstonecraft analogized the irrationalist grounds of such sexism to those of the evil we call racism:

> Why subject her to propriety—blind propriety, if she be capable of acting from a nobler spring, if she be an heir of immortality? Is sugar always to be produced by vital blood? Is one half of the human species, like the poor African slaves, to be subject to prejudices that brutalize them, when principles would be a surer guide, only to sweeten the cup of man? Is not this indirectly to deny woman reason? for a gift is a mockery, if it be unfit for use.[26]

Wollstonecraft was undoubtedly influential on emergent American feminist thought,[27] but the influence was infrequently acknowledged by nineteenth-century American feminists except by more radical and outspoken advocates like Margaret Fuller[28] and Lucretia Mott.[29] Even while insisting on Wollstonecraft's importance to American feminism, Mott noted that "[h]er name was cast out as evil" (like other moral prophets like Jesus); and Fuller accurately diagnosed the problematics of Wollstonecraft for Americans not in her work but her life[30] as it had been frankly told by her husband, William Godwin.[31] Godwin published his *Memoirs of the Author of a Vindication of the Rights of Woman* the year after his wife's death after giving birth to a daughter (whom we now know as Mary Shelley).[32] The events of the narrative included Wollstonecraft's passion for a woman (Frances Blood),[33] her passionate though abortive love for a married man (the painter Fuseli),[34] her love affair with Gilbert Imlay (resulting in a child born out of wedlock),[35] her suicide attempt when the affair ended,[36] and her love affair with Godwin and resulting pregnancy, whereupon they married.[37] Further, Godwin made quite clear that, for Wollstonecraft, passionate sexual love between men and women was "the principal solace of human life,"[38] indeed was "sacred,"[39] and was to be pursued "with perfect fidelity to that affection when it existed,"[40] whether the couple was married or not (only sex without love was forbidden by virtue).[41] From the perspective of mainstream nineteenth-century America, Wollstonecraft's work and life accordingly stood for the unacceptable principle of free love, and most forms of nineteenth-century feminism would, until late in the century, distance themselves from acknowledging any such principle. Even then, frank acknowledgment of the principle would be repudiated by most mainstream feminists with consequences I shall shortly investigate; I shall call this reactionary response, when it shall later occur, the Wollstonecraft repudiation, marking a central and continuing normative struggle for moral identity within American feminism.

## The War on Free Love

No aspect of this struggle was more central for our purposes than the increasingly powerful alliance of suffrage feminism with the attack on free love in general and Victoria Woodhull in particular. In effect, suffrage feminists warred on a principled interpretation of the basic right to intimate life. This basic human right was, as leading abolitionist thinkers like Weld and Channing made clear, a right that was conspicuously and flagrantly abridged by failure to respect either the right to marry of African American slaves or the right to custody of their children.[42] Elizabeth Chandler in her poems and essays brought women's moral experience prominently to bear on such atrocities; and abolitionist feminists from the Grimke sisters to Harriet Jacobs had explored the pivotal role abridgment of such basic human rights played in the dehumanization of African Americans (in effect, treated on the same terms as economically remunerative breeding cattle).[43] When Lydia Maria Child offered her important antiracist criticism of the Massachusetts antimiscegenation law, she identified the inalienable human right at stake as the "power to control the affections, any more than the consciences of citizens,"[44] "a connexion which, above all others, ought to be left to private conscience and individual choice."[45] We turn now to the further elaboration of this argument for a basic human right (the right to love) in the wake of the Civil War. I focus on such a rights-based challenge to conventional marriage (by, among others, Elizabeth Stanton, Victoria Woodhull, Stephen Pearl Andrews, Ezra Heywood, and, in a different form, Lysander Spooner); the sharp repudiation of that argument by increasingly conservative suffragists and their allies (including the purity and antipolygamy movements); the resulting political war on contraception, abortion, and prostitution; and the censorship of serious discussion of these matters when both Emma Goldman and Margaret Sanger sought to raise them in the period in the early twentieth century leading directly up to the ratification of the Nineteenth Amendment. The voice of rights-based abolitionist feminism, on issues central to the emancipation of women and others, was decisively stilled largely by conservative suffragists and their allies en route to their morally problematic prohibitionist victory in 1919 and their morally vacuous suffrage victory in 1920.

The argument for free love was associated in the antebellum period with Mary Wollstonecraft and was largely repudiated as much for the way of life as for the arguments of its proponents. In particular, Mary Wollstonecraft, a towering figure in the development of rights-based feminism, could not be acknowledged as such because Godwin's memoir frankly exposed a life of premarital affairs, pregnancies, and suicide attempts that shocked conventional morality. Godwin emphasized that Wollstonecraft firmly believed in sexual fidelity when in love, and Wollstonecraft herself defended long-term relationships when based on rationally based friendship and mutual affection. But these points hardly assuaged American horror at Wollstonecraft's theory and practice of successive changes in sexual love objects and her flat and antiromantic acknowledgment that sexual love in women (as in men) was in its nature quite short-lived. American attitudes to sexual love in the nineteenth century were nothing if not highly (even religiously) idealized and romantic;[46] as Harriet Beecher Stowe wrote to her husband Calvin about her "almost insane love" before they married, "I loved you as I now love God."[47] Such religiously idealized sentiments were outraged by Wollstonecraft's sadly quotidian and deflationary picture of marriage as, at best, mutual lust followed by a coolly rational friendship.

To forestall such objections, any plausible American defense of a basic right to love had to situate its argument in the role of sexual love as a romantically imaginative expression and sharing of moral personality with the beloved.[48] It is no accident that Lydia Maria Child, when she prefigured later arguments for this right, grounded it on an inalienable right to feel and act on affections that she associated with the inalienable right to conscience: for nineteenth-century Americans, love, like religion, was a central expression and authentication of one's free moral personality fulfilled in tender and caring relationship to the value placed on other personalities.[49] Thus understood, an argument for a right to love might take its place among other basic human rights, securing to all persons appropriate respect for so basic a right.

Abolitionist feminism, which distinctively placed such emphasis on the unjust abridgment of women's basic rights to conscience and speech, could reasonably be elaborated as well to criticize the unjust abridgment of women's rights to free moral personality in intimate life. Elizabeth Stanton had controversially pressed such arguments in the antebellum period in service of reforms of marriage and divorce; and she continued to do so, equally controversially among fellow suffragists, after the Civil War. In 1869, Stanton thus publicly embraced the right to free love as the ground for securing to women the right to divorce, "freedom from all unnecessary entanglements of concessions, freedom from binding obligations involving impossibilities, freedom to repair mistakes."[50] Denying that free love meant promiscuity, Stanton adduced Mary Wollstonecraft as an example that "true free lovers are among the most progressive, the most virtuous of women and of men."[51] Marriage, unless reformed consistent with respect for this right, was slavery, and thus such reform "is the same issue as that of immediate or gradual emancipation in the slavery question."[52] Abolitionist feminist arguments for women's suffrage "mean logically . . . that the next logical equality and next freedom is in a word 'free love.' "[53]

Unfortunately, the argument for free love in this period became associated in the public mind with one of the great scandals of the era, the Beecher-Tilton affair,[54] and the role played in that affair of certainly the most notorious advocate of free love of that time, Victoria Woodhull.[55] Woodhull had a sordid past before she came to national attention: one of ten children in a flamboyant family that staged a traveling road show, Woodhull played a psychic healer; she was married at fifteen to a physician and drunkard, Canning Woodhull, they had two children before the couple separated, and Victoria returned to her family, specializing with her sister, Tennessee, in spiritualism.[56] After the Civil War, Woodhull married her lover, Dr. Blood, but kept her first husband's name. Following a vision, Victoria brought her extended family to New York City in 1868. The recent widower, Cornelius Vanderbilt, was smitten by Tennessee and established the sisters as financial speculators and stock brokers; Vanderbilt leaked them information, and they were financially successful. In 1870, Woodhull declared herself a candidate for president of the United States, and published with her sister *Woodhull and Claflin's Weekly*. More strident and extreme, though better financed than Stanton and Anthony's short-lived (two and a half years) *Revolution*,[57] the *Weekly* advocated free love, short skirts, and legalized prostitution; it also printed the first translation of the Communist Manifesto in America. Woodhull practiced as well as preached free love, having various love affairs, and her domestic arrangements included living with both her first and second husbands.[58] The Wollstonecraft repudiation was to apply, a fortiori, to Woodhull: her publicly notorious arguments for free love in particular were read in light of the scandals of her life and easily discredited (Stanton notwithstanding) for that reason. We need first to understand her arguments and then the scandals that discredited them.

Woodhull played an important public role in the early suffrage movement. On her own, she presented a suffrage petition to Congress in December 1870 and had been invited to testify before the House Judiciary Committee in January. Her hearing was scheduled on the same day as the opening session of the National Association convention being held in Washington, D.C. (its leaders were Isabella Beecher Hooker, the sister of Catharine

Beecher and Harriet Beecher Stowe, and Susan B. Anthony). Hooker and Anthony interrupted their proceedings to attend Woodhull's testimony. Both were impressed with her intelligence and beauty and invited her to attend their convention, joining them on the platform. Woodhull argued before the committee and the convention that a women's suffrage amendment was otiose. Using an argument Stanton had made the year earlier (interpreting the text, consistent with radical abolitionist constitutionalism, to enforce the best reading of human rights),[59] she claimed that the Fourteenth Amendment already gave women the right to vote and run for political office.[60] Woodhull's cogent presentation of Stanton's case was well received and led suffragists for several years to pursue this line of argument rather than the federal amendment route.[61] On the basis of this argument, Woodhull ran for president in the 1872 election.[62]

Woodhull made the case for the principle of free love in a speech delivered in 1871.[63] Consistent with the abolitionist feminist approach discussed earlier, Woodhull grounded her argument in the idea of inalienable human rights central to the Declaration of Independence, an idea that made each person "self-owned."[64] Echoing Lydia Maria Child, Woodhull argued that "[g]overnments might just as well assume to determine how people shall exercise their right to *think* or to say that they shall not think at all, as to assume to determine that they shall not love, or how they may love, or that they shall love."[65] The state owed each person protection "in the *free* exercise of his or her *right* to love,"[66] an *inalienable, constitutional,* and *natural* right"[67] as basic to moral personality as the right to conscience,[68] indeed an aspect of it ("Free Love will be an integral part of the religion of the future").[69] Woodhull used the right as the basis for the criticism of the economic imperatives that compelled women of her age to marry as "legalized prostitution";[70] conventional women thus have no "right to . . . sit in judgment over our unfortunate sisters."[71] Marriage institutions, which violated this right, were "slavery";[72] enslaved women had a right to emancipation.[73]

Woodhull's argument for free love was derived from (indeed was ghostwritten by) her then intellectual mentor, Stephen Pearl Andrews[74] (Andrews's views also centrally shaped those of Elizabeth Stanton on free love, marriage, and divorce).[75] Andrews developed and published his pathbreaking arguments for a basic moral, political, and constitutional principle of free love in the antebellum period, drawing upon radical abolitionist arguments in general and the abolitionist feminist theory of moral slavery in particular.[76] While clearly influenced by Fourier,[77] the originality of Andrews was to make the case for free love, drawing on the religiously idealized American conception of romantic love that would alone give the argument any appeal in America, in terms of a principled elaboration of the argument for toleration.[78] "Freedom of the Affections,"[79] as an inalienable human right, was thus grounded, for Andrews, on the same basis as (indeed, reflected aspects of) the other such rights of conscience,[80] thought,[81] speech,[82] association,[83] and of action expressive of these rights.[84] Respect for such an inalienable human right[85] should be accorded the same scope as that for other such rights like religious liberty, namely, free exercise of the right "*provided* he assails nobody else's Liberty, or Life, or Property."[86] Within the just scope of such rights, persons must "judge for themselves what is moral, and proper, and right for them to do or abstain from doing."[87] For the same reason that the state may not judge what is religious for a person to believe, it may not make or enforce judgments in the sexual arena:

> for me to aid in sending you or another man to prison for Fornication, or Bigamy, or Polygamy, or a woman for wearing male attire, and the like, is just as gross an outrage in kind, upon Human Rights, as it would be to aid in burning you at Smithfield for Protestantism or Papacy, or at Geneva for discarding the doctrine of the Trinity.[88]

Women were owed respect for this basic right on equal terms with men as a condition of their normative self-ownership.[89] Failure to accord them respect for this right in conventional marriage was moral slavery,[90] and made of marriage a kind of prostitution.[91] Securing respect for this right would guarantee the only form of love that could reasonably be called romantic and therefore pure,[92] and was, Andrews suggested, the most fundamental right owed women as a matter of basic justice.[93]

Neither the power of Andrews's argument (including its use of the American conception of romantic love) nor Woodhull's beauty and eloquence in making it could impact a public opinion that interpreted the argument against the background of the national scandal that shortly erupted around Woodhull. Woodhull was arrested in 1872 on a federal obscenity charge brought by Anthony Comstock for a defense she had published of her living arrangements that included a revelation of an extramarital love affair with a leading preacher of the age.[94] Woodhull defended her arrangements as a legitimate exercise of her right to love, for which she made no apology. In contrast, she now publicly pointed to the moral hypocrisy shown by a leading preacher of the age (Henry Ward Beecher, brother of Catherine Beecher as well as Harriet Beecher Stowe and Isabella Hooker), who privately accepted the right to free love (having an affair with Elizabeth Tilton, wife of Beecher's protege, Theodore Tilton), but refused to defend it in public.[95] Woodhull named Elizabeth Stanton as the source of her story and publicly demanded a confession of adultery by Beecher (in fact, Woodhull herself had had an affair with Theodore Tilton[96] and probably with Henry Ward Beecher as well).[97]

Woodhull's accusations were true, but she had underestimated Henry Ward Beecher's egotism and influence and the capacity of ideologically self-deceiving Americans (including his influential sisters Catharine and Harriet, though not Isabella)[98] to blink at reality in order to hold men and women to a double standard of sexual morality. Beecher was tried twice: first, by a church board he appointed (that acquitted him); second, by a civil court (the jury was unable to reach a verdict). Beecher had dismissed Woodhull and her sister as "two prostitutes,"[99] and they were vilified by his supporters in the press and in public (eventually going to Britain, where they married wealthy men and adopted conservative lifestyles). Beecher, frightened by what Stanton knew (she never denied Woodhull's story), launched a campaign against her and Anthony as advocates of free love. Stanton, in fact, accepted the principle of free love as a legitimate one when grounded in romantic love and monogamy.[100] Stanton, disgusted at Beecher's moral duplicity, published her own account of the events and was the only public figure to criticize the two jury verdicts.[101]

The principle of free love, as a crucial component of feminist civil liberties, was also forthrightly defended during this period by Ezra H. Heywood.[102] Heywood crucially grounded his argument, like Andrews and Woodhull, in the principled elaboration of "the right of private judgment, which is conceded in politics and religion . . . to domestic life."[103] Abridgments of so basic a right could no more be legitimately justified on sectarian grounds than abridgment of any other such basic right; "priests and magistrates [should not] supervise the sexual organs of citizens any more than the brain and stomach."[104] A universal human right, grounded in the Declaration of Independence, "is now legitimately claimed in behalf of sexual self-government."[105] In particular, each woman has "a right to herself,"[106] including emancipation from the moral slavery that conventional marriage now imposed on her.[107]

The important antebellum radical abolitionist constitutionalist, Lysander Spooner, made a more general argument in 1875, suggesting limits of the rights-based principle to the intrusion of criminal law into a number of areas.[108] Spooner's essay articulated a general right to experience, acquire knowledge, and learn from mistakes, central to respect for a free person,[109] and the inadequacy of abridgment of this right either on paternalistic,[110] or sectarian theological grounds.[111] Spooner's essay was published as part of an effort to resist arguments, like those of the WCTU (Woman's Christian Temperance Union), for liquor prohibition,[112] but he noted that it would condemn as well criminalization of sexual crimes like prostitution[113] and fornication.[114]

Suffrage feminism, particularly after its alliance with the WCTU, increasingly resisted both the general form of Spooner's argument and, in the wake of the Woodhull scandal, the specific application of the argument by Heywood and others to a right of free love alleged to be central to women's rights. Indeed, the increasingly repressive moral temper of the nation was reflected in the federal obscenity prosecution brought unsuccessfully by Anthony Comstock against Woodhull[115] and the recurrent such prosecutions against Heywood for publication of his free love essays, two of which led to convictions. Although the first was presidentially pardoned, the second conviction resulted in a punishment of two years at hard labor; Heywood lived only one year after his release in 1892.[116] Free love advocate Lois Waisbrooker was also repeatedly arrested for her publications, both under the federal obscenity law and comparable state laws, culminating in her prosecution at the age of seventy-six for the publication of her article, "The Awful Fate of Fallen Women," which a Washington state court judged obscene in 1902.[117]

Harriet Beecher Stowe, who had converted to suffrage feminism by 1869,[118] nonetheless demonized Woodhull in a way she had never attacked proslavery apologists, even at the height of her most passionate indignation.[119] If the Comstock Law and related state laws were silencing Heywood and others by criminal sanctions, Stowe was doing so in the court of public opinion by her forceful Wollstonecraft repudiation of Woodhull and her ilk.[120] Stowe made her point by defending her brother, who was in fact a moral and sexual hypocrite in precisely the way Woodhull had charged, "as a sexless angel."[121] Stowe's defense bespoke the repressive ideological power of the conception of gender roles (women's higher morality) increasingly central to suffrage feminism. Men and women were to be held to the same standard, but one "holding men to a standard even more virtuous than that of the Victorian woman."[122] Stowe affirmed such unreasonable standards in response to the first publicly serious argument of a human right to love specifically urged by and on behalf of women in the United States. Precisely at the time when the traditional orthodoxy of women's general roles had been subjected to reasonable doubt, Stowe polemically demanded that all discourse conform to the orthodoxy, repressing precisely the arguments and claimants the public most reasonably needed to hear. The Wollstonecraft repudiation thus worked the worst ravages of the paradox of intolerance on American feminism: precisely the discourse most reasonably needed to challenge unjust gender roles was repressed, and an insular and parochial epistemology of gender roles distorted political reality to its own unjust terms. A man who was a moral and sexual hypocrite became a sexless angel; a dissenting woman, who fairly subjected his hypocritical conduct to criticism, was demonized as a "witch"[123] or, in the terms used by Henry Ward Beecher of Woodhull and her sister, "two prostitutes."[124] As the terms of insult indicate, prostitutes were to be the primary scapegoats of this ideologically embattled repression of reasonable doubt and discussion.

# The War on Commercial Sex

The purity movement, which was an ideological outgrowth of temperance, powerfully enforced this repressive political ideology at large, including its impact on suffrage feminism. The idea of purity was historically allied to temperance;[125] prohibitionist attitudes to liquor were thus naturally extended to prostitution understood as sexual intemperance.[126] Liquor consumption was associated with loss of inhibitions, including sexual restraints. Frances Willard captured the worry of temperance women when she spoke of "intemperance and impurity" as "iniquity's Siamese Twins."[127] The worry, however, cut deeper: impurity reflected "pollution beliefs in which certain practices were prohibited because they obscured the clarity of the division between evil and good."[128] Among these was sex not for the purpose of procreation, long a matter of concern to Christian morality; but another of particular importance to Americans in general and American women in particular was sex that was not an expression of religiously idealized romantic love. Americans in the nineteenth century did not use purity to refer to the asexual or passionless;[129] both men and women could regard their sexual relations as pure (including premarital relations) if they were sexually legitimate, and one ground for such legitimacy was its romanticism,[130] often religiously idealized.[131] Frances Willard would thus effectively describe women's purity in marriage not as asexuality, but as a sexual life in which she has "undoubted custody of herself," including Willard's euphemism for the timing and quality of sexual relations (determining "the frequency of the investiture of life with form and of love with immortality").[132]

The prohibition on prostitution became an obsessional aim of the purity movement because its very existence rendered indeterminate the kind of reactionary line the movement wanted to draw between legitimate and illegitimate sexual relations. In the antebellum period, when abolitionist women like Lydia Maria Child and the Grimke sisters were exploring their common ground with the slave and the black, they identified and explored their common ground as well with women prisoners and prostitutes,[133] each, as Child put it, within "a hair's breadth" of being the other.[134] Women, under the impact of the theory of moral slavery central to abolitionist feminism, confronted "the enslaving ethos of the woman-belle ideal."[135] The Grimke sisters, Harriet Jacobs, and Sojourner Truth had underscored the unjust force this ideal played in sustaining not only slavery but also racism and sexism more generally. Not only were black women, on the basis of a racialized conception of the ideal, not regarded as women, but any woman who seriously demanded basic human rights was also condemned as not a woman, even as unnatural, in a way no man was for his demand of such rights on equal terms. The abolitionist feminist challenge was at its core a critique of this ethical double standard as a way of degrading women from their status as bearers of universal human rights, and thus of the role that the woman-belle ideal unjustly played in this degradation. The injustice of the treatment of prostitutes was, from this perspective, yet another instance and example of this injustice from which all women (as sisters) suffered. Their treatment rested on the unjust double standard of the belle-femme ideal, which did not regard prostitutes as women. Prostitution was thus a natural symbol for this wider injustice.[136]

This charitable and rights-based approach to prostitution was the ground for Judith Butler's successful opposition in the late 1860s to the introduction of the licensing of prostitution into Great Britain.[137] Butler's advocacy importantly built upon and elaborated the opposition of prostitutes themselves to the forms of police control over women's sexuality contemplated by the Contagious Diseases Acts,[138] indeed encouraging prostitutes to organize to resist the act.[139] Butler thus underscored the lack of legal safeguards of the basic rights of women under the system,[140] and worked within a framework that accepted the right of these women to control their persons.[141] Consistent with this position, Butler opposed attempts to repress prostitution itself.[142] In particular, in 1897 Butler warned against "the soundness of principle of those engaged in social purity work" which, while discoursing in public "of the divinity of womanhood . . . [was] yet . . . ready to accept and endorse any account of coercive and degrading treatment of their fellow creatures, in the fatuous belief that you can oblige human beings to be moral by force."[143]

Butler's opposition to licensing was influential in the United States, but her warnings about a repressive social purity movement went unheeded.[144] Under the leadership of Frances Willard and the WCTU,[145] the evil of prostitution was redefined "as sexual intemperance"[146] and thus subject to the same prohibitionism advocated for alcohol. The rights-based approach of antebellum abolitionist feminists to prostitution was repudiated, indeed warred upon. In a particularly vivid example of the political irrationalism wrought by the paradox of intolerance, a conspicuously sectarian view of woman's higher morality repressively enforced its claims at large on the basis of an ostensible attack on the double standard when its own normative stance (woman's higher morality) expressed and reinforced precisely the ethical double standard that it had been the aim of abolitionist feminism to expose and criticize. Where abolitionist feminism underscored the moral continuities among all the injustices experienced by women (including prostitutes), increasingly conservative suffragists, like Willard, drew a Manichean line between the idealized experience of organized mother-love and the depraved conduct of other women, of which an example must be made.

Willard's leadership gave political expression to a movement of repressive suffrage feminism endorsed as well by Harriet Beecher Stowe, and the prostitute was its scapegoat. Its normative attitude was centrally shaped by its reactionary opposition to and repression of abolitionist feminism as a theory and practice of feminist emancipation on grounds of universal human rights.

Abolitionist feminism in the antebellum period was largely a form of moral criticism within radical moral abolitionism.[147] It was only in the wake of the triumph of political abolitionism in Lincoln's 1860 election, the Civil War, and the growing public appeal of radical moral abolitionism as the background of the Reconstruction Amendments that abolitionist feminism would come to stage center as a credible form of political abolitionism. Abolitionist feminism called, however, for a rights-based criticism of the theory of gender roles endorsed by Catharine Beecher, Horace Bushnell, and Frances Willard in terms of abridgment of at least four areas of human rights: conscience, speech, intimate association, and work. The theory of moral slavery, central to abolitionist feminism, argued that abridgment of basic human rights in all four areas on inadequate sectarian grounds was central to the unjust dehumanization of both African Americans and women. Basic rights of conscience had thus been abridged by imposing on women a normative conception of gender roles based on a misogynist interpretation of basic religious and other cultural texts in which women had never been permitted to participate as scholars, teachers, and ministers on equal terms. To accomplish this, basic rights of free speech (and ancillary rights of education) had not been fairly extended to women on equal terms, as the experience of the Grimke sisters dramatically attested. Rights of intimate association had not been extended to women on equal terms because the terms of marriage (including custody of children) were fundamentally unfair. Finally, women had not been extended their basic rights to work and the economic independence to which exercise of that right would lead.[148]

Such abolitionist feminist criticisms subjected to reasonable doubt, on the basis of fundamental conceptions of rights-based American political and constitutional morality (that had been saliently reaffirmed in the texts of the Reconstruction Amendments), the theory and practice of American gender roles as they were conventionally understood. In particular, the analysis raised questions about what had been unquestionable, destabilizing a normative conception of women as essentially centered in private, intimate family relations. If women had been unjustly deprived of basic human rights as the abolitionist feminist theory of moral slavery alleged, then basic questions about the traditional normative conception had to be raised. The unjust political power of sectarian religious beliefs over their lives had to be contested by their own increasingly morally independent minds and in their own public voices as the Grimke sisters, Lucretia Mott, and Elizabeth Stanton had insisted; marriage and divorce would have to be reexamined and reformed, as Stanton urged, on terms of justice; an economic structure of work that deprived women of basic rights to work would be contested and its opportunities competitively made available to women, as Mott argued.

If abolitionist feminism arose as a principled elaboration of the argument for toleration on the same platform of human rights, repressive suffrage feminism sought sharply to truncate the force of this argument by the enforcement at large of precisely the sectarian political epistemology of traditional gender roles about which abolitionist feminism had raised reasonable doubts. Consistent with the paradox of toleration, the traditional orthodoxy polemically enforced its sectarian claims in precisely the areas under challenge by abolitionist feminism. Its normative measure was sectarian religion; the scope of debate was limited to the terms of the orthodoxy, repressing dissenters through obscenity prosecutions, censure (as with Stanton's *Woman's Bible*),[149] and the like; women's traditional role in the family was the source of a politically enforceable higher morality that was to stand judgment over the ethics of human rights (rather than conversely); women's idealized moral role rendered them superior to the competitive world of work.

No person was a better scapegoat for this repressive ideology than Victoria Woodhull, with her theory and practice of free love and its confusion in the public mind with prostitution. Woodhull defied the ideology at each of its reactionary points: she not only challenged the role of traditional religion in politics, but spoke in her own morally independent public voice; she criticized women's role in the family as inconsistent with the human right to love, condemned marriage as legalized prostitution, lived and justified living on the basis of free love, and took objection to hypocrites like Henry Ward Beecher who lived but would not justify free love; and she worked as a successful stockbroker. Free love, in the view of some (though not all) of its advocates (Stanton), had nothing to do with promiscuity, and little with commercial sex. But, the repressive ideology of gender roles was not interested in making distinctions, but giving effect to an embattled political ideology of gender roles. To do so, the political epistemology of gender, concerned to maintain conventional norms of good and bad women, ferociously attacked the role for women that Woodhull put on offer, one that obscured the ideological clarity of the division between good and bad women as conventionally understood. Nineteenth-century condemnation of prostitutes crudely could include all sexually active women outside marriage,[150] or women who engaged in sexual intercourse not for propagation,[151] or, most generally, who misused any power or function;[152] the condemnation reflected as well opposition to sexual autonomy and economic independence in women[153] in circumstances of growing urban anonymity and commercialism.[154] Woodhull did not agree with any of these grounds or forms of condemnation. Indeed, her theory and practice of free love and feminism would wholly destigmatize women for love affairs outside marriage, for loving without propagation, and for being sexually and economically independent; she also questioned legal and even abusive moral condemnation of women who engaged in commercial sex on the ground that they were within their rights and the condemnation rested on "an assumed right to thus sit in judgment over our unfortunate sisters,"[155] i.e., questioning whether there was a defensible moral line between their situations and that of many conventional women who marry.

The polemical force of the purity leagues arose as a political reaction to this kind of challenge to traditional gender roles, namely, to condemn and indeed abolish the evil of prostitution in order to quash the very idea or imag-

ining the idea of the legitimacy of Woodhull's theory and practice, in particular, her suggestion that traditional marriage was not only moral slavery[156]
but legalized prostitution.[157] Purity occupied the space of a politically
enforced pollution ritual meant to reaffirm traditional certainties about good
and evil that were, in fact, very much in reasonable doubt; from its perspective, the prostitute's "life style, attitudes, and behavior were ominous signs of
change in the feminine ideal, which would ultimately influence all
women,"[158] and the reactionary defense of the threatened ideal saw abolitionist condemnation of prostitution as the dyke against the flood of disas-
trous changes it feared. To achieve its abolitionist ends, as it successfully did
in the early twentieth century,[159] the purity movement symbolically transformed prostitution, which had been a metaphor for the situation of all
women in the antebellum era and thus for appropriate charity and sisterhood,[160] into an evil radically discontinuous from the experience of conventional women. Where abolitionist feminists had developed a general theory
of moral slavery for all women, purity advocates tendentiously used prostitution as a "master symbol"[161] that inverted the general theory of moral slavery,
ascribing such slavery only to prostitution on grounds that were, in fact, quite
dubious and known to be dubious (ascribing prostitution to economic necessity,[162] to exploitation of immigrants,[163] to force and kidnapping,[164] and the
like). In effect, precisely the sectarian normative conception of gender roles,
which abolitionist feminism subjected to such profound rights-based criticism
on the basis of the argument for toleration, was not just immunized from the
reasonable public criticism and debate it needed, but was in fact idealized as
the source of a higher morality that was politically enforceable at large as the
sole measure of legitimate discussion of issues of gender. On this basis, not
only were prostitutes demonized as not women and barely persons, but the
ideology repressed precisely the speakers and speech, grounded in abolitionist feminism, that raised the larger questions of principle about patterns
of injustice that were intractably rooted in conventional gender roles. Conventional gender roles became an unquestioned and unquestionable
national political religion, and suffrage feminism was its minister.

By the early twentieth century, as it neared its constitutional victory in
1920, suffrage feminism was decisively now the instrument of the repressive
conception of gender roles that we have now studied at some length. Suffrage
feminism was no longer the solution to American sexism; it had become part
of the problem. The consequences were catastrophic for the pioneering feminists of this period, like Emma Goldman and Margaret Sanger, who not only
made forms of the free love argument but interpreted it to extend to basic
rights like contraception, abortion, and even consensual homosexuality.

There was evidently in nineteenth-century America a lively practice
among American women of use of various contraceptive techniques and contraceptives and of abortion services, but this practice was supported by little

self-conscious public theory or argument.[165] The books of Robert Dale Owen and Charles Knowlton made the discussion of reproductive control a more public matter in the 1830s;[166] Knowlton, however, suffered several obscenity prosecutions; two resulted in convictions (one leading to three months at hard labor), the other in hung juries.[167] In this environment, even leading advocates of free love like Victoria Woodhull and Ezra Heywood expressly condemned contraception.[168]

The importance of Emma Goldman and Margaret Sanger was to interpret the principle of free love, as we have so far studied it, to encompass contraception and much else. Of the two women, Goldman offered the more profound rights-based interpretation of the principle; but Sanger, precisely because of her narrower focus (on contraception), had the more enduring impact on American culture and law. Both endured criminal prosecutions for their advocacy of free love; Goldman, who had immigrated to the United States from Russia in 1885, was ultimately deported in 1919.[169]

Goldman's remarkable moral voice, more than any other of her generation, indicted the state of suffrage feminism (in particular, its support of the purity movement) from the perspective of a rights-based feminism self-consciously aligned with the Garrisonian moral abolitionism that gave rise to abolitionist feminism.[170] Goldman's anarchism, like Garrison's, affirmed the primacy of a rights-based moral discourse, grounded in "the sovereignty of the individual"[171] and the argument for toleration,[172] that empowered persons to claim their basic rights of moral personality against the unjust political orthodoxies that traditionally stifled and silenced them.[173] Goldman's opposition to electoral politics was not only that it was ineffective in securing people's rights,[174] but that it also demoralized the moral competence of persons to come to know and demand their rights as free people.[175] Her indictment of suffrage feminism, in her two essays "Woman Suffrage"[176] and "The Tragedy of Woman's Emancipation,"[177] was precisely that the obsession with securing suffrage, with all the political compromises of principle that struggle required, had rendered suffrage feminism not only morally vacuous (because not rights-based), but, in fact, aggressively hostile to realizing the rights of women. Rather than subjecting to criticism the sectarian ideologies that traditionally crippled the capacity of women to come to know and demand their human rights, suffrage feminists, through their political deals with the WCTU, the purity movement, and Anthony Comstock, were themselves the enforcers of such ideologies,[178] "strengthening the omnipotence of the very Gods that woman has served from time immemorial."[179] In fact, the right to vote has a very different normative status, Goldman argued, than the more fundamental human rights of the person; indeed, it was not a right in the latter sense at all, but at best an instrument by which such more basic rights may be secured.[180] The tragedy of suffrage feminism was its obsession with an amoral means at the expense of betraying its only defensible moral ends.

The crux of this tragedy was suffrage feminism's Wollstonecraft repudiation of women's basic human right to love. Goldman grounded this right in the source of all human rights, the self-originating claims of one's moral personality. To understand herself as a bearer of human rights, a woman must assert "herself as a personality, and not as a sex commodity,"[181] which includes "refusing the right to anyone over her body; by refusing to bear children, unless she wants them; by refusing to be a servant to God, the State, society, the husband, the family, etc., by making her life simpler, but deeper and richer."[182] Against the background of a conspicuously unjust conscription of women's soul and body for the sexual and reproductive uses of others, "the most vital right is the right to love and be loved"[183] on one's own terms as a woman, to "listen to the voice of her nature,"[184] and bravely "to acknowledge that the voice of love is calling, wildly beating against their breasts, demanding to be heard, to be satisfied."[185] Echoing the abolitionist feminist theory of moral slavery, Goldman underscored how "truly enslaved" women are by their "own silly notions and traditions,"[186] and that "[s]uffrage can not ameliorate that sad fact; it can only accentuate it, as indeed it does."[187] To truly emancipate themselves from such moral slavery, women must be guaranteed the moral, educational, and personal resources to defy the "internal tyrants, whether they be in the form of public opinion or what will mother say, or brother, father, aunt, or relative of any sort; what will Mrs. Grundy, Mr. Comstock, the employer, the Board of Education say? All these busybodies, jailers of the human spirit."[188]

The abolitionist war against prostitution had recently been defended by Jane Addams on the basis of the need for state-imposed curbs to realize "chastity and self-restraint"[189] in the anonymity and temptations urban environments[190] particularly offered immigrants;[191] Addams had endorsed the common abolitionist case for liquor and prostitution,[192] the purity movement's analogy of prostitution to slavery,[193] and the role of female suffrage in securing these aims.[194] In her important essay, "The Traffic in Women,"[195] Goldman, very much in the spirit of antebellum abolitionist feminists and of Victoria Woodhull, insisted that prostitution be regarded as raising an issue (treating women exclusively as a sex object and economically bargaining for them on that basis) central to the moral subjugation of all women, including conventionally married women.[196] This deeper issue of moral slavery was not only evaded, but also, Goldman argued, perversely reinforced by ascribing to prostitution an evil wholly discontinuous with the experience of other women on grounds that would not bear examination. In fact, "it is merely a question of degree whether . . . [a woman] sells herself to one man, in or out of marriage, or to many men."[197] The abolitionist case made, by Addams and others, rested on both distortions of fact and of value. Overwrought factual distortions included ascribing American prostitution to immigrants and coercive white slavery[198] as well as, monocausally, to economic factors.[199] These distortions, in turn, reflected a sectarian conception of value ("a perverted conception of morality"[200] whose unjust political enforcement very much entrenched the interests of a politician like "the future Napoleon of America, Theodore Roosevelt");[201] that conception rested and indeed legitimated the abridgment of human rights, in particular, the denial to women in general of their human right to love. This conception kept women "in absolute ignorance of the meaning and importance of sex" rendering "the entire life and nature of the girl . . . thwarted and crippled."[202] And deviation from this repressive and unjustly defined gender role led to stigmatization of a girl who sought love before marriage or outside marriage as a fallen woman and thus a prostitute, in effect, unjustly creating the status that it now would further condemn."[203] The consequence of such an unjust enforcement through law of a sectarian ideal of puritanical gender roles was "the perversion of the significance and functions of the human body, especially in regard to woman."[204] Suffragist women, like Addams, thus forged a deeply flawed conception of the emancipation of women: one calling for "a dignified, proper appearance, while the inner life is growing empty and dead," "a compulsory vestal, before whom life, with its great clarifying sorrows and its deep, entrancing joys, rolls on without touching or gripping her soul."[205]

In contrast, a rights-based feminism condemned, Goldman argued, the abolitionism of both the purity movement[206] and the WCTU,[207], and the suffrage feminism that now supinely served these movements.[208] Its agenda must include protections of the rights of conscience and speech of a Mary Wollstonecraft and Oscar Wilde[209] against the unjust political repression led by an Anthony Comstock;[210] Roger Baldwin, the founder of the ACLU (American Civil Liberties Union), admired, assisted, and learned from Goldman in her insistence on organizing to protect basic civil liberties.[211] It must address, as Elizabeth Stanton and Edward Carpenter more recently had urged,[212] basic injustices not only in marriage as an institution but also in lack of economic opportunities that deprived women of economic independence.[213] Finally and crucially, it must address the rights-based principle of free love. Goldman not only, as we earlier saw, defended the principle, but also clearly pioneered its application to the right to contraceptives.[214] She also suggested that it might apply to abortion,[215] and evidently defended in speeches and elsewhere its application to consensual homosexuality.[216] On the last point, Goldman not only, as we have seen, condemned the trial of Wilde and cited a leading British advocate of the rights of homosexuals, Edward Carpenter,[217] but even enthusiastically claimed Walt Whitman as an influence on her views on free love.[218]

Goldman's life was at least as sexually radical as Victoria Woodhull's, and her political life more so.[219] She was neither a politician nor interested in politics, for which she had a rights-based contempt worthy of Garrison. The entire point of her anarchism was, very much like antebellum radical moral abolitionism, to confront the American public mind in general and American suffrage feminism in particular with basic issues of conscience rooted in the argument for toleration. She, more than any feminist of her generation, spoke in the authentic ethical voice of antebellum abolitionist feminism, and, in that voice, cogently indicted suffrage feminism for the shrunken and decrepit thing it had made of its rights-based heritage.

Margaret Sanger's early public career rested on principles as radical as and quite similar to Goldman's, but she eventually focussed them much more narrowly on the issue of women's rights to contraception.[220] Sanger's 1914 monthly journal, aptly named *The Woman Rebel*, offered a theory of woman's moral slavery by unjustly politically enforced sectarian conventions of gender in marriage and elsewhere that was quite as radical as Goldman's,[221] and similarly grounded in a basic human right, namely, that "[a] women's body belongs to herself alone."[222] But, even at this early rather radical period of her career, Sanger focussed the argument on "the importance of our fight for birth control."[223] Sanger was indicted in 1914, in part under the federal anti-obscenity Comstock law, for her publication of *Woman Rebel*: her arrest was followed by that of her husband, who had, in his wife's absence, sold her pamphlet on *Family Limitation* to a Comstock agent. Sanger's response was to go to Europe (her husband was convicted and served a prison term in her absence); here Havelock Ellis, the important British student and advocate of sexual reform (including decriminalization of homosexuality)[224] became perhaps the closest mentor of her life and, for a period, her lover.[225] Sanger returned to the United States when she saw that confronting such prosecutions might lead to building public support for women's rights to contraceptives. Growing public outrage at her prosecution led to the charges being dropped, but Sanger was criminally convicted in 1916 under New York's Comstock law when she opened a birth control clinic in New York. Her conviction and prison time enormously enhanced her growing reputation.[226] Sanger made an essentially political decision to build gradually a movement centering only on the issue of contraception rights, suppressing not only many of her other more radical views (for example, about a right to sexual variety)[227] but also, in contrast to Goldman's honesty, the facts of her sexually quite unorthodox lifestyle (usually conducted in Europe).[228] Sanger also became anti-abortion (changing the views of her *Woman Rebel* days);[229] and her associate in her New York City birth control clinic, Hannah Stone, condemned homosexuality.[230]

Nonetheless, in one of her two most articulate defenses of her position, Sanger's argument opened with a quotation from Whitman,[231] and cited the work of Havelock Ellis repeatedly.[232] Sanger rested the case for a woman's right to use contraceptives on a more general right of love, expressing "a new conception of sex, not as a merely propagative act, not merely as a biological necessity for the perpetuation of the race, but as a psychic and spiritual avenue of expression";[233] and, like Goldman, she regarded this "natural right of woman to the control of her own body, to self-development and to self-expression"[234] as more fundamental than the right to suffrage,[235] freeing women, as it would, from "[t]he barriers of prurient puritanism."[236] The unjust abridgment of this basic human right had, echoing the abolitionist feminist theory of moral slavery, made of maternity a kind of slavery,[237] not a motherhood freely expressive of moral personality but a kind of unjust conscription or compulsion,[238] not a life expressive of "a vigorous, constructive, liberated morality" but the "role . . . of an incubator and little more."[239] Abridgment of such a basic human right required, consistent with the argument for toleration, a compelling secular justification, but there was none in contemporary circumstances. In fact, a highly sectarian normative conception of women, one in which "women have been so degraded that they have been habituated to look upon themselves through the eyes of men,"[240] has been unjustly imposed on women. Such a sectarian normative conception rested on the failure to allow women to develop "their own self-consciousness," and thus "the exercise of judgment, reason, or discrimination," "the exercise of self-guidance and intelligent self-direction" of "that inalienable, supreme, pivotal [moral] power"[241] which they, as persons, possess. Only the removal of such "moral taboos" as the measure of public law can "free the individual from the slavery of tradition, remove the chains of fear from men and women. . . . Free, rational and self-ruling personality would then take the place of self-made slaves, who are the victims both of external constraints and the playthings of the uncontrolled forces of their own instincts."[242] The consequence for women would be that, for the first time in human history, they will be accorded the respect due them as persons, including the ultimate human right to be an individual. Woman's ethical role was not set, as Catherine Beecher and her suffrage feminist followers supposed, "by self-sacrifice but by self-development."[243] Respect for moral personality, which included the human right to love, will awaken "woman's interest in her own fundamental nature," "[f]or in attaining a true individuality of her own she will understand that we are all individuals"[244] and, as such, held to what Sanger's abolitionist feminist forebears would have called the same standards of universal human rights on the platform of human rights. There was, for Sanger, no higher morality than the ethics of respect of persons. The ethical challenge for women was not to idealize a sectarian tradition which, in fact, degraded them, but to reconstruct themselves and their societies on the terms that would dignify their transformative moral powers as ethically responsible agents and bearers of human rights to construct a more reasonable morality of sex and gender.[245] That, Sanger argued, was "their pivotal function in the creation of a new civilization."[246]

When she tried to express and act on these convictions, Sanger, however, was made to suffer criminal prosecution, conviction, imprisonment under obscenity laws she condemned as the unjust political repression of women's struggle, self-consciously in the tradition of American revolutionary constitutionalism, for basic human rights.[247] Goldman was also arrested, convicted, and imprisoned for public birth control lectures in 1916.[248] Goldman's broader interests led her to oppose conscription to raise troops for America's entry into World War I, which was the subject of her prosecution, conviction, and imprisonment under a federal law for obstruction of the draft in 1917.[249] The government, anxious to be rid of so troublesome a critic, shortly thereafter successfully had her deported on the ground she was not and never had been a citizen.[250] One District of Columbia attorney observed: "With Prohibition coming in and Emma Goldman going out, 'twill be a dull country."[251]

The events, as we have seen, were not unconnected. Goldman, the severest critic of suffrage feminism, was deported as an outcast from America at precisely the time suffrage feminism was to achieve its final victories in 1919 and 1920. The price paid was repression of some of the arguments of human rights that feminists and the nation most needed to hear.

## The Scapegoating of Commercial Sex Today

What relevance, if any, does this interpretive history have to contemporary debates and concerns? If suffrage feminism was morally bankrupt in the ways I have suggested, surely contemporary feminism has embraced a robust understanding of the right to intimate life in a number of areas (contraceptive use, abortion services, consensual adult homosexuality), and indeed secured constitutional legitimation of its claims in several of these areas (contraception,[252] abortion[253]) and almost secured recognition in others (homosexuality).[254] So, one reading of this interpretive history may be that contemporary feminism has precisely learned from the mistakes of suffrage feminism and achieved the advances it has made precisely by the more robustly principled understanding it has urged of the basic right to intimate life both in its own terms and as a central component of the struggle against sexism as a political and constitutional evil.[255]

Contemporary feminism is not, however, monolithic, and certain strands of divisive controversy among feminists (let alone the reactionary ideological backlash to feminism as such)[256] reflect, I believe, the uncritical continuing force for much of the interpretive history I have discussed. That interpretive history centered on the force of the paradox of intolerance that, precisely when rights-based feminism raised reasonable doubts about the unjust force that gender stereotypes had been permitted to enjoy in the distribution of rights and opportunities, repressed the forms of dissent that most reasonably advanced such reasonable debate and discussion; in effect, debate was truncated to the measure of the sexist orthodoxy under attack, repressing the persons and views who most fundamentally challenged the orthodoxy as unworthy outcasts. The force of this paradox persists under contemporary circumstances in a particularly insidious and vicious form that remains largely invisible to critical debate and discussion, surely an indication of how much unjust political force it retains.

The force of the paradox may have had some shred of rational appeal during the historical period I earlier discussed when women in fact enjoyed little economic independence from men and no acknowledged rights of free love; at least in such circumstances, the condemnation of commercial sex reflected a conventional (albeit uncritical) way of life that limited women to a romantic domesticity sexually and economically dependent on men. It at least made sense, against the background of such a politically enforced idealization of such domesticity, to condemn commercial sex as, in all its variant forms, in its nature essentially degrading of women (men or women, homosexual or heterosexual, experiencing sex in violation of the romantic domestic ideal of womanhood and thus of manhood). However, in contemporary circumstances, the persistence of such views, as the basis of criminalization and stigmatization, must be deemed even more irrationalist against the background of increasingly acknowledged basic rights of women, on a par with men, both to economic independence and to many of the rights (contraception, abortion, consensual homosexuality) associated with the right of free love as a basic right to intimate life. To the extent such rights are now acknowledged and even (to a significant degree) constitutionalized, surely the persistence of such views (in the continuing criminalization and condemnation of commercial sex) must be regarded as having even less rational basis than they previously may have had. Indeed, to the extent a dominant consensus uncritically acquiesces in such criminalization and condemnation, it must be regarded as even more deplorably grounded in the injustice central to the paradox of intolerance as I have discussed it. A dominant consensus condemns sex workers, as outcasts from basic rights now freely accorded other persons, on an ideological basis (degrading women) rejected everywhere else as a just basis for law, and one that rationalizes the very degradation it claims to condemn. Such nescience rationalizes injustice, ideologically inverting reality to maintain an ideology of gender roles now conspicuously under reasonable attack everywhere else.

My point may usefully be made in terms of Freud's observation about the role played by the narcissism of small differences in the European political irrationalism of anti-Semitism.[257] Freud observed that the political irrationalism of anti-Semitism was most in evidence when it came into play during an assimilationist period when, in fact, the differences between Jews and the dominant society approached the vanishing point. What I call the paradox of intolerance was precisely the irrationalist and unjust political construction of difference (building on historical patterns of unjust intolerance and subjugation) in service of conceptions of national identity now conspicuously subject to reasonable doubt; the Jews were the scapegoats of European national self-doubt in the same way African Americans had been in the United States.[258] In the same way, the paradox of intolerance exercises powerful hold on our public imagination today precisely when the line between now-acknowledged conceptions of basic rights (including the right to intimate life) and other areas approaches the vanishing point. Whatever may have been the case during the heyday of the alliance between suffrage feminism and the purity leagues, we certainly no longer regard it as politically or constitutionally legitimate in many domains to enforce through public law a conception of mandatory gender roles based on the abridgment of basic rights to fair economic opportunity and sexual autonomy. Nonetheless, the dominant political consensus either sharply questions or wholly rejects the application of the right to intimate law in certain domains. Three such applications are notable: the repudiation by antipornography feminists of any application of the right to intimate law to pornographic materials, the rather overwrought repudiation by dominant politicians of all parties of the very idea of same-sex marriage, and the failure to take seriously commercial sex as a domain to which basic human rights fully apply.

## Antipornography Feminists

Historically, as we earlier saw in the case of Emma Goldman and Margaret Sanger, no group suffered more from censorship under America's federal and state obscenity laws than dissident American women, challenging the dominant pro-natalist gender and sexual orthodoxy of their age. Nonetheless, an important strand of contemporary American feminists has defended a revised conception of such laws not on the ground of traditional obscenity law (that all erotic material is without value), but on the revised ground that certain such erotic materials in their nature degrade women.[259] Once, however, one gets the state in the business of making judgments of this sort there is, of course, no principled limit on the scope of state censorship (as indeed occurred in Canada when its Supreme Court's acceptance of such a view led to toleration of the sorts of heterosexual pornography that antipornography feminists despise, and censorship of gay and lesbian materials which such feminists claim to want protected from such censorship).[260] The very fierceness of unreason with which the antipornography view is maintained suggests the force of the paradox of intolerance in an age of considerable reasonable doubt about conventional gender roles. It is precisely because there is no principled line between the imaginative erotic material the antipornography feminists want protected and unprotected that the condemned material is so easily demonized, and reasonable inquiry into evidence of what causes misogynist attitudes so blithely ignored (including the more intellectually and ethically responsible inquiry into the deeper religious and economic sources of sexism). It is because there is no difference between the erotic materials in question that the repressive force of the paradox of intolerance must create a difference, one that irresponsibly distracts us from the kind of reasonable inquiry we need into the real sources of and remedies for the structural sexism of our public and private culture.

## The Repudiation of Same-Sex Marriage

We can discern a similar moral blindness in the conventional public attitudes that condemn the very idea of same-sex marriage.[261] Homosexual unions, as complex and various as heterosexual unions, are now very much part of our cultural landscape, and many American states including the highest court of my own state New York[262] (though not yet the Supreme Court of the United States) regard gay and lesbian sexuality as fully protected by the right of private life now liberally extended (by the United States Supreme Court) to almost every stage of heterosexual sexuality (including not only contraception and abortion, but family relationships,[263] marriage,[264] and divorce[265]). Most impartial empirical studies find that both homosexual and heterosexual relationships increasingly share many common features (including shared economic contributions to the household, interest in sex as an expressive bond central to the love and friendship that the relationship fosters, several partners over a lifetime, lessened interest in children as the basis for the relationship, and, when there is an interest in children, only in few of them);[266] and some studies suggest that, if anything, homosexual relationships more fully develop features of egalitarian sharing that are more often the theory than the practice of heterosexual relations.[267] It is precisely because there is a vanishing difference between homosexual and heterosexual unions that the force of the paradox of intolerance erupts to construct a political difference (namely, not extending marriage to gay and lesbian couples), one that demonizes a culturally marginal group and thus evades reasonable discussion and debate about the larger issues of gender stereotyping in contemporary marriage. The other contemporary issue about gay rights (gays in the military) has many similar features.[268]

## The Demonization of Commercial Sex

Both antipornography and anti–same-sex marriage arguments subliminally raise the question of commercial sex, which is my main topic here. The antipornography argument thus assumes that the commercialization of sexual services in the pornography industry must render it unseemly and disrespectable for the same reason that commercial sex is; and a longstanding trope in Anglo-American stigmatization of gays and lesbians has been that such a lifestyle is a kind of prostitution, a fallen man or fallen woman, as the case may be, and thus stigmatized on the ground that prostitutes are stigmatized.[269] Whereas important feminists now attack antipornography feminists[270] and defend the legitimacy of gay and lesbian relations as a feminist issue,[271] few embrace commercial sex as a domain calling for protection on grounds of basic human rights. Prostitutes remain and are the ideological scapegoats whom most (both on the left and right) love to hate.

The persistence of this ideological scapegoating today requires explanation, and it is best explained, in my judgment, by the reactionary force of the paradox of intolerance against the background of both the elaboration of basic human rights in many areas and the sharper constitutional questioning of the uncritical political force of gender stereotyping in our law and social and economic practices. It is precisely because we have come so far both in extending basic rights in a principled way and questioning gender stereotyping (based on the abridgment of such rights) that our political environment has become so easily inflamed by the reactionary force of the paradox of intolerance, as applied here to a traditionally despised and stigmatized cultural minority. From the perspective of a principled elaboration of basic rights of intimate life and of work, one would have thought that public law could no longer reasonably demarcate gender roles in terms of unjustly stereotypical conceptions of either sexuality or of work. We now recognize the right of women autonomously to define and explore their sexual lives and imaginations in as free a way as men always have, and to work as well in any employment in which they choose to exercise their talents and energies, on equal terms with men. How can sexual services, in principle, not equally be subject to these basic rights? We surely have no more right to impose on all persons highly personal, often sectarian ideals of romantic love than we have to impose ideals of religious belief or ritual or sectarian food practices, and the like. We can no more justly impose gendered conceptions of roles in sexuality or in employment against sex workers (whether women or men, heterosexual or homosexual, or whatever) than we may in sexual and employment practices more generally. The claims now justly and indeed constitutionally made on behalf of both women and men to acknowledge their basic rights free of unjustly imposed gender stereotypes applies equally to sex workers, whether male or female. The claims they are making cannot reasonably be distinguished from claims now made and accepted by and on behalf of all other persons. We so ferociously exclude sex workers from the civility of our political and constitutional discourse precisely because their claims are, on grounds of principle, so reasonable.

Such sex workers are, in their claims to basic rights of intimate life and of work, no different from the rest of us. If we regard our rights to intimate life to compass sexual imaginations and lives that answer to our personal erotic needs and rebel against mandatory gender roles (for example, that our sexuality must be procreational or conventionally masculine or feminine or whatever), surely sex workers must equally have the right to explore their own sexual lives in the same way and to render sexual services to others on the same fair terms. If we question on grounds of justice the enforcement of gender stereotypes through public law that limit freedom in both public and private life (including the freedom to explore different conceptions of gender and sexuality and to engage in economic competition on fair terms), surely we must, on grounds of principle, question as well the enforcement of such unjust stereotypes to delegitimate the commercial availability, on fair terms, of sexual services. Much of the traditional condemnation of such services by the purity leagues rested, as I earlier argued, on an idealized conception of women's roles in the family (enforcing an idealized sphere of romantic domesticity that sharply demarcated women's sexual and maternal roles in the family from any suggestion of independent agency either in private or public life). We now see in many domains the constitutional and statutory rejection of the enforcement of such an idealized conception as a just measure of rights and responsibilities either in public or private life.[272] Women in private life as much require protection from unjust forms of abuse and economic exploitation as they do in public life; and they perform important services there that are as much economic as they are personal or sexual, and many of them may reasonably be assessed in terms of standards of fair contribution and reward that apply in the public sphere as well. Further, nothing in the fair understanding of intimate life debars women or men from participating as well in public life on fair terms either in the economy or politics; in particular, we are increasingly skeptical of the role gender stereotypes have traditionally played in the unjust distribution of rights and opportunities in public as well as in private life. To the extent the idealized conception blinded us to these elementary claims of justice, such a pedestal put women, in Justice Brennan's eloquent words, "in a cage"[273]—a sectarian ideology unjustly used to limit reasonable freedom in both private and public life.

If we reject this sectarian ideology as a just measure of rights and responsibilities, surely we must reasonably reject as well the enforcement through public law of the reprobation of commercial sex that turned, as we saw, on the enforcement of the romantic ideal of domesticity. Surely, much of the best feminist discourse inspired by Elizabeth Cady Stanton[274] and Charlotte Perkins Gilman[275] has made quite clear the crucial role of unjust economic and sexual inequality in both public and private life as the root of American structural sexism.[276] The enforcement of the idealized gender stereotype of romantic domesticity crucially immunized from reasonable public scrutiny and debate both the devalued economic and sexual roles women played in marriage and the prohibition and stigmatization of such roles outside the home. The condemnation of commercial sex played a crucial symbolic role in the unjust demarcation of these economic and sexual roles precisely because commercial sexual services by women doubly challenged the dominant stereotype (women acting as autonomously sexual and economic agents). Such condemnation as much rests on the unjust enforcement and construction of gender inequality as the now-discredited condemnation of working or sexually active women (or, for that matter, mothers), and should be rejected, as a matter of principle, on similar grounds. Sex workers, on this view, challenge today, as they have in the past, the structural injustice of gender inequality precisely by insisting on both sexual and economic independence. Their insistence on independence, in their sexual and economic lives, poses a stark challenge to the residual force the gender stereotype of romantic domesticity retains in our private and public lives: sex workers (both women and men) insist precisely that their sexuality will advance their own ends (as well as those of others) and that their sexual work will receive a fair return for valuable services rendered. Such independence challenges the unjust force of the gender stereotype (of mandatory sexual and economic dependence) at the core of the structural injustice we call sexism, warping, as it does, the fair distribution of rights, opportunities, and resources of men and women in public and private life. We cannot reasonably understand, let alone remedy, such injustice if we continue to acquiesce in the anachronistic contempt for persons who may most reasonably challenge the unjust political force gender stereotypes continue to enjoy in a constitutional culture now committed to the condemnation of such stereotypes.

Our collective social and political intelligence suffers from the continuing force such unjust stereotypes continue to exert over our public and private lives. Such scapegoating expresses, at bottom, irrationalist, indeed reactionary political impulses that disable us from reconstituting our sense of personal and political identity on terms of justice. Rather than thinking about the continuities in personal claims of justice in diverse domains and taking appropriate steps to reconstruct our practices on grounds of justice (for example, demanding basic norms of mutual respect and fair dealing between equals in all relationships, sexual and economic), we engage in a sterile, self-defeating scapegoating of traditionally despised minorities. We degrade what we should respect on the irrationalist ground (popularized in uncritical American public opinion by the success of the purity leagues) that we thus protect women from degradation; such self-deception (degrading on the ground of protecting from degradation) cripples our moral intelligence in matters of sexuality and gender, rationalizing our culpable failure to attend to or engage in the painful but necessary reasonable criticism of and discourse about the structural injustices of race and gender that should have a paramount claim on our political conscience. The irrationalist political force of such scapegoating precisely rests on the reactionary impulse to suppress the reasonable claims of justice of groups (to respect and protection in terms of applicable norms of security and fair dealing) as much entitled to claims of basic rights as all persons are. We have nothing to lose and much to gain from resisting the force such political stereotypes unjustly continue to enjoy in our public and private life. The struggle for human rights under law in the United States, which has achieved so much in challenging the unjust role of stereotypes of race and gender in American public and private life, must reflectively ground its claims on arguments of principle that enable us to recognize the common humanity of all persons as claimants of basic human rights. We need now to acknowledge that our common struggle for recognition of human rights must no longer unjustly stigmatize commercial sex as outside the civility of our constitutional and political discourse, but as very much at the core. It is time to acknowledge that the argument of constitutional principle, which protects intimate personal life from state abridgment by anything less than a compelling secular justification, must embrace, on equal terms, the claims of sex workers and their clients to respect for their human basic right of intimate life as well as all their other basic human rights. The inclusion of such unjustly stigmatized minorities in our common principles confirms the transformative moral power of such struggle. Through it, such traditionally stigmatized cultural outcasts dignify their lives as free and equal moral persons and, at the same time, enlarge and deepen our reasonable sense of the critical demands of moral community in a free and democratic constitutional republic.

# Notes

1. See David A. J. Richards, "Commercial Sex and the Rights of the Person: A Moral Argument for the Decriminalization of Prostitution," 127 *U. Pas. L. Rev.* 1195 (1979); *Sex, Drugs, Death and the Law: An Essay on Human Rights and Overcriminalization* (Totowa, N.J.: Rowman and Littlefield, 1982).

2. One such example is the pending case brought on behalf of Jane Roe II by Elliot Shaw, more fully discussed by Elliot Shaw in his contribution to this volume.

3. See, for fuller discussion of this theme in these various contexts, David A. J. Richards, *Toleration and the Constitution* (New York: Oxford University Press, 1986); *Foundations of American Constitutionalism* (New York: Oxford University Press, 1989); *Conscience and the Constitution: History, Theory, and Law of the Reconstruction Amendments* (Princeton, N.J.: Princeton University Press, 1993); *The Constitution, Feminism, and Gay Rights: The Struggle for Justice on the Platform of Human Rights* (forthcoming, University of Chicago Press or Stanford University Press).

4. See John Stuart Mill, *On Liberty*, ed. Alburey Castell (originally published 1859; reprint, New York: Appleton-Century-Crofts, 1947).

5. For fuller discussion of the arguments of Lydia Maria Child in this connection, see Richards, *Conscience and the Constitution*, 82–83; *The Constitution, Feminism, and Gay Rights*, chs. 2–3.

6. For fuller exploration of this theme as the background to the proper inter-

pretation of intimate life as a basic American constitutional right of the person, see Richards, *Conscience and the Constitution*, 224–32.

7. For fuller discussion, see Richards, *Toleration and the Constitution*; *Foundations of American Constitutionalism*; *Conscience and the Constitution*; *The Constitution, Feminism, and Gay Rights*.

8. I discuss this problem in depth in my forthcoming book, *The Constitution, Feminism, and Gay Rights*; my argument in this paper develops themes taken from that book.

9. See Richards, *Constitution, Feminism, and Gay Rights*, chs. 3–4.

10. For fuller exposition and elaboration of this idea, see Richards, *Conscience and the Constitution*, 67, 72, 85, 129, 158–60, 163, 168–69, 183, 187, 194.

11. See Janet Todd and Marilyn Butler, eds., *The Works of Mary Wollstonecraft*, vol. 5 (originally published 1790; reprint, New York: New York University Press, 1989), 5–60.

12. See Janet Todd and Marilyn Butler, eds., *The Works of Mary Wollstonecraft*, vol. 5 (1792; reprint 1989), 65–266.

13. See Richard Price, "A Discourse on the Love of our Country," reprinted in *Richard Price: Political Writings*, ed. D. O. Thomas (originally published 1789; reprint, Cambridge: Cambridge University Press, 1991), 176–96; Edmund Burke, *Reflections on the Revolution in France*, reprinted in *Burke's Politics*, ed. Ross J. S. Hoffman and Paul Levack (New York: Knopf, 1959), 277–400 (originally published 1790). For commentary, see Virginia Sapiro, *A Vindication of Political Virtue: The Political Theory of Mary Wollstonecraft* (Chicago: University of Chicago Press, 1992), 12–13, 186–222.

14. For Price's appeal to Locke, see Richard Price, "Two Tracts on Civil Liberty, the War with America, and the Debts and Finances of the Kingdom: with a General Introduction and Supplement," *Price: Political Writings*, ed. D. O. Thomas (originally published 1778), 20, 81–82, 87, 97.

15. See Richard Price, "The Importance of the American Revolution," in *Price: Political Writings*, ed. D. O. Thomas, 125–30.

16. Ibid., 130–37; Richard Price, "The Evidence for a Future Period of Improvement in the State of Mankind" (originally published 1787), ibid., 160.

17. See Richard Price, "The Importance of the American Revolution," in *Price: Political Writings*, Thomas, 119.

18. See Wollstonecraft, *Vindication of the Rights of Woman*, in *Works of Mary Wollstonecraft*, Todd and Butler, 66.

19. See ibid., 67.

20. See ibid., 157.

21. See ibid., 68.

22. See, for example, ibid., 91, 101, 105, 112, 113, 116, 145, 161, 182, 215, 222, 236, 239.

23. Ibid., 220.

24. Ibid., 225.

25. Ibid., 182.

26. Ibid., 215.

27. The important influence of Lucretia Mott in shaping the feminist theory and practice of Elizabeth Stanton included, as Stanton made clear, Mott's 1840 con-

versations in London with Stanton about the work of "Mary Wollstonecraft, though . . . tabooed by orthodox teachers." See Anna Hallowell, *James and Lucretia Mott: Life and Letters* (Boston: Houghton, Mifflin, 1884), 186.

28. See S. Margaret Fuller, *Woman in the Nineteenth Century*, ed. Madeleine B. Stern (originally published 1845; reprint, Columbia: University of South Carolina Press, 1980), 62–63, 66.

29. See Lucretia Mott, "No Greater Joy Than to See These Children Walking in the Anti-Slavery Path" (speech delivered December 3–4, 1863), reprinted in *Lucretia Mott: Her Complete Speeches and Sermons*, ed. Dana Greene (New York: Edwin Mellen Press, 1980), 270.

30. See Fuller, *Women in the Nineteenth Century*, 62.

31. See ibid., 66.

32. See William Godwin, *Memoirs of the Author of a Vindication of the Rights of Woman* (London: J. Johnson, 1798).

33. Godwin calls Wollstonecraft's love for Frances Blood the "ruling passion of her mind," ibid., 19; see also ibid., 21, 46, 109.

34. Ibid., 85–92, 97–99.

35. Ibid.

36. Ibid., 127, 132–5, 146.

37. Ibid., 148–58.

38. Ibid., 91.

39. Ibid., 106.

40. Ibid., 92.

41. "She conceived that true virtue would prescribe the most entire celibacy, exclusively of affection, and the most perfect fidelity to the affection when it existed," ibid., 92.

42. See Richards, *Conscience and the Constitution*, 59–93.

43. For fuller discussion, see Richards, *Constitution, Feminism, and Gay Rights*, ch. 3.

44. See Lydia Maria Child, *An Appeal in Favor of that Class of Americans Called Africans* (originally published 1833; reprint, New York: Arno Press and the New York Times, 1968), at 196.

45. See Milton Melzer and Patricia G. Holland, eds., *Lydia Maria Child: Selected Letters, 1817–1880* (Amherst: The University of Massachusetts Press, 1982), 110.

46. For an important study on this point, see Karen Lystra, *Searching the Heart: Women, Men, and Romantic Love in Nineteenth-Century America* (New York: Oxford University Press, 1989), especially 237–58.

47. Reprinted in Nancy F. Cott, "Passionlessness: An Interpretation of Victorian Sexual Ideology, 1790–1850," *Signs* 4 (winter 1978): 219–36, especially 234.

48. See Lystra, *Searching the Heart*, 75–77, 80–83.

49. On the pervasive analogy between love and religion, see Lystra, *Searching the Heart*, 237–58.

50. See Elizabeth Stanton, "Speech of Marriage and Divorce, 1869," reprinted in Beth M. Waggenspack, *The Search for Self-Sovereignty: The Oratory of Elizabeth Cady Stanton* (New York: Greenwood Press, 1989), 121–25, at 122. The speech is also reprinted, here dated 1870, in Ellen DuBois, "On Labor and Free Love: Two Unpublished Speeches of Elizabeth Cady Stanton," *Signs*, 1, no. 1 (1975): 265–68.

51. See Waggenspack, *Search for Self-Sovereignty*, 123.

52. See ibid.

53. See ibid., 124.

54. See Altina L. Waller, *Reverend Beecher and Mrs. Tilton: Sex and Class in Victorian America* (Amherst: University of Massachusetts Press, 1982).

55. See, in general, Johanna Johnston, *Mrs. Satan: The Incredible Saga of Victoria C. Woodhull* (New York: G.P. Putnam's Sons, 1967); Lois Beachy Underhill, *The Woman Who Ran for President: The Many Lives of Victoria Woodhull* (Bridgehampton, N.Y.: Bridge Works Publishing Co., 1995).

56. For an important study of the connections between spiritualism and woman's rights in nineteenth-century America, see Ann Braude, *Radical Spirits: Spiritualism and Women's Rights in Nineteenth-Century America* (Boston: Beacon Press, 1989).

57. See Elisabeth Griffith, *In Her Own Right: The Life of Elizabeth Cady Stanton* (New York: Oxford University Press, 1984), 131–33, 148–49.

58. See, in general, Johnston, *Mrs. Satan*; Griffith, *In Her Own Right*, 148–49.

59. Griffith, *In Her Own Right*, 25–26, 136, 147–48.

60. See "Congressional Reports on Woman Suffrage," reprinted in *The Victoria Woodhull Reader*, ed. Madeleine B. Stern (Weston, Mass.: M & S Press, 1974), 40a–112. See also Victoria Woodhull, "A Lecture on Constitutional Equality" (delivered 1871), reprinted in Stern, *Victoria Woodhull Reader*, 3–33; Tennie C. Claflin, *Constitutional Equality a Right of Woman* (New York: Woodhull, Claflin & Co., 1871).

61. See, for example, Susan B. Anthony, "Constitutional Argument" (1872), reprinted in Ellen Carol DuBois, *The Elizabeth Cady Stanton–Susan B. Anthony Reader: Correspondence, Writings, Speeches*, rev. ed. (Boston: Northeastern University Press, 1992), 152–65.

62. See Griffith, *In Her Own Right*, 151–52.

63. See Victoria Woodhull, "A Speech on the Principles of Social Freedom" (New York: Woodhull, Claflin, & Co., 1871); reprinted in Stern, *Victoria Woodhull Reader*, 3–43.

64. Ibid., 6.

65. Ibid., 16.

66. Ibid.

67. See ibid., 23.

68. Ibid., 40.

69. See ibid., 23.

70. Ibid., 17; cf. ibid., 34, 35.

71. Ibid., 32.

72. Ibid., 29, 35, 36.

73. Ibid., 37–38.

74. See Johnston, *Mrs. Satan*, 65–66; Madeleine B. Stern, *The Pantarch: A Biography of Stephen Pearl Andrews* (Austin: University of Texas Press, 1968), 116–21.

75. See Elizabeth Battelle Clark, *The Politics of God and the Woman's Vote: Religion in the American Suffrage Movement, 1848–1895* (Ph.D. diss., 1989; Ann Arbor, Mich.: U.M.I. Dissertation Information Service, 1992), 94–97, 123, 125, 133–45, 176–99, 270–71.

76. See Henry James, Horace Greeley, and Stephen Pearl Andrews, *Love, Marriage, and Divorce* (originally published 1853; reprint, New York: Source Book Press, 1972).

77. For acknowledgment of the influence, see ibid., 17–18, 35, 62, 76, 127. See Jonathan Beecher and Richard Bienvenu, *The Utopian Vision of Charles Fourier* (Boston: Beacon Press, 1971); Jonathan Beecher, *Charles Fourier: The Visionary and His World* (Berkeley: University of California Press, 1986).

78. Andrews thus invoked the Protestant principle as central to his argument; see James, Greeley, and Andrew, *Love, Marriage, and Divorce*, 11–14, 62, 68.

79. Ibid., 106.

80. Ibid., 86, 108.

81. See ibid., 89.

82. Ibid., 66.

83. Ibid., 32–33.

84. Ibid., 89.

85. Ibid., 95, 107.

86. Ibid., 108.

87. Ibid., 107.

88. Ibid.

89. Ibid., 65, 67, 69, 95–96, 119.

90. Ibid., 10, 31, 35, 67.

91. Ibid., 29.

92. Ibid., 28.

93. Ibid., 96.

94. For fuller discussion, see Johnston, *Mrs. Satan*, 156–92; Underhill, *Woman Who Ran for President*, 220–46.

95. On Woodhull's concern at Beecher's belief in free love but refusal publicly to acknowledge his belief, see Johnston, *Mrs. Satan*, 173; Walker, *Reverend Beecher and Mrs. Tilton*, 93, 112–13, 136.

96. See Johnston, *Mrs. Satan*, 112–19.

97. Ibid., 124–25.

98. On Harriet Beecher Stowe's hostility to Woodhull, including a fictionalized portrait of her in Stowe's novel, *My Wife and I*, and her passionate defense of her brother's innocence, see Joan D. Hedrick, *Harriet Beecher Stowe: A Life* (New York: Oxford University Press, 1994), 371–79; on Catharine Beecher's hostility, see ibid., 375. On Isabella Beecher Hooker's skepticism about her brother's conduct and defense of Woodhull's right of free speech, see Jeanne Boydston et al., eds., *The Limits of Sisterhood*, 292–327.

99. See Griffith, *In Her Own Right*, 157.

100. See ibid.

101. See ibid., 158.

102. See Ezra H. Heywood, *Cupid's Yokes* (originally published, 1874), reprinted in Martin Blatt, ed., *The Collected Works of Ezra H. Heywood* (Weston, Mass.: M & S Press, 1985); *Uncivil Liberty* (Princeton, Mass.: Cooperative Publishing Co., 1871), reprinted in Blatt, ibid. For useful commentary on the free love movement in general and Heywood's role in particular, see John C. Spurlock, *Free Love: Marriage and Middle-Class Radicalism in America, 1825–1860* (New York: New York University Press, 1988).

103. See Heywood, *Cupid's Yokes*, 22.

104. See ibid.

105. Ibid., 23.

106. See Heywood, *Uncivil Liberty*, 16.

107. Ibid., 20–21.

108. See Lysander Spooner, *Vices Are Not Crimes: A Vindication of Moral Liberty* (originally published 1875; reprint, Cupertino, Calif.: Tanstaafl, 1977).

109. See ibid., 4–5, 15, 32–33.

110. See ibid., 17.

111. See ibid., 18.

112. See ibid., xiii–ix.

113. See ibid., 17.

114. See ibid., 22–3.

115. The charge was eventually dismissed. See Johnston, *Mrs. Satan*, 60–64, 183, 196.

116. See Spurlock, *Free Love*, 226–29.

117. See Braude, *Radical Spirits*, 139–40.

118. See ibid., 358–62.

119. See Hedrick, *Harriet Beecher Stowe*, 377.

120. See ibid., 378–79.

121. See ibid., 377.

122. See ibid.

123. See ibid.

124. Quote reprinted at Elisabeth Griffith, *In Her Own Right*, 157.

125. See David J. Pivar, *Purity Crusade: Sexual Morality and Social Control, 1868–1900* (Westport, Conn.: Greenwood Press, 1973), 33, 81, 99.

126. See ibid., 100.

127. Quote reprinted Ian Tyrrell, *Woman's World, Woman's Empire: The Woman's Christian Temperance Union in International Perspective, 1880–1930* (Chapel Hill: University of North Carolina Press, 1991), 192.

128. See ibid.

129. See, in general, Lystra, *Searching the Heart*; but cf. Cott, and for Britain, see Michael Mason, *The Making of Victorian Sexuality* (Oxford: Oxford University Press, 1994); *The Making of Victorian Sexual Attitudes* (Oxford: Oxford University Press, 1994).

130. See Lystra, *Searching the Heart*, 75–77, 80, 83.

131. See ibid., 237–58.

132. See Frances Willard, *Glimpses of Fifty Years: The Autobiography of an American Woman* (originally published 1889; reprint, New York: Source Book Press, 1970), 614.

133. See Barbara J. Berg, *The Remembered Gate: The Origins of American Feminism: The Woman and the City, 1800–1860* (New York: Oxford University Press, 1978).

134. See ibid., 219; see also ibid., 219–22.

135. See Berg, *Remembered Gate*, 174.

136. See ibid., 179–80, 207, 219–22.

137. See, in general, Judith R. Walkowitz, *Prostitution and Victorian Society: Woman, Class, and the State* (Cambridge: Cambridge University Press, 1980); Barbara Caine, *Victorian Feminists* (Oxford: Oxford University Press, 1992); Sheila Jeffreys, ed., *The Sexuality Debates* (New York: Routledge & Kegan Paul 1987), 111–89.

138. See Walkowitz, *Prostitution and Victorian Society*, 8–9, 128; on the strong female subculture during this period, see ibid., 25–26.

139. See ibid., 138.

140. See ibid., 93.

141. See ibid., 117, 137.

142. See ibid., 140–41, 146–47.

143. Quoted at ibid., 252.

144. See Pivar, *Purity Crusade,* 65–66, 87, 111.

145. See ibid., 117, 174–75.

146. See ibid., 100.

147. See Richards, *Conscience and the Constitution,* ch. 3.

148. For further development of these points, see Richards, *Constitution, Feminism, and Gay Rights,* chs. 3–4.

149. For fuller discussion of this point, see Griffith, *In Her Own Right,* 210–13.

150. See Christine Stansell, *City of Women: Sex and Class in New York, 1789–1860* (New York: Knopf, 1986), 175.

151. See Pivar, *Purity Crusade,* 35.

152. See ibid.

153. See ibid., 190–91.

154. See Ruth Rosen, *The Lost Sisterhood: Prostitution in America, 1900–1918* (Baltimore: Johns Hopkins University Press, 1982), 40–41.

155. Woodhull, "Speech on the Principles of Social Freedom," 32.

156. Ibid., 29, 35, 36.

157. See ibid., 17, 34, 35.

158. See Mark Thomas Connelly, *The Response to Prostitution in the Progressive Era* (Chapel Hill: University of North Carolina Press, 1980), 47.

159. For useful studies of this era, see Connelly, *Response to Prostitution in the Progressive Era;* Rosen, *The Lost Sisterhood;* Barbara Meil Hobson, *Uneasy Virtue: The Politics of Prostitution and the American Reform Tradition* (Chicago: University of Chicago Press, 1990); Timothy J. Gilfoyle, *City of Eros: New York City, Prostitution, and the Commercialization of Sex, 1790–1920* (New York: W. W. Norton, 1992). For background see Pivar, *Purity Crusade.*

160. See Rosen, *Lost Sisterhood,* 8–9.

161. See Connelly, *Response to Prostitution in the Progressive Era,* 6.

162. On the contemporary lack of support for the economic deprivation theory of prostitution, see Connelly, *Response to Prostitution in the Progressive Era,* 33–34; Rosen, *Lost Sisterhood,* 137–68.

163. Contemporary studies showed that immigrants were, in fact, underrepresented in the prostitute population; see Connelly, *Response to Prostitution in the Progressive Era,* 62–64; Rosen, *Lost Sisterhood,* 140–41.

164. On the lack of support for the claims made for white slavery as the cause of American prostitution, see Connelly, *Reponse to Prostitution in the Progressive Era,* 124–35; Rosen, *Lost Sisterhood,* 112–35.

165. For important studies, see Linda Gordon, *Woman's Body, Woman's Right: A Social History of Birth Control in America* (Harmondsworth: Penguin, 1976); Janet Farrell Brodie, *Contraception and Abortion in 19th-Century America* (Ithaca: Cornell University Press, 1994).

166. See Brodie, *Contraception and Abortion,* 89–106.

167. See ibid., 95–96.

168. See Gordon, *Woman's Body,* 97, 101–103.

169. For a good general study, see Richard Drinnon, *Rebel in Paradise: A Biography of Emma Goldman* (Chicago: University of Chicago Press, 1961).

170. For Goldman's identification with Garrison, see Emma Goldman, *Anarchism and Other Essays*, Richard Drinnon, ed. (originally published 1896; reprint, New York: Dover, 1969) 76.

171. See Goldman, *Anarchism and Other Essays*, 67.

172. For Goldman's use of the analogy of the Reformation, see ibid., 74–75.

173. For further development of this point (the foundation of Goldman's anarchism on the demand for the right to conscience central to the argument for toleration), see Drinnon, *Rebel in Paradise*, 105–11.

174. See ibid., 62–63.

175. See ibid., 64.

176. See ibid., 195–211.

177. See ibid., 213–25.

178. See ibid., 170.

179. See ibid., 52.

180. See ibid., 197–99.

181. See ibid., 211.

182. See ibid.

183. See ibid., 224.

184. See ibid., 222.

185. See ibid.

186. See ibid., 208.

187. See ibid.

188. See ibid., 221.

189. See Jane Addams, *A New Conscience and an Ancient Evil* (New York: Macmillan, 1913), 190, 210–11.

190. The very secrecy of urban life now required, Addams argued, more state controls to secure chastity; see ibid., 206, 212. Addams was particularly concerned by the temptations (or opportunities) now open to working women living alone (outside the control of their families) in such environments; see ibid., 28–31, 55–59, 64–71, 72–73, 77, 79, 89–90, 143.

191. See ibid., 28–30.

192. See ibid., 112, 188.

193. Ibid., 3–13, 197.

194. See ibid., 191–98.

195. See Goldman, *Anarchism and Other Essays*, 177–94.

196. See ibid., 20, 24–25, 26–27.

197. See ibid., 179.

198. See ibid., 189–93.

199. See ibid., 184.

200. See ibid., 25.

201. See ibid., 29.

202. See ibid., 24.

203. See ibid., 185–88.

204. See ibid., 171.

205. See ibid., 217.

206. See ibid., 173–74.

207. See ibid., 175.

208. See ibid., 195–225.

209. See ibid., 168.

210. See ibid., 169–70, 174.

211. See Drinnon, *Rebel in Paradise*, 140–41.

212. On Goldman's citation of Carpenter, see Emma Goldman, *Anarchism and Other Essays*, 229.

213. See, in general, Goldman's "Marriage and Love," ibid., 227–39.

214. See ibid., 172. For Goldman's crucial work to defend this right, see Drinnon, *Rebel in Paradise*, 165–72.

215. See Drinnon, *Rebel in Paradise*, 172–3.

216. See Alix Shulman, "The Most Dangerous Woman in the World," in Emma Goldman, *The Traffic in Women and Other Essays on Feminism* (New York: Times Change Press, 1970), 13; Bonnie Haaland, *Emma Goldman: Sexuality and the Impurity of the State* (Montreal: Black Rose Books, 1993), 164–76; Jonathan Ned Katz, *Gay American History: Lesbians and Gay Men in the U.S.A.* (New York: Meridian, 1992), 376–80, 530–38.

217. For Goldman's amused comments on her later meeting with Carpenter and his domestic arrangements with his lover, see Richard and Anna Maria Drinnon, eds., *Nowhere at Home: Letters from Exile of Emma Goldman and Alexander Berkman* (New York: Schocken, 1975), 127–28.

218. See Drinnon, *Rebel in Paradise*, 60–62. For Goldman's own later comments on the importance of Whitman's homosexuality to his greatness as a poet and rebel, see Richard and Anna Maria Drinnon, *Nowhere at Home*, 140–41.

219. On Goldman's personal life, see, in general, Drinnon, *Rebel in Paradise*. With respect to her political radicalism, I have in mind her complicity with the attempt of Alexander Berkman, her then lover, to murder Henry Frick. See ibid., 41–54.

220. For an excellent general study of Sanger, see Ellen Chesler, *Woman of Valor: Margaret Sanger and the Birth Control Movement in America* (New York: Anchor, 1992).

221. See Alex Baskin, ed., *Woman Rebel* (New York: Archives of Social History, 1976), 16, 20, 40.

222. See ibid., 25.

223. See ibid.

224. See Havelock Ellis and John Addington Symonds, *Sexual Inversion* (London: Wilson and Macmillan, 1897).

225. See Chesler, *Woman of Valor*, 111–25.

226. See ibid., 102–103, 109, 126–27, 128ff., 138–40, 150–60.

227. See ibid., 96.

228. See ibid., 110, 249, 315.

229. See ibid., 271; but cf. ibid., 300–303.

230. See ibid., 306.

231. See Margaret Sanger, *The Pivot of Civilization* (originally published 1922; reprint, Elmsford, N.Y.: Maxwell Reprint Co., 1969), 1. See also Margaret Sanger, *Woman and the New Race* (originally published, 1920; reprint, Elmsford, N.Y.: Maxwell Reprint Co., 1969).

232. See Margaret Sanger, *Pivot of Civilization*, 50–51, 78–79, 141–42, 183, 186, 211, 243. Indeed, Ellis wrote the preface to Sanger's *Woman and the New Race*, vii–x.

233. See Sanger, *Pivot of Civilization*, 140; see also ibid., 211–19, 259. For a similar argument rooted in a basic human right of moral personality and control of one's body, see Sanger, *Woman and the New Race*, 53–56, 59, 68, 94, 193–94, 197, 211; for the new imaginative value placed on sex, see ibid., 108–12, 117, 167–70. Like Goldman, Sanger argued that this right was a more basic right central to the emancipation of women, ibid., 94–95, 210–11, and that marriage, without guarantees of this right, was a kind of prostitution, ibid., 112.

234. See Sanger, *Woman and the New Race*, 68.

235. See ibid., 2, 94–95, 210–11.

236. See ibid., 211.

237. See Sanger, *Pivot of Civilization*, 24–25, 38. See also Sanger, *Woman and the New Race*, 28–29, 45, 53, 55, 59, 64, 70–71, 72, 93, 94, 179, 183.

238. See Sanger, *Pivot of Civilization*, 28, 30.

239. See Sanger, *Woman and the New Race*, 226.

240. See Sanger, *Pivot of Civilization*, 209; see also Sanger, *Woman and the New Race*, 98–99, 210.

241. See Sanger, *Pivot of Civilization*, 209.

242. See ibid., 232.

243. See ibid., 272.

244. See ibid., 273.

245. See Sanger, *Woman and the New Race*, 167–85.

246. See ibid., 272. For the role of women in creating a new morality of sex, see ibid., 167–86.

247. See ibid., 186–97, 210–25.

248. See Drinnon, *Rebel in Paradise*, 168–69.

249. See ibid., 184–205.

250. See ibid., 206–23.

251. See Drinnon, *Rebel in Paradise*, 223.

252. See *Griswold* v. *Connecticut*, 381 U.S. 479 (1965).

253. See *Roe* v. *Wade*, 410 U.S. 113 (1973); *Planned Parenthood of Southeastern Pennsylvania* v. *Casey*, 505 U.S. 833 (1992).

254. See *Bowers* v. *Hardwick*, 478 U.S. 186 (1986) (denying, by 5–4, application of right of constitutional privacy to consensual homosexuality); but cf. *Romer* v. *Evans* 522 U.S., 116 S.Ct. 1620 (1996) (striking down Colorado Amendment Two, which constitutionally forbade any antidiscrimination protections for homosexual sexual preference). If *Romer* impliedly denied that populist moral disapproval is sufficient to deny rights to gay and lesbian persons in a case involving antidiscrimination protection, *Bowers* (involving a graver incursion into personal liberty, namely, criminalization, on grounds of populist moral disapproval) may be impliedly overruled.

255. For further development of this theme, see Richards, *Constitution, Feminism, and Gay Rights*, ch. 5.

256. See, for example, Susan Faludi, *Backlash: The Undeclared War Against American Women* (New York: Doubleday, 1991).

257. On "the narcissism of small differences," see Sigmund Freud, in chapter V of *Civilization and Its Discontents*, James Strachey, ed. and trans., *Standard Edition of the Complete Psychological Works of Sigmund Freud* (London: Hogarth Press, 1961), 21: 114; see also *Moses and Monotheism*, ibid., 23 (1964): 91.

258. For elaboration of this point, see Richards, *Conscience and the Constitution*, 80–89, 156–70.

259. See Catharine A. MacKinnon, *Only Words* (Cambridge, Mass.: Harvard University Press, 1993).

260. See, for fuller discussion of this point, Nadine Strossen, *Defending Pornography: Free Speech, Sex, and the Fight for Women's Rights* (New York: Scribner, 1995).

261. For more extended criticism of these attitudes, see William N. Eskridge Jr., *The Case for Same-Sex Marriage: From Sexual Liberty to Civilized Commitment* (New York: Free Press, 1996); Mark Strasser, *Marriage, Family, and the Constitution: Domestic Relations Jurisprudence and Same-Sex Unions* (forthcoming, Cornell University Press); Richards, *Constitution, Feminism, and Gay Rights*, ch. 8.

262. See *People* v. *Onofre*, 51 N.Y.2d 476, 415 N.E.2d 936 (1980).

263. See *Moore* v. *East Cleveland*, 431 U.S. 494 (1977).

264. See *Zablocki* v. *Redhail*, 434 U.S. 374 (1978).

265. See *Boddie* v. *Connecticut*, 401 U.S. 371 (1971).

266. On the continuities among heterosexual and homosexual forms of intimacy in the modern era, see, in general, John D'Emilio and Estelle B. Freedman, *Intimate Matters: A History of Sexuality in America* (New York: Harper & Row, 1988), 239–360; Anthony Giddens, *The Transformation of Intimacy: Sexuality, Love, and Eroticism in Modern Societies* (Cambridge, U.K.: Polity, 1992); Philip Blumstein and Pepper Schwartz, *American Couples: Money, Work, Sex* (New York: William Morrow, 1983). See also Barbara Ehrenreich, Elizabeth Hess, and Gloria Jacobs, *Remaking Love: The Feminization of Sex* (New York: Anchor, 1986); Anne Snitow, Christine Stansell, and Sharon Thompson, eds., *Powers of Desire* (New York: Monthly Review Press, 1983); Carole S. Vance, ed., *Pleasure and Danger: Exploring Female Sexuality* (Boston: Routledge & Kegan Paul, 1984).

267. On this point, see Susan Moller Okin, "Sexual Orientation and Gender: Dichotomizing Differences," in David M. Estlund and Martha C. Nussbaum, eds., *Sex, Preference, and Family: Essays on Law and Nature* (New York: Oxford University Press, 1997), 44–59.

268. See Richards, *Constitution, Feminism, and Gay Rights*, ch. 8.

269. On this point, see George Chauncey, *Gay New York: Gender, Urban Culture, and the Making of the Gay Male World 1890–1940* (New York: Basic Books, 1994), 61, 67, 69–70, 81–85, 97, 185–86, 286.

270. See Strossen, *Defending Pornography*.

271. See, for example, Sylvia A. Law, "Homosexuality and the Social Meaning of Gender," 1988 *Wisc. L. Rev.* 187; Adrienne Rich, "Compulsory Heterosexuality and Lesbian Existence," in Catharine R. Stimpson and Ethel Spector Person, *Women: Sex and Sexuality* (Chicago: University of Chicago Press, 1980), 62–91.

272. See, in general, Richards, *Constitution, Feminism, and Gay Rights*.

273. See *Frontiero* v. *Richardson*, 411 U.S. 677 (1973), at 684.

274. See DuBois, *The Elizabeth Cady Stanton–Susan B. Anthony Reader*.

275. See Charlotte Perkins Gilman, *Women and Economics*, Carl N. Degler ed. (originally published 1898; reprint, New York: Harper & Row, 1996).

276. For fuller discussion of the development of contemporary rights-based feminism, see Richards, *Constitution, Feminism, and Gay Rights*.

# Appendix B
## ABOUT THE EDITORS AND CONTRIBUTORS

**Chris Atchison** is in the School of Criminology of Simon Fraser University in Burnaby, British Columbia, Canada.

**Renee Blake,** photographer, was the chair of the art exhibit for the International Conference on Prostitution '97 and resides in southern California.

**Jacqueline Boles, Ph.D.,** is a professor of sociology at Georgia State University in Atlanta, Georgia.

**Judith Bradford** is a graduate student at Fordham University in New York.

**Gwen Brewer, Ph.D.,** is an emeritus professor of English at California State University, Northridge.

**Sarah Bromberg** is a member of COYOTE in San Francisco, California.

**Helen Buckingham** is a well known former madam from the United Kingdom.

The late **Bonnie Bullough, R.N., Ph.D.,** was a professor of nursing at the University of Southern California and distinguished professor emeritus at the State University of New York at Buffalo.

**Vern Bullough, R.N., Ph.D.,** is a visiting professor of nursing at the University of Southern California and distinguished professor emeritus at the State University of New York at Buffalo.

**Rosie Campbell** is the coordinator of women's studies, Deanery of Hope in the Community, at Liverpool Hope University College in Liverpool, United Kingdom.

**Elizabeth Clement, Ph.D.,** resides in Philadelphia, Pennsylvania.

**Sarah Crosby** is the service manager for MASH (Manchester Action on Street Health) in Manchester, United Kingdom.

**Dwight Dixon, J.D., Ph.D.,** is a researcher in San Diego, California.

**Joan K. Dixon, Ph.D.,** conducts research with her husband in San Diego, California.

**Joyceline Elders, M.D.,** is a former surgeon general of the United States under the Clinton administration.

**James E. Elias, Ph.D.,** is the director of the Center for Sex Research, California State University, Northridge, and a professor in the department of sociology.

**Veronica Diehl Elias, Ph.D.,** is a professor of sociology and a member of the Center for Sex Research at California State University, Northridge.

**Kirk Elifson, Ph.D.,** is a professor of sociology at Georgia State University in Atlanta, Georgia.

**Amy Flowers, Ph.D.,** resides in La Mirada, California.

**Kimberly-Anne Ford** is a professor in the department of sociology and anthropology at Concordia University, Montreal, Canada.

**Laura Fraser** is in the School of Criminology, Simon Fraser University, Burnaby, British Columbia, Canada.

**Delores French** was prosecuted in a high-profile prostitution case in Atlanta, Georgia.

**Robert Gemme, Ph.D.,** is a professor, researcher, and cofounder of the department of sexology at the University of Quebec at Montreal in Montreal, Canada.

**Timothy Gordon** is an artist known for his art of the Old West.

**Richard Green, M.D., J.D., MRCPsych.,** is a visiting professor at Charing Cross Hospital, Westminister Medical School, and is also a senior research fellow at the Institute of Criminology, Cambridge University. He is an emeritus professor of psychiatry at University of California, Los Angeles.

**Wan Yan Hai** is a visiting scholar to the University of Southern California from the department of health and anthropology at Beijing Management College in Beijing, China.

**Marti Hohmann, Ph.D.,** is editor-in-chief of *Masquerade* magazine in New York City.

**Xaviera Hollender** is the "Happy Hooker" and resides in the Netherlands.

**Gordon Isaacs, Ph.D.,** is a professor at the University of Cape Town in South Africa.

**David E. Kanouse, Ph.D.,** is a member of the RAND Corporation in Santa Monica, California.

**Michael P. Knox** is in the School of Law, Social Work and Social Policy at John Moores University in Liverpool, United Kingdom.

**Jim Korn** resides in San Francisco.

**Janet Lever, Ph.D.,** is a member of the RAND Corporation in Santa Monica, California, and a professor at California State University, Los Angeles.

**Jacqueline Lewis, Ph.D.,** is a professor in the anthropology department of the University of Windsor, Windsor, Canada.

**Hugh Gene Loebner, Ph.D.,** is a businessman from New Jersey.

**John Lowman, Ph.D.,** is a professor in the School of Criminology at Simon Fraser University in Burnaby, British Columbia, Canada.

**Tim Madigan** is the editor of *Free Inquiry* magazine in Buffalo, New York.

**Wendy McElroy** is a writer and researcher who resides in Toronto, Ontario, Canada.

**Kathryn Norberg, Ph.D.,** is a professor in the history department of the University of California, Los Angeles.

**Cynthia Payne** is a former English madam who has had several films such as *Personal Services, Wish You Were Here,* and *House of Cyn* made about her life and her life in prostitution.

**Mary Elizabeth Perry, Ph.D.,** teaches at Occidental College in Pasadena, California.

**Shane Petzer** is the coordinator of the Sex Worker Education and Advocacy Taskforce in South Africa.

**Ignasi Pons, Ph.D.,** is a professor in the Department de Sociologia i Methodologia de Ies Ciencies Socials at the Universitat de Barcelona in Barcelona, Spain.

**Priscilla Pyett** is a research fellow in the Centre for the Study of Sexually Transmitted Diseases at La Trobe University in Carlton, South Victoria, Australia.

**David A. J. Richard, J.D.,** is the Edwin D. Webb Professor at New York University School of Law in New York City.

**Wendy Rickard, Ph.D.,** is a professor in the department of health sciences at the University of East London, London, United Kingdom.

**Maria Del Carmen Santos-Ortiz, Ph.D.,** is with the School of Public Health on the Medical Sciences Campus of the University of Puerto Rico in San Juan, Puerto Rico.

**Sibyl Schwarzenbach, Ph.D.,** is a professor at Baruch College and the Graduate Center, City University of New York.

**Victoria Serra, Ph.D.,** is a professor in the Department de Sociologia i Methdologia de Ies Ciencies Socials at the Universitat de Barcelona in Barcelona, Spain.

**Craig Seymour** is in the department of American studies, University of Maryland.

**Elliot P. Shaw** is an attorney in West Palm Beach, Florida, who is best known for his work in the Jane Roe II case and the federal *Roe II* v. *Butterworth* case.

**William Simon, Ph.D.,** is a professor of sociology at the University of Houston, Houston, Texas, and a member of the Center for Sex Research at California State University, Northridge.

**Annie Sprinkle** bills herself as the "Notorious Prostitute/Porn Star turned Sex Guru/Performance Artist."

**Margo St. James** is the founder of COYOTE (Call Off Your Old Tired Ethics), serves on the Prostitution Task Force, and resides in San Francisco, California.

**Elroy Sullivan, Ph.D.,** is a social psychologist residing in Houston, Texas.

**Coral Velisek** was the subject of a notorious prostitution prosecution in Florida, where she resides.

**Deborah J. Warr** is a sex researcher who has worked in collaboration with the Prostitutes' Collective of Victoria, Australia.

**D. J. West, M.D., LittD., FRCPsych.,** is a professor in the Institution for Criminology at Cambridge University, Cambridge, United Kingdom.

**Judy Whitehead, Ph.D.,** is a professor in the department of anthropology at the University of Lethbridge in Lethbridge, Alberta, Canada.

**Masumi Yoneda** is a lecturer in international human rights law, Kyoto Women's University, Kyoto, Japan.